Jess Willard

Jess Willard

Heavyweight Champion of the World (1915–1919)

ARLY ALLEN *with the assistance of* JAMES WILLARD MACE

Foreword by Tracy Callis

McFarland & Company, Inc., Publishers
Jefferson, North Carolina

All the photographs in this book
were supplied by James Willard Mace.

LIBRARY OF CONGRESS CATALOGUING DATA ARE AVAILABLE

Names: Allen, Arly, author. | Mace, James Willard, author.
Title: Jess Willard : heavyweight champion of the world (1915–1919) /
Arly Allen with James Willard Mace ; foreword by Tracy Callis.
Description: Jefferson, North Carolina : McFarland & Company, Inc.,
Publishers, 2017. | Includes bibliographical references and index.
Identifiers: LCCN 2016047955 | ISBN 9781476664446
(softcover : acid free paper) ∞
Subjects: LCSH: Willard, Jess, 1881–1968. | Boxers (Sports)—United
States—Biography. | African American boxers—Biography.
Classification: LCC GV1132.W55 A55 2017 | DDC 796.83092 [B] —dc23
LC record available at https://lccn.loc.gov/2016047955

BRITISH LIBRARY CATALOGUING DATA ARE AVAILABLE

ISBN (print) 978-1-4766-6444-6
ISBN (ebook) 978-1-4766-2637-6

Front cover, left to right: Jack Dempsey, Jess Willard,
Jack Johnson (photographs and design courtesy James Willard Mace)

Printed in the United States of America

McFarland & Company, Inc., Publishers
Box 611, Jefferson, North Carolina 28640
www.mcfarlandpub.com

To all the great boxing scholars
who labor in forgotten fields

Table of Contents

Foreword by Tracy Callis

I remember listening to Murray Woroner's Computerized Heavyweight Tournament back in 1968. Jess Willard met Joe Louis in that one and it took 12 rounds for the Brown Bomber to lick Big Jess. What? Twelve rounds? Why, Jack Dempsey, in real life, stopped Jess in three rounds. But it took Louis 12 on Woroner's computer. Now that was something very surprising, not that I consider Louis better than Dempsey, I do not. But a man lasting that many rounds with Joe in his prime is quite a feat. I had to learn more about this man, Jess Willard.

Out came the sports books, boxing books, record books, etc. Off to the library I went in search of microfilm, old newspapers, and the like. Hour after hour, I spent going through all of these items, reading about the big Kansan. I learned lots but never did I learn as much about Big Jess as when I read through Arly Allen's work on Mr. Willard.

As the author writes, "The men he fought, Jack Johnson and Jack Dempsey, are remembered today as great American heroes. But like an old book between two elaborate bookends, Willard is now forgotten." How can this be? The young Jess knocked out the experienced and slippery Johnson and the older Jess took everything the pulverizing power-hitter Dempsey could throw and kept going as long as he could. Big Jess needs to be credited for being what he was—a big, strong, tough man who was a very able fighter.

Standing 6'5" and weighing something like 225 pounds to 250 pounds during his career, Willard was a giant for his time. Somehow, someway, he has been written off over the years as a big oaf with average talent, a man whose size enabled him to accomplish what he did. This is not true. For a man of his size, Jess moved very well during the early and prime years of his career. In addition, he carried a very hard punch and possessed a sturdy chin, accompanied by the mental attitude that makes a fighter truly tough.

Over the years, doubt has been cast upon his knockout of Johnson. Arguments have been presented that Jack was not knocked out but took a dive and a photo of the black champion lying on the floor with his hand shading his eyes from the sun suggests this was the case. The author devotes a chapter to discussing the facts surrounding the incident and contends that Jess did, indeed, score a knockout of the great fighter. He includes a picture showing Johnson being picked up off the floor by Tom Flanagan while the crowd mills around him in the ring. This is in contrast to the assertion by the Associated Press that Johnson hopped up on his own shortly after being counted out.

The views and words of many reliable sources as well as those of the author himself are used to describe the time in which Willard lived, his life and family, a number of happenings that took place and the status of boxing during this time. All of these are talked about in an interesting and informative manner. A number of familiar names are mentioned and various incidents regarding these men are discussed. They are brought to life. In addition, many unfamiliar names and people are discussed too.

Regarding the life of Jess, a number of many new facts are revealed. For example, Willard was a champion sprinter and swimmer. He was a champion bronco-buster and horse trader too. Further, he married his childhood sweetheart and his marriage lasted for 60 years, in contrast to Johnson and Dempsey who had multiple affairs and several marriages.

A most interesting chapter is that which discusses Willard's encounter with Jack Dempsey. The author argues that Dempsey did not follow the rules of the time, and had he done so, he would not have beaten Willard. The popular position that Dempsey was not afraid of anybody is contested and the assertion made that he was afraid that Willard might kill him.

The author contends that Dempsey's fear of Willard led him (and Doc Kearns) to want to win at any cost. Whether this meant that Jack had plaster of Paris in his gloves is not known but it is true that Dempsey ignored the rule on allowing Willard to get up after a knockdown, ignored the rule against kidney punches, and got away with leaving the ring before the fight was over.

In my view, Jess Willard was a much better fighter than many historians and boxing analysts give him credit for being. A detailed biography of Big Jess is long overdue and with his book, Arly Allen has provided this. There is an abundance of rare facts about Jess, various men associated with the sport, and other interesting incidents. The knowledge of the reader will be enriched regarding this former heavyweight champion, his time period and other related happenings.

Tracy Callis is the director of historical research for www.cyberboxingzone.com, an elector to the International Boxing Hall of Fame, a member of the advisory board of Steve Lott's Boxing Hall of Fame in Las Vegas and a member of the executive board of directors of the International Boxing Research Organization. He is the author of A Brief History of the Heavyweights, 1881–2010 *(WIN BY KO, 2013).*

Preface

It is now more than 100 years since Jess Willard first surprised the world by defeating the heavyweight champion, Jack Johnson. During that time many books and articles have appeared about Jack Johnson, but none have been written about Jess Willard. In the same way, Willard was defeated by Jack Dempsey in 1919, and since that time the account of his defeat has become well known through the many books and articles about Jack Dempsey, but no one has written about it from Willard's perspective. This book is an attempt to correct the historical record.

As such, this book challenges a number of long-established myths about Jess Willard and his boxing battles. Jack Johnson was considered unbeatable, yet Jess Willard beat him. Jack Dempsey was called a man-killer, yet Jess Willard, not Dempsey, had actually killed a man in the ring. And Dempsey, whom many believe feared no man in the ring, entered his battle with Willard afraid that Willard might kill him as well.

Willard was born in Kansas in a little town north of Topeka called St. Clere. Yet he was not able to box in Kansas, nor even show motion pictures of his abilities in Kansas. Willard had to move to Oklahoma and Missouri to begin his early boxing career. There are very few memories of Willard in Kansas. Later he spent much of his life in California where he was better known and remembered. But while there, he was also responsible for the destruction of championship boxing in that state.

Had he been lucky, Jess Willard might have become a policeman. He applied twice and was turned down twice. Had he gotten a job with the police, he might have had a normal middle-class life. But because he was not lucky he became a boxer, and ultimately the most famous man in America.

The life of Jess Willard was full of contradictions, the most extreme being that Willard became the heavyweight boxing champion while professing to hate boxing. He engaged in a profession in which he had to beat up other men, while being unwilling to hurt his opponents. Unlike most fighters, Willard did not like to fight. Most of his opponents enjoyed the sport of boxing and were happy to destroy their opponents in the ring. This was particularly true of Jack Johnson and Jack Dempsey. Willard did not, and often said that if his opponent was not hurting him, he saw no reason to hurt his opponent. For this he was criticized repeatedly by sports writers which gave rise to the myth that Willard was not a great champion. Yet Willard was a great champion and was considered unbeatable in his time. As you read this book, you will find out how this could have been.

This work would not have been possible without the help of James Willard Mace, one of Jess Willard's grandsons. Jim Mace has been a constant help to me in developing this biography. In truth this book is really his book. He has provided me with a copy of his own life of his grandfather which he wrote in 1980, but never published. He has also provided me a memoir which his grandfather dictated to John Patrick before he died. And he has provided me with several hundred family photos which chronicled Jess Willard's career.

I owe Jim Mace and his wonderful wife, Marilee, a debt which I can never repay.

I was drawn to Jess Willard's life by memories of my own father telling me that my town, Lawrence, Kansas, was once home to the world heavyweight champion when my father was a boy. The fact that there is no memory preserved in Lawrence of Jess Willard created an incentive for me to attempt to introduce Willard to his former town and state. What began as a small effort has since grown into a book which you hold in your hands. I can only hope that you enjoy reading it, as I have enjoyed writing it.

In addition, I want to thank Tracy Callis, Tony Gee and the other members of the International Boxing Research Organization. The IBRO is a wonderful organization of international experts in the field of boxing ably managed by Dan Cuoco who publishes their quarterly *Journal.* This organization has members who are knowledgeable in the smallest details of boxing history from the date of the first recorded boxing match (1681) to the training regime of the most recent champions. I owe a particular debt to Tracy Callis who was kind enough to read all of these chapters and to correct them for grammar and substance. I also owe a debt to Tony Gee, the British Prize-Ring Historian, who critiqued chapter 1 on Jack Johnson and chapter 9 on Jack Dempsey. And I owe a great debt to many individual members of the IBRO whose contributions I have tried to cite in the footnotes.

It goes without saying, and yet I will say it, that none of the above named is responsible for any of the errors that might be found in this book. I alone am responsible for any errors, as well as the interpretations which I have placed on events. Every historian engages in a retelling of history, and the best histories tell you something you did not know about the past. I hope you will learn something you did not know about the past in this book.

I have recently learned from my good friend and high school classmate, Marsha Henry Goff, that in 1954 the head of the Lawrence Chamber of Commerce, George "Bus" Zook, planned to erect a statue of Jess Willard in Centennial Park, which is located on the land where Jess had his home. Unfortunately that did not happen. There still is no monument to Willard in Lawrence.

1

The Defeat of Jack Johnson and the Triumph of the Great White Hope

In 1915, a tall Kansas bronco-buster named Jess Willard became the most famous man in America. Like Charles Lindbergh after him, Willard appeared out of nowhere to capture the attention of the American public, and through it, the world. Willard was a shy, basically gentle man, who nonetheless engaged in one of the roughest sports in the world: boxing.

It was an accident of history that Willard became the most famous man in America. Flashing like a comet, he entered the ring in 1911, fought for 12 years and then disappeared. Although he lived until he was 86 in 1968, after the year 1923, when he retired from the ring, he faded from the American memory. The men he fought, Jack Johnson and Jack Dempsey, are remembered today as great American heroes. But like an old book between two elaborate bookends, Willard is now forgotten. People no longer remember his name. At best, they remember his nickname: "the Great White Hope."

Race Relations and Boxing at the Beginning of the Twentieth Century

By the beginning of the twentieth century, the sympathy for the Negro expressed during the American Civil War had vanished.[1]

Slavery had codified the position of blacks in America. Whether they were slaves or freemen, their position was inferior to that of whites. This very inferiority made many in the North sympathetic to them. Large numbers of northerners wished to see them set free and become equal with whites. On the other hand, despite wishing blacks to be free, most northerners did not wish them to be living near them. Generally, the northern legislatures attempted to forbid free blacks from entering their states. In 1856 the supreme court of Indiana convicted a Negro male for bringing a Negro woman into the state in order to marry her. "The policy of the state is ... clearly evolved. It is to exclude any further ingress of negroes, and to remove those already among us as speedily as possible."[2]

In the South, so long as slavery existed, many southerners were comfortable living with and working with freed slaves. Freemen posed no threat. However, the elimination of slavery in the South led to the deterioration in the relationships between black and white. Alexis De Tocqueville had foreseen that as legal barriers to equality fell, social barriers would rise. "Thus, in the United States the prejudice that repels Negroes seems to grow as Negroes cease to be slaves, and inequality is engraved in mores in the same measure that it is effaced in the laws."[3]

After the war, as the country industrialized and blacks moved out of the south looking for jobs and new places to live, they encountered waves of Europeans who were seeking the same jobs and the same living places. Competition bred contempt. As foreign immigrants competed with freed slaves for jobs and living spaces, a virulent animosity developed between the two groups. The innate reluctance of the northern white elite to rub shoulders with the urban Negro was reinforced by the struggle between the white immigrants and the black migrants. This led to the era of segregation.[4]

Segregation became the dominant condition of the American Negro. In every aspect of life, from jobs to housing, from schools to churches, blacks were systematically excluded from white society. In nearly every section of society the black man was prevented from competing with whites on an equal basis.

In the whole of American society there was only one place by the early 1900s where whites and blacks could meet and compete equally. That was in the sport of boxing.[5]

Boxing was an outlaw sport. As such, it provided a haven for rejects from normal society. Blacks and whites had long competed in boxing matches. Indeed, the first American to gain fame as a boxer, Tom Molineaux (1784–1818), was a Negro. Molineaux traveled to England, the home of boxing. There he twice challenged the English champion, Tom Cribb, once in 1810 and again in 1811. Although Molineaux lost both fights, the bouts attracted wide public attention and demonstrated the inherent role of "fair play" which always has prevailed in boxing.[6]

From 1880 to 1910, the very years during which society and sport were building the walls of segregation, boxing welcomed numerous black fighters at the highest levels of the sport. The only barrier to black fighters in boxing was the "color bar" drawn by the most famous heavyweight champion, John L. Sullivan. As John Lardner, the son of Ring Lardner, noted: "The [color bar] was almost never applied outside the heavyweight division; race honor became an issue when the scales reached one hundred and seventy-five pounds."[7]

John Lawrence Sullivan was a second-generation Irish immigrant from Boston. Sullivan won the heavyweight "Championship of America" by defeating Paddy Ryan outdoor on the turf in Mississippi City, Mississippi, in a bare-knuckle bout in 1882 carried out under the London Prize Ring rules. He lost his title to James J. Corbett in 1892 inside the Olympic Athletic Club in New Orleans, fighting according to the Marquess of Queensberry rules using gloves. As heavyweight champion Sullivan made the Irish proud of him and of themselves. He was the first "mass cultural hero in American life." Although boxing was still an outlaw sport, by the time Sullivan finished his career, it had become so popular that it triumphed over the law. By adopting the Marquess of Queensberry rules, John L. brought boxing into the modern world.[8]

At the same time the Irish were, like the Negroes, scorned and relegated to the lower levels of society by the white establishment. In part this was because many were illiterate farmers who had no useful skills, and in part it was because their Catholic religion appeared antithetical to American democracy. In the 1850s as Irish immigration was reaching the flood stage, white Protestants created a political party known as the Know-Nothings to attack and drive out the Irish Catholics. Then, in 1863, believing that the Emancipation Proclamation gave Negroes special advantages, Irish men and women rebelled in what became known as the New York Draft Riots. Irish mobs destroyed the

Colored Orphan Asylum on Fifth Avenue and attacked and killed a number of Negroes. The violence between the Irish and the blacks was such that the only solution, suggested one English historian, was for every Irishman to kill a Negro and then be hanged for it.[9]

"John L." did not kill any Negroes, but he did his best to kill their chances in the ring. As a great promoter of boxing, he toured the entire country issuing a public challenge offering to fight any man. But when confronted with Peter Jackson, a Negro who had come from Australia specifically to fight him, Sullivan amended his statement to say he would take on "all fighters—first come first served—who are white. I will not fight a negro. I never have and never shall."[10]

By his refusal to fight Peter Jackson, Sullivan created the "color bar" which many future heavyweight champions would follow. James J. Corbett defeated Sullivan at the Carnival of Champions in New Orleans in 1892. Although Corbett had fought Peter Jackson to a no-contest decision after 61 rounds before he held the title, he refused to fight him after he had won the title. Neither did Jackson receive an opportunity to fight for the title when Robert Fitzsimmons, who took the title from Corbett, and James J. Jeffries, who defeated Fitzsimmons, won the championship.

Peter Jackson died in 1901 without ever getting a shot at the title. He was succeeded by a more flamboyant fighter by the name of John Arthur Johnson, more commonly known as Jack Johnson. Johnson was an American Negro, born in Galveston, Texas, on March 31, 1878. The son of a former slave, Henry Johnson, and his wife, Tiny, Jack had lived through the ferocious hurricane which destroyed that city in September 1900. At that time he was 22 years old and weighed 168 pounds and was a superior boxer. Seeking a better life than that available in Galveston, by 1904 Johnson had progressed to the point where he thought he could challenge the undefeated reigning champion, Jim Jeffries.

Jeffries, like the other heavyweight champions before him, drew the color line. Although Jeffries himself had fought the blacks, Bob Armstrong, Hank Griffin and Peter Jackson, prior to winning the championship, and fought Hank Griffin in an exhibition after he won the title, he refused to risk the title in a bout with a black man. He said he would have fought Johnson too, had he not been champion, but he refused to fight Johnson in a championship bout. "The title will never go to a black man if I can help it," he told *The Milwaukee Free Press* in September 1904.[11]

The problem was that Jeffries had run out of white opponents. So superior was Jeffries to the competition that there was no one left to fight him except Johnson. Thus, in an unprecedented move, Jeffries retired from the ring and left the title to those who would claim it. He gave his blessing to a fight between the former light heavyweight champion, Jack Root, and a reasonably good heavyweight, Marvin Hart. On July 3, 1905, with Jeffries serving as referee, Hart defeated Root and claimed to be heavyweight champion of the world. To solidify his claim, Hart pointed out that he had also defeated Jack Johnson earlier in his career. But few people credited Hart with being champion and soon a new man appeared who defeated Hart and laid claim to the title. This was the "Little Napoleon of Boxing," a Canadian named Noah Brusso, but who fought under the name Tommy Burns.[12]

Tommy Burns was the smallest heavyweight champion of the modern era. Only 5 feet, 7 inches tall and weighing between 160 and 180 pounds, he was a born fighter. Like Napoleon Bonaparte, whom he resembled, he was willing to tackle long odds. Burns recognized that most boxing fans did not consider him to be a legitimate champion. As a result, he sought out every white fighter of promise and defeated them one by one. After winning all his fights in the United States, he traveled to England and defeated the English champion, James "Gunner" Moir, in December 1907. In March 1908, he went to Ireland and defeated Jem Roche, the heavyweight champion of Ireland. He then went on tour of Australia where on August 24, 1908, he defeated Bill Squires, the former Australian champion, for the third consecutive time. Then in another bout in September Burns defeated Bill Lang, the reigning Australian heavyweight champion. At that point Tommy Burns had exhausted all his opponents, save one: Jack Johnson.

Unlike his predecessors, Tommy Burns did not draw the color line. Instead he insisted that he would fight any man if the price were right. This gave Johnson his opportunity. Reversing the tactic used by Peter Jackson in trying to corner Sullivan in the U.S., Johnson followed Burns to Australia in 1908 and succeeded in obtaining a match with him on the day after Christmas.

The day after Christmas was traditionally known in most English-speaking countries outside of America as Boxing Day, the day in which people give Christmas boxes or presents to their servants. But it took on a different meaning in 1908, for the Burns-Johnson boxing match became a world sensation. Not only was the match a sensation because Burns had agreed to fight Johnson, it was a sensation because of the terms. Burns agreed to fight for $30,000 win, lose, or draw. This was the largest purse in boxing history at that time, and it became a touchstone for Johnson for the rest of his life. He insisted on the same terms when he fought Jess Willard in 1915.[13]

The Burns-Johnson fight was held in a special stadium built on Rushcutter's Bay outside of Sydney, Australia. Earlier, a large number of American sailors had witnessed Tommy Burns defeat Bill Squires on August 24, 1908, in this same stadium. The sailors were from the American "Great White Fleet." This fleet had been sent around the world by President Theodore Roosevelt to demonstrate America's coming of age, especially to Japan which represented the "Yellow Peril." In 1904–1905, Japan had defeated Russia in the Russo-Japanese War. This was first time in modern history a non-white nation had defeated a white European nation in war. It proved to be an analogue to the fight between Johnson and Burns in which a black man ultimately triumphed over a white man. These two events influenced public thinking in a strange and unusual way: They gave birth to a new crusade in which a boxing match was seen as a symbol of political domination.

Jack London, who was at the Burns-Johnson fight and reported it for *The New York Herald*, was the first to express this concern. London had wanted Burns to win: "Personally, I was for Burns all the way. He was a white man and so am I. Naturally, I wanted to see the white man win.... But one thing remains; Jim Jeffries must emerge from his alfalfa farm and remove that smile from Jack Johnson's face. 'Jeff,' it's up to you."[14]

London's concern mirrored the concern of the white Anglo-Saxon world. It was more fully expressed by the British magazine *Boxing*:

> The coloured races outnumber the whites, and have hitherto only been kept in subjection by a recognition on their part of physical and mental inferiority....
>
> Here we are, the hitherto dominant race, compelled to recognize that an American negro, the descendent of an emancipated slave, is the principal figure, our acknowledged master at the one great physical sport in which actual personal superiority can ever be authoritatively tested. Does anyone imagine for a moment that Johnson's success is without its political influence, an influence which has only been checked from having full vent by the personality of Jim Jeffries?

Having laid the scene, the editorial came to its climax: "Jeff may smash Johnson when they meet … and by so doing restore us to something like our old position. We shall never quite regain it, because the recollection of our temporary deposition will always remain to inspire the coloured peoples with hope. While, if after all, Johnson should smash Jeffries—But the thought is too awful to contemplate."[15]

Although he did not want to return to the ring, James Jeffries was ultimately persuaded by an appeal to his patriotism and by a purse of $101,000, the largest prize in the history of boxing at that time, to agree to a title fight with Johnson. Both Jeffries and Johnson were compelled by forces outside their control to make this bout. The comments above indicate the pressure placed on Jeffries. The pressures on Johnson were not less great.

In the first instance, many white people still did not consider Johnson the real champion. Certainly he had defeated Tommy Burns, but Tommy Burns, despite his great efforts, had not really deserved the title. He had not defeated Jeffries; he had merely defeated Marvin Hart. And Marvin Hart had defeated Jack Johnson. Johnson's defeat of Burns simply completed the circle, but it was a circle of mediocrity, not excellence. Jeffries remained the undisputed, undefeated heavyweight champion.[16]

The Light and the Dark Side of a National Question; Postcard issued prior to the Jeffries-Johnson fight, July 4, 1910. This fight set off the quest for the Great White Hope.

Secondly, Johnson stood tall in the black community but his role there was incomplete as well. He was described as a Moses ready to lead his people out of Egyptian bondage, if only pharaoh, in the guise of Jim Jeffries, would let him. Just as John L. Sullivan had given hope and pride to the downtrodden Irish by his victories, so too did Jack Johnson give hope and pride to the downtrodden Negroes by his. "Success is counted sweetest," Emily Dickinson had written, "by those who ne'er succeed." And American Negroes were a textbook example of failure. Jack Johnson's boxing skills were their greatest hope. His victory became their victory.[17]

Once the match was made, the fight promoter, George "Tex" Rickard, did everything he could to stir up public interest. Every day from October 29, 1909, when the papers were signed, until the day of the fight, July 4, 1910, newspapers all over the Anglo-Saxon world were full of information about the upcoming fight. Rickard's aggressive publicity made the fight a topic of daily comment. As *The New York Times* was to print the day after the fight:

> For weeks if not months it [the prizefight] has been the foremost topic of conversation among all sorts and conditions of men—and women. Its prominence as a news topic has been enforced by public opinion. The people who most strenuously denounce prizefighting have closely followed the daily accounts of the preparations for the battering match. They have deplored the publication of the reports and read every word of them.[18]

In small towns as well as big cities, the question of the day was Jeffries or Johnson? Newspapers, like the Lawrence, Kansas, *Journal*, printed the betting odds on Jeffries and Johnson daily on the front page for a month before the fight. In Hutchinson, Kansas, as well as Washington, D.C., and all over the south, black churches held special services to pray for Johnson's victory. Booker T. Washington, who thought Johnson was a disgrace to his race, nonetheless had a special telegraph line brought to the Tuskegee Institute so that the entire school could read the blow-by-blow account. The day of the fight, *The Chicago Daily Tribune* printed the following adaptation of Henry Longfellow's lines from the poem "The Building of the Ship":

> Punch on! Punch on, O Heavyweight!
> Punch on, O Jeffries, strong and great!
> The Paleface Race, with all its fears,
> With all the hopes of future years,
> Is hanging breathless on thy fate![19]

The Reno fight was a watershed moment in American social history. Boxing had transformed an athletic event into a political and social crisis when Johnson decisively defeated Jeffries on July 4, 1910.

If American society was fixated on the concept of color, boxing was color blind. The boxing fraternity believed in fair play and let the best man win. They were not disturbed by Johnson's victory. There were no riots in Reno. But elsewhere both blacks and whites were indeed disturbed by Johnson's victory. The Reno fight triggered the first nationwide race riots in American history. Hundreds of people were wounded and 26 people were killed.

Unexpectedly, common people faced an uncommon problem: How were they to live with the consequences of Johnson's victory? Blacks were pleased and excited by the victory. They took to the streets to celebrate a new kind of pride they had not known before. Whites, on the other hand, felt a new kind of fear that they had not known before. As a result the joyous parades of Negroes were met by angry white mobs which feared that blacks would now seek to emulate Jack Johnson.

In an attempt to stifle the new pride Johnson had provided them, *The Los Angeles Times* immediately attacked the black population. They should not expect Johnson's victory to have any meaning in their lives: "Remember you have done nothing at all. You are just the same member of society you were last week.... You are on no higher plane, deserve no new consideration, and will get none.... No man will think a bit higher of you because your complexion is the same as that of the victor at Reno."[20]

Then, in a spontaneous reaction to the riots and the fight, towns and cities all over America banned the showing of the fight films of the Johnson-Jeffries bout. It was feared that the films, if shown, would trigger further riots. The idea of banning the films of Jeffries' defeat began as a genuine grass-roots movement, but eventually, in 1912, the United

States Congress passed a law outlawing the interstate transportation of all fight films. This ban lasted until 1940.

There were even suggestions that newspapers should cease to carry fight news and especially news of fights in other localities. Both Theodore Roosevelt and William Jennings Bryan predicted the Johnson-Jeffries fight would mean the end of boxing all together.[21]

But boxing did not die. Instead the Reno bout stimulated it. The defeat of Jeffries led to one of the most exciting periods ever recorded in the history of boxing: "The White Hope Era."

All over the English-speaking world the call went out for a new champion, a new white man who could defeat Jack Johnson and bring the title back to the white race where it belonged. "Professor" Billy McCarney was one who had a unique perspective on this new era. He was a boxing promoter, sportswriter and onetime manager of Jack Johnson before the Reno bout. It was his belief that between July 5 and December 31, 1910, over 1,000 white heavyweights took up boxing in order to defeat Jack Johnson. As John Lardner later wrote: "In the heat of the search, well-muscled white boys more than six feet two inches tall were not safe out of their mothers' sight."[22]

According to McCarney, the phrase "White Hope" was coined by Otto Floto, a Denver and Kansas City sportswriter. It was a way of expressing the need for someone to defeat Johnson after he had defeated Burns. Floto first applied the phrase to Jim Jeffries as the man who could come out of retirement to wipe the smile off Johnson's face. But with the defeat of Jeffries, it was applied to any white boxer who would to take up the challenge to defeat Johnson. The "Original White Hope" was Carl Morris from Oklahoma City and Sapulpa, Oklahoma. But the phrase was also a way of drawing attention to this new era of boxing and enhancing its market value. Following Morris, there was a sudden flood of young boxers who quit their jobs to take up boxing.[23]

The phrase "the Great White Hope" was to be applied to the man who could defeat Johnson. It was patterned on the title "the Great White Fleet" of battleships which President Theodore Roosevelt had commissioned. This linkage between military power and boxing power was not accidental. Indeed, the military was one of the few places where boxing was legal in the years prior to 1920. Many boxers of the time, such as Gunboat Smith, Gunner Moir, Bombardier Wells, Sailor White and Soldier Kearns, had learned their skills in the military. But more important, it was viewed by many as a patriotic duty for white boxers to step forward to try to dethrone Jack Johnson. Winning back the title from the Negro was a patriotic act.[24]

The first step, of course, was to decide what constituted a "white hope." John Lardner's definition was the best: "Roughly speaking, at that time a white hope was a white heavyweight who had not recently been knocked out by another white heavyweight."[25]

White hopes could be from any of the Anglo-Saxon countries. Most were from the United States, but there were also white hopes from Canada (Arthur Pelkey), South Africa (George "Boer" Rodel), England ("Gunner" Moir and Bombardier Wells), Ireland (Jem Roche), Australia (Bill Squires and Bill Lang), and even Georges Carpentier from France. But even such loose rules were made to be broken by the lure of money. The Japanese put forward a "brown hope," the Chinese put forward a "yellow hope." A Navajo Indian, George Near, sauntered out of Arizona and into the Western Athletic club in Los Angeles seeking to become the white hope. Sam Langford, one of the great Negro fighters of the time, might have won the title of "white champion of the world" when he knocked out Gunboat Smith in late 1914, save for the fact that Smith had already lost that title in July to the Frenchman, Georges Carpentier. The ultimate winner of this strange sweepstakes was Eddie Robinson, Carl Morris' early manager. Robinson proposed to create "The International White Hope Association" with the job of finding the ideal candidate for this title. In describing the qualifications for the White Hope Champion, Robinson was forced to admit that "setting aside Johnson's color," Jack Johnson himself was the ideal candidate for the job.[26]

Organizing the Fight and Getting to Havana

It was a long and tortured path to that moment in April 1915 when Jess Willard stepped into the ring in Havana, Cuba, with Jack Johnson and knocked him to the canvas. It took Willard five years to learn how to box and then achieve the status of a man worthy to fight Johnson. During those years Johnson had followed his own tortured path. He had lost his first white wife to suicide; he had been robbed of his business, the Café de Champion, in Chicago; before his first wife died, he had been indicted for smuggling jewels; after she died, he had been indicted, tried and found guilty of White Slavery (the Mann Act). In June 1913 he had fled the United States with his new white wife, Lucille Cameron. Johnson had then taken up residence in Europe as an outlaw in exile. But no sooner had he settled in Europe than that continent exploded into World War I on August 1, 1914.

After a dangerous ride across France with thousands of refugees fleeing the German invasion, Johnson was able to escape mainland Europe and come to rest in London. There, Jack Curley, a promoter, met him at his apartment in St. Mary's Mansions and discussed a championship fight while Johnson, who prided himself as a chef, cooked dinner. They dined on homemade biscuits, fried chicken and corn while they negotiated. Since Johnson was still a fugitive from United States law, the fight could not be held in America. Nor could it be held in England since Europe, as well as Canada and Australia, were embroiled in the world war. On the other hand, Mexico and South America were neutral. Mexico was naturally the closest place to the United States. Thus by January 9, 1915, *The New York Times* could announce that the next heavyweight championship fight would be in Juarez, Mexico, at the race track.[27]

But Mexico had problems of its own. In 1911 the dictator, Porfirio Diaz, had been overthrown and the Mexican Revolution, the first of the great twentieth-century revolutions, had begun. Although Mexico was divided between warring factions, Jack Curley had made an agreement with Hipolito Villa, brother of Francisco "Pancho" Villa, the general who temporarily controlled this section of Mexico. Villa was interested in having the fight in his area, since it would bring many tourists and lots of money, which would help him in the war effort. Putting his faith in these revolutionary rascals, Curley had signed an agreement to have the fight occur in Juarez on March 6, when a cattleman's convention was to be held in El Paso.

Jess Willard was given the opportunity to fight for the championship by chance. According to the report given to sports reporter Robert Edgren by Willard, Jack Curley was visiting H.H. "Harry" Frazee, a New York theatrical man, seeking some passes to shows. Frazee (who would later gain sport infamy by buying the Boston Red Sox and trading their pitcher, Babe Ruth, to the New York Yankees) happened to be reading about Willard in the papers. Frazee and his partner, L. Lawrence Weber, another theatrical producer, were interested in the possibilities of finding someone who might dethrone Jack Johnson. The article suggested that Willard might be that man. When Curley sent his business card up to Frazee's office, Frazee remembered that Curley knew Johnson and had promoted his fight with "Fireman" Jim Flynn in 1912. He asked Curley, "What do you think of a match between Johnson and this fellow Willard? Any white man who can whip Johnson now can get a mint of money. Would he have a chance?" Curley thought he might.[28]

The moment was opportune. Although Willard had turned down previous offers to fight Johnson believing he was not ready, he now needed the work. Willard had been put on trial in January 1914 in Los Angeles for prizefighting. This case had grown out of a bout in which he killed John "Bull" Young in the ring. Although he was found innocent of the charges of murder and manslaughter, Young's death had put championship boxing out of business in California. Willard and Tom Jones, his manager, had faced multiple lawsuits and were out of money. Curley, now representing the Frazee-Weber syndicate, contacted Willard and Jones to see if they were interested.

Curley asked Willard to come to Kansas City. There, sitting in the railway station, he offered Willard a championship fight with Jack Johnson. It seemed like a gift from heaven. Jones and Willard returned to New York with Jack Curley and met with Harry Frazee. Jones was offered cash to sell the contract he had for Willard's services to Frazee, Weber and Curley, while he remained Willard's manager. Jones agreed to do this. This left him with a financial stake in the fight, but without the full financial responsibility. Willard, on the other hand, was promised nothing. He was told that Johnson would get the lion's share of the money:

> "You understand," said Frazee, "that Johnson has to have his $32,000 [Jack's fee was $30,000 plus training expenses of $2,000]. The other expenses will be heavy, the receipts may be small, and when the fight is over, you may not get a dollar."
>
> "I'll fight Johnson for a straw hat or a drink of water," said Willard. "I'll make my money after I whip him. I'll buy my own railroad ticket down to El Paso, return trip, and so if I lose I'll never bother you again. You won't need to pay me a red cent."[29]

With this background, Curley took a boat to England. There, on November 14, Curley got Johnson to sign the contract to fight Willard. In order to seal the deal, Curley paid Johnson's way to Buenos Aires, Argentina, from which port he was supposed to go to Mexico. Curley then returned to New York with the fight arranged.[30]

Willard and Johnson had actually met in Chicago at Bill O'Connell's gym in 1912, prior to Johnson's fight with "Fireman" Jim Flynn. At the time, Johnson had asked Willard to spar with him, but Willard had turned him down. As Willard later told sports columnist Ed W. Smith:

> One day I was tugging at the pulley weights and otherwise working myself into shape, when Johnson, who had trouble getting suitable sparring partners, walked up to me and said very pleasantly:
>
> "Come on, young man; box with me, will you?"
>
> The suddenness of the request and the matter of fact tone in which it was uttered rather took me off my feet and I started to stammer. But I gathered myself and finally managed to say:
>
> "No, I can't do it, Mr. Johnson."
>
> "Why, what's the matter?" he asked, flashing that old golden smile of his. "I never try to hurt anybody who works with me."

> "It isn't that," I managed to tell him, and then summoning up my courage, I blurted out:
> "You see I'll have to fight you some day for the championship and it wouldn't be right or fair to box you now."
> If you ever saw a man taken off his feet it was the champion that afternoon.
> "What, you too?" Then he looked at me and smiled in a kindly way. I knew then that he didn't take me seriously, but somehow I seemed to have gained his respect and attention.
> "Well, well, boy," he said and shook my hand. "That's the way to talk, anyway, and I certainly wish you plenty of luck."[31]

Although Jack pretended not to remember Willard, he nonetheless knew he was big, strong and impervious to pain. Thus, while the world waited for Johnson to turn up in Juarez, Willard and his party arrived and set up shop and began training.

Compared to Johnson's, Willard's trip to El Paso was relatively easy.

Willard was in New York City on January 8 and 9, 1915, where he spent the day at the Fairmont Athletic Club in the Bronx making a movie. There, from 2 p.m. to 5 a.m. the next day, Willard and a cast of actors were involved in making *The Heart Punch*, a film written and directed by Stuart Paton of Imp Universal Studios. The film was completed in one day and was shown on January 14 at Universal Studios which was then located at 1600 Broadway.[32]

The idea for the film came from Paton who persuaded Tom Jones and Jack Curley that a movie was the best way to introduce Willard to the public. The need for this introduction was demonstrated by Universal Studios itself when they declared Willard the "Arkansas 'White Hope.'"

Tom Jones and Jack Curley both played themselves in the film which centered on a fighter, Willard, whose wife (played by Marie Wierman) did not want him to box. But his young daughter (Katherine Lee) was ill and there was no money in the house. While in a bar Willard had a fight which attracted the attention of a promoter, Curley, who offered him money to fight a professional heavyweight. Despite his wife's concerns, Willard left his sick child, fought and won the battle and then hurried home with money to help his child get well.

Once the filming of *Heart Punch* was over, instead of going to Arkansas, as Universal would have had it, Willard and Tom Jones went to Kansas City, Missouri, where Willard trained in Lou Cutler's gym at 1208 Main Street. On January 21, Willard boxed a four round exhibition at the Kansas City Convention Center with Al Norton who had recently beaten Tom "Bearcat" McMahon. As *The Kansas City Times* had it: "The gloves were big and the rounds were short, but Al found time to hit the canvas on several occasions.... Jess really looked like a regular hope."[33]

While Willard was making his slow trip to El Paso, Johnson was making even slower progress. After leaving England at the end of November 1914, Johnson had taken a boat to Buenos Aires. Despite the fact that this was a dangerous trip, as German U-boats were beginning to sink allied merchant ships in the Atlantic, Johnson did not encounter any trouble on the seas. But he did encounter problems on the land. While Mexico was his final destination, the troops of Venustiano Carranza held the only ports on the Caribbean where Johnson could disembark. Carranza had declared those ports barred to Johnson. This was part of an agreement with the United States to capture Johnson and turn him over in return for guns and ammunition to fight Pancho Villa. Villa, in return, planned to invade Carranza's territory and capture Tampico on the Caribbean side of Mexico, thus allowing Johnson to enter.[34]

Advertising poster for *The Heart Punch*, the first motion picture starring Jess Willard, 1915.

The wars between the Mexican generals were beginning to concern the American tourists whose money was needed by all parties. So, on January 27, Pancho Villa published a guarantee of protection for all who came to Juarez for the fight.[35]

Willard accepted these assurances and arrived at El Paso on January 25. He had filled out his training camp by hiring Walter Monahan, a former sparring partner of Johnson, Tom Kennedy, a New York heavyweight, Jim Savage, also of New York, as well as Jack Moran. In addition, Jack Hemple and Tex O'Rourke later became sparring partners. Missing from his camp were "Fireman" Jim Flynn, who had broken his hand, "Uncle Tom" McCarey, who had run the Vernon fight center when Jess killed "Bull" Young, and former champion James J. Jeffries, who had wanted to train Willard if he fought Johnson. These last three had promised to be in Jess' corner, but, for some reason or other, did not show up.[36]

After leaving Argentina, Johnson landed in Barbados on February 7 to the surprise and delight of the local population. He tarried there seeking a secure route to Juarez. He attempted to charter a ship to Mexico, but all that did was to embroil him in a law case in Barbados. He even considered flying into Juarez in an airplane, but that proved impractical. He could find no way to avoid Carranza's armies. Then, astonishingly, the papers announced that Johnson somehow had escaped Carranza's blockade and had landed in Mexico. The fight was on.[37]

The report of Johnson's arrival in Mexico was premature. In fact, the boat which took Jack and his wife, Lucille, from Barbados landed in Cuba, not in Mexico. And there Johnson stayed. The difficulty of getting to Mexico and the uncertainty of his welcome there made him decide not to leave Cuba. And if the fight was going to occur at all, it had to be postponed.[38]

In an interview he gave to Robert Edgren in Havana, Johnson revealed deeper concerns which kept him from Mexico. Although Jack Curley was convinced that the Mexican bandits would keep their word and not harm the tourists, Johnson was not.

> Johnson told me he never thought of getting to Mexico after finding that he might have trouble getting to Juarez. He said he even doubted that he'd ever have fought in Juarez under any circumstances because Villa or some other Mexican gentleman with a long rifle and a short conscience would probably kidnap him after the fight and hold him as long as Johnson could raise a dollar to save his life.
>
> "No sir," said Jack, "I didn't want to decorate the interior of some dark cave for three or four years, with some fellow sending my fingers and toes and ears out for souvenirs."[39]

The confusion over Johnson's whereabouts and the uncertainty of the fight created a ruckus in Jess Willard's camp. Temperamental in the best of times, Jess was upset by the delays and confusion about Johnson's arrival. In an argument with Tom Jones in the lobby of a hotel in El Paso, he announced that he had ceased training and would not train any more until Johnson arrived on the scene. Willard and Tex O'Rourke then left on a hunting trip. Jack Curley, the promoter, went to Havana to find Johnson. Tom Jones, on the other hand, had drawn a line in the sand: "There will be no fight unless it is held in Juarez." And with Johnson in Cuba and no way to get him to Juarez, it seemed likely that there would be no fight at all. But this was not really what Jones or Willard wanted. Once again, Johnson was calling the tune.[40]

This long, drawn-out saga of "Where's Jack Johnson?" began to tell on those who made their living as sportswriters. Johnson's bout with Frank Moran in Paris in 1914 had been a fiasco and had flattened the interest in any bout in which Johnson might appear.

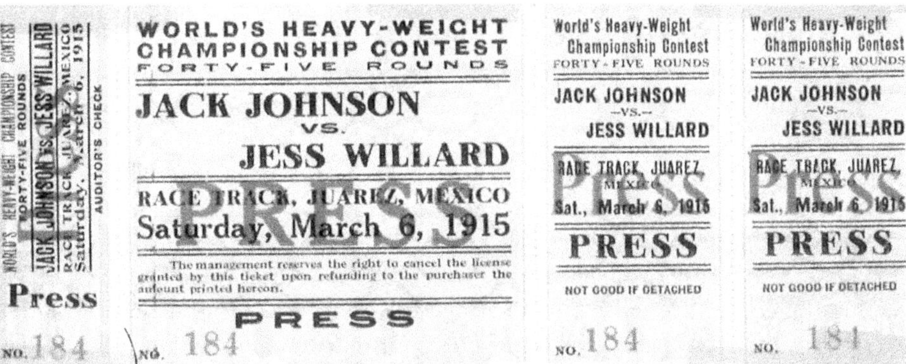

Tickets printed for the Johnson fight in Juarez, Mexico, March 6, 1915. This fight was transferred to Havana, Cuba.

Willard, on the other hand, could not excite crowds on his own. As Grantland Rice once wrote: "The tall White Hope carries as much magnetism as a carload of sawdust."[41]

Even if Johnson and Willard did get together in the ring it might not be a very good fight. "In his ring career to date," wrote one writer, "Willard has never shown aggressiveness in the ring, and boxes with a sort of slow, diffident style which leaves much to be desired if he is considered a championship possibility." If Willard was slow and diffident, Johnson was reported to be out of shape. He seemed not to be taking the fight seriously. Pictures taken of Johnson in Cuba before the fight showed him seriously overweight. Both fighters left their public concerned. Small town papers such as *The Evening Star* of Independence, Kansas, noted, "Little Interest in the Fight: Havana Mill stirs no excitement." Writers for larger papers published articles with headlines such as "Willard-Johnson to draw a Poor House" and "Jack Johnson in No Condition for Grueling Battle in Ring."[42]

Jack Curley arrived in Havana on March 2 and, after meeting with Johnson, sent a telegram to Tom Jones in El Paso, asking what it would take to get Willard to fight Johnson in Havana. Jones responded that he had already invested $18,000 in having the fight in Juarez and could not see it being any place else. At that news, Willard left El Paso for Los Angeles where his wife and family now lived. Ed Smith of *The Chicago Evening American*, who had been scheduled to be the referee, returned to Chicago, and even Jones himself left El Paso. Curley's telegram, despite Jones' reply, had been a blow to the solar plexus of Juarez's hopes.[43]

By March 6, *The Chicago Daily Tribune* announced that Johnson had won the argument and that the fight would occur in Havana the first week in April. "I could not convince Johnson that it would be safe for him to go to Mexico," Curley declared. Curley then cabled Willard to come to Havana with or without Tom Jones. Jones said he would not send Willard to Havana unless he was given a suitable guarantee. By this he meant that he needed money to get them there. According to Willard's later story, this money was advanced by Colonel Martin J. "Matt" Winn who headed the syndicate which ran Churchill Downs and the Kentucky Derby. With the help of Winn's money, by March 10, Willard and Jones had agreed to terms and were on their way to Havana.[44]

Everybody involved breathed a sigh of relief. The organizers did not have to worry about bandits and kidnappers troubling the fighters or their fans. General Mario Garcia Menocal, who had become president of Cuba in 1913, was in support of the event. Menocal was a graduate of Cornell University and ran the country with the assistance of the American government. By Cuban standards he was scarcely corrupt. But that did not mean that everybody was pleased. A group of planters, headed by Capitan Cushman A. Rice, head of the National Sporting Club in Havana, worried that permitting bi-racial bouts would create trouble. "There will be no fight between Jack Johnson and Jess Willard in Havana, or between any other black and white. There is no racial strife there now, and I do not intend to have any stirred up by having a Caucasian pitted against an Ethiopian if I and my friends can help it."[45]

In fact, the racial divide in Cuba was similar to that in the United States. In 1910 Cuba was among those countries which had banned the fight films of Johnson beating Jeffries for fear of riots. In 1912 a black revolt broke out in Oriente province and threatened Havana. And when Johnson arrived in Havana in February 1915, he and his party were thrown out of their hotel as undesirables. At the end of March, Johnson's white wife, Lucille, had gotten into a hair-pulling fight with a manicurist who refused to do her nails because Lucille had married a black man. The potential for riots was so strong that President Menocal decided to station a company of infantry and another company of cavalry at ringside. And on the day of the fight the streets were full of Cubans carrying little flags to show their support: the whites carried white flags for Willard while the blacks carried black flags for Johnson. The Johnson-Willard fight was possible in Cuba only because of the fame it brought to the island, but normal boxing matches between black and whites were banned. Still, Cushman Rice and the planters were unable to ban the Willard-Johnson fight.[46]

Boxing was an English sport and spread throughout the British Empire. It was not native to Spain or the Spanish-American colonies. As such, it was a new introduction to Cuba and most Cubans did not really understand its rules and rituals. Nonetheless, through the efforts of George M. Bradt, the publisher of *The Havana Daily Post*, and the North American planters, including Cushman Rice, Havana had enjoyed a number of boxing bouts. At the beginning of February, Bradt had built a new boxing arena known as the Stadium, in Maine Park on the waterfront. The grand opening on February 13 was a boxing match pitting Young Ahearn vs. Willie Lewis for the middleweight championship of the world. In an article published on February 2, Bradt had listed the fighters he was importing to Cuba, including Sam McVey, "Battling" Jim Johnson, and John Lester Johnson from New York, and Colin Bell from Australia. "It needs but the name of Jack Johnson to complete the list of crack heavyweights of the day," wrote Bradt. The unexpected arrival of Johnson was an answer to Bradt's prayers. And when it became known that the heavyweight championship was to be held there boxing was raised to a level of excellence unknown before. The local population went into a frenzy.[47]

By the end of March *The Florida Times-Union* of Jacksonville carried the Associated Press report:

> Havana is fight mad. Nothing but pugilism is being discussed in the clubs, hotels and homes by men and women of the city.... The task of educating the Cuban people to a full understanding of boxing now is under full headway. Boxers are gathering here from all parts of the United States and bouts are scheduled for every night this week. Windows and billboards are filled with fight cards and posters. Pugilists parade the streets, followed by crowds of boys and men. About the training camps groups of negro youths spend all day sparring.[48]

George Bradt had also brought in a large vaudeville group which played for a short time in the Stadium. While this did not prove successful, it did provide an interesting interlude when one of the vaudevillians, Miss Cecilia Wright Keith, proved to be a great fan of boxing. Miss Wright convinced Bradt to let her cover several of the boxing bouts which he had booked for the Stadium. She soon became a fixture of the boxing scene and stayed in Cuba to cover the Johnson-Willard fight when her troop left the island. She, not Nellie Bly, proved to be the first woman to cover a championship prizefight. As we shall see, she initially occupied a ringside seat at the Johnson fight until Johnson requested that she be moved. Then she wrote a fine article describing the fight from the perspective of Lucille Cameron Johnson.[49]

With politics out of the way, the sportswriters could finally get down to analyzing the prospects of the fight. And right off the bat they got things wrong. It was assumed that Willard was either 27 or 28 years old, or ten years younger than Johnson. This gave Willard a new advantage to add to his weight, height and length of reach. In fact, Willard was only three and one-half years younger than Johnson. He was 33 compared to Johnson's 37. In boxing terms, this made the fight between two elderly gentlemen. Other writers argued that the fight would be a mismatch because both Willard and Johnson were defensive fighters and no one would be the aggressor. Tommy Burns, despite previous experience, still believed that Johnson was basically yellow. But he did have one thing right when he told Willard: "If he lands a blow or two and doesn't hurt you he gets discouraged. If you play your cards right you'll surely be the next champion."[50]

Jack Curley, who had money invested, was concerned that there was not enough enthusiasm for the fight and worked vigorously to build up interest. He was delighted to see that the white Cuban aristocracy was quickly supportive of Willard. According to *The Havana Daily Post*, Willard's party was met at the dock by nearly 7,000 Cuban sport fans and "cheers for Willard were loud in the air." *The Havana Daily Post* stated that Willard "has been received with open arms and no doubt will have a following of thousands within a short time." The American papers noted many women in these large crowds attending the training camps. In fact, President Menocal's wife planned to give a tea for the society women in her box before the fight. With publicity finally going his way, Curley sent a letter to Charles Brill, the sports editor of Oklahoma City's *The Daily Oklahoman*, where Willard had begun his boxing career, telling him that Willard was certain to win the fight. He repeated this in other papers.[51]

Still the sportswriters noticed that there was little betting on the fight and that few of the seats in the stands at the Oriental Race Track were selling. Partially, the slow sales were due to the thought that Willard could not defeat Johnson, and partially they were due to the fact that the fight had originally been set for 11 a.m., Easter Sunday morning, April 4. Why this date was chosen is not clear, but gradually as sales resistance increased, it was decided to change the date from Easter Sunday to Monday, April 5. The promoters believed that they would sell 5,000 more tickets if the fight was moved from Sunday. President Menocal was persuaded to declare Monday a governmental holiday after 11 a.m. and insist that all of his government officials attend the fight.[52]

By March 26, the advanced ticket sales for the fight had reached over $50,000 with the promoters hoping that total receipts might reach $325,000. The Oriental Race Track could accommodate 10,000 people in the stands with another 10,000 in the infield. The same day it was announced that Jack Welsh of San Francisco would be named referee.[53]

Initially, there had been some fear that the fight might be fixed, but by the end of March it seemed clear that the fight was going to be an honest one. Both Willard and Johnson had trained themselves to be in fighting trim. The public still had faith in Jack Johnson and the betting odds were 3 to 1 and 2 to 1 for Johnson and against Willard.[54]

Experienced sportswriters began to pour into Cuba during the last week in March and the quality of analysis markedly improved. The Cubans were excited about the battle, and gradually those in the United States became excited as well. Some 5,000 spectators witnessed Willard work out at the Palm Garden at the Miramar Hotel where a ring had been set up, while 3,000 watched Johnson do his workouts at the Havana Stadium on the waterfront. And gradually the odds began to shift in Willard's favor.[55]

In a sagacious article published in *The Washington Post* on March 30, both Willard and Johnson laid out their strategy for the fight. Willard said that he did not plan to rush Johnson, but rather let Johnson come to him. The contract had allowed Curley to set the length of the fight anywhere between 20 and 45 rounds and Curley chose to have the fight 45 rounds. This was tailor-made for Willard.

> This isn't any hurry-up fight, and my chances will increase with each passing round. This is something of an endurance contest, and I think that after 20 rounds or so Johnson will be winded and worn to a point where I can go in and beat him into unconsciousness.
>
> One thing is that I won't rush Johnson—not for fifteen rounds or so. I'd be a fool to do so. If I did, I'd be playing right into Johnson's hands. I know his game. It's a waiting one—but I can outwait him.[56]

Johnson recognized Willard's plan as a good one, but said that there were ways he could force Willard into an aggressive posture, even if he did not want to do so.

> You know that there's tricks in all trades and in this ring trade there's a trick by which you can force the other fellow to rush you whenever you want to. If Willard doesn't voluntarily rush me as soon as I want and as often as I like, why, I'll just have to work that little trick of mine and get him rushing—and rushing fast, too. Jeffries wasn't going to rush me, you know. He was going to wait back until I rushed him. But Jim did the rushing—and he started early, too.[57]

In retrospect, Johnson made a bad mistake in signing for a 45-round fight. He clearly believed that he could out-box Willard and dispose of him within 20 rounds. Had the fight lasted only 20 rounds, Johnson would have won. But the fact that it was scheduled for 45 rounds was his undoing. Jess Willard was stronger and more durable than Johnson realized and the extra length of the fight was the thing that made Willard champion.[58]

Both men felt that they would win by a knockout. Willard was recognized to have a powerful punch and had knocked out a number of men, while Johnson was not a fighter who normally knocked out his opponents. Still Johnson planned to do it this time. Johnson mentioned his two best punches, a blow to the stomach and a right uppercut when the other fellow comes into a clinch. He tried both of these, but they did not work on Willard. Willard, on the other hand, said his best punch was a right to the jaw. This, indeed, proved to be the blow that knocked Johnson out. As always it is difficult to predict in advance the outcome of a fight, but clearly Willard's strategy proved the correct one. It was interesting to see how prescient his description of the fight would prove.[59]

By April 1, the serious training was over. It was silly time again. Willard had reached his fighting weight of about 240 pounds and Johnson was about 225. On his birthday, March 31, Johnson celebrated by running five miles, pushing a steam roller and then wrestling a bull. The next day, Willard went him one better by running six miles, wrestling with a mule and jumping over a five foot high rail fence. Then Nature intervened. Heavy rains fell in Cuba which caused Johnson to curtail his training. The storm moved north and became a rare April hurricane which traveled along the East Coast of the United States. Three people were killed in Richmond, a massive blizzard buried New York City in ten inches of snow, and 19 inches fell on Philadelphia. An 80 mile per hour gale struck Cape Cod accompanied by the blizzard. The "Eve of Easter" storm of 1915 showed that even a world championship fight had to take a back seat to Nature.[60]

In Europe, the war, which the French General Joseph Joffre had predicted would be over in a few months, dragged on. It had settled down into bloody trench warfare. And in an unexpected way, the prize fight between Willard and Johnson took on universal significance. It was no longer just a battle between white and black; now it became a battle between good and evil. The fight between Johnson and Willard became an analogue to the fight between Germany and the Allies and gave encouragement to the soldiers. Even in the darkest moments, sport can offer men relief from tragedy.[61]

Grantland Rice too, was astonished by the fact that in the midst of the war, European soldiers were focused on the Havana fight. He drew a contrast between their war and the Big Fight.

The Big Fight

("Thousands of troops in the European trenches have been waiting eagerly to hear the result of the big fight between Johnson and Willard." Cable)

Above their heads the shrapnel shrieked
Its blood-red song of hate;
The 12-inch guns rang down the field
The anthem of their fate;
Blood-clotted in the stinking trench
Across the livid night,
Between the crashing of the guns
They talked about—The Fight

They stood among the Million Dead
Beneath the rotting loam;
But no one dreamed of peace again—
And no one talked of home;
But where the blood of thousands left
A carmine trail of blight,
They talked of jabs and uppercuts
They talked about—The Fight

Between their trenches in the mud
The disappearing dead
Showed here a hand and there a foot
And here a mangled head;
And so with blood and bones and skull
On through the waning light
They sowed their Crop of Death, but still
They talked about—The Fight.[62]

Jackson Stovall, writing in the Negro paper, *The Chicago Defender*, continued the parallel with the European war:

> Should Willard ... send the pugilistic Napoleon to the canvas for the count of ten, the vast assemblage which is sure to gather would go into a frenzy. The defeat of Germany in her struggle with the allies would pale into insignificance, so to speak, in comparison.
>
> The Caucasian race throughout the domain of Uncle Sam would celebrate his passing and a wave of depression would sweep over the loyal members of Ethiopia.[63]

Then, with everybody focused on the final preparations for the fight, Johnson astonished them all when he announced that he planned to put on a six-round exhibition with the Negro, Sam McVey. McVey was a legitimate champion candidate. Before Jack became champion, McVey and Johnson had three fights, all of which Johnson won. But once he was champion, Johnson attempted to behave exactly as the white heavyweights had done. He refused to give any of the other great Negro fighters such as McVey, Sam Langford, Joe Jeannette and Jeff Clark a chance to dethrone him. Johnson effectively invoked the color bar like all of his predecessors since John L. Sullivan. The one exception to this occurred on December 19, 1913, while in Paris, after fleeing the United States, when Jack fought another Negro, "Battling" Jim Johnson, to a draw. Jack took the fight because he was broke and needed money. Although Jim Johnson was not the type of fighter who would ordinarily give Jack trouble, Jack nearly lost the fight because he broke his forearm sending a blow to Jim's head in the third round. Jack fought the rest of the ten rounds with a broken arm. Jack made certain that the McVey fight not have similar problems. As a result, Johnson and McVey agreed to a sparring match and the fight itself was billed as an exhibition, which meant that the championship was not at stake.[64]

Still, Jack Curley was afraid that Johnson would be hurt in his bout with McVey, or even worse be knocked out, and that would ruin the fight with Willard. But in fact the event turned out to be a powder puff sparring match and no damage was done to either man.[65]

The day before the fight most newspapers carried the particulars of the fighters and the fight arrangements. The locale was the Oriental Race Track at Marianao, ten miles outside of Havana on a streetcar line. The day of the fight was to be Monday, April 5, 1915, and was supposed to begin at 12:30 p.m. The fight was to be according to the Marquess of Queensberry rules using five-ounce boxing gloves. The ring was originally to be 19 feet square, but Johnson objected to that as being too small. It then was expanded to 20 feet square with a 3-foot apron all around. The fight was to be a maximum of 45 three-minute rounds (making it potentially the longest championship fight since Joe Gans defeated Battling Nelson in 42 rounds at Goldfield, Nevada, in 1906). Johnson was to receive his money upfront for the fight plus expenses. Willard was supposed to receive $10,000 after the fight and all expenses were paid. But since prizefight promoters were not very good accountants, in reality, this meant that Willard would get nothing. His payoff was to be from future events, and Willard knew that. Jack Welsh of San Francisco was to be the referee and the stakeholder was a wealthy wine salesman, "Pommery" Bob Vernon of New York. Jack Johnson weighed approximately 230 pounds while Willard weighed approximately 240 pounds, but the official weigh-in was to be in the ring just before the fight. Willard stood 6 feet, 6¾ inches high and Johnson 6 feet ½ inches. Johnson had a reach of 73¼ inches while Willard had a reach of 83¼ inches. Johnson was 38 while Willard was supposedly 28 but was in reality 33 years old.[66]

One other fact of importance: Lucille Cameron Johnson, Johnson's wife, was with him in Havana. It was her job to get the money for the fight before it was over, so that there would be no question of chicanery by Bob Vernon or Jack Curley. But it was also her fate to rise and fall with her husband. As they had no children, his fate was her fate.[67]

Harriet Evans Willard, "Hattie," Jess Willard's wife, was not in Havana. Very rarely did she attend any of Jess' fights. She was at home in Los Angeles with her four small children, Zella (7/8), Francis (4), Jess Jr. (16 months), and Enid (5 months). The day before the fight was to begin Hattie Willard sent Jess a telegram. She was trying to think of something to say when Jess Jr. tottered up to her and said, "Da da." Immediately she sent the wire saying, "Little Jess is waiting for you to win."[68]

Unlike many fighters, Jess Willard was a true family man. Their welfare was critical to him. He was fighting for them. "It is a case of must with me. After this fight, if I lose, there can be nothing for me in the fight game. I have a wife and four children waiting for me, praying for me in Los Angeles. I can't get a dollar if I lose; if I win I can clean up a fortune though later work. It's my only chance."[69]

The Fight and the Immediate Aftermath

The day of the fight, Monday, April 5, 1915, dawned partly cloudy. The rains that had swept over Havana in the past few days were gone, but several dark cloud banks hung over the sea as late as 11 a.m. By 12:30 p.m. when the match was supposed to start the sky had cleared and although the day started cool, by the end of the fight the temperature had reached 70 degrees.[70]

Prior to the fight the Cuban military did a search of the grounds. Several companies of soldiers were stationed around the grounds as well as two troops of cavalry who surrounded the field. Outside of the race track on a circle of green hills soldiers were stationed on the higher points to keep pirate film crews from creating pictures of the fight.

By 11:30 several thousand fans had arrived and filled in most of the cheaper seats, but the more expensive seats remained unoccupied until later. The stands and the infield gradually filled with whites wearing white straw hats. The outskirts filled in with blacks, many of whom Curley let in for a dollar a ticket. The betting odds had shifted from 2 to 1 for Johnson to 7 to 5 in favor of Willard. Attendance at the ring was estimated by the American papers at 15,000 to 20,000 with a few of the $20 seats still unsold. *The Havana Post* estimated that 32,000 people watched the fight of which only 5,000 were Americans.

At 12:30, the ring announcer and motion picture entrepreneur, Fred Mace, presented to the crowd Johnson's receipt for $29,000, the balance due him for the fight after payments for expenses and travel had been deducted. Although the fight was supposed to begin at 12:30 and Johnson himself had arrived at 12:25, he did not step into the ring until 12 minutes past 1 p.m. He was dressed in a gray bathrobe which, when removed, revealed bright blue trunks with no belt or particular colors. This was unusual as during the previous century it had been common for boxers to wear a flag or a pennant as a belt to show their allegiance to their country or cause. Johnson showed no allegiance to anyone. Once in the ring his only concern was to look to where his wife, Lucille, was sitting.

Four minutes later, wild cheering from the crowd exploded and Jess Willard appeared dressed in a heavy red sweater, blue trousers and a black hat. He stripped to reveal dark blue trunks with an American flag as a belt. The men shook hands in the center of the ring. Johnson noted the presence of the woman reporter, Cecilia Wright Keith, in the press row at the edge of the ring and asked that she be removed. His stated reason was that he did not want a woman to hear what he might have to say during the fight. But he may also have been concerned about the fact that in both the Burns and Jeffries fights, those sitting next to the ring had been splattered with blood, as Johnson destroyed his opponent. For whatever reason, Miss Keith obligingly retired to an adjacent box further back.

Both men were then weighed in the ring. Willard weighed 238 pounds and Johnson weighed 225. After weigh-in both boxers put on their bandages and gloves in the ring. They shook hands again, the ring was cleared and time was called at 1:28 p.m.[71]

According to the written reports, Johnson began the first round aggressively with a series of uppercuts to Willard's jaw. To those who watch what remain of the fight films, it appears that Willard tried to land the first blow and that he crowded Johnson around the ring until the end of the round when Johnson launched a flurry of blows to Willard's head. The round was awarded to Johnson.

The New York Herald writer contrasted Johnson's behavior to that of Willard. Johnson was cheerful and laughing when he entered the ring and had a carefree manner which contrasted with the solemn, frightened appearance of Willard. "Willard went through the first two rounds as though he did not know exactly what was happening." After the bell, Johnson told his seconds, "I can hit him any place at any time I want to."[72]

In the second round he attacked Willard's body and then drove him to the ropes with a series of blows to the face. Willard, on the other hand, found Johnson hard to hit in the head and so drove for his body. Willard tried a hard right swing in the third round but missed and both men laughed. When Johnson then landed a hard left to Willard's body, Jess asked: "Is that the way you do it?" Willard tried to hit Johnson in the fourth round but Johnson merely laughed then landed several blows to the body and one to the face that cut Willard's lip. First blood to Johnson. Johnson was, in Willard's view, boxing superbly.

In rounds five, six and seven, Johnson continued to pound Willard's body with both fists and drove him back upon the ropes. Johnson rubbed the laces of his gloves against Willard's cut lip. Willard appeared rattled initially and only at the end of round seven did he seem to be able to hit Johnson. However, despite all of Johnson's efforts, Willard showed no real damage. His lip was cut and his body showed red welts where he had been hit, but he was still standing.

By the beginning of round eight Willard seemed to be gaining confidence.

"The fighters battered each other across the ring. The negro having the better of it. Willard landed on Johnson's mouth. Johnson uppercut Willard over the heart. Willard bounced off the ropes and landed a left to the jaw. Round ended with the negro swinging blows to Willard's head. Slight advantage to Johnson."[73]

Round eight was a mental turning point in the fight. Johnson had made an incredible effort to wear Willard down and put him out. But as Tommy Burns had predicted, once Johnson found that his punches had no real effect upon Willard, he began to get discouraged. Willard, on the other hand, was encouraged. Having survived the early rounds and finding that the best blows Johnson could throw at him did little harm, Willard began to move from defense to offense. As he put it: "By the eighth round I had the feel of the fight and figured I was on to anything Johnson could do. I mixed with him and felt I could handle him in any department. I was hitting him with double punches when I got an opening and felt I could win any time now. My advisers told me to keep up the wearing-down process and I heeded what they said."[74]

Jess shaking hands with Jack Johnson before the fight, with Jack Welsh, the referee, standing between them, April 5, 1915.

In round nine Johnson hit Willard hard, and started one of his ears bleeding. But Johnson's blows appeared to lack power. The crowd sensed that Johnson was weakening, and shouted, "Kill the black bear!" Johnson immediately rallied and hit Willard with three hard driving hooks to the stomach. Willard responded by driving a left to Johnson's face and causing his mouth to bleed. Then Johnson drove Willard to the ropes with a series of hard blows. Slight advantage to Johnson in the round.

In rounds 10, 11 and 12, Johnson continued to hammer Willard on the body and the face, but despite his best efforts, his blows were having little effect. At the beginning of round ten, Johnson was slow to leave his corner, but he rallied to knock Willard to the ropes again and staggered him with a right chop to the head. With the crowd jeering at him, he tried to rattle Willard by talking to him. Willard angrily answered in kind. In round 12 Johnson was able to cut Willard's cheek, but the body and head blows seemed to have no effect and despite the beating he was taking, Willard walked spryly to his corner at the bell. Had Willard been a lesser man or had this fight been a modern championship bout of no more than 15 rounds, Johnson would have won handily. Johnson was far ahead on points and Willard still had not shown championship skills.

By round 13 Willard's entire body was red with welts from the blows he was receiving. Willard drove Johnson to the ropes, but then Johnson jarred him with a left hook to the jaw, followed by two left hooks to the body. In round 14, Johnson remained the aggressor. Willard missed a right uppercut and Johnson slammed him on the mouth with his left. Willard laughed. Johnson began to miss some of his leads and Willard drove a hard right to Jack's ear. Johnson continued to pound Willard's body. In round 15, with the crowd taunting Johnson, he rushed Willard to the ropes again and delivered five hard blows. Then he remarked, "What a grand old man," to Willard. Jess grinned at the remark and at the blows Jack delivered. At the end of the round both men were slugging it out toe to toe in the center of the ring. As Willard recalled the struggle: "Johnson was landing

The Oriental Race Track at Marianao, ten miles outside Havana, Cuba, where the Johnson fight ultimately occurred on April 5, 1915.

a lot but the punches lacked steam and did no special harm. My cheeks and lips were cut but he couldn't put any solid stuff on me. The hard training I had done was paying off. I felt he was getting weaker and I was getting stronger as the bout progressed. In the 14th round I started using my uppercut. Johnson's leads were beginning to go astray."[75]

By round 16 Johnson had lost much of his strength. Nonetheless, he had not given up. He missed a left to the head. Thwarted, Johnson said, "Willard is a good kid." Johnson then rushed him to the ropes and landed two terrific swings to Willard's side. Jess was slightly unsteady as he walked to his corner. Hattie Willard, reading the telegraph reports in California, recalled being concerned at this time.

Willard recovered and began round 17 with a right to Johnson's body and a left to the head. Jack drove Willard to the corner and landed two blows to the head and a hook to the body. Then he followed up with two blows to the head, but the round was basically even. As Jess remembered it: "In round seventeen I reached him with several solid punches and his counters didn't bother me at all."[76]

In the 18th round Johnson hammered at Willard's chest and stomach and then hit him twice in the jaw, but nothing seemed to work. Willard, after many attempts, landed a straight left to Johnson's face and a right to the jaw. Johnson won the round but he was beginning to lose the fight.

The 19th round was the last round Johnson won. Willard ceased to be on defense and became the aggressor. Johnson stood in the middle of the ring and blocked Willard's blows. As a result, few blows got through and no real damage was done. But it was clear that Johnson could no longer lead, and that his power was gone. When Willard got back to his corner, his manager, Tom Jones, asked: "Does he seem tired, Jess?" "I could throw him over the ropes," said Willard. "I can beat him now any time."[77]

Willard opened the twentieth round with two light blows to Johnson's head to which Johnson said: "Lead again, kid." Willard smiled and someone in the crowd yelled, "Hurry up, we want to see the races," referring to the fact that races were to follow the fight. Willard landed a hard blow to Johnson's jaw. Johnson immediately cut loose and they battled across the ring, while the crowd went frantic. Then Willard drove a hard right and left to Johnson's body at the bell. This was the first round Willard had won. As he described in his autobiography: "I felt Johnson was ready to go about the 20th round but my corner men told me he might be stalling and cautioned against taking chances. I could see that Johnson was definitely weakening but I continued to fight as I was told."[78]

Johnson too felt that he was ready to collapse. He asked Harry Frazee to bring Jack Curley to his corner as soon as possible. Curley was in the box-office counting the receipts and only made it to Johnson's corner by the 25th round. Johnson leaned down: "Take my wife to the gate, Jack. I'm going fast and I don't want her to see the finish if I am to be knocked out."[79]

In both rounds 21 and 22 the pace slowed considerably. Johnson made a few attempts to hook to Willard's body, Willard directed a blow to Johnson's face, and they fell into a clinch. Johnson walked around the ring unmolested while Willard tried a right-hand swing and missed. Both fighters laughed. Round 22 began with more clinching. Johnson was clearly tired and showing the effects of the battle. "In the 22nd round I hammered at his body with heavy punches and knew he felt the effects of the blows," said Willard later.[80]

In round 23 Willard immediately rushed into a clinch with Johnson and threw his whole weight on his opponent. When he broke the clinch he shot two lefts to Johnson's face and then added two more and clinched again. Johnson did not throw a blow in the entire round. In round 24 Willard repeated the same pattern, clinching and throwing his weight upon Johnson. Johnson tried a few weak blows only to be met by a left smash to his face at the bell. In round 25 it was clear that Johnson was attempting to hold on and win the fight on points at the end of round 45. However, Willard was dictating the pace at this time. He forced Johnson to fight and then hit Jack a massive blow to the heart which shook Johnson. Willard then hit Johnson with a fast left to the jaw and a left to the mouth. Johnson staggered back to his corner at the bell. The heart punch, with which Willard had won his motion picture fight for Universal Studios in January, won the real fight with Jack Johnson. After Willard hit Johnson with that blow in round 25, Johnson was all in. As *The New York Herald* reported:

> Just one look which "Jack" Johnson of Texas, shot in the direction of his wife, who occupied a seat near ringside, told the story of his impending defeat here to-day. As he left his corner at the beginning of the twenty-sixth round he knew he was a beaten man, but his wife still continued to yell encouraging words, serenely confident that he was merely deferring the overthrow of the giant "Jess" Willard....
>
> Johnson walked forward a few steps, then looked pitifully toward his wife. That glance was meaningless to most of the spectators, but it warned others that at last Johnson had come to his "swan song." His expression was so hopelessly one of despair and helplessness that those who saw it will never forget. It was as though Johnson had called aloud to his wife:—
>
> "The end has come. They've been clamoring for it this last five years. Now they've got me."[81]

Willard's comments were similar: "In round 23 I battered and cuffed Johnson about and he did not strike an effective blow in return. He had found that he couldn't knock me out and was trying to conserve himself for a decision win. In the 25th round I hit him hard—almost at will—and sensed that he was about ready to go."[82]

Willard had opened the 26th round with a smash to the body. Johnson tired to clinch. When Jack Welsh, the referee, broke the clinch, Willard smashed Johnson with a right and a left to the body. Johnson clinched again and looked over his shoulder to where his wife had been sitting. Willard then smashed Johnson again with a right to the jaw. Johnson tried to clinch and hold on to Willard as he was falling, but Willard stepped away, and Johnson fell backwards to the canvas and out. As he fell, his right arm went up over his face, as if to shield his eyes from the glare of the sun while Jack Welsh counted him out. The fight was over.

As Willard remembered it:

> I went to him fast in the 26th round and rammed lefts and rights to his body. He tried to clinch and I broke free and bobbed his head with a right. We worked into center ring and I pushed another right into his head. He drooped and I lined up another shot which landed solidly on his jaw. He went down, almost without staggering. Referee Jack Welsh counted Johnson out and raised my hand as victor after one minute and twenty-six seconds of the 26th round. All I could think of at the time was how good it would be to get out of that hot ring and into the shade again.[83]

According to Robert Edgren, "That was as hard a knockout as ever was seen in the ring. After it Johnson's arms, legs and whole body quivered as he was helped to his corner, and were still quivering when he stumbled from the ring 10 minutes later."[84]

The writer for Richard Fox's *National Police Gazette* also argued that Johnson had been knocked out: "This punch [to the point of the Jaw] won the championship of the world, for the negro dropped unconscious to the floor and was counted out." He also rejected any thought that the fight had been faked.

"Taking it all in all it was one of the most satisfactory fights that was ever contested for the title of champion, and all suspicion of the result being prearranged was removed by the vicious manner in which every round was contested and the way in which Willard achieved his victory at the end."[85]

In his analysis of the fight, Edgren noted three things that had usually worked for Johnson that in fact did not work this time. Typically in clinches, Johnson was able to pull down the arms of his opponent, and throw his weight upon him, thus wearing him down. But when fighting Willard,

> when Johnson tried to pull Willard's arms down and "lie" on him, Willard let his arms go and jumped up a few inches, throwing his whole weight on Johnson until the black man managed to wriggle away from beneath that 247 [238] pounds. After that, Johnson didn't try to use his weight.
>
> And in wrestling—his favorite stunt—the black champion had none the best of it. He tried to hold Willard close—too close to use the body punch. Willard punched anyway. Johnson held him and smiled to the crowd. Willard kept on punching. Johnson lost his smile and broke away. Another old stunt of his gone wrong.[86]

The third thing which usually worked for Johnson was subduing his opponent with a flurry of punches from all angles. Johnson was not a knock-out fighter, but because of that he was a brilliantly clever boxer. He had power in his blows which, when combined in groups, generally brought his opponent to the canvas. This too he tried on Jess Willard, and this too failed him.[87]

It was slightly after 3 p.m. when Johnson was counted out in the ring. It had been the longest heavyweight championship fight in modern boxing history. The crowds could not be contained and suddenly poured into the ring to congratulate Jess Willard. They ignored Johnson who was lying on his back and was in danger of being trampled. According to William H. Rocap of *The Chicago Daily Tribune,* Johnson's seconds, led by Sam McVey, had some difficulty dragging him to his corner. A picture printed in *The St. Louis Post-Dispatch* showed one of Johnson's seconds bending over him attempting to pick him up as fans fill the ring. *Sic transit gloria mundi.*[88]

The Cuban military flooded the ring to protect Willard and drive the spectators out. They drove him back to Havana through cheering crowds. The road was lined with whites who celebrated Willard's victory. Among the cheering throng were many Negro children waving black flags thinking that Johnson had won again. But it was not to be.

The Associated Press version of these last events was significantly different. According to their version, Johnson did not have to be dragged by his seconds to his corner. Instead, "a second or two after Jack Welsh, the referee, had counted to ten, Johnson quickly got up. It was well he did so, for a moment later a rush of spectators to the fighting platform all but smothered the pugilists." This version is not confirmed by the films of the last round which, in fact, show members of the crowd standing by Johnson's head and walking around him as he lay flat on his back on the floor of the ring. There is no picture of Johnson leaping to his feet to go to his corner.[89]

Further, it was the Associated Press' opinion that Jack Johnson had not actually been knocked out.

"There is much discussion tonight, and probably will be for a long time, among the followers of the fighting game as to whether Johnson was really knocked out. In the sense

The confusion in the ring after Jack Johnson was knocked out. Note Johnson lying on his back on the ring floor and being helped up by his second, Tom Flanagan.

of being smashed into unconsciousness he certainly was not put out. The consensus of opinion is that Johnson expected and knew that there was no possibility of his winning; so when knocked down he chose to take the count rather than rise and stand further punishment."[90]

This "consensus of opinion," plus the fact that when Johnson fell his arms came up over his face as if to shield his eyes from the sun, has tarnished Jess Willard's win. The old cries of "fake" which had been raised before the fight when Johnson seemed to be out of condition had died away during the fight when he demonstrated that he was in superb condition for nearly 20 rounds. At the end of the fight a single cry of "fake" rang out as Johnson tried to escape Willard's blows. But the cry was not taken up by the crowd.

More importantly, the Associated Press recalled that "Johnson had often stated that fighting was a business and that he would not foolishly submit to repeated knockdowns when he found he had met his master." On the other hand, in an interview three days before the fight, Robert Edgren asked Johnson what he would do if he lost: "Why, I don't think there's much chance of that, although we all get it some time. If Willard beats me he'll have to knock me cold to do it, and if he knocks me out the first thing I'll do when I get over it, will be to congratulate him. If any man can beat me I won't hold a grudge against him. I'll show them I'm a sportsman even if they won't let me come home to my own country."[91]

Willard proved to be Johnson's master, and Johnson behaved exactly as he told Edgren he would. But did Johnson decide to lie down when he realized that he had no hope? That is a question that remains still today.

The Associated Press version rests on two points, the first being that the statement that Johnson was back on his feet "a second or two after Jack Welsh, the referee had counted to ten." This is demonstrably false based upon the surviving footage of the motion picture film and the picture in *The St. Louis Post-Dispatch*. Although the film does not show exactly how and when Johnson got to his feet, the picture in *The Post-Dispatch*, and other testimony shows that he had to be helped to his feet by his seconds and that he clearly was not faking the knockdown. Herbert Bayard Swope, the editor of *The New York World* and member of the Algonquin Roundtable, who was at ringside, wrote that "perhaps five seconds after the counting stopped, Johnson's seconds managed to pull him to his feet and half carry him to his corner." *The New York Herald* had a similar story:

> There was no time, nor no thought for the loser. He still lay prone on the canvas as Willard's newly made admirers swarmed about him like a pack of flies. Johnson's wife had screamed in anguish as the negro toppled over and "Tom" Flanagan, his trainer, cursed roundly at the turn of fate. Flanagan was one of the first to reach the prostrate form of the fallen champion....
>
> Whether the blow struck by Willard had dulled his senses or whether the physical exhaustion was so complete as to make him speechless it is hard to say, but the defeated champion never uttered a word as Welch [sic] and Flanagan pulled him to his feet and managed to get him to his corner.[92]

Johnson's supposed agility in getting up off the floor has been used to support the second point: "In the sense of being smashed into unconsciousness he certainly was not put out. The consensus of opinion is that Johnson expected and knew that there was no possibility of his winning; so when knocked down he chose to take the count rather than rise and stand further punishment." This judgment cannot be supported or denied by the film evidence.

Had Johnson pretended to be knocked out, the argument would then have been strengthened by the picture of Johnson hopping to his feet as soon as the count was over. But he manifestly did not do this. He still could have pretended to be knocked out and lain on the canvas for a longer time. But when the crowd surged into the ring and nearly stepped on his head as he lay on the floor, had he been pretending, he would have naturally reacted. But we do not see that in the films.

The "consensus of opinion" which held that Johnson lay down rather than face further punishment is contrary to all boxing experience. It assumes that Johnson was not as great a champion as his predecessors, John L. Sullivan, Gentleman Jim Corbett, Robert Fitzsimmons, James J. Jeffries, and Tommy Burns. All of them refused to lay down when confronted by a greater man. The real consensus is that champions never give up. They fight until they are defeated and can fight no more. It is this which makes them champions in the first place.

Jack Johnson might be the exception to this rule. He might have been, as Tommy Burns thought he was, yellow at heart and afraid of punishment. But this is not the picture we have of him fighting 26 rounds. He fought his heart out. He was a gallant warrior who earned a warrior's fate. He did not give up. He gave it all he had. It is an insult to his memory to think that he quit when he still had fight in his body.

The day after the fight, Johnson himself confirmed the fact that he fought as hard as he was able, and that he was knocked out.

> I met a better man and was beaten. I did the best I could and put forth the best that was in me to win, but despite the rain of blows Willard seemed unaffected though I hit him hard enough and often enough in the first twenty rounds to floor ten ordinary heavyweights. One consolation I have is that I proved to my friends that I was in condition. This was shown by the fight up to the twentieth round. No man could have tried harder than I to win, but I was up against a man who wouldn't crumple when I hit him and whose right to the jaw was powerful enough to take the championship away from me.[93]

There is simply no truth to the speculation that Johnson quit in the ring.

Grantland Rice aptly summed up Johnson's defeat in verse:

> Gone are the golden molars
> That flashed on a world at bay;
> Gone is the regal bearing
> That sticks with the champion's sway;
> Flat on his back in the resin
> With the tale of his glory done—
> Merely a middle-aged fat man
> Blinking up in the Cuban sun.[94]

The Most Famous Man in America

The Havana fight had made Jess Willard the most famous man in America. The quest to find the man who could bring back the heavyweight crown to the white race was over. Jess Willard had become "the Great White Hope." The Cubans were the first to react. After bringing him in a cavalcade to Havana under military escort, they tendered him a dinner and a reception the day after the fight at the Stadium. They remained enthusiastic over the new champion and could not do enough for him. Everywhere Willard went he was met by cheering crowds. Both Willard and Johnson were presented with gold watches by the citizens of Havana, while Willard and Jack Curley presented Johnson a loving cup. But it was Willard who was the hero of the hour.

The decision in Havana triggered celebrations all over America. William H. Rocap commented, "The scene of jubilation which followed the victory by Willard was one that has never been equaled in America at any fight," while Herbert Bayard Swope wrote: "Never in the history of the ring, which stretched back hundreds of years, was there such a wildly, hysterically, shrieking enthusiastic crowd as the 14,000 men and women who begged Willard to wipe out the stigma that they and hundreds of thousands of others, especially in the South, believe rested on the white race through a negro holding the championship."[95]

The joy of the white Cubans was replicated in the streets of many American cities. Sid Keener, sports editor of *The St. Louis Times*, described the "thousands and thousands of fight fans as well as thousands and thousands of ordinary citizens who flooded the downtown streets waiting for the final decision." When the verdict was in, "the thousands and thousands screamed 'Willard wins.' They acted like crazy people."[96]

According to *The New York Tribune*, "The roar which arose from the crowd which packed Park Row yesterday afternoon when The Tribune bulletin board proclaimed that Johnson had been knocked out would have done credit to a Presidential victory. For a moment the air was filled with hats and newspapers. Respectable business men pounded their unknown neighbors on the back and capered about like children."[97]

In Anadarko, Oklahoma, John Willard, Jess Willard's older brother, was the center of a mob of happy farmers who congratulated him at his brother's victory. The whole community was rejoicing that the championship belt had come back into white hands.[98]

The next day, April 7, Willard was about set to sail on the steamer *Governor Cobb* back to Key West, when Johnson came to see him off. The crowd that had assembled to see Willard was so large that it delayed the sailing for two hours. But it fell silent when the two men met.

> "I'm glad to see you, Jack," said Willard.
>
> "Glad to see you again, boy," said Johnson, looking up at the face of the man who had torn his title away. "I just came down to say good-by and say I wish you all the luck in the world. I hope good luck will follow you all of your life. I hope you'll keep the championship as long as you want it. Take good care of yourself and save your money. Then when you're old you won't have anything to be sorry for."
>
> Johnson shook hands with many friends who were going away with the Willard party. Turning, he started down the gangplank, hesitated and turned back again.
>
> "Boys," he said, "you're the lucky fellows. You're going home. It's hell to come down here to the boat and see you going back to the good old United States and not be able to go along."
>
> Then as Johnson turned to go, the immense throng, which had been silent during the meeting of the ex-champion and champion, burst into cheers for the conquered as well as the conqueror.
>
> Willard was affected by this meeting as was the crowd. "What do you think," asked Jess, "of Johnson coming down to see me off? That fellow ought to have been white. I know lots of white men who wouldn't have done that. I'm almost sorry I beat him."[99]

When the *Governor Cobb* steamed into Key West harbor later that day, it was met by a flotilla of ships of all kinds, flying flags of welcome, with their crews lining the decks cheering. Several government torpedo boats turned on their sirens to salute the new champion. Despite a bout of seasickness, Willard appeared the conquering hero as he stood on the upper deck of the *Governor Cobb* waving his sombrero in reply. When he came down the gangplank to the shore, the crowd, held back by the police, broke through the barriers and rushed towards him.

"Soon Willard was surrounded by a throng of cheering, jumping, gesticulating persons, and he was half carried to another end of the pier, where a committee from the board of trade bundled him into a carriage for a parade up to the town. A band headed the procession to Willard's hotel, and he was given an enthusiastic greeting all the way."[100]

Robert Edgren agreed with this assessment: "If he had saved the country he could hardly have received more frantic applause from the white citizens of Key West who were massed to meet him. They rushed from every side to shake his hand or touch his coat sleeves, or even to get near enough to see him clearly."[101] The next day, April 8, Willard's party hired a Pullman railroad car to carry him north to New York: "The day's trip was made amid a succession of spontaneous receptions. Word of the approach of the new champion was flashed ahead and everywhere flags and bunting were flying, bands playing and hundreds waiting in the heat at stations between Daytona, Florida, and Savannah, Georgia. At every crossroad and depot were throngs numbering from a few score to thousands."[102]

In an interview with Robert Edgren on March 30, Johnson made a prediction about the fight and its aftermath: "I'm going to win this fight. And then I'll never fight anybody again. This is positively the last one. I'm going to buy a farm in France, about 14 miles out of Paris, as soon as the war is over, and then I'll settle down. I'll raise my own chickens and hogs and fodder, and be the only real retired heavyweight champion of the world."[103] This boast that he would retire to a farm in France was a romantic notion of Johnson's and might well have been what he intended, but the war did not allow it. It also conflicted with other statements that he had made about his plans once the fight was over. On March 19 he announced that he planned to buy a hotel in Havana. "I will become a citizen of Cuba and settle down here for life." The next day he announced to the press that he would return to Chicago immediately after his fight with Willard. "I am getting tired of knocking around. As soon as I have whipped Willard, I will come back to Chicago and take my medicine as the government has fixed it for me." In truth, Johnson did not know what he would do after the fight, and neither, we will learn, did Jess Willard. The outcome was a surprise to both of them.[104]

Jess Willard was totally unprepared for the reception that awaited him. Before the fight he was just an ordinary man, a bit taller than most, but still nothing special. And had he lost, that is what he would have remained. But because he had won, he became a famous celebrity. Willard did not know how to handle his fame. He often said that if he were a speaker, he would not have become a boxer. But on the train trip to New York, he was asked for a speech at every stop. He manfully answered every request to speak to the crowds, but by the end of the first day, his responses grew slower and slower and his speeches shorter and shorter. In addition, after shaking hands with hundreds of individuals, he began to wrap his right hand in bandages and later put his arm in a sling, as his hand was becoming sore from all those who wanted to shake the hand that knocked out Jack Johnson.[105]

As he made his triumphant journey north, he was besieged not only by well-wishers but by offers to fight new challengers as well as offers to go on the stage. At a time when the average wage in the country was only about $600 per year, it was said that Hammerstein's Victoria Theatre in New York City had offered him $5,000 for a week's engagement. He was supposedly offered $100,000 for his share of the theatrical receipts for the coming year.[106]

Then there were the crazy stories. According to the savants of Paris, Willard did not become the champion by defeating Jack Johnson, since Johnson was to have fought Sam Langford, another Negro contender, and did not do so. Thus Langford supposedly had a claim to the title, having never beaten either Willard or Jack Johnson in the ring.[107] Then, when the train reached Jacksonville, Florida, Frank Laznicka, a policeman who had fought and lost to Willard in Elk City, Oklahoma, in 1911 under the name of Frank Lyon, challenged Jess to step off the train and fight a return match.[108] Another story was that Jess Willard himself was an imposter. His real name was Arthur Brittingham, son of a well-to-do Missouri farmer. "Willard is merely a fighting name," said Frank Brittingham, his supposed cousin. He argued that Brittingham almost killed a coal miner in Kansas in a prizefight and as a result, changed his name to Jess Willard.[109] Next, the Old Trail Drivers' Association, composed of cattlemen and cowboys who followed the trail prior to 1883 when Jess was two years old, made Willard a life member.[110] Finally, as a joke, an old friend of Jess', the president of the Oklahoma State Board of Agriculture, offered Willard the job of State Cattle Inspector. This job might actually have been useful to him, for it was something that he understood better than what fame had in store for him.[111]

Fame plays many tricks on the unwary, and Jess Willard was the most unwary of all.

He had apparently believed that once he had defeated Jack Johnson, he could go back to his job on the farm. But he had no farm and no job. It was now up to him to turn his fame into cash. He was "the Great White Hope," the most famous man in America, the heavyweight champion of the world, and he was broke.

2

Growing Up in Kansas and Boxing in Oklahoma

Jess Willard had been broke before, but he had never been famous. Who was this fellow, Jess Willard? Where did he come from? What was his background? What made it possible for him to become the Great White Hope and the most famous man in America?

Jesse Myron Willard was born on the Willard farm outside St. Clere, Kansas, on December 29, 1881. He was the fourth son of Myron B. and Margarette (Maggie) Bailey Willard.

Myron Bacon Willard was born in Hayesville, Ashland County, Ohio, on October 11, 1844. Myron's father was Luman Willard, a sea captain who died in Hayesville. His mother was Emily Willard, who had married Luman in 1835, when she was 20 years old. Myron was the second of three children and the only boy in the family. He served in the Union Army in the Civil War, and was mustered out at Fort Leavenworth, Kansas, on September 16, 1865. He got a job working as a store clerk in Leavenworth for Joseph P. Bauserman for $18 per month. By 1869, he had met Margarette Belle Bailey who would become his wife. The two were married on March 9, 1869, in Leavenworth. Their first son, Marion Loren Willard, was born there on December 25, 1869. In 1870, Willard was living at Stranger (now Linwood, Kansas) and running a general store as well as selling horses to the United States government. Their second son, John Albert, was born in Stranger on March 26, 1872. In December 1873, Myron and his wife decided to leave Leavenworth County and move west to the unincorporated site of St. Clere to get land to raise cattle. There, they built a house on the banks of Cross Creek, one-half mile east of the site of the hamlet of St. Clere. Their third son, Robert Orlando, was born there on January 27, 1875. On July 1, 1879, Myron was appointed postmaster for St. Clere. In the census of 1880, Myron was listed with his wife and three children, Marion, age 10, John, age 8 and Robert, age 5. He died on October 29, 1881, and is buried in the Emmett/St. Clere cemetery. He was later joined there by his wife, Margarette.[1]

St. Clere was located in Pottawatomie County, four hours north of Topeka by buggy. The settlement was officially incorporated on January 6, 1880, on land donated by a farmer, John Le Clere, but it never really amounted to much. There were no houses in the town; it simply served as the central market and post office for the farmers who lived in the county. In its prime, the town consisted of two stores, a blacksmith, a post office, a Baptist church and a small school. The real town, once the railroad came through, was Emmett, five miles to the south. Thirteen miles further south was the town of St. Marys, a Catholic mission established to minister to the Pottawatomie Indians.[2]

The Pottawatomie were forest Indians and Kansas was pure prairie. From the border of Missouri west, stretched vast rolling plains of grass which were inhabited by buffalo, infested with grasshoppers and regularly swept by prairie fires. The buffalo, the grasshoppers and the fires all devoured the grass. But each in their own way contributed to the vitality and variability of the native prairie. Most particularly the buffalo and the prairie fires kept the land free of weed trees and stimulated the rebirth of the grasslands each year. The only trees that survived grew along the banks of the rivers. The rivers flowed clear and clean, but there were very few of them. As a result, this land was known to the few whites who traversed it as "the Great American Desert." Surely, the Pottawatomie must have considered it such as well.[3]

As the Pottawatomie were driven westward to Kansas territory, they were joined by two groups of missionaries. The first group was Protestant led by Johnston Lykins and Robert Simerwell who created a Baptist mission south of the Kansas River. The second group was Catholic led by Father Maurice Gailland, S. J., who created a mission north of the River. The Protestants were centered on Uniontown, while by 1853, the Catholics created a small town named St. Marys (always spelled without an apostrophe) around their mission. With the beginning of the Civil War in 1861, the Protestant mission went out of business and Uniontown disappeared. That site is now occupied by the Kansas State Historical Society to the west of Topeka. The Catholic mission survived, and by northeast Kansas standards, St. Marys became a wealthy town. The Federal Government provided a monthly payment to the Pottawatomie who used this money to purchase their supplies in town. This guaranteed government payment supplied ready cash to an area where cash was rare. It made St. Marys the most prosperous town in the surrounding area, and so it remains today. In 1856, at the instigation of Dr. Luther R. Palmer, one of the first settlers in the area, the land around the Indian reservation was named Pottawatomie County. By 1880 much of the Pottawatomie reservation was sold off and what remains of the reservation now lies in the bounds of next door Jackson County. Still, Pottawatomie County, where the Willards settled, preserves the tribe's name.[4]

By 1880, St. Marys had the Catholic mission and the government payments to the Pottawatomie. Emmett had the railroad line. But, St. Clere had nothing, save farmland and a few creeks. Still, once the town was established, Myron Willard was recognized as one of its first citizens. He appears in a record book in June of 1880. He ultimately acquired four building lots in the town worth $650.[5] On October 28, 1880, he bought an additional lot for $65.[6] He also bought a farm of about 160 acres, the first half of which he bought for $45.90 at a tax sale on October 25, 1880, and the second half of which he bought on January 29, 1881, for $50.[7]

Willard called himself a general merchant in the Census of 1880. He was 35 years old and his wife was 30. His primary business was to run a general store in St. Clere, but he also served as schoolmaster and ran the post office. In addition, he also planned to raise corn and cattle on his farm in addition to hogs, geese and chickens. He was industrious and in 1880 he had two employees, a clerk named Albert Page, and Margarette's sister, Mary Bailey, both of whom lived with the Willards. By the time of his death on October 29, 1881, he had an estate worth $3,000. He was a deacon in the Baptist church, a Mason, and a member of the Grand Army of the Republic (GAR), the veterans' organization of the Civil War. He left behind three sons, Marion, now age 11, John, aged 9, and

Robert, age 6, along with his widow, Maggie B. who was pregnant with their last son, Jesse Myron.[8]

The family home, which burned down sometime after 1994 but whose foundations can still be seen, was about one-half mile east of the settlement of St. Clere and backed up on Cross Creek. Maggie lived there with her four children until Jess was 11. She then married Elisha Leonard Stalker on March 2, 1893. Stalker had eight children of his own, but most of them were grown and had moved away by that time. Jess lived with the youngest Stalker children, a boy, Winfred, and a girl, Addie, on the Stalker farm in Adrian, next to the Pottawatomie Reservation. It was here that Jess began his relationship with the Pottawatomie Indians. In the fall of 1900, his mother and stepfather moved to 2518 Clay Street in Topeka, Kansas. At that time, Jess became the ward of his older brother, Robert, and they both lived in St. Clere. In their later years, the Willard children too spread out: Marion went to work for the Post Office in Topeka and lived at 625 Buchanan Street; John went into farming near Fort Cobb in Caddo County, Oklahoma; Robert became a grocer and farmer at Holy Cross in Pottawatomie County. Jesse Myron, the youngest, moved to Emmett and bought a livery stable.[9]

As a child, Jess was far more interested in horses than he was in school. He was a big, fat, good-natured boy who always had a smile for everyone. Horseback riding was his passion, but as he grew bigger, he found it difficult to find horses he could ride. He then shifted to driving a buggy. When he sat on a buggy, the seat was his throne and the whip his scepter. He was king of all he surveyed. But when he was seated in the class room, it was a different story. His step-father considered Jess a champion at skipping school: "There was a strip of timber between my house and the school house, and his

The four Willard boys at the time of their mother's funeral, February 1908. Left to right: John, Marion, Jess and Robert.

mother used to take a switch and follow him part way to school to make sure he wouldn't play hooky. But when he reached that timber, Jess would disappear and we would not see any more of him until after school hours."[10]

When he did go to school, he was whipped frequently by his teachers. One, A.L. Bell, later wrote about this in the St. Marys paper. But by the time he was 12, Jess was big enough to make his teachers think twice. As he remembered it: "My formal education ended when I was about ten or twelve years old. The German schoolmaster was going to make an example of me with a hedge-switch with briars on it but I reached the door before he reached me and never returned."[11]

With his schooling at an end at age 12, Jess got a job herding cattle for an Indian named Woodchuck. He had to furnish his own saddle horses and earned $30 a month. At the same time, he started riding broncos and worked on various ranches as both a cow-herder and a bronco-buster. The ranches around St. Clere were smaller and quite different from the wide-open spaces of the Southwest. And although Jess was often called a cowboy, he was better described as a horse-trader or as a bronco-buster.

> His prowess at breaking horses, not only for riding but for driving and work teams, probably accounts for the reference to him as a cowboy. But Jess Willard never rode the range, and while he may have herded cattle on his farm or while his older brothers did the plowing, he was never an actual cowpuncher with the big outfits.[12]

He began horse trading when he traded off his pony, "Dyke." He then developed the skill of breaking wild horses to the plow and saddle. He told the story that when he was 12 years old, there was a bad mustang on a farm that no one could ride. One day, when all of the men were idling about, someone dared Jess to try to ride the bronco. He climbed up on the back of the vicious little horse and for five minutes the mustang kicked

Jess Willard at about 17 years old with his horse Dyke.

and reared and tried to shake him off. He clung on to the pony for dear life and stuck until the mustang was tired out and subdued. After breaking that pony, he gained the admiration of the other fellows. Before long, he became recognized as one of best horsemen of the area. Initially, he bought wild horses from the Pottawatomie, broke them and then sold them to farmers in the area. Then, in 1901 when he was 19, he used money inherited from his father to travel to Idaho and Wyoming to bring back wild mustangs to break and sell. Even after he won the heavyweight championship, the subject he most wanted to talk about was horses: "Didn't know did you, I was considered one of the best horse traders in Kansas?" he said with a big laugh. "Well, I was and there isn't anything in the world I know quite as well as I know horses, and I'll be breeding them soon, too."[13]

Apart from school and work, there were few formal activities available for boys growing up in northeastern Kansas in the early 1900s. They made up their own games. Jess was a good athlete. He excelled at high-jumping and weight-lifting. He was proud of the fact that he was an excellent swimmer and able beat any of the other boys in both short and long distance swimming. And he was a great runner: "I could go out any time and turn off 100 yards in eleven seconds. This was fast enough to beat any of the lads in that section of the county, and I took many prizes at the county fairs."[14]

Jess also played first base on the Emmett baseball team. The story was told that when Emmett went to play Maple Hill, a nearby town, Jess could not go. The game turned out badly for Emmett. They not only were beaten on the field, but they were chased out of town, having to leave their gloves, bats and gate receipts behind. A few weeks later, Maple Hill, augmented with the toughest fellows available, came to Emmett to play a rematch. This time Jess was present. When the Maple Hill team took to the field they were ready for a fight. But Jess pushed his way through the crowd, picked up the Maple Hill manager by the shoulders, and set him down before the manager of the Emmett team and demanded that he apologize. He promptly did. Then Jess got a camp chair, placed the Maple Hill manager in it and demanded that he sit there during the rest of the game. He did that too. There was no more trouble with Maple Hill.[15]

Jess was an all-round athlete. But the one sport about which he knew nothing was boxing. He assumed that all fights were with bare fists. One of the blacksmiths in Emmett, Bert McAnerney, had been a semi-pro fighter and may have taught some of the local boys how to box. It is possible that Jess may have been initially schooled by McAnerney. But Jess had never seen either boxing gloves, a boxing ring or a boxing match until he went to Oklahoma City in 1910 when he was 28 years old.[16]

Growing up, he had few fights with the other boys. His large size made most boys want to leave him alone. He boasted that he had never been in a rough and tumble fight. However, one of his friends reminded him that when he once took "Hattie" Evans to a dance and was insulted by a group of rowdies, he knocked them all down and they fled. Hattie told the same story, but as she remembered it, the fight was not over her but over a horse.[17]

Jess was willing to fight over horses. When he was 16 he rode his horse into St. Clere and tied it at the hitching rack. When he came back, his horse was not there. He waited and eventually Walt Perry, a 22-year-old, rode up on it. Jess lit into him and they fought for a while until both were exhausted. They paused. Then they started again and continued for sometime. Finally, Jess stopped and said: "I'm not going to fight all day." He put on his coat and walked away with his horse. Walt Perry did not object.[18]

He also remembered a fight he had with a boy named Kelly whom he knocked out. Such activities led to him being considered a strong man who was not afraid of fighting. But since he was not interested in fighting, he became the trusted referee in most local bouts. Being a referee in the days of bare-knuckle fighting was often more dangerous than being a fighter. The fighter had only to worry about his opponent; the referee had to worry about everyone at the fight. If one fellow seemed to be getting the worst of it, his friends might step in and even things up. As a result, bare-knuckle fights often turned into brawls. But when Jess was the referee, things went peaceably and the fights were honest. He was too big to be intimidated by the friends of the boys fighting. He ensured that any fight he refereed was fairly fought and that the best man was allowed to win.[19]

By 1906, at age 25, Jess earned enough money to buy the livery stable in Emmett for $360. On June 2, 1906, he borrowed $747.85 from the Emmett State Bank to increase his business. On April 9, 1907, Jess bought another livery stable in Delia, Kansas. He also owned a dray or hauling business which was run for him by Frank Searcy. Although Jess did not know how to shoe a horse, he nonetheless bought a blacksmith shop, possibly the one run by Bert McAnerney. He also provided contract harvesting for various farmers. In addition, he sent four teams of horses to help build the railroad that was going through Onaga in October of 1907. In all these activities Jess had become an entrepreneur. He appeared to be one of the most active men in the neighborhood. He was well on the way to becoming one of the most important men in the area. Despite all of this, Jess suddenly became distracted. On June 4, 1907, he sold the livery stable in Delia. Then on January 7, 1908, he sold the livery stable and dray business in Emmett to Gottleib Sigg and others for $1,600. He was disinvesting in Emmett. The local newspaper was not pleased. "Emmett is unwilling to say much about Willard's business enterprises. The consensus of opinion of the country folks is that Jess was plain lazy."[20]

What happened? We really do not know. On February 10, 1908, Jess' mother died at her home in Topeka of pneumonia after an illness of three months. She was buried in the St. Clere cemetery beside her first husband, Myron. This cut Willard's main tie to the area. Then, on March 13, Jess Willard and Harriet (Hattie) Bailey Evans eloped to Leavenworth and were married there. They immediately left for Texas. According to a story Willard told as late as 1967, he was offered an opportunity to become a land agent in Texas and that led to him to selling his livery stable and moving out of Emmett. But we have reason to doubt that.[21]

Jess and Hattie had known each other from childhood. They also had been seeing each other for some time. The Evans farm was a quarter of a mile from the Willard home. But, Barnus B. "Barney" Evans was not impressed by Willard. Barney Evans was one of the most prosperous and successful area farmers. Jess was not. He was big enough, but not serious enough. The Evans also considered Jess an unscrupulous horse-trader. At one time, the local constable had to serve him papers for mortgaging a team and buggy for which he had not yet paid. Furthermore, Jess was often broke. When he was broke, he would have what he called "Collection Day." He would go around and collect money that was owed him. When Tom Gideon told Jess he did not have any money, Jess simply picked him up by his feet and dangled him upside down until gold coins fell from his pocket. Jess then picked out the coins that paid the debt and walked away.[22]

Despite the fact that people in Emmett considered Willard to be a poor businessman, Hattie loved him. After her father forbade her to see him, and even built a high board

Jess and Hattie's wedding portrait, March 1908.

fence around the yard and locked the gate to keep him out, Hattie would run out when he drove up in his buggy, climb the fence and jump in and the two would race off together. When Jess asked for Hattie's hand, Barney Evans turned him down. After they became married, Jess was always referred to as "Hattie's husband" or "Mrs. Evans' son-in-law." It was only after he won the heavyweight championship that Barney Evans began to refer to him as "my son-in-law."[23]

Mrs. Evans summed up the family's view of Jess: "We did not like Jess at first, but he proved to be a good husband. He is a great man for children and nothing pleases him better than to romp with their four while his wife goes shopping. It just shows a girl has to take a chance, and this time she won."[24]

The marriage was only a surprise in its suddenness, for Jess and Hattie had a secret. To hide it from their friends and family, they took the train south from Kansas City as far as it would go. They ended up in the new town of Palacios, Texas, which was just being built on the Gulf of Mexico, and settled there. Hattie, it turned out, was pregnant. On April 23, 1908, their first child, Zella Margaret Willard was born.[25]

Jess and Hattie remained in Palacios for over a year, boarding with Mrs. Lyda Williams. During that time, they enjoyed the pleasures of being parents. But, they kept their families in Kansas ignorant about Zella's existence. While Hattie took care of Zella, Jess took a variety of jobs, including working for Clyde Randolph at the ice plant and selling real estate for the Burton D. Hurd Land Company which was just opening up a suburb called "Collegeport." Although initially promising, the real estate job did not pan out. Those people who purchased land from Burton Hurd soon found out that Hurd was merely an agent for the Able B. Pierce Ranch, which owned the land. Pierce refused to give the buyers title to the land until he had been paid by Hurd. The delays left Willard, as a salesman, with a series of unhappy clients and without his commission. With the real estate business not working out, Jess went to work for the Pierce ranch, The Ace of Clubs, as a cow-puncher.[26]

The Willards' days in Palacios were pleasant ones. Everyone there remembered Jess as a big, lanky fellow who had a smile for everyone. Jess, in turn, liked the people he met in Palacios and kept in touch with them over the years.[27]

Oil was being discovered in the Palacios-Bay City area at the time the Willards were there, and Jess might have found work in the oil fields had he stayed. But in the summer of 1909, a hurricane hit Palacios and Bay City. Jess and Hattie decided to leave the area and return north with their daughter Zella. They did not return to Kansas, however. Instead, they moved to Oklahoma. And although Jess' brother, John, and his family lived near Fort Caddo, Jess and Hattie chose to go further west to Elk City. There seems to have been no special reason for going to Elk City other than to keep Zella's true age a secret from their family. In fact, Hattie and Jess never revealed that Zella had been born in 1908. To the end of her life, Zella believed that she had been born in Palacios on April 23, 1909.

Oklahoma had been Indian Territory prior to 1907. It became a state in that year and by the time the Willards arrived it was developing a number of settled towns. In 1910, Elk City was becoming a decent sized town on the western plains. The land around Elk City was devoted to the growing of cotton and broom corn. When he arrived, Jess got a job driving a six-mule wagon as a teamster. The little village of Hammon was being built just north of Elk City and Willard hauled construction materials to the town and cotton back from the area. Early on, Willard gained a reputation for prodigious strength. When his wagon, carrying a bale of cotton weighing around 640 pounds, tipped over on the road, Jess righted the wagon and then reloaded the bale by himself and drove into Elk City.[28]

Nineteen ten was a watershed year for the Willards. Jess was facing a crisis at work as the railroads took away the freight business. And Hattie was facing her own crisis: Zella was two and Hattie was pregnant again. But, while the Willards struggled to make a living and deal with their growing family, an even greater crisis occupied the country at large.

As we have seen, the most important event in the English-speaking world in the summer of 1910 was the boxing match between the black champion, John Arthur Johnson, and the previously undefeated world champion, James J. Jeffries. This event altered Jess Willard's life. Jess had just driven his wagon into Elk City when he heard of Johnson's victory over Jeffries. Jess claimed that he had not been sufficiently interested in the fight to read about it in the papers. However, a friend of his, Harvey Payne, a postal clerk, told him the news and then added, "Jess, you're big enough to lick this nigger. Why don't you do it?" Jess had never boxed professionally in his life. But, with the overland freight business being closed down by the railroads, and with a second child on the way, Jess was ready for a new career.[29]

Most men, when they get involved in boxing, have been involved in fights and violence during their childhood which prepared them for the rigors of the ring. Boxing, in fact, was often their best alternative to prison. But, as we have seen, Jess Willard was different. Jess was a gentle giant. His strength was prodigious, but his temper was mild. "How did I happen to get into boxing?" he responded to Herbert Bayard Swope in 1915.

"Why I never had any thought of it until Johnson beat Jeffries at Reno five years ago." Once he gave it some thought, however, Willard embraced it wholeheartedly. His first words to his wife that evening were "I'd rather beat that fellow Johnson than be President of the United States." As he was to later write: "God made me a giant. I never received an education, never had any money, and my folks, God bless them, never had any money. I knew I was a big fellow and powerful strong. I just sat down and figured out that a man as big as me ought to be able to cash in on his size and that was what started me on the road to boxing."[30]

Jeffries' failure to defeat Johnson in Reno had created a social problem. Boxing had created the crisis by allowing Johnson to gain the championship, now it was up to boxing to solve the crisis. All over the world, big, strong white boys began to learn to box so that they could defeat Jack Johnson and become "the Great White Hope." Jess Willard was soon to become one of them. As he told Ed Smith, sports editor of the *Chicago Evening American*, "I confess right here that I was fired with ambition such as I never had before. I pictured myself as the real candidate for the title held by Johnson, and in my dreams could see myself crowned the king of them all." But Jess was slow off the mark.[31]

One of the first men to gain a reputation in the fall of 1910 was Carl Morris, an engineer on the St. Louis and San Francisco Railroad, known as the Frisco Line, operating out of Oklahoma City. Morris had boxed while in the army and had some knowledge of the sport. He had just pulled his engine into the Oklahoma City yard when he learned that Johnson had beaten Jeffries. He climbed down from his cab, quit his job and beat up the first Negro he saw.

Morris stood about 6 feet, 4 inches tall and weighed nearly 315 pounds. He was big and slow and more suited to be a wrestler than a boxer, but boxing was the sport of the hour and Morris immediately went into training. He worked out with Frank Carsey at the Carsey Athletic Club in Oklahoma City under the direction of Kid Bruno, a lightweight boxer from Chicago. Together, Carsey and Bruno were able to teach Morris some boxing skills and to get his weight down to about 235 pounds. But then things changed and Carsey was effectively driven out of Oklahoma City and his athletic club closed down. In his place, a former insurance salesman, John David (J. D.) Brock took over. Morris did not get along with Brock and left Oklahoma City for Tulsa. It was in Tulsa, and the little town of Sapulpa next door, where Morris earned the title "the Original White Hope."[32]

While Carl Morris was gaining fame in Oklahoma City and Tulsa, Jess Willard was beginning to box in Elk City. Harvey Payne set up Jess' first fights in a barn with the local town tough. In the first fight, Jess was knocked out. In the second fight three weeks later, Jess knocked the tough out. This was a beginning, but Elk City did not have any real training facilities, nor did they have any trainers. For that he would have to move to Oklahoma City. In December 1910, Willard sold his mules and he, Hattie and Zella moved to a small house in Oklahoma City "where things had to be better—they couldn't be much worse." There, his second daughter, Frances, was born.[33]

When he arrived in Oklahoma City, Willard initially sought a job as a policeman. "I figured that possibly I could get on the police force there and this would be an improvement over my past employment since it would at least provide a steady income." But things did not go his way and the police job fell through. As he walked downtown, seeking employment, Jess met W.T. Yoder, the owner of the Auditorium, the location for the fights that were held in Oklahoma City. Looking at Willard's size, Yoder immediately took him to meet the promoter, J.D. Brock. Brock had just returned from a trip to Kansas City where he had gone to try to find fighters for his Union Athletic Club. Having lost Carl Morris, who now was the most famous white heavyweight in the country, Brock was desperate to find someone who could be the focus of the Oklahoma City club.[34]

When Yoder brought Willard into the Union Athletic Club on December 21, 1910, it was the answer to Brock's dreams. Jess stood 6 feet, 6 inches in his bare feet, weighed 225 pounds and claimed to be able to run the 100 yard dash in 11 seconds. His only drawback was his age which was actually 28, although he claimed it was 24. His first words to Brock when he walked into the gym were "I want to learn to fight and then whip Jack Johnson." The following day, Brock signed Jess to a contract which promised to pay him $15 per week and train him to become a boxer. Brock, Willard and Oklahoma City were all delighted. As Charles Brill of *The Daily Oklahoman* wrote on December 22, "Oklahoma City has a New Hope." The next day Brill wrote another article which proved to be truly prophetic.

> After a conference lasting throughout the day Thursday (December 22), agreement was made between President J.D. Brock of the Union Athletic club and Jesse Willard, the "Oklahoma City hope," whereby Willard will train in Oklahoma City with the expectation of whipping Carl Morris and all the other heavyweight aspirants, and finally knocking the crown from Jack Johnson's head.[35]

In one brief paragraph, the paper summarized Jess Willard's future boxing career. It also gave Hattie and Jess one of the best Christmases they ever had.[36]

Although hired as a boxer, Willard had never actually seen a boxing match. It so happened that Brock had a match scheduled between Clarence English and Harry Brewer, two decent welterweights, on New Year's Eve. Willard attended and began to learn what boxing was all about. "I was lost in admiration at the speed those boys showed and I made up my mind then and there, that if I could ever get anywhere as good as they were, I could whip Johnson. Neither of them was a champion, but believe me, I thought them about as wonderful as could be turned out. I could not sleep that night for thinking about that fight and my ambition became a raging storm within me."[37]

The euphoria that Jess Willard and J. D. Brock may have felt at the end of December 1910 was dashed with the dawn of the New Year. Although "prizefighting" (which meant professional, public boxing matches) was outlawed in Oklahoma, a gentleman's agreement between the county attorney, E. E. Reardon, Frank Carsey, and then J. D. Brock, had allowed boxing matches to take place in the Auditorium. However, the election in the fall of 1910 brought into power a new county attorney, Judge Sam Hooker. Hooker was part of the Progressive movement. Beginning on January 1, 1911, Judge Hooker ordered Brock to close down the Union Athletic Club and stop all boxing.[38]

Brock tried to negotiate with Hooker to find a way to continue his business but could not. Brock lost most of the fighters he had brought to Oklahoma City and the Union Athletic Club was closed down. Nonetheless, Willard stayed in Oklahoma City as he had no where else to go.[39]

In an attempt to reactivate his business, Brock decided to hold his matches outside of Oklahoma County which was the jurisdiction of Sam Hooker. Thus, on February 15, Brock matched Willard with Louis Fink, a sparring partner of Carl Morris in Sapulpa, Oklahoma, Morris' new home town.

Fink was the former heavyweight champion of Colorado and had been boxing since

1909, while Willard had been training for one and one half-months. Fink stood 6 feet tall and weighed 180 pounds. His record was 13–1 with nine knockouts. Fink completely outmatched Willard in terms of knowledge and skill, but Willard weighed 54 pounds more than his opponent and stood six inches taller. Fink had come to Oklahoma to fight Carl Morris. Though that did not happen, he had stayed to serve as one of Morris' sparring partners. J. D. Brock had wanted to match Willard against Morris but Morris would not allow it, so Brock settled on having Willard fight Fink. This was fortunate for Willard since Fink could not hurt him with his blows.[40]

The fight was the main event and scheduled for 15 rounds, an extraordinary number for Willard who had never appeared in the ring before. Although the fight was fast and furious, both fighters proved to be inept; Fink because he was overmatched due to Willard's size and reach, and Willard because he was confused by the noise of the crowd. According to *The Sapulpa Evening Light*, J. D. Brock had insisted that they break clean during the fight. This suited Fink perfectly. Given Willard's size advantages, Fink's strategy was to jab with his left or swing with his right and then clinch or get out of the way. But since Willard proved faster on his feet than expected, Fink could not get out of the way easily, and was forced to continually clinch. As a result, the two fighters frequently grappled with each other, forcing the referee and seconds to separate them at the close of each round.

Willard drew first blood by hitting Fink on the nose in the second round. He then knocked Fink to the canvas in round three, although it was ruled a slip. By the end of the round, Willard was out of breath. By round four Fink began to hit Willard and then clinch. From round four to round seven, Willard was plainly out of breath and wobbling from exhaustion. Fink was in no better shape. In round six, Willard hit Fink with an uppercut and nearly knocked him out. In rounds seven and eight, Fink was groggy. In round nine, both men grappled and fell to the floor. In round ten, after a series of warnings against hitting in the clinches, the referee, Al Venn, finally disqualified Willard for throwing Fink to the floor. "Willard probably did not mean to foul, but he was so ignorant of all ring methods that he could not help it," wrote *The Sapulpa Evening Light*, the next day. "It is doubtful," the paper continued, "if Willard will ever appear in the ring again, at least until he can improve greatly over what he showed to fans last night."[41]

Jess Willard in 1911 as he was when he began boxing in Oklahoma City.

The fight demonstrated Willard's inexperience. He had never been in a refereed ring fight before his fight with Fink. He had never even seen a refereed boxing bout before he attended the one put on by Brock on December 31, 1910. Halfway through round two, Willard quit fighting and walked to his corner, thinking the round was over. Then, during the fight, he would stop and turn whenever anyone in the audience shouted his name. At the end of the fight he went over to one man who had been calling to him during the fight and held out his hand: "I guess I have met you," he said, "but I don't recall your name. You were calling to me during the fight, but I was too busy to do more than look at you. What do you want?" As *The Daily Oklahoman* was later to admit, while "Willard looked good physically, there was also a unanimous vote that Willard behaved in a most ignorant manner in the ring.... His action in the ring demonstrated that he probably knew less about what he should do than any boxer that ever stepped inside the ropes."[42]

This loss did not dampen Willard's spirits. Instead, he considered his "pugilistic coming-out-party a success." Despite the loss, Brock too believed Willard had great potential. No sooner had he returned to Oklahoma City than Brock was quoted in *The Daily Oklahoman* as offering to bet $1,000 that Willard could knock Fink out in three rounds in a return match. The Morris camp immediately took up the challenge. Brock was forced to retreat claiming that he had Willard lined up to fight Charles Cavanaugh, a fighter from Dayton, Ohio. Cavanaugh was also scheduled to fight Carl Morris. Despite later claims, I have not been able to confirm that Cavanaugh fought either fighter. Instead, Willard fought Ed Burke, a sparring partner of the famous "Fireman" Jim Flynn.[43]

"Fireman" Jim Flynn was actually an Italian named Andrew Charniglioni, who had worked on the railroad in Pueblo, Colorado. Like many, he changed his name in deference to John L. Sullivan who had made the Irish the archetypical boxers in America. He got his nickname "Fireman" after he stole a switch-engine from the Pueblo yards while fleeing from the police. Flynn was a skilled and dangerous boxer who had already fought and lost to Tommy Burns, the former heavyweight champion, and Jack Johnson, the current champion. Although Flynn would fight Johnson again in 1912, he could not beat him. Instead, he earned the title of "the white hope crusher" since, while not good enough to defeat Johnson, he was good enough to defeat many of the "hopes" who sought to meet Jack Johnson.

Flynn was a feared competitor with a lot of fight knowledge. He had come to Oklahoma at the request of Eddie Robinson, who was serving as a promoter for Carl Morris' manager, W. T. Stone, in the fall of 1910. However, at the end of January 1911, before Flynn arrived, Robinson left the Morris camp. As a result, when Flynn arrived in Oklahoma City on February 14, expecting to fight Morris on February 22, his bid was rejected. Flynn then settled in Oklahoma City for several months while negotiating for a fight with Morris. While there, he worked out with Jess Willard at the Benevolent Athletic Association (BAA), the new name Brock had given his club.[44]

According to the newspapers, Eddie Robinson and Carl Morris had a falling out over the Mike Schreck fight which Robinson wanted to hold in Muskogee on January 30. However, the same day the dispute was announced, it was also announced that W.T. Stone had sold Morris' contract to an oilman, Frank B. Ufer, for $25,000. Ufer chose to put Con Riley, from Cincinnati in charge of Morris, and Robinson went to Muskogee on his own. With the departure of Robinson and Stone, the miracle career that had propelled Morris to the top, ended. Morris now became the stepping stone upon which better boxers stood to gain attention. When Morris and Flynn did finally meet in Madison Square Garden on September 15, Flynn proved vastly superior to Morris, beginning Morris' downward slide into mediocrity.[45]

Sparring with Flynn was highly valuable to Willard. Flynn was notorious for attempting to knock out his sparring partners and the rough treatment that Willard got from Flynn was very helpful to him. Although Flynn was later to claim that he had knocked Willard out while they were sparring, the reverse may have been true. And we do know that after several weeks of training with Flynn, Willard was a much better fighter. He had gone into the fight with Fink "gloomy and worried, fearing his ability to stay fifteen rounds." But, that bout and his training with Flynn, gave him confidence. Before he left for El Reno for his second fight, "he declared that he had not the slightest doubt that he would be returned the winner in the early stages."[46]

The fight with Ed Burke occurred on March 7 at El Reno, a town of about 3,500 people outside of Oklahoma City. Willard knocked Burke out in three rounds. According to a local reporter, Willard could easily have beaten Burke in the first round, but chose not to. "At times Willard left his guard down and Burke landed on both the body and the head. Willard declared afterward that he had wanted to see if it hurt, and that while each blow was a stinger, those to the head did not daze him and those to the body had no effect."[47]

The fight with Burke also showed another side of Willard that is often overlooked. Willard was not a born fighter. He did not have the killer instinct that the greatest boxers have. As he said, he was primarily interested in the money. But he was also interested in providing the public with its money's worth as well. This he explained in summing up his reaction to his second refereed fight. "I am sorry Burke was not a larger man. He looked much larger in street clothes than when stripped, and I regretted that we were forced to continue the contest. I think I could have settled him in the first round, but I wanted to give the crowd as much for its money as possible. I felt entirely at ease and no panic threatened me at any time."[48] Willard's comments showed a more concerned and diffident person than is often found among fighters. Willard approached fighting as a workman does his job. He took pride in himself and his work, but did not seek to embarrass his opponents, as for example, Jim Flynn and Jack Johnson did.

The training with Jim Flynn and the bout with Ed Burke convinced J. D. Brock that Willard was ready for the return bout with Louis Fink. Before that bout would take place, Brock scheduled Willard for an additional training fight with "Big Six" Warner, a heavyweight from Galveston, Texas. The ten-round bout was to take place at the Majestic Theatre in Shawnee, Oklahoma, on March 13. Warner was a much smaller man than Willard and weighed 175 pounds to Willard's 230. As a result, Brock promoted the fight as a boxing and sparring match, not a knockout fight. Brock and Willard went to the theatre and watched the preliminary fights and then about ten minutes before the Willard-Warner bout was to take place, Willard walked out through the back door. A call to his hotel revealed that he had apparently hopped a freight train back to Oklahoma City. The fight with Warner never took place.[49]

If the training with Flynn and the bout with Burke had taught Brock something about Willard, it taught Willard something as well. He clearly felt that Warner would not provide much competition for him. As *The Shawnee Daily News* reported at the time: "Before he left he is said to have remarked that he had been given to understand that it was to be a knockout fight, and as it wasn't to be such, he didn't care to stay as he was no boxer." Although Willard had only had two bouts by this time, he felt that Warner would not have been a challenge. On the other hand, *The Shawnee Daily Herald* was outraged: "The action of Willard brands him as a quitter and in the future he will probably never receive any recognition from promoters of boxing exhibitions."[50]

Willard was certainly no quitter. He felt embarrassed at being involved in a fight which would not allow him to do his best. To Jess Willard, "to box" meant to pull your punches and not to fight to your ability. He believed that the Warner bout would have been a repeat of the Burke fight. Knowing that he could easily dispose of Warner he may have felt it was a waste of his time and unfair to the paying public. However, because he dodged the Warner bout, the Morris camp assumed that Willard was not "game," and that made them eager for the return bout between Willard and Louis Fink.

The second Willard-Fink bout occurred on March 24 in Oklahoma City. In choosing this location, Brock was taking a big risk, for Judge Hooker was looking for an opportunity to close down prizefighting in the city. But, with a bet of $1,000 on Willard to knock Fink out in three rounds, and with the Warner fiasco so fresh in his mind, Brock no doubt felt he needed the fight held on friendly ground. He had also taken precautions to have the fight held under the auspices of the Benevolent Athletic Association (BAA).[51]

In 1909, County Attorney E.E. Reardon, taking note of the fact that the bouts in Oklahoma City were inside and according to the Marquess of Queensberry rules, using gloves, permitted boxing in Oklahoma City as long as it was "simply an exhibition of cleverness." "What we are after," said Reardon, "is to eliminate the brutality that comes with prize fights and thus distinguishes them from boxing exhibitions."[52]

Boxing promoters, like J. D. Brock, tried to convince the legal authorities that all of their bouts were "scientific exhibitions of boxing and sparring" rather than "prize fights." And since the public liked boxing and tended to support the matches, most police turned a blind eye to the events or even became spectators themselves.[53]

There was, in addition, a general understanding that boxing bouts held in chartered athletic clubs for the private entertainment of their members were legal, even in states where public prizefights were illegal. This view had developed out of the movement of Muscular Christianity.[54]

However, the Progressive movement, to which the new governor, Lee Cruce, and the new County Attorney, Judge Sam Hooker, belonged, rejected the arguments of the Muscular Christianity movement and held all boxing and prizefighting to be illegal. It was Jess Willard's misfortune to become embroiled in these first legal contests over boxing versus prizefighting in Oklahoma.

J.D. Brock was counting on the view that exhibitions of boxing, held for the members of the club, would be considered legal when he created his Benevolent Athletic Association (BAA). It was his hope that the bout between Willard and Fink would be recognized as a "boxing or sparring exhibition" and not a prizefight. In this way he hoped to escape the wrath of the county attorney. Had this occurred everything would have worked out perfectly, for Willard knocked Fink out within three rounds and Brock won his bet of $1,000.[55]

At this point, things seemed to be working out well for both Willard and Brock. Brock had won $1,000 betting on Willard while Willard had successfully begun a new career. Hattie was tending the family, and Jess had avenged his first loss and was gaining confidence in the ring. More importantly, he had a way to support his family. As he would later write to a friend: "So I got this boxing game into my head. I never liked it; in fact, I hated it as I never hated a thing previously, but there was money in it. I needed the money and decided to go after it."[56]

But the law intervened. Immediately following the second Fink fight, Judge Sam Hooker issued warrants for the arrest of Willard and Fink for prizefighting. Fink fled the county back to Sapulpa and Willard was forced to surrender to Oklahoma County Judge John W. Hayson. His bond was set at $500 and he was scheduled for trial later. "Anybody would think I waylaid Fink on the street," said Willard, "the way they are after me." He then returned to training for his next fight.[57]

On March 29, Willard and Brock along with Jim Flynn went to Sapulpa to see Carl Morris fight Mike Schreck from Cincinnati. Morris easily defeated Schreck in six rounds. Before the fight, Flynn mounted to the ring and posted $1,000 to meet Morris. His challenge was met with great applause by the crowd but Ufer, Morris' new manager, refused to accept the challenge.

The day after the fight, Brock also posted a challenge for Willard to fight Morris for $1,000. It was then announced that Willard was to meet "Battling Brit" at El Reno on April 11 for his next fight followed by Joe Cox, the Missouri Hope, at the end of April at Monett, Missouri.[58]

"Battling Britt" had already fought and lost to both Carl Morris and his brother, Ulric. Jess was reluctant to fight Britt, just as he had been reluctant to fight Burke and Warner. Willard declared: "I wish I was not matched to fight this man Britt. I saw him at Sapulpa, when I met Fink after my initial engagement and he fought the semi-windup with Ulric Morris. I anticipate having little trouble with him, but it will really do me little good as what I need is big strapping fellows that I can tear into." Britt agreed with Jess. He took one look at Willard and decided not to fight him. He then pronounced Willard better than Morris: "He [Britt] said Willard looks more formidable than does Morris, and he believes that Willard is the best man."[59]

No police interference occurred at El Reno, so Brock scheduled another fight, this time again in Oklahoma City with a serious figure, Al Mandino. Mandino was a heavyweight from Knoxville, Tennessee. He had already fought "Fireman" Jim Flynn in Muskogee and had lost in four rounds. He then came to Oklahoma City to fight Willard, while Jim Flynn served as referee. Mandino weighed 200 pounds to Jess' 212 and was considered an "aggressive and wicked fighter" by the newspaper and represented the toughest test of Willard's abilities so far.

Brock held the bout in the BAA gymnasium in hopes that Judge Hooker would not interfere. The fight was announced for the night of April 14, 1911. Willard proved his worth in this fight, for at the beginning of the fourth round, he knocked Mandino down three times in rapid succession. "The last blow was a terrific one. It broke two of Mandino's teeth, tore open his jaw on the inside, also his lips, and he went down like a log." Willard had knocked Mandino out in less time than it had taken Flynn. Mandino said that the blow was the hardest he had ever received. Nonetheless, *The Daily Oklahoman* criticized Willard for refusing to attack his opponent. Commenting about Willard's jabs in the first round, the newspaper noted that they lacked force: "In fact this was the flaw in the character of Willard's fighting; he did not use his strength in landing his blows." Further, as he had done in other fights, Willard passed up opportunities to knock his opponent out early. Jess' reluctance to fight men smaller than himself and his reluctance to put real power into his blows, even with big men, was a trait that would be consistent throughout his career.[60]

Following the fight, Sam Hooker issued another set of warrants for the prizefighters, showing that holding the fights in the BAA gym offered no protection for Brock and his fighters. Mandino left town and Willard remained to face the music.[61]

According to Willard's life story, "How I won the title," as told to the sports editor of the *Chicago Evening American*, Ed W. Smith, Brock was able to put on one more fight in Oklahoma City at this time. "Two weeks later Joe Cavanaugh fought me in the same ring in Oklahoma City and he did a little better [than Mandino], managing to stick through to the eleventh round before I got him on the chin with a hard one that got him out for the full count."[62]

The fight with Cavanaugh (be it Joe or Charles) is a will-o-the wisp. There is no record of this fight in the local papers. Given Judge Hooker's attack on heavyweight boxing, it may have been hushed up by the newspapers to avoid prosecution. Despite not being able to find any record of this fight, I feel we must give credit to Willard's memory and say that it is likely that the Cavanaugh fight did take place at this time. It is difficult to argue against Willard's own testimony. But since Willard and Brock faced two warrants for prizefighting at this time, I think we can argue that to avoid further legal difficulties, the fight was not publicized.

On the other hand, Brock was now forced to realize that his plans to continue holding heavyweight fights in Oklahoma City had come to an end. He restricted the fights in the BAA gym to lightweights and under. He then joined with the town of El Reno to build an outdoor arena midway between El Reno and Oklahoma City on the inter-urban line. This would allow people to easily attend the heavyweight fights, but place them outside the boundaries of Oklahoma County and Sam Hooker's jurisdiction.

The next fight scheduled was between Willard and Bill (Bert) Schiller for May 15. Schiller was from Louisville, Kentucky, and was an old time fighter. He had fought twice with Marvin Hart, the former heavyweight champion. Schiller, like most of the heavyweights, had originally come to Oklahoma to fight Carl Morris. But, like many of them, he had failed to get a bout. Jess Willard was second best, but he too was gaining a reputation, and Schiller really had no hope of defeating him.

In order to give some excitement to the fight, it was announced well in advance. This allowed the police to become aware of it and nearly ensured police involvement. A large number of people were likely to attend thinking that they would see the police arrest the fighters. At the same time, Brock ruled that the bout would not be a knockout fight. Instead, Willard would have to spar and box (hit without intending to do any serious damage to his opponent). Brock also decreed that the bout would last no more than four rounds. It was commonly thought that four rounds constituted a legitimate length for a boxing or sparring match and that if an exhibition went four rounds the public could not demand their money back. Thus, in his planning, Brock hoped to make the bout long enough to be legitimate and short enough to escape police punishment. In this he was successful, for the police did not interfere and nobody was arrested.

Still, the fight was uninteresting. Schiller had trained with Willard prior to the fight and knew what was expected of him. At the beginning of the fourth round, Willard rushed Schiller who sank to a knee as if exhausted. Patsy Corrigan, Willard's trainer, who was also serving as referee, rushed Schiller to his corner and declared Willard the victor.

Later, Schiller told the crowd that he could have continued the fight. Willard agreed: "While I think Schiller undoubtedly would have been able to return to the contest, I know I had him beaten and could have beaten him in one or two rounds had we been fighting, but our instructions were to box and that is what we did."[63]

In a later account of this fight, Jess revealed that he received a broken knuckle. The cause of the injury was the fact that the boxing gloves were too small for Willard's hands. Since they were the only gloves available they had to be used. But, when they were cut off his hands at the end of the fight, he found that he had broken the first knuckle on his right hand. This experience led him to require specially made gloves once he began to earn enough money in his later fights.[64]

Despite the legal problems he faced, J.D. Brock was eventually successful in getting a decision from the Morris camp to fight Willard. Carl Morris and Jess Willard were now the most famous heavyweight fighters in Oklahoma. A fight with Carl Morris could mean sudden fame for Jess Willard if he won. This is what Brock had been working for since Willard had walked into his club in December. The fight was scheduled for June 10 at Tulsa and had it occurred, it would have been the most famous boxing match in the history of Oklahoma. But the fight did not occur.[65]

Before the Willard-Morris fight could occur, Willard was arrested again and put on trial for "prize fighting." J. D. Brock was forced out of the prizefight business and resigned as president of the BAA, turning the club over the Patsy Corrigan. He was forced to sell his contract with Willard to two real estate men, A.W. Phillips and A.H. Cutrell for $7,500. He also was forced to testify against Willard in court.[66]

Willard was not the only boxer to go to trial in Oklahoma at this time. In Muskogee, the fight between Joe Gorman and "Knockout" Brown erupted in a riot when someone fired a gun causing a stampede. The county sheriff arrested the promoter, the referee and Joe Gorman and put them on trial. Then, the authorities declared that "there will be no more prize fighting in Muskogee." Eddie Robinson, who had set up his shop in Muskogee and who had promoted the Jim Flynn-Al Mandino fight there, was forced out and ended up in Fort Smith, Arkansas, where he began promoting fights.[67]

Another legal battle occurred in Tulsa when Governor Cruce prevented the fight between Carl Morris and Jim Flynn on July 4. Initially, the fight was to occur in Tulsa or Sapulpa, but the governor threatened to send in the militia to stop it. Frank Ufer then took the fight to New York City. Cruce had effectively driven out of the state the two most famous boxers in its history. Oklahoma would never again command the attention of the boxing world as it did at that time.[68]

In a further sidelight to the Flynn-Morris fight, once it was removed to New York, it too became embroiled in a legal battle. Bat Masterson, the famous Kansas lawman, who was at the time a sports writer for *The Morning Telegraph*, wrote a column on September 10 in which he suggested that the fight might not be on the square since Ufer was financing both fighters. He concluded his column with the statement "The Flynn-Morris contest is a frame-up and should not by any means be permitted to go on." Ufer then replied with a paragraph in an article in *The New York Globe and Commercial Advertiser* of September 15, in which he said that Masterson had "made his reputation by shooting drunken Mexicans and Indians in the back." Masterson sued for libel. Masterson prevailed and was awarded $3,500 and costs of $129.25. Despite the trial and Masterson's fears, the fight did go on and Flynn handed Morris the first defeat of his career.[69]

Back in Oklahoma City, in a trial on May 31, the county jury found that the second Fink fight had been a prizefight and not a boxing match. Willard was found "guilty of violating the Oklahoma statutes on prize fighting, the specific instance being the alleged knockout of Louis Fink before the Benevolent Athletic Association, March 24."[70]

Because he was a married man with two children, Willard was let off lightly. He had faced a fine of up to $500 and a year in jail. Instead, he was given a simple fine of $100. Still, this was well beyond his means. Jess asked J.D. Brock for the money but Brock had already sold his contract to Phillips and Cutrell. Phillips and Cutrell refused to pay because they had not been involved in the events. With no way to pay his fine, Willard and his wife and daughters fled back to Elk City. According to Willard's later testimony, later in the summer, he asked A. W. Phillips for money to send Hattie and the children back to Kansas but, again, Phillips refused. As a result, Hattie had to pawn her watch to get the fare to get back to her parents.[71]

We do not know much about the Willard's time in Elk City in 1911. The family apparently lived there between the middle of June and the end of August. Jess must have engaged in odd jobs. It is also possible that the family moved to Sayre, a town 20 miles to the west. There is a report that the Willards rented rooms from Mrs. Walter Jenks in the summer. Hattie apparently took in washing while Jess looked for work. According to J.M. Grady, who lived in the same rooming house with the Willards in Sayre,

> Jess was undoubtedly the laziest man when it came to physical labor I ever met. He had a wife and a child when I knew him: it was said he would not make a move to support them. He just rested and rested. Things went from bad to worse until he was arrested as a vag, but just before the officers started to jail him his wife took a roll of bills from her stocking totaling $700 and paid the fine. No one knew until then that the family had a cent.[72]

While in the west, Jess had at least two more fights. On July 4, he met Frank Lyon (Frank Laznicka) from Jacksonville, Florida, in a ten-round bout in Elk City. Lyon was one of the many "white hopes" who was trying to get noticed by touring the country and taking on all-comers. He was 26 years old, weighed 230 pounds, and had a reach only ¼ inch shorter than Jess' own. Lyon was nearly as tall as Jess at about 6 feet, 5 inches. Jess, at this time, was 29 years old, stood 6 feet, 6¾ inches and weighed about 230 pounds as well. As Jess said of the match, "He was a little tougher than the average run of fighter they had in that section, and I had to work hard to get the decision at the end of ten rounds." The match was nearly even and as a result the fight was slow and cautious. Jess broke Lyon's nose in the first round but then remained cautious for the rest of the fight. Willard won on points with only one round, the sixth, going to Lyon. Nonetheless, Lyon believed that he could have beaten Willard in a return bout. Later, in 1915, when Jess was returning from Havana after beating Johnson, his train passed through Jacksonville and Lyon, who was then a policeman on the Jacksonville force, challenged him again. The return bout did not occur.[73]

The Daily Oklahoman article about the Lyon fight said that Willard was to fight a W.O. Stuckey in Cheyenne, a small town northwest of Elk City, on July 5. I have not been able to find any trace of this fight in the newspapers of the time. There was also the claim by Harold Wallace, president of the State National Bank in Ardmore, Oklahoma, that he fought with Willard in Ardmore at some undisclosed time before Willard became famous. This claim cannot be verified.[74]

On August 10, Jess did apparently fight another bout, this time in Hammon, the small town to which he had carried freight in 1910. This fight was puzzling, both because of the name of his opponent, Mike McKimminsky, "the Irishman with the Russian name" as the newspaper had it, and because the paper seems to have printed a report of the fight before it happened. Mike McKimminsky may have been a local boy of whom nothing else is known, or he may have been Con Comiskey, a well-known "white hope."[75]

Willard's fight in Hammon was scheduled for the evening of August 10, 1911, when the town held its first anniversary celebration. Jess was well-known in Hammon from his freight-hauling days and would have been the local favorite. The confusion in the name of his opponent may have been due to the quality of the newspaper reporting. The following is the report exactly as it appeared on page 1 of *The Hammon News* of August 10:

> In the evening after a few preliminary, the State scrap lecature the white mans hope, and the Irishman with the Russian name was pulled off—in about ten round Jess got tired trying to keep up with the other fellow and cease to rinn him around the ring. The gaiety of the dance kept up till a late hour. It was estimated that there were 2500 people present all having a good time, a special train from Elk City was run arriving in time to see the fight bringing quite a crowd of people.[76]

Since the fight was scheduled for the evening of August 10 and apparently continued for ten rounds and a "late hour," either the article, such as it is, was written before the fight was concluded or the actual publication date of the paper was August 11, not August 10 as printed. In either case, it appears that Jess won the bout at the end of ten rounds on the basis of a popular decision.

Despite his legal problems, Jess Willard was gaining a reputation as a prizefighter. The fact that Frank Lyon and, perhaps, Con Comiskey had traveled to Elk City and Hammon for a chance to fight him was recognition that he merited serious attention. Carl Morris had also finally been persuaded to sign for a fight with Jess, which suggested potentially equal billing with the most famous of the "white hopes." On August 6, *The Daily Oklahoman* announced that a promoter named O.H. Stacy, from the Knickerbocker Athletic Club of Albany, New York, planned to come to Oklahoma City to seek out Willard. Stacy claimed to represent a group of promoters on the East Coast who were interested in providing Willard with bouts there. Stacy apparently met with Phillips and together they made a deal for Phillips to bring Willard to New York. This, at least, is what Phillips told Jess later. But the problem was that Willard was nowhere to be found.[77]

Following his appearance in Hammon, Willard disappeared. It appears that he sent his wife and children back to Kansas to live with her parents, while Jess himself hopped a freight and traveled farther west. We next catch a view of him in Boone, Colorado, in the late summer where he obtained a job picking chili beans on the E.H. Smith farm for a dollar a day and room and board. The men there remembered him, both because he could do the work of about two men during the day, and because in the evening he told them stories about boxing and his plans to defeat Carl Morris. George Lovern, who was running the Smith farm at the time, remembered that Jess "certainly impressed all of us that he was a genuine athlete and handled his mitts like an expert." Willard stayed on the farm through the harvesting and threshing of the bean crop and then said that he was going back to Oklahoma.[78]

Still, this proved to be a low point in Willard's life. His wife and daughters had been sent back to Emmett to live with his in-laws. While this gave Barney Evans and his wife, Edith, their first chance to become acquainted with their grandchildren, it confirmed Mr. Evans' view of Jess as a ne'er-do-well who needed to get a steady job. And although Jess' reputation as a fighter was growing, he was not aware of it. He had been reduced to the status of an itinerant farm hand, separated from his wife and children, with no apparent prospects for getting back together with them. The fall of 1911 was a tough time for the Willards.

3

The White Hope Era (1911–1912)

Joplin and Springfield (Fall 1911)

Suddenly there was hope!

When Jess Willard returned briefly to Oklahoma City in late September 1911, his new manager, A.W. Phillips, informed him of the opportunities awaiting him in New York. This seemed like the break Willard needed, but Phillips apparently wanted to test Willard's skill with some local talent before heading to the East Coast. Since Jess was likely to be put in jail if they stayed in Oklahoma City, Phillips took him to Joplin, Missouri, where a local boy, Joe Cox, was making a name for himself as a "white hope."[1]

Joe Cox was from Ebenezer, and was a graduate of Drury College in Springfield, Missouri. He was recognized as the best all-round athlete in college and had a time in the 100-yard dash of 9.8 seconds, just short of the world record. He stood 6 feet, 2 inches tall and weighed 185 pounds, making him a perfect candidate for a "white hope." Cox knew about Willard and, in fact, had been in the crowd that witnessed Jess' first fight with Louis Fink in Sapulpa. Already, at that time, even before Cox had one bout, he was being billed as "the most promising Missouri heavyweight."[2]

Cox began fighting at the Business Men's Athletic Club (BMAC) in Joplin. Prizefighting was outlawed in Missouri, just as it had been in Oklahoma, but the gentleman's agreement which permitted "sparring and boxing exhibitions" in chartered athletic clubs for the benefit of their members was honored by the police. Jimmy "Bowtie" Bronson owned the BMAC and generally ran a clean and honest operation. This made the club an ideal place for Cox to launch his career. At the time, the most famous boxer at the Joplin club, was Jeff Clark whom Bronson had named "the Fighting Ghost." Clark was a light-skinned Negro who was so slight that Bronson was initially afraid that he could not measure up. But Clark proved to have world-class talent being both fast and very clever. He was a fighter with the potential of Joe Gans, the former lightweight champion, who had died in Baltimore that very year. Clark was the most famous member of Bronson's club until Cox showed up.

Cox signed a contract with Clarence C. "C.C." Warren from Monett on February 20, 1911. It was Warren's hope that Cox could begin his career by fighting Jess Willard, just as J. D. Brock had wanted Willard to begin his career with a fight with Carl Morris. But, in each case, the manager's ambitions had to give way to boxing reality. Cox was not ready for Willard, any more than Willard had been ready for Morris. Instead, Cox's first bout was on February 28 with a wrestler named Al Allegar from Joplin. Their exhibition of three rounds, which Cox won, was fought at the club as a preliminary bout. Still, on the strength of this exhibition and his daily work-outs, *The Joplin Globe* declared "Joe Cox may be Champion of the World Some Day."[3]

On March 16, Cox met Louis Fink in a bout at the Monett Athletic Club. Cox proved to be a superior boxer to Fink and knocked him out in the 14th round. This proved to some Missourians that Cox was superior to Willard. In fact, *The Springfield Republican* ran as a headline for their version of this fight: "Joe Cox Whips Willard." Jess Willard was gaining and losing a reputation in Missouri without even knowing it.[4]

On April 18, Cox fought Tim Hurley who had lost to Carl Morris the previous fall. Just prior to this fight, "Fireman" Jim Flynn had come to the Joplin Club from Oklahoma City to fight Jeff Clark. As he trained for the Clark fight, Flynn took Cox on as a sparring partner. Flynn was famous for battering his sparring partners, and he quickly knocked Cox to the floor and put him temporarily out of commission. Cox recovered and was able to meet Tim Hurley and knock him out in the third round of their fight. But the public anger at Flynn's beating of Joe Cox, plus the skill that Jeff Clark demonstrated, caused Flynn to leave town and go back to Oklahoma City. Flynn never fought Jeff Clark, but he did raise questions about Joe Cox's abilities.[5]

Cox's victory over Tim Hurley led to rumors that Cox would now fight Jess Willard. The victor of that battle would then fight Carl Morris. Indeed, J. D. Brock had considered having Willard fight Cox in Monett. At the same time, both Brock and C. C. Warren were also trying to get a fight with Morris as well. C.C. Warren was so proud of Cox that he offered to bet $2,000 on Cox to defeat Morris. J. D. Brock, however, was able to get the deal for Willard to fight Morris first. Joe Cox was left to fight an unknown, George Paylock of Carthage, on May 23 in Joplin. Paylock was completely out-classed and quit in the fifth round of their six round bout, giving Cox the victory.[6]

With his record now 4–0, Cox was riding high. Again his manager tried to get a fight with Morris. By this time, things had deteriorated in Oklahoma City, and the match between Willard and Morris had been cancelled. It seemed like a good time for Cox to make his move. Still, the new manager of Morris, Frank B. Ufer, refused the bout and Cox had to settle for a match with another one of Morris' sparring partners, Harry Wuest. Wuest was a heavyweight from Cincinnati and was the best man in the Morris camp. He was undefeated in his own right and hoped to have a career as a "white hope" candidate. He was clearly the best fighter Cox had faced, with the exception of Jim Flynn, and Flynn had flattened Cox when they sparred together. Further, Cox had to fight Wuest in Sapulpa, not in the friendly confines of the BMAC in Joplin.[7]

The fight occurred on May 29. Cox held his own through the first seven rounds, but in the eighth round Wuest knocked Cox down for a count of seven. After that the fight belonged to Wuest, who won by a knockout in the 14th round. Cox fought a good fight but he was out matched. Papers from Tulsa to Springfield chronicled Cox's defeat, and for some of them, this fight ended Cox's career. In keeping with John Lardner's rule that "a white hope was a white heavyweight who had not recently been knocked out by another white heavyweight," Joe Cox was no longer a "white hope." "This eliminates another promising young scrapper from the race," wrote *The Tulsa Democrat*.[8]

The demise of Joe Cox coincided with the decline in fortunes of boxing in Joplin. A new governor, Herbert Spencer Hadley, had been elected in 1910. Beginning in 1911 he, like his colleague in Oklahoma, Lee Cruce, began to crack down on boxing. Governor Hadley refused the BMAC permission for a fight between the black, Jeff Clark, and the white, Jack "Twin" Sullivan, and the club was shut down. Joe Cox then transferred his allegiance to the Springfield Athletic Club which was chartered on June 13, in keeping with the new rules issued by the governor. A fight with Jim Harper of Kansas City was planned for July, but this did not occur. Instead, C. C. Warren had Cox train on a farm for the rest of the summer. He did not return to the ring until the fall, when he was scheduled to fight Mike Schreck on September 4.[9]

Schreck was from Cincinnati and had been boxing since 1902. He had beaten Marvin Hart and Tommy Burns, both of whom had later claimed the heavyweight title. But Schreck's best days were behind him. He had recently lost to both Carl Morris and Harry Wuest. Schreck's manager, "Professor" Billy McCarney, hoped that Schreck could regain some prestige by beating Cox. Following a strategy that he would use often in his career, McCarney wrote a newspaper article which was published in *The Springfield Leader*, praising Cox and declaring that he was a coming prospect. This article persuaded Cox to get back into the ring and led to the fight with Schreck.[10]

The outcome of the fight was not what either fighter wanted. Cox proved a good boxer and a match for Schreck. At the same time, Cox was not good enough to knock Schreck out. The local papers were divided on the result with *The Springfield Leader* declaring it a draw, while *The Joplin News Herald, The Joplin Globe* and *The Springfield Republican* declared Cox the winner. Still, the local fans had doubts about Cox's abilities, while Billy McCarney concluded that his man had come to the end of the line and dropped him. Schreck went back to Cincinnati and continued to fight until 1915. McCarney stayed in Springfield and "horned in" on the Springfield Athletic Club where he eventually became the promoter.[11]

Willard and his manager, A. W. Phillips, arrived in Joplin in the middle of September in hopes of meeting Cox and getting Willard's career back on track with a victory. They were greatly surprised when they found that the local fans favored Willard over Cox, and wanted to bet that Willard could beat the local boy. This caused Phillips to develop the idea that he might make more money on the fight if Willard should lose to Cox. When he proposed this idea to Willard, Willard refused. Phillips then cut off Willard's funds and left him in Joplin without any money. Willard had to borrow money from Jimmy Bronson to eat. Bronson, noting that it would cost him a great deal to house and feed Willard, sent him on to Billy McCarney at the Springfield Club. Bronson had a great fighter in Jeff Clark, while the Springfield Club had only Joe Cox, whose disappointing effort against Wuest and then Schreck prompted them to search for a better fighter.[12]

"Professor" Billy McCarney, 1911.

Willard arrived in Springfield on September 23, 1911, with the intention of fighting Joe Cox, before moving on to New York, where he had been promised several bouts with big men, including Jim Flynn. Jack O'Leary, the manager of the new Springfield Athletic

Club, was to be the promoter of the Cox-Willard fight. With frightening rapidity, what seemed to be a simple thing, turned into a complex tangle of troubles.[13]

The troubles began slowly with the appearance in Springfield of a vaudeville act known as the Romano Brothers. The Romanos were physical culturists who painted themselves white and posed as Greek statues. Both of them were also heavyweight boxers and as a finale to their act, they gave a boxing match in which they demonstrated famous punches of past champions of the ring. Paul was the older of the two brothers at 24. He stood 6 feet, 3 inches tall and weighed 218 pounds. His brother Carl was 22 and also stood 6 feet, 3 inches tall and weighed 210 pounds.[14]

On September 26, McCarney and Willard were sitting in the Springfield Athletic Club when Paul Romano walked in. Romano told McCarney he was a boxer and that he had fought six rounds with the current champion, Jack Johnson, and one round with the former champion, Robert Fitzsimmons. On top of this, his father was an English Archbishop and he and his brother were traveling under an assumed name to avoid embarrassing the family. Romano then announced that he was here to fight Joe Cox, whom he had heard was the best man in the area.

Believing this to be the most outlandish braggadocio, Billy McCarney responded that unfortunately, Cox was not in town, and that the fellow sitting next to him also wanted to fight Cox. He therefore suggested that Romano and Willard put on gloves and fight for the right to fight Cox. Romano agreed and in a few minutes they were in the ring giving one of the best exhibitions ever seen in the club, with only Billy McCarney and the janitor as audience.[15]

Romano proved to be a very good boxer, but not quite good enough to defeat Willard. Thus, at the end of four rounds, he left with a black eye and the decision to let Willard fight Cox. But, the surprising thing was that everything Romano had said was true: He had fought six rounds with Jack Johnson on March 10, 1910, after Johnson had won the title from Tommy Burns. He had fought one round with the former champion, Bob Fitzsimmons. He was the son of the Episcopal Archbishop of South Africa, and he was traveling with his brother under an assumed name in a vaudeville act playing at the Jefferson Theatre. Paul Romano's real name was Victor McLaglen, and he would later become famous in the movies, winning an Academy Award for Best Actor in 1935 for *The Informer*. He also played opposite John Wayne in many movies, most notably for boxing enthusiasts, *The Quiet Man* (1952). Years later, when Jess Willard lived in Los Angeles, he and McLaglen renewed their acquaintance and became drinking buddies.[16]

Having disposed of Paul Romano, who then left Springfield to become a sparring mate of Carl Morris, Willard began training for the Cox fight. But three days later, Willard found himself in jail.

Having left Willard in Joplin and cut off his funds, A.W. Phillips was surprised to learn that Willard had come to Springfield and made friends with "Professor" Billy McCarney at the Springfield Athletic Club. Willard, thinking that Phillips no longer had any interest in him, asked McCarney to take over as manager. Phillips, who had paid $7,500 for Willard's contract, was not about to allow McCarney to take Willard from him. When he learned of Willard's actions Phillips came to the Springfield club with a gun and demanded to see "the Professor."

McCarney was the only man in the club at the time Phillips arrived with gun in hand. McCarney quickly explained that "the Professor" was out of town and would not be back until the next day. After Phillips left, McCarney called the police who arrested Phillips, took his gun and threw him in jail. Phillips then told the police that Willard was a prizefighter and was wanted in Oklahoma for having skipped bail on a prizefighting charge. The call went out for Willard and he too was thrown in jail, pending the arrival of the warrant from Oklahoma City.[17]

While Willard was in jail, he apparently discussed the possibility of his fight with Joe Cox with the police. The Springfield police, unlike the folks in Joplin, were proud of Joe Cox and wanted him to win. Although they let Willard out of jail, they apparently told him that if he actually defeated Cox in the ring, they might arrest him again for prizefighting in Missouri. Then, when the sheriff's deputy from Oklahoma City arrived in Springfield he admitted that the warrant he carried was for a misdemeanor, and, as such, Jess was not required to go back to Oklahoma City.[18]

The next day, October 1, 1911, *The Springfield Republican* announced that an agreement had been made for Cox and Willard to box a ten-round bout the following week at the Springfield Athletic Club. Due to his troubles with Oklahoma, Willard decided that he would no longer be known as the "Oklahoma City Hope." Now he called himself "the Kansas Giant." While this was not nearly as colorful as his later title of "the Pottawatomie Giant," it demonstrated that Willard, and not his manager, was beginning to call the shots in his career.[19]

No sooner had the Cox-Willard bout been announced than a new challenge appeared upon the scene. Once again, Willard was sitting in the club rooms, this time with Jack O'Leary, the manager, and "Professor" Billy McCarney, when in walked two men asking for O'Leary. The shorter of the two men introduced the taller man as "Tim O'Neill from Chicago." "O'Neill" asked for a fight with Joe Cox or any big man in the neighborhood. Billy McCarney had been in Chicago and knew the real Tim O'Neill and recognized that this was not the genuine article. Still O'Leary told "O'Neill" that if he wished to try someone out, he could try his hand with Willard. When the two saw Willard's size they began to back down, but goaded on, they finally agreed to a match.

Willard and "O'Neill" were soon dressed in gym togs and in the ring. For the first few minutes they were at it "hammer and tongs" until Willard delivered a solid left followed by a right to the jaw. "Tim O'Neill" was out on his feet. Willard then stepped back and refused to fight any more: "One tap would have dropped him out for good, but Willard was man enough not to land it when there was nothing at stake." "O'Neill" and his manager quickly left the club for parts unknown. *The Springfield Republican* summed up the event with the following observation: "If he [Willard] shows half the class against Joe Cox that he did against Romano and 'O'Neill,' then it is goodbye and a slow curtain for the local lad."[20]

The newspaper report of this bout had a damaging effect on Willard's training. The reputation Willard had earned from the two impromptu fights with Romano and "O'Neill" had placed him in a very difficult position. He was already wanted for "prizefighting" in Oklahoma. The police in Springfield had made their interest in Cox clear to him and suggested that he might be arrested for "prizefighting" in Missouri if he defeated Cox. And finally, the governor of Missouri, Herbert Spencer Hadley, who opposed prizefighting, had come to Springfield on the eve of the Cox fight and was considering closing down the Springfield Athletic Club. This was only prevented by the City Prosecutor, James H. Mason, who assured the governor that he would have sufficient policemen in the audience so that "any violation might be throttled 'right there.'" As a result, Governor Hadley allowed the Cox-Willard bout to proceed.[21]

Given this situation, Willard was not positively motivated for the fight. He had left A.W. Phillips over his suggestion that Willard let Cox win. Now, he was forced to reconsider his position. He had to find a way to lose so as not to end up in jail again. The problem proved too great for Willard to solve. According to one only partially apocryphal story, Cox hit Willard a solid blow to the stomach in the fifth round. At that point, Jess picked up the little referee, Jimmy Bronson, and with Bronson kicking and screaming, held him like a shield between himself and Cox and backed out of the ring. Billy McCarney, his manager, jumped into the ring and shouted: "What are you quitting for? You're not hurt, you big oaf!" "I know that, Mr. McCarney," Jess is supposed to have said, "but it's a wise man who quits before he is hurt."[22]

The real story is only slightly different. After closing one of Cox's eyes in the second round, Willard dropped his guard in the succeeding rounds and let Cox hammer away at will. Then, in the fifth round, "with a sickly smile upon his face that much resembled an infant's grin after taking half an ounce of paregoric, Willard turned to Bronson and throwing up both hands yelled: 'I'm in no condition to fight!' Willard then left the ring leaving the audience stunned."[23]

Willard's behavior in the Cox fight was a black mark against him for the rest of his life. He was constantly hounded by those who considered him a quitter. Unlike the Warren fiasco in Shawnee, which did little damage, the Cox fiasco stripped him of his chances to move into the big time fights in New York. Further, it deprived him of the services of Billy McCarney, who might well have made him into a champion years sooner. Instead of help from McCarney, Willard earned his enmity. McCarney never forgave Jess for walking out on the Cox fight. Later, when Willard might have been considered for participation in Tom McCarey's White Hope Tournament in 1912, McCarney appears to have used this performance in Springfield to keep him out. This led to the rise of Luther McCarty who, save for an accident of fate, might have become the Great White Hope.

The promise that existed in September for Willard had vanished by October. He was without a job, without a manager, and without an income.

Chicago Days (1912)

When Jess Willard walked out of the ring in Springfield, Missouri, on October 9, 1911, he walked into obscurity. In his later accounts, Jess says that he went to St. Louis and then to Chicago. In October, there was a strike of the shop workers on the Illinois Central Railroad. Willard went to St. Louis and got a job as a deputy United States marshal to protect the strike breakers. When not on duty, Willard put together a small gym in the East St. Louis roundhouse where he worked out on a punching bag and sparred with other strike breakers. It was here that Charles Cutler discovered him on February 1, 1912. Cutler was a world class wrestler who had come to St. Louis on January 26, where he defeated a German wrestler known as "Sampson the Champion." Cutler met Willard while he was in St. Louis.[24]

Cutler was well-known in Chicago at that time. He had been a protégé of the great John L. Sullivan and boxed under the name "Kid" Cutler. Sullivan had hoped Kid Cutler would knock out Jack Johnson when they were matched in 1908. But after Johnson knocked him out, Cutler switched to wrestling. When he bumped into Willard, he decided that any man who stood 6 feet, 6¾ inches and weighed 210 pounds had some value in the ring, either as a wrestler or a boxer. Cutler took Willard under his wing and brought him back to Chicago with him. There, he put him to work at Wicker Park Hall gym as a sparring partner for an Italian middleweight boxer named Hugo Kelly, as Kelly prepared for his fight with a Greek named George "Knockout" Brown.[25]

At the beginning of February, Cutler had badly wrenched his knee in a bout with Jess Pedersen, a Danish wrestler. This put him out of action for more than a month, giving him time to devote to getting Willard started in Chicago.[26]

One of the first things Cutler did was to get a large photo of Willard published in *The Chicago Evening American*. The photo showed Jess standing with his left arm extended straight out and Charley White, the featherweight boxer, standing underneath it. The photo and the article brought Willard instant attention from the Chicago promoters and revived his career.[27]

Prior to Willard's arrival, the Chicago papers had been musing over the heavyweight scene. Tex Rickard, who had promoted the Jeffries-Johnson bout in Reno, argued that the public was really only interested in the heavyweight crown, but he did not see anybody who could defeat Johnson on the horizon. Jim Corbett, the former champion, suggested that Al Palzer might be an answer, but even Palzer's manager refused to consider him worthy at this time. James Wood "Sunny Jim" Coffroth of San Francisco, was quoted as saying that there was no sense in worrying about big cards, as new idols seemed to drop out of the sky just when no one expected them.[28]

Jess wrestling with Charley Cutler in 1912.

As "Sunny Jim" predicted, Willard seemed to drop from the sky just as the boxing world was prepared to admit that Jim Flynn was the best "white hope" they could muster. Jim Flynn had signed to fight Johnson on July 4, 1912, two years after the Jeffries fight. But if Johnson vs.

Jeffries had been "the Fight of the Century," Johnson vs. Flynn was to become "Boxing's Greatest Fiasco." Flynn had fought and lost to Johnson already, and Jack had no doubt that Flynn would lose again. The rest of the boxing world was also convinced that Flynn could not carry the day. The only people in favor of the fight were the mayor and citizens of Las Vegas, New Mexico, who ultimately bankrupted the city to put on the show.[29]

Shortly after his arrival in Chicago, Cutler put Willard into training in Bill O'Connell's gym. This was Johnson's home gym and he apparently got reports on Willard's arrival and his progress. As a result he gave praise to Willard although they had never met.[30]

Willard gave O'Connell credit for teaching him how to use his left hand to give a straight jab which kept his opponents off balance. Prior to this time, Willard used a wide swinging punch with his left hand, which both telegraphed the blow and reduced the impact. By learning how to throw a straight jab, Willard felt that he was finally learning how to box. In addition, O'Connell taught him to stand up straight and use his tremendous reach to his advantage. The report from the gym was that he was "awkwardly clever, but is remarkably fast and handles himself well."[31]

By the end of March, Cutler had recovered from his injury with Jess Pedersen and returned to wrestling and he now had less time to help Willard make his way in the world of boxing.

Although he felt that Willard was ready for some action, none came his way. As a result, Cutler put Jess in the wrestling ring with the Polish grappler, Zbyszko. Jess lasted 2 minutes and 30 seconds. Wrestling was not his game.[32]

On May 9, Johnson announced that he would train for the Flynn fight in Chicago and was looking for some heavyweights with whom to work out. In his biography, written after his battle with Johnson in Havana, Willard says that he first met Johnson at this time at O'Connell's gym.[33]

On May 9, the same day Johnson announced his decision to train at O'Connell's, Willard was to have his first fight since arriving in Chicago. He was scheduled to fight Frank Ryan, an unknown, at East Chicago, Indiana. The East Chicago police chief, Leo McCormick, threatened to prevent the fight and the fight was called off.[34]

On May 22, Jess went to Fort Wayne for the first of his three fights with John Washington "Bull" Young.

John Young came from Wyoming to Chicago in October 1911. He was under the management of Sig Hart, Jack Johnson's former trainer. He was 6 feet ¾ inches tall and weighed about 240 pounds. He was, said Ed Smith, columnist for *The Chicago Evening American*, built like a battleship with "his weight lying down close to the waterline." Young's father had been a bare-knuckle boxer in Lancashire, England, prior to coming to Wyoming and he urged John to get into boxing. John got his nickname "Bull" from the fact that a promoter had supposedly seen him plowing a field without any oxen. He had massive hands, a deep chest and an exceptionally large jaw. His arms were long and his legs seemed short for his body. He fit the public's picture of a prizefighter: ape-like, hulking and brutish.[35]

What was not known at the time was that Bull Young suffered from acromegaly. This was a disease in which the pituitary gland becomes over-active, creating an enlargement of the hands and feet, a protruding jaw, thickened ribs leading to a barrel chest and coarse facial features. All of these features could prove beneficial in the prize ring; hence it was sometimes called "the prizefighter's disease." What was not so beneficial was the fact that these features were often accompanied by degenerative arthritis, joint pain, and an enlarged heart which might lead to an early death. Bull neither knew nor cared about these drawbacks. His goal was the same as Willard's, to win enough fights so that he might have a chance to defeat Jack Johnson and become "the Great White Hope."[36]

The first fight between Young and Willard was in Fort Wayne. Both were big men and both had strong punches, and both could take a punch. There were two fundamental differences between them: Young was much slower than Willard and Willard had a longer reach. Throughout his career, Willard preferred to be a defensive fighter. This forced his opponents to accept a great deal of punishment as they attempted to reach him. "Young could reach him only by boring in at close range and by swinging out and up. Each time John did this he placed himself at the mercy of his tall opponent and it was under these circumstances that Willard drove home his hardest raps." Young was knocked down once in the first round, once in the fourth round and knocked out in the sixth round. "The blow that put John away in the sixth was an awful jolt, well directed and with all the power Jess could place back of it. It lifted Young into the air and he went down with a thud. That the Wyoming bear can stand all sorts of punishment is evidenced by the fact that he got up shortly after the count of ten and walked unaided to his corner."[37]

The fight in Fort Wayne was a success for Willard. It revived his career. The Fort Wayne fans were so impressed that they would later claim that Jess had begun his career in their ring. The same was not true for Young. He clearly had dreams of becoming "the Great White Hope" and this defeat by Willard had given him a set-back. Young was sure that he could do better if they were to meet again.[38]

Willard was next sent against Frank Bowers (or Bauer) from Ontario who was billed as the heavyweight champion of Canada. Bowers was sponsored by Harry and Fred Gilmore and trained in their Chicago gym. Their first fight was to be in St. Charles, Illinois, on May 30. Within three rounds, Willard had Bowers in such trouble that his seconds threw in the towel. Gradually, Willard was making a name for himself.[39]

On July 2, Jess Willard and John Young got back in the ring again. This time the battle occurred in Chicago. Since prizefights were illegal in the city, the bout got no publicity. It was, according to *The Chicago Evening American*, "a privately conducted fight." The results, however, were the same. The fight was scheduled for 15 rounds but Jess knocked Bull out in five rounds. With this success, Jess was finally ready for the east coast and the fights that he had lost due to the Cox debacle.[40]

Despite his success in Chicago and Fort Wayne, Willard was still an unknown when he reached New York. The story goes that his manager, Charley Cutler, was able to get a small notice in the papers in early July, when he arrived, but the New York promoters were hard to impress. To show what he could do, he was put to work at the gym in Mount Vernon, New York. There he knocked out three heavyweights in one afternoon. This convinced Billy Gibson, newly appointed head of the Madison Square Garden Athletic Club, to match him against Arthur Pelkey in a "White Hope" elimination tournament.[41]

The story Willard told was that he arrived in New York without any manager and without any money. Cutler had returned to wrestling and was concentrating on his own career. Willard tried to get an appointment with Billy Gibson of Madison Square Garden but could not. He finally got in contact with Gibson's brother-in-law, Billy Hector. Hector agreed to serve as Jess' manager for one fight and got him the bout with Arthur Pelkey. Robert Edgren, sportswriter for the Pulitzer papers and famous boxing authority, wrote a life of Jess Willard up to 1915 and described this same situation. In his account, Billy Gibson's brother-in-law was Billy Hedkley, and it was Hedkley who set up the fight with Arthur Pelkey.[42]

Arthur Pelkey was a French-Canadian from Ontario whose real name was Pelletier. He was fighting out of Chicopee, Massachusetts, and was reputed to be a good boxer. Since Willard was unknown, Pelkey was given the odds of knocking Willard out. This was despite the fact that Pelkey was shorter than Jess by several inches and outweighed by 20 pounds.

According to Robert Edgren, who witnessed the fight, "Jess came into the ring as unconcerned as a postman about to deliver a letter." Throughout, Willard smiled at the crowd and seemed to think the fight was a joke. "Pelkey, lean-jawed and grim, broad-beamed and burly, started the fight in his usual rushing style. And to the astonishment of the crowd, Jess just jabbed him away and laughed. Jess wasn't worried in the least."[43]

The fight progressed slowly until the sixth round when Pelkey began a savage attack on Willard's midsection. Normally Willard had not suffered much from body blows but Pelkey succeeded in weakening him. In the seventh round, Willard returned the favor and delivered a series of right-hand upper cuts which knocked Pelkey back and forced him to clinch. By the tenth round, neither man was doing much, but Willard still won the newspaper decision although no decision was rendered in the ring. As Jess remembered it: "I didn't get him knocked out, but I did almost take his head off. It was a no-decision fight but the papers gave me the win." As a sign of the new and modern times, there were, *The Chicago Daily Tribune* reported, three women present to watch the match.[44]

Under the terms of the Frawley Act, which governed New York boxing from 1911 to 1917, bouts were restricted to no more than ten rounds and no decision could be rendered in the ring. Thus, all fights in the state were "no decision" bouts and recorded as ND in the record book. However, ND really meant "newspaper decision," as each bout was actually decided by the sportswriters who covered the event. This led to the strange situation that fighters had to read the newspapers the next day to find out whether they won or lost their match.[45]

This no-decision rule was tested by the National Sporting Club in May of 1912. At the end of a bout on May 9, between Jim Stewart and Edward "Gunboat" Smith, the referee, Patsy Haley, held up Stewart's arm as a sign that he had won the contest. The following week, the New York State Athletic Commission ruled against Patsy Haley and the National Sporting Club, and deprived both of their licenses. On May 24, the New York Supreme Court upheld the Athletic Commission's decision. As a result, the National Sporting Club was shut down and Haley was prevented from being a referee until he was reinstated by the Commission on June 6. The rule of no decisions in New York fights lasted until the Frawley Law was repealed in 1917.[46]

Willard's next fight was on August 19, before a capacity crowd in Madison Square Garden. In this bout he was matched against Martin Luther McCarty.[47]

Luther McCarty was now under the management of "Professor" Billy McCarney, who had managed Willard at the time of the Cox bout. Luther was McCarney's dream pupil. He stood 6 feet, 2 inches tall, weighed about 205 pounds and was fast and powerful. McCarney had discovered him working out, together with Bull Young, in Chicago under the direction of Sig Hart. Hart thought so much of McCarty that he planned to adopt

Martin Luther McCarty, 1912.

him as his son. But, he carelessly loaned him to McCarney for a fight in Springfield, Missouri, with Joe Cox. In order to protect McCarty's reputation, McCarney billed him as Walter Monahan when he fought Cox. After McCarty easily defeated Cox, McCarney decided that Luther was a true "white hope" and began to use his real name. McCarney refused to send him back to Chicago, and kept him in Springfield, training at the athletic club. After a series of bouts, McCarney succeeded in getting Carl Morris to come out of retirement to fight Luther in Springfield. Luther won the fight and immediately drew the attention of the Eastern fight promoters. Thus, he had arrived in New York to work in the same tournament as Jess Willard.[48]

While Willard only admitted to carrying a grudge into one fight, that with Carl Morris, it is clear that Billy McCarney carried a grudge against Willard. He had not forgotten Willard's behavior during the Cox fight and used it every chance he got to downgrade him as a boxer. To McCarney, and to Springfield, Willard was a "Yellow Hope" who lacked what old time boxers called "bottom," what the fans of 1910 called "game" or "sand," and what we call "courage" or "stamina." And McCarney was nearly right, because Willard was without a manager in New York and on the verge of giving up.

Just before the bout with McCarty, Willard met with Johnny Dunn, a veteran fight promoter. He told Dunn that he felt sick and could not go on. Dunn asked him if he had any money, and Willard replied, "Not a cent." Dunn then asked him what he would do if he were walking along Broadway and McCarty should come up and punch him in the nose, even if he was sick. Willard replied, "Why, I'd punch him back again." Dunn then told him to get into the ring and feel exactly the same way. Willard did.[49]

McCarney believed that when pressed hard, Willard would give up, as he did with Cox. Thus, he counseled Luther to hammer Jess hard. This McCarty did. But to Luther's surprise, Willard gave back as good as he got. The two giants stood toe-to-toe for round after round and hammered away at each other. Luther nearly closed Jess' eyes at the beginning of the bout, but Jess hung in and broke Luther's nose shortly afterward. Jess was able to stagger Luther repeatedly in the fifth and sixth rounds. As Robert Edgren remembered it:

> Once he [McCarty] landed a hard swinging right on Willard's left cheek bone. A red spot appeared, and for a round or two the big fellow's eye looked puffy. Jess, stung, stopped smiling around at the crowd, and paid attention to McCarty and as Luther came rushing in to follow his advantage, nearly lifted him off his feet with a crushing right uppercut on the jaw. I remember the clash of Luther's teeth still. He shook his head and stayed up, but it was a close call.[50]

In a pattern that now became familiar to his opponents, Willard was able to lash out with his straight left jab to keep McCarty away, and follow up with a right uppercut which staggered him when he came in close. Neither fighter was knocked down during the ten rounds but both were damaged. McCarty left the ring with a broken nose and both eyes swollen closed. Willard's eyes were swollen and he had a large bruise on his cheek. *The New York Times, The Chicago Evening American, The Trenton Evening Times* and *The Daily Oklahoman* gave the decision to Willard while *The New York Tribune* and *The Chicago Daily Tribune* called it a draw. But nobody gave the fight to Luther McCarty.

According to *The Chicago Daily Tribune*, "It was a great fight and the crowd went crazy over it." Only Billy McCarney ended the evening with ashes in his mouth. He had hoped McCarty would knock Willard out. This would have made Luther a star and would have sent Willard back to Kansas where he belonged. But, it was not to be. Jess Willard proved that he was a better fighter than Luther McCarty. Unfortunately for Willard, Charley Cutler did not prove to be as good a manager as Billy McCarney. Despite his victory over McCarty, Willard would get no new fights for months, while Luther became the best known white heavyweight in the world.[51]

Following the bout with Willard, McCarney took his fighter to the West Coast where they hoped to repair their fortunes. Willard was apparently left by his manager alone in New York without any money. As a result, he began to look to others for help. He first turned to the veteran manager, Tom O'Rourke, who was handling another white hope, Al Palzer. Palzer was suing the head of the New York State Athletic Commission at the time for failing to match him with Jack Johnson. With one heavyweight giving him a headache, O'Rourke didn't really need another.

However, he agreed to take Willard on for 50 percent of Willard's earnings. Jess turned him down. Next, he then returned to Billy Gibson at the Madison Square Garden Athletic Club. Gibson again turned Willard over to his brother-in-law, now known as Billy Heckler (formerly Hedkley or Hector). Heckler scheduled him to fight Glen Coakley, a middleweight from Fort Wayne, on September 2, but nothing seems to have come of this. Willard then asked Gibson to match him with Al Palzer. There was some hope of this bout occurring. Then Palzer was given a chance to appear in Tom McCarey's tournament and turned down the fight with Willard.[52]

Heckler and Gibson then planned to match Willard with Edward "Gunboat" Smith in New York on October 28. But Willard objected to fighting for six percent of the gross and asked for 15 percent. They laughed at Willard's request and when he said he would not fight for less, Heckler suggested he leave town since he would get no work in New York. Willard returned to Chicago. Smith, who was a more agreeable fighter, stayed on and had four bouts between September and December, while Willard sat idle. In the meantime, a series of events occurred involving Jack Johnson which dramatically altered the boxing world.[53]

Johnson had agreed to fight Jim Flynn for the heavyweight title on July 4, 1912, two years to the day after his victory over Jim Jeffries. As mentioned above, few people were excited by this bout and few thought Jim Flynn could win. Nonetheless, the fight took place and, as predicted, Johnson won. The fight was notable for the fact that Flynn used his head to butt Johnson throughout the fight. Head butting was illegal, dating back to the London Prize Ring Rules of 1838. The crowd was incensed. The sheriff stopped the fight in the ninth round and awarded the verdict to Johnson as a knockout. But more important than the victory were some of the events surrounding the fight.[54]

For sometime the public had been grumbling about Johnson. *The New York Times* felt that he should have defended his title against one of the other Negro fighters such as Sam McVey or Sam Langford. Because Johnson refused to fight any other Negro, the Madison Square Garden Athletic Club, which had the rights to put on bouts in Madison Square Garden, decided to bar Johnson from fighting there. At the same time, the Masons in England revoked Johnson's membership and censored the Dundee, Scotland lodge for initiating him. And, the United States Treasury Department indicted Johnson for smuggling a diamond necklace into the country.[55]

All of these issues paled in comparison to the problems Johnson had with his wife. Although married to a white celebrity woman, Etta Terry Duryea, Johnson had a casual attitude towards his marriage vows. He had brought Etta with him to his training camp in New Mexico. Nonetheless, he attracted the attention of several white girls from the town of Las Vegas. This greatly disturbed his wife, as well as disturbing the families of the girls, who were not used to having Negroes fraternize with their daughters and sisters. Although Jack Curley, the fight promoter, was able to soothe the feelings of the girls' families, he could not soothe Etta's feelings. After the fight, on the trip back to Chicago, Etta tried to commit suicide by throwing herself off the train. Johnson was able to prevent this, but still, when Etta arrived back in Chicago, she was a very unhappy woman.[56]

Upon arrival back in Chicago, Jack opened his Café de Champion, a wonderfully furnished restaurant and drinking establishment designed to attract both blacks and whites. For Jack, this was a dream come true. While he had gained a fortune boxing, his real goal was to gain acceptance into white society. Everything he did, from his interest in classical music, to Shakespeare, race cars and airplanes, to his marriage to a white woman, to the creation of the Café de Champion, all were part of his effort to break down the color barrier. It was as if he thought, that by winning the heavyweight championship he had become a white man.[57]

These things did not endear him to white society. Even worse, they served to alienate him from black society. Etta was the first to feel the effects of this. Initially, very much in love with Jack, she knew that her marriage would isolate her from her white friends and family. What she did not expect was that she would be shunned by black society women as well. They resented her for marrying one of the really exciting black males in the country. Jack's own family thought she married him for his money. Etta eventually discovered she had no friends, save Jack. Then, when she realized that Jack was radically unfaithful to her, her world fell apart.[58]

The trip to Las Vegas had jarred her, but the return to Chicago sealed her doom. Jack installed her in a lavish apartment on the third floor over the club. In an apparent attempt to placate Etta, on July 31, Jack announced that he was retiring from boxing and planned to devote his time to running the Café. But, Jack did not plan to give up his other women. In fact he maintained a separate apartment on the second floor of his club, just below Etta's apartment where he entertained both white and black women. Newspaper cartoonist Thomas A. Dorgan (TAD) once spent a day in the Café and watched a string of women make their way upstairs to the private dining room where Johnson held court. "I made it seven in twelve hours," Dorgan said, "not counting repeaters."[59]

All of this was too much for Etta to bear and on September 11, she asked her maids to pray for her, locked herself in her room and shot herself.

Jack was devastated by her death. The whole city joined him in his grief. Sermons were given in black churches shaming the parishioners for having shunned Etta and blaming them for her death. Her own mother, however, had a different view. She attributed Etta's death to a rare moment of extra-lucidity when Etta suddenly realized how isolated she had become by marrying Johnson. Still, Jack wept for Etta and the world wept with him.[60]

All of that changed in October, when Jack began to take another white girl, Lucille (Lucile) Cameron, out in public wearing Etta's furs and jewels. Suddenly, all those who had sympathized with Johnson over Etta's death turned on him. Both blacks and whites were disgusted by his behavior and Jack now found himself isolated. Criminal proceedings had already been pending against him for smuggling. Now they began to be urged against him for kidnapping Lucille for the purpose of "white slavery" (transporting women across state lines for immoral purposes). The City of Chicago ordered the Café de Champion closed. Respectable Negroes in Chicago considered him an embarrassment to the race and asked Johnson to leave town. Ada Banks, a light-skinned black woman who had left her husband for Jack, supposedly shot Jack in the foot for having taken up with Lucille. Ada's estranged husband then sued Johnson for alienation of affection. Offers for him to fight in New York, California, and Australia dried up. His step-brother, Charles Johnson, turned against him. And, Tom McCarey of the Vernon arena in Los Angeles, decided that Johnson was no longer worthy of his title.[61]

With the retirement of George "Tex" Rickard, "Uncle Tom" McCarey became the most famous boxing promoter in the United States. McCarey's decision to strip Johnson of his title came on October 17, after a conversation with Harry Carr, a sports columnist for *The Los Angeles Times*. Carr had seen a wire story about how Johnson had supposedly taunted the mother of Lucille Cameron and told her that he intended to marry her daughter. Mrs. Cameron-Falconet collapsed into tears and said she would rather that Lucille spend her life in jail than be married to Johnson. Reading this, Carr called Tom McCarey and asked him to come to *The Times* office. There, Carr suggested that McCarey declare Johnson's title vacant and that he offer a diamond belt for the new heavyweight champion of the world. Astonished at the plan, McCarey immediately asked: "But what would the sporting writers say about taking away Johnson's title?" Carr said that no sport writer would dare defend Johnson after his affair with this white girl. Thinking it over, McCarey agreed and the next day he announced his White Hope tournament.[62]

Harry Carr had been right in his view that stripping Johnson of his title and awarding it to a white fighter would meet with universal approval. No fighter could claim to be champion without the respect of the fans. It was the fans, not the title, which made a man a champion. Johnson, by showing off Lucille and then marrying her, had lost the respect of the fans. He no longer could be considered champion. "Jack Johnson can blame Jack Johnson and no one else for his present position," wrote Ray C. Pearson in *The Chicago Daily Tribune*, "for his actions outside the ring have brought his downfall."[63]

By the end of 1912, Tom McCarey's tournament had taken on a life of its own. It was a given that Johnson was no longer world champion. McCarey began his selection of contestants from among those well known to the prizefighting community. His first choice was "Fireman" Jim Flynn, the perennial "white hope crusher." McCarey knew that Flynn could not beat Johnson, as he had proved by losing to him twice. But, he also knew that any man who wished to replace Johnson had to be able to beat Flynn. Thus, Flynn became the filter McCarey used to test unknown men.

The first of these unknowns was Luther McCarty who had just beaten Al Kaufman, a former sparring partner of Johnson's, in San Francisco. Since McCarty was on the coast, he got the first shot at Flynn. There were many other candidates for the tournament, most notably Edward "Gunboat" Smith and Jess Willard, but Billy McCarney, had issues with both of them and may have been instrumental in having them left out. Thus, McCarey's choice fell on Al Palzer, a tall and powerful Iowa farm boy. Since Palzer was not on the West Coast, he became the choice to fight the winner of the McCarty-Flynn bout.[64]

The "White Heavyweight Tournament" began on December 10, when McCarty knocked out Flynn. Then, on January 1, 1913, McCarty knocked out Al Palzer and became the "White Heavyweight Champion," and the logical successor to Jack Johnson. Immortal fame had settled upon the boyish brow of Martin Luther McCarty.

While McCarty was flying to the height of pugilism, Jess Willard was toiling in the trenches. After beating McCarty in New York, he had languished in Chicago without work. Although Charles Cutler, his manager, continued his career as a wrestler, he was either unable or unwilling to find fights for Jess. According to a later report by the former lightweight champion, Ad Wolgast, during the fall of 1912, Willard was living off the free lunch in saloons and sparring with "pork and bean" type fighters in Chicago. When nothing turned up there, Willard himself contacted a promoter named Marvin Smith, who lined him up with a fight in Buffalo.[65]

The fight in Buffalo was with "Sailor" White on the night of December 2. White was from Brooklyn and a capable fighter. He had participated in a "White Hope" tournament in New York City in 1911. He had been beaten by Al Palzer on February 12, 1912, in New York, but had beaten a number of other "hopes" including Alfred "Soldier" Kearns and Jim Barry. Willard was unknown in Buffalo and the fight was not well publicized. Still, the crowd that attended was curious to get a look at the giant from the west. He was, as the local newspaper noted, "the biggest man ever to box in a local ring." When Willard knocked the Sailor out in two and one half minutes of the first round, the crowd was astonished. White was no competition, despite the fact that he was a skilled boxer and weighed 200 pounds to Willard's 214. As *The Buffalo Evening Times* noted, "Willard is tall, but not so tall that he is awkward. He has a wonderful punch and his foot work is smart. He simply smothered White with a variety of wallops from all distances. He used good judgment, measuring before he struck and invariably landed what he tried.[66]

Having knocked out "Sailor" White, Willard gained some reputation around Buffalo. Then, when Luther McCarty knocked out Jim Flynn on December 10 in Tom McCarey's tournament at Vernon, California, and it was realized that Willard had beaten McCarty in New York during the summer, Willard's stock rose to new heights. Willard had been angling to fight a middleweight, Tony Ross, in Pittsburgh but when he knocked out White, Ross backed out of the fight. Marvin Smith, the local manager, then negotiated for Willard to fight George "One Round" Davis. Davis was a light-heavyweight and considered the champion of Buffalo. Instead, Davis was matched to fight "Soldier" Kearns in New York City on December 18. As a result, Willard went back to Chicago where he spent time sparring with Marty Cutler (Charley Cutler's brother). When Kearns knocked Davis out in one round, Willard lost interest in Davis and signed to fight Kearns on December 27 in New York City.[67]

Kearns proved more of a challenge than Sailor White had been, but Jess beat him in eight rounds with a KO.[68]

The New York Times gave a description of the Kearns fight which gives us a better picture of Willard the fighter at this time.

> Muscles bulged out on Kearn's back and arms such as are usually found on wrestlers, and he gave the appearance of abnormal strength. Willard, without an ounce of superfluous flesh on his tall frame, also showed a wonderful pair of shoulders. From a boxing standpoint, Willard was the ideal build, but Kearns carried so much strength that he offset considerable of the other advantages which the Texan enjoyed.
>
> The early rounds showed Willard at his best, and his work was most impressive. He assumed a position that is decidedly strange in boxing circles, holding his head far back so that it was very difficult to reach. His great height made the task especially difficult. He had all of the appearances of an experienced athlete, using good judgment in his method of attack, and he showed the grace and ease of a finished boxer, at the same time always remaining cool.[69]

Originally, in Oklahoma, Willard's stance had him leaning forward, knees bent and arms out so that his jab lacked power. As *The Daily Oklahoman* put it:

> When Willard was learning he stood in an awkward position. His knees were bent forward as if he were going to sprint. His left jab was sent in a half crooked, uncertain manner. Now it is different as the big fellow stands up and makes the most of his 6 feet 6 inches. His feet are planted firmly when he stabs with his left hand, he moves about the ring without any effort, and when he hits, the blow travels true as a bullet.[70]

By the end of 1912 Jess had adopted an upright posture with his arms held in close to his sides. This allowed him to put far more power in his blows and time his attack more accurately. He had gained what the old fighters called "time and balance."

From his earliest days, beginning when he fought Ed Burke, Willard had demonstrated that he could take a hit and not be fazed. He had also demonstrated that he had enormous power when he hit his opponent. But, his talents were often overlooked or misinterpreted by writers who were used to smaller and more aggressive fighters. Willard was never very aggressive. When fighting, he preferred to have the opponent be the aggressor and then take advantage of his mistakes. This strategy served him well in his fight with Johnson for the championship, but it annoyed the spectators and sportswriters looking for more action. His behavior in the ring proved strange and unusual, and he was often judged to be an inexperienced or weak fighter. Initially, this was true, but Willard was a quick learner in boxing and by the end of 1912, he had become a cool and knowledgeable fighter.[71]

But there were other aspects of Willard's personality in the ring that disguised his abilities. He disliked fighting those he considered unworthy of him, such as "Big Six" Warner and "Battling" Britt in Oklahoma. He dreaded the police and did not like to fight if there was a possibility of getting arrested again, as in the case of Joe Cox. And, as we shall see, he was deeply concerned that he might seriously injure one of his opponents. This led him to be slow and tentative in the ring. That he was not physically slow or tentative is attested to by many writers. That he was not afraid of any of his opponents is equally true. He was not afraid of what his opponents might do to him, but what he might do to them. This trait led to many unsatisfactory fights, beginning with Ed Burke and Bill Schiller in Oklahoma and continuing through his title bout with Jack Dempsey in 1919.

"One Round" Davis was one of those that Willard did not want to fight. Davis was not a bad fighter. He had defeated the heavyweight Jim Stewart and would also gain a decision over the heavyweight, Dan Daily, who, at 6 feet, ½ inch, was tall enough to be worthy of Willard. Davis had bounced back from his knockout by Soldier Kearns and had defeated a good middleweight, Jack "Twin" Sullivan, on December 26 in Buffalo. Davis believed that he would then fight the winner of the Willard-Kearns fight. Now that Buffalo knew something about Willard, the prospect of a Willard-Davis fight on January 1 ensured a big crowd. Buffalo fans were very anxious to see Jess in action against their home-town champion. According to *The Buffalo Evening Times*, there was "more interest in this battle than any that the local promoters have put on." *The Times* fondly imagined that the victory over Sullivan had raised Davis' reputation in Willard's eyes. This was wishful thinking. Jess had no respect for Davis after his loss to Kearns. Although Marvin Smith, the local manager, signed a contract in Jess' name, Willard left the east coast and returned to Chicago, skipping the fight with Davis. From Willard's standpoint, there seemed no point in fighting a person like Davis whom he could easily defeat. Furthermore, he objected to fighting for 20 percent of the gross of the fight, saying that Davis was not as good a card as before. But, things looked different from the standpoint of the boxing club in Buffalo. They had been hoping to get another look at Willard and, at the last minute, they were left with an empty date on one of the most important fight nights of the year. Although they were able to get Dan Daily from Pittsburgh to substitute, they were furious with Jess for skipping out on them. Their local champion, "One Round" Davis, won a ten-round decision over Daily, but the crowd was not the size that they would have had for Willard.[72]

This type of behavior, which had been evident in the "almost" fight with "Big Six" Warner in Oklahoma, was one of the things which made it difficult for promoters to schedule Willard. His exceptional size made few men want to fight him; his non-aggressive style led to boring fights; his temperamental habits made him a manager's nightmare. It was no wonder that he had so few fights. In the meantime, Luther McCarty, who was more modest in size, more aggressive in temperament, and more predictable in his behavior, shot to glory as the "White Heavyweight Champion" and the logical successor to Jack Johnson. It was clear what 1913 would bring: McCarty would become the darling of the press and Willard would be ignored.

4

1913: A Year of Consequences

McCarty as Champion and Willard in the Weeds

On January 1, 1913, Luther McCarty, the Nebraska Cowboy, defeated Al Palzer, the Iowa farmer, to become the "White Heavyweight Champion of the World." Suddenly, a new white, clean world of boxing had dawned and was personified in Martin Luther McCarty. The new champion was tall, strong, attractive and boyish. He was the object of every woman's dreams and the son every father wanted to have. It was as if the sun had suddenly come out from behind a cloud and revealed the earth as new and exciting. The long, dark era of Jack Johnson, was over.[1]

Jack Johnson might be undefeated in the ring, but no one cared. He had announced his retirement in July after the Flynn fight and now he had no further say in the matter. As *The Kansas City Star* commented: "And the strange part of it is the fact that there has been no wail from the rightful holder of the title. The grueling mixups with the federal authorities, the death of his wife and his recent acquisition of another 'blonde' seems to have John Arthur thoroughly cowed. We have been expecting a chirrup for some time, but not a wail from Chicago. Even Jack Curley has forsaken him."[2]

Luther was not "the Great White Hope," for he had never met or beaten Johnson. Instead, he made "the Great White Hope" unnecessary. His victory and his presence meant that Johnson and the other Negro fighters, Sam McVey, Joe Jeannette and Sam Langford, were now removed as contenders in one quick stroke. For Tom McCarey had made it a condition of his tournament that the winner of the prize belt must never fight a Negro. The color line drawn by John L. Sullivan back in 1882 was reestablished in 1912. "When I accepted the heavy-weight championship belt," said McCarty, "I agreed to an unwritten clause that I should never fight a negro. The idea of this series of scraps was to pick out a white champion and keep the title in the white race. Well, I'm going to live up to my contract."[3]

The calamities that followed upon Johnson's courtship and marriage to Lucille Cameron altered the public perception of Johnson for all time. But I believe that there were two which hit Johnson the hardest.

The first occurred on December 31, 1912, New Year's Eve. Johnson took Lucille to a ball put on by the 8th National Guard Regiment, an all black organization which represented the cream of black society in Chicago. The couple was met at the door with some hostility but was allowed to enter. But, when they stepped on the dance floor, the band ceased to play and the other dancers left the floor. Lucille and Jack were shunned by the black elite of Chicago and eventually left the ball. As they did so, the band began to play again and the other dancers returned to the floor.[4]

The second event occurred a few days later on January 9, 1913, and involved Jess Willard as a ringleader.

On January 8, Johnson had been in Bill O'Connell's gymnasium where he boxed six rounds with Ned Carpenter, a potential "white hope" from Wisconsin. There was a large crowd there, from champions to novices, for O'Connell's gym was the meeting place for all of the boxers and fighters in Chicago. It was their home away from home, the place they felt most comfortable. Jess Willard and his manager, Charley Cutler, were also there. And after boxing with Carpenter, Johnson boxed three rounds with Marty Cutler, Charley's brother, who served as sparring partner for both Johnson and Willard. Willard himself gave a boxing exhibition with Cleve Hawkins, a black heavyweight, and George "Knockout" Brown a white middleweight. As usual, the sparring was vigorous but friendly. At the end of the evening, a group of the white fighters, led by Jess Willard, Charley Cutler, Packey McFarland, a welterweight, and Charley White, a featherweight, went to Bill O'Connell and said that unless Johnson was barred from the gym, they would be compelled to move to another location to train. They announced that they would no longer train in the same quarters as Johnson.[5]

This ban was personal, not racial. The whites made it clear to O'Connell that they did not want the other black fighters, such as Cleve Hawkins and "Kid" Cotton, barred. Their objection was solely to Johnson "the man who had disgraced the 'profession' by his conduct." Bill O'Connell then told Johnson the news. "Johnson when told over the 'phone of his being persona non grata is said to have been almost broken-hearted. He had never before realized how deep-seated was the feeling of men of all walks of life and all colors against him."[6]

Six days later, on January 14, Johnson and his wife Lucille boarded a train at 2 a.m. with one-way tickets to Toronto. Johnson was, at the time, free on $30,000 bail imposed in October by Judge Kennesaw Mountain Landis for having "kidnapped" Lucille. When the train stopped in the middle of the night at Battle Creek, Michigan, Johnson was arrested. Johnson swore that he had no intention of fleeing the United States, but the evidence was all against him. Johnson was brought back to Chicago and placed under arrest again. Judge George A. Carpenter, who was later to preside over Johnson's trials, accepted Johnson's explanation that he was not trying to flee the country, probably because the charge of kidnapping and white slavery had become moot. Once Johnson married Lucille, the case fell of its own weight, since his wife did not have to testify against him.[7]

It is clear, however, that the rejection by the 8th National Guard Regiment and his ban from O'Connell's, provided the impetus for him to flee the country and take up his residence in Europe. The black community was now against him. Worse still, the boxing fraternity had turned against him and announced that they no longer wanted to associate with him. The bastion of bi-racial boxing was denied him. And Jess Willard, who had gained Johnson's respect as a challenger worthy of note, had led this movement.

As momentous as this was for Johnson, for Willard this was a minor incident. Johnson was no longer the focus of his life, Luther McCarty was. Since Willard had already been in the ring with McCarty in New York and had, by most accounts, won the decision, he assumed that he would have another chance to fight McCarty and gain the title of "White Heavyweight Champion."

But this was not to be. Billy McCarney, McCarty's manager, had no desire to have Luther lose the title just as soon as he had won it. So he kept Luther away from heavyweights who might threaten his crown and two in particular, Edward "Gunboat" Smith and Jess Willard. The day after his victory in "Uncle Tom" McCarey's tournament, McCarty announced that he was willing to fight all comers and promised that Jess Willard would be the first one he would fight. Like most boxers, McCarty was anxious to defeat those who had defeated him, so as to wipe his record clean. But the next day McCarney stepped in and announced that Willard would not get a chance to fight McCarty until July 4 at the earliest. Prior to that, McCarney planned to have McCarty fight a series of people he knew Luther could beat. This led him to reschedule a bout with "Fireman" Jim Flynn in April and Arthur Pelkey in May. McCarty had already defeated Flynn in December 1910, while Arthur Pelkey was a competent but not highly regarded heavyweight. Later in the year, perhaps, after Smith and Willard had fought each other, McCarney might have allowed one of them to fight Luther for a large purse.[8]

Jess Willard recognized part of McCarney's strategy and, as a result, he turned down an offer to fight "Gunboat" Smith in California on February 1. "I have refused the offer to meet Smith because I know that I can beat him, and the terms offered me would not make the trip worth while. One of my hands is sore and I want it to heal properly so that if I get a chance to meet McCarty I will not have any excuses to offer if he beats me." Naturally, Willard did not expect McCarty to beat him, but he also did not wish to risk losing his match with McCarty by losing again to Gunboat Smith.[9]

But there were other issues on Willard's plate at this time which made his situation more complicated. After the victory over McCarty in the summer of 1912, Charley Cutler had not been able to get Jess any bouts. Although Willard and Cutler had never had a written contract, Willard owed a lot to Charley. Cutler had rescued him from obscurity in St. Louis and brought him to Chicago. He had set him on the path to fame. Even though Willard's victories over Arthur Pelkey, Luther McCarty, Sailor White and Soldier Kearns did not owe much to Cutler, he had helped Willard go from being a "nobody" to becoming the most famous boxer in Chicago after Jack Johnson. As *The Los Angeles Times* noted: "Willard has become an idol at O'Connell's gymnasium [with] fans crowding to the place each day to watch him work."[10]

Cutler's inability to offer more help to Willard at this time brought other promoters to the fore. A syndicate of Chicago business men offered Cutler $10,000 to turn Willard over to them. Willard was agreeable but responded that it was up to Cutler whether to accept the syndicate offer or not. "If he [Cutler] is too busy to take care of my career and desires to accept their proposition, I will go with them in a minute. Otherwise no offer could induce me to quit him." Willard's statement was designed to assure Cutler that he would stick with him if Cutler could help him get good bouts, especially one more with Luther McCarty. But Cutler misread this, and seemed to believe that Willard would stay with him no matter what happened. This led Cutler to continue with his plans to make himself the world heavyweight wrestling champion, ignoring Jess. As a result, when nothing developed, Willard began to consider seeking out a new manager. As he was to recall later, "It was along about this time that I began to bethink myself of securing a regular manager who could push my claims and handle business the way I thought it should be handled."[11]

One of the people most interested was Tom Jones, the manager of Ad Wolgast, the former lightweight champion. Jones knew what it took to make champions and Willard looked like a champion to him. Wolgast had suggested that Jones take Willard up during the fall of 1912 when Willard was sitting idle. Although nothing came of it at that time, by the beginning of 1913, Jones returned with a suggestion that he become Willard's manager. Jones offered Cutler $2,500 for an unconditional release of Willard, but Cutler refused the offer.[12]

Even though he could not get a new fight with Luther McCarty, Willard did attract a great deal of attention in the boxing community. The papers were now full of opportunities. On January 7 it was announced that the National Sporting Club of London had offered $75,000 to Cutler for three fights for Willard in England. Then Billy Gibson, head of the Madison Square Garden Athletic Club, wanted to get Willard and McCarty in the ring for another fight in New York. In addition, it was reported that James W. "Sunny Jim" Coffroth of San Francisco offered Willard fights with several opponents. Suddenly, Willard seemed to be going places.[13]

It is hard at this distance to evaluate the reason why none of these offers worked out. Possibly they were simply part of the hyperbole that accompanied the fight game, puffery designed for newspaper consumption and not reality. Or possibly it was due to Cutler's lack of ability as a manager. Whatever the reason, all of these offers proved illusory.

More realistic and closer to home, George Biemer, fight promoter of the Summit City Athletic Club in Fort Wayne, wanted to have Willard fight in his ring. Apparently Cutler felt safe with this idea, and so he signed Jess to fight Frank Bowers and Jack Leon in Fort Wayne. Neither was among the first rank of heavyweights and it was hard to understand why they were chosen. Perhaps these men, whom Ad Wolgast had contemptuously called "pork and beaners" were the best Cutler could do. Whatever the reason, at least they got Willard back into the ring.[14]

The fight with Bowers was scheduled for January 22 and the fight with Leon after that. Willard had already fought and defeated Bowers once on June 29, 1912. However, due to confusion over the spelling of his last name (Bowers, Bauer and Bauers), it seemed to many that Frank was a new competitor. The only thing that made this fight seem like a challenge was that Bowers had just come off a three round fight with "Fireman" Jim Flynn, which ended in a draw. Bowers' trainers apparently believed that he had improved enough to test Willard again.[15]

As a further attempt to cement his relations with Willard, Charley Cutler arranged for some vaudeville appearances for him before the Bowers fight. These were to take him to Minneapolis and St. Paul. Then, after the Bowers fight, he was to go to Kansas City, Omaha, Milwaukee and St. Louis. Cutler also supposedly planned for a motion picture crew to film Jess roping steers in the Chicago stockyards. While this was not Jess' strong point, a man named Miller did appear at O'Connell's gym and asked if Jess would be willing to ride an untamed horse for $100. This was more in his line and so the motion picture crew supposedly filmed him taming the wild outlaw horse. Finally, as part of the consideration for Willard staying with him, Cutler agreed to retire from wrestling after his fight with Jess Westergaard in Dallas, and to devote his time to Willard's career. All of these acts demonstrated that Cutler was trying to prove that he was interested in Jess. But still, he left it to his brother, Marty, to second Willard in Fort Wayne while Charley went to Dallas to wrestle Jess Westergaard.[16]

The fight with Frank Bowers was won by Willard in the fifth round. Although Bowers was strong and able, he went to the canvas in the third round when Jess hit him with a hard right hand. Unfortunately, that blow broke the knuckle of Willard's middle finger and tore some ligaments and it took two more rounds before Jess could knock him out. The last blow was fortunate, since the police were poised to stop the fight, just at the moment of the knock out.[17]

The Bowers fight illustrates the differences of opinions held by sports writers on Willard's ability at the time. Ray C. Pearson, writing for *The Chicago Tribune*, saw Willard, as many others did, as unschooled and unimpressive.

> The fact that it took Willard five rounds to dispose of Bauer, of whom nobody ever heard until he was matched with Jess, makes one thing stand out plainly, and that is that Willard's offensive fighting ability is extremely weak.
>
> One thing appears certain, and that is that Willard is not ready for McCarty.[18]

This view was widely held. But Eddie Santry, former featherweight champion, and the referee of the fight in Fort Wayne, had a different view.

> He's about the best there is right now, though still green. I was in the ring and right close to the men all the time and will say that Willard hits harder than any heavyweight in the game today. Fitzsimmons, when his hands were good, could not hit with more pile-driving force than this fellow. Jess was under wraps all the way with Bauer for fear of injuring him, but at that he shot over a couple of right-hand uppercuts that would have stopped less gamer ringmen than the St. Charles heavy.
>
> I never saw a boxer improve as fast as has Willard. He's got a nasty left hook developed, the short kind, you know, that does not have to travel far to hurt. And his right uppercuts and crosses are stunners. He does not waste punches, either, and when he starts one it's a good bet it will land. There is none of the old-woman style of milling with him. He did not pull a punch from his hips in the fight. All of them were of the snappy kind that you see champions use.
>
> I do not hesitate to say that I think Willard can trim Jack Johnson in the latter's present condition.
>
> I saw McCarty fight a couple of times, and if Willard can't beat him, then I never had a boxing glove on. Willard is bigger and tougher and a harder hitter than McCarty, and I actually believe he can out-box him too.[19]

Another observer, Robert Ripley of *Believe It or Not* fame, then a sports writer and cartoonist, had a similar view.

> Luther McCarty, the cowpuncher, may rightfully claim the world's heavy weight title, but one Jess Willard, also a cowpuncher, may rightfully claim a victory over the self same Luther.... And what's more, Jess hints that he can repeat the same, and all he wants on earth is just one little chance to prove it.
>
> Instead of boxing with a wide open guard and swinging his hands away from his body, as is usual with most big fellows, Jess works somewhat like Fitzsimmons. He waits for the other fellow to get to close quarters and then rips up either hand with great power. His right "upper-hook" is particularly dangerous. Besides being naturally clever he knows more about ring science than the average white heavy weight, and just dotes on meeting a man who will come to him and slug.[20]

The link in these articles between Willard and Bob Fitzsimmons, the former middleweight and heavyweight champion, was more than just happenstance. According to an article written before the Soldier Kearns fight, Fitzsimmons had spent some time in the fall of 1912 working with Willard to teach him these very techniques. Supposedly Fitzsimmons had taught him the art of the short powerful punch, how to keep his arms close to the body when fighting, and how to let his opponent come to him. Whether he learned these techniques from Fitzsimmons himself or not, they fit naturally with Willard's style and he adopted them.[21]

Jess Willard had become a genuinely good fighter with championship potential. But his unusual behavior both in an out of the ring made him appear much less formidable than he actually was. He had, for example, appeared in Fort Wayne for the Bowers fight dressed in an "English Walking suit" carrying a cane. Proud of his success, Jess was putting on "the Big Time." Even when normally dressed, Willard did not look like a fighter. Now, according to *The Fort Wayne Journal Gazette*, he looked like "just about the most cultured looking being to be found any place." His manager now called him "Gentleman Jess." To others he just looked like a dandy. This led many in the fight crowd to discount his real abilities. Still, despite fighting second-rank opponents, he had gone from being a complete unknown at the beginning of 1912 to one of the top ranked heavyweight fighters in the world by the beginning of 1913. And for this, Charley Cutler was largely responsible.[22]

Even though Charley Cutler did not accompany Jess to Fort Wayne, Tom Jones did. Although Jones supposedly was there to arrange a fight for Ad Wolgast, his real reason was to see Jess fight and evaluate his prospects. Apparently neither Willard nor Jones was impressed with each other at this time, and no deal was made. According to *The Los Angeles Times*, Jones felt that Jess would need a lot of polishing before he could hope to win the title from Luther McCarty. But this may have been sour grapes, and merely a way to disguise Jones' failure to secure Willard's contract.[23]

After the Bowers fight, Cutler took him on the second part of the vaudeville tour which had been set up in December. Willard and Cutler were in Kansas City at the Century Theater for the week of February 9, 1913. This act consisted of Willard taking on all comers in boxing and Cutler taking on all comers in wrestling.[24]

The Kansas City stay led to a series of interesting encounters. The first of these was the announcement that Jack Johnson was going to box Willard at the Century Theater. It turned out that this was a good black fighter known as the "Kansas City" or "Topeka" Jack Johnson, who praised Willard's ability:

> This fellow is very deceptive. I figured when I saw him box that I could outpoint him easily. But he punches straight, has a good left hand and is so tall and long armed, that he is able to use his cleverness to much better advantage than a shorter fighter. He hits harder than it appears to the spectators and is much harder to hit than it appears. I believe he will make a good heavyweight if he possesses gameness and I do not believe his gameness has been tested fully. Personally, I think he will develop into a great heavyweight.[25]

Secondly, Jess took the opportunity to call-out Clarence Ferns McCubbins. McCubbins was a little man with a big mouth from Perry, Oklahoma. Ferns was a welterweight (145 pounds). He had been fighting under the name "Kid" Ferns when Willard arrived in Oklahoma City in December 1910. Ferns quickly took over training Willard. Ferns was a better boxer than a teacher, and a quarrel broke out between the Kid and Willard. Ferns later claimed that he had knocked Willard out in training and caused him to quit the ring. In fact, it was Ferns' tongue, and not his fists which had irritated Jess. After being berated by Ferns for not learning quickly enough, Willard had stomped out of the ring. Willard remembered how Ferns had taunted him when he was just beginning in Oklahoma. By the time Willard got to Kansas City he had enough of Ferns' bragging and proposed a three or four round bout to let Ferns prove his skill. Naturally, Ferns declined.[26]

Then it was announced that Ad Wolgast and Tom Jones had dissolved their partnership. Wolgast had accepted a match with "Harlem" Tommy Murphy against the advice of Jones. Wolgast had recently had an appendix operation and Jones wanted to keep Wolgast out of the ring, but Wolgast refused. The first fight with Murphy was a 20-round draw which left both men severely battered. Not willing to leave well enough alone, Wolgast accepted a return bout in which he was beaten by Murphy. This was the beginning of Wolgast's decline and made it even more important for Jones to sign Willard to a contract. Jones knew that Willard had the makings of a potential champion, while Wolgast had passed his prime.[27]

Finally, Ed Cochrane, a sport columnist for *The Kansas City Journal* interviewed Jess about the Joe Cox fight in Springfield. Cochrane had served as referee for Luther McCarty's victory over Carl Morris in Springfield and had probably heard the story of Willard's fight with Cox from Billy McCarney. He wanted to get Jess' side of the story. Jess admitted to Cochrane that he had quit rather than fight Cox. Willard said that after being arrested in Springfield, the police had told him that if he let Cox win they would let him out of jail. This admission was picked up by papers all over the nation and became the topic of the day. Just when things seemed to be looking up for Jess, the Joe Cox fiasco came back to knock him down. The admission about the Cox fight kept Willard from getting his fight with McCarty, and made it more important from Willard's perspective to reconsider Tom Jones as a manager.[28]

Following the vaudeville tour in Kansas City, Cutler and Willard moved on to Omaha and then returned to Chicago on February 21. Billy McCarney and Luther McCarty were in Chicago at the time. McCarty also had been touring in vaudeville, but had announced that he was tired of it and wanted to get back to fighting. In addition, both "Gentleman Jim" Corbett, former heavyweight champion, in his column, and W.W. Naughton, the west coast columnist, in his, had been shaming McCarty for not fighting Willard. It seemed an ideal time for Cutler to get a contract.[29]

Luther and Jess met face to face.

> "Hello, Luther," said Willard, "You're looking fine!"
> "Feeling great," was McCarty's answer, "and I'm ready to fight any time."
> "Well, nothing would suit me better than to settle that little quarrel we had in New York," was Willard's reply.
> "I'm on," answered McCarty. "But all arrangements will have to be made by my manager. You were pretty lucky to stick around for ten rounds, and if ever I get you back into the ring again they will have to carry you to your dressing room."
> "I'm willing to take that chance," was Jess' retort.

McCarthy then said, "Now, let's cut out this rough talk, and get down to brass tacks. I'm willing to meet you in a finish fight at any time, provided you will go out and win just one good fight first. That is all I ask of you. I honestly believe that I will kill you if ever I get you in the ring for a long fight." Willard had no fear of McCarty, but he did agree to a preliminary fight.[30]

Back in December, Charley Cutler had signed an agreement for Willard to fight a heavyweight, Jack Leon. Leon, while not of the first rank, was billed as the "champion of the Pacific Coast." He was apparently a Russian who had come to the United States as a wrestler. Then he had taken up boxing. On November 24, 1910, he had knocked out Billy Dunning in the fifth round of a fight at Presque Isle, Maine. Dunning had died 24 hours later. While not well-known, Dunning was a heavyweight lumberman who had fought Jack Johnson to a ten-round draw on September 3, 1906. For Leon to have killed Dunning gave him the reputation of being a tough and dangerous man.[31]

Although the early reports from Fort Wayne suggested Willard was out of shape and might have a difficult time with Leon, the reverse proved to be the case. Willard started slowly but by the fourth round he overwhelmed Leon and knocked him down for a count of nine. Leon rose to defend himself. Willard sent forth a right uppercut and the fight was over. All Leon could say after the fight was "Did he knock me out?"[32]

However, if Willard thought that by beating Leon so quickly he might have improved his stature with McCarty, he was mistaken. The day after the fight, the "Sporting Notes" column of *The Fort Wayne News* had the following comment: "If Bill McCarey [*sic* for McCarney], Luther McCarty's manager, saw Willard fight last night, Jess is farther than ever from a match with the 'champion.' No manager would want to stand a paper champion up where he might get his mug in the way of that right uppercut."[33]

This proved to be the case. There was really nothing Willard could do to get another fight with McCarty, save bide his time. If he defeated other heavyweights he merely made himself less attractive to McCarney and McCarty. If he lost to them, it would show that he was not worthy of a bout. Furthermore, very few heavyweights wanted to tangle with Jess. He was just too big and just too good for anybody to be interested in fighting him. There was nobody in Chicago now who would step into the ring with Willard. He had also been banned from fighting in New York State due to his refusal to fight "One Round" Davis in Buffalo. So he went to the west coast in hopes of finding employment.[34]

In the meantime, the ranks of the truly great heavyweights were thinning. With Johnson out of the contest, and the racial ban reinforced, the other Negro fighters like Sam Langford, Sam McVey, Joe Jeannette and Jeff Clark no longer counted. They were in a separate competition. The fact that they were better than most white fighters also made them unattractive for fights. What white fighter wanted to lose to a Negro, when he had the possibility of fighting for the championship with Luther McCarty?

This left the field to the best white heavyweights. This list no longer included Jim Flynn, "the White Hope Crusher," who had been crushed by McCarty. It no longer included Carl Morris "the Original White Hope," who had also been defeated by McCarty. Nor did it include any foreign fighters. The best of the British was Bombardier Billy Wells, but he had been beaten first by Al Palzer and then by Edward "Gunboat" Smith. France had a contender in Georges Carpentier, but he had been beaten by two American middleweights, Billy Papke and Frank Klaus. Australia's best was Bill Lang, but he had been beaten by Jack Lester, a mediocre American heavyweight, and also beaten by the two touring Negroes, Sam McVey and Sam Langford. Canada had potential contenders in Arthur Pelkey and even in Tommy Burns, the former heavyweight champion. But Burns was not a serious prospect and Pelkey had been defeated by Jess Willard in a no decision bout in New York in 1912. In short, according to the dean of the west coast sports writers, W.W. Naughton, there were really only three or four white heavyweights worthy of the championship: McCarty the Champion, Jess Willard, Gunboat Smith and possibly Al Palzer.[35]

Since Al Palzer had already been beaten by McCarty, this really left only Willard and Gunboat Smith as legitimate contenders. As we have seen already, Billy McCarney had successfully kept Willard and Smith out of Tom McCarey's White Hope tournament due to issues McCarney had with both of them. McCarney thought Willard a "Yellow Hope" for running out on the bout with Joe Cox. And he apparently had a problem with Jim Buckley, the manager of Gunboat Smith, for some slight the latter had done to him years ago in New York. Thus, neither Smith nor Willard was likely to get a chance to fight McCarty if Billy could keep them away. This meant that there seemed no one of first-rate caliber with whom McCarty could fight. Still, McCarty wanted to fight and Billy could not continually avoid the challenge and the money that fighters laid before him. The issue was how to choose a time and a place and a fighter that Luther could defeat with the least possible trouble.

McCarney had one ace in the hole which he played that spring. This was to schedule, as part of the vaudeville tour, a series of exhibitions which did not count as genuine fights. Between January and April, McCarty fought a series of exhibitions, but by April, the public was getting restless and McCarney had to find a person with whom Luther could have a regular bout. He decided on a rematch with "Fireman" Jim Flynn, whom Luther had beaten in Vernon, California, in the opening round of Tom McCarey's tournament. To be sure no problems arose this was to be a no decision bout lasting only 6 rounds. *The Chicago Daily Tribune* described it as a fight matching "a magnificent specimen of mankind, handsome and mighty" against "a little man, strong of heart but lacking in physique." There were no knockdowns. McCarty won despite the fact that Flynn "took all of McCarty's punches with a smile." Luther then fought a ten-round, no-decision bout with Frank Moran in New York. Moran was considered to be a trial-horse, but he gave McCarty a tough fight, and demonstrated that McCarty lacked a true knock-out punch. Still, Luther survived the ten-round battle and won a newspaper decision according to *The New York Times*. Another three-round exhibition with an unknown, Fred Fulton, a heavyweight born in Kansas and raised in Minnesota, occurred on May 15. Finally, McCarty and McCarney traveled to Calgary, Alberta, Canada to fight with Arthur Pelkey for the heavyweight title.[36]

The fight with Pelkey was a clever calculation by McCarney. Luther had fought some of his first fights in Calgary in 1911 and thus had the home-town crowd with him. The contest was for the title, but Professor Billy made sure that there was really no risk in losing it. All Luther had to do was spar ten rounds with Pelkey and he retained the title. There was no pressure on him to knock Pelkey out or even make much of a show. All he had to do was remain standing at the final bell and he would win the match. And the money was good. Tommy Burns was trying to build Calgary into a prizefight center. Although the sport was illegal in the town, Burns had built a new arena just outside the city at the end of the streetcar tracks. All he needed was a few good fights to build a reputation for quality so that the crowds would come. Luther McCarty was the biggest draw available, so it seemed to be a win for everyone concerned.[37]

The best laid plans of mice and men *gang aft agley* as the poet Robert Burns wrote. And so it was with the Pelkey fight. McCarty smiled as he entered the ring on May 24, 1913, while Arthur Pelkey looked grim and determined. A few blows were thrown, but nothing of consequence. McCarty smiled, turned slightly and fell flat on his back in the ring. The cheers of the crowd quickly turned to silence as McCarty did not move. Suddenly, as McCarty lay in the ring, a brilliant ray of sunshine pierced the gloom of the arena and covered him with an ethereal light. Martin Luther McCarty was dead. It was an astonishing end to an astonishing career.

McCarty's death was front page news around the world. It was the first time in history that a champion had been killed in the ring. It was also the first time any boxer had been killed in the ring in Canada.

Everybody connected with the fight suffered. Billy McCarney, and the referee, Ed W. Smith, *The Chicago Evening American* sports editor, were arrested. Tommy Burns, the promoter, was indicted for manslaughter. Arsonists burned down his new arena. Boxing was banned in Alberta and Burns' dream of turning Calgary into a prizefight center went up in smoke. But even more than McCarty, perhaps, the one who suffered most was Arthur Pelkey. On learning of McCarty's death "Pelkey broke down and cried like a child all the way to the police barracks. 'I killed a man, I killed a man' were the only words that passed his lips for over an hour."[38]

Pelkey was arrested and charged with manslaughter. Even though he was absolved from blame, the shock of having "killed" McCarty in the ring ruined Pelkey. His wife, who had accompanied him to Calgary, cried hysterically for a week and had to be sent home to Boston for her health. Bad luck seemed to follow him. He became sort of a boxing freak, a man whose presence in the ring or gym brought shudders to those who recognized him. He became an uncomfortable man to have around. "But for the untimely turn of the hand of Fate, he might have been one of the most famous men in the world, enjoying the plaudits of the mob and the attendant financial benefits." Instead, he is remembered in boxing history as the man who killed Luther McCarty.[39]

By the rules of boxing, if Luther McCarty had been the champion when he went into the ring in Calgary, then Arthur Pelkey was the champion when he walked out of the ring. But champions are really made by the public, and nobody was ready for Pelkey to be champion, most of all Pelkey himself. "Some people say that I am a fluke champion.

Arthur Pelkey and Luther McCarty before their bout in Calgary, May 1913.

Maybe I am; perhaps I'm the real thing. I don't know the answer myself but we will soon find out all about it. I claim no credit for beating poor Luther McCarty, but the title has been forced on me and I'm going to defend it."[40]

Others, such as "Spark-Plug M'Closky," were more direct: "Pelky is no champion of the world. He happened to be in the ring when the champion of the world dropped dead from heart disease, or hip disease, or spontaneous combustion or something. Eddie Smith, the newspaper guy, who refereed the bout, was in the ring too. He is just as much champion of the world as Pelky. Eddie Smith is the real champ."[41]

Eddie Smith was of course not the real champ, but nobody knew now who the real champ was. To add to the confusion, Jack Johnson, who had been convicted of "white slavery" in June, had fled the country and taken up residence in France. From there he proclaimed both his innocence and his right to the title. Although no one wanted to accept this claim, now there was no one to say him nay.

The sunlight illuminating the body of Luther McCarty in the ring in Calgary 1913.

Tom Jones Takes Over as Manager and Disasters Follow

Before McCarty's death, Gunboat Smith and Jess Willard were attempting to find a way to force Luther into the ring with one or both of them. Willard had moved to California to seek some fights. In the process, he had finally cut his ties with Charley Cutler. As early as January 10, 1913, there were newspaper articles about Tom Jones taking over management of Willard. By the end of March Willard had decided to switch to Tom Jones. He claimed that he would do right by Cutler, but business was business. "Cutler and I are not only good friends, but we are old cronies. I like him and he likes me, but just the same we have not made much progress as a team. This is the time when I should be getting matches and making money, and I find myself idle most of the time. I need someone who knows the managerial game and who can further my interests as well as his own." Needless to say, Charley Cutler was not happy losing his "meal ticket."[42]

In addition to cutting his ties with Cutler, Jess also had an operation to remove a growth in his nose which restricted his breathing. This operation was successful, but it kept him out of the ring until May. However, at the beginning of May, Jones negotiated a fight for Jess with Gunboat Smith which was initially scheduled to be held on May 17, but then delayed to May 20.[43]

By the middle of May the San Francisco papers were full of the coming Willard-Smith fight. A great deal was riding on this bout. Many people thought Luther McCarty was committed to fighting the winner on July 4 in San Francisco, with the winner of that bout becoming the White Heavyweight Champion. Although McCarty was to fight in Calgary on May 24 with Arthur Pelkey, there was no doubt that he would win that fight and be ready for a serious world championship fight on July 4. Since so much was riding on the Willard-Smith fight, "Sunny Jim" Coffroth, who controlled the boxing scene in San Francisco, introduced an innovation. He held the bout at night in a new outdoor arena built on Eighth Street in downtown San Francisco. The new electric lights worked perfectly and made the fight as bright as day.

Tom Jones, Willard's manager, circa 1914.

Willard was, as usual, taller and heavier than his opponent. But strangely the odds favored Gunboat Smith 10 to 7. In part this may have been because Willard was an unknown quantity on the west coast. But since he weighed 50 pounds more than Smith and stood six inches taller, the odds should have favored him. But the odds makers seemed to know something that the public did not. The odds makers proved correct. Willard lost the fight to Gunboat Smith on a 20-round decision.[44]

Harry B. Smith, a sportswriter from San Francisco, attributed Willard's loss to his inexperience. "The Kansas cowboy proved last night that he knows so little about the game as to be styled an absolute novice." Willard suffered from his characteristic lack of aggression. "The Kansas man displayed no knowledge of the art of attack, and that cost him a chance to smash Smith down with his greater weight." Gunboat also had problems: "Handicapped by the size of Willard, who towered over the smaller man and held him off at long range, Smith had fairly to leap from the canvas in order to score." There were no knock-downs and neither fighter was seriously injured, although Smith opened a cut on Willard's ear which had been damaged in training.[45]

Deeper in Harry Smith's analysis was a hint at what went wrong. Tom Jones had just taken over Willard's training, providing new instructions and an entirely new set of trainers and corner men for this fight. Willard's "inexperience" was due not to his lack of knowledge, but due to advice that contradicted that which he had formerly received. Watching the fight, Harry Smith noticed this but attributed it to Willard's "inexperience."

> Willard showed quite enough to make many friends for himself, but there is one thing that he must develop if he wants to be a great fighter. And that is the knack of thinking fast and of putting his thoughts into action. It was hard to tell last evening whether Willard was slow to take advantage of his many openings because he lacked experience or because he was slow in deciding what to do.... More than once he staggered the Gunner with lefts and sent him up against the ropes, but there the novice would stop, look around the ring as if inviting assistance, and then allow Smith to come to a protecting clinch.[46]

Only after the fight did the public learn what the odds makers already knew: Tom Jones and the new corner men did not know how to handle Willard. Their disagreements and contradictory advice upset Jess and made him indecisive in the ring.

> During the latter part of the bout Willard's seconds started a wrangle in Jess' corner, and Tom Jones almost pulled Charley Anslinger's scalp off during the minute's rest between the twelfth and thirteenth rounds. Anslinger had made some observations to Willard that did not please Manager Jones, and Jones went for him, grabbing a handful of Anslinger's hair and almost pulling it out.
>
> Another thing that bothered Willard was the conflicting instructions he received. Jones would tell him something and Willard would try to follow the instructions. But while he was trying to follow Jones' instructions some one in his corner would counterman the order and Jess would stop still, open his mouth and look around to get the signal.[47]

Willard was not a novice. By rights he should have beaten Smith easily. But the confusion in his corner caused him to lose a close decision in a crucial fight that really mattered. The winner of this fight stood to be the next man to have a chance to fight Luther McCarty for the title, and Willard had lost. Gunboat Smith now stood as the premier "white hope" after McCarty. Had things gone as planned, Smith and McCarty might have settled the matter on July 4 in San Francisco in the very arena in which Willard and Smith had fought. But things did not go as planned. McCarty died in Calgary on May 24 and the boxing world changed once again.

Although he lost the fight, Willard gained the praise of the west coast sports writers. Harry B. Smith said, "It was a defeat that carried with it no disgrace, and the same crowd that last night laughed because of Willard's inexperience, may be applauding him twelve months from now." Jack Welsh, the west coast referee who would later handle the Johnson-Willard fight, told Robert Edgren in Havana, "If I had been the referee I'd have given the decision to Willard. In my opinion he won all the way." And W.W. Naughton, who believed that Willard should have at least had a draw, stated that there was no question of Willard's gameness: "he is true blue in the matter of courage." Still, damaged by the defeat, Tom Jones decided to be cautious in matching Willard with other fighters for the while.[48]

Willard's next fight was with Charley Miller on June 27 in San Francisco. Miller was 25 years old and had already been beaten by Jim Flynn. On the other hand, he had defeated Al Kaufman, Jim Barry, "Battling" Jim Johnson and Jack Geyer, and though they were all past their prime, Miller had at least gained some experience. But Miller had yet to gain a real reputation. "He is simply a husky with an ability to withstand punishment and with little ring sense," wrote *The Washington Post*.[49]

Willard entered this fight expecting an easy time. Instead, he would later admit that "Charley Miller, the western heavyweight fighter, gave me the hardest battle I was ever in and ever expect to be in."

> I was completely fooled by this bout. They told me it was to be only four rounds, so I decided that it wouldn't be at all necessary to train much for the affair. Twelve minutes of boxing seemed so easy to me that, after I got thinking about it for a time, I decided that I did not need any special preparation at all for the thing.
>
> How horribly I was mistaken in the matter was made plain to me before I had been in action with Miller for a couple of minutes.
>
> Miller rushed me around the ring as if I was the cheapest novice in the business, and to make matters worse, I played right into his hands by slugging away with him, hoping to win on a knockout in great style.
>
> Well, I knocked him down a couple of times, but couldn't hit him squarely on the jaw. He simply wouldn't stay down, and in the third round I was so tired that I could scarcely get out of my chair.
>
> They called the fight a draw at the end of the fourth round, and I can truthfully say right now that I never was so glad to hear anything in the world as the sound of that final gong.
>
> It was with difficulty that I dragged myself to the corner at the finish, and all I could gasp out to Tom Jones in my corner was something about "never again."[50]

The draw with Willard was a feather in Miller's cap and black mark on Willard's record. It proved the truth of the criticism leveled at Willard that he did not seem to take fighting seriously enough. As *The New York Times* would later say, "In all of his bouts he has shown a disposition to regard boxing something as a joke." Willard's physical ability carried him to victory, but his mental attitude left him vulnerable to defeat. Had his mental outlook matched his physical talents, he might have been the greatest heavyweight in the history of the sport. But such was not the case. And the Charley Miller fight proved it.[51]

Following the Miller fight, Jones matched Willard with Al Williams of Cleveland. One of the peculiarities of the fight game was that boxers often took pseudonyms or changed their names from time to time. The real name of "Tommy Burns," the Canadian heavyweight, who lost the title to Jack Johnson, was Noah Brusso. "Fireman Jim Flynn's" real name was Andrew Chiariglione. "Wildcat" Ferns, whom Jess knew in Oklahoma City as "Kid" Ferns, was really Clarence Ferns McCubbins. So too was "Al Williams of Cleveland" really the Al Mandino of Tennessee whom Jess had fought and knocked out in Oklahoma City on April 14, 1911. After that fight, Mandino changed his name and became a sparring partner for numerous fighters, notably Jim Flynn in his battle with Johnson in Las Vegas, New Mexico.

Williams as Mandino was no match for Willard in Oklahoma City in 1911; and Mandino as Williams was no match for Willard in Reno in 1913. After eight rounds, with Williams sprawled on his hands and knees in the ring, the referee raised Willard's hand in victory without even counting Williams out. The fight was disappointing to the crowd because it was so one-sided. And Willard was again criticized for "a certain reluctance to properly punish his adversary when occasion offered." But this was typical of Jess who disliked fighting men who were not his equal. He found no glory in punishing a man like Williams who was already beaten.[52]

Following the Williams fight, Tom Jones tried to match Jess with Sam Langford, the great Negro fighter, whom many considered second only to Jack Johnson.

Langford had been fighting in Australia for the last two years. He returned to the United States and found that the color line was drawn against him and that fights with whites were difficult to find. Willard had initially said he would not fight any Negroes save Jack Johnson, but when he found it difficult to get bouts, he changed his mind. A fight was scheduled as a four round exhibition in San Francisco. It was prevented when the local supervisors refused to allow a permit for the fight. The reason was that one of the fighters (Langford) had a "world wide reputation as a prize fighter." Since "prize fighting" had been outlawed in California since 1850, he could not be allowed to fight in San Francisco. Willard was disappointed, but Ring Lardner thought Jess was lucky not to have to get into the ring with Langford: "Jess Willard must have friends among the San Francisco supervisors, who refused a permit for the scheduled four-round bout between him and Langford." In point of fact, what this incident proved was that while fighters and promoters often had no trouble in engaging in biracial bouts, boxing was becoming more segregated. The sport of boxing had always been color-blind. But the public had come to see boxing between blacks and whites as no longer acceptable. Willard had sparred with black fighters from his earliest days in Oklahoma City and had great respect for them. He considered Jack Johnson a gentleman and a clean fighter. But *alia tempores, alia mores*, and he began to learn that he could no longer fight black fighters other than Johnson.[53]

Instead of fighting Sam Langford, a true challenge, Jones next inked Willard to fight John "Bull" Young, who was no challenge at all.

Willard had already fought Young twice before, knocking him out both times. The only reason for scheduling a third fight with Young was that the loss to Smith and the draw with Miller caused Jones to fear putting Willard in with truly good men until he had more "schooling." Hence he signed for fights with Williams (Mandino) and Young, both of whom Willard had beaten before. It was not that Willard needed more "schooling." Rather it was Jones and his team who needed more schooling. They needed to learn more about Willard's temperament and boxing style. Willard was a complex man who had all of the physical tools to win the championship, but he was moody and could easily be discouraged if not handled properly. And so far, Jones had not handled him well.

There was also another reason for this bout. Young had been Luther McCarty's sparring partner during the White Hope tournament at the Vernon ring. Young himself had ambitions of greatness and had been pestering Tom McCarey to allow him to take up where Luther left off. So far McCarey had refused to let Young box in his ring, but Young had been insistent. Now that McCarey planned to hold a new white hope tournament to develop a successor to Luther, Young wanted to be involved. Since Willard had also been left out of the first tournament, the idea appealed to McCarey that Willard and Young might be the first group in an elimination round. The second round was to be the Arthur Pelkey-Charlie Miller bout scheduled for September 23. The winners of the first two rounds were to fight in October, with the winner of that bout to fight Gunboat Smith in November. The final winner would then be the new "White Heavyweight Champion."[54]

The Willard-Young bout, was scheduled at the Vernon Arena for Friday, August 22. Vernon, California, was a small industrial area totally surrounded by Los Angeles but with its own municipal government. In a gesture of independence, when Los Angeles outlawed boxing in 1907, Vernon allowed Jim Jeffries to build a boxing arena there. The Jeffries Athletic Club began holding 25-round bouts with decisions in 1908. Beginning in 1910, the Vernon arena came under the new leadership of "Uncle Tom" McCarey and his referee, Charles Eyton. It became the center for boxing in Los Angeles and remained so up until January 1915. Unexpectedly, the Willard-Young fight served to destroy championship boxing in California and put Tom McCarey out of a job.[55]

For Jess Willard, the bout was to be another training fight designed to get Willard and his manager working together. Both knew he could fight, but they needed to find a way to improve Willard's abilities rather than confuse them. In addition, a win by Willard might put him on the road to becoming the next "White Heavyweight Champion" to

Jess Willard and John "Bull" Young at the beginning of their fight in Vernon, California, August 1913.

replace Luther McCarty. While the outcome could boost Willard's chances, Bull Young lacked the experience and history of a Fireman Jim Flynn. He was not likely to become Willard's stepping stone to greatness. Still, Willard did not expect to lose.

For John Washington "Bull" Young, the fight was more critical. He had already lost two bouts to Willard in 1912, but they were the only losses on his record. He knew that he had to win this fight to stay in boxing. He had already made plans to marry a girl he had met in Venice, should he win. But also he had made plans to quit the ring forever and return to Glenrock, Wyoming, if he lost. It was "make or break" time for Bull Young.[56]

Bull had support for his cause from many in Los Angeles. De Witt Van Court, a boxing trainer and the most knowledgeable writer in Los Angeles, wrote that in his opinion the new champion would be one of four men: Jess Willard, Bull Young, Al Palzer or Arthur Pelkey. Two were going into the ring that night and one, Pelkey, was ringside. In addition, Noah Young, Jr., Bull's brother, was in his corner, while his father, Noah Young, Sr., had been instrumental in persuading Tom McCarey to put Bull in the ring again. As *The Los Angeles Times* noted, "When Bull Young meets Jess Willard in the Vernon Arena August 22, the world at large will be able to know the answer to the old riddle about what happens when an irresistible force meets an immovable object. It certainly looks like sure death for the first man who becomes the recipient of a love tap from the other." The stage was set for a fight which was to have major consequences for all the parties involved.[57]

Willard was six inches taller than Young and had a much longer reach, but they weighed about the same. From the beginning, Jess controlled the fight, keeping Bull at bay with his long left jab. Still, Willard would not follow up on his advantage. It was a typical Willard fight, and according to De Witt Van Court, "the contest was slow and uninteresting throughout." Finally, in the tenth round Bull claimed to have discovered a weakness in Willard's defense. He told his corner that he was going to rush inside Willard's jab, and though he might get hit, he felt he could take Willard down. At the beginning of the 11th round Young showed renewed determination as he rushed Willard. Jess was taken aback by Bull's sudden aggressiveness. As Bull rushed in Jess met him with a solid left hook to the jaw followed by a terrific right uppercut to the chin. "It was the hardest punch I have ever seen delivered in a boxing ring," wrote Van Court. "Bull doubled up like a rag, fell back on his haunches and then on his back, completely out."[58]

"When Bull fell there was a deathly stillness in the house, and many immediately rushed to ringside, but were held off by the police. Drs. Griffin, Scroggs, and Houghton entered the ring and administered several injections of stimulants and Young rallied slightly for a short time. He was then taken to the hospital for treatment."[59]

The scene at the Clara Barton Hospital was memorable. The three doctors who had been at the ring were personal friends of the fighters. With them in the operating room were Noah Young, Jr., Bull's brother, Jack Davies, his second, and Earl Rogers, the most famous defense lawyer in Los Angeles. Rogers was a leader of what in earlier years had been called "The Fancy." "The Fancy" was a mixture of wealthy aristocrats and urban lowlife who were united by their love of boxing and gambling. Rogers was elegant in dress, brilliant in court, and dissolute in his private life. He had defended Clarence Darrow for jury tampering. He was a drinking buddy of Jack London, and was the model for Earl Stanley Gardner's "Perry Mason." He had been at the fight with the doctors, but he was in the operating room to provide the defense for Uncle Tom McCarey, Jess Willard and all of boxing.[60]

Downstairs, in the dimly lighted main hall, were other members of The Fancy. These were Bull's friends, "nervous, awed, in sporty checks, diamonds, in glaring colored sweaters, hatless and disheveled. Tears flowed from eyes and hearts of strong men who were brave enough to make no excuses. Each of the half-dozen chairs in the reception room contained a figure whose shoulders heaved over a bent head."[61]

Outside in the dark, afraid to even to come into the hospital, stood two more: Walter Monahan, Bull's sparring partner, and Jess Willard. When some one suggested they go in to see Bull, Monahan replied: "See him.... I can't stand it.... I was up there in that white room.... I saw him. He's dying, I tell you. He's dying. Our Bull's gone."

The doctors worked all night over Bull. By 2 a.m. it seemed as if he would pull through. "He looks well enough to set up and get back into the ring and finish the fight," said one of the doctors. Relieved, the crowd went home. "But there was one who did not go home. All night long, a lonely, worried figure hung around in the street in front of the Clara Barton Hospital. It was Jess Willard, the big, gentle-hearted cowboy whose blow had felled Bull Young." Thus when death came to Bull Young at 9:35 a.m. on August 23, it was Jess Willard who first learned the news.[62]

Immediately upon learning of Bull's death, Jess Willard went to Earl Roger's office to give himself up. There he met Noah Young, Jr., who had just learned the news. Willard faltered, "I-I want to go in. I want to tell I am sorry. He stepped through the door and tried to say something but his voice choked. He put his arms around Bull's brother and they cried on each other's shoulders like two heart-broken big boys—which they were, the tears streaming down their faces, neither saying a word."[63]

The day of Bull's death, August 23, a man named Malcolm McLaren filed a criminal complaint against everybody involved with the fight and had them arrested and charged with manslaughter. The trial was set for 10 a.m., August 29 in the Justice of the Peace Court before Justice J.W. Summerfield. Willard was given bail of $5,000 while all of the rest, Tom McCarey, Al Greenwald, his partner, Harry Gilmore, Jr., Young's manager, Tom Jones, Willard's manager, Charles Eyton, the referee and later head of Paramount Films, Al Harder, timekeeper, Walter Monahan and Jack Davies, Young's seconds, and Charles Anslinger, Eddie Webster and Jim Cameron, Willard's seconds, were all given bail of $1,500 each. Since no one had so much money available on short notice, a call was made to former champion, Jim Jeffries, who came and bailed them out.[64]

Two days later at the coroner's inquest Willard was found "unintentionally" responsible for Young's death. In addition, it was revealed at the inquest for the first time, that Young's massive physique was due to a thyroid condition known as acromegaly, accompanied by an enlarged heart. The doctors' testimony at the inquest revealed that while Willard's blow to the chin had undoubtedly knocked Young out, it may not have been the cause of death. Dr. A.D. Houghton, who had been at the fight, gave the following testimony: "Young was, in my opinion, rendered unconscious by the blow Willard struck. But I do not believe the blow killed him. By falling, rigid on his spine, he might have suffered injury serious enough to cause death."[65]

This seemed good news for Willard and the others, but Chief Deputy District Attorney, W. Joseph Ford, declared that as far as he was concerned, the manslaughter charges still stood. He asked that the parties be bound over for trial in the Superior Court of the County of Los Angeles on new charges of prizefighting and second degree murder.[66]

By amending the complaint to include prizefighting Ford entered the complicated field of prizefight law. English law had been the basis for prizefight law in the United

States for more than a century. The Earl of Halsbury summarized the matter in this fashion:

> Amicable contests in wrestling or boxing are not unlawful, and a person who unintentionally causes the death of another in the course of such a contest is not guilty of culpable homicide; but a prize fight, or any contest either for money or otherwise in which the lives or health of the combatants are endangered, or in which the intention is to continue the contest until one of them is disabled or subdued by violent blows, is illegal, and if death results, the survivor and those who are present and encourage the fight are guilty of manslaughter.[67]

By declaring the fight at Vernon a "prize fight" Ford was girding himself for a battle.

Against the dicta of the Earl of Halsbury and Chief Deputy District Attorney Ford stood California law. During the nineteenth century, prizefighting was considered one of the four deadly sins of society in all Anglo-Saxon countries. Strenuous efforts were made to prohibit prizefighting, as well as gambling, prostitution and alcoholism. But despite the efforts to curb these social sins, they persisted. In the case of prizefighting, between 1835 and 1900 virtually every state, as well as the federal government, had outlawed it. California had passed its first law against prizefighting in the first state legislature of 1850.Yet, for the most part, these laws were ignored.[68]

Beginning in 1890, moreover, laws began to be passed which allowed licensed athletic clubs to hold sparring and boxing matches. Such an amendment to the law was passed in California in 1899 at the request of James J. Groom, a boxing promoter. Nonetheless, prizefighting, as distinct from sparring matches, remained illegal. Just what the difference was between them was not clear. In 1911, Judge Frank R. Willis of the Los Angeles County Superior Court decided that a fight between George Memsic and Ad Wolgast at Vernon was a boxing match and not a prizefight. Earl Rogers argued that this decision should control the case against Willard. The Young case resolved itself into two parts: (1) Did the blow by Willard kill Young, or did the fall or even the later operation at the hospital kill Young? and (2) Was the fight at Vernon a legal sparring match, in which case the death would be considered an accident, or was it an illegal "prize fight," in which case the death was manslaughter (if done without malicious intent) or murder (if done by premeditation and intent)? The Young case was made more complicated by the fact that the records of Judge Willis' decision seemed to have disappeared from the court.[69]

By the beginning of October, Chief Deputy District Attorney Ford was forced to drop the manslaughter charges against Willard and the other men because he decided he could not get a conviction. However, he planned to continue with the charge of "prize fighting" despite the Willis decision. Acting in the name of District Attorney J.D. Fredericks, Ford took the revised case to the Superior Court of the County of Los Angeles and placed it before Judge Gavin W. Craig, Jr. All 12 men were now accused "of the crime of engaging in, aiding and encouraging a fight, commonly called a Ring or Prize Fight, a felony."[70]

While the court case was going on, boxing came under attack on another and more dangerous front. For a number of years State Senator William E. Brown, a lay reader of the Christian Science Church, had been leading a crusade to outlaw or severely restrict professional boxing. So far his efforts had been unrewarded, but his acts threatened the future of the sport.[71]

Now, the death of Bull Young had given new support to Brown's cause. Aided by the Church Federation of Los Angeles, spearheaded by Attorney Nathan Newby, chairman of the "Civic Righteousness Committee" an initiative was undertaken to get 50,000 signatures for a referendum against prizefighting. By September 11, the Reverend Eli Talbott had been appointed to lead the referendum campaign. He now began an initiative petition to put the issue on the ballot for a state election.[72]

The Pacific Athletic Club, run by Tom McCarey at Vernon, was licensed to hold "sparring exhibitions." Because the District Attorney had charged McCarey with holding prizefights, all boxing had ceased at the Vernon ring. Those boxers in town began to leave. Even friends turned against McCarey. De Witt Van Court slammed him for poor management in an article in *The Los Angeles Times* of August 24. *The Los Angeles Examiner* came out against prizefighting in an editorial on August 27 and again on September 15. On August 26, the Board of Supervisors of Los Angeles condemned prizefighting in the city and called for it to be outlawed in the county and the state, neglecting to note that this was already the case. Venice voted to close down boxing in that town. The City Council of Riverside announced that it opposed prizefights. When McCarey suggested he might reopen his club with a fight on October 14, the Church Federation collected thousands of signatures to oppose it. When he invited the pastors to actually see the fights, he was again attacked. The stress of these events was too much and McCarey collapsed. The days of his business were numbered.[73]

Tom McCarey had been careful to follow the rules based upon the Willis decision which permitted legal boxing or sparring bouts at Vernon. The problem was that the California law of 1872 (section 142) did not define what constituted a prizefight, nor did the amendment of 1899 describe what constituted a legal sparring match. The events of the Memsic-Wolgast fight of March 18, 1911, were determined by Judge Willis not to be a prizefight. This agreed with the view of Tom Jones, Ad Wolgast's manager, who, when asked, "Wasn't the training for the boxing match, as you call it, similar to the training for a prize fight?" responded, "I don't know. I never saw a prize fight and I know nothing about training for one."[74]

Based on the Willis decision, Earl Rogers demurred against the charge of prizefighting and argued that "the facts stated in the said information do not constitute a public offence." While it was unfortunate that John Young died as a result of a fall in the ring, the District Attorney had already recognized that no murder or manslaughter had occurred. Hence, the events in the Vernon ring were not criminal and "the court has no jurisdiction over the offense attempted to be charged therein."[75]

Judge Craig took this under advisement and then on October 21, overruled the demurrers. In so doing, he sent a signal that he intended to settle the issue of what constituted prizefighting, once and for all.[76]

After analyzing the prizefight law of 1872, which had supplanted that of 1850, Judge Craig turned to the amendment of 1899 which said:

> Provided, however, that sparring exhibitions, not to exceed a limited number of rounds with gloves of not less than five ounces in weight may be held by a domestic incorporated club upon the prepayment by such club of an annual license to be fixed by the board of supervisors of cities and counties, or by the city council or other governing bodies of incorporated cities. Said exhibitions must comply with the rules and regulations as the said supervisors, city councils or other governing bodies of cities and towns shall prescribe by ordinance.[77]

Craig tackled first the issue of why prizefighting should be a crime. He first argued that the aim of the law was to protect the public, not the fighters. "A law making body does not adopt this plan out of tender solicitude for the feelings, bodies or morality of the fighters, but to protect the public at large from debasing and demoralizing influences." Prizefighting was a crime because it was damaging to public morals, not because it damaged the fighters themselves. Up to this point, Judge Craig was following the conventional path of prizefight law.

The judge then reversed himself and decided that the legislature did indeed have a tender solicitude for the feelings, bodies and morality of the fighters. That is why sparring was legal but prizefighting was not.

> To this end the sparring exhibition allowed by the amendment must be one in which two persons attempt through skill and science to strike one another or to avoid being struck, but in which contest no serious physical injury is attempted to be inflicted by one upon the other. The incentive to win must not be a reward as the result of knocking out or rendering unconscious for a limited period one's opponent, but rather the fruit of the use of skill in boxing.

There was nothing in the California law which allowed Judge Craig to leap to this conclusion. Indeed, he was forced to admit, "It's true that this statute has been on the books in its present form since 1899, and has not previously been construed to prevent the acts complained of in the information."

But Judge Craig then turned the law upon its head and declared "it is equally true that the statute has not been construed by any court of appeal as permitting such acts."

With this statement, Craig stepped out of the realm of law and into the realm of theology. The idea that "whatever is not permitted is forbidden" was directly out of Calvinist theology and the Westminster Catechism. It was based upon the view that what was not specified in the Scriptures was forbidden. As such, it directly opposed the basic precepts of United States law where whatever is not forbidden by law is permitted. In making this pronouncement, Judge Craig showed himself to be an adherent of the new twentieth century philosophy of Progressivism being introduced by the reformers such as Senator Brown. His definition of what was permitted in a sparring match essentially quoted the language of the referendum that was being proposed by the churches. Theology was trumping the law.[78]

The ancient law of sport has always been *volenti non fit injuria* (consent negates crime). All types of acts, which if they occurred in regular life might be considered crimes of assault or negligence, are ignored when they occur in sport. Even death occurring in a sport played by the rules is forgiven. The ancient law, to again quote the Earl of Halsbury, was that "amicable contests in wrestling or boxing are not unlawful, and a person who unintentionally causes the death of another in the course of such a contest is not guilty of culpable homicide." The truth of this had been demonstrated in the boxing deaths of both Luther McCarty and John Young, for in both cases the prosecution found it impossible to convict anybody of either murder or manslaughter. The fighters' deaths were not the result of a crime. Both had entered the contests willingly and as a result no crime had occurred. But the reformers were intent upon creating a new law, and that law held that any damage done to the fighters, even with their consent, was reason enough to outlaw the sport.

Since Young had died as a result of the fight, Judge Craig assumed that the fight had been a prizefight and ordered a jury trial to settle the matter. Willard, McCarey and the rest were required to await trial on January 7, 1914, for the crime of "prize fighting."

Judge Craig was like a tuning fork struck by the hammer of Progressivism. He reverberated with the ideas of his times. The election of 1912, which brought Woodrow Wilson to the presidency and made Hiram Johnson governor of California, was changing the country. Despite the fact that Governor Johnson's own son had taken up boxing, the conventional view of a large portion of the population in California was that professional boxing should be banned. In the new world of the Progressives, unless the law specifically permitted boxing, it became a crime. And "no one," said Judge Craig in his famous dictum, "can acquire a prescriptive right to commit a crime." *The Los Angeles Times* went even further when it editorialized that "the public cannot consent that murder shall be made a spectacle and a pastime."[79]

Ring Lardner took that thought as his text and made a poem about it:

With Apologies to Pete

"Bull" Young was a most willing youth;
for punishment a pig.
They matched him with Jess Willard, who's
not quite three times as big.
"Bull" carelessly got killed; his "friends"
were very sorry then,
And feared the public might not like the
murdering of men.

St. Patrick's Day—all holidays—meant
money on the coast;
Rich fodder for promoters—lobster, pheas-
ant, quail on toast.
They'll have to go to work once more and
dine on redhots when
They pass a horrid law against the murdering of men.[80]

The boxing community was held in suspension from the end of October to the beginning of January in California.

Back to Boxing and Beginning Again

The tension of waiting for the settlement of the court case wore on Willard. Finally, after saying he would never fight again, Jess decided that he had to get back into the ring. Tom Jones was quite clear about the reason: "This big fellow can lick anybody in the world. And we are going after all the heavyweights. We have to. We both need the money. This expensive prosecution has just about broke us both."[81]

The expense of defending themselves in court had forced Tom Jones to borrow money from Ad Wolgast. In return, Jones and Willard signed a contract with Wolgast giving him 15 percent of Willard's future earnings. Wolgast forgot about the contract until Willard defeated Jack Johnson in 1915. He then reminded Jones of the contract. In November 1915, Willard, Jones and Wolgast met and Ad agreed to tear up the contract for a direct payment of $10,000.[82]

On November 1, 1913, while training at Jack Doyle's camp in Vernon, Willard received a telegram from Tom Jones saying that he had a fight lined up with Carl Morris in Milwaukee. Despite their early history together in Oklahoma, Willard and Morris had never actually met in the ring. Now Jess was broke and Morris was no longer the most important of the White Hopes. The fight lacked the excitement and importance it would have had years earlier. Yet, the time seemed right for them to meet and decide who the better man was. As was usually the case with Morris, problems intervened. First, the fight was delayed and transferred from Milwaukee to New York, in hopes of a bigger draw. Then, since Willard was still banned from boxing in New York State, the fight was further delayed until he could sort out his differences with the New York State Athletic Commission.[83]

Because of the problems with fighting in New York, Jones signed Willard to fight George "Boer" Rodel, a South African White Hope in Milwaukee on November 17. Fighting Rodel would allow Willard to keep busy while Jones worked out the details of the Morris fight. Rodel had won a large number of fights in South Africa as an amateur and had some success on the east coast as a professional. He was managed by James Joy Johnston, commonly known as the "Boy Bandit of Broadway," due to his ability to steal controversial decisions for his fighters. Rodel was scared to death of getting in the ring with Willard who had just killed the last man he faced. The "Boy Bandit" therefore persuaded his fighter that the bout was fixed for him to win. As Johnston later told the story:

> So in the dressing room just before the fight while I am examining Jess' bandages I whispered to him: "Go easy on Rodel tonight."
>
> "I'm gonna knock him out as quick as I can," Jess snarled back.
>
> "I wouldn't do that Jess," I said. "I'd be careful. You just killed one man and this Rodel has a weak heart just like Bull Young had."
>
> Willard blanched and then muttered, "You mean if I hurt your man I might get mixed up with the police again?"
>
> "Sure and if you kill Rodel you might go to jail for the rest of your life because you've already killed one man."[84]

With this advice ringing in his ear, the fight turned into a disaster for Willard. Milwaukee had just become open to boxing and the Rodel-Willard fight was the first heavyweight bout to be offered. *The Milwaukee Free Press* announced that the "earth will shake when hopes arrive!" and predicted a capacity crowd. A special train was scheduled to bring fans from Chicago to see the fight. Willard was in excellent condition as was Rodel. The fight was scheduled for ten rounds. Then, when Johnston came back from talking with Willard, he told Rodel that all he had to do was sail in and batter him and Willard would collapse. That is what Rodel did and that is what Willard did. As John Lardner had it, "Willard's behavior in the fight was a model of tenderness. He might have been Rodel's mother."[85]

"Milwaukee boxing fans last night had their first glimpse of the modern day white hopes in action—and they're still holding their noses." So wrote J.A. Ermatinger of *The Milwaukee Free Press*. "As a boxer, Willard is the biggest joke that has appeared here in a decade," he continued. "Rodel was the aggressor throughout. He was mighty careful though to keep out of the way of the comparatively few hard swings that Willard turned loose." Willard showed only one flash of aggressiveness in the fight in the seventh round when he had staggered Rodel with a right to the face, but the bell rang and saved Rodel. "This was the only round when Willard really retaliated for the blows Rodel landed." By the tenth, and final round, the crowd was booing Willard.[86]

The Los Angeles Times was kinder to Willard. According to their account, Willard won a draw. But they too noted that "it was an unsatisfactory mill and the crowd hissed the Kansas man out of the ring at the finish." Willard took the fight as a joke and fought only in spots, "and these spots were few and far between." "Between almost every round, Referee Duffy stepped over to each corner and told the principals that they must fight."[87]

As we have seen repeatedly, Willard was neither slow nor hesitant when he wished to fight. Nor was he awkward or easily hurt. His stamina was astounding and his strength prodigious. It was not his body that let him down, but his mind. Johnston's clever strategy was precisely correct for that moment. Willard was concerned about the possibility that he might harm Rodel, whom *The Milwaukee Free Press* had described as a kindergarten kid in the presence of the school bully. Willard had sworn that he had no idea that his blow to Young's chin was so powerful. He had acted instinctively when Bull had rushed in, and he was afraid that he might do the same with Rodel. "'Well,' laughs James J., 'Rodel wins the fight hands down without any trouble, because whenever Jess made a motion to throw his ponderous right he'd see me looking up at him from the ringside, wagging my finger and pointing to my heart in warning. Jess was afraid to throw a punch the whole fight.'"[88]

The fight with Rodel was a disappointment to Jones and Willard, all the more because Charley Cutler had come back to haunt them. When Jones had gone to Chicago in early November, he and Frank Gotch, the former world wrestling champion, were talking in the Morrison Hotel when Cutler came up. As Jones moved to shake his hand, Cutler hit him with a hard right to the jaw, knocking him back against the wall. Cutler attempted to follow up but he was stopped by Gotch. Jones tried to explain, but Cutler was having none of it. Cutler also said he would be at ringside at the Rodel fight and planned to challenge Willard to a 10- or 20-round fight. "I have no hopes of becoming heavyweight champion," said Cutler. "All I want to do is show the public that Willard is not the fighter he is credited with being. I made him what he is, and brought him to the front by matching him with a number of 'dubs.' I want to fight him over any distance, and I know I can beat him. Then I will be satisfied." Although the fight with Cutler did not come off, Charley did not go away.[89]

In addition to the problem with Cutler, the fiasco with Rodel nearly cost Willard his one chance to fight Carl Morris. His bad showing led the New York promoters to decide to substitute Rodel for Willard in the Morris fight scheduled for December 2. In an attempt to salvage some respectability, Jones matched Willard with Jack Reid (Jack Read, Frank Reed) of Toledo, Ohio. Reid had boxed Luther McCarty to a draw and defeated a number of other heavyweights. Although he was not well-known, he was a fighter of some reputation. Their fight was to be in Fort Wayne, a location that had always been kind to Jess. Success here meant that the fight with Carl Morris would take place; failure and Morris would refuse to fight Jess yet again.[90]

Because of the bad showing Willard had just made, Jones sent to Chicago for Cleve Hawkins, Willard's Negro sparring partner. In addition, Tom Jones brought in the infamous Joe Cox, from Springfield, Missouri, to serve as a sparring partner, along with a middleweight from Fort Wayne, Glen Coakley. Cox's appearance was interesting and suggests that Tom Jones was beginning to use some psychology as well. Having Cox spar with Willard daily may have driven out the doubters, who thought Willard was yellow. Instead of having to live down the Cox fiasco, now Willard had to live down the Rodel fiasco, and having Cox on his side may have helped. At any rate, they promised that the fight with Reid would not be at all like the fight with Rodel, which Willard himself admitted was the worst of his career. As a result, when Willard stepped into the ring he was confident and well trained. This showed immediately. The fight had hardly begun, when at the beginning of the second round, he sent a hard right to Reid's ribs followed by a left to the jaw and Reid went down. Although he was not knocked out, he called it quits. According to *The Fort Wayne Sentinel*, it was Reid who was haunted by the image of Bull Young in this fight, not Jess Willard.[91]

The Reid fight made it possible for Jess Willard to fight Carl Morris. Although they had been scheduled to fight in Oklahoma in 1911, both had been driven out of the state by Governor Lee Cruce. Their paths had then diverged, and now for the first time they were to come together. Only one stumbling block remained in the way: Jess was still barred from fighting in New York State, due to his failure to keep his date to meet George "One Round" Davis in Buffalo. But on December 1, 1913, the New York State Athletic Commission rescinded the ban they had placed on Willard. This was done, based on an agreement that Willard was to meet Davis in Buffalo, at the Queensberry Athletic Club, on December 16. The way was finally cleared for Jess and Carl to meet in Madison Square Garden in New York City.[92]

For years Jess Willard had wanted to get into the ring with Carl Morris, and for years Morris' backers had claimed Carl would whip Jess if he got the chance. On December 3, both got the chance they had waited for since January 1911. It was the one fight in Jess Willard's career which could properly be called a grudge match. As Willard recounted later, "The one man I took pleasure in beating was Carl Morris, who started out from Oklahoma about the same time I did.... I felt I had a grudge against him when I faced him in New York. And I quickly discovered that I could beat him. And believe me it was one pleasure to do it. Every time I stuck a glove into him it made me feel good and I couldn't help laughing all the way through."[93]

It is one of the certainties of boxing that the build-up to a fight is often greater than the fight itself. Occasionally grudge matches yield great fights, as each fighter does his best to defeat his rival. But this was not the case in the Willard-Morris fight. Despite their dislike for each other, the two men put on a lousy fight. Damon Runyon was there that night and summed the action up in a headline: "Only Referee William Joh in Peril when Heavy Aspirants Mix."

> It was a decidedly thrilling experience for Mr. Joh, because there were frequently moments when it appeared certain that either Morris or Willard would fall and squash him. Then too, there were times when a wild swing might have struck Mr. Joh in the jaw, for all Mr. Joh knew, or for all Morris or Willard knew, either, for that matter. They did not feel that it was their business to exercise control over their swings after they had started them. They just wished their swings well and let them go, and Joh had to do the dodging.[94]

The net result of the fight, Runyon reported, was to make George Rodel, "the Boer from Australia," as he was introduced by Joe Humphries, champion of something or other. Jimmy Johnston, Rodel's manager, claimed that Willard won. And since Rodel had beaten Willard, that made him champion of something. What? Runyon did not know.[95]

The Los Angeles Times, after predicting Morris would win, summed up its verdict in its headline: "Gee! What a Rotten Fight."[96]

The day of the fight *The New York Times* had listed Willard, Gunboat Smith and Carl Morris as the top three candidates for the heavyweight title and predicted that the Willard-Morris fight would eliminate one of them. Three days after the fight they revised their analysis: "It eliminated not one but both men from any consideration as successors to Jim Jeffries at the head of the white heavyweights." Speaking of Morris, the paper said, "In his bout with Willard, however, Morris proved conclusively that he will not measure up to a champion." This proved true, as Morris never rose to championship status. Of Willard, the paper was equally prescient:

> Willard can box well for a man of his size, and there is no denying that he can put his great weight behind his right-handed punches. At the same time he carries little or no aggressiveness and tires easily. In all of his bouts he has shown a disposition to regard boxing something as a joke. He lacks the heart of a real champion, and gives the impression that he would be out of place in a bout against a hard-hitting opponent.[97]

Most often the newspapers were confused by Willard's style and his behavior in the ring, but this writer for *The New York Times* got it right. Willard did lack the real heart of a champion, if by that, one meant the killer instinct to go after his opponent and when he had him down, keep him down. Willard's natural instinct was to let up when he had an opponent down. Willard himself admitted this: "When I knew I hurt the other opponents, I felt sorry, and often I have deliberately let up on them." And Willard was afraid of his own power. Very rarely did he unleash his full might on any opponent. He was, as Charles Samuels was later to write, "as gentle and sensitive as Ferdinand the Bull." These two weaknesses could be fatal when Willard met a hard-hitting opponent such as Jack Dempsey who did have the killer instinct. Fortunately, these fighters were very rare.[98]

Having finally settled his score with Carl Morris, Willard now had to settle with George "One Round" Davis in the unfriendly confines of the Buffalo Queensberry Athletic Club. Despite the fact that he felt Davis was not worthy of a match, Willard had no choice. The New York State Athletic Commission refused to allow him to box in New York until he had fulfilled his obligation to the Buffalo club. Thus, in the presence of a record-breaking crowd, Willard knocked Davis out. Davis had begun the fight with confidence and had hit Willard with a series of lefts and rights in the first round. But, at the opening of the second round, Willard hit Davis in the mouth, splitting his lip. He followed this up with another right to the mouth, followed by his patented right upper cut which had killed Bull Young. Davis went to the floor and was out for several minutes after being hit. The Buffalo fans had their fight, and it had ended just as Willard knew it would. What he did not realize was that the fight would draw a record crowd and that the take would be $8,500. This gave Jess $1,700, the biggest sum of money he had ever seen in his life. In addition, the score was settled, and now he could fight in New York whenever he chose.[99]

In keeping with *The New York Times* observation that Willard seemed to take boxing as a joke, before the fight he was walking down the street in Buffalo when he overheard two men debating the up-coming fight. He interjected himself into their discussion and ended up betting one man $25 that Davis would knock Willard out. Neither man recognized Willard until he climbed into the ring. Then the man, who had bet on the fight, screamed, "The fight is fixed!" and nearly fainted. He revived in the second round when Willard knocked Davis out.[100]

There was one more score to settle before the end of the year. This was with George "Boer" Rodel. Since the disastrous debacle in November, Willard had learned that Rodel did not have a bad heart and that Jimmy Johnston had made a fool of him. Tom Jones had wisely made it possible for Jess to get back in the ring with Rodel to rectify the mistake. They met in New Haven, Connecticut, on December 29. "After the first two rounds," wrote *The New York Times*, "there was no question of Willard's superiority." In the fifth round Rodel rushed in and landed a right to Willard's face, but Willard returned the favor and sent Rodel to the mat for a count of nine. In the seventh round, both fighters fought hard, but Willard knocked Rodel down for a count of one. In the eighth round, Jess chased the Boer around the ring and hit him with a punch right over the heart that sent Rodel down for another count of nine. Then in the ninth round, Willard landed his patented right upper cut and Rodel was out. Willard only admitted to one grudge match in his life and that was his fight with Carl Morris, but it certainly seems as if he might also have had something to prove in his second bout with George Rodel.[101]

The year 1913 had begun with the triumph of Luther McCarty and with the hopes that Jess Willard might fight him for the championship. McCarty's death threw the heavyweight class into turmoil. There were now many claimants to the throne, and nobody gave credit to any of them. There remained only one person who could settle the matter and that person was Jack Johnson.

5

1914: The Rise of Willard and the Destruction of Championship Boxing in California

The end of 1913 was a time for wrapping up loose ends. Willard had finally beaten his longtime rival, Carl Morris. He had taken two rounds to knock out "One Round" Davis in Buffalo, but the outcome had been what he had expected. And he had redeemed himself by decisively defeating "Boer" Rodel. There was now only one matter left to deal with, but it was one that Jess dreaded. He had to go to trial in Los Angeles as a result of the death of Bull Young.

Jess Willard on Trial

The trial of Jess Willard began on January 7, 1914, in the Superior Court of Los Angeles County. Initially, the charge had been manslaughter, then it changed to second degree murder, then the murder charge was dropped entirely. The only charge that remained was whether the fight was a prizefight, and therefore illegal under California law. Originally there were 12 defendants. Then the prosecutor dropped the charges against everyone else, leaving Willard alone in the box. Jess had an innate fear of the police dating back to his days in Oklahoma, where he had been convicted of prizefighting, and in Missouri where he had been put in jail for prizefighting. Now it was the *People vs. Jess Willard.* He was the lone defendant and he was not happy. "He was sure," wrote one analyst, "that if he were not executed he would spend the remainder of his days in prison."[1]

Since the other 11 men had been released from the indictment, they now became witnesses for the prosecution. Charles F. Eyton, the referee, said that it did not appear to him that the blow that hit Young was particularly severe. In an effort to enhance the good name of boxing, he added that many boxers (and here he mentioned Packey McFarland, the welterweight, by name) did not try to win by knockouts. When W. Joseph Ford, the Chief Deputy District Attorney, brought forth a record book showing that Packey was credited with a great number of knockouts, Eyton was astonished. The good name of boxing was returned to its normal, questionable status, when Harry Gilmore, Jr., Packey's manager, admitted that he made up most of the knockouts to make Packey's record seem more impressive. Eyton then stumbled again when he described the fight round by round and stated it was so tame that the spectators considered it a farce. Since

Young had died due to his beating in the ring, those in the courtroom who had not seen the fight must have wondered what a serious battle might look like.[2]

Following on this testimony, Willard took the stand and swore that at no time did he hit Young with his full strength. It is certainly true that usually Willard did not hit his opponents with his full power, but whether or not this was true of the fatal blow, no one knows. Eyton had testified that the blow that knocked Young out travelled no more than six inches; Tom McCarey estimated eight. But it was well-known in boxing circles that short blows are often the most powerful. A well-delivered blow of six or eight inches may carry far more power than a blow that travels a long distance, for the latter loses much of its power by the time it connects.[3]

After hearing this testimony, the jury debated the issue all night, and on January 13, they brought in a verdict of not guilty. The bout had been a sparring match, not a prizefight. This was a great relief for Jess Willard, but it left Judge Gavin W. Craig, Jr., dissatisfied. He viewed the trial as a test of California prizefight law. All it achieved was to show that the distinction between a sparring or boxing match and a prizefight was just as confused as it had always been. If the fight in which Bull Young was killed was not a prizefight, what did a prizefight look like?

For the promoters things had become much clearer: Every bout was a legal sparring match and prizefights, it they existed at all, did not occur in California. For Judge Craig and reformers like State Senator William E. Brown, prizefights did occur, and knockouts were proof positive of a prizefight. Judge Craig's unstated assumption was that every professional fight was a prizefight. And, Judge Craig instructed the jury, "no compliance with the regulations for sparring exhibitions, no matter how complete the compliance may be, can convert a prize fight into a sparring exhibition."[4]

The jury had taken to heart Judge Craig's words but had scrambled their meaning. They agreed with the judge that there was no way a prizefight could be converted into a sparring match. But they began with a different assumption. The jury believed that every fight in Vernon was a boxing or sparring match, just as the judge believed that they were not. If the fights at Vernon were sparring matches, using Judge Craig's own instructions, they could not be converted into prizefights; hence no prizefights had occurred. So they declared Jess Willard innocent.[5]

It was irritating to the judge to have things so clear and then have the jury come to the wrong conclusion. Even worse, Chief Deputy District Attorney Ford announced that in light of the jury's verdict he would no longer prosecute prizefight cases. The reformers decided that if there could not be a legal settlement of this issue there needed to be a political settlement. 1914 was an election year. Although Jess Willard had won the battle, the reformers swore that they would win the war.[6]

Back to Boxing

Once the trial was over, Jess was able to get back to boxing. On January 1, 1914, Edward "Gunboat" Smith knocked out Arthur Pelkey in San Francisco. Pelkey had carried the title of "white heavyweight champion" having left the ring alive in Calgary when Luther McCarty had died. When Smith knocked out Pelkey, this made Smith the white heavyweight champion. But the title, which Georges Carpentier later described as a "ridiculous pomposity," had little meaning following the death of Luther McCarty. Indeed, *The New York Times,* in an article praising Smith, assumed that once again the real champion was Jack Johnson. "Whether Smith can and will regain the title for the white race is a question of the future, but there can be no disputing the fact that the Gunner has proved that he is a logical candidate for the task."[7]

Naturally, stories like this gave Jess Willard and Tom Jones heart palpitations. Willard knew that he could beat Smith easily, and Tom Jones, now that he had more experience with Willard, knew it too. Thus, they sought a return bout with Smith. By January 18, a return fight had been arranged for San Francisco on July 4. For Willard this was another chance at redemption; for Smith it was also designed as a defining moment. Despite his decision over Willard the previous year, there remained doubts about Smith's ability. After watching Smith fight Pelkey, west coast writers did not feel Smith was really championship class. *The Washington Post* also felt Smith had to prove himself against Willard before he would be ready for Johnson: "The long, awkward figure of the giant Kansan looms up like Banquo's ghost at the championship feast that Smith now is enjoying." The contest for the real heavyweight title now was to be decided between Willard, Smith and Johnson. The quest for "the Great White Hope" had returned.[8]

The people, who had doubts about Smith, also had doubts about Willard. W.W. Naughton, dean of the west coast writers, wrote, "Willard came west and secured matches and, by the same token, forfeited all the good opinions that were formed of him by coast sports before they saw him. As a fighter he went from bad to worse and was regarded as one of the jokes of the white hope movement." But De Witt Van Court saw reason to hope. "Personally," he said, "I look for Jess Willard to be the next champion of the world." But both Smith and Willard now recognized that for either to claim the title they had to take it from Jack Johnson.[9]

Once again, without doing anything special, Jack Johnson held the attention of the boxing world. "Now that I am recognized as the white heavyweight champion, there is nothing that would please me more than to go to Paris and restore the heavyweight title to the white race," announced Gunboat Smith in January 1914. Willard had the same idea. But first each was supposed to meet the other in the ring in San Francisco on July 4.[10]

On March 26, Charley Cutler reentered Jess' life once again. Cutler now sued him for $2,150 for unreimbursed expenses including $500 for room and board between February 1, 1912, and June 1, 1912. This lawsuit establishes the time when Cutler began his training of Willard. It indicates that Jess was on his own between October 10, 1911, when he walked out of the Joe Cox fight ,until February 1, 1912, when he met Cutler in St. Louis. And although Charley Cutler did many good things for Jess Willard's career, his behavior after they parted company was very distracting.[11]

Policemen and lawsuits tended to reappear in Jess Willard's life with disconcerting frequency. And usually they spelled trouble for Jess. He had a built-in fear of both and did not do well when confronted with either. We have seen his troubles with Judge Sam Hooker in Oklahoma City in the spring of 1911. We have seen his problems with the Joe Cox fight in Springfield in the fall of 1911. We have seen his problems with Judge Gavin Craig in Los Angeles in 1913 and 1914. Each of these events seems to have left an invisible scar on Willard. The very threat of involvement with the police seemed to affect his performance and leave him distracted.

On March 27, the day after being sued by Charley Cutler, Jess took a fight in Youngstown, Ohio. The fight originally was between Battling Levinsky, whom John Lardner described as "an agile but peaceable boxer," and Tom "Bearcat" McMahon, a fighter with modest ambitions. Levinsky's manager, "Dumb Dan" Morgan, had said of Levinsky: "He couldn't knock your hat off, and he knew it." But Levinsky became sick with gastritis following a bout with Bob Moha, a slightly better boxer, and for the first time in his career, Jess Willard stepped in as a substitute. It was a mistake. Jess weighed 220 and McMahon weighed 176, a difference of 44 pounds. Physically, Jess was the better man, but intellectually he was not. Whether he was affected by the lawsuit, or whether it was his old fear of harming a lesser opponent, once again, Jess seemed to wilt in front of a determined smaller man.[12]

The fight took place before the largest crowd ever assembled in the Youngstown opera house. The New Castle, Pennsylvania *News*, McMahon's hometown paper, turned it into a thing of romance. Jess, the giant, outweighed Tom by "over fifty pounds" and towered over him by "nearly two feet." "The New Castle man was forced to jump into the air at times to land on the face or the head." According to John Lardner, "Dumb Dan" Morgan, Levinsky's manager, gave McMahon some advice before the fight: "This bum just sticks out his left hand. Ignore it." McMahon did and got a cut lip and a bloody nose for his efforts. Willard was unmarked in the fight. But McMahon was the aggressor all evening while Willard remained on the defensive. According to the *Youngstown Telegram,* the fight was a draw, but according to the *Youngstown Daily Vindicator,* the *New Castle News* and the *New York Times,* Willard lost the fight on points. "Seemingly amazed at the ferocity and tenacity of McMahon, Willard did little but stand in the center of the ring and wait for the Bear Cat to approach."[13]

It is difficult to account for Willard's poor showing against Tom McMahon. We know that Willard disliked fighting smaller men. This worried him in Oklahoma and it continued to worry him his entire life. As he wrote to a friend in his later years, "In the fights I engaged in I never could do anything to the other fellow in the way of damage. I simply couldn't do it. Harming the other fellow seemed to me to be cruel, and so long as the other fellow didn't harm me much I couldn't see any reason why I should hurt him."

The speed of Tom McMahon and Gunboat Smith certainly aided each of them in their battle with Willard, but Jess' own diffidence aided them more. He knew that he could beat them, but fear of harming them kept him from doing his best. Simply put, Jess Willard lacked the killer instinct of a great fighter.[14]

Despite the unsatisfactory outcome of the Bearcat McMahon fight, three weeks later Jess was in the ring again with another native of New Castle, Pennsylvania. This time it was a man more his own size: Dan Daily (Tom Daly), who stood over six feet tall. Jess was supposed to have had a bout with Daily in January of 1913, but had dropped out due to a finger broken in the second Frank Bowers fight. The rematch was to occur on March 17, 1914, but it actually occurred on April 13 in Buffalo, New York. Using his patented right uppercut, Willard knocked Daily out for the first time in his career in the ninth round of their bout.[15]

Then two weeks later, on April 28, in Atlanta, Georgia, Jess Willard again met George "Boer" Rodel. Boxing writers and managers were better known for their knowledge of ring skills than geography or history. Jimmy Joy Johnston, Rodel's manager, named him "Boer" and billed him as the "Hero of Ladysmith." This was a battle in the South African Boer War which was fought when Rodel was 12 years old and in which he bravely took no part. Joe Humphries, the famous ring announcer, compounded the confusion when he introduced Rodel at the Willard-Morris fight as being from Australia. Humphries knew that Rodel was from far away, and Australia was as far away as he could imagine. And since no dub would come all the way around the world, he had to be the champion in his home country. Thus, through the magic of malapropism, by the time of the third Willard fight, Rodel had earned the title of Champion of Australia, having never fought on or even visited that continent.[16]

This fight was the rubber match between Rodel and Willard. They had met twice before and each had won once. Rodel had won the first bout when J. J. Johnston, the "Boy Bandit," had tricked Willard into believing that Rodel had a bad heart. Willard had won the second bout when he realized that he had been tricked. So unlike the McMahon fight in which he did nothing, Willard promised to make the third Rodel fight "a slam-bang affair." Rodel stood 6 feet, 2 inches tall and weighed 215 pounds to Willard's 6 feet, 6 inches and 220 pounds. Since there were only four inches difference in height and five pounds difference in weight, there was no need for him to hold back as he did with smaller men. Rodel too was willing to slug it out with Willard, and, since the winner was to face Gunboat Smith, there was a good deal riding on the result.[17]

Willard had predicted that he would defeat Rodel in eight rounds, but it took him only six to knock him out. Once again hyperbole filled the newspaper columns. Willard stood "at least seven inches taller than Rodel and weighed at least fifty pounds more." If Willard had actually lost a bout to Rodel, as reported, "the big cowboy must have had one hand tied behind his back." "The result was forecasted from the time the men stepped into the ring.... It was a shame to let the men get together." Even though he won, Willard was not in the championship class: "We hate to think of what Johnson or Sam Langford would do to him. Shades of Corbett, Jeffries and Fitzsimmons, where is the class of the heavies if Jess Willard is a sample of the best? All in his favor is his size."[18]

In many ways, Willard was his own worst enemy. As Tex O'Rourke, his sparring partner in El Paso, was later to say, he hated notoriety. He lacked charisma and the magnetism which might make him an interesting subject for writers. But equally, sometimes he could not get a square break. He was rightly panned when he let a smaller man pummel him in the ring. But it seemed unfair when fighting a larger man near his own size that he should be panned as well. Rodel was not precisely Willard's equal in size, few men were, but he was close enough so that Willard's superiority should not have been held against him. If he lost, he was a dub; if he won, "it was a shame to let the two men get together in the ring." But as Jack Johnson was to later say, on the day they fought in Havana, no man in the world could have beaten Jess Willard.[19]

Although the way was now clear for the July 4 fight between Willard and Gunboat Smith for the white championship it ceased to hold any interest for Gunboat. Since Smith had already beaten Willard once, after Willard's unsatisfactory bout with Tom McMahon, Smith entered into discussions with Georges Carpentier, the European heavyweight champion for a bout to consolidate their two titles. The Carpentier fight took precedence over the fight with Willard and by June 1, Smith was in London and the Willard fight was officially off.[20]

Then Frank Moran, a heavyweight from Pittsburgh, went to Paris and landed a championship fight with Jack Johnson for June 27, 1914. The Johnson-Moran fight pushed everything else into the shadows. The Smith-Carpentier fight was delayed until the middle of July, and Carpentier took the job of being the referee for the Johnson-Moran fight. Although the French were naturally excited about Carpentier's prospects, the Johnson-Moran fight seemed like an opportunity to elevate Paris to the level of Sydney and Reno as a famous prizefight location. If Moran could defeat Johnson and reclaim the title for the white race, Paris would be pleased. With an excess of Gallic pride the magazine *L'Auto* predicted that "this battle of June 27 will become at once the most sensational, the most memorable of boxing history which will rank among the gigantic duels of Sullivan and Corbett, of Fitzsimmons and of Jeffries." Suddenly, all other fights seemed a waste of time.[21]

Both Smith and Willard were delighted when Moran lost the decision to Johnson in 20 rounds. As C.F. Bertelli, reporting the fight from Paris, wrote: "There was never a second during that period [of 20 rounds] in which a victory by Moran could have been said to have been in the realms of possibility."[22]

Johnson was out of shape, and gave Moran his chance, but still Moran could not beat him. Johnson had only taken the fight because he was out of money and needed the cash. But neither Moran nor Johnson got a penny out of the fight. Dan McKetrick, Moran's manager, tied up the funds from the fight so that only the Bank of France got the money, which it enjoys up to the present day. Moran had taken a beating and Johnson had risked his title for nothing.[23]

The Smith-Carpentier fight now occupied center stage. The bout occurred in London on July 16. Once again the American white hope failed. Smith lost his title to Carpentier. For Carpentier to win the title of "White Heavyweight Champion" was considered a great triumph at the time. The French, like the English, were just as anxious as the Americans to take the title away from Johnson and bring it back to the white race. The French newspaper *Sporting* declared on July 17 that "Carpentier was the true white hope." Upon his return to Paris from London, he was welcomed by a joyous crowd of 20,000 people. But Carpentier had only a few days to enjoy his triumph. On August 1, 1914, World War I broke out and France suddenly had much more important things to worry about. Carpentier enlisted, survived the war and became a French war hero and nobody ever mentioned the "white heavyweight" title again.[24]

War had yet to come to America, so the struggle with Johnson continued. With the defeat of Gunboat Smith, all of the talk was now about Willard fighting Jack Johnson. Moran had been eliminated as a contender for a while; Smith was out of the running, and Jess Willard now stood alone as the last of the white hopes with a chance to beat Johnson. On June 28, the day after the Johnson-Moran fight, William A. Brady, "Gentleman Jim" Corbett's former manager, announced: "In the twenty-four hours that I have had to think over the Johnson-Moran bout, I have decided that there is one man who can whip the negro. He is Jess Willard." Then, on July 15, while visiting Gunboat Smith's training quarters outside of London, Johnson was in a talkative mood. He said to Brady,

"So you think a man like Jess Willard can trim me do you?" When the writer said yes, Johnson's eyes flashed and he said: "Now that I can go back to America, I will give you the commission to match me against the Los Angeles heavyweight [Willard] for six rounds in Philadelphia in November or any other place you may select."[25]

This, like many of Johnson's comments, needed to be taken with a grain of salt. According to an article in *The Milwaukee Free Press* of April 15, 1914, and repeated in *The Times* of London on April 16, 1914, a United States Court of Appeals had reversed the decision handed down by the lower courts in Johnson's conviction under the Mann Act. It was ruled that Johnson had not been proven guilty of trafficking in vice. This merited a new trial which was to have been held within 30 days from April 14, at which Johnson needed to be present. Johnson could not make it back on such short notice, but he planned to return to Chicago after his fight with Frank Moran to face a new trial. These newspaper articles led to Johnson's belief that he would be back in the country in November of 1914 in order to fight Willard. However, at some point in time Johnson must have discovered that these articles were untrue, for he did not return.[26]

Johnson knew from watching Willard in Chicago that there was no way a fight between the two could be for only six rounds. Nor would such a bout yield Johnson the money he needed. For both his financial needs and his self-esteem, Johnson wanted the same deal that Tommy Burns had gotten at Rushcutter's Bay: $30,000 win, lose or draw.[27]

Unless a Willard-Johnson fight was scheduled for at least 20 rounds, it would neither test the two, nor draw the type of money Johnson wanted. Ad Wolgast, the lightweight fighter, made the same observation when he heard Johnson's comments. Ad offered to promote the fight himself if it were a longer bout, even if it meant buying a fight club to do so. Uncle Tom McCarey announced that he wanted to accompany Willard to wherever the match would occur. The next day, Jim Jeffries announced that he wanted to second Willard when he fought Johnson. "If Jess Willard is matched to meet Jack Johnson I would like to train Jess," said Jeffries. "I feel that if properly trained, Jess can whip the champion."[28]

Both Jones and Willard were happy with the news that Johnson wanted to fight Willard, but Willard, himself, had wanted to fight Gunboat Smith and Tom McMahon first. He still was embarrassed by his losses to those two fighters and wanted to clear his record. De Witt Van Court agreed with Jess' decision: "If Willard is to meet Jack Johnson he is right in stating that he is willing to try and wipe out all decisions in meeting both McMahon and Gunboat Smith if he can do so. If we are to have a white man meet Johnson to uphold the white race, we surely want the best that we can have."[29]

But Smith and McMahon were not the only blots on his record that Willard wanted to expunge. He also wanted to fight Carl Morris again to wipe out the memory of a truly dreadful fight. Tom Jones made an offer of $4,000 to Morris to meet Willard in Kansas City on Labor Day. And just like in the old days in Oklahoma City, Morris turned it down. This made "Knockout," a columnist for *The Chicago Daily Tribune*, shake his head and mumble about the more modest purses of days gone by. Instead, Morris fought and beat Fireman Jim Flynn in Kansas City on October 29, avenging his defeat years ago in New York. But it was too little, too late for Morris.[30]

By August 25, with a Johnson-Willard match becoming more likely, the Frazee-Weber syndicate was put together. Acting through Jack Curley, they purchased the rights to Willard from Tom Jones for $25,000 and turned over promotion of the fight to Curley. Tom Jones still remained Willard's fight manager, but the strategy of getting fights now rested with the syndicate and Jack Curley. Their initial intention was to take Willard and Fireman Jim Flynn over to Paris where Jess would fight Johnson and Flynn would fight Georges Carpentier. The fight would be a double card and would ensure gigantic purses for all involved. There was only one small problem. As the article in *The Milwaukee Free Press* noted: "It is understood that no fights can be held in Paris while the war is in progress."[31]

The day after the Johnson-Moran fight, June 28, Archduke Franz Ferdinand of Austria-Hungary was assassinated in Sarajevo, triggering World War I. Johnson continued on with his business going briefly to London for the Carpentier-Smith Fight and then to Sweden and finally to St. Petersburg. While in Russia he was hoping to make money by appearing in theatres and charming the Russian public who found blacks to be exotic creatures. Thus, he was not in Paris, when on August 2, the Germans launched the Schlieffen plan. The plan's main objective was to sweep through Belgium, turn south and engulf Paris in one swift blow. Although Johnson avoided the panic that swept Paris, he soon found that Russia was in the war as well. Once the Germans launched their attack on Belgium, the Russians launched an attack on East Prussia. By August 20 Russia had conquered Gumbinnen and threatened Konigsberg on the Baltic. Then in a swift reversal of fortunes the Russians lost their entire Second Army near Tannenberg (August 26–30, 1914). Shortly thereafter, the police knocked on Johnson's door and told him that he had to leave the country. As he remembered it, "They invoked the five-and-ten law. That means five minutes to pack, and ten minutes to get out of town."[32]

Johnson and his party made it back to Paris only to find the city in chaos. He found one of his cars in storage and drove it to Boulogne over roads crowded with troops and fleeing families. He made it across the Channel to the relative safety of England, where he remained popular. He obtained a number of week's booking in the music halls in London and elsewhere and supposedly was scheduled to leave England for Brazil on October 15. Then, just at the critical moment, he learned that Jack Curley was coming to London with a proposition for him.[33]

Johnson and Jack Curley went back a long way. Curley had been a boxer in the 1890s and had then turned promoter. He had been the matchmaker of one of Johnson's first fights in 1899 in Chicago with "Klondike" an older fighter. Johnson was promised $25 if he won and $10 if he lost. He lost, but the promoter, Paddy Carroll, head of the Phoenix Athletic Club where the fight took place, refused to pay Johnson. Johnson was flat broke, so Jack Curley and Sig Hart, both of whom worked for Carroll at the time, pooled their resources and gave Johnson $3 for food and board. Later, when Curley was managing Fireman Jim Flynn, he promoted the fight in Las Vegas, New Mexico. He had offered Johnson $30,000 plus training money and film rights. Since Johnson was broke as usual, Curley's offer was accepted, even though everyone in the fight business knew that Flynn had no chance. The fight was a fiasco, it broke the town of Las Vegas, and Jack Curley lost money. Nonetheless, he made good on his promises to both Johnson and Flynn. Johnson got $31,000 while Flynn got a new car which had been promised only if he won. Johnson was aware that Curley made up the payments out of his own pocket and treasured him as an honest man. Thus the appearance of Jack Curley with a proposition once again interested Jack Johnson.[34]

The Frazee-Weber syndicate, for which Curley now acted as spokesman, offered Johnson the same inducements that he had always demanded: $30,000 and training money, win, lose or draw. For Johnson the $30,000 figure which Tommy Burns had demanded in Australia in 1908 had become a talisman. It represented the epitome of wealth and control. Burns had demanded this sum as champion and Johnson adopted the position that what was good enough for the white champion was good enough for the black. Even the fabulous purse which he won in the Jeffries fight (estimated between $100,000 and $200,000) could not erase the magic figure of $30,000 and training money.

Johnson agreed to sign with Curley to fight Jess Willard. Although Johnson had known Jess from Chicago, he played coy with Curley: "And who is this WeeLARD you want me to fight?" "Don't pull that Parisian accent on me you mug," said Curley, "plain American, 'Willard.' He's a big mule-skinner from Kansas. He's six-feet-seven-inches tall, weighs 260 pounds, has dynamite in either hand, and can't be hurt." The fight was set. Now the only problem was where it would occur.[35]

With Europe plunged into a world war there was no possibility of the fight being held there. Canada and Australia were equally out, since as members of the British Empire, they too were involved in the war. The United States was neutral and was the ideal place to have the fight, but Johnson was still under sentence for the crime of white slavery (not with Lucille Cameron, but now with a white prostitute named Belle Schreiber) and so could not return to the country without being arrested. This left Latin America as a neutral and potentially friendly fight location. The closest place would be Mexico, which shared a long border with the United States.[36]

In an article dated November 5, "Knockout," a sports columnist for *The Chicago Daily Tribune*, authoritatively announced the terms of the match and the members of the syndicate who were backing it. But in a smaller article on the same page, a more ominous headline appeared: "Vote on Coast Indicates Boxing will be Killed."[37]

The Death of Boxing in California

The death of Bull Young and the inability of the courts to properly punish the pugilists and promoters rankled the Progressives in California. The churches had obtained enough signatures to place Proposition 20, to outlaw boxing bouts of over four rounds, on the ballot for the November election. Under the terms of the new law, no winner of any bout could receive a prize worth more than $25. The idea was to eliminate "prizefighting" and make boxing a purely amateur sport in California. *The Los Angeles Times*, which was then very conservative in outlook, urged the citizens to vote *No* on this item. The day after the election the matter was still in doubt. Despite the opposition of *The Los Angeles Times*, the people of Los Angeles voted 145,045 in favor of the ban, and 124,166 against it. At the same time, Angelinos voted against prohibition and in favor of prostitution. In Los Angeles boxing was viewed as more dangerous to public morality than either drinking or public prostitution. But it took some time to count the votes in the entire state.[38]

The election of November 1912 had unleashed a "purity campaign" which swept across the southern part of the state. The "puritans" introduced local ordinances to outlaw the free lunch in bars, ban cigarettes, outlaw betting on horse racing, forbid the theatre production of *Salome*, forbid the "Turkey Trot," ban poolrooms, outlaw narcotics and prevent the marriage of diseased or defective persons. These local prohibitions were passed in the November 1914 state-wide general election. They were part of a concerted program to remake Southern California into a New Jerusalem.[39]

When the final statewide returns were in, prohibition was not adopted; the eight hour law was defeated, as was a proposition against the eating of wild game and the Sunday rest law. The state did gain control of water rights which it retains to this day. The poll tax was abolished and the minimum wage law was adopted. And both prostitution and championship boxing were outlawed.

The ban on championship boxing in California meant that beginning on January 1, 1915, there could be no more 20-round bouts in either the Vernon ring or in San Francisco. "Uncle Tom" McCarey and "Sunny Jim" Coffroth, the two most famous of the west coast promoters, were out of business. The great history of championship boxing in California gave way to what was to become known as the "Four Round Era." Only in 1925, during the era of Jack Dempsey, did longer bouts return to the state as boxing made its resurgence throughout the United States. In the meantime, the death of Bull Young killed championship boxing in California.[40]

Despite having unleashed the torrent of protest against championship boxing in California and being ultimately responsible for its death, Willard himself was largely untouched. Beginning in late August, the newspaper columnists began to tout Willard as the best of the White Hopes and the man to defeat Johnson. In an article by "Ringside" Reagan which was printed all over the country, the author cited the failure of Frank Moran to defeat Johnson in Paris in June, and the failure of Gunboat Smith to defeat Georges Carpentier in London in July, as proof that Willard was the sole remaining white hope capable of defeating Johnson. Willard, Ringside believed, had all the attributes necessary to become champion save one: "One thing in his disfavor is that he must be thoroughly aroused before he will put forth his best effort. He is lackadaisical and will not allow his temper to become ruffled while an opponent is not annoying him with hard blows." Therefore Willard must allow Johnson to force the fight and lead. If Willard could make Johnson lead, Jess would likely be able to win by a knockout. And this is what happened.[41]

In November, Otto Floto, the man who gave birth to the phrase "the White Hope" also came to the decision that Jess was the only man who could beat Johnson. "He's got the size, height, reach, weight and knows how to box. If a man of his proportions can't turn the trick—well, then commend us unto the vast unknown to seek for a yet undiscovered Moses that will lead the white race out of the wilderness and restore to them the crown that Johnson snatched from Jeffries' head."[42]

A similar article had appeared in *The Chicago Daily Tribune* on August 26, entitled "Groom Willard for Title Bout." This article gave the behind the scenes discussion of the negotiations between Tom Jones and the syndicate headed by Jack Curley which ultimately put together the fight. This was followed up by an article in *The New York Times* about the syndicate and their offer to Johnson, which was ultimately accepted.[43]

Jack Curley went to England to meet Johnson in early November carrying with him the documents Willard had signed in New York. Curley met Johnson and Johnson signed on November 17. Each of the fighters deposited $1000 in earnest money. The location was to be Juarez, Mexico across the river from El Paso. The date was to be in March 1915 and the fight was to last from 20 to 45 rounds.[44]

The enthusiasm for the fight was not total. There were those who raised cautionary flags. The first to do so was De Witt Van Court in Los Angeles. In an article on October 18, Van Court noted that both Willard and Johnson were defensive fighters and as such were likely to spend most of their time waiting for the other fellow to lead. "In my opinion it would be one of the poorest contests for a championship that one could witness." Van Court also anticipated difficulty with Juarez as a fight location and suggested either Tijuana, south of San Diego, or Havana, Cuba, where English boxing was beginning to take hold.[45]

Jack Skelly, who had fought and lost to George "Little Chocolate" Dixon in the Tournament of Champions in 1892 in New Orleans, was quoted in *The Chicago Daily Tribune*, as opposing Van Court's view. Boxing was based on defense, not offense. Skelly wrote: "The ability to evade punishment helps to make the successful boxer. Boxing has been known for hundred of years as 'the manly art of self-defense.' The great past masters of the science were men who knew how to safeguard themselves and fought mostly at their important combats ... in a defensive manner, not with wild aggressiveness."

Far from boring, the fight between Willard and Johnson was likely to be a superior fight based on the science of defense. "We must all give Jack Johnson credit for being a great scientific boxer and possibly the greatest defensive fighter the ring has ever known.... Jess Willard will possibly discover this fact if he clashes with Johnson on March 17." From the standpoint of boxing Jack Skelly, not De Witt Van Court, had it right. The art of boxing is to hit without being hit. This was what the greatest boxers from John Broughton to Jack Johnson had made their standard. Jess Willard would have learned this as well, especially if he had trained with Bob Fitzsimmons. Far from being dull, the fight between Johnson and Willard was likely to be an outstanding one, if it was on the square.[46]

The question was, would the battle between Willard and Johnson be an honest fight? On November 22, "Ringside" Reagan wrote another article which speculated that it might not be. A headline placed over the article in *The Daily Oklahoman* carried the message: "Johnson can Win by being Beaten." "Ringside" professed to believe that Willard could beat Johnson in a fight to the finish, since he was younger than, and as strong as, Johnson. But he noted that Johnson was to get 50 percent of the movie rights to the bout, which "Ringside" estimated would be worth $500,000 "should Johnson be knocked out." "Ringside" suggested that Johnson might get knocked out and give up the title to obtain such a marvelous payday. Although "Ringside" knew that boxing films had been banned in the United States and many other countries after the Johnson-Jeffries fight, he assumed, as did many others, that if Willard were to win, the ban would be lifted. Although this did not happen, it gave credit to his idea that Johnson might throw the fight.[47]

Johnson sailed from England on November 25 bound for Buenos Aires, Argentina, where he was to spend Christmas. From there, he was to make his way north to Mexico, where the fight was to be held.[48]

Although Johnson was obliged by the contract not to fight anyone prior to his bout with Willard, it was well known in December that he had contracted to fight Sam McVey in Havana, Cuba in early 1915. Supposedly this was to be after he fought Willard, but due to the delay of the Willard fight, it actually occurred before Johnson fought Willard. Willard, himself, was willing to fight any white hope available prior to the Johnson fight, beginning with the winner of the Gunboat Smith-Jim Coffey fight.[49]

Smith fought Coffey in New York City on December 15. The fight went ten rounds, and because it was in New York, it was a no decision fight, which meant that the sportswriters determined who won. The newspaper consensus was that Jim Coffey, the Dublin Giant, had defeated Smith. By rights, Willard should then have fought Coffey. But Billy McCarney, who was a lost soul after the death of Luther McCarty, now was managing the once-great Carl Morris. McCarney supposedly offered Willard a guarantee of $6,000 to fight Carl. Willard would have been happy to fight Morris again, but his new management rejected McCarney's offer and said that Morris had to fight Jim Coffey first.[50]

After making this pronouncement, Willard reversed course. He declared that he wanted to have a tournament in which he would fight all of the major white heavyweights one a day for seven consecutive days. But this, like his earlier pronouncements, led to nothing. Compared to his contemporaries, Willard fought very little and only had a few exhibitions before his title fight with Johnson.[51]

Underneath the posturing of fights and challenges a new pattern of boxing behavior was emerging. Boxing had been the one sport where blacks and whites were free to compete in public on a regular basis. Jack Johnson had been only the most visible of black champions. With the notable exception of Tommy Burns, every heavyweight champion since had drawn the color line, including Jack Johnson. Jack Johnson did allow one black, "Battling" Jim Johnson, to fight for the title in Paris in 1913. Still, no other colored fighters were given a chance to fight for the heavyweight title between 1908 and 1937. But this was not new.

What was new was a growing reluctance to have blacks and whites fight each other in the lower weight classes and in non-title fights. Following the race riots of 1910 after the Johnson-Jeffries fight, the white public became even more wary of the Negro population than they had been before. While boxers, like Willard himself, had no problem training with blacks and using them as sparring partners, the general public began to object to public contests between blacks and whites. Boxing was ceasing to be colorblind. The refusal of the Board of Supervisors in San Francisco to permit the fight between Willard and Sam Langford was merely one example of this. As *The Daily Oklahoman* was to write:

> The day of the black pugilist as a national figure is near the end. The passing of Johnson, Sam Langford, Sam McVey and others who now are past their zenith probably will be the exit of the negro from the ring. All over the world black-white matches are being frowned upon and in the states where the boxing game has advanced to that point where boxing commissions have charge of affairs, black-white bouts are being outlawed.[52]

Boxing was coming of age. It was becoming more regulated, and that meant it was becoming more segregated.

6

Show Business

The Trip Home from Havana

Jess Willard defeated Jack Johnson to win the World's Heavyweight Boxing title in Havana, Cuba, on April 5, 1915. This made him the most famous man in America, but he still did not have any money. He had won the heavyweight crown from Jack Johnson, but he got nothing for it save fame. As Jack Curley was to tell his Cuban creditors, "We didn't make enough to cover expenses." And Jess Willard did not even count as an expense. Jess now had to find a way to make money from his fame.[1]

Although the fight was a social success and brought the title back to the White Race, it was not a financial success. We have seen that the original choice of having the fight in Juarez, Mexico, failed, and money was lost making the shift to Cuba. We need not believe Tom Jones' statement that he had invested $18,000 in the Juarez fight, for promoters and managers were notoriously loose with the truth. But something was spent setting up quarters there, and not all the bills were paid. Further Jones had to get a loan from Colonel Martin J. "Matt" Winn, who headed the syndicate which ran Churchill Downs and the Kentucky Derby, to pay for passage of Willard and his sparing partners to Havana.[2]

The night after the fight Curley issued a gracious statement to the newspaper expressing his gratitude to the people of Havana for their kindness:

> Long after Havana forgets the event, Jack Curley will remember the loveable treatment towards all of us by all of the people of Havana. Today indeed was the greatest and happiest day of my life. Words can never express the feeling that comes in connection with such a tremendous undertaking ending successfully as this one did.... Up to this hour I have not even inquired as to the gate receipts: in fact, I don't care anything about them. Willard's victory more than repays the trouble and tribulations of nine months' hard work.[3]

The next evening, April 6, the residents of Havana held a reception in the Stadium for Willard, Johnson and Curley which was managed by Fred Mace, the movie man. Willard, Johnson and Curley were all presented gold watches by the citizens while Curley and Willard presented to Jack Johnson a beautiful silver loving cup.[4]

That night Jack Curley was arrested and thrown into jail. According to *The Havana Daily Post*, "The cause of his arrest was the overlooking of certain important debts contracted here in connection with Monday's fight, and the fear that he might absent-mindedly leave on the morning's steamer without having observed the formality of paying the said bills."[5]

Also arrested with Curley were Jack Johnson and John R. Robinson, publicity agent for the fight. Robinson was an innocent bystander who had been tasked by Curley with obtaining necessary support items for the fight. This included renting a number of automobiles for the day of the fight. Payment for renting those cars was not forthcoming. Johnson also was responsible for a bill for several hundred dollars for 40 days of car rental. Johnson had planned to go to Jamaica leaving the bill unpaid. But, with cash in hand, he quickly paid up once the matter was brought to his attention.

Curley was in a different fix. He had originally reported that the receipts for the fight were $110,000. In fact, they appeared to be closer to $60,000. Of that Johnson had received $32,000, leaving about $28,000 for all other expenses. L.L. Weber, Curley's boss and one of the original backers, had put up about $25,000 of his own money by the time Willard and Johnson entered the ring. In addition Harry Frazee, the other member of the syndicate, had put up $10,000. If Curley's statement that the revenue from the fight was only $60,000 is accurate, it was clear that the expenses far exceeded the amount earned.[6]

The next day, Curley was somehow able to escape police custody and make his way through a gauntlet of creditors to the *Governor Cobb* at the docks. His departure was widely mourned. Those of his creditors, who took a policeman with them to meet him at the docks, were paid. But not even these financial discussions went smoothly as Curley found it necessary to punch one policeman on the nose. Curley had also promised to meet a number of other creditors at various locations throughout the city at or after the time the boat sailed. These bills were not paid. Curley was particularly agile in palming off most of his debts on John Robinson and Richard Klegin, both of whom ended up in jail. Curley then joined Willard on the *Governor Cobb* and sailed to Key West.[7]

The Havana Daily Post noted the contrast between Curley's actions and those of Johnson following the fight in an editorial entitled "A Sermon in Black and White."

> With the white men, or better stated, with the men with white skins, creditors had to rush down to the dock and with policemen to get their bills paid. The ones who got there late were left in the cold. Jack Johnson, on the other hand, has stayed behind and paid every bill that he owed, and also out of his own private funds he has liquidated the bills of men who were left stranded because of the double dealing of others. Every obligation he had contracted has been settled and when he leaves next week for Europe there will not be any who can say that he ran away without paying his debts or that he ever tried in any way to obtain the possessions of another. There is some contrast![8]

Jack Johnson had not stayed behind in Havana for purely altruistic reasons. While we can admire the contrast he provided the Cubans in comparison with Jack Curley, he stayed because he was trying to get his hands on the fight films that Fred Mace had prepared of the battle. Everyone counted heavily on the money to be made from the fight films. Johnson's agreement was that he was to have the exclusive rights to the films for foreign countries, including Europe and South America. Johnson initially tried to sell his rights to the fight films to Harry Frazee for $200,000. Frazee apparently agreed but wished to pay the money over time. Johnson, believing that cash deferred was cash denied, refused and kept the rights. But rights are one thing, having the films in one's hand is a totally different thing, and Johnson did not have the films.

He had heard, however, that some films of the fight were going to be shown in the Havana theatres. He immediately tried to get a court injunction to stop this. He appealed to the police and the police referred it to a judge. And there it stopped. Johnson ran smack into the most dreaded of all Latin American words: "Mañana."

"But when can I find out what you are going to do about it?" queried the big ex-champion. "Mañana, maybe," answered the judge.[9]

The next day, Johnson again met with the judge, and again found that mañana had not yet arrived. In fact, Johnson never was able to stop the pirated version of the fight film which took over the entire Cuban market. Nor was Johnson able to get his hands on the Mace version of the real fight films before he left Cuba.[10]

When Johnson eventually arrived in Europe, he found that those who promised to send him the real films from Cuba tried to cheat him and leave him with nothing. He was able to stop the European distribution of the pirate version from being marketed. And he was able to get hold of the original film and make additional copies and distribute them to South America, Australia and South Africa. But in doing so, he found himself in competition with Eddie Weil, who represented Weber and Frazee. Weber and Frazee now claimed the exhibition rights of the films for the whole world. Seemingly ignoring Johnson's rights, Lawrence Weber announced in an ad in *Variety*: "Warning to Exhibitors, any and all motion pictures of the Willard-Johnson world championship fight excepting those advertised herewith, and under my direction, are UNAUTHORIZED, signed L. Lawrence Weber." Johnson got something from the films, but whether he ever received $200,000 worth of revenue, we do not know.[11]

Willard was offered $100,000 for his theatrical rights for the next year, but he too rejected the offer. Although the interstate transport of fight films had been banned by the United States Congress in 1912, Curley and others believed that with a Willard win, this ban would be lifted. No one could object to seeing Willard defeat Johnson. It was like objecting to the display of the American flag. But with an absence of patriotic fervor, the Federal government refused to permit the films to enter the country and be shown. Another of Curley's financial strategies went amiss.[12]

The loss of the fight film rights in the United States was a major blow to the syndicate. Not willing to give up on showing the films, Weber and Frazee attempted having them shipped to Newark, New Jersey, for distribution in New York. The films, however, were impounded by Frederick S. Freed, Deputy Collector of Customs at Newark. In a case that ultimately went to the United States Supreme Court (*Weber v. Freed* 239 U.S. 325, 36 Sup. Ct. Rep. 131 p.308) the decision went against Weber. The Supreme Court upheld the power of Congress to prohibit the introduction of foreign articles into the United States and specifically fight films based upon the act of July 31, 1912. This made illegal the introduction of "any film or other pictorial representation of any prize fight or encounter of pugilists, under whatever name, which is designed to be used or may be used for purposes of public exhibition."

This decision was obviously flawed. Photographers could bring in and publish still pictures of the fight in newspapers, but Weber could not bring in and distribute moving pictures of the fight. Public exhibition of still pictures were permissible; public exhibitions of moving pictures were not. As if to prove this point, the Gayety Theater in Kansas City, Missouri, advertised on April 25, 1915, "Pictures of the Willard-Johnson Fight." In smaller type below they said: "Slides Depicting all the Important Scenes at the Ring Side." Clearly they were stringing together a series of still photos to show the action of the fight. Since moving pictures were themselves made up of a series of still photos, the legal question should have been at what point does a series of still photos legal for distribution, become moving pictures and therefore illegal?[13]

This question never came up, since the real goal of the law was not to ban the films *per se*, but to prevent riots like those in 1910. Had Johnson not defeated Jeffries, and had the riots not occurred, Congress would not have passed the law of 1912 banning the transportation of fight films in interstate commerce. This was a prime example of how a congressional act could be twisted totally out of shape to create an unintended consequence. A law originally passed to prevent riots had now become a law designed to outlaw moving pictures. Still, outlawing motion pictures was not something entirely foreign to the mind of the Supreme Court. In a stunning decision, in *Mutual Film Corporation v. Industrial Commission of Ohio* (236 U.S. 230 [1915]), Justice Joseph McKenna had argued that the power of amusement and education provided by motion pictures "make them the more insidious in corruption by a pretense of worthy purpose." Further, "there are some things which should not have pictorial representation in public places and to all audiences." The court unanimously decided that motion pictures were not protected by freedom of the press or the right of free speech.[14]

In the Weber case, speaking for the Court, Chief Justice Edward Douglass White, used an argument which explains, in part, the reason for upholding the ban. In reaching for a suitable analogy, he noted that "the white slave law, so far as it is directed against transportation of women for use as a source of profit is analogous to the statute at the bar; for in both cases the object of transportation is the use of the thing or person transported, as capital from which income is to be derived, rather than as an object of sale."[15]

The white slavery analogy was a not-so-subtle attack on Jack Johnson, who stood convicted in Illinois of the crime of white slavery. This analogy was Chief Justice White's way of expressing bias against Johnson on other grounds than just prizefighting. He appears to have been saying to the public: Prizefighting and prostitution are crimes, and Jack Johnson has been involved in both. Since the law could penalize Johnson for transporting prostitutes across state lines, the law could also penalize Johnson for transporting prizefight films across state lines. Given the confusion and the restrictions placed upon the film distribution both Johnson and the Weber-Frazee syndicate lost money on the fight films. The interstate commerce clause had become the most efficient mechanism for censorship in the United States.

Vaudeville (1915)

With revenue from the prizefight films eliminated, there were two other ways by which Jess Willard could profit from his accomplishment. The first was in championship fights and the second was by going into show business.

Since the days of John L. Sullivan, the preferred alternative to fighting was to go on the stage. All of the previous heavyweight fighters, including Johnson himself, had participated in vaudeville and theatre shows. When Jess won the title, one of the first groups to contact him was the vaudeville circuit. Two days after his victory, *The New York Times* announced that he had an offer of $5,000 per week to play at Oscar Hammerstein's Victoria Theatre located at 1481 Broadway in New York. As *Variety* later reported, the $5,000 figure was what Willard's handlers had asked, but since the Palace, Hammerstein's rival, refused to bid for Willard's services, the actual amount was compromised at $4,000 per week. Still, given the fact that a working man's yearly income was around $600 per year, the average wage was 33 cents an hour and a new Ford automobile cost about $500, for the first time in his life, Willard was making good money.[16]

Variety was certain that Frazee and Weber would "clean up" by sending Willard on exhibition in vaudeville. But here again they were mistaken. While great crowds came to the theatres to see Willard, they did not buy tickets. In Baltimore Willard was mobbed by the public when he got off the train, but only 600 people came to see him in a theatre which could seat 2,000 people. In New York, "although 5000 people were around the St. Nicholas Rink in New York last Saturday night when Willard walked in there, but a bare 200 paid admission to see him inside."[17]

When Willard appeared in Atlantic City, New Jersey, to give a sparring match on April 11, he was met by a crowd that was larger than the one which greeted the three American presidents, Roosevelt, Taft and Wilson combined, when they visited the beach in 1913. But the Progressives robbed the crowd of the chance to see Willard spar with his trainers by notifying the police that such a performance was illegal on Sunday due to the Blue Laws recently enacted.[18]

It is difficult to understand why Willard did not draw in the East Coast theatres. Certainly the crowds loved him. Perhaps politics was against him. The Progressive politicians who had come into power in 1910 and 1912 had succeeded in eliminating championship boxing in California. Now, they had their sights set on New York. It would take them until 1917 to eliminate boxing in New York. But, in the meantime, they successfully sought ways to make it difficult to convert the enthusiasm of the crowds into cash for the promoters.

Willard, himself, was partly to blame for his lack of theatrical success. As Grantland Rice pointed out, Willard had no personal magnetism. He was overwhelmed by the size of the crowds and he lacked the ability to banter with the public. Unlike Johnson, he was not a natural showman. Johnson could charm theatregoers with singing and dancing as well as quick repartee. Willard could do none of this. In his vaudeville acts with Charlie Cutler in 1913 in the Midwest, Willard was able to box challengers from the audience, while Cutler took on wrestling challenges. But on the East Coast, his act was emasculated by removing the sparring exhibitions and the fight films. As a result there was very little to interest the paying public other than to just look at him. As he told *The New York Times*, after being welcomed by parades and the adulation of thousands, "This life is new to me, and I don't like it. I'm not an actor; I'm a fighter. I'm anxious to get away from it all, but I am tied down. Little did I ever think what this wave of popularity would mean."[19]

In addition, there was at least one instance where Willard himself refused to carry through on an obligation to his fans and let them down. Willard and Tom Jones made an agreement for Willard to box four rounds before the Westchester Athletic club in White Plains. About 300 fans had paid their money to see Willard cap off an evening of boxing. But when Willard and Jones drove up and saw the size of the crowd they realized that there was not enough money there to meet their guarantee of $750. As a result, they turned around and drove back to New York leaving many angry fans.[20]

If Willard himself was partly to blame for damaging his reputation with the fans, perhaps even more responsible were his managers. *The New York Times* noted: "Tom Jones guards the world's champion as if he were solid gold. He spirited him into the theatre over the roof and spirited him out and rushed off in a curtained limousine. Willard knows no freedom. He is guarded and followed and watched more closely than the heir apparent to a throne, and Willard just says, 'It all makes me sick.'"[21] Although the management recognized that Jess could not handle large crowds, they over did the need for privacy. Jess did very well in small groups and when interviewed by the press. Uniformly the reporters complimented him on being modest, cheerful, always smiling and generally friendly. Again, as *The New York Times* reporter saw him: "He is bashful, and shrinks from the blare and tumult of the admiring throng. In the big blue eyes is a kindly look, a look that you never think could be changed to the cold brutal stare of a prizefighter. The boyish smile about his mouth is always at play."[22]

Although Willard opened to a packed house at Hammerstein's the net result of his act was a failure. It began with a few still photos of the situation at Havana, including a few photos of the fight itself. After that, Loney Haskell, "the champion announcer of Broadway," came on and introduced all of the people associated with the fight in Havana, finishing up with Tom Jones. Jones then introduced Willard's sparring mates, "Jack Temple [sic]" and "Walter Moynihan [sic]," and then Jess himself to wild applause.

"When the noise had run out on him, Jess said that as a talker he wasn't there, immediately proceeding to a light exercise on the ropes, then shadow dancing, after which he held out his stomach for Temple and Moynihan to throw the medicine ball at. They never missed him nor the stomach with it. That's something new in stage exhibitions, using a stomach for a target. Jess should take his stomach to some of these dancing cabarets and give it a real test. When the medicine ball had had enough of a work-out, Willard displayed his favorite punches. They weren't many, but they included the double one he used on Johnson in the 26th."

The reviewer then summed up the evening's entertainment:

> It doesn't make any difference what kind of an "act" Willard presents, although a sparring match couldn't hurt. Anybody who pays to see him on the stage just wants to see him, and he is some little guy to look up at standing above everyone.[23]

Perhaps another reason why Willard's vaudeville career on the east coast was a failure was that the public was presented with a man who was withdrawn and unhappy. He was a square peg being placed in a round hole. He simply was not a good fit for vaudeville. He was much more at home on a ranch.[24]

Willard's engagement at Hammerstein's lasted one week. The following week was to see him in Boston at a rate of $2,000 for one night, and then on to Kansas City where he was guaranteed $4,000 for a week.[25]

Willard arrived in Boston on April 19. It was the perfect time for him to appear since the Boston Marathon had been scheduled for the day before. It was estimated that 150,000 people would be lining the route to see the race. Unfortunately for those in charge, Willard could not be persuaded to join the crowd at the finish line. His presence would have enhanced the race, while the race patrons would have given him publicity and might have attended his performance. But, as Walter E. Hapgood said in his column "Along the Sport Trail,"

> Don't imagine for a moment that as has been intimated, Jess Willard, who crowned himself world's champion two weeks ago this afternoon, will be found in the crowd at the finish of the Patriots' Day Marathon run. Willard will be in town all right but he is here distinctly on business. His business consists of displaying himself at the Arena, this evening, at one, two and three dollars a throw to those who are anxious to see what the new white champion looks

like, how he measures up, and to get first-hand Willard's own story of his triumph. For this Willard has been guaranteed $2000, and it would be mighty poor business policy, in view of all this, for Jess to give the public a free peak at him.[26]

The policy of keeping Willard out of the public eye backfired, and another opportunity was lost. The day of the performance, *The Boston Herald* carried two unflattering articles about Willard. The first described how he had failed in his debut at Hammerstein's in New York and the second was about how uncomfortable he was to perform on stage. With no positive publicity, only 500 people showed up to hear John L. Sullivan introduce Willard in glowing tones and predict he would be one of the most popular champions ever. The house fell way short of the $2,000 guarantee. Willard's popularity was fading fast.

The shift of the tour from Boston to Kansas City was a blessing. Kansas City was home territory for Willard. It allowed him to get back among friends and relations. As he told Otto Floto, "Gee, I am getting closer to the wife and kids every day."[27]

Still it was not Los Angeles, where his family now lived. When asked when he would see his family or when he would fight again, Willard shrugged his shoulders, smiled and said: "I am in the hands of my enemies—my managers, I mean, excuse me, merely a slip in conversation." He then went on to say that he would do whatever the "enemies" wanted him to do: if they wanted him to fight, he would fight; if they wanted him to tour he would tour. His main objective, he said, was to keep the respect of the public and not do anything that would disappoint them with his actions. However, "I would rather fight than tour in exhibitions because I feel I can beat them all and want to prove it."[28]

A different view of things was presented by Al Rosenthal, an Oklahoma City merchant, who saw Willard at Hammerstein's and then traveled with him to Chicago and on to Kansas City.

Stories of Willard's great popularity are not embellished. A packed house at Hammerstein's that first night cheered fully five minutes after he first appeared on the stage. Every time we stopped on the way from Chicago to Kansas City the train found thousands at the stations to see the big man. Cries of speech, speech, greeted him every time. He would show himself but he replied to the demands for a speech that he didn't know how to make one. He "kidded" them a little and called out goodbye as the train started. Photographers snapped him hundreds of times.[29]

When Willard passed through Chicago on April 21 on the way to Kansas City, he met up once again with Charley Cutler, his former manager. Cutler had obtained a judgment against Willard for expenses incurred from February 1 to June 1, 1912. The judgment was for $2,500, but when they met in Chicago, Cutler cut the amount in half, and Willard paid up.[30]

Willard arrived in Kansas City to play at the Gayety Theater from April 21 to 24, 1915. Things went better there. Just as in other places, the crowds were enthusiastic to meet him. A reporter from *The Kansas City Times* noted: "the populace followed him from the Union Station to the Edward Hotel, accompanied him upstairs in the elevator, and, when shooed out of his bedroom, did him the homage of trying to look over the transom while he combed his hair." Unlike on the east coast, this enthusiasm carried over to the theatre performances as well.[31]

The Gayety was located in Missouri and Missouri laws allowed Willard to box several rounds each show with his sparring partners. The difference was astonishing. Unlike the stops on the east coast, in Kansas City the crowds accepted the increase in ticket prices and filled the 1000 seat theater to overflowing. He performed both at matinees and in the evenings and filled the house at every show. "Saturday night [April 24] extra chairs were placed in every vacant space, even the scenery being removed from the stage to make room for extra scores." The receipts were $7,500 of which Willard and his management team was said to have gotten $4,000, or $1,000 per day.[32]

While in Kansas City, Willard was also invited to attend a Rotary Club luncheon. There he met and impressed the local business community who found him far removed from the class of rowdy prizefighters who gave the sport a bad name. Instead, after giving him a five minute standing ovation, they found him an interesting conversationalist well versed in scientific farming methods. "Willard," wrote Edward Cochrane, sports columnist for *The Kansas City Journal*, is "not a prize fighter of the low brow type, but a well educated, clean living, family loving man."[33]

J. A. Boyle, of *The Kansas City Post*, had a similar surprise:

> Many interviews with Willard give the impression that the new champion is slow-brained and dull-witted—a giant physically and a pigmy mentally. A greater mistake could not be made. Among friends where he is at ease Willard's reticence and monosyllabic conversation vanishes and in a jiffy the man appears to you in a new and unsuspected guise. He has a laugh and a return sally for every jest, a philosophy of life when the talk touches a serious vein that is proof of thought and study and sober contemplation, and last, but most important of all, if you are seeking to picture Willard the man, he has a clear, concrete plan for raising a family, typical of the very best American manhood that convinces you that Jess Willard is as much entitled to admiration as an American citizen as he is a fighter.[34]

The show then traveled to the Gayety Theatre in Omaha on April 25 for three days which was a repeat of the Kansas City success and the pay was the same, $1,000 per day.[35]

> Despite the success of the "west of Chicago" circuit, Willard remained a reluctant vaudevillian. As Al Rosenthal told it, "There is no doubt that he would rather be on the farm than in vaudeville, yet he had sense enough to know that it is on the stage and in the ring that his fortune is to be made. In fact he told me that he wished he were away from the crowds, but he knew the thing for him to do was to stay with the boxing game and that later he would retire to the farm to enjoy life."[36]

Willard returned from Omaha to Topeka, Kansas, and then to Oklahoma City, Oklahoma. Although these towns were his old stomping grounds and full of friends and family, he had no more financial success than he had on the east coast. People filled the streets around his theatres, but few people paid admission to see the show. People were thrilled to see the champ, but most could not afford a ticket to see his act. As *The Topeka Daily Capital* noted when Jess played there: "The audience at the two performances yesterday fell short of expectations, possibly for the reason that Willard's management charged grand opera prices."[37]

Kansas had very strict laws against boxing and would not allow any sparring or boxing demonstrations at all. This fact, perhaps more than the high prices, destroyed the audience. Willard and his troop put on an evening and then a matinee performance at the Grand Theatre in Topeka on May 1 and May 2 to a small crowd full of people from Emmett and the surrounding towns who knew him. Once again the crowds outside the theatre were bigger than those inside. After the matinee, while Jess visited with friends and family, Tom Jones and the rest of the troop went to Oklahoma City. Jess followed later that day and arrived in Oklahoma City the next morning.[38]

Universally, the news reports of Willard's visits were favorable. He was constantly described as a likable over-grown boy with a smile for everyone. Despite the fact that Willard was uneasy with the crowds back East, he was comfortable with the crowds in the West. When questioned about a crowd of about 75 people following him in Topeka, he shrugged it off.

> Crowds? They don't have crowds in this part of the country. That bunch here don't bother me a bit.
>
> Why you ought to see them in New York. Fifteen thousand people would pack a street and it would take dozens of policemen to make a way for me to get out.... Those fellows there grabbed onto me every time I left my hotel. I was lucky to get away with my clothes.[39]

Mishandling by his management plus the restrictions on his ability to box exhibitions meant the ultimate failure of his vaudeville tour.[40]

At the same time Jess' film *The Heart Punch* was having a hard time getting through the censors of the State of Kansas. The board of censors deleted the boxing match from the film, and specifically the section which showed the blow which gave the film its name. The producers appealed the case to an appeals board consisting of the governor, the secretary of state and the attorney general. The producers hoped that they could get a favorable ruling to show the film while Jess was in Kansas. The governor at that time was Arthur Capper, editor of *The Topeka Daily Capital* newspaper, and presumably a person the producers hoped would be sympathetic. Unfortunately, one of the members of the board objected to not only the fight scene, but the scene where Jess Willard abandons his dying daughter to go to fight in the prizefight in hopes that he would win enough money to save his daughter. Another objected to a bar room scene where Willard attracted the attention of the fight promoter. As a result, the film was not approved for distribution before Jess left the state. In its place, the Orpheum in Topeka showed a one reel film taken in February of Willard's training camp in Texas.[41]

In Oklahoma City, Willard was booked for the night of May 3 at the Auditorium, whose former manager, W.T. Yoder had been the man who introduced Jess to J.D. Brock in December 1910. The Auditorium was now managed by Sammy Samson, and it was he who persuaded Jess to come back for one show. With Jess came Tom Jones, Walter Monahan, his sparring partner, and two wrestlers who were managed by Jack Curley Americus (August John Schoenlein) and Yussif Hussane. There was also a trapeze group called the Leon Sisters and Billy Tucker, the champion bag puncher of the world. Jess had learned something since his debut on Broadway and now had his act together.[42]

Still, there remained a serious disconnect between Willard's popularity and the numbers of paying customers at the shows. We can see why this was by recounting the visit to Oklahoma City.

When Willard arrived in Oklahoma City at 9 a.m. on Monday morning May 3, he was immediately sent to his hotel. This caused him to bypass a gala reception that had been planned in his honor. Tom Jones then turned down an invitation for Willard to umpire a baseball game between Oklahoma City and Denison, Texas, saying that Willard did not understand the game well enough to make good decisions. In addition to not wanting people to see Willard for free, Jones worried that he might be hit by a foul or batted ball and permanently injured. Later Jones sealed him off from the public in his hotel:

> The demand to see and talk to him was so great that it was necessary to discontinue telephone connections to his apartment. No one was permitted to go to his room. When he drove up to the Auditorium Monday night, the jam at the door was so great that it was with difficulty that an aisle through the crowd was opened. When the exhibition at the Auditorium was over, Willard was hustled out the back door into a waiting automobile.[43]

It was easy to see why, despite the public enthusiasm for Jess on the street, inside the Auditorium the crowd "was not nearly as large as had been anticipated." Tickets to see Willard were priced at $1 to $2 compared to motion pictures which were priced at five cents and ten cents a seat. A stage show, "Officer 666," had evening box seats at 75 cents and all matinee seats at 25 cents. As a result, in his old home town, where Willard was most popular, Sammy Samson, the promoter, lost money. Although Tom Jones acknowledged Samson's loss, he refused to take the blame: "Sammy, you lost on us here last night. It wasn't our fault and it wasn't yours." Nonetheless, with the same situation being repeated in town after town, it is hard to find anybody else to blame. Tom Jones and the syndicate were simply too greedy, and as a result, Willard's vaudeville tour failed.[44]

There was one other bit of business that Jess needed to attend to in Oklahoma City. He was still responsible for the $100 fine that had been levied against him in 1911. At that time he had been convicted of prizefighting and with no money, he and Hattie and their two daughters, Zella and Frances, had to flee town and move to Elk City. Judge Sam Hooker, the previous county attorney, had been serious about getting Willard to either pay his fine or serve time in jail, and even sent a deputy to serve him papers in Springfield, Missouri, in the fall of 1911 when Jess was fighting there. As a result, although his friends argued that the fine was not lawful, when Jess returned to Oklahoma City, he was forced to pay before his show could go on. Jess was also sued for $40 for a tailor-made suit that he ordered in Oklahoma City and for which he had not paid by the time he left.[45]

Unexpectedly, Jess was also served with papers by A.W. Phillips and A.A. Cuttrell, the real estate men who had purchased Jess' contract from J.D. Brock in 1911. Phillips and Cuttrell sued Willard for $20,500 for breach of contract, arguing that Willard had walked out on them by refusing to fight in Joplin and Springfield. They also claimed that they paid his $100 fine in Oklahoma City and some tailor bills for his clothes. However, since both these bills had not been paid by the time Willard returned to Oklahoma City, it is clear that Phillips and Cuttrell had overstated their expenses. In another surprise, the day after suing Willard, Phillips himself was bound over by a federal grand jury on a charge of "White Slavery." He was accused and ultimately convicted of paying for Georgia King, 22, from Fort Smith, Arkansas, to come to Oklahoma City for immoral purposes.[46]

Surprised by Phillips lawsuit, Jess fled to his railroad car and refused to let Fred Saunders, the deputy sheriff in to serve the papers. Saunders had to break through a window before he could reach Willard who was hiding in a bathroom. This suit could not be settled at this time. Jess was given until June 1 to respond, but in fact the issue did not go to trial until November.[47]

From Oklahoma City the tour went to Wichita, Kansas, and then to Colorado Springs, Denver and Pueblo, Colorado. When he tried to take his vaudeville act to Wichita, Kansas, on May 4 he found that the local sheriff, Frank Sarver, would not allow him to spar with Monahan nor show the blows that defeated Johnson. Once again the act was emasculated. And once again the theatre was not filled to capacity. As *The Wichita*

Beacon put it: "Outside the fact that it was the world's heavyweight champion performing on stage Willard's act was about as exciting as a high school callisthenic drill."[48]

As the vaudeville tour was falling apart, Willard was thrown a lifeline by the Miller Brothers' Circus. After the stop in Omaha, on April 28, and before the vaudeville tour was over, the syndicate of Weber, Frazee and Curley, signed a contract with Edward Arlington on behalf of Colonel Joe Miller for Willard to join the Miller Brothers 101 Ranch Wild West Show for the remainder of the 1915 season. One version of the 101 Ranch Show, with Colonel Miller at the head, had come to Kansas City on April 25, just after Jess Willard and his vaudeville act had closed. Miller had heard of Willard's success in Kansas City and was prompted to want him to join the show. It was an ideal arrangement for both men. The 101 Ranch Show needed a new attraction while Willard needed a new way to present himself.

The 101 Ranch Wild West Show (May to October 1915)

In 1915 there were actually two 101 Ranch Shows on the road. The first show had opened on February 20 in San Francisco at the Panama-Pacific Exposition, but it had not been as successful as the Millers had hoped and Colonel Miller decided to close it on June 14 and move east. Miller had also opened a second show in Hot Springs, Arkansas, on April 10. This show moved north and arrived in Kansas City on April 25. Although Willard's vaudeville success in Kansas City was not easily repeated elsewhere, it did give him the right to demand $1,000 a day from the 101 Ranch Show. At the same time, Joe Miller was not buying a pig in a poke. He established a unique arrangement in which Willard traveled with the 101 Ranch Show, but was not actually part of it. Instead, Willard had a separate show with a separate admission. The two shows traveled together and shared publicity, but Willard's performance started after the main show finished. This brought enormous extra value to the 101 Ranch Show without involving much extra expense. The arrangement benefited both organizations.[49]

Jess with Colonel Joseph Carson Miller of the 101 Ranch, 1914.

Jess Willard was to join the second 101 show in Minneapolis on May 10. The two shows merged at Eire, Pennsylvania, on June 25 and finished the season as a single unit. The united show was now known as "The 101 Ranch Wild West Show with Jess Willard."[50]

According to the terms of the deal with the Miller Brothers, Willard was to appear daily in the grand entrance parade into the Big Top, but he did not have to appear in the street parade as the show entered each new town. Willard's show had special billing, and required a separate 25 cents admission fee. This meant that to cover his $1,000 a day fee, Willard needed to bring in 2,000 paying customers for each matinee and evening show, or a total of 4,000 people per day. There were no Sunday shows. Apparently, attracting the crowds proved no great problem, for Willard easily generated his own income and more. In addition, the Millers provided Jess and his entourage with a private railway car, a chauffeur and an automobile as well as a chef and porter and others, for a total staff of eight. But the most important thing was now, for the first time in all his travels, he had Hattie with him.[51]

Generally Willard had led a nomadic life. Aside from when they were in Texas and Oklahoma starting out, Hattie and the children had lived apart from Jess as he moved from one town to another. In the summer of 1911, when Jess went to Colorado to pick beans, Hattie and the children moved back to her parent's farm outside of St. Clere. In March 1913, anticipating restarting his career in the west, Jess moved Hattie and the children to California. There they had purchased a bungalow at 5838 Gregory Ave in Hollywood. Hattie and the children were living there when he defeated Jack Johnson in Havana. It remained their home until December 1915, when they moved to Rogers Park in Chicago.[52]

Hattie had thought about moving the family to New York when Jess went into vaudeville, but felt uncomfortable about giving up their California home. "I think, personally, there could be a better place for a home than New York, and maybe after his theatrical tours we can return to California to live," said Hattie. In fact, the first thing Jess had done with the money he made following the Johnson fight was to pay off the mortgage on their California home. Still, Hattie and Jess had hoped that they would ultimately be able to buy a ranch home for themselves and the children. Then, when the Millers offered a job with the Wild West Show and a private railcar, the *Jenny*, things began to fall into place. This special railway car had seven separate suites, one for Hattie and Jess and another for Tom Jones and his wife. In addition, there was a dining room and a parlor.[53] If the Wild West show was not the real thing, it was closer to Kansas and a ranch than Hammerstein's theatre on Broadway. The summer of 1915 became one of the best times the Willard family ever had.[54]

Once he had joined the 101Ranch Wild West Show, Jess announced that he would wear his fancy cowboy outfit and ride a horse in the Grand Parade which opened each show. When Edward Arlington, who managed the production of the show, offered to secure suitable clothes for Willard "the big champion smiled good naturedly": "Why," he said, "out home I have a whole room full of that stuff, left over from the old days when the boys used to say that I could hold my own with any of them on a bucking broncho or in a round-up of wild cattle."

Thus, instead of being billed as the world heavyweight boxing champion, he was billed as "a cowboy from Kansas, crack rifle and revolver shot, expert swimmer, [who] never drinks or smokes," all of which was true. Naturally in his special section of the show, Willard reverted back to the heavyweight champion. He and Walter Monahan gave boxing demonstrations and entertained the crowds with their act from Havana. Unlike the situation back east, the crowds loved it and extra performances were soon being booked to accommodate the fans.[55]

Willard toured with the 101 Ranch Show all summer and finally left the show in New Orleans in late October as his contract dictated. There were several special moments, however.

The first occurred just after the Willards had joined the 101 Ranch Show in Minneapolis on May 10. On May 14, the show stopped in Rochester, Minnesota, for one day. There a local plasterer named Fred Fulton challenged Willard to a three round boxing

Jess and Hattie standing with Mr. and Mrs. Tom Jones at the end of their private railway car, 1915.

Poster advertising Jess Willard dressed in his cowboy attire for his appearance in the 101 Ranch Show, 1915.

exhibition. Fulton, like Willard, had been born in Kansas and stood 6 feet, 4½ inches. He was lighter than Willard and weighed about 220, but he actually had a longer reach by 1½ inches than the champion. Fulton had already fought Luther McCarty and now was trying to get a name, so challenging the champion was a great idea.

Willard agreed to the exhibition and in the second round of the three-round bout, Fulton caught Willard with a blow on the jaw, knocking the champion flat on his back. This was something that no one else had been able to do, and it gave Fulton an immediate boost of confidence. As a result of this punch, Fulton began to camp on Willard's trail and repeatedly sought championship bouts.[56]

The second was in June when the papers carried story that doctors in Buffalo said that Hattie Willard had tuberculosis. There were only two things wrong with this story. The first was that it was not true, and the second was that it did not come from Buffalo. Once it was realized that there was no confirmation in the Buffalo papers, the story eventually disappeared.[57]

Then in Allentown, Pennsylvania, on August 18, Tom Jones got into an argument with Edward Arlington, the general manager of the Wild West Show. Arlington and Jones had a dispute over the time Willard's performance was to begin. The quarrel developed to the point where Willard was ready to accept an offer from a rival show for more money for the rest of the summer. Ultimately the quarrel was patched over and Willard remained with the 101 Show until the end of the tour. It was said at that time that Willard was getting a salary of $6,000 per week of which Jess got to keep 60 percent and the syndicate got 40 percent.[58]

In addition to the difficulties Jess encountered in vaudeville, he was soon embroiled in two serious lawsuits. The first we have seen was the one by Phillips and Cuttrell in Oklahoma City which alleged breach of contract in not fighting in Missouri. This lawsuit was finally settled with a trial in Oklahoma City in November 1915.

The second one was a breach of contract lodged against him in New York on June 12, 1915, by Robert Edgren who believed he had obtained the exclusive contract to publish Willard's life in the papers. Edgren and his syndicate were embarrassed to find that Willard had made a similar agreement with Ed Smith of *The Chicago Evening American*, and that Smith had published a parallel life based upon his interviews with Willard. Willard was hopeful of receiving $26,000 from the Chicago paper, but Edgren sued Willard for $27,333.33 with the goal of preventing him from being paid by Smith's paper. In addition, the suit entailed whatever property Willard had in the state of New York.[59]

Although the Willards had no property in the state of New York at the time, when the 101 Ranch Show stopped in Detroit, Willard bought a new six cylinder Studebaker. It was a seven passenger machine which was added to the show train and was parked on its own flatbed railroad car. This was a similar car to the one which had driven him to the fight in Havana, and Willard had fallen in love with it. Although he could not buy one in Havana, by the time he reached Detroit, he thought he could afford one. Initially he had a chauffer to drive the car, but both Jess and his wife announced that they intended to drive the car themselves while they were on the trip. Still, Tom Jones was nervous. He had bet everything he had on Willard's success in Havana. Had Willard lost, Jones would have been wiped out. This made him anxious to get as much out of the vaudeville tour as possible, and when that looked like a failure, he was deeply concerned. The switch to the Ranch 101 Show was a Godsend for Jones as well as Willard. But Jones remained worried that if they spent their money too fast, everything could go wrong. As he remarked, "We had all our diamonds soaked, and although we have since got them out, they are still damp from the experience."[60]

After leaving Michigan, the show moved on to New York. But we do not find that any attempt was made to seize Jess' new car. This suggests that the Edgren lawsuit was settled by this time.

In August Hattie Willard left the show as it was time to get the children back in school. She first returned to her parents' home in St. Clere, where the children may have been staying, for a visit. Then she went to the Willard home in Hollywood, where she put the children in Colegrove school in September, while Willard continued on with the show.[61]

Then, in September, when the 101 Show was in Indianapolis, Jess visited the Cole Motor Car Company and bought a Cole "8" car for Hattie. He had the car delivered with a chauffeur to their house.

Manager Ed F. Harris of the Cole Motor Company, Los Angeles, accordingly took the car and driver out to Mrs. Willard's bungalow and asked Mrs. Willard if he might show her a Cole eight—and possibly demonstrate it to her.

> "Oh," said Mrs. Willard, "what a beautiful car; but it would be no use for me to ride in it, as I do not believe that we can afford one."
>
> "Well, if that's the case," said Mr. Harris, "since you appreciate the beauty of the Cole eight so much, I believe I ought to give it to you; so please consider it absolutely yours and the chauffeur there will be at your order from now on."
>
> Mrs. Willard gazed at Mr. Harris blankly—and then he told her of the surprise present Jess had arranged for her.
>
> "You may think," said Mrs. Willard to Harris, when he was leaving, "that Jess is a great champion—but I know that he is even greater as a husband."[62]

After the conclusion of the 101 Ranch tour, Willard returned to California to his wife and children. At the end of November, it was announced that the tour had averaged receipts of about $1,200 per day and that Willard had worked 140 days. This generated $168,000 for the summer. In addition he got $25,000 for the life stories that were published in the newspapers, plus $20,000 from his vaudeville tour. Although he had earned nothing from the fight in Havana itself, he had earned approximately $213,000 since he defeated Jack Johnson in Havana. And this excluded any revenues from *The Heart Punch* film and the fight films.

But there were expenses. The syndicate of Jones, Weber, Frazee and Curley had taken 40 percent of the revenue, leaving Willard with 60 percent or about $127, 800. Then it cost $33,000 to buy out Weber and Frazee, although Jones paid some of that cost. This left Willard with revenue of around $100,000 for the victory over Johnson and the tours. From this he had paid off the mortgage on his house in California, paid for the cars for himself and Hattie, plus living expenses for himself and Hattie and the children. He was still worth around $50,000 at the end of November. This was not bad for a man who was broke at the beginning of April. Willard's willingness to fight Johnson for a straw hat or a glass of water had paid off.[63]

Although some boxing writers criticized him for not getting right back into the ring, Jess and Hattie finally had the money for which they had hoped. And if Jess had made his $100,000, the Miller Bros show had made over $200,000 for the season. Everybody had prospered.[64]

But this prosperity was partly an illusion. The war in Europe had created an insatiable demand for horses and mules, as well as agricultural products. The United States prospered by selling supplies to Great Britain and the Allies, and normal people had money in their pockets. In addition, wealthy Europeans immigrated to America and brought their money with them.

It was Colonel Joe Miller's belief that this prosperity would not last and that eventually the war might involve the United States. Already, while touring England in August 1914 with his show, Miller had his livestock confiscated by the British Government for the war effort. He only managed to salvage his trick horses through the direct influence of the King. Then, in 1915, Zach Miller found that the military was commandeering shipping and he had to buy his own steamship in order to be able to ship horses he had sold to Italy. On April 17, George Miller was forced to hold up a shipment of 1,046 war horses worth $100,000 to the Greek Government for lack of payment. The scheme to ship horses to Europe had begun to unravel when, on May 7, 1915, the German U-boats broke a gentleman's agreement and sank the Cunard liner, *Lusitania,* which they claimed was carrying war supplies. The passenger ship sank with the loss of 1195 lives including 139 Americans. The war, which had started as a dynastic conflict in Europe, was expanding to include the whole world. The prosperity of 1915 was not to be repeated.[65]

By the month of November everything seemed to be going well for Willard and his family. Along with other athletes and movie stars, Willard was asked to be one of the key events in the Christmas Charity Fund Benefit, which was being put on by *The Los Angeles Examiner* for the poor of the city. Willard was to box a number of rounds for charity as was James J. Jeffries. The paper was full of his pictures and his praise. In addition, each Sunday, *The Examiner* devoted a full page to a series entitled "How to Have Health and Muscles Like Mine" by Jess Willard. By the end of November, this series had reached 28 installments "Written for this Paper by the Physical Champion of the World."

On the negative side, November was a month of lawsuits for Willard. He had hired the famous defense lawyer, Earl Rogers, to go to New York to put an end to two matters which had troubled him. As we have seen, the law suit against him by Robert Edgren was apparently settled by the time Willard toured New York State with the circus. But Willard himself had launched a lawsuit against the people who put out the rumor that Hattie had tuberculosis. Beyond the story that Willard told in Oklahoma City, it appeared that the instigators of the rumor had wanted to get Willard involved in a charity bout which would have benefited them. When Willard refused, they then published articles designed to damage Willard's reputation by saying, "Notwithstanding his wife's illness, Jess Willard continues to show himself in the circus ring twice a day." According to Earl Rogers, there was not one atom of truth to this story and he went back to New York to institute a damage suit against these people.[66]

At the same time, his Kansas lawyer, A. T. Crane of Atchison and Topeka, was busy solving the lawsuit which Phillips and Cuttrell had brought against him in Oklahoma City. All of these were ultimately settled in favor of Willard, but each in their own way left a mark. He remained concerned and sensitive about policemen and lawsuits throughout his life. Still, being home with his family after nearly a year of traveling promised Willard a period of peace.

The Houdini Disaster (November 29, 1915)

On Monday, November 29, Jess Willard went to the Orpheum Theatre, located at that time at 630 South Broadway in Los Angeles, to see a performance by Harry Houdini, the escape artist. According to Houdini's usual custom, he invited members of the audience up on stage to witness the act up close. Having heard that Willard was in the audience, he made a short speech inviting the champion up on stage. Willard was seated in one of the balcony loges. Willard's response to Houdini's request that he join a group of men on the stage was not what anyone expected: "Aw, g'wan with your act. I paid for my seat here." Houdini tried to entice him down. He turned to the audience and said: "Those who are in favor of having Mr. Willard on the stage please signify by applauding." Willard sat silent while the audience applauded for him to join the act. When the audience's applause quieted down, Willard leaned forward and said: "Hey, if you will pay me what you are paying those seven men, I'll come down."

The audience was incensed at this and began to hoot and hiss. Houdini accepted the challenge from Willard and remarked: "All right, you come down and I'll pay you exactly what I am paying these gentlemen, which is nothing, for I have never seen any of them before in my life; so kindly make good and come right down."

Willard yelled from his box: "Go on, you faker. You're a four-flusher, and I know it. Certainly you're a four-flusher."

Houdini dashed down to the footlights and shouted back: "Look here, I don't care how big you are; you have thrown down the gauntlet and I will not let you get away with that slur. I want to tell you one thing and that is that I will still be Harry Houdini and a gentleman when you are no longer champion of the world."

The audience went wild with excitement and shouted and applauded for ten minutes. Willard tried to shout down to Houdini but the noise from the audience drowned him out. "Every time Willard tried to speak they hissed and hooted him.... Willard after trying ineffectually to make himself heard, got up and left the theatre."[67]

Willard, who was used to winning in the ring, had just lost a major decision in the public arena. As H. M. Walker in his column "An Ear to the Ground" noted, "Right then and there the Houdini party fell heir to a wave of press stuff that sent Press Agent Ham Cline home cheering for joy." Willard had given Houdini's press agents an enormous windfall at his expense.[68]

Initially Willard was only booed in the theatre. As Houdini wrote to his sister Gladys: "Nothing like this howling mob of refined ladies and gentlemen ever crossed my vision of success.... Instead of a place of entertainment, it was a seething, roaring furnace." But then Houdini realized that as the theatre crowd departed they spread the word of Willard's humiliation far and wide. For all his public indignation, Houdini was privately delighted. As he again wrote to Gladys: "I have received at least a million dollars' advertising space from this fray." Now when he walked down the street, Houdini, not Willard, was given the greeting: "Hello, Champ!" Three months later, when Houdini was playing Milwaukee, a newspaper article by J.J. Delaney in *The Milwaukee Sentinel* announced, "The world's heavyweight champion is in Milwaukee this week." Houdini had knocked out Jess Willard.[69]

Sports columnist, H. W. Walker, writing in *The Los Angeles Examiner* recounted that he received some eight or nine letters berating Willard and demanding that he, not

Houdini, apologize. In an attempt to recover lost ground, Willard wrote to *The Los Angeles Examiner* to present his side of the story. He complained:

> When I declined to come down to the stage, this should have settled the matter and the stage "hero" should have gone on about his work. The only reason in the world he "worked up a scene" was because he knew my name would be a boost for him. I understand the management of the theatre claim it is the "biggest press job" they have ever put over in months. Possibly this is true. But why should I pay the freight?
>
> As a paid patron of the theatre I was entitled to decent treatment. And after the performer had "baited" me the least the management could have done would have been to write me an apology instead of using my name as a target for their press agent junk.
>
> When my attorney, Earl Rogers, returns to this city, I shall put the entire matter in his hands. I do not believe that the laws of California permit the theatrical management singling out a patron for the abuse that I have had to stand. Knowing that the "Examiner" is the one fair paper in Los Angeles, I address my side of the case to you.
>
> Sincerely, Jess Willard
> World Heavyweight Champion[70]

Willard had a point. He was expecting to be entertained, not become a focus of the entertainment. He also had been imbued with Tom Jones' concerns about having his name used by others for their benefit. Furthermore, he was naturally a private and shy man and when surprised he became defensive and aggressive. He felt rightly abused.

On the other hand, Willard had not realized that once he became a famous figure it required sacrifices on his part. He could not expect to be recognized in public and not have the public take an interest in him. He had not learned the rule: *Noblesse Oblige*. Had he learned how to banter with the public, he might have deflected Houdini's request, or he might have acquiesced with better grace. His behavior was not acceptable for the most famous man in America. It appeared boorish and ill-mannered. Houdini had indeed knocked him out and left him lying on the canvas.

Needless to say, Willard did not apologize, either to Houdini or the public. As a result his continued residence in Los Angeles with his family became uncomfortable. As he was often to do in later years when his actions made him socially unattractive, Willard moved.

One month later, by Christmas 1915, he had moved his family from California to Chicago, where he was to live for the next several years.

The Sells-Floto Circus (1916)

The success of the Wild West Show tour in the summer of 1915 made Willard want to repeat that again. On January 19, 1916, it was announced that Jack Curley had signed up Jess Willard and Frank Gotch to tour with the Sells-Floto Circus. Gotch was the world champion wrestler, and was to earn $1,250 per week, while Willard, as the reigning world champion heavyweight, was to have a guarantee of $500 per day. The circus season was to start early in April with Willard giving a brief riding exhibition and then boxing five or six rounds each day with his sparring partner. Tom Jones was to be the announcer for the athletic events, while Jack Curley was to be the advance man.[71]

Harry Heye Tammen and Frederick Gilmer Bonfils were running the Sells-Floto

Circus out of Denver, as one of their businesses. Tammen and Bonfils were the owners and publishers of *The Denver Post* and *The Kansas City Post*. Several years earlier, they had bought the Sells Circus which had combined with the Floto Dog and Pony Show, making the Sells-Floto Circus. In 1913 they had bought the rights to Buffalo Bill's name and equipment when his Wild West Show had gone bankrupt. Thus Buffalo Bill's name was carried on the sides of the circus, even though Buffalo Bill Cody was not part of the 1916 show. Instead Cody had joined the 101 Ranch Show for 1916, replacing Jess Willard as the special attraction. With Willard and Frank Gotch, working for the Sells-Floto Circus, Tammen decided to call the show the "Champion Shows of the World" and to show Jess Willard and Frank Gotch shaking hands encircled by the words "Sells-Floto Circus and Buffalo Bill." The Sells-Floto Show started out in Denver on April 23 with the official opening in Wichita, Kansas, April 29, 1916. Save for Wichita, the route hit different towns from those Willard had visited in 1915 and did a great business.[72]

Despite the bad publicity Willard had gotten from the Houdini fiasco the previous year, he had re-burnished his reputation by defeating Frank Moran in a championship bout in New York City in March 1916. This was Willard's first fight since winning the title from Jack Johnson. It left the public convinced that no one could defeat Jess Willard. He was invincible.

Following the Moran fight in New York, Willard returned to Chicago where his family was now living. Then, on April 24, he arrived in Wichita, in a private railway car, to join the circus. This time he had left Hattie at home in Chicago. She was still recovering from the birth, on April 13, 1916, of their fifth and last child, Alan Willard, who weighed eight pounds. Once the circus schedule began, although the newspapers were full of articles about further fight opportunities, there were in fact no more fights planned until the fall. "Willard is making us too much money; I cannot afford to release him," is the way owner Tammen of the Sells-Floto Circus explained his position in the matter."[73]

Although Tammen and Bonfils owned the Circus, Jack Curley still had contract rights over both Willard and Frank Gotch the wrestler. In an attempt to generate more publicity in Wichita, he negotiated with A.M. Ebright, the president of the Wichita baseball team, to have Willard and Gotch serve as pitcher and catcher and throw out the first ball of the season. Unfortunately, despite advertising this fact, neither Willard nor Gotch turned up at the ballpark for opening day. This got the circus season off to a bad start.[74]

A second problem arose for Willard when he again ran into Sedgwick County Sheriff, Frank Sarver. Both Gotch and Willard were supposed to take on all comers as part of their acts in the circus. There was nothing illegal about Gotch doing this since there was no law against wrestling in Kansas. In fact, Gotch advertised that he would pay $100 to any man who could stay 15 minutes with him in the ring. But there was the law against boxing or sparring in public in Kansas which had tripped Willard up in 1915. As a result, once again, Willard was barred from showing his boxing skills in Kansas, his home state.[75]

In addition to the circus, there were other sorts of income for Willard that showed up periodically. These came from local print advertisements. In November 1915, Kelly-Springfield Tires ran a picture in *The New Orleans Times-Picayune* with the headline "Two Champions: Kelly Springfield–Jess Willard" with Jess encircled with a tire and a copy of a letter from Jess thanking them for their service. In Wichita, a men and boys clothing store called The Hub ran an advertisement with Jess Willard's name at the top: "Jess Willard 'is a good'eal like our Clothes' The Best Ever." While these were purely local ads, a national ad for Nuxated Iron ran regularly in many newspapers around the country. This claimed that "Nuxated Iron" was responsible for Willard's immense strength. This print ad attracted attention by showing a picture of Willard in a fighting pose above a statement saying, "I consider that plenty of iron in my blood is the secret of my great strength, power and endurance," signed Jess Willard. And at the end of 1915, Willard had a Sunday column in the *Los Angeles Examiner* showing how one should exercise and keep oneself fit and strong. Income of this type added to Willard's total revenue for the year, but this too was dependent upon his winning championship fights.[76]

For most of the time life with the circus was enjoyable and uneventful. But since the Willards had a private railway car, it naturally became the target of well-wishers who would stop by and knock on the door to get a look at the champion. Often this was done in the early morning, which woke Jess up. In order to get some privacy, Willard took the sign "Champion of the World" off his railway car and placed it on the tent where the Negro "canvasmen" slept. In addition Willard and his wife or friends might go for a drive in the countryside near where the circus was parked. Occasionally, these drives themselves became noteworthy events, as in May, when Willard was arrested for speeding in Boone, Iowa. Once it was known that Willard had a court date, the entire population of Boone turned up at the court house to see Willard tried for speeding. They were disappointed. Willard posted a bond of $5 and failed to appear in court. The circus moved on, leaving Boone $5 richer and its population without a show.[77]

Working in the circus continued to be profitable. In August, the Sells-Floto Circus set a record taking in $11,000 for the matinee and evening performance combined, when it played a single day stand in Denver. According to *Variety*, "Jess Willard was the side attraction and is credited with drawing the greater portion of the big receipts."[78]

But not everything went smoothly. On July 18, while giving a wrestling exhibition in Kenosha, Wisconsin, Frank Gotch broke a leg. Willard and Tom Jones, who were watching at the time, carried Gotch to an automobile and took him to the hospital. It proved to be a bad fracture and Gotch was forced to drop out of the show. Then on October 20, in Riverside, California, two new hands were killed when they unfastened the wrong rope on a main pole of the tent and it fell inward on top of them. This damaged the circus and was a memory that bothered the Willards the rest of their lives. Finally, at the beginning of November, when the show stopped in El Paso, Texas, Charles Knoblauch, who had rented Willard his ranch for a training camp when the Johnson fight was to be held in Juarez in 1915, attached his new car. When Willard and Tom Jones abruptly departed El Paso for Havana in 1915, they were in such a hurry that they left a number of bills unpaid, Knoblauch's among them. Knoblauch bided his time, and when the circus came through, he seized Willard's car, forcing him to hop a freight train to get out of town.[79]

The 1916 Sells-Floto Circus closed in Fort Worth, Texas, on November 13. Immediately the papers were full of speculation about Willard's plans. *The Daily Oklahoman* declared that Willard had no rivals and might retire undefeated. Gabe Kaufman, a local promoter in Kansas City, wanted Willard to fight the winner of the Battling Levinsky vs. Carl Morris bout scheduled for November 16. In Denver, Jack Kanner, head of the National Athletic Club there, wanted to hold a series of bouts with Jess fighting the winner of the elimination rounds in May of 1917. Tom Andrews, head of the Cream City Athletic club of Milwaukee, came up with an offer for Willard to fight Fred Fulton. And

Dominick Tortorich, who had worked hard to get Willard in a championship fight in New Orleans at Mardi Gras in early 1916, was back again with a similar offer for the spring of 1917.[80]

The Buffalo Bill and Wild West Show with Jess Willard (1917)

Willard seemed far more reluctant, in the fall of 1916, to fight than he had in the previous spring. He had gone back home to be with his family in Chicago. He denied that he had retired, but admitted that he had gained a lot of weight and said he now weighed 270 pounds. The newspaper men suggested that he looked 20 pounds heavier. If he was going to get back in the ring, it would take a lot of training and time to get back in shape.[81]

Furthermore, the circus had once again proved profitable, and he looked forward to another year of touring in 1917. He had made far more money in the 101 Ranch Wild West Show and the Sells-Floto Circus than he ever made in the ring. He found the world of the Wild West shows congenial and wanted to continue traveling with them. But he did not have the foresight of Colonel Joe Miller.

Colonel Miller had predicted that you could not get something for nothing. The prosperity that the war brought could not long last. Miller believed that the war would soon engulf the United States and that the days of the Wild West Show were over. As a result, at the end of 1916, Miller sold off his stock and equipment to Edward Arlington and closed up the 101 Wild West Show. The Miller brothers then turned their attention to their giant farm enterprise, which they knew would profit from the need for food and animals that the war would bring. Unfortunately, Arlington and Willard did not have anything like the management skills of the Millers. They assumed that the fountain of prosperity from which profits flowed into the circus would continue through 1917.[82]

On February 23, it was announced that Willard had signed on with the circus route for another year. This year it was to be the Buffalo Bill and Wild West Show, now run by Edward Arlington. The year began with two bad omens, however, for Buffalo Bill Cody died on January 10. Then on January 23, Cody's son, Lieutenant Frank Cody, was shot down by German planes as he flew for the Royal Flying Corps. Nonetheless, Arlington had rented Cody's name for the 1917 season and placed Johnny Baker, Cody's adopted son, in charge of the circus. In 1917, the show was to begin in Norfolk, Virginia, and run from April 11 to November 3, traveling north along the East Coast, then west along the Great Lakes, south to Fort Worth, Texas, and east to Georgia and then ending up in Jacksonville, Florida, on November 3. Willard was to get his customary salary of $1,000 to $1,200 per day. He was to perform twice a day and take on all comers in boxing exhibitions. In addition, a clause in the contract allowed him to cancel the circus performances with three weeks notice to engage in a boxing contest. It promised to be another year of prosperity, with an income of $100,000 for the Willards.[83]

Willard had not really counted on there being a war. At the end of March, Willard sounded more like he was planning to retire. When he visited Oklahoma City on March 20, he said he was looking for a ranch and livestock. Retirement, not championship fighting, seemed to be on his mind. "My contract with my managers also runs out in about six months and then I will be a free agent. I will then be able to get away from the crowded thoroughfares of the large cities and can once more get out where it is free."[84]

Willard's plans for retirement were disrupted by President Wilson's declaration of war at the beginning of April. Willard had no real idea of how that would affect his life. Despite having volunteered to join the military in the first flush of patriotic enthusiasm, Willard really assumed that he would continue with the circus during 1917. While the circus was profitable for the month of April, by May things had gone off track. At the end of April, *Variety* reported that the theatrical business was bad all over the country. The public was distracted by the idea of a war. In addition, the Wilson administration proposed levying a ten percent tax on all entertainments. Show business in the Midwest was having a tough time, while in the east heavy rains kept the crowds at home. Circus managers were concerned that they might have to cancel their routes during the summer time. The demand for soldiers threatened to strip the circuses of workers. Ringling Brothers particularly feared heavy government taxes and began canceling contracts with several of their acts. On the other side of things, Newport, Kentucky, banned circuses until the end of the war. Many advance men found it difficult to line up space for the circus to set up since towns were turning empty fields into garden space. And gradually, the military was taking control of the railroad system. The war was changing the circus world along with everything else. By the end of May it had become apparent that Edward Arlington was going to have to close the circus. Suddenly Jess was out of a job.[85]

There were many things Willard could have done at that time. He could have retired from the circus and taken up farming, as Colonel Joe Miller had done. He could have gone back into boxing and fought Carl Morris or Fred Fulton. He could have joined the army or the navy, as Frank Moran and many other boxers did. He could have traveled the country giving exhibitions as a recruiter. But he did none of these things. Instead, just about the time Arlington decided to sell the circus, business began to turn up. As a result, Willard decided to buy the circus from Arlington, pay off its debts, and run it himself. Even in wartime, Willard believed that "the show must go on!"[86]

The purchase of the Buffalo Bill Show, with its two trains of cars and over 200 horses, led to many complications which Willard had not expected. Initially he had to spend $105,000 to buy the show. Then he found that he had to hire a number of people to run it. He hired Edward Arlington back to schedule the show on the road. He hired Melville B. Raymond, a New York showman, to manage the show. The purchase of the show had been completed by Ray O. Archer, who was described as a life-long friend of Willard's and a banker. And in fact, while Archer and Willard were good friends dating back to Emmett, Kansas, days, Archer was a druggist, not a banker. And although Willard felt comfortable with him, Archer lacked the talents that Willard would need in the next few years.

Willard felt that he could make more money in the circus than in the ring. The only problem was that in order to be a success in the circus, he had to be a success in the ring. A championship victory was necessary each year in order to draw in crowds to the circus. His victory over Jack Johnson made his 101 Wild West Show a success. His victory over Frank Moran made his Sells-Floto tour a success. But there was no victory in 1917 to make the "Buffalo Bill Wild West Show with Jess Willard" a success, and it was not.

This was not entirely Willard's fault. It took skill and knowledge to manage a circus. Edward Arlington could do that, but Ray Archer, Willard's secretary, and Melville Raymond, could not. By the middle of July, Willard's circus was bumping into the Hagenbeck-Wallace Circus and the Ringling Brothers Circus. For some reason, the Buffalo Bill show and the Ringling Brothers Circus played the same Midwest town only two days apart. This was bad for both parties. Then on July 27–28 it happened again in Detroit where Willard's circus and Barnum & Bailey played at the same time. By this time Melville Raymond and Johnny Baker had left Willard and moved on, although Edward Arlington remained. Still, this left Ray Archer in charge, and Archer knew nothing about managing a circus.[87]

Coupled with these scheduling problems, which should have been sorted out by Arlington, an even more difficult problem arose. The public was dissatisfied with the performance of Willard himself. People had always complained about paying a fee to see the circus and a second fee to see Willard perform after the main show. But given the fact that Willard had done nothing in 1917 to enhance his image, and several things related to the War that tarnished it, the double billing began to irritate. As a result, *Varsity* noted the following: "The Willard show has been getting some unfavorable reviews from the newspapers en route, several avowing that the show carried a sideshow attraction in Willard and that the wild west exhibition was not up to the former Buffalo Bill show standard."[88]

As a result of this criticism, Willard had to make himself more available to the public. He also decided to keep the show on the road much longer with the plan of closing up in Florida about January 1, 1918. This was designed to generate more money, but it could not bring Willard back into the good graces of the public.[89]

Despite his plans of keeping the show on the road until January, in the fall of 1917 Willard was forced to sell off much of his stock and close shop early. All of the circus hands were able to find work easily and many of the horses became property of the United States Army. All of the wild animals were sold to a firm in Kansas City who serviced zoos. Willard again reaped a financial harvest, but his career under the big top had come to an end.[90]

Willard was still the world champion heavyweight boxer, but even that suffered as the public had become concerned with more important things. Willard's multiple streams of income began to dry up and he, like Colonel Miller, began to turn his attention to farming. Willard's future became very different from his past.

7

Back to the Ring: 1915–1916

Jess Willard had made his money in show business. That had brought him the prosperity that he and Hattie had sought. But he had made his reputation as a prizefighter. Now that he had beaten the unbeatable Jack Johnson, he had a sense of confidence in the ring that he felt nowhere else. Show business was merely a break between ring engagements. Before he left Havana, he told the reporters: "In time I will meet all my challengers, picking out the real contenders first. They need not worry, for as long as they are not colored, I shall not bar any of them." He asked for a summer in show business and then said that he would defend his title against any white man at any time and at any place.[1]

Fight promoters are greedy fellows and they cannot wait to get their paychecks back in the ring. The day after the fight in Havana they began bombarding Willard with new offers to fight. But the syndicate of Weber, Frazee and Curley who controlled Willard's destiny at this time wanted to have him earn easy money in vaudeville without endangering his earning capacity with a new fight.[2]

Now the boxing battles swirled around Willard as they had swirled around Johnson previously. Each challenger and his manager sought to position himself as the only true contender for Willard's title. Jim Coffey fought and defeated Carl Morris. Charles Weinert, in a controversial decision, defeated Gunboat Smith. Then Frank Moran defeated "Bombardier" Billy Wells in England. Even though Willard had stepped away from the ring to concentrate on earning money in show business, the fact that there was a new white champion stimulated boxing.[3]

Willard's syndicate had high hopes for vaudeville into which they now had sent him. But they had not properly prepared him for the tour, nor had they counted on the barriers facing him. Willard's strength was that he was slow to arouse. He had a mild disposition which was better suited to the farm than to the city. There remained a conflict between Willard's native instincts and the desires of the Weber, Frazee, and Curley syndicate to recover from their losses in Havana and with the fight films. Weber and Frazee wanted him to generate money in show business, which they understood, rather than have him go back to boxing, which they did not. Since the syndicate had claim on 40 percent of the revenue Willard made, they wanted to have a successful show business run before he got back into the ring. Vaudeville was a failure, but when they finally signed him with the 101 Ranch Wild West Show, they succeeded in placing Willard in the right spot. Finally, everybody could prosper.[4]

Willard had repeatedly shown himself uncomfortable in show business, but he did recognize that in the Wild West shows he could make more money than fighting. There was no question that it was easier to make $100,000 during the summer in the Wild West

Show than to make $30,000 in a championship fight. From the syndicate's standpoint, Willard should stay in show business as long as possible and have as few fights as possible. And he agreed. He was willing to stay with the 101 Ranch through his contract period to the end of October 1915, even though there were numerous requests for him to fight during the summer. But once the summer and the contract were over, Willard wanted to get back into the ring.

On August 28, Willard and Jones began to lay out their strategy for the fall. They announced that Willard would fight all of his challengers one at a time with Willard's fee $30,000 per bout (the same fee established by Tommy Burns in 1908), allowing three weeks between bouts. It seemed simple. All that was necessary was that his challengers get their money together for the fights to come off. In fact, it proved anything but simple.[5]

Trying to Get Back into the Ring

No one took up this challenge at the time. Willard still had two months to run on his contract, but he had thrown down the gauntlet. Then, on September 20, 1915, in Milwaukee, Tom Jones purchased Harry Frazee's interest in the Willard syndicate. Gradually the Havana syndicate was breaking down, and within a month, Willard and Jones had bought all the parties out. Frazee and Weber had moved back to show business. Everyone had gotten their money out of the deal, based not on the fight itself, but on Willard's performance twice a day in the 101 Ranch Wild West Show. Only Jack Curley remained hanging around, hoping to be involved in the future fights.

The same day that Jones made the purchase of Frazee's shares, he told a group of sportswriters that he had not received a single offer for Willard to box since the fight in Havana. Although this was manifestly untrue, it was true that Jones had not been able to accept a single offer, both because he did not control Willard's destinies and because Willard was under contract to the 101 Ranch until the end of October. This was acceptable to most of the sportswriters, for they understood the economics of the situation. As "Ringside" Reagan, a columnist for *The New York Mail*, had said in April, "The boxing contingent is perfectly willing that Willard should earn a little easy money—for above five or six months. But after that Jess must fight the most logical of contenders." And this was what Jones planned for him to do.[6]

In October the pace began to pick up. When the 101 Ranch Show arrived in Oklahoma City on October 4 for a one day stay, Tom Jones announced that Willard was ready to get back into the ring and fight after November 1. He even announced that the fight would be held in New Orleans and was to be a 20-round bout. Everything was arranged. There was only one small problem: Willard had no opponent.

"Willard will be open to meet any one after November 1," Jones said. "He will not require much training for he has kept in condition all summer. Just who his first opponent will be I do not know. Coffey and Moran have been talked of, but neither has made a definite proposition."[7]

The next day, Richard C. Klegin, a rather shady character who had assigned himself the title of managing director of the Willard-Johnson fight in Cuba, turned up in Oklahoma City. Klegin offered $50,000 for Willard to fight the winner of a Coffey-Moran bout which was scheduled in New York on October 18. According to Klegin, Willard would get $32,500 while the challenger would get $17,500. This deal sounded good. Its only weakness was that Klegin did not have either Coffey or Moran under contract, nor did he have any location in which to hold the fight, nor did he have any money of his own. Still, Jones listened attentively to Klegin and then said that he would decide after meeting in New Orleans with the resident promoters there, Dominick Tortorich and his new partner, the former heavyweight champion, Tommy Burns from Calgary.[8]

The following week, Billy Gibson, who now had returned as manager of boxing at Madison Square Garden, made Willard the same offer to fight the winner of the Jim Coffey vs. Frank Moran bout that Klegin had proposed. Gibson's offer had much more credibility than that of Klegin, for Gibson was actually Coffey's manager and had Madison Square Garden as a location. Still there were a few problems with Gibson's proposal as well. The Frawley Law was still in effect in New York, which meant that no bout could go more than ten rounds, and no decision could be given in the ring. This rule would have worked strongly against Willard in the Johnson fight, but it actually worked in his favor in any future fight. The only way Willard could lose a bout was if he were knocked out or died, as Luther McCarty had done, in the ring. If Willard walked out of the ring alive, it is likely that he would retain his title in New York. A second problem was that as Coffey's manager, Gibson, was not allowed to act as the promoter as well. If Coffey lost to Moran, Gibson could promote Moran's fight with Willard, but if Coffey won, he could not. Thus Gibson's proposal was not really any more solid than that of Richard Klegin. Both needed a good bit of work to make them acceptable.[9]

Then, on October 18, Coffey and Moran met in Madison Square Garden for what amounted to a semi-title fight, with the winner supposedly to have a title fight with Jess Willard after November 1.

The Coffey-Moran fight was unusual in a number of ways. First of all, Frank Moran demanded that he be paid his share of the gate before he got into the ring. He had his reasons. When he and Jack Johnson fought in Paris in 1914, Dan McKetrick, the fight promoter tied up the receipts in such a way that neither Moran nor Johnson was ever paid. Both Johnson and Moran learned from that experience. Johnson refused to get into the ring in Havana until he had been paid. Moran refused to get into the ring in Madison Square Garden until he had been paid. When Gibson refused, Moran got dressed and walked out of the building, leaving 10,000 people waiting for a bout that might never occur. Frederick A. Wenck, chairman of the New York State Athletic Commission, was called in. Faced with the situation, he agreed that Moran should be paid before the fight. They sent runners out to find Moran, who was walking up Fifth Avenue by that time, and he returned, was paid, and the fight went on.[10]

The second oddity was that Jim Coffey lost the fight by a knockout, even though he was up and walking around the ring, at the time.

Coffey and Moran were evenly matched. Moran weighed 200 exactly while Coffey weighed 201. Coffey had a glass jaw, while Moran cut easily and was a bleeder. It looked like the battle could go either way.

Coffey began like a champion. He looked cool and was boxing superbly. "Moran could do practically nothing, and looked like a cart horse against a thoroughbred." Moran was beaten by repeated punches and at the end of round one he was bleeding from a cut lip and a broken nose. In round two, Moran looked groggy. Coffey hit him with innumerable rights and lefts, while few of Moran's punches seemed to reach Coffey. "Suddenly came the bolt from the blue. Coffey went in to slug and he left an opening. Up came that right of the Pittsburgh man and it crashed against Coffey's jaw. His knees sagged and he tottered to the ropes. Coffey wobbled about the ring very unsteadily, but he managed to evade punishment in the few seconds that remained before the bell rang."

At the beginning of round three, Moran attacked Coffey with a left followed by a hard right. "The Irishman crumpled up and staggered toward Moran as if to clinch. Moran measured him with his right and caught him full on the jaw. Coffey dived headlong forward and fell flat on his face."

Coffey was knocked out. But he did not remain down on the canvas. Instead he got up quickly, but had no idea what had happened nor where he was. Moran was astonished, as was the referee, Bill Brown. As Coffey stood looking aimlessly out at the crowd, Moran decided to renew the bout. He swung at Coffey but missed. Brown suddenly stepped in and declared the fight over. Coffey's corner protested, thinking their man might make a comeback. "Although Coffey was able to stand, he was out cold as if the referee had counted a dozen over him, and it was merely what the psychologists call reflex action of the muscles which enabled him to rise at all." Moran had won the fight by a knockout. Frank Moran was now the acknowledged challenger for Jess Willard's crown.[11]

At the end of October in New Orleans, Willard's contract with the 101 Ranch Wild West Show expired. By November 6, Willard was back home at 5838 Gregory Avenue in Hollywood, California. When Willard arrived back home, he had been away so long, he found the children were not exactly sure who he was. Zella was perhaps old enough to remember him, but Frances, age four, was particularly wary. When Jess attempted to get her to behave, she ran to her mother and said: "Mother, do I have to do what that man says?" Having Daddy home required some adjustment.

When Harry Williams arrived and knocked on the door of the Willard bungalow things had settled down. He found the champion and his family making popcorn.

> The Willards are farm folks, ranch people, and can find enjoyment in old-fashioned things like popping corn. The simplicity of the whole thing was simply delightful.
>
> Usually, it is difficult to associate a ring champion with anything except cafes, footlights and bright lights generally. Here was real home life—home life that went straight to the heart. Surely there could be no savagery in this man popping corn with his kiddies. And there isn't.
>
> Soon the children shyly ventured in. They were a lot more afraid of the newspaper men than they were of the champion. Such is the power of the Press. Zella, aged seven, Frances E., four, Jess Jr., two, were soon clustered around their large lumpy daddy. Then came Enid, crawling. Enid is one year old, and it was her birthday anniversary. Daddy got home just in the nick of time to help her celebrate.
>
> It was like a litter of puppies frolicking and tumbling over a great good-natured Newfoundland.[12]

While Willard was enjoying the reunion with his family, a trial was going on in Oklahoma City. When he had returned there in early May, he had been served with papers by A.W. Phillips and A. H. Cuttrell for breach of contract arising out of the Joe Cox affair in Springfield, Missouri. In a deposition in November 1915, Willard admitted that he had signed a contract for Phillips to manage him. He argued, however, that Phillips had breached the contract when he wanted Willard to throw the fight with Joe Cox. When Willard refused, Phillips reported him to the police in Springfield and had him put in jail. This, in Willard's mind, effectively broke the contract. After a rather long deliberation the jury held that the contract Willard had signed with Phillips was invalid. Ten out of the 12 jurors admitted that Phillips had some claim on Willard but they awarded Phillips and Cuttrell only one dollar in damages against Willard. The other two jurors would not admit that Willard owed anything. This put an end to the long and damaging issue of the Joe Cox fight.[13]

Back in New Orleans on November 1, Tom Jones met with about 2,200 boxing fans at the New Orleans Athletic Club and announced: "You will see Jess Willard fight for the heavyweight championship of the world in New Orleans next February or March. Everything has been arranged but the opponent." To back this up, on November 3, before Willard left for Los Angeles, Tom Jones signed a contract with Dominick Tortorich and Tommy Burns, for Willard to fight "any white opponent in New Orleans, La. some time during the months of February or March 1916 for the consideration of thirty-two thousand, five hundred dollars ($32,500) at the Tulane Athletic Club."[14]

This announcement was amplified by Tommy Burns, the former heavyweight champion, in an article that appeared in *The Los Angeles Times*. According to Burns, although Moran was the logical contender, they needed to have an elimination tournament, because a new fighter had appeared upon the scene by the name of Fred Fulton.[15]

Like Willard, Fulton had been born in Kansas. He was from the small town of Blue Rapids, near Manhattan, and stood nearly as tall as Willard, at 6 feet, 4 inches. He weighed 220 pounds. Fulton had a reach of 84½ inches or 1¼ inches longer than Willard himself. To top it all off, Fulton now lived in Rochester, Minnesota. As we have seen, when Willard and the 101 Ranch Show visited Rochester on May 14, Fulton had challenged Willard to an exhibition. "In the second round of their three round exhibition, Fulton caught Willard flush on the jaw, knocking the champion on his back, something that Jack Johnson could not accomplish in the 26 rounds that he boxed in Havana."[16]

The addition of Fred Fulton into the mix confused things. Burns wished to have Fulton fight Jim Coffey, who had been eliminated by Frank Moran and then have the winner of that bout fight Moran again. The idea of an elimination tournament had some value, but ultimately it only served to fill the newspapers with speculation and to delay the production of a real fight. Several sportswriters stepped away from the flurry of daily newspaper articles and asked, even if there was an elimination bout, did any of the challengers pose a serious threat to Willard? George R. Holmes of the United Press concluded that "there is no heavy now looming up on the pugilistic horizon capable of giving the champion a real championship battle." After looking over the candidates, he summed up his analysis: "Jess, it appears, is king of all he surveys."[17]

Sam C. Austin, writing in the November 27 issue of *The National Police Gazette*, had a similar view. He summed up his article with the headline: "Willard's Title Disputed by a Bad Lot of Fighters." Austin had no praise for Frank Moran. Moran, he said, "was never looked upon as a great fighter, only a mediocre performer and a good trial horse for the promising heavies." But who else was there? "It is said that the first of these will be Fred Fulton, and something within me urged the question, who in h--- is Fred Fulton?" "Right along it has been the opinion of this writer, and a great majority of those who have seen Willard perform, that any white heavyweight to-day would stand no chance with the conqueror of Jack Johnson." According to both Holmes and Austin, Willard had fallen into the same trap as Johnson and Jeffries before him. He had run out of credible challengers.[18]

Given the paucity of good white fighters, a Boston syndicate suggested that Willard might be willing to fight Sam Langford, the best black boxer after Johnson, for a purse of $50,000. Unlike many other places in the country, Boston had not yet banned biracial bouts. But this fight never occurred. Instead, Langford fought another Negro fighter, Harry Wills, on December 3 in Harlem. And Willard kept his vow never to fight another black fighter in the ring.[19]

Following up on the articles by George Holmes and Sam Austin, De Witt Van Court, now the dean of the West Coast writers, wrote a long article in *The Los Angeles Times*, praising Willard. Van Court had earlier predicted that Willard would one day be champion. Now that he was champion, Van Court simply was gushing in his praise. "He is one of the most perfectly built men for his size in the country." Van Court praised his speed and stamina and commented that Willard had "one of the most perfect body defenses I have ever seen." He kept his arms next to his body ready to absorb blows while holding his hands ready to hit back. "This is real old-school stuff and the correct and safest way to protect the body." When his head was attacked, Jess would coolly pull his head back just far enough to miss the blow. "This was the Jim Corbett, Joe Gans and Abe Attell style of avoiding dangerous swings aimed at the head and proves skill of the highest class." In short, "judging from the great improvement Jess Willard has made in his boxing since his last appearance here," Van Court wrote, "it will be many years before he will be defeated for his title of champion of the world."[20]

At the beginning of December 1915, it was generally agreed that Jess Willard was the supreme heavyweight boxer in the country and without peer. Nonetheless, since he needed to get back into the ring, he would probably fight Frank Moran for the championship in a 20 round bout in New Orleans during Mardi Gras. It was also recognized that although Moran was not truly championship class, he was the best heavyweight available. So, on December 3, Tom Jones signed a contract with the New Orleans promoters for Willard to fight a championship bout on March 4, 1916, with Fred Fulton. Fred Fulton? What was going on?[21]

Tommy Burns had insisted on his tournament strategy in which Fulton and Coffey were to fight the first bout and Moran was to fight the winner of their battle. But Coffey did not comply with Burns' wishes and instead signed to fight Gunboat Smith on November 28. Burns then tried to get Moran to fight Fulton, but Moran refused. This left Burns with Fulton as his only fighter, so by default, Fulton became Willard's challenger for the New Orleans bout. In addition, Willard's fee of $32,500 was likely to take all of the receipts from the bout, just as Jack Johnson's had done at Las Vegas and in Havana. While Willard had been willing to fight for nothing, Frank Moran wanted $10,000. This left Burns in a quandary. He felt that he could not afford Frank Moran as a challenger. Nor could he get Moran to fight Fulton in an elimination bout. He had persuaded Tortorich that there would be three sell-out battles in New Orleans, culminating in a world championship bout just before Mardi Gras. Now there was only one battle scheduled between the champion and an unknown, Fred Fulton. Burns and Tortorich began to get cold feet.[22]

This led to a break between Tortorich and Burns. On December 10, Dominick Tortorich sold his interests in the Tulane Athletic Club to a newspaper man, Wm. F. Steele from Denver. Tortorich ended his partnership with Burns, leaving Burns and Steele as partners in the Tulane Athletic Club. But Tortorich still remained shareholder in the Willard-Fulton fight.[23]

This had a disconcerting effect on the Willard-Fulton fight. On December 14, Tom Jones and Michael Collins, Fulton's manager, met in Chicago to sign the papers for the fight, but there were no papers to sign. Since the original contract had specified that the fight would be held in the Tulane Athletic Club, the break up between Tommy Burns and Dominick Tortorich meant that new contracts were needed. Amazingly, however, two days later the papers were ready to be signed with Tom Andrews of Milwaukee signing for Tortorich and Burns as if no break had occurred. The fight was to be on March 4, 1916. Willard was to get his $32,500 while Fulton was to get $7,500 and 15 percent of gross and 25 percent of the motion picture rights.[24]

But all was not well in Willard's camp. The Houdini fiasco occurred on November 30. Three weeks later, on December 21, Willard had left his house on Gregory Avenue in Hollywood and moved the family to Chicago. There his wife bought them a house for $13,000 in Rogers Park for Christmas. Willard gave as his reason for making this move that he wanted to have his family near him, and California was too far away. But before he left Los Angeles, he had given the sports columnist H. M. Walker a long list of the injustices inflicted upon him by the boxing community. He felt he had been abused. Willard was really upset and not in the mood to play games.[25]

Tommy Burns, on the other hand, had been too clever by half. In the contract signed on December 15, he had insisted that Willard fight Fred Fulton. But on December 24, he sent a telegram to Tom Jones suggesting that Fred Fulton be removed and Frank Moran be substituted in his place. He now considered Fulton too much of a risk and did not feel that the public would support the fight in a way that would allow them to make their guarantees. "When we signed Jess Willard up for a 20-round championship match, he agreed to meet any white heavyweight selected and we made it plain that we would pit him against the man favored by the sport writers of the country. Fred Fulton is not that man, we have decided, and we therefore have resolved to offer the match to Frank Moran, who seems the popular choice."[26]

Furthermore, Jim Coffey had signed to fight Moran a second time in New York on January 7, 1916. Coffey believed he could show that Moran's victory in their first bout was a fluke and that he, Jim Coffey, was the better fighter. Perhaps the real championship fight could now be between Willard and Coffey. Either way, if Willard fought Coffey or Moran, the promoters and the public were assured of a better fight than if Willard fought an untested Fulton. But Burns had reckoned without Tom Jones.[27]

When Willard and Jones learned that the New Orleans promoters now wanted to substitute Moran for Fulton, Jones exploded. He called Mike Collins, Fulton's manager, and told him that since they had signed a contract, Willard and Jones would keep their word. "I have wired Tortorich and told him to take the match or leave it; we are going to box Fulton first and will go elsewhere if necessary. I am awaiting his reply." Then, on December 28, Tommy Burns reversed course again. He agreed to stage the Fred Fulton-Jess Willard bout as originally scheduled. He sent the following wire to Tom Jones in Chicago: "Tortorich did not want to go through with the match, so I have today taken over his interest and I will go through with the Willard-Fulton match myself. Get here yourself as soon as possible. We can sign new articles when arrive. Tommy Burns."[28]

On December 29 it was announced that Tom Jones and Tom Andrews, the Milwaukee promoter, were to arrive in New Orleans that day. Tommy Burns was waiting for them. In a newspaper article that day, he reverted to his previous position that (1) Fulton should participate in an elimination battle to prove his worth, before being matched with Willard and (2) that Moran had been asked to fight Willard, but that his demands were too high to make him acceptable to Burns. Nothing seemed to have changed since November.[29]

But nothing in boxing is ever as it seems. No sooner had this appeared then it was announced that the bout between Willard and Fulton in New Orleans was off. Instead Willard had signed to meet Fred Fulton in a ten round bout in Milwaukee. Then Burns telegraphed Ike Dorgan, Frank Moran's manager, and offered Moran $7,500 to fight Willard in New Orleans on the original dates of March 4 or March 6, 1916. And, in a stunning turnabout, Tom Jones agreed for Willard to fight Moran in New Orleans if Moran defeated Jim Coffey on January 7: "I have agreed [for Willard] to take on Moran here, or in fact, any of the others and to do this too with less than two weeks after meeting Fulton in Milwaukee."[30]

It is hard to understand the convoluted thinking of boxing promoters. It appeared that Thomas S. Andrews, a local promoter in Milwaukee, had offered Jones $25,000 for a ten round bout between Willard and Fulton in Milwaukee on February 22. Although this was less than the normal amount Willard expected, it was an alternative to the New Orleans offer. Since neither Jones nor Burns wanted to back down, the Milwaukee bout represented a compromise to which each could agree. Thus, having turned down Burns' final offer, Jones sent a telegram to Andrews: "Am ready to do business with you."[31]

Things seemed to be going Andrews' way. According to *The Washington Post*, "when Andrews announced his plans to stage the bout to five Milwaukee business men today [December 30], they immediately placed orders for $100,000 worth of tickets for the scrap." This meant that money for the fight was secured. Then, the next day, January 1, 1916, *The Post* announced that the fight had been called off. The reason given was due to a problem with the division of money. What that meant was that there was not enough money to go around and the news reports were sheer puffery. Willard did not fight Fred Fulton then, or ever. Instead, Fulton signed the next day, January 2, to fight Dan "Porky" Flynn in New Orleans on January 28. That fight actually occurred and Fulton defeated Flynn in 20 rounds.[32]

All of this negotiation meant one thing: While Moran and Coffey and Fulton all got their chance to box, Willard did not. He had not had a bout since April 1915 and now it was January 1916. The man who had promised to be a fighting champion had done no fighting. If Willard was ever to get a chance to defend his title something had to change.

The Arrival of Rickard

That change occurred on January 12, when George Rickard entered the picture. Here was a man who could carry through on his promises and under whose direction good things happened in boxing. Rickard was born in Kansas City, but his family moved to Sherman, Texas, when he was four years old. Growing up in Texas led to his nickname "Tex." Although basically a gambler and a rancher, Tex Rickard had promoted two championship fights which became classics. The first fight was between the lightweight champion, Joe Gans, and Battling Nelson at Goldfield, Nevada, on September 3, 1906. The fight was really a promotion to sell shares in the mines at Goldfield, but due to Rickard's native abilities it attracted wide attention. To prove the prosperity of Goldfield and to show that they had the money to back up the fight, Rickard had the purse of $30,000 in gold coins piled in the window of a local bank for a week before the fight. Stimulated by the gold, Gans and Nelson battled for 42 rounds of brutal boxing. Finally Nelson was disqualified for low blows and Gans was given the decision.

The second championship fight was "The Fight of the Century" between Jack Johnson and undefeated former champion Jim Jeffries. Rickard overcame enormous odds, including having to move the fight from San Francisco to Reno at the last minute. Yet his genius for publicity made this a battle in which the whole Anglo-Saxon world was interested. As we have seen, the fight on July 4, 1910, led to nationwide race riots in the United States and set in motion the entire "white hope" movement. In addition it provided the largest purse in boxing history prior to 1920. Rickard, Jeffries and Johnson all made a fortune out of this fight.

Following the fight, Rickard had traveled to Paraguay in South America. There he created one of the largest cattle ranches in the world on five million acres running 50,000 cattle. He returned from Paraguay a few days after Johnson lost the title to Willard in Havana. He was in New York City when all of the turmoil was going on about getting a championship fight for Willard. Although Rickard had never met Willard, he decided to step in and offer $45,000 for Willard to fight Moran in New York City.[33]

The appearance of Tex Rickard as a promoter of a Willard-Moran bout made it an event worthy of attention. Neither Willard nor Moran was a charismatic fighter. Even collectively they could not excite the New York sportswriters. But when Tex Rickard took over, a ten round, no-decision fight, with two unexciting battlers, it became something special. Harry A. Williams of *The Los Angeles Times* commented: "A few years ago this pair would have been fortunate to receive a guarantee of $10,000 for that number of rounds. So when he [Rickard] begins talking in terms of $45,000 or thereabouts for a ten round spat between Willard and Moran we are all bound to sit up and take notice."[34]

Williams, like most sportswriters, did not think much of Frank Moran. "Moran while heretofore regarded as a second or third rater is generally accepted as the only white man entitled to a match with the big fellow. In short, it appears to be the best match possible under the present circumstances." To be fair to Moran, he had improved his position by knocking Jim Coffey out a second time, in nine rounds on January 7, 1916. This meant that his first victory (strange as it was) was no fluke. Indeed, Moran felt he was riding high. He believed his 20-round fight with Jack Johnson in Paris was a victory, even though no one else did. Coupled with his two recent knockouts of Jim Coffey, he announced to the world: "I am the equal, if not superior, of any heavyweight in the game."[35]

Before Rickard announced his offer, the major question had been: Was there any way a bout featuring Willard could make money? There was nothing electric about Willard. He was a big farm boy who loved his wife and family. While this was admirable, it was not the sort of thing that sold tickets. Many promoters felt that it would be difficult to put together a fight that would generate the $30,000 which Willard expected and which all recognized as the going rate for a championship bout. A cartoon by Robert Ripley in the January 6, 1916, *The New York Globe* summed up the situation before Rickard made his offer. It showed Willard sitting on a stool in his dressing room saying: "$30,000 win-lose-or draw—Or I don't fight! In the back at the door are the promoters and the crowd saying, 'The Fans are tired of Waiting' and 'There isn't that much Money in th' House.'"

Rickard, by offering $45,000, had answered this money question in dramatic fashion. He had thrown chum into the waters and stirred up the sharks. Suddenly other promoters were now convinced that there was money to be made. The prizefight waters began to roil and churn as promoters, scenting prey, brought forth counter offers.

First and foremost of these sharks was James Joy Johnston, the "Boy Bandit of Broadway" who had tricked Willard in the first Rodel fight. Johnston was now the manager of Madison Square Garden, having displaced Billy Gibson. He was in an enviable position, as the Garden was the largest indoor arena in New York City and vital if one wanted to obtain the largest crowds. Johnston offered $35,000 for Willard and $20,000 for Moran, for a total of $55,000 compared to Rickard's $45,000.[36]

Next was Jack Curley, who had put on the Havana fight. Curley was known to both Jones and Willard, but he also had lost money for many people on his last two championship fights. He had forced the town of Las Vegas, New Mexico, into bankruptcy after the Johnson-Flynn fight in 1912, and had left numerous creditors unpaid in Havana, including Jess Willard himself. Further, his offer was only $32,000 plus 45 percent of the total gate receipts. Had this been Rickard's offer it might have meant something, for as Jack Dempsey was to later say: "In every fight Rickard ever put on, he himself furnished at least fifty percent of the box office draw. Regardless of who the fighters were, they never dragged in more than fifty per cent. Sometimes it was much less than that." Rickard could build a box office and make the 45 percent of revenue mean something. But Jack Curley could not. It was likely that, as it had in Havana, the percentage of the box office revenue would simply vanish. As Jess Willard might have said, "Jack Curley couldn't draw flies."[37]

Following these men were the also-rans. The old-time fighter, Jack Skelly, offered $52,000 for a fight in May at the Empire City Race track. This avoided the problem of trying to get Madison Square Garden away from Jimmy Johnston, but it ran into another problem. Willard was scheduled to join the Sells-Floto Circus in Wichita, Kansas, at the end of April. The fight needed to be in March at the latest.[38]

Philadelphia Jack O'Brien, the former fighter and now a promoter, offered $50,000 for a six-round battle in Philadelphia. Billy Gibson, back as manager of Jim Coffey, offered Willard $25,000 to fight Coffey in Madison Square Garden. While Barney Oldfield, the famous race car driver, joined with Sunny Jim Coffroth, to offer a fight in Tijuana, Mexico, since championship bouts longer than four rounds were now illegal in California.[39]

While all of this was going on, Tom Jones once again did the unexpected and signed a contract for Jack Curley to promote the bout. This astonished Rickard, who had advanced a much better offer than Curley, and it left the boxing community puzzled. In response, Rickard increased his offer to $49,500, agreeing to pay Moran $17,000 and Willard $32,500. Moran wisely accepted this offer and agreed to join with Rickard. But Tom Jones was not to be moved: "I have signed with Jack Curley and that ends the matter."[40]

It was now the end of January and no fight had been agreed upon. Rickard and Jones had reached a Mexican stand off: Willard had signed with Curley while Moran had agreed to be with Rickard. To add insult to injury, Curley said that he would only offer Moran $15,000 and that if Moran would not sign for that, Curley would find another person to fight Willard. This was not a good strategy to use with Moran who was stubborn and not willing to be pushed. And given the difficulty in getting Willard and Moran together in the first place, the public was not likely to be impressed if once again the contestants were changed.[41]

All this squabbling wore Rickard out. He knew most of the parties and doubted that they could carry through on their offers. Curley, he knew, was most likely to find that at the end of the day there would be very little in box office receipts to share with the other parties. He also knew that Jimmy Joy Johnston would live up to his nickname and rob anyone who asked to rent the Garden for the fight. For that reason, Rickard proposed to have the fight in March and to rent a large circus tent in which to hold the crowds, while Curley planned to have the fight in April in a baseball park.[42]

Throughout his life Willard remained loyal to those he trusted. He had remained loyal to J.D. Brock, his first promoter, until Brock abandoned him when he went on trial for prizefighting in Oklahoma. He remained loyal to A.W. Phillips until Phillips had him put in jail in Missouri. He had remained loyal to Charles Cutler until Cutler abandoned him in New York to pursue his own career. He trusted Tom Jones even when it nearly ruined his career both in the ring and on the vaudeville circuit. Willard's native instincts were to get into the ring and fight his opponents. But now he could not do that. Instead, months had been wasted in futile negotiations over bouts that never occurred. So when Tex Rickard appeared with a *bona fide* offer it is hard to understand why Jones turned it down. But he did.

And time was running out. Delaying the fight into April, as Curley planned, would conflict with Willard's circus schedule. Willard knew it too. He knew that if he was to have a fight in the spring, he needed to get started now. Even though no date had been set and no opponent announced, on January 18, Willard began training.[43]

Willard's action may have forced Jack Curley's hand. Without notifying Jones, Curley signed Willard to fight Jack Dillon, a light heavyweight, who stood 5 feet, 7½ inches tall and weighed about 175 compared to Willard's current weight of 260. This was the type of fight Willard abhorred. Ike Dorgan, Frank Moran's manager, heard about this first and called Jones in Chicago. Jones said that a fight with Dillon was ridiculous and that he, Jones, was the only person allowed to sign for a fight on Willard's behalf.[44]

As if to prove his point, the same day he learned of the Jack Dillon match, Jones repudiated it and signed a contract with Dave Lewishon, the Chicago representative for Tex Rickard. Willard was now signed to fight Frank Moran on March 17 with Rickard as promoter. Further, both Willard and Jones said that they would not honor the contract signed by Jack Curley with Dillon. From this it would appear that Curley was in deep trouble. But such was not the case. In fact, Curley's signature appears as a witness on the typed contract for Willard to fight Moran which was presented to Lewishon on February 3, 1916.[45]

Jones, it turns out, had been playing a serious game of poker with a master poker player. Jones had signed his contract with Curley in an attempt to force Rickard to increase his bid for Willard's services. He knew that Curley could not equal the crowds Rickard could draw. He also knew that Curley could not easily force Moran to take less for the fight than Rickard had offered. The key ingredient which made Curley's action understandable was that Jones had been conducting a bluff. Using Curley as a stalking horse, he had forced Rickard to increase his offer to Willard. Instead of guaranteeing Willard

$32,500 for the fight, the new contract now stated that Willard would get $47,500 plus 51 percent of the moving picture returns. The total value of the contact had increased from $49,500 on January 20 to $67,500 on February 3, all because Jones and Curley had beaten Rickard at his own game.[46]

Despite the arduous efforts everyone had made to create this fight, it was not settled yet. On February 9, both *The New York Times* and *The Washington Post* announced that the fight which had been scheduled for March 17, was now scheduled for March 8. There was only one place to hold the bout in New York City, and that was Madison Square Garden. But the Garden had already been leased for March 17 (St. Patrick's Day), so a new date of March 8 had to be set. Jimmy Johnston, true to his reputation, had increased the rent to Rickard from $1,500 a night to $7,500 for the night of the bout. In addition, when the final contract was signed with Willard and Moran, the total pay to the fighters was $70,000 with Willard getting $47,500 and Moran getting $22,500.[47]

Due to the increased costs, Rickard had to undertake a remodeling of the Garden, if he was to be able to get a profit. Ordinarily the Garden would seat 10,000 people, but Rickard planned to increase that to 13,000. Even so, he thought he would have to charge $50 for the box seats with $3 for the far rear seats. It was estimated that the average seat price would be $9, an astronomical price for a ten-round boxing match in 1916.

As if these financial stresses were not enough, both Jones and Willard came down with medical ailments. Jones was confined to his New York hotel room due to an attack of rheumatism, while Willard, who was still in Chicago, was forced to stop training due to an attack of the grip. Willard admitted to a sore throat but he did not consider his health a problem. Despite that, the malady lingered on.[48]

By February 14 Willard's health had not improved and he was still unable to train. He weighed 262 pounds, 24 pounds more than he had when he fought Jack Johnson a year earlier. He was clearly out of shape. Since he could not seem to shake the cold that had been troubling him, he told Tom Jones that Jones should call off the bout. He knew he could not get in shape by the March 8 deadline.[49]

A number of reasons were given for delaying the fight. Hattie Willard said Jess had a severe cold. Robert Edgren, the sports writer, said that Willard's indisposition was an attempt to get more time to train. Willard himself wrote an article in *The Washington Post* saying that he wanted to delay the fight from March 8 to March 25 because March 8 was Ash Wednesday and many of his friends would not attend a fight on Ash Wednesday. Tom Jones then jumped in and said that if anybody was going to ask for a delay in the fight, it should be him: "He [Willard] can't decide anything in this matter. I'm his manager, and if a postponement is necessary I myself will ask for it." But when it was finally announced that the fight had been postponed until March 25, everybody seemed to approve. Willard had more time to train, as did Moran, and the New York fans seemed to show more interest in the bout than they had with the earlier date.[50]

Then on February 20, Willard had a relapse and was ordered to bed by his physicians. The next day, Tom Jones showed up in Chicago and announced that Willard was in fine trim: "All these stories about Willard being out of condition are pure bunk," Jones said.

"Right now, all that's the matter with Willard is the after affects of a cold. It has really helped him in one way. He weighed about 255 pounds when he stopped training. He now weighs around 250.

"It will be mighty easy for him to drop off another 5 or 10 pounds before March 25, and that is all he has to lose, for he will fight at 243 or 245."

Robert Edgren announced in his column that the bout could not be postponed again. Not only would the public not stand for it, but there were no more open dates at Madison Square Garden. The fight had to be now or never.[51]

Tickets had now gone on sale and the sales were averaging $9,000 per day with a large number of tickets being sold to women. This surprised *The New York Times* reporters who wondered if having women at prizefights would become a usual occurrence. It also caught the box-office managers unawares.

"Two women walked up to the box office at the Garden yesterday and asked for two $25 tickets in the section reserved for women and their escorts. It was a new experience for the seasoned ticket sellers to sell fight tickets to women and they stood at the window at least half an hour asking all kinds of questions before they finally bought the pasteboards. And after they paid for them they demanded a long explanation as to why they should cost so much."[52]

On February 24, Willard left Chicago for New York. He appeared fully recovered from the effects of his cold and ready to go to work. "This will be the first time Willard had put in a long siege of training in New York. Before he won the title it was his habit to drop in over night for his bouts in Gotham. In those days he needed little preparation. All he needed was a chance to stretch his long legs after stepping off the train."[53]

When he arrived at Grand Central Station on February 25, he was met by a massive crowd, similar to the type of crowds that met him in the previous April. But more importantly, he met Tex Rickard for the first time. Rickard was probably the most astonished person in the crowd. His first words to Willard were "Has Moran seen you yet?" When Willard admitted that they had met, Rickard continued: "Well, all that I can say is that Moran is about the gamest man I know of. One glimpse of you, and I would have looked for a lonely cabin above the timber line."[54]

Not only Rickard, but the reporters were astonished by Willard's appearance.

> Willard is a fighter, but few could guess his secret by looking at him.
>
> Today Willard is a finished product. His face has filled out, matured, and he is almost handsome. Even more massive than before, and admittedly heavier, he does not seem so big, as he is groomed to the minute and carries himself with the confidence of one sure of himself.[55]

Although Willard had estimated his weight at 260 pounds and Tom Jones had placed it at 250, in fact, when he was weighed by Joseph Cramer (Kramer), the official physician for the New York State Athletic Commission, he weighed 272½ in his street clothes. Still, despite being seriously over weight, Cramer pronounced him fit for the fight. Furthermore he was cheerful. As Robert Edgren reported, "If Willard has any fear of losing his laurels to Frank Moran he doesn't show it. On the contrary, he is cheerful over the coming affair."[56]

In keeping with his reluctance to fight in Havana on Easter Sunday and in New York on Ash Wednesday, Willard also refused to spar and work out in the gym on Sundays. Instead he took long walks in Central Park. He was a firm believer that walking was the best exercise one could get and was happy when he was out walking with his sparring partners.[57]

One thing Willard did not like to do was to be interviewed by social columnists, particularly women social columnists. As soon as he got to New York one of them, Nixola

Greeley-Smith, descended upon him and sought to ferret out his innermost secrets. Protected by Tom Jones, Willard manfully faced his opponent in a conversational bout which lasted nearly an hour. "It was exceedingly painful to both of us," wrote Miss Greeley-Smith. "For the champion admitted frankly that he was not used to talking with women and they scared him. I don't mind admitting, for my part, that the champion scared me."

As an opening conversational gambit, Willard was asked if he liked music. When he said he did, he was quickly hit with a low blow: "Ragtime or Chopin?" He covered up and immediately claimed a foul. It turned out that he liked band music, but more than that he could not say. In politics he said he was neutral and let the best man win. He was against fighting, particularly with guns and suggested that talking was the way to settle disputes:

> "I'm no believer in violence. Now in bringing up kids, I say, 'What's the use of spanking them just because they make noise?' If you spank 'em they only make more noise. Talk is the thing: talk that's what makes every big man afraid of the littlest woman. Take my wife, now. She's only 5 feet 6, and look at me! But she's my boss, I can tell you, and little Jess Willard is her boss. The littler they are the more bossy—that's the way it goes. I'm such a big fellow that even in the ring I never have to duck away from the tallest man, but I tell you, I duck from the littlest woman—yes, I do. And when Mrs. Willard comes after me with a rolling pin, or even a line of talk, I tell you I don't duck—I run."
>
> Do not believe for one moment that Mr. Willard said all of this without prodding. He is the kind of man that simply won't wind up for more than five words at a time....
>
> "Is Mrs. Willard a good cook?" I asked.
>
> "She's a crackerjack," replied the champion enthusiastically. "And I can tell you I'm a pretty good cook myself. I can boil water without burning it. I can make biscuits and fry bacon. And say, you just ought to taste the fried beefsteak with milk gravy that I cook. Can you make milk gravy?" asked the champion eagerly.
>
> I lied to Jess Willard. You see, I had labored so hard to find the "open sesame" to the champion's soul—and behold, the magic word was—gravy.
>
> "Yes, of course I can," I said.
>
> "Then you know how," Mr. Willard said approvingly. "You just put a little milk and seasoning and flour in the beefsteak grease and keep on stirring and never let up, because if you let up the gravy will get lumps in it. Gee, but that's good."
>
> So I left Mr. Willard, his face alight.[58]

Beginning on March 1, Willard began to be concerned that perhaps he was over working his main sparring partners, Walter Monahan and Jack Hemple, and that he might need some new fellows to offer different styles of boxing. This idea was taken up by Fred Wenck, Chairman of the State Athletic Commission as well, who argued that Willard was not fully preparing himself for the fight with Moran. Yet when Willard put a call out for sparring partners only one person showed up. Tom Jones tried to get contenders Al Reich and Jim Coffey to work out with Jess but they too refused. As Jones noted: "It's all right until they get a lamp at him close up—then good night."[59]

Government Interference

By March 5, Tex Rickard announced that the advanced ticket sales had passed $100,000. Despite the fact that the ticket sale was going well, there were clouds on the horizon. Fred A. Wenck's visit to Willard's camp was not one of benign support. It grew out of the attempt by Martin G. McCue, an old time prizefighter, and now a member of the New York Assembly, to put a stop to the Willard-Moran fight. McCue had seen Willard when he first arrived in New York and was convinced that Willard would never be able to lose enough weight to make a good fight. Working from this information, McCue assumed that the fight was fixed. He put pressure on Wenck and the New York Athletic Commission to do everything they could to hinder the fight, while he, McCue, tried to get a bill passed in the assembly to halt the fight. McCue failed in his attempt to get the fight banned, but he did succeed in focusing the public's attention on Willard's weight and his training methods. Wenck, in an unprecedented move, insisted that Willard be weighed before he even started training. When Willard refused to strip to be weighed, they weighed him with his clothes on and found that he weighed 272½ pounds. This supposedly demonstrated that Willard was not in shape to fight.[60]

Robert Edgren was initially pulled into this dispute and contrasted Moran's training methods with those of Willard. Moran had set up his headquarters in Saratoga, while Willard set up his camp in the Pioneer Athletic Club near his hotel in Manhattan. Moran had spent his time outdoors chopping wood and taking long trips through the snow and ice-boating, while Willard was cooped up in a hot and restricted space suitable to a dance academy. Willard's choice of training location seemed to confirm that he was not taking the fight seriously and that something was amiss.[61]

Gradually, Edgren and the other sportswriters began to realize that the attack on Willard's weight was part of a subtle campaign on the part of McCue and Wenck to destroy the bout. When Willard had requested on his own, additional sparring partners, Wenck approved that choice as showing that Willard was serious. Jones hired George "Boer" Rodel as a sparring partner and that worked out. But when Tom Jones mentioned in print Jim Coffey and Al Reich as additional partners and that did not work out, Wenck used that as a weapon against Willard and Jones. Wenck revoked the license of the Pioneer Athletic Club and banned Jones from charging 25 cents a person for all those wanting to see Willard train. Wenck's argument was that Willard and Jones were defrauding the public by implying that Willard would spar with Reich, when in fact he did not. Willard was incensed that the Athletic Commission wanted to determine how he trained and with whom he sparred; Jones was incensed that the Athletic Commission had deprived him of a source of revenue by preventing him from charging 25 cents a head for those who wanted to see Willard train. Although both Jones and Willard considered leaving New York over this interference, they were persuaded to stay and complete the fight with Moran.[62]

The attack on the fight had actually been launched on many fronts, but it focused specifically on Willard's weight. Assemblyman McCue used the fact that Willard weighed more than any heavyweight had ever weighed going into a championship bout as proof that the fight was a fraud. Although this argument was rejected in Albany, it got a lot of press in New York. "I looked at Jess Willard a few days ago," said McCue. "He is no more in condition to fight than I am. To permit this fight to be held will be the death knell of boxing in New York." Assemblyman McCue's comments began to sound uncomfortably like those that Senator Brown had issued in California, prior to the elimination of championship boxing in that state in 1914. And in fact, in 1917 the Frawley law was repealed and championship boxing was eliminated in New York.[63]

Whether or not he realized what was going on, Robert Edgren, who now carried the by-line "World's Greatest Sporting Writer," switched sides and began to support Willard and Tex Rickard in this battle to preserve boxing in New York. The same day McCue made his statement, Edgren published a column in which he argued that Willard weighed no more now than he did before the Havana fight. Another writer picked up the thread and found that Willard felt he was only about five pounds heavier than he wanted to be with several weeks of training still to go. Then Edgren issued another column which carried an explicit threat that any attempt to deprive New York of this championship fight would be politically unpopular.[64]

Wenck and McCue had attempted to insinuate that not only was Willard not serious in his training, but that Tex Rickard was not trustworthy. Wenck wanted the Commission to take control of the fight revenues to protect the public. Edgren argued strongly against this. He pointed out that one of the reasons why this fight was so popular was precisely because it was being promoted by Tex Rickard. "Rickard," Edgren wrote, "is an extraordinary sort of fellow. He keeps his word. His honesty isn't measured in dollars. Nobody who ever knew Tex Rickard is going to be in sympathy with any attempt to intimate that his contract isn't as good as any certified check, and that the money in his hands isn't as safe as in the hands of any stakeholder in the world, whether 'known to the boxing commission' or not."[65]

Edgren's campaign succeeded. Wenck had tried to get the other members of the commission to meet in New York and take over control of the money Rickard had raised. They were to create a new, secret stakeholder, to replace Bob Vernon, who had also served as stakeholder for the Willard-Johnson fight. But the other two members of the commission did not show up. Those two commissioners effectively vetoed Wenck's plan and the money and control of the fight remained in Rickard's hands.[66]

McCue and Wenck had overplayed their hands. The idea of Wenck seeking to "protect" Rickard's reputation by taking the money was ridiculous. It appeared to be the crudest form of blackmail and Rickard would have none of it.[67]

Having failed in their attack on Rickard, and on Willard's training methods; a new attack was launched, this time against the rules. B.A. Jessup, a candidate for a position on the state athletic commission, argued that the law required the use of eight ounce gloves, rather than the five ounce gloves normally used. Jessup argued that using eight ounce gloves would "reduce the passage at arms to a display of science and skill, thus eliminating any element in the way of roughness that might possibly be introduced." This was a common argument used by those whose basic goal was to eliminate boxing entirely. Rather than take on boxing directly, they sought to hide their attack under the shield of compassion for the welfare of the boxers. But this objection was ignored and, even though the fight was fought according to the rules of the commission, five ounce gloves were used.[68]

Back to Basics

Having put an end to the efforts to get the fight banned, it appeared that things should proceed smoothly. Willard had gotten his weight down to 252 or 253 and felt in fighting trim. Moran had been forced to delay more training as he was already honed to a fine edge and there were still ten days before the bout. In fact, both boxers now were threatened with becoming stale and the fight was still days away.

Robert Edgren then wondered if the two fighters were not doing an unusual amount of training for a ten-round bout. Rather than not training hard enough, as McCue and Wenck tried to suggest, Edgren believed they were training too much: "As a plain matter of fact each has gone through preparation enough to fit him for a hard 20 rounds. Boxers are usually content with a week or two of training for a short contest. Yet Moran, figuring on a possible chance to win the championship, has worked as hard for this fight as Bob Fitzsimmons and Jim Corbett worked for the finish fight at Carson."

Willard too seems to have worked as hard as he worked for the 45-round bout in Havana. True, he trained for about three months for the Havana fight, but much of that was to learn the game better and improve his skills. He had the skills now, and the only purpose of training was to get into physical shape. Normally that would take a couple of weeks: "Yet he trained a couple of weeks in Chicago before coming East, and on the 25th will have gone through just a month of training in New York. That's enough to put any clean living man into fighting trim, in spite of the 'expert opinion' of our friend, Marty McCue."[69]

Then, a few days before the fight was to take place, Frank Moran was involved in an impromptu battle between his old fight manager, Dan McKetrick, and his current lawyer, Frank S. O'Neil.

Dan McKetrick, who later told John Lardner, "I'm as bitter a man as there is in the world," had initially chosen Moran to fight Johnson in Paris with the idea of cheating Johnson out of his title. Moran, who was an honest fighter, was not aware of McKetrick's plans. Instead Moran believed in trust, and refused to sign contracts with anyone, and that included McKetrick. McKetrick saw sinister motives in this action and made a vow that he would tie up the funds of the fight so that no one would get anything out of it. This he did. The fight in Paris ended with a decision for Johnson, who retained his title. And true to his word, McKetrick tied up the funds and they remain in the Bank of France to this day. But when McKetrick returned to New York, he again sued Moran for funds he had advanced him.

The jury decided that Moran did not owe McKetrick anything. The funds paid out to him were proper expenses of the fight. After the decision, Moran and his party went to Whyte's chophouse on Fulton Street to celebrate, only to have McKetrick and his party show up as well. Manager McKetrick made a remark to Lawyer O'Neil to which O'Neil took offense. McKetrick followed up with a fist to O'Neil's eye, while O'Neil struck McKetrick on the jaw. Tables were overturned; dishes smashed and recriminations were hurled. Moran stood on the sidelines and acted as peacemaker. As Moran later said to John Lardner: "The rarest bliss that can befall a pugilist, is the sight of managers and lawyers punching each other, for nothing."[70]

On March 20, Fred Wenck once again sent Dr. Joseph M. Cramer (Creamer) to examine Willard and Moran in preparation for their fight. Cramer commented: "I am satisfied Willard is ready right now to go ten rounds at top speed with Moran or anybody else, and that his present condition is a fine tribute to his training methods, despite any criticism to the contrary." He found that Moran was "bristling with vigor and ready to fight when he returned here from Saratoga two weeks ago. If possible, he is even better today." This seemed to put a quietus to all of the complaints by Wenck and McCue.[71]

The fact that the fight was occurring in New York City not only meant a great crowd, but also meant that the papers were full of comments from past champions. Heavyweight champions James J. Corbett and James J. Jeffries wrote columns praising both fighters, but allowing Willard the better chance. Corbett even wrote that Willard was as good as or better than Jeffries was. "Sunny Jim" Coffroth on the other hand remembered when Willard lost to Gunboat Smith and Charley Miller in his arenas and said he believed Moran would win if he did not get scared. Kid McCoy, former middleweight champion, was all for Willard: "Jess Willard is a real champion in the fullest sense of the word. He is an extraordinary man and it will take a man slightly better than extraordinary to beat him. If Willard lived in my day and trained the way the oldtimers did, he would have conquered any man in the game. This is a bold, broad statement, but it is my honest opinion."[72]

Everyone realized that Willard was bigger, taller and more skilled as a boxer than Moran. Everyone agreed with Corbett when he summed up the fight: "Willard has many advantages over Moran. He is the biggest man that ever held the heavyweight championship. And he knows how to make his size count. Willard is the quickest man of his size with his hands that ever climbed into the ring. He is quicker with his hands than Moran too. Jess is 50 pounds heavier and 6 inches taller than Frank. And that is a big advantage."

But Moran had one advantage that Corbett saw: Willard was not aggressive and did not try to knock his opponents out. He had been pulling his punches in his training which Corbett saw as a mistake. This meant that when he actually tried to swing full speed his arms were likely to get tired and heavy. As a result, Corbett saw the fight going all ten rounds unless Moran got lucky and scored a knockout of his own. If he did, he would win. If he did not, Moran would lose. It was that simple.[73]

The day of the fight it was announced that the battle was a sell-out. Rickard had increased the number of seats to 13,000 and there were to be 1,000 standing room tickets sold as well. The list of box-holders was a list of all the most important people of business and Broadway. There were Whitneys, Goulds, Morgans and Vanderbilts in attendance, as well as George M. Cohan, Weber and Fields, Enrico Caruso, John Philip Sousa, Diamond Jim Brady and even Honest John Kelly and Mayor Curley from politics. "Never before had New York been so worked up over a glove contest," wrote *The New York Times*. "Last night on Broadway, in the restaurants and in the theatres, the leading topic of conversation was: 'Are you going to the fight?'" Even Tex Rickard himself was surprised at the excitement the bout had caused. "I have done everything in my power to make this bout an attractive one, and the only thing that remains is for the boxers to do their share."[74]

The fight was more interesting for the crowd outside the ring than for the fighters in it. Normally, most society men and women would not be seen out in public after dark in anything but evening dress. For men, this meant the standard evening clothes: black suits, white ties, white shirts, waistcoats or vests. For women, it meant evening or ball dresses. And indeed, at the fight, most of the men and a few of the women were so dressed. But prizefights still were illegal in most places, and even those conducted under the Frawley law, carried with them the frisson of wickedness. The more daring young men came dressed in the new casual tuxedoes with black ties, while the daring young women came in "smart new Spring suits which fill the city's finery shops." In addition, because boxing matches skirted the border of legality, they had always attracted a mixed crowd of the crude and the cultivated. "The Fancy," as the wealthy contingent was called, were content to rub shoulders with the bruisers, the shoulder-hitters and the rogues. But in this fight, Tex Rickard had filled the entire house with "the Fancy" and left the rogues outside. He was altering the culture of boxing, making it more respectable, and, at the same time, more profitable. He was laying the foundation for the million-dollar gates. This was something only he was able to achieve.

Nonetheless, the rogues and rabble would have their revenge. As we shall see, in the future, the New York Athletic Commission, under a new director, William Muldoon, would place a limit on the price of tickets to boxing matches. The Moran fight would be the last time, for many years, that anybody could charge $50 for a ringside seat. Boxing was not yet ready to become a sport exclusively for "the Fancy."

As for the fight itself, it turned out just as Gentleman Jim Corbett had predicted. There were no knockouts and not even any knock downs. Willard was aggressive enough to provide the public with thrills without doing any major damage to his opponent, while Moran was battered and bleeding at the end, but not broken. The seventh round was the highlight of the fight. Willard sprang forward as if ready to end the fight. Moran was cov-

Jess shaking hands with Frank Moran prior to their championship fight in New York City, March 25, 1916.

ered with cuts on his face. He tottered back and forth as if ready to drop under the crashing blows from Willard's fists.

> A fighter never took such a beating more gamely than Moran in that round. When the round was nearly over the challenger, instead of doubling up and crumpling under the punishment, showed his indomitable courage. His eyes lost their dullness. Anger flashed at the mighty man who was beating him. With his arms at his side, weak and limp, Moran proved his gameness. He had the heart of an ox.
>
> The ambition of a lifetime was going away from Moran rapidly when his limp right fist clinched and he drove it up against the champion's jaw with a terrific crash. Willard, stunned under the power of the smash, backed against the ropes, but he could not get away. With head down, Moran fought desperately and sent his left against the other side of the champion's head.
>
> Willard was so much surprised that he forgot to raise his guard to his face, and again Moran's wicked wild swing jarred the point of the giant's jaw. Willard did not smile now. A worried look came over his big boyish face, and Tom Jones was dumbfounded. Half a dozen times Moran smashed the champion in the greatest rally of the bout, and he still had Willard against the ropes punishing him when the round ended.[75]

This last burst of effort was the end of the fight for Moran. Moran had taken everything Willard was prepared to give and lasted. He could not win the fight; there was no question among the sportswriters that Willard had won the bout decisively, but Moran had fought a game fight and won the hearts of the crowd.

There were many comments after the fight about why there were no knock downs or knockouts. Moran tried his hardest in the seventh round but his blows were not powerful enough to bring Willard down. Willard, on the other hand, gave several reasons for not knocking Moran out. He first said that in the second or third round he broke his hand on Moran's elbow which got in the way of an upper cut. This proved to be true. After the fight Willard had an x-ray which revealed that he had broken a finger on his right hand and had a bad break of the *os magnum*, a bone in his wrist. As a result he did not follow up on many opportunities he might have had to knock Moran out. But then, after some consideration, Willard amended his comment to say that he "did not knock out Moran because a knockout would have had a bad effect on the fighting game in New York, and there is enough feeling against it now."[76]

Harry Carr, from *The Los Angeles Times*, who had come all the way to New York to see the fight, had a different view. Willard, he remembered, was not one to deliver undeserved punishment. If he had not been hurt, he did not want to hurt his opponent. It was Willard's native concern for the other fellow which prevented him from knocking out Moran. According to Carr: "Jess seemed to be reasonably interested in the fight, but he could not manage to get excited about it." On leaving the Garden, Carr overheard a society lady say to her companion: "It doesn't seem to me that Willard tried to punish him much." Carr agreed: "Lady, I string with you. I don't think that Jess tried very hard. He was satisfied with an evening of good exercise in which he kept the championship in the family."[77]

Robert Fitzsimmons, the former heavyweight champion, was of a similar opinion.

> Every minute of the ten rounds was Jess'. His cleverness enabled him to block most of the vicious swings that the yellow-haired Irishman shot at him, and when one of them did land, Willard's strength enabled him to take it with a laugh. Moran never had a chance with him.
>
> Outclassed is the only word for it. Frank never had a right to be in the same ring with the

champion.[78]

These opinions were shared by the crowd as well. They cheered more loudly for Moran than for Willard. They wanted the smaller man to win. Although they expressed dissatisfaction at the lack of a knockout, they really did not want to see Moran knocked out by the giant, Willard. And Willard, sensing their feelings, stopped short of knocking Moran out.

The Washington Post summed up the fight this way: "The two men gave of their best. Not a single round was drab or dreary. There was a feeling every minute that something out of the ordinary might happen, but while this something never came, there was action every minute."[79]

Just before the fight, Jess had a long-distance call from his wife in Chicago wishing him well. He also got a chance to speak to his eldest daughter, Zella, who was eight. "Hope you win, daddy," was Zella's message. "Good-by; I'll be home early next week and bring you the largest doll in New York," said her father. As Jess had said in Havana, the reason that he got into boxing was to provide for his family. They were the force that drove him on.[80]

Willard accomplished a great deal when he defeated Frank Moran. Robert Edgren interviewed Charlie White, the referee in the Moran fight. White praised Willard as one of the greatest ever.

"He's remarkably quick to see blows coming and to block them or avoid them. He has skill in hitting and he has a great natural knack of hitting from straight in front without drawing back his hands. He's wonderfully supple and loose-jointed for a big man. If he had begun boxing when he was a boy he'd be the greatest marvel the ring has ever known."[81]

A similar article which appeared in *The Daily Oklahoman* the next day declared that "Willard's Crown is Absolutely Safe." This article suggested as well that Tom Jones should continue the strategy of using the circus for the summertime and fighting in the wintertime. This generated the most money for all parties. Victories in the ring enhanced Willard's stature in the circus, and the circus brought people who could not see Willard in the ring but would pay for the privilege of seeing him in the summer.[82]

The only slightly negative comments came from Frank Moran who said what many had realized, that Willard did really not like to fight.

"He is a great fighter," said Moran, "but he is not a marvel for the simple reason that he does not like to fight—that is, he hasn't the fighting spirit. I don't want to be immodest, but to use myself as an example: If Willard had my fighting spirit with his boxing ability and great physical strength he could lick any three men in the world."[83]

1916–1917

At the end of the 1916 circus season, there was a constant drumbeat of boxing challenges. Once again Willard's attention turned to getting back into the ring. Frank Moran had been disposed of. Frederick Fulton had gained stature over the summer and he seemed to be the natural challenger. Fulton stood almost as tall as Willard himself and had a great record of defeating most of the other white heavyweights. And, as we have seen, he had already knocked Willard himself down in an exhibition in May of 1915. Fulton had defeated Al Reich in New York on April 28, 1916, by a knockout in the ninth round. Since Fulton had entered the ring, he claimed that he had 38 fights and won 34 knockouts. This, he believed, entitled him to fight Willard for the championship.[84]

Tom Jones seemed to agree, for it was announced on May 14 that Willard would fight Fulton on Labor Day. But this date was killed by Harry H. Tamen, owner of the Sells-Floto Circus who said succinctly: "Willard is making us too much money; I cannot afford to release him."[85]

This decision caused Robert Edgren to suggest that it was likely that Willard might never fight again. For Willard to turn down an offer of $45,000 for a fight with Fulton convinced Edgren that Willard was ready to get out of the business.

> Willard is a very unusual sort of a champion. He is undoubtedly a great heavyweight fighter—one of the best that ever held the title. Personally he's a very agreeable person—a good-natured, clean-minded, decent sort of fellow who fills his position as a champion with credit. This, and the fact that the whole country feels grateful to him for putting Johnson into the discard, will make him popular for a long time, even if he doesn't fight again.[86]

Having said this, Edgren reversed course a couple of weeks later when he argued that unless Willard did accept a challenge soon, "the fans will come to the conclusion that Jess is growing too fat to fight." In response, Willard admitted, that although he exercises everyday and did not eat between meals, "I have found that I take on weight rapidly." On the positive side and likely to keep Willard out of the ring longer was the fact that he was reputed to now be worth $200,000. This led Frank Menke to predict that unlike past years, Willard would probably skip any fights during the winter season of 1916–1917. Since his real reason for fighting had been to provide for his family, and with this amount of money saved, there seemed to be no reason for Willard to go to the effort to get back into the ring.[87]

Publicity photograph for Jess Willard as champion, 1918.

Menke was correct. Willard passed up the opportunity to have a championship fight during that winter. According to rumors he had increased in weight to 300 pounds, and by turning down fights, he gave the opportunity to Fred Fulton and Battling Levinsky to claim the title without the inconvenience of fighting for it. Jack Curley came to his aid and predicted that Willard would defend his title, should any legitimate challenger appear on the scene. But when Harry

Carr interviewed him at the time the Sells-Floto Circus came to Los Angeles in October, he found that the only topic Willard wanted to talk about was livestock. Willard really did seem to be thinking seriously about retiring.[88]

Still, Willard was as popular at the end of 1916 as he ever had been. He had many opportunities to fight beginning in November of that year. Gabe Kaufmann of Kansas City wanted to put on a bout between him and the winner of the fight between Battling Levinsky and Carl Morris. Jack Kanner, head of the National Athletic Club in Denver, wanted to set up an elimination bout which would ultimately pit Willard against Fred Fulton. A new syndicate was in charge of Madison Square Garden in New York and they sought Willard's services for a bout on New Years' Day. Dominick Tortorich hoped once again to have Willard fight in New Orleans during Mardi Gras. And Tom Andrews of the Cream City Athletic club of Milwaukee again offered to have Willard fight Fred Fulton.[89]

The Daily Oklahoman declared, "Jess Willard in Class by Himself; May Retire Undefeated Champion." But Tom Jones said that Willard was willing to get back into the ring with the right man (which really meant the right price). Willard said he would fight whomever Tex Rickard wanted him to fight but Rickard said that he could not get Willard's signature on a contract. In addition, Willard admitted to weighing 270 pounds, while those who saw him said he looked 20 pounds heavier.[90]

Then at the beginning of December it was announced that Willard might fight Georges Carpentier in a French War Relief bout in New York. This bout was backed by Miss Anne Morgan, the daughter of J.P. Morgan, and Tex Rickard. But it fell through for a variety of reasons. The French Army would not give Carpentier leave to train and fight. Willard required several months to get into fighting trim. Carpentier preferred to continue flying for the French Aviation Corps rather than get back into the ring. And Tom Jones objected to the amount of money Willard would get for the fight. Les Darcy of Australia was chosen to fight Carpentier. Ultimately, the fight broke down. Willard withdrew, Les Darcy died in Memphis of Septicemia, and Georges Carpentier returned to war. Only after the war would Carpentier return to the United States to fight Jack Dempsey in the first million dollar gate in history.[91]

Meanwhile, Fred A. Wenck, Willard's old enemy from the New York Athletic Commission, was hauled into court on a charge of fist-fighting. This was the beginning of the end for Wenck's rule of the Athletic Commission.[92]

Nineteen sixteen proved to be one of the most profitable years the country and the Willards ever had. Woodrow Wilson had been reelected president with the slogan "He kept us out of the War!" The United States was importing prosperity by selling its produce and products to the Allies. And Willard had defended his title easily and demonstrated that he was truly an unbeatable champion. His strategy of fighting a championship battle in the winter and then touring with the circus in the summer pleased both Jess and Hattie. The championship fights and the circus tours nicely complimented each other and generated massive amounts of income for the Willard family. Everything was going so well that Willard saw no reason for it ever to change. And yet, it did.

8

The World War and Fred Fulton

Following his victory over Frank Moran in March 1916, Willard returned to the comfortable confines of the Sells-Floto Circus. He and Hattie spent the summer and early fall traveling with the circus and again earning more money than he could earn in the ring. His reputation had been burnished by his victory over Moran. He was now considered unbeatable. He seemed to have found the ideal lifestyle: take the winter off to fight a championship battle, then travel with the circus during the summer to earn money and let the public see him. Had he been able to follow this pattern, he might have gone on for several more years and retired undefeated. But circumstances beyond his control proved to make that impossible.

Following the end of the circus tour in 1916, Willard had many offers to fight. A proposed fight with Georges Carpentier, the little French aviator, proved to be a red herring which continued to be discussed into January 1917, when it died a natural death. The most attractive challenger was Fred Fulton, the Rochester, Minnesota, plasterer, who had knocked Willard down when they met in 1915. Fulton, who was nearly Willard's size, continued to move through the ranks of the heavyweights with great effect. On October 26 he defeated Andre Anderson in Eau Claire, Wisconsin, in one round. On January 9, he knocked out Tom Cowler, an Englishman, in one round, in Brooklyn. On February 12 he knocked out Charley Weinert in two rounds in New York. By then, Fulton had done a good job of gaining Willard's attention by knocking out all of the other contenders seriatim.[1]

Fulton's brief flurry of fame disappeared on April 4 when he lost a bout with Carl Morris on a foul. Morris was ahead in the fight up until the fifth round because he kept crowding Fulton, preventing him from using his long reach. Fulton believed that Morris was fouling him by head-butting and, as a result, lost his temper and hit Morris a low blow. Although Morris won the bout, it was widely believed that the fight was rigged in some way, and that both men were in the wrong. The net result of the fight was that for the time being, both fighters had eliminated themselves from contention for Willard's crown. As *The New York Times* saw it:

> Out of the recent bout between Carl Morris, the Oklahoma heavyweight, and Fred Fulton of Minnesota, one fact looms more clearly than any other, Jess Willard, heavyweight champion of the world, is in no immediate danger of being shorn of his laurels. Neither Morris nor Fulton showed ability enough in their uninteresting fiasco of Wednesday night to be entitled to further serious consideration as a championship possibility.[2]

Morris and Fulton may have been knocked out of heavyweight contention, but it was Willard who really lost in this bout, for he had lost his opportunity to have a championship fight prior to going back to the circus that spring. Then, the unexpected happened and boxing was forced to take a backseat to real fighting.

On April 2, 1917, President Woodrow Wilson asked Congress to declare war on Germany. It did so in an overwhelming, but not unanimous fashion. There were many first-generation Germans living in the United States, still speaking German. Indeed, representatives of one-half of Kansas, Jess Willard's home state, voted against the declaration. The president, whose campaign slogan had been "He kept us out of the War," had gotten us into the war. The prosperity which the United States had enjoyed as a neutral nation began to evaporate.

Suddenly, the world of the young was divided in two: The men who went to fight in Europe; and those who stayed home. The country was gripped with a patriotic fervor. That month, George M. Cohan, the Broadway showman, produced the defining American song "Over There!" It began with the stirring and bellicose lines "Johnny get your gun, get your gun,"

Johnny get your gun, get your gun, get your gun!
Take it on the run, on the run, on the run!
Hear them calling you and me,
Every son of liberty.
Hurry right away,
No delay, go today,
Make your daddy glad to have had such a lad.
Tell your sweetheart not to pine,
To be proud her boy's in line.

Over there, over there,
Send the word to be heard over there-
That the Yanks are coming, the Yanks are coming,
The drums rum-tumming everywhere.
So prepare, say a prayer,
Send the word, send the word to beware.
We'll be over, we're coming over,
And we won't come back till it's over
Over there.[3]

The same anxious desire which had consumed their grandfathers at the beginning of the Civil War now gripped these young men. They were in a hurry to join up before the war was over. They wanted to get into the fight. Even Jess Willard, who was one of the least bellicose of men, immediately sent a telegram to President Wilson: "I'm ready to fight! Where do you want me?"[4]

But the early fervor, which burned with a white-hot heat, soon spent itself. In Jess Willard's case, he gradually realized that he was 35 years old, and had a wife and five little children under ten. True, he was in excellent physical condition, but the idea of fighting in the trenches began to lose its appeal. Still, there were many other men of his age who did enlist in the war effort. Grantland Rice, the famous sportswriter, was 36 years old. He was married and had one daughter, but he chose to enlist as a private in the army. In Britain, Winston Churchill, who, as First Lord of the Admiralty, had been responsible for the disastrous defeat at Gallipoli, resigned from the British Cabinet and joined the army at age 41. Frank Moran, Willard's opponent in 1916, joined the army and served as a boxing instructor with the troops, as did many other fighters. But Willard did not.

Nor did he choose the more peaceful way of serving as an army or navy recruiter. More important was the fact that virtually everything Willard did from this point on seemed to backfire on him. It began when he left his home in Chicago and joined the circus.

Immediately after sending the telegram to Wilson, Willard left his home in Chicago for Norfolk, Virginia, the first stop of the 1917 circus tour. As a result he did not get the response sent to his home by Captain F.R. Kenney, the local recruiting commander for the army, offering him a Lieutenancy in the Officers Reserve Corp. Kenney hoped to use Willard in the recruiting drive which was underway with the idea that once the army was up to strength he would be put in charge of a fighting contingent.[5]

Nonetheless, when Willard got to Norfolk, he was immediately co-opted by the navy to help them with their recruitment. He was asked to walk the deck of a battleship and put on a boxing exhibition and advise young men to join the navy. Willard was willing to help:

> I am ready for service whenever I am needed. I have received no word since offering my services, but you can bet your life that I am ready if they will accept me.
>
> I tried to enlist at the recruiting station in Chicago before I left home, but after I weighed in, I was told I was too large and too heavy and they would not have me. If they can find a place for me I will be right there and do my share in whatever capacity they want me.[6]

By the time the circus got to Washington, D.C., Willard's comments about enlisting in the army began to change. Ignoring Captain Kenney's telegram, in an interview on April 23, Willard was quoted as saying: "I never said I had endeavored to join the army and was rejected because of my size, nor did I receive any word that enlistment conditions would be waived in my case." By the time the show got to New York, Tom Jones further modified Willard's comments about enlisting in the army: "I know personally that the big fellow is ready and eager to enlist for service at the first call for married men, and he has often told me he was going as soon as this call is sounded." The patriotic fervor which swept the nation at the declaration of war was beginning to be tempered by reality.[7]

April 1917 was a time of chaos in the United States. German agents were attempting to get Mexico to invade the United States. At the same time, other agents were attempting to stir up discontent among American Negroes. Pacifists besieged the United States Capital, leading Senator Henry Cabot Lodge to knock one of them, Alexander W. Bannwart, down with a blow to the jaw. Many universities eliminated all sports events for the duration of the war. And large groups of Apaches, Comanches, Kiowas and Wichitas, whose fathers and grandfathers had fought against the United States Army, now volunteered to fight for it.[8]

But volunteers could not provide enough enlistees for the military. On June 5, the first draft registration began and even more men were called into the military. All males aged 21 to 30 were required to register for military service. Since Willard was older than 30, he was not required to register. But ultimately both his labor force and his audience were affected, as the war effort took priority over pleasure.

As the country turned its attention to the European war, less time and money was spent paying attention to the circus. In the first instance there was a sudden labor shortage among the men who worked to put the circus on the road. Then, as we have seen, Edward Arlington chose to sell the circus in June and Willard chose to buy it. This had disastrous results. Suddenly, instead of having a comfortable income, Willard was faced with major management and cash-flow problems. In order to solve his short-term problems, Willard fired Tom Jones and Jack Curley. Willard explained it this way:

> As long as I was working for a salary Jones and Curley got their percentage of my earnings. But the war and bad weather hurt the show business, and I received notice that my contract was to be cancelled. That would leave me out in the cold, so I bought the circus.
>
> As owner of the show and not an employee I could not see where Jones and Curley should be entitled to any part of the gross receipts, so I discharged them.[9]

This proved to be a very bad move for Jess Willard, although it would take a while for it to become apparent. It altered the course of Willard's life and may have cost him his heavyweight title.

While Willard had many talents, he was not agile with words. He was comfortable talking with friends, but lacked the ability to debate with antagonists. In the past, he had always relied upon Tom Jones and Jack Curley to deal with verbal negotiations. But once he had fired them, not only did he not have them to help him, now he had to deal with them as opponents. This left Willard naked before his enemies.

It did not take long before Willard began to realize some of the problems this move had created. The break occurred while the circus was in Buffalo. The next day, Jack Curley petitioned the New York Supreme Court to enjoin Willard from giving circus performances in the state. He claimed that he had a contract with Willard that was good through September 15 and that the firing was a breach of contract. Tom Jones claimed the same contract obligations and, exercising his power as manager, signed two contracts to fights to take place before September 15. But these attempts to sabotage Willard did not work. By July 15, Curley's suit had been denied by Justice Peter A. Hendrick of the New York Supreme Court, and Willard was able to continue on with his circus schedule. And on August 8 Willard put on a boxing exhibition with Sailor Kearns for 5,000 soldiers training in Pittsburgh, for which no payment was made.[10]

By November, with the failed circus year behind him, Willard considered fighting again. The trouble was that Morris and Fulton seemed to be the only opponents available. This led, Arthur Struwe, writing in the *Milwaukee Free Press,* to assume that Willard might retire.

> The prize ring has no further lures for Jess Willard. The champion of the world is about to retire. And he will be the first heavyweight champion who will leave the ring still wearing the highest toga in pugilistic circles.
>
> Lack of suitable opponents to test his merits in the ring is also one of the reasons why the champion wants to get out of the game. Another thing is his propensity for taking on weight. Jess at the present time tips the bean mark over the 300 mark. It would require months of hard training for him to reduce if a match for the championship was to be made.
>
> The champion wants $50,000 for his end if he is to appear in the ring again. No promoter would give that figure for a contest between Willard and either Fred Fulton, Carl Morris, Jim Coffey, Bill Brennan or Billy Miske, the latter a light heavyweight.
>
> Outside of Fred Fulton there isn't one of this quintette [sic] who could even make Willard extend himself.[11]

Struwe's analysis irked Willard, who denied that he was ready to retire. He claimed that he was ready to fight but it was his belief that the public was not ready for it. "I do not believe that the public wants a heavyweight contest at this time, but should I find I am mistaken and that public sentiment is to the effect that it will prove beneficial to the country, I am ready and willing to defend the title, provided a suitable purse is guaranteed."[12]

When asked who he would prefer to fight, Jess immediately answered that he preferred to fight Georges Carpentier. This led the sportswriters to wonder how serious Willard was, since it was clear that Carpentier could not get free from his military obligations in France. A few days later, J. V. Fitzgerald resurrected Fred Fulton from the graveyard of forgotten favorites and pointed out that since his losses to Carl Morris and Jack London in April, Fulton had won seven fights, including a bout in September with Morris and just recently a fight with Gunboat Smith on November 27. "Willard has stated there is no public demand for his appearance. He has asserted Georges Carpentier is the logical man for him to meet. In that Willard appears to be wrong, for Fulton seems to be the logical man and the public seems ready for the bout."[13]

Given this contradictory advice, and having been criticized by Tom Jones and the public for making it too difficult to find suitable opponents due to his demands for large purses, Willard did something remarkable. He declared that he would defend his title against any person, at any time, as long as all of the proceeds went to the Red Cross. Willard preferred that the fight be held in the spring of 1918 so that it could be in the open air and they could get the largest crowd possible. Further, he offered to make all the fight arrangements himself so that all of the revenue would go to charity. He intended this magnanimous gesture to show that he was not dodging any fighter. He hoped it would help him regain some of his popularity with the public. But once again, Willard found that no good deed goes unpunished.[14]

Willard predicted that this fight might generate $1,000,000 for the Red Cross. He was pleased that the Chamber of Commerce of Sacramento offered to have the fight held in their town, forgetting that California law only allowed four-round bouts at this time. New Orleans, which allowed 20 round fights, also wanted to have the bout in their city. He was also pleased that Sam Langford, Bill Brennan, Frank Moran, Harry Greb and Fred Fulton all volunteered to be his opponents.[15]

All of this backfired on Willard when J. V. Fitzgerald of *The Washington Post* announced in an article on December 20, that the Red Cross might refuse Willard's offer. "There is practically no chance of the organization accepting an offer from the title-holder to engage in a championship fight for its benefit, it was learned." The reason given for this astonishing attitude seemed to be that the officers of the Red Cross were put out that Willard did not consult them first before making his offer public.[16]

The following day, Fitzgerald attacked Willard for restricting the bout for the Red Cross to only ten rounds and wanting it to be a no-decision affair. From Willard's standpoint these were perfectly reasonable conditions. They were the same conditions imposed by the State of New York when he fought Frank Moran for the championship in 1916. But then apparently Willard added another restriction which was not so benign: The bout would not be for the title. It would not be a championship bout. Fitzgerald considered these restrictions as proof that Willard had no intention to carry through with his offer of a charitable fight for the Red Cross.

> There isn't one chance in 1,000 of the Red Cross accepting the offer of the heavyweight champion anyhow, so the talk of a benefit bout will be nothing more than talk. Were Willard sincere in his offer to aid the Red Cross he would have consulted that organization before heralding his "patriotism" far and near. Likely he figured his proposal was an impossible one from the Red Cross standpoint and from the standpoint of his rivals.[17]

From Willard's standpoint, this criticism from the press and the Red Cross was inexplicable. He had made an offer in good faith and was astonished that it was turned down. Lacking the sophistication of a promoter like Tex Rickard or even Tom Jones, Willard had no idea that he should have presented his ideas to a board of directors prior to announcing it in public. He was stunned to find people turning down his offer to fight a charity bout when all the revenue went to them. This was a classic case of why he needed a manager. Had he had Tom Jones on his side, this offer to benefit the Red Cross might have worked out well for everyone. As it turned out, it did not work out well for anybody. It left a bad taste in his mouth and weakened his interest in charity bouts.

By the end of 1917 the United States had shifted to a war economy. Despite Willard's best efforts, he did not seem to be able to participate in the war effort. His circus tour had failed. His chances at a heavyweight bout, even for charity, were turned down. He had fired Tom Jones and Jack Curley and now they were working against him. Despite the fact that at the beginning of 1918, the papers were discussing the various ways to get Willard involved in a championship fight, neither he nor the country seemed to be enthusiastic about this. Tex Rickard, who had promoted the Willard-Moran fight in 1916, announced that although a fight between Willard and Fred Fulton would probably draw an immense crowd, it would not be worth the trouble at this time. Then Fulton tried to claim the championship without fighting for it. According to Fulton's manager, Mike Collins, Willard had given up his right to the title by not defending it when Fulton wanted to fight. Despite all of the negatives, Arthur Struwe could still say that "Willard Stands alone among Heavyweights."[18]

To add to Willard's troubles he was sued by one Victor J. "Tex" Dowd for $25,000 for an injury incurred in a wrestling match in Rome, Georgia, while he was employed by the circus. Tex Dowd had been a member of Willard's staff since the Havana fight, and undoubtedly felt that he had a claim on Jess. Willard felt otherwise and refused to pay. Although seemingly a small event, such things as the Dowd suit greatly upset Willard. Instead of accepting the papers, Willard barricaded himself in the second storey of his house in Chicago for three hours while the sheriff and his men tried to reach him. "'My men will stay until Willard comes down or jumps out of a window,' declared the sheriff as he left the arena." Such behavior, when coupled with articles suggesting Willard had been offered $75,000 for a 45 round bout in Nevada, made it easy for the sports fan to reject him. Willard saw his popularity gradually vanish. By the beginning of 1918, *The Washington Post* columnist J. V. Fitzgerald could write: "Jess Willard is an unpopular champion, perhaps the least liked of the holders of the heavyweight crown." Willard had replaced Jack Johnson both as heavyweight champion and as public pariah.[19]

Willard's dilemma was personal. It did not mirror the dilemma of boxing itself. Boxing remained a popular sport in 1917 with close to 1,100 bouts held, despite the fact that Willard did not participate. It continued to be practiced during 1918, as well as being one of the sports promoted by the military services. Many professional boxers, like Frank Moran, Walter Monahan, George "Knockout" Brown and Benny Leonard joined the army to teach soldiers to box. But though boxing remained popular, the public was in an ugly mood. There was a growing reaction to seeing healthy young athletes of all types, engaging in sport, while lesser men were enlisting in the army and navy. A new word was used to describe those who refused to join the military and who stayed home. They were called "slackers" and they could be subject to arrest. In some cases, these men were properly censored, but in other cases the law may have been too severe. William Harrison "Jack" Dempsey, the 23-year-old boxer, who was in fighting trim, was rightly called a "slacker" for refusing to go to the army, but he was not arrested. On the other hand, Fred Toney, a star pitcher for the Cincinnati Reds, was arrested for refusing to go, even though he was the sole support of his elderly mother and invalid brother. Jess Willard was not called a "slacker" in print, but he was widely resented due to the great wealth he had accumulated and the fantastic purses that were offered for his services. He was hailed as a great physical specimen but he chose not to join up to help the war effort. The public no longer held him in esteem.[20]

There were other things on Willard's mind at this time. He was still trying to dispose of the remnants of his circus. More importantly, Willard had been embarrassed by the sheriff's deputies who chased him out of his house in Chicago. In a behavior pattern that was becoming too familiar, Willard fled Chicago and went to Jacksonville, Florida, where the remnants of his circus were stored. Then, on February 13, he and Hattie went to Lawrence, Kansas, to visit with Mr. and Mrs. Nathan Bailey, Hattie's aunt and uncle. While there, they looked at property, and on February 27 they bought one of the finest homes in Lawrence from Joseph G. Cummings at 1700 West 9th Street for $15,000. As part of the deal, Willard gave Cummings his home and furnishings at 5838 Gregory Avenue in Hollywood. The Lawrence house was surrounded by 56 acres of land and stood on a high promontory overlooking the Kaw River Valley on the north, the Wakarusha River Valley on the South and the town of Lawrence on the East. The property straddled the Oregon Trail (now Iowa Street). The house was on the east side of the Trail and it fronted on Ninth Street. It backed up on Seventh Street, which was also known as "The Fort to Fort Road." This was an old military road which linked Fort Leavenworth in the east, on the Kansas River, with Fort Riley in the west near Manhattan. It was the ranch home that both Hattie and Jess had always wanted. In addition, it offered them the chance to be near the University of Kansas, where, if all went well, their children could go to college. College was an experience they had never had, but hoped to provide for their children. It was just this link with the university, plus being near their families in Lawrence and Topeka, that attracted the Willards to Lawrence.[21]

While Willard was occupied with his affairs in Lawrence, Jack Dempsey and Fred Fulton continued to box. Dempsey had already fought a total of 36 battles and had been credited with nine one-round knockouts. On February 12, Jack "Doc" Kearns, who managed Dempsey, announced that Dempsey and Willard would meet in a championship fight in Cheyenne, Wyoming, on July 4. This bout was to be worth $100,000 to be split between the two fighters. The challenge was relayed to Willard in Lawrence. It caught Willard by surprise: "That is the biggest joke I ever heard," declared Willard. "I know of no arrangements for a meeting with Dempsey. Besides Fulton looks pretty good now, doesn't he?" Willard proved correct: The Cheyenne bout proved to be a joke and the offer was withdrawn on February 23. Then, on February 25, Fred Fulton knocked out Frank Moran in the third round of their scheduled 20-round bout in New Orleans. This verified Fulton's right to meet Willard in a championship bout.[22]

Fulton then defeated Jim Harper of Kansas City, one of the early victims of Carl Morris, on March 1. He then signed again to fight Tom Cowler on March 11 and knocked him out in the fifth round.[23]

With these other fighters continuing to be active and popular, Willard was faced with

Jess and Hattie in their new Fiat car in front of their house in Lawrence, Kansas, 1918.

a fundamental choice: Either to retire or to get back into the ring. The move to Lawrence appeared to most people as a statement that Willard planned to retire. Boxing was outlawed in Kansas, while Chicago had long been Willard's boxing home. It seemed logical that had he wanted to stay in boxing and participate in championship fights, he would have stayed in Chicago. All the training facilities were there, as well as a supply of sparring partners. Lawrence had nothing to match. But in a move that surprised many, Willard decided not to retire and instead, on March 11, he signed a contract with Colonel Joseph Carson Miller of the 101 Ranch, for Miller to replace Tom Jones as his manager. Under this contract, Miller was Willard's partner. They agreed to split costs and income on a 25–75 percent basis, with Miller getting the 25 percent end. Although Willard was dubious, Colonel Miller believed that the public wanted to see Willard back in the ring. Miller immediately announced that he wanted to arrange a championship fight between Willard and Fred Fulton for July 4. If that could not be achieved, he would seek to arrange a championship fight with Jack Dempsey.[24]

As soon as Colonel Miller had been announced as Willard's new manager, Dominick Tortorich proposed a Willard-Fulton 20-round bout in New Orleans with a purse of $100,000. This offer did not go anywhere. Then, when Colonel Miller met with Michael Collins, Fulton's manager, in Kansas City they immediately ran into trouble and could not agree on terms. Miller offered Fulton $10,000 for his share of the fight. Collins refused to sign for less than $20,000. Miller objected but the following day it was announced that Willard and Fulton were signed to fight in a championship battle on July 4.[25]

Initially the fight was praised by the newspapers. *The New York Times* noted that the news of the fight "was received with satisfaction throughout the country." Fulton was nearly Willard's equal in size and reach. Fulton had been fighting continually during the past two years, while Willard had been idle. Further, as we have seen, when they had met previously just weeks after Willard had defeated Jack Johnson, Fulton had knocked Willard down. Since Willard was out of shape and now estimated to weigh between 300 and 350 pounds, there was a real chance that Fulton might defeat Willard. On the other hand, J.V. Fitzgerald of *The Washington Post* believed that it would not take Willard long to get back into shape. He was sure that Willard "will put up a real fight before he surrenders his heavyweight crown." He had opposed Willard fighting for the Red Cross, but seemed to find no fault in him fighting for himself. Even the hometown *The Lawrence Daily Journal-World* was pleased to announce that "Lawrence Soon to be Fighters Mecca." The fact that Willard would be doing part of his training in Lawrence, and putting on some training bouts for the soldiers at Camp Funston near the current Fort Riley, was sure to attract "delegations of Willard fans to Lawrence to pay their respects and watch the champion in action."[26]

Influenza Appears

That same month, a little cloud only the size of a man's hand, rose out of the plains in western Kansas. It would ultimately darken the skies and strike fear into cities and towns. It would alter the strategy of holding championship boxing fights and bring whole nations to their knees. This little cloud, not the warriors, would bring World War I to an end. The public first learned about it on March 16, 1918, when *The Junction City Daily Union* carried a small item on the front page: "Wesley Cook, one of the well-known young men of this city, died suddenly this morning at his rooms on West Fifth street, after an illness of 24 hours. Mr. Cook was taken sick yesterday with pneumonia and passed away early this morning." Wesley Cook, who had just gotten married a few weeks before, was one of the first publicly recorded victims of the great influenza epidemic.[27]

The very first inkling that something was going terribly wrong was when Dr. Loring Miner in Haskell County, Kansas (southwest of Dodge City), began to be flooded with patients in late January and early February. These patients showed signs of a virulent kind of influenza. Influenza was common in Kansas in the winter time and presented with aches and pains and fever and runny noses. And normally it was over in a week or two, having done nothing more than send its victims to bed for several days or a week. But this new type of influenza could be fatal. It often presented as pneumonia and killed its victims rapidly. Another unusual aspect of this disease was that it did not strike the elderly or children as was usually the case. It was not a disease of the weak. Instead, it struck the young, the strong and the most robust of the population. Like Wesley Cook, they were the ones who were taking on the early responsibilities of adult life.

Kansas was a rural state full of small towns and small farms. In normal times, such an epidemic would have sputtered and flamed and then died out for lack of fuel. But these were not normal times. The war in Europe had led to the creation of a massive army training deployment, Camp Funston, in the center of Kansas. Funston had just been built in July 1917. It was a city of barracks and tents on the Kansas plains next to Fort Riley and Junction City. By July 1918, it had a population of 38,000 men with the goal of growing to 60,000 by August 1918. The winter of 1917–1918 was particularly cold. At Camp Funston, the Army reported that "the barracks and tents were overcrowded and inadequately heated, and it was impossible to supply the men with sufficient warm clothing." As a result, the men crowded together around the camp stoves to keep warm. Camp Funston acted as the narrow waist of an hour glass drawing in boys from the farms and towns all over the west, concentrating them together and then sending them out to many other areas around Kansas and the wide world. Some of these boys were from Haskell County and brought with them this new type of influenza.[28]

By mid-March the influenza epidemic had disappeared in Haskell County, but it was just beginning in Junction City and Camp Funston.

> On March 4 a private at Funston, a cook, reported ill with influenza at sick call. Within three weeks more than 1100 soldiers were sick enough to be admitted to the hospital and thousands more-the precise number is not recorded-needed treatment at infirmaries scattered around the base. Pneumonia developed in 237 men, roughly 20 percent of those hospitalized, but only 38 died. While that was a higher death toll than one would normally expect from influenza, it was not so high as to draw attention, much less than the death rate in Haskell, and only a tiny fraction of the death rate to come.[29]

The Difficulties of Boxing in Wartime

Like most people, Jess Willard and Colonel Joe Miller were unaware of the threat that this new disease posed to their plans to hold a championship boxing bout. Their problems focused on trying to find a place to hold the bout. It had been hoped that it could occur in Milwaukee. But Fulton had some difficulty with the Wisconsin boxing authority and it seemed likely that they might object to the fight. Thus, Willard suggested that the fight be held in Minnesota, Fulton's adopted home state. I. H. Herk, a local theatrical manager in Minneapolis, then offered $125,000 for the fight. Then, the Louisiana Auditorium Company in New Orleans offered $130,000 for the Willard-Fulton bout if it were held there in November. On March 25, George Biemer, the Fort Wayne promoter, offered $140,000 for the fight. The same day in Chicago, Willard signed the agreement for the fight. This guaranteed him 75 percent of the net profits of the bout, while Fred Fulton was guaranteed $20,000. Suddenly things seemed to be working out for Willard.[30]

But things were not working out so well for the rest of the country. The headlines in the papers during March told of a massive German offensive that had broken through the Allied lines and which nearly drove the British army into the sea. Paris was also threatened. On the home front, *The Lawrence Daily Journal-World* carried articles about the shortage of food. The double effect of removing most of the young men from the farms and the towns, combined with the demand for food for the troops created a food shortage all over the country. In Lawrence, this led to the formation of Mother-Daughter Canning Clubs to preserve food. Kansas was an agricultural state, where wheat and cattle were ubiquitous; yet people were forced to endure "wheatless" and "meatless" meals. On March 23, it was announced that two nights a week were to be "lightless." This meant that all stores which were not open for business were to have all of their lights turned off on Sunday and Thursday night until further notice. In addition, those people who had automobiles were being asked to loan them to the Red Cross for their activities. The war was thus brought home to the smallest towns as stories were carried about the local boys being drafted into service. Then, in a small item on the front page of *The Journal-World* on March 25, it was noted that a Lawrence businessman, Charles L. Wall, had died suddenly in Topeka after a short sickness with pneumonia. Influenza had escaped from Camp Funston and now had spread to the general population, miles away.[31]

On March 27, Jess Willard and Colonel Joe Miller visited Baltimore to sell some horses left over from Willard's circus and to see if that might be a site for the upcoming championship bout. They were surprised when the president of the police board told them that, in his opinion, the general public would oppose holding a fight between Willard and Fulton there. After being turned down by Baltimore, Miller moved on to New York, but New York had outlawed boxing again in 1917, so no fight could be held there. Although there were a number of places offering payment for the bout, none of them seemed exactly right.[32]

At the beginning of April, it was believed that the fight would be held either in Denver or in New Haven. In anticipation of the fight, Willard began training by walking five miles a day. The same day that the possibility of Denver was mentioned, the Ford Motor Company announced that 200 people a day in its Detroit plant were falling ill with a mysterious epidemic resembling grip. It was estimated that 2,000 people had already been affected there. The war news was better than in March. The Allies were barely holding onto the Western Front after being reinforced by the first American troops. On the home front, the University of Kansas baseball team had only one returning letterman from last year's team, while the track team had lost virtually all of its members. There was a massive gap between the plans for a $100,000 prizefight and the environment in which most people were living.[33]

By the middle of April, *The New York Times* carried an article with the headline "Places Available for Bout Decrease." "A feeling against the bout as it is at present planned is growing in various parts of the country. The latest to deliver a rebuke to the two heavyweights and those behind the contest is Governor Boyle of Nevada, who, in stating that the contest could not be held within his jurisdiction, admonished the prospective principals in the encounter to direct their fighting energies to the war."[34]

In addition to being turned down by Nevada, Colonel Miller also had been rejected by Governor Lindsey of New Mexico. *The Times* went on to predict that the nature of the bout would have to change if it was held at all.[35]

The following day, J.V. Fitzgerald of *The Washington Post* announced that the governor of Colorado had also decided to prevent the fight in his state. Fitzgerald summed up the situation: "Now that Jess Willard and Fred Fulton are all dressed up for battle for the world's heavyweight championship it begins to look as if they will have no place to go."[36]

At this point Colonel Miller shifted his plans back to Minnesota, which had been Willard's original suggestion. He was able to get the governor's permission to hold the fight in Minnesota, and even got the permission to have the referee issue a decision at the end of the fight. However, he was hindered by the fact that state law did not permit a bout longer than ten rounds. Although both St. Paul and Minneapolis had rejected having the fight in their cities, Miller decided to have it on land between the two cities. This gave him a location and a date for the fight. But then he made a tactical blunder. He decided that he needed a commitment from the local business community for $10,000 in order to build a new outdoor arena. "The situation is now flatly up to the Twin Cities. If my proposition is agreeable and the bonus is raised, the fight will be held somewhere in St. Paul or Minneapolis. I have several offers from other cities in various parts of the country, but because boxing is legalized in Minnesota, I prefer to stage the fight here."[37]

The decision to ask for financial help from the business community raised a storm of protest from the Minnesota population and delayed support for the fight. In the meantime, J.V. Fitzgerald in his column in *The Washington Post* and Jess Willard, himself, questioned the value of a ten-round fight to determine the heavyweight championship. As these concerns were being raised, the Minnesota Safety Commission, which had regulatory power over the fight, began to have second thoughts. At the same time, a political cartoon was published on the front page of *The Lawrence Daily Journal-World* which showed Uncle Sam with money for Liberty Bonds sticking out of his pocket, while Willard and Fulton approached him. The caption read "Don't Let Them Pick His Pockets." The fact that Willard's hometown paper was turning against the fight was a sign of the difficulties faced.[38]

Since no decision had been made by the Minnesota Safety Commission, the fight remained in limbo. The lack of a positive response by the Commission led Miller to abandon his plans to hold the fight in Minnesota. The question remained: Could the

"Don't let them pick his pockets."

fight be held at all? *The New York Times* began to have its doubts: "With each succeeding day doubt grows concerning the holding of the proposed heavyweight championship bout between Jess Willard, title holder, and Fred Fulton, the Rochester, Minn., plasterer."[39]

Then, on May 11, Miller called off the bout. "Public opinion is against holding this contest. There is no use opposing public opinion: that I have found out. But before I have always gone through with what I started: this time I am yielding to sentiment. Conditions due to the war have brought about changes in sentiment, and so I decided to call off the fight."[40]

The fact that the bout was cancelled caused little surprise. J.V. Fitzgerald, who seemed to have had a personal animus against Willard, had a subhead in his column stating that the "Public Doesn't Mourn Calling off the Big Fight." *The New York Times* printed a long article with the title "Failure of Title Bout No Surprise." And Ray Pearson of *The Chicago Daily Tribune* announced that "Jess Willard has quit the ring." As proof of this, Pearson pointed out that Willard had sold off all his Chicago real estate and sent his family to live in Lawrence. To add insult to injury, Fred Fulton announced: "I have a contract with Col. Miller and I shall claim the championship and the $1,000 forfeit money if Willard does not fight."[41]

Fulton did not claim the title or the forfeit from Willard; instead he almost immediately signed to fight Jack Dempsey on July 27. While public opinion was against Willard fighting, it was not against boxing itself, nor initially against the idea of a Fulton-Dempsey fight. Further, both Fulton and Dempsey had just fought a common opponent, Billy Miske, in the St. Paul Auditorium, Fulton on January 18 and Dempsey on May 3. There had been no public outcry or protest against these fights. If these fights could be held in St. Paul, why had there been such difficulty in placing the Willard fight there, or any where?

The simple answer would seem to be that Willard had antagonized the press and the public so that they no longer supported him. This certainly was true in retrospect.

But there was more to the issue than that. The prize for heavyweight championship fights for Tommy Burns and Jack Johnson had been $30,000 win, lose or draw. In 1908 and 1915, $30,000 had seemed like all of the money in the world. Fight fans had been astonished by such a figure when most bouts had generated purses in the $100, or, at best, $1,000 range. Now, however, promoters were talking about $75,000 to $100,000 per fight, of which Willard was likely to get 75 percent. This was a radical change in economics in three short years. At the same time, there was a decrease in the earning power of the normal American family as a result of the war. This put Willard, as champion, far beyond even the imagination of the boxing fan. Willard had been praised by the press in 1915 as a smiling, boyish champion, who came from humble beginnings to defeat the black giant, Johnson. That same Willard was now perceived as a greedy plutocrat who could earn 100 times the yearly salary of a working man in one boxing bout. To people who were submitting to meatless meals and lightless nights, who were sending their sons to fight in a war from which many of them would not return, and who themselves were fearful of the epidemic of influenza, Willard's situation seemed out of touch with reality.

Fulton and Dempsey, on the other hand, were still fighting for modest purses. The entire gate in St. Paul, when Fulton fought Miske, was $18,000. The gate when Dempsey fought Miske was $13,400. When Fulton fought Dempsey, they were each promised $12,500. While these were large numbers to the normal fan, they were still comprehensible. Willard's demands were not.

Public Stress

The stress of the war was bad enough, but as people began to learn more about the impact influenza was to have on their lives, the public developed an angry mood. They began to strike out in various directions. In Lawrence, to take a couple of examples from *The Journal-World*, the Reverend Mr. Gastrock of the Worden German Lutheran Church was taken from his home on the night of May 8, stripped to the skin and coated with tar. The reason given was that Reverend Gastrock gave his sermons in German and refused to make English sermons on the Red Cross drive and the Liberty Loan campaign

"Another Dead One."

when asked to do so. In the same edition of *The Journal-World,* the front page editorial cartoon entitled "Another Dead One" showed Uncle Sam digging a grave for a coffin labeled "German Language." A little figure in the corner says: "Not a Bloomin' Mourner in Sight."[42]

The second example concerned an order sent by Lawrence Mayor George L. Kreeck, himself of German ancestry, to the chief of police to arrest any man found not working. "I intend to see that the vagrancy ordinance on the city statutes is forced to the very letter this summer. A man who is not working in these times is not only a slacker but worse than a slacker-a traitor to his country. He is eating food and wearing clothes which some one else has produced. No matter how much money he may have, it is his duty to work."[43]

Mayor Kreeck's warning may not have been directed at Jess Willard, but, on the other hand, it may have been. When Jess returned to Lawrence he immediately told the public that he had not come to play the part of a gentleman of leisure. A couple of his new friends helped him in this regard. The day after he arrived back in town, Edward T. Riling, an attorney, and his next-door neighbor, immediately named him as an appraiser in a property suit in the County District Court. This met with the approval of Judge C.A. Smart, who remarked that he too would do his best to help Willard to realize his ambition to become a useful citizen. The alternative was to be sent to prison or to the military.[44]

Then, on May 31, it was announced that Fred Fulton would box Jack Dempsey on July 4 in Danbury, Connecticut. The fight was to be for 20 rounds with 10 percent of the receipts as well as the motion picture revenue to go to war charities. "Honest John" Kelly was to be the official stakeholder.[45]

Two days later, *The New York Times* suggested that the fight was not a sure thing. The promoters had not been able to raise the necessary finances to support the Willard-Fulton bout when Colonel Miller had approached them, and it was not clear that their condition had improved. Further, the governor of Connecticut had opposed the planned Willard-Fulton fight and it is "problematical whether he will recede from this attitude in the case of the proposed Fulton-Dempsey contest."[46]

The Connecticut fight failed and the promoters turned to Baltimore. Once again, Baltimore turned down the heavyweight bout. It seemed that perhaps the same reservations were held about the Dempsey-Fulton fight as had been held about the Willard-Fulton fight.[47]

The fight was finally allowed to take place in the Federal League Ball Park in Harrison, New Jersey, on July 27. It was promoted by Jack Curley and once again, Curley was unable to draw the crowds. As Dempsey remembered it:

> Various reform groups who were attacking alcohol and tobacco now criticized us, saying it was morally wrong to pay for a fight while the country was at war. The Spanish influenza was reaching epidemic proportion. And some claimed it would get even worse if masses of people sat together at a prizefight. Doc [Kearns] paid no attention and made another publicized donation to the Red Cross. Suddenly, certain factions did an about-face, saying that sports were badly needed, at home and abroad, for entertainment and morale-especially when portions of the purses were given to the Red Cross.[48]

The ball park had a seating capacity of 25,000 but there were perhaps no more than 7,000 spectators. Most of the high-priced seats were empty and Curley was forced to cut back on the guarantee he had promised both fighters. While there were numbers of servicemen at the fight, there were very few women and almost none of the notables either from New York City or the fight world. The times were not auspicious for championship boxing bouts.[49]

Before the fight began, Fulton, in checking Dempsey's bandages, complained about his use of blacktape on his hands. Dempsey refused to remove the tape but told Fulton to put as much of the tape on his hands as he wished. Fulton decided not to. The fight began with Dempsey refusing to look directly at Fulton as they stood in the ring. According to Nat Fleischer, Dempsey had won the fight before it was even begun: "He took all of the fight out of Fulton by saying before the gong, 'Let's shake now-then we can come out fighting.' That remark and Fulton's acceptance of the proposition spelled his doom."[50]

The fight began with Fulton advancing on Dempsey. He swung his left at Dempsey, who ducked under the blow and slammed his right fist into Fulton's chest, just over the heart. He followed up with a left hook to Fred's stomach, causing Fulton to bend over. Then Dempsey hit him on the jaw and Fulton fell back to the floor and the fight was over. According to the referee, it took Dempsey 23 seconds to knock Fred Fulton out. According to Robert Edgren, the fight lasted 18⅗ seconds. In either case, it was one of the shortest heavyweight bouts in history. Fred Fulton towered over his opponent and outweighed him by 20 pounds but he never landed a blow on Dempsey. Fred Fulton had ceased to be a contender for Willard's crown. Now there was only one contender: Jack Dempsey.

In the meantime, Jess Willard had settled down to growing alfalfa on land south of his home in Lawrence. He kept his hand in boxing, however. On June 29, it was announced that he would take part in a boxing carnival at Fort Riley on July 4. There he boxed a six- round exhibition for the soldiers, with all proceeds going to the Red Cross. On July 27, when he learned of Dempsey's victory, he was not impressed. "I am not surprised at the result," Willard commented. "All you have to do is to hit Fulton to have him down." Still, Willard wanted to meet Dempsey, but not before the end of the war. He had learned that, save for exhibitions for the troops, boxing in wartime was a losing proposition. "Just as soon as the war is over I am going to take on Dempsey or any other claimant. I have not retired from the ring, and I have no intention of doing anything of the sort."[51]

Dempsey too had learned that the country was not ready for a championship boxing bout. The poor crowd in New Jersey and the criticism that had preceded it taught him that now was not the time to reach for the crown. He also personally was worried that he might be tried as a "slacker." He announced after the Fulton fight that "he was going back to the West next week to resume his trade in shipbuilding and will not fight in the ring until the war has ended." In point of fact, Dempsey was not a shipbuilder even though he occasionally dressed up like one. In order to make it appear that he was doing his bit for the country, Doc Kearns gave him a pair of overalls, which he put on over his regular clothes, and handed him a rivet gun. The photos appeared in newspapers all over the country and were a tremendous embarrassment. They showed Dempsey wearing patent leather shoes beneath his overalls. The public recognized the fraud, and Dempsey became an object of ridicule.[52]

Although not a shipbuilder, Dempsey did volunteer his services for various boxing exhibitions and, in this he was more successful than Willard. But then he made the same mistake that Jess Willard had made in 1917. According to a *Chicago Tribune* writer, Dempsey said he was going to enlist and carry a gun in France. "Dempsey expects shortly to shoulder a gun and go to France for the real fight. 'When they call me I'm ready and willing to go,' he said. 'Perhaps I shall enlist before that time comes. There isn't any money to be made in the boxing game now, so I'm thinking of bigger things.'"[53] Of course, he did not enlist. Instead, he got an exemption from service, saying that he was the sole support of his entire family: his wife, his mother, father, widowed sister and three brothers.[54]

Basically, Dempsey kept out of the war by engaging in charity boxing bouts. He was scheduled to appear in a boxing exhibition to benefit the Salvation Army in Chicago on August 10. Willard too was scheduled to appear at the same benefit. Then, abruptly, the Acting Chief of Police called off the show and declared that there would be no boxing for charity in Chicago. This was seconded by the Major General of the Army who forbid boxing at Fort Sheridan. This decision cost the Salvation Army about $50,000, plus the chance to see the best boxers in the country in action. Even charity boxing had fallen into disrepute about the country.[55]

On September 5, Ed W. Smith, *The Chicago American* sports editor, wrote a column which attacked Willard for apparently breaking his word to Jack Kearns, Jack Dempsey's manager. This was ironic since Willard had a reputation for being honest and Kearns had a reputation for being a cheat and a liar. After the collapse of the Salvation Army boxing benefit, Kearns supposedly asked Willard to fight Dempsey in Philadelphia. As noted before, Willard refused and said that he would not fight until after the war was over. Initially, Kearns publicized the fact that there was a possibility of a Willard-Dempsey fight in Philadelphia. Later, when it became clear that Philadelphia was caught in the influenza epidemic, Kearns denied that Willard had agreed to anything. Then, when Willard went to visit a friend in Colorado Springs and it was reported that he might be willing to fight a charity bout there with Dempsey, Kearns immediately took to the press. He so agitated the Philadelphians that he turned them against Willard. Why, they said, would Willard fight in Colorado Springs and not in Philadelphia? Ed Smith, who should have known better, supported Kearns and used his column to besmirch Willard's reputation. In point of fact, Willard denied agreeing to fight in either place until after the war. Kearns was simply acting as an *agent provocateur* attempting to make Willard look bad to the public. In this activity, Ed Smith became his willing assistant.[56]

Clearly Willard was caught in a dilemma. He could not defend his title in a legitimate championship battle. His efforts to find a place to fight Fred Fulton had demonstrated this. Equally, he had been turned down when he tried to fight for charity, as his attempts to fight for the Red Cross and the Salvation Army had shown. His charity bouts at Fort Riley and Camp Funston attracted no attention outside the local area, so they did not count. Nor could he return to his Kansas farm and simply ignore boxing. As Ed Smith said in another column, Willard's title was one of the nation's greatest assets. It was, Smith said, wasteful of Willard not to exercise his title. Using the same threatening warnings that had been directed at German-Americans and slackers, Smith concluded his column: "In a word, he should be made to parade it [his title] where the parading would do the most good for the soldiers and sailors of this country. There is no half-way ground in this matter at all." Ed Smith may have thought that he was benefiting the cause of the Army and Navy, but he was not. In fact, he was promoting the cause of Jack Kearns and Jack Dempsey.[57]

Jack Kearns was doing everything he could to focus the public on a Willard-Dempsey bout. In addition, by attacking Willard, Kearns was attempting to distract the boxing world's attention from a recent defeat that Dempsey had suffered at the hands of Willie Meehan in California on September 13. Dempsey had taken the fight with Meehan too lightly. But instead of admitting that, Kearns declared that Dempsey had been robbed by a poor referee. According to Kearns, the decision "was scandalous and the less said about it the better." Saying little about the fight and keeping the decision out of the paper was exactly what Kearns wanted to achieve. He did not want the public to know that this was the second time Meehan had beaten Dempsey. Out of five meetings, Dempsey only won only one. Meehan won two and there were two draws. Naturally, for Kearns, the less said in the press about Dempsey's loss the better. He wanted the public to think that Dempsey was unbeatable. This was the only way Kearns could get Willard into the ring with Dempsey. So Kearns worked continuously to ensure that when the war was over, Dempsey was the first fighter Willard faced.[58]

J.V. Fitzgerald agreed that it was best that Willard and Dempsey delay their championship battle until the war was over. In the middle of October, "Sunny Jim" Coffroth, who was hanging on as a promoter in San Francisco following the elimination of championship boxing in 1915, proposed a boxing carnival for the war effort. He proposed a series of contests to be held in Madison Square Garden in New York City which would pit the champions of each weight class against their best opponents. He expected to have Willard meet Dempsey in this carnival. The idea had a lot of merit, save for the fact that boxing was now outlawed in New York and this was the height of the influenza epidemic. Boxing had also been banned in both Pennsylvania and New Jersey due to the fear of contagion. Influenza had knocked out boxing all along the east coast.[59]

On October 22, the boxing committee of the United War Work campaign sent Willard a telegram requesting his participation in the charity event. On October 25, Willard telegraphed that he would gladly box for the war work fund. At the same time, Willard suggested that he box either Willie Meehan, who had just defeated Jack Dempsey, or Walter Monahan, Willard's former sparring partner. Once Willard agreed to fight, Jack Kearns notified Coffroth that Dempsey would also agree to fight, especially if he could fight Willard. *The New York Times* predicted this would be one of the greatest boxing carnivals of all time.[60]

Then, with the abruptness of a bombshell, it was announced that the boxing program had been cancelled.

> John D. Rockefeller, Jr., told the committee that protests against boxing as a means of aiding the war fund had been received from ministers in all sections of the country. This action means that the country-wide program which had been planned by James W. Coffroth of California will have to be canceled unless the boxing promoters decided to conduct the benefit boxing shows through independent committees of their own.[61]

Once again Jess Willard's attempt to participate in a charity event through boxing was thwarted.

However, despite the ban placed on this major event, Willard himself went ahead and did organize a smaller charity bout. The same day Coffroth's boxing carnival was cancelled Willard accepted an invitation from Fort Worth to box there for charity. He sent to Fort Oglethorpe, Georgia, and was able to get Walter Monahan, his former sparring partner, released to fight at Fort Worth. Monahan had been training soldiers in boxing in Georgia and was in splendid condition. Willard asked Billy Sunday, the evangelist, to referee. On Sunday, November 9, he and Monahan put on a great show for the troops.

After the bout, Monahan declared that he felt so good he wanted to go a few rounds with Dempsey himself. Willard quickly replied,

> No, save him for me. Men like Dempsey were especially made for me. If the public wants the bout, some promoter will quickly get the inspiration and we can talk business. We all must be assured that there will be no interference, for I have a wife and kiddies, and they must be protected. Dempsey will not have to languish for an opponent long, although he has not beaten any man of class in good condition. The Fulton 18-second victory was more or less of a fluke. It is not likely Dempsey could repeat it if given eighteen rounds. So tell the people in the North to save Dempsey for me. Don't let some second-rater brush him off.[62]

The Background to the Armistice

Willard's difficulty in getting in a charity boxing event must be understood, not only in the light of the war effort itself, but also in the light of the influenza epidemic which was raging at the same time.

It had taken the Americans nearly a year of strenuous effort, from the declaration of war in April 1917, until the first armies were sent to France in April 1918. But influenza organized its forces much more rapidly. We have seen that it was in Haskell County in January 1918. By March, it had infected Camp Funston. Despite the fact that thousands of recruits became incapacitated by the virus, and hundreds were dead, the Army ignored the threat and shipped the soldiers out to Brest, France. The demand for additional manpower by the Allies was so great that sick or not, the American forces were needed.

The Americans arrived just as German General, Erich Ludendorff, had begun a massive offensive in the west. Germany and the Central powers recognized the threat posed by the new American armies. They recognized that unless they could defeat the British and the French before the Americans were on the ground, Germany herself might be defeated. Fortunately for the Germans, the Russian Revolution and the Treaty of Brest-Litovsk, which was signed on March 3, had ended the war in the east. This relieved them of the pressure of fighting a two-front war, even though they still kept 50 divisions on the Eastern Front. Ludendorff developed a multi-pronged offensive for the Western Front which was designed to drive the British into the sea near Ostend and then encircle Paris. His strike began on March 21. The final great battle of the war had begun.

Great success rewarded his efforts. By April 12, the German forces had broken through the Allied lines and threatened to destroy the British forces. Desperate, the British General Haig issued his famous order of the day: "With our backs to the wall and believing in the justice of our cause each one of us must fight to the end." The situation for the Allies looked grim. Then, by the end of April, the German drive began to slow. Influenza had begun to affect the war effort.

The American troops infected with influenza landed at Brest about the first of April. Then, as fast as the troops moved, the epidemic moved even faster. It spread outward from Brest in concentric circles. By April 10, it had entered the French army. By late April it had reached Paris and Italy, and the first cases appeared in the British Army. By late April, too, it had reached the German Army. Dr. Harvey Cushing, an American serving with the British, reported the success of the early German offensive and then noted that the offensive had stalled: "The expected third phase of the great German offensive gets put off from day to day.... When the next offensive will come off no one knows. It probably won't be long postponed. I gather that the epidemic of grippe which hit us rather hard in Flanders also hit the Boche worse, and this may have caused the delay." This was confirmed by Ludendorff himself: "It was a grievous business having to listen every morning to the chiefs of staff's recital of the number of influenza cases, and their complaints about the weakness of their troops."[63]

Due to wartime restrictions, none of the warring armies wanted to release data on the progress and effect of influenza on the troops. Only Spain, which was neutral, reported the effect, and as a result, gave the disease its name: Spanish Flu. But we now know the effects on some of the armies. Between June 1 and August 3, 200,825 British Soldiers in France, out of two million, or about 10 percent, could not report to duty. Although there were a number of deaths, generally the disease was benign. The danger of this first iteration of influenza was that it was so debilitating. Every hospitalized soldier required the services of doctors and nurses to keep him from becoming a fatality.

After a hiatus during August, in September a new and more virulent form of influenza exploded in Europe. Again we do not know the direct effect upon the German army, but we know that it devastated the American army. Conditions were so bad in America that two planned military drafts were cancelled and a meeting was held with President Wilson about halting the shipping of any further soldiers to Europe. On average, in the army camps, 20 percent of the soldiers who caught influenza developed pneumonia. Of those who developed pneumonia, nearly 40 percent died.[64]

The situation at Camp Grant, Illinois, illustrates the effect influenza had on the American military. Influenza hit Camp Grant on September 21 with 70 men admitted to hospital. The next day new admissions rose to 194, then 370, then 492, and it reached a high of 788 on September 29. "So sudden and appalling was the visitation that it required the greatest energy and cooperation of every officer, every man, and every nurse to meet the emergency," wrote one observer. Barracks were converted to hospital wards and the capacity was expanded from "10 occupied beds to a capacity of 4,102 beds in six days." Every department was overrun, nor were the medical personnel immune. "Eleven of the 81 medical officers fell ill, three civilian and three army nurses died." Ten days after the epidemic hit, the numbers of new admissions began to fall off, but the number of deaths began to climb. On October 1, there were 14 dead; October 2, 30 deaths; October 3, 46; October 4, 76; October 5, 100; and on October 6, 117. The mortuary was designed to handle only 4 deaths a day. The place filled up with bodies so fast that the camp had to hire trucks to haul them away. All in all, Camp Grant had 10,713 influenza victims, including 1,060 deaths in a population of 40,000. One must add to this the camp commander, Colonel Charles B. Hagadorn, who committed suicide as the dead bodies piled up. The recruits from these camps who survived were not fit and healthy to travel overseas. Between September 1 and the end of November 1918, "influenza and pneumonia sickened between 20% and 40% of U.S. Army and Navy personnel." The American military campaign nearly broke down.[65]

The situation among the civilian public was equally grim. In Philadelphia during the week ending October 16, the disease killed 4,597 people. This was the very time and place where Jack Kearns hoped to have Willard fight Dempsey. Mortuaries were crowded with bodies and there was a shortage of people to bury the dead. The streets of large towns were deserted as businesses closed and people tried to avoid others who might spread the disease. In San Antonio, 53.5 percent of the population was struck by influenza and 98 percent of all homes in the city had at least one person sick with the disease. In the United States, influenza infected 28 percent of the civilian population. So severe was the infection among the general population that it lowered the average life span by ten years.[66]

We only have partial figures for Germany, but in Frankfurt the mortality rate of those hospitalized with influenza was 27.3 percent. That meant that if you were sent to a hospital, you had only had three chances out of four of returning home alive. In Cologne, the mayor, Konrad Adenauer, who would become German chancellor after World War II, summed up the situation: the disease had left thousands "too exhausted to hate."[67]

Adenauer's comment revealed the truth of what brought the war to an end, and why it ended in an Armistice. On November 11, 1918, on the 11th hour, of the 11th day, of the 11th month, the guns fell silent. Europe and America were exhausted. No one could continue the fight. The United States, the last best hope for reinforcements, could no longer find healthy troops to send to battle. The war had killed millions of young men from France, Germany and Great Britain. The war had only killed 48,909 American soldiers. Influenza, however, killed 62,000 American soldiers. On the American home front, out of the range of the guns, 675,000 people died, more than ten times as many as were killed in the war. Worldwide the death toll was perhaps 50,000,000 people. Influenza proved far more deadly than war.

Because of the disease, World War I, "the war to end all wars," came to an end, not with a bang but a whimper. The influenza epidemic did not. After its violent outbreak between September and October 1918, it went into remission, only to return in January 1919. However, the outbreak of 1919 was not as severe as that of 1918, and gradually the fire of contagion sputtered and died out. By 1920 the world was returning to normal again.

9

1919 and the Battle with Jack Dempsey

Back to Normalcy

The end of World War I brought changes to the world of boxing. Jack Skelly, the old-time fighter, saw it as a benefit to Jess Willard. Jess had not fought in three years. He had the ranch that he and Hattie had always wanted. His children were growing up. He had plenty of money. He was in a perfect position to retire undefeated, unlike his predecessors who had all suffered defeat in the ring. As wise as this advice was in retrospect, Willard chose not to take it. J.V. Fitzgerald, *The Washington Post* columnist, who was not Willard's closest friend, urged him to come out and fight. The war was over, now was the time to get back into the ring.

> If Jess Willard is going to come out of his shell and defend his heavyweight championship, as he says he is, it is high time for him to give some consideration to the claims of Jack Dempsey.... It isn't reasonable to suppose that Willard can come back now and fight as he could three or four years ago. Since he conquered Johnson, Jess has engaged in only one fight. That was with Frank Moran in March 1916.... But he has loafed since then. He has boxed often, to be sure. He has not neglected keeping his body in excellent condition, and yet he has never since been tuned up to fighting pitch.... Maybe he can do it successfully. Certainly he will leave no stone unturned to be at the top of his form when he defends his title. His years of clean living will stand him in good stead. But his three years of almost uninterrupted rest are bound to tell against him against a rushing, hard-hitting fighter of the Dempsey type.[1]

Following his charity bout with Walter Monahan in Fort Worth in November, Monahan thought to challenge Jack Dempsey for a match. However, Willard told Monahan to leave Jack Dempsey to him. Monahan then announced in Philadelphia that Willard was ready to fight Dempsey. The stage was set for the bout to develop. All that was necessary was the agreement from Dempsey, a site and a promoter.[2]

On January 24, 1919, Tex Rickard had signed Willard to a contract for a championship fight with any opponent Rickard selected. The fight was to be up to 40 rounds and was to be on July 4. Willard was to get $100,000 for his end of the fight. This was an extraordinary amount of money. To put it into perspective, Ted "Kid" Lewis, the world champion welterweight, was guaranteed $1,250 to meet the former world champion, Jack Britton in a 12-round bout originally scheduled for February 24, but actually fought on March 17. At the same time, Battling Levinsky was matched to fight Harry Greb, for $500 in Buffalo on February 17. All of these were at one time or another world champions and all became Hall of Fame boxers. The money paid to Willard, was not only far beyond what the normal working man could hope to earn, it was also far beyond what other

Jess visiting with Tex Rickard in 1919.

boxing champions could hope to earn as well. It was even more than the $75,000 that President Wilson earned a year.[3]

Although Rickard did not immediately name a challenger for Willard, most people assumed that it would be Jack Dempsey. Before Willard signed his agreement with Tex Rickard, Doc Kearns had signed Dempsey to fight Billy Miske in a 20-round bout in New Orleans in March. Miske was one of the few fighters Dempsey had faced who had not succumbed to his power. This made the bout in New Orleans a significant hurdle which could have tripped Dempsey up. To avoid that, the fight with Miske was cancelled and in its place, Kearns lined up a number of journeyman fighters whom Dempsey promptly defeated in a series of one-round knockouts. Still, Rickard was uncertain as to whether to choose Dempsey or the Frenchman, Georges Carpentier, as Willard's opponent.[4]

Carpentier was an authentic French war hero who was twice decorated for bravery. Dempsey and Willard, on the other hand, had not participated in the war at all. This made them unpopular in their own country. Dempsey's lack of a war record, as well as being too small to fight Willard were, in Rickard's eyes, two strikes against Jack. Willard, on the other hand, antagonized his public when he treated the championship fight just as a business proposition. He said,

> I presume some people will think I demanded the earth to box. Rickard met my terms and I accepted. I want to say that I didn't get a cent for fighting Johnson in Havana. In fact, I had to borrow money to get back in the United States. The man who meets me will have the same opportunity that I did to make money. I am making money in the oil business and I did not care whether I ever fought again.
>
> I don't care who is selected to meet me. The purse is the thing. I am not boxing for fun. It's business with me.[5]

Honesty is a virtue, but candor is not. Willard had reached the point where his candor was becoming destructive. Sports fans realize that sport depends upon money to make great matches and games. Nonetheless, they also want to believe that their heroes are playing for something more than money; they want to believe they are playing for the spirit of the game. Sport is more than money. It links fan and athlete in a joint effort to achieve glory and honor that neither can achieve by themselves. The country made that clear when the 1919 Chicago White Sox threw the World Series for the money offered by Arnold Rothstein. Willard did not make a corrupt bargain with gamblers. But when he said: "The purse is the thing. I am not boxing for fun," he lost most of the good will that he had left in the community. Boxing has never been purely business. In response to his statement, we can hear the echo of the fan's cry: "Say it ain't so, Jess."

Complicating Rickard's problem was the fact that Doc Kearns, Dempsey's manager, detested Rickard, and the feeling was mutual. Kearns was a hustler, a swindler and a con man. He thought nothing of cheating others. But he hated it when someone got the better of him. Kearns had been out-maneuvered by Rickard when Les Darcy, the Australian middleweight, had come to the United States during the war. Kearns thought that he had a deal to be Darcy's manager, but Rickard got to Darcy first. Even though Darcy died of septicemia before he could fight in the United States, Kearns never forgave Rickard for stealing Darcy from him. Nonetheless, Kearns needed to get Rickard's approval for Dempsey to become Willard's challenger.

While Rickard was considering who should fight Willard, he made a visit to Dempsey's hotel in New York.

> Dempsey was lying on the bed. "Every time I see you Jack," he said, "you look smaller to me."
>
> As usual, Dempsey let Doc do the talking. "What did you come down here for, Tex," Kearns asked, "a beauty contest? When this guy nails them, they stay nailed. They end up looking down their own backs."
>
> "He's too small for Willard," said Tex.
>
> "Too small! Too small! He punches Carl Morris inside out. He puts away Fulton with the first solid blast. Bill Brennan can stay only six rounds with him!"
>
> Tex said that the world was ready for a big fight but that Dempsey against Willard would not draw enough. "Jack was lucky with Morris and Fulton," he said, "but they weren't champions. Willard's a better champ than people think."
>
> "Why, this kid here will knock that big yellowbelly of a bum right out of his shoes."
>
> "Willard will take a lot of knocking out," insisted Tex.
>
> "He'll get a lot of knocking out," shouted Doc, jumping up and down. "Dempsey will be the greatest champion that ever lived."
>
> "You're sure, Doc, that he'll be the next heavyweight champ?"
>
> "Tex, it's a lead pipe cinch."
>
> "Then he should be willing to fight Willard for nothing."
>
> "He should, but he won't," said Kearns, reacting like a man stabbed.
>
> Tex reached for his hat. "It's a gamble, but maybe I could let you have expenses."
>
> "What are you, Rickard, a promoter or a piker?" snorted Doc. "If you wanta get in on big things you gotta take chances. There's lots of other guys bidding for Jack. About all we're doing now is sitting around, listening to offers."
>
> "But none of them have Willard, eh, Doc? What would Jack fight for?"
>
> "Fifty thousand dollars."
>
> Rickard laughed. "I guess you've been reading French magazines, Doc, and have fancy figures on the brain. There is no use us talking until you sneeze the dust out of your head."

"It's fifty grand or nothing," insisted Kearns.
"Well, that's it, boys. It's nothing." Ignoring Kearns, Tex turned to Jack. "So long, Jack."[6]

However, when it became apparent to Rickard that he could not get Carpentier in time to meet the July 4 fight date, he returned to Kearns and Dempsey. This time Kearns seemed more agreeable. He told Tex:

"I don't want to argue no more with you about dough. We'll take fifteen thousand for our end if you'll go ahead and announce the match."
"I ain't signed you guys yet."
"Well, you got my word on it."
"Why are you in such a hurry about my announcing it?" asked Tex suspiciously.
Doc Kearns put his head down. He took out his handkerchief and dabbed at his eyes. "Its on account of my mother," he choked out. "Her birthday's this week and if she could read in the papers that I was going to match a guy fighting for the heavy title-well, Tex, this would be the best present I could give her."
Tex announced the fight the next day. On seeing the newspaper story, Kearns rushed off, gurgling, to Rickard. "Okay, sucker," he told him, "now you can give us fifty grand for our end."
Tex blew his top.
"Why did you announce the match?" Kearns demanded. "You ain't going back on your word, are you?"
"Why not? You went back on yours"
Kearns laughed lightly. "Yeah, but I never prance around posing like some honest John."[7]

Getting Ready for Toledo

Tex Rickard did indeed announce the bout in the newspapers on January 30, 1919. But he hedged his bets. He told the reporters that "he wanted to arrange with Jack Dempsey to meet Jess Willard, providing Dempsey sustains no injuries between now and next July." It was a lukewarm announcement without the usual fan-fare and trumpet blasts, and occupied a small corner of *The Washington Post* on January 31, 1919.[8]

It was not until February 5, after extensive negotiations, that it was finally announced that Dempsey would indeed fight Willard. He was to get the sum of $27,500 and one-third of the motion picture rights. This figure was the result of a vote by the newspaper men who were in the room during the negotiations between Kearns and Rickard, neither man trusting the other. The choice of referee was left up to the two fighters, but, in case they could not agree, Rickard would make the choice and his decision would be final. This would later prove to be a critical decision. No site had yet been chosen for the fight, and that proved to be critical as well.[9]

Immediately after the fight was announced, the newspapers were full of opinion on who might win. Tom Jones declared Willard would win; John "the Barber" Reisler, one of Jack Dempsey's former managers, picked Dempsey; and Fred Fulton announced that his fight with Dempsey had been a fake.[10]

Fulton's announcement was designed to sabotage Dempsey's chance at the Willard fight. Dempsey's defeat of Fulton was one of the things that had propelled him into the battle with Willard, and Dempsey immediately denied Fulton's charge, as did Jack Kearns. This was to be expected from both of them, since so much was riding on the championship bout. Kearns' word was not to be trusted, but Dempsey said he was willing to fight Fulton again, if Rickard would let him. In the meantime, Georges Carpentier turned down the fight with Willard. He declared that he could make enough money without having to fight a man of Willard's size. With only one real candidate to fight Willard, Rickard turned down Dempsey's request to fight Fulton again and let the Willard-Dempsey bout proceed. The only long term effect of Fulton's announcement was to have New Jersey question his qualifications as a fighter, now that he was an admitted faker.[11]

About the same time, another fighter attempted to sabotage the bout. Jack Johnson had returned to Havana, Cuba. While there he announced that he was paid to lie down and let Willard win the title. According to Johnson's claims after the fight Willard was to arrange things with the Federal authorities so that Johnson could be allowed back into the United States to look after his property and see his mother. Further, the fight was to end at the end of the tenth round, but because Willard was making such a poor showing at that time, Johnson supposedly carried him to the 26th round. Now, "unless Willard agrees to fight within a reasonable time, which he should to prove, if he can, that he beat me fairly, I shall claim the world's title."

In 1915, Willard was in no position to convince the Federal Government to let Johnson back into the country. At the end of their fight it was Johnson who had all of the money, while Willard was broke. And as for the claims that Johnson lay down, Willard's response was that was nonsense: "If Johnson made any sort of deal in that fight four years ago, he made it with someone else than me and I never knew about it. If he sold the championship, he sold himself with it. He is down and out. He is a convicted and confessed criminal. His wishes and his states should be taken by the public just as a convict's testimony is taken in court-for a lie." Tom Jones, Willard's former manager, was quoted as saying: "I was closer at that time to Willard than any other man in the world and what Johnson says is absolutely the worst kind of bosh."[12]

Two days later, in an editorial, W.C. Simons, of Willard's hometown newspaper, *The Lawrence Daily Journal-World* took up Johnson's comments. Although not a fan of prizefighting, Simons could not let Johnson's remarks pass unchallenged.

> Now let us examine Willard's character for a little bit and size up the man. He is still living happily with the only wife he has ever had and has a fine little family of boys and girls growing up, to whom he is going to give the advantage of a good education. Instead of spending his money in saloons and brothels he has invested in a home and in property which brings him an income. He has not sought prominence through the sport columns, but has gone ahead as a man to do a man's part in the development of his country and in the building of his own fortune.
>
> There has been absolutely nothing in Willard's character or actions to cause one to accept as true for a single minute the accusations that have been brought against him. We do not believe he is a crook, we do not believe there was any bargain when he met Johnson, but rather that he went in where other fighters were afraid to go and won the victory because he was the best man.[13]

The Journal-World's judgment has stood the test of time.

While all of this was going on, both Rickard and Willard were being distracted by activities in the Oil Patch. Both of them had made investments in Texas oil, and for both of them it was ironic. Willard had gone to Texas in 1908, just after marrying Hattie. He

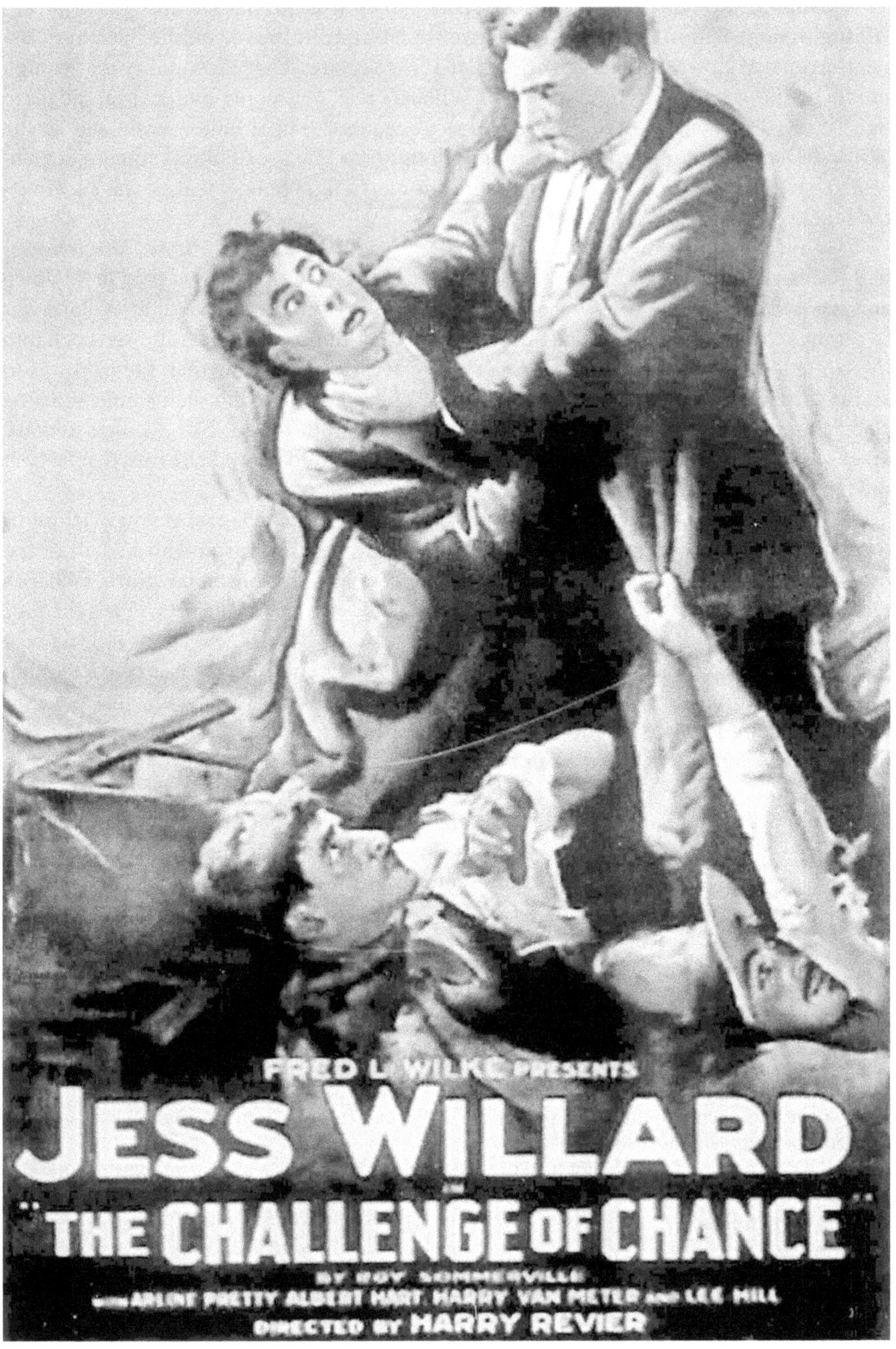

Poster for Jess Willard's second motion picture, *The Challenge of Chance*, 1919.

had lived there for a year, but had left just as the oil boom was starting. Had he remained, he might have become an oil man, not a boxer. As it was, Willard's oil lands were so extensive that he spent nearly all his time dealing with them. He claimed he only agreed to the championship fight due to his friendship with Rickard.

Rickard too had left Texas before the oil boom started. He had been a cowboy, riding across land that he later found covered with oil derricks. "I have played the game of fortune up and down and across the board, and everything considered I have done pretty well during the last twenty-five years. Think of what I might have made, however, if I had stayed right here and drilled oil wells instead of chasing the end of the rainbow to the furthermost parts of the earth."[14]

In February, Willard finally was able to sell off the last of his circus equipment. He had sold his circus animals in 1918, now he sold his circus train and other equipment for $47,000 to the Horm Amusement Company of Kansas City. In addition, he had begun acting in a new film, *The Challenge of Chance*, which was planned for theatre release the month before the championship bout. This film, plus his ranch near Lawrence, his oil fields and his championship title were his future sources of revenue.[15]

While Rickard was seeking a place to hold the bout, Willard was already in training on his farm in Lawrence. He built a gymnasium on his ranch, as well as spending hours running on the roads nearby. He did not plan to take Dempsey lightly. But there were two missing elements to his training: He lacked sparring partners in Kansas and he lacked a manager. The papers often referred to his friend, Ray O. Archer, as his manager, but Archer had really no experience with boxing. He was not a trainer, nor did he know how to deal with boxing issues. Although he was supposedly Jack Kearns' counterpart in the Willard camp, he was a puppy compared to Kearns' bulldog. Kearns had forgotten more about boxing than Archer ever knew. Instead, Willard really acted as his own manager.

Willard recognized these short-comings, but was unable to overcome them. Tom Jones, whom he had fired in 1918, would have rejoined his camp, had he been asked. But he was not asked. Instead Willard asked a boyhood friend, William B. Welch, who now lived in New York, to serve as his manager: "I've got some good boys with me; none better. They are honest and loyal, but I would like a man with me to talk to me like a brother, to keep track of every move and run all my finances during the time I am training. You can do it for me. I want you by May 1: no later." The problem was, although Willard trusted Welch and Archer, neither knew anything about boxing. Welch disappeared after this mention and played no part in Willard's defense of his title. Later, Willard was to write that his biggest mistake was not to have asked Kid McCoy to serve as his manager. "Kid McCoy tried to work in my corner but at that time I did not see fit to accept his services-something I will always regret.... McCoy knew all the tricks, and had practiced most of them during his fistic career, so it would have taken more than a Kearns or DeForest [Jimmy De Forest, Dempsey's trainer] to fool McCoy since De Forest had taught the Kid a great many of the ring tricks he knew."[16]

One of those tricks was that Kearns and Dempsey developed a propaganda war against Willard. Dempsey argued in his autobiography that Willard did not like black sparring partners and had adopted a strong dislike for the Negro race. This is not at all true. As we have seen, Willard had respect and admiration for Jack Johnson after the fight in Havana. In addition, from his very earliest training in Oklahoma, he had used

Ray Archer and Jess Willard circa 1918–1919.

black sparring partners. In Chicago, when he and others had objected to training with Johnson, he had specifically stated that he did not want the black fighters, Cleve Hawkins and Kid Cotton, barred from the gym.[17]

One other man who did know boxing and whom Willard could have used at this time was his former sparring partner, Jim Cameron. Cameron was a Negro heavyweight living in Los Angeles. He was 6 feet, 2 inches and had fought most of the famous men of his time, including Fred Fulton, Sam Langford, Harry Wills and Frank Moran. He would have been an ideal member of Willard's team. Unfortunately, at the beginning of April, Cameron got into an altercation with a friend of his, Elleyett Bly, whom he believed wanted to kill him. They met on the street in Los Angeles, Bly pulled a knife and Cameron shot him dead.

Then Cameron went home, dressed in a new shirt, walked to the police station and turned himself in. Following his confession to the police, Cameron told them he had no ill-will against Bly and hoped that they would allow him to be a pallbearer at Bly's funeral.[18]

The next month, Willard went to Los Angeles to complete work on *The Challenge of Chance*. Willard attempted to help Cameron while he was there, but he could not. Nor could Cameron help Willard at this time. For both it was an opportunity lost.[19]

On May 6, it was announced that Tex Rickard had chosen Toledo as the site of the championship bout. Ohio law limited the fight to no more than 12 rounds with a decision. One unusual rule about boxing in Ohio at that time was that the match was technically an exhibition, not a prizefight. Prizefights were illegal in Ohio, as they were in many states. According to Ohio law, a prizefight was when two men fought for a purse or prize. Willard and Dempsey were being paid their fees win, lose or draw, by Rickard. They were not fighting for a purse and their payment did not depend on who won. This made the fight legal in Ohio.

Rickard was drawn to Toledo due to the large railroad net which linked the city to the rest of the country. He claimed that Toledo was within fifty miles of seven million people. He estimated that the contest should draw $400,000 leaving him with $225,000 after taxes and expenses. So confident was he that the fight would be a financial success that he agreed to pay the government war tax for each admission from his own pocket. "I believe when a man is asked to pay $50 or $60 for a ticket that is enough." Rickard's estimate was not far off. On July 9, he estimated the crowd at 20,000 and the receipts at $452,000. Toledo received $31,500, while the United States war tax was $41,000.[20]

Everything was now set for the fight, and Rickard notified Willard and Dempsey that they should be in Toledo by May 20 and that they were to complete their training in Toledo. Willard immediately wired back that he needed to complete shooting *The Challenge of Chance* in Los Angeles and could not arrive in Toledo until May 24. In point of fact, Willard did not arrive until June 1, after stopping off in Lawrence to see his family. That was agreeable with Rickard and Dempsey, and it gave Jack Kearns extra time to make Dempsey the hometown favorite. Dempsey's training routine benefited this strategy. He was to work hard for one week, then lay off for a week by playing baseball with the kids on the beach, telling them stories about his adventures and generally making himself agreeable to the local people. While Dempsey was ingratiating himself, Kearns was spending all his time with the press tearing down Willard and explaining how Dempsey was going to be the next heavyweight champion of the world. This one-two punch nearly knocked Willard out before he even arrived in Toledo.[21]

When Willard did arrive in Toledo, he astonished those who had been listening to Doc Kearns comments by appearing in splendid condition. He had trimmed down to 258 pounds and expected to weigh no more than 243 when he entered the ring. This was only a few pounds more than he had weighed in Havana when he fought Jack Johnson. Further, Willard had yet to hire a trainer. "I'll train myself and then I'll have no one to blame if I'm beaten," Willard told the newspapers. "I never was very far out of shape. I've been training since February and believe my condition will cause surprise when I start boxing."[22]

There was one major difference between Willard's training in Toledo and that in New York and Havana. He was much rougher on his sparring partners. He had not attempted to knock down any of his sparring mates in the past, and indeed was concerned when he accidentally did so. But at Toledo, Willard seemed to take his cue from Dempsey, who routinely knocked down his sparring partners. Despite the fact that Willard pulled most of his punches in training, an action for which T.A. Dorgan (TAD) had criticized him in the Moran fight, in his first sparring match he knocked Jack Lavan through the ropes and in the second knocked Walter Monahan out in the ring. Then, using 14 ounce gloves, he knocked Soldier Stanton, who had formerly boxed Dempsey, out in ten seconds. It appeared that consciously or unconsciously, Willard was training for a more brutal fight than in the past. As his antagonist, J.V. Fitzgerald of *The Washington Post* admitted, Willard had lost his paunch but he had regained his punch.[23]

The Fight Preliminaries

Fitzgerald was one of the few sportswriters who looked beyond the outward show to see below the surface. Willard was in top shape, but he had aged.

> In other words, time has put its mark on the champion. He has aged since he won the championship and since he scored over Moran, the last time he was in a real battle. It doesn't show in his immense frame; it isn't visible in his eye, that tell tale mirror of the athlete's condition, but it is evident in a certain sagging of the facial muscles. Jess confesses he is 35 years of age-the chances are that he is nearer 40, if appearances count for anything.[24]

Fitzgerald was correct. Willard was 37 and would be 38 in December. He was facing a man of 23 and who would celebrate his 24th birthday on June 24 in Toledo before the fight. If the age difference between Willard and Johnson of 4 years had been critical to Johnson's defeat, the age difference of 13 years between Dempsey and Willard was even more a factor. Yet aside from J.V. Fitzgerald and Grantland Rice, very few sportswriters seemed to comment on this.[25]

Willard's early training had showed that he was short of wind, so he had to concentrate on that. Otherwise, he seemed in great shape. Ray Archer hired an ex-football player, Joe Sullivan, as one of his sparring partners. Sullivan weighed about 175 and was just about Dempsey's height. When Willard got into the ring with him, he let down his guard and Sullivan rushed Willard continually. "Jess allowed Sullivan to plant half a dozen punches on his chin. He made no effort to block them, pushing his face out for Sullivan to take aim at. The blows did not bother him a bit apparently."[26]

This was exactly the behavior Jess had used in the ring with Ed Burke back in Oklahoma in 1911, and it achieved the same result. It convinced Willard that he could take a punch to the jaw and not be hurt by it. Since this was one of Dempsey's favorite punches, this type of training helped convince Willard that Dempsey could not hurt him.

Willard's efforts led to a shift in public opinion about the fight. Before he arrived in Toledo, public sentiment was 100 percent for Dempsey. He was younger, more agile and, based upon his previous fights, possessed of a superb knockout punch. But once Willard got into the ring and began pummeling his sparring partners, sentiment shifted to him.

> The wise "ring birds" saw Willard allowing his sparring partners to welt him on the jaw and on the body with all the power they could put behind their punches while Jess simply stood unprotected in front of them. This was the punch-assimilating test for Big Jess, and he showed no evidence the punches hurt or weakened him.
>
> Some of these fans said: "It is easy enough for Willard to take the punches, but there's a big difference between the punches of these sparring partners and Jack Dempsey."[27]

Perhaps there was, but few of these "ring birds" would have done what Willard did. Willard's actions worried Doc Kearns. Dempsey was used to knocking his opponent out in the first rounds. He was not prepared for a long distance fight. Suppose Dempsey hit Willard with his best shot and Willard did not fall? Dempsey and Kearns were both concerned.[28]

After the fight there were many who argued that Willard's defeat by Dempsey was a foregone conclusion. But before the fight neither Willard nor Dempsey felt that way. Instead, Willard felt supremely confident, while Dempsey wondered if he had challenged the one man he could not beat. On June 15, with the temperature climbing to 110 degrees, Willard boxed 6 rounds with his sparring partners, Jack Hempel and Walter Monahan. Sailor Bill Ketchel, a young 195 pound heavyweight, who was hired as a stand-in for Dempsey, went one round with Willard took a blow to the midsection and decided to return to New York. If there was any weakness to Willard's training it was that he could not keep additional hard-hitting sparring partners.

Willard then announced to the crowd of about 1,000 people that he had invited his wife to come to Toledo to watch the bout. "This move on the part of the champion, boxing experts said, is the real test of his confidence because, they said, he would not think of permitting his wife to witness the spectacle if he thought he would be defeated."[29]

On June 16, *The New York Times* announced that Willard now weighed 248 and was lighter than he was when he fought Moran. He expected to reach 245 by the time he entered the ring with Dempsey. He had his toughest workout yet before a crowd of 2,000 to 2,500 people who paid 25 cents each to watch him work. He was delighted to add a new sparring partner, Jack Heinen, with whom he had been matched in 1913, but had never fought. Heinen "boxed savagely and earnestly" with Willard, but was knocked out twice in one round. The next day, Heinen did better and boxed three rounds with Willard. In addition, Ray Archer added Joe Chip, the brother of former middleweight champion, George Chip, to the mix. Joe was a middleweight as well and gave Willard a fast-paced workout over two rounds. Willard used 14-ounce gloves to spare his partners.[30]

Bathing in Brine

While Willard had been losing weight, Dempsey had been gaining weight. Due to a cut over his eye, and bruised ribs, Dempsey had not been sparring for the last two weeks. His workouts had been much lighter than those of Willard and his meals heavier. It was a surprise to the public that when he stepped on the scales in bathing trunks and boxing shoes, he weighed 201 pounds. According to the reporters, Dempsey looked in perfect shape, although he was "copper color as a result of weeks of exposure to the sun." Another reporter noted "his sun blackened shoulders and arms shed rain like a piece of tanned leather." Willard, who had equally been exposed to the sun, retained his light complexion.[31]

The secret to Dempsey's dark color was not the sun, but his use of brine to harden his skin. Ad Wolgast, Tom Jones' first champion, was also a believer in bathing in brine. He did it for exactly the same reason that Dempsey did. "When he is hot and sweaty and the pores of his skin are open, he bathes his face in salty water. This has gradually toughened his skin until it is hard for any opponent to break his skin."[32]

The use of brine to toughen the skin of the hands and face is no longer practiced by boxers wearing gloves. Indeed, some modern boxers argue that the use of brine causes the skin to crack and be more prone to cuts. But it is clear that bare-knuckle fighters, such as Dempsey was in his bar-room days, and even glove boxers such as Ad Wolgast, swore by the use of brine or other pickling substances to make the hands and face hard and leather-like. Combined with hard work, a fighter using brine could make his face as tough as leather and his fists as hard as stone. Tom Sharkey, like Dempsey and Wolgast, also used brine to harden his hands. When people examined his fists, they were willing to bet they were covered with leather.[33]

The Question of Bandages

On June 20, Willard announced that he was not happy about the possibility of Dempsey entering the ring with bandaged hands. He proposed that the fighters have their hands bandaged in the ring, as he and Jack Johnson had done in Havana. Dempsey had a reputation for using heavy bandages on his hands. W. O. McGeehan, writing about this, noted that it was Dempsey's habit was to bind his hands so that they looked like the old Roman *Cestus*. "When the maulies are thus reinforced they naturally carry an added kick. A couple of wallops from the well-bandaged mitts of Dempsey disposed of Fulton in short order."[34]

The rules of the Boxing Commission in Toledo specified soft bandages. Willard declared that he planned to use plain cotton bandages with a couple of layers of surgical tape to hold the bandages in place. "That is all I care to use, and I think Dempsey should feel the same way about it. I believe it always looks bad to the spectators to see a boxer come into the ring with his hands looking as hard as a club because protected by some heavy material."[35]

Jess Willard in the ring before the Dempsey fight, 1919. You can see the very light bandages on his hand, before the gloves were put on.

On July 1 the matter was settled. "Jess Willard and Jack Dempsey will go into the ring for the heavyweight championship contest here Friday with bare hands, and all the bandaging and taping will be done in the view of the spectators and seconds of the heavyweight rivals. This announcement was made today by Tex Rickard, promoter of the contest."[36]

Jack Kearns protested against this. The next day Tex Rickard reversed his decision and announced that the fighters would tape their hands in their dressing rooms in the presence of a representative of the rival camp. The change occurred, Doc Kearns said "because of the blazing heat." Another reason given was that to tape in the ring would create unnecessary delay. Either way, Dempsey entered the ring with his hands heavily wrapped in tape and Willard had lost a critical battle to Doc Kearns.[37]

Handicapping the Fight

One week before the fight, the wise men of the boxing world had no idea who would win. Willard appeared supremely confident that he would defeat Dempsey. Although Dempsey did not evidence the same confidence, he was honed and ready to fight. Many people believed him to be the better man. Tex Rickard, who was selling the tickets, publicly considered it a toss-up. In private, Rickard had deeper concerns: He was afraid that Willard might kill Dempsey. He admitted this to Dempsey, but he could not admit this to the public. Frank Moran, Frank Erne, former lightweight champion, Mike Gibbons, Sam Langford, Ring Lardner, Bat Masterson, W. O. McGeehan, Harry Cross of *The New York Times,* Tom Jones, Jim Nasium of *The Philadelphia Inquirer*, Fred Turbyville of the *Newspaper Enterprise Association*, and Weed Dickinson of *The New York Telegraph* all believed Willard would win. Jack Curley had bet a lot of money on Dempsey, as had Tad Dorgan. Hype Igoe, Jack Knox of *The New York Telegram*, Walter St. Denis of the *New York Globe*, H.C, Hamilton of *United Press*, Bill Wathey of the *New York Telegram,* Otto Floto of the *Denver Post* and Rube Goldberg of *The Cleveland Plain Dealer* were all for Dempsey. J.V. Fitzgerald was sure that Dempsey would go into the ring as the favorite. Both sides believed that their man would win.[38]

Grantland Rice would sum up the match in this way:

> If Willard wins it will be easy enough to see why Dempsey could not spot his rival fifty pounds of fighting flesh and have a chance. Fifty pounds plus 5 inches in height and 6 inches in reach. If Dempsey wins it will be easy enough to see why a middle aged man around forty who hadn't boxed in three years (in competition) had no chance against a fast, game youngster around 23 who had been hard at it for the last two years. And so it goes.[39]

With the most knowledgeable boxing critics uncertain about the outcome, it remained to the amateurs to make news at Toledo before the fight. One group came from Lawrence, Kansas, Willard's new home town, prepared to make a splash. Headed by W. G. "Billy" Hutson, owner of the Eldridge Hotel, they arrived in Toledo with $6,000 worth of $1 bills. Each bill was wrapped with a paper band saying on one side "Kansas Jayhawk" and on the other side: "We train with Jess. Sure we will win. There's lots more where this came from. We make it everyday of the year in Lawrence, Kansas, the home of Jess Willard, our champion."[40]

Then there was the disaster of the concessions. "Professor" Billy McCarney, Willard's old nemesis, along with his partner, Thomas V. Bodkin, bought all the concessions and then sold them off to suckers. The ice cream concession melted in the heat; the ham and cheese sandwiches turned into a pile of goo; the lemonade concession (which McCarney absent-mindedly sold to two different men) was ruined when the old fighter, "Battling" Nelson took a bath in one of the barrels. The only concession, which did well, and which McCarney did not control, was water. A number of enterprising boys sold it for ten cents a glass. "In the end," McCarney recalled, "none of the concessions made a quarter, so to speak. It was appalling the way the whammy fell upon those folks." It was amateur time in Toledo.[41]

While not an amateur, Grantland Rice took a distinctly unique outlook in the fight. Rice had enlisted in World War I as a private although he was 36 years old in 1917 and was married and had one daughter. He had little sympathy for either Willard or Dempsey, since neither had enlisted. He ridiculed the promotional material which pronounced them "the world's two greatest fighting men."

"For neither Willard nor Dempsey is a fighting man in the 1914–1919 meaning of the phrase. Between these two dates more than fifty million donned the harness of battle, but neither Willard nor Dempsey was on the list."

"There is," Rice summed up, "no touch of glamour around either man."[42]

There were many critical things said about Jess Willard before the Dempsey fight, some were true and others not. The most honest was that Willard pulled his punches when sparring with his partners, and that he seemed to lack the killer instinct when in the ring. As Dempsey reported: "To Doc, he lacked the animal instinct, the inner fury and the all-important lust for battle." This was correct. It was Willard's natural instinct to let up on his opponent if his opponent seemed to be hurt. The opposite was true of Dempsey. When he had weakened an opponent, that was the time he was most ferocious. Willard was protected by his size and his prodigious strength. It was very difficult for his opponents to harm him in any way. And because few could hurt him, Willard felt no particular need to hurt his opponents. This made Willard a naturally defensive fighter.[43]

Dempsey was perpetually concerned about being hurt. This made him constantly on the offensive in his fights. His success rested on his aggressive nature and vigorous attack. Dempsey could not think of pulling his punches, for it would mean his defeat. Dempsey was called the "Man-killer" by Carl Morris, but it was not the hyperactive Dempsey, but the larger, more powerful Willard who had actually killed a man in the ring. Willard went into the fight worried that he might kill Dempsey in the ring. He even asked Rickard for legal immunity should he kill Dempsey. Tex Rickard and Dempsey himself also worried about the same thing.

The day before the fight with his whole future depending upon the success of his big show Tex dropped over to Dempsey's camp. Going into Jack's dressing room, he waited until they were alone. Then he told him:

> "Son, this Willard is a great fighter. I am worried about you because I am afraid he might kill you. He killed one man, you know."
>
> "Yes," said Dempsey, "I know he did, Tex."
>
> Rickard chewed on his cigar as he searched for the words he wanted to say next. He was very nervous as he went on:
>
> "Well, here's what you do. You get in there and fight him the best you can. But if he hits you hard and hurts you a lot, and you thinking he is going to kill you, you just go down and stay down. Don't think about me. It will be all right with me. I don't want you to get killed."[44]

Dempsey, Rickard and Willard all approached the July 4 fight fearing that Willard might kill Dempsey in the ring. This had a paradoxical effect on the fighters. Willard was hesitant as he went into the ring. He was confident that he could defeat Dempsey and that Dempsey could not hurt him. He was prepared to fight a normal bout of 12 rounds and win a decision, as he had done with Frank Moran. He did not want to slam into Dempsey and hurt him and certainly he did not want to kill him. Willard's hesitancy was based on

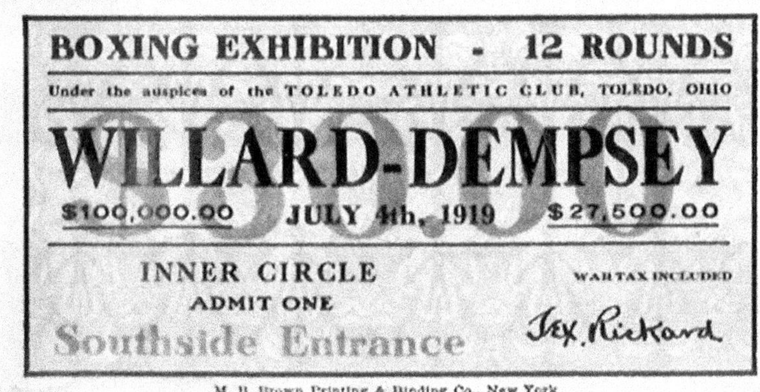

Ticket for Willard-Dempsey fight, July 4, 1919.

his concern as to how he might fight Dempsey, win the decision and not harm the younger, smaller man.

Dempsey's concern was more acute. He was astonished at how big Willard appeared in the ring when they were face to face. He was, as he admits, terrified that Willard might indeed kill him. So Dempsey did what he had done often in the past when faced with big and dangerous men, he attacked with all his might. He was prepared to ignore the rules. His goal was to knock his opponent out in the first round so that he himself would not be hurt. He was ready to do whatever he needed to do to get out of the ring alive. Dempsey's aggression grew out of fear; Willard's hesitancy also grew out of fear. And in this case the fear was the same on both sides: how to avoid killing Jack Dempsey.

The Fight: July 4, 1919

On July 4, 1919, at 3:30 p.m., Dempsey met Willard in the ring in Toledo. Willard entered the ring confident and self-assured. On the other side of the ring, while he was prepping Dempsey for the fight, Kearns told him that he had bet $10,000 (which he did not have) at 10 to 1 odds that Jack would knock Willard out in the first round. This bet gave Kearns the incentive to do whatever it took to win the fight. As Kearns was later to admit: "I had schemed and connived over too many years to let anything go wrong with a bet like that, let alone with the championship of the world. The hell with being a gallant loser. I intended to win."[45]

Then, just before Jack climbed into the ring, Doc Kearns gave him some additional advice:

> "Don't show no emotion, no anxiety, no nothing, kid. The press is just waiting for you to crack-it'd be good copy. Be careful!"
>
> Doc had a point. I made sure that I didn't even look into Willard's face for fear my eyes would give me away. Staring at my own feet was safer. I couldn't take a chance of being psyched out.
>
> Once our gloves were slipped on, we stepped toward each other to shake hands. As Willard moved away I realized I wasn't just fighting for a title, I was fighting for my life.[46]

Both Kearns and Dempsey now had the incentive to do anything necessary to win this fight, and to try to win it in the first round: Kearns had a $10,000 bet he could not cover and Dempsey felt he was fighting for his life.

Roger Kahn, in his interviews confirmed Dempsey's concern when he met Willard in the ring before the fight.

> He [Willard] stepped into the ring doffed his robe, and turned his back on Dempsey, and held both hands aloft.
>
> "I thought I was going to be sick to my stomach," Dempsey said. "Willard's back was a solid wall. His fists looked like they were as high in the air as I was tall. I saw muscles standing out on his back. Fat? He was in terrific shape. I said to myself, 'This guy is liable to kill me. I'm twenty-four years old, and I might get killed.'"[47]

The referee was Oliver Thomas Pecord, a welterweight who fought under the London Prize Ring rules in the 1880s. Pecord had refereed many local bouts in and around Toledo, but had not refereed anything even approaching a championship fight. Willard had strongly opposed having Pecord referee. He preferred having Tex Rickard be the third man in the ring, but once again he was overruled and Pecord was given the role.[48]

Once he was given the role, Pecord profoundly underestimated the complexity of the job before him. As he said before the fight:

> My work today in the title fight is plain. The rules of the Toledo Boxing Commission are not complicated and are thoroughly understood by both Willard and Dempsey. Each man wants only fair treatment. And wanting it they must give it. There shouldn't be the slightest question of honest boxing. Willard and Dempsey are in the front rank of the heavyweight division and to hold their profession and the championship contest on a high level, must be gentlemen in the ring.[49]

Being a gentleman in the ring was the last thing in Dempsey's mind at the time. He felt he was fighting for his life. This made him an extremely dangerous animal. But Pecord was oblivious to the nature of the coming events. He had never seen a fighter with the ferocity of Dempsey, and he had no idea what such a fighter might do in the ring. Instead, Pecord was a man who embodied the *Peter Principle*: He had been raised to his level of incompetence. As W.O. McGeehan put it, "his status before the elevation was that of a bartender in a dry town." Two years later, Pecord would burn down his own house by using a lit match to locate a gas leak. He was lucky he wasn't killed. This was the man whose decisions determined the outcome of the fight.[50]

Establishing the Rules

At the beginning of the fight it had been agreed that the fighters would follow some special rules put down by the Toledo Boxing Commission. These rules consisted of (1) No rabbit punches, (2) No kidney punches, (3) Fighting in the clinches was allowed as long as one arm was free, and (4) Breaking cleanly at the word of the referee. "Otherwise, straight Marquis [sic] of Queensberry rules will be followed." Then, on July 2, the rules again were changed and the prohibition on rabbit punches was dropped. Only kidney punches were forbidden. This was seen as a victory for Willard who wished to be able to box as long as one arm was free.[51]

Jess Willard went into the ring weighing 243 while Dempsey weighed 187. Both had lost weight in the last few days of training. The fight was to be a 12-round bout fought with special five-ounce gloves. Willard, however, used six-ounce gloves since the five-ounce gloves would not fit his hands. The ring was to be 20-foot square instead of the standard 24 feet, so as to allow room for more seats ringside. And the dressings on the hands were to be soft bandages with a reasonable amount of tape to hold the bandages on. Ring time was to be 3:30 p.m., but in fact it was nine minutes after 4 p.m. when the fight began. The sky was clear and the temperature was 110 degrees. The betting on July 4 was 10 to 8 in favor of Jess Willard.[52]

When the bell rang to start the fight, no one heard it. Willard, standing in his corner, looked around wondering when the bell would sound. Finally, W. Warren Barbour, the time keeper, blew a whistle to start the fight. This was a bad beginning.

Willard, not Dempsey, opened the fight by sending two lefts into Dempsey's face. Dempsey dodged and weaved out of distance from Willard's reach. He seemed to be sizing Willard up. Then he came in and they clinched. Willard, demonstrating his strength, swung Dempsey around and then broke the clinch, holding his arms up in the air. The agreement in the rules had been clean breaks, and Willard intended to do so. Dempsey swung a left to the jaw and a right and left to the body. Willard answered with a left to the mouth and a right to the eye. Again they clinched and again Willard broke with his arms high in the air. Dempsey kept his head down and his eyes seemed focused on Willard's chest. Flailing his arms, he drove in under Willard's guard and hit him with everything he had, rights and lefts in a whirlwind fashion. Willard grabbed him and

The James Montgomery Flagg painting of Willard towering over Dempsey at the beginning of their fight in Toledo, July 4, 1919, was commissioned by Jack Dempsey for his New York City restaurant located on Broadway between 49th and 50th streets.

walked him around in a circle then broke the clinch. Dempsey charged back in with rights and lefts pounding. Suddenly, a blow landed on Willard's jaw and the Champion went down for the first time in his career.

This was something for which Willard had trained. He had let several of his sparring partners hit him as hard as they could squarely on the jaw. He felt impervious to blows either on the jaw or on the body. Yet Dempsey's blows were something different. As Grantland Rice wrote: "He fell before a man who must be able to hit harder than any man who ever lived."[53]

Willard looked dazed and had a silly grin on his face. He started to get up. Dempsey hit him as soon as he had regained his feet, knocking him back into the ropes. Again Willard fell to the canvas. He rose and Dempsey attacked for a third time, flailing with both fists and again knocking Willard to the ground in Dempsey's own corner. This time Willard rose but only partially. He was bent over with his hands on the floor. Before he could stand up, Dempsey attacked and knocked him into the ropes with repeated blows to the head. For the fourth time Willard fell to the canvas. As he rose again, he tried to grab Dempsey and slow the flailing fists. Dempsey again drove him back again into Dempsey's own corner. This time Dempsey hit him in the kidneys from behind and delivered repeated blows to the head. Willard fell for the fifth time. Once again Willard got to his feet and tried to grab Dempsey, but Dempsey refused to let him clinch. Willard tried to use his arms to ward off Dempsey's blows and struggled across the ring to a neutral corner while Dempsey hit him repeatedly with blows to the head. Willard slumped to the canvas, holding on to the ropes. He was down on the canvas for the sixth time. Willard pulled himself up with the ropes for a seventh time. Before he could stand, Dempsey hit him again from behind in the kidneys and the head knocking him down into a sitting position in the neutral corner.[54]

The bell rang, but a rope on the canvas fouled the bell and prevented it from being heard. Willard was saved by the bell. But none of the officials save Warren Barbour, the timekeeper, were aware of this. Ollie Pecord, the referee, who thought he had counted Willard out, was distracted by the flood of people pouring into the ring. Instead of trying to keep order, he backed up and leaned against the far ropes to the left of Willard's corner. Doc Kearns ran across the ring to Pecord and talked to him in an agitated manner asking him to declare Dempsey the winner. Jimmy DeForest, who remained in Dempsey's corner, was yelling to Kearns to wait a minute that there was something wrong with the bell. "Shut up!" said Kearns. "For $100,000 who the hell cares if there's something wrong with the bell! Pecord! Pecord! Raise Jack's hand! Raise his hand! He's the new champ!"[55]

While they were talking, Barbour got Pecord's attention and told him the fight was not over.

For Kearns the possibility that he might have had Pecord raise Dempsey's hand was equal to the deed. He persuaded a number of newspaper reporters that in the confusion, this had indeed happened. Dempsey also said it occurred.

> And Ollie raised my hand, grinning. I was stunned. Doc rushed up to me, threw his arms tightly around me and told me to get out of the ring. I did, as people started to climb into the ring, Jimmy told me to move faster. We were by the press seats when Jimmy half turned and saw that the ring was in a state of chaos. Doc, half in and half out of the ropes, was frantically waving me back. Ollie had told him that the fight wasn't over, and Warren Barbour, the offi-

cial timekeeper, screamed over the confusion that if I didn't get back into the ring I'd be disqualified.[56]

Dempsey's account does not match the films of the event. Despite Kearns' assurances that Pecord raised Dempsey's hand as a signal that he had won, there is no sign of this at this time in the fight films. The most we see is Pecord pushing Dempsey back from the fallen Willard, before Pecord walks across the ring to the far side away from the camera. Then we have the picture of Kearns rushing over to argue with Pecord on the far side of the ring, in plain view of the camera, while Dempsey is led out of the ring, presumably by De Forest. Suddenly Pecord rushes across to Willard's side of the ring where Warren Barbour was seated. He bends down and learns that the fight is not over. Pecord is followed by Kearns, who, upon hearing the news, rushes towards Dempsey's corner (which is in the lower left hand of the screen) and (standing half in and half out of the ring) calls Dempsey back into ring.

Presumably Kearns knew earlier from Jimmy DeForest that the round had ended before Willard was counted out. Due to the $10,000 bet he had on Dempsey, Kearns was trying to finesse a one-round knockout. It was, as Charles Samuels said, the "maddest swindle" of Kearns' life. Had he been able to get Pecord to declare Dempsey the winner at the end of the first round, Kearns would have won $100,000, Dempsey would have been the champion, and Willard, if he complained at all, would have been nothing but a sore loser. As it was, Pecord did not raise Dempsey's hand and Dempsey was forced to return to the ring under the threat of being disqualified and losing the match. Barbour knew the rules, even if the referee and the judges did not. Kearns actions at this time show clearly that he was trying to steal the championship and that Dempsey was willing to go along.

Breaking the Rules

Kearns was lucky. "Pecord was an inexperienced home-town referee, or he would have disqualified Dempsey for leaving the ring before the fight was officially over. In the confusion, however, he permitted the fight to continue. That was the one reason that Kearns' recklessness did not cost his man-killer the title."[57]

Damon Runyon put a threatening spin on this. Writing the next day, he said the following: "Some have suggested that Dempsey's leaving the ring might have constituted a technical infringement of the rules, but no one would have had the nerve to advance such a technicality after that first round. It was obvious that Willard was whipped."[58]

Interestingly, at least one reporter did have the nerve to declare that Dempsey should have lost the fight at that point. This was Nellie Bly, the sport butterfly who covered the fight for *The New York Evening Journal*. In her report the day after the fight she stated:

According to all rules and precedents Dempsey forfeited the fight when he left the ring and did not return to his corner to await the order of the referee.

It was boyish and impulsive. But it was strictly unethical, and had the referee been alert he would never have permitted it to happen.[59]

Although her voice was a whisper in the wind, Nellie Bly understood the rules of the ring better than Damon Runyon and most of the male reporters, and she was not afraid to say so. Furthermore, Willard was not whipped. He came back to battle for two more rounds. Runyon's comments reflect his close association with Dempsey and with Doc Kearns. He made Willard into a "ponderous fellow" with a "doughlike body" who did not deserve to be in the same ring with "the young mountain lion in human form." For Runyon, it was inconvenient when Willard did not lie down quietly at the end of round one. It was equally inconvenient for anybody to suggest that "technically" Dempsey should have been disqualified.

Although there was plenty of reason to do so, no challenge was urged that Dempsey had defaulted by leaving the ring before the fight was over. Had Willard had a manager like Tom Jones or Kid McCoy working in his corner, they might have demanded that Dempsey be disqualified. It was well established by the London Prize Ring rules of 1853 (which were eventually incorporated in the Marquess of Queensberry rules of circa 1865), "That any pugilist voluntarily quitting the ring previous to the deliberate judgment of the referee being obtained, shall be deemed to have lost the fight."[60]

By voluntarily quitting the ring, Dempsey should have lost the fight. On the other hand, had Kearns gotten Pecord to lift Dempsey's hand in triumph that would have qualified as a "deliberate judgment of the referee," and would have legitimized Dempsey's departure. But this did not happen. Willard was his own manager at the time, and he was otherwise engaged, as were all his corner men. Since no one in Willard's corner complained, Kearns hustled Dempsey back into the ring, and the fight went on.

None of the reporters were aware, or seemed to be aware, of the numerous other things that might have disqualified Dempsey in this fight. According to the Toledo rules, kidney punches had been outlawed. Yet, it appears that twice Dempsey used kidney punches to disable Willard. No reporters commented on these blows.[61]

These mistakes were not the only ones Pecord made in this round. A more comprehensive mistake lay in the way Pecord handled Dempsey when Willard fell to the canvas. We often hear that in 1919 there was no rule requiring Dempsey to go to a neutral corner when Willard fell. This is true as far as it goes. But it does not go far enough. It is true that the neutral-corner rule was only introduced in the Tunney-Dempsey fight of 1927. But prior to that, between 1865 and 1927 there was a rule which governed all bouts fought under the Marquess of Queensberry rules and which should have been second nature to Dempsey and Pecord. Rule 4 in the Marquess of Queensberry rules of 1865, states: "If either man fall through weakness or otherwise, he must get up unassisted, ten seconds to be allowed him to do so, *the other man meanwhile to return to his corner, and when the fallen man is on his legs the round is to be resumed*, and continue until the three minutes have expired."[62]

This was the same exact wording of the rule which governed the fight between John L. Sullivan and James J. Corbett and all the heavyweight championship fights from 1892 on. To argue that Dempsey was not aware of this rule is ridiculous.[63]

Dempsey ignored the new rule to which he had agreed in the second Tunney fight, just as he ignored the old rule to which he had agreed in the Willard fight. This was typical of Dempsey. Paul Gallico described Dempsey's behavior in the ring with Luis Firpo which mimicked his behavior in the ring with Willard:

> According to the rules he [Dempsey] was not even a fair fighter and in the heat of the battle the niceties of ring comportment went by the board. Often many of the blows he sprayed from his weaving, catlike crouch were low. Against Firpo, half maddened by battle lust, he stood over the fallen challenger when he knocked him down, instead of retiring to a corner for the count and slogged him again when he had barely regained his feet. And once, even stood behind him and hit him on the rise. The referee, himself, stunned by the fury of the fight in which he found himself involved, let Dempsey get away with it.[64]

Dempsey got away with these actions against Firpo, just as he had gotten away with them against Willard.

Dempsey's predilection to ignore the rules was well known at the time. Damon Runyon, writing before the Willard fight, while praising Dempsey, explained that "Dempsey cares mighty little about the form of the rules." This was clear in Dempsey's behavior. Ignoring the rules in 1919 won him the championship; ignoring the rules in 1927 cost him the championship. He robbed Willard in 1919 and he may have robbed himself in 1927. What goes around comes around.[65]

Arthur Daley, writing in 1965, reviewing the Joe Stone film about Willard's life, noted that

> One observer counted six distinct fouls [by Dempsey]. It was like a barroom fight and Ollie Pecord, the referee, never raised as much as a little finger to check the flagrant misbehavior.
>
> "Pecord didn't referee the first round," wryly commented Big Jess on the sound track. "He just witnessed it."[66]

Despite the fact that none of the male reporters had the nerve to suggest that Dempsey should have forfeited the bout for technical reasons, several were brave enough to suggest that Willard should have lost sooner for technical reasons. Frank Menke and Otto Floto, both writing in *The Kansas City Post*, suggested that the delay caused by Dempsey leaving the ring had actually benefited Willard. Frank Menke noted that it took two minutes and four seconds to get Dempsey back in the ring and start round two. Otto Floto declared it was two minutes and 46 seconds. This gave Willard extra time to recuperate. They did not complain that Dempsey left the ring illegally, but they did complain when he was gone so long that Willard gained an advantage. They choked on the gnat and swallowed the camel.[67]

In addition, Floto and Menke both complained that Pecord took too long to begin his counts when Willard went down. Floto noted that on the first knockdown, Pecord "walked clean across the ring to where Jess fell before he began to count." This allowed Willard 15 seconds to recover. Menke faulted Pecord for taking too long to count during the sixth knockdown when Willard was hanging on the ropes in a neutral corner. His view was that Willard was in "a position that the Marquis [sic] of Queensberry, as well as the Toledo Boxing Commission rules specify as reason for the referee to begin counting. But Pecord did not count." According to Menke, Willard wobbled on the ropes for about eight seconds and then dropped to the floor. "Then—and only then—did Pecord start his count." Floto further argued that there were 16 seconds left when the bell rang to end the round, so Dempsey should have won then.[68]

Everyone admits that Pecord was a bad referee. We cannot address the amount of time on the counts, given the fact that Pecord was certainly not following the rules. But he was not wrong in the last case Menke cites. Menke was referring to no. 5 of the Queensberry rules, which reads: "A man hanging on the ropes in a helpless state, *with his toes off the ground,* shall be considered down." Willard was indeed hanging on the ropes, but his feet were not off the ground, and Pecord was correct not to begin counting until Willard actually dropped to the floor.[69]

Overall, Menke blamed Pecord for allowing the fight to go on when he knew the bell was malfunctioning. This, Menke believed, was the major mistake of the fight. But Menke was wrong again: the major mistakes that Pecord made were to not require Dempsey to return to his corner when Willard went down and to not penalize Dempsey when he left the ring before the fight was over.

The Effect of the Fight

To be fair, it was not really Dempsey's responsibility to keep track of the rules. That was the responsibility of the judges (Tex Rickard and Major Anthony J. Drexel Biddle) and the referee, Ollie Pecord. When Dempsey hit Willard and knocked him to the canvas the first time, Pecord should have required him to go to his corner and allowed Willard to rise. This did not happen. And when Pecord ignored the rule, the two judges should have declared a foul. All three of them should have insisted that Dempsey obey the rule. But they did not. Nor did any of them protest when the same thing happened after all the other knockdowns. The fight films clearly show Ollie Pecord having to shove Dempsey away from Willard so that Pecord could start his count. Dempsey crowded Willard and stood so close to him that the very second his knees left the canvas, and even before he was on his legs, Dempsey was ready to hit him again. Had judges or Pecord followed the Marquess of Queensberry rules (as they said they planned to do) Willard would not have been knocked down so many times in the first round. Either that, or Dempsey would have been disqualified.[70]

The only innovation which occurred in 1927 was that the rule now specified that instead of going to *his* corner, Dempsey had to go to a *neutral* corner at a knockdown. But in 1919, Dempsey did not leave Willard's side. The only time Dempsey went to *his* corner was when Willard happened to be knocked down in that corner. Most of the time the rules did not apply. Even given all of this, Willard's strength was such that though Dempsey ignored the rules and knocked Willard down seven times in the first round, he could not knock him out.

Willard's own description of his situation at that time is of interest:

> Writing about the fight various boxing reporters have said that Dempsey's punches landed against my face and body had the sound of a blackjack or a baseball bat striking flesh when they landed. After Dempsey's first effective punch landed to my head I felt as though I had been hit with a swift moving brickbat-the shocking power was that great. For the first time I went down from a blow received in a ring fight. This punch left me shaken and dizzy for the rest of the fight-an easy target for scores of other punches delivered by Dempsey. I got up after the first knockdown, trying to gather myself together after the crushing blow I had received. My memory of what happened after that is understandably vague.[71]

Clearly, Dempsey hurt Willard badly in the first round. Willard himself admits it. But Willard's stamina was so great that he was able to go two more rounds with Dempsey despite his beating. Earlier in this narrative, we have mentioned that in the first fight between Jim Coffey and Frank Moran, Coffey was counted out even though he was up and walking around in the ring. It can happen that the reflex to get up and continue the battle is so great that even fighters who are out on their feet can continue to fight. However, in Coffey's case, he had lost the power to defend himself despite being up on his feet. Coffey stood gazing aimlessly around at the crowd and had no idea he was in the ring. He could not protect himself against Moran's blows, so the fight was properly stopped. Willard, however, never lost the ability to defend himself. Although he did not remember his own actions, he continued to stand and fight back against Dempsey's blows. Try as Dempsey might, he could not knock Willard out, nor could he even knock him down after that first round. Indeed, Dempsey later admitted that several of Willard's blows in these following rounds rocked him.

Willard's comments about the last two rounds show his determination, despite his beating.

> The things that happened in the next two rounds I have been told of, read about or seen in the uncut version of the motion picture of the fight. The knockdowns and punishment I had taken in the first round had messed me up pretty bad. If any thought kept me going it must have been that I always felt that I could knock out any fighter I got a chance to hit and that sooner or later I would get a chance to unload against Dempsey. It was reported that I did get to him with a couple of good punches in the third round, but I have no memory of it. After the third round my seconds ended the fight.[72]

Walter Monahan, in an interview with T.A. Dorgan (TAD), confirmed this.

> When I picked him off the floor at the end of the first round he said to me "What's the matter? What? What is this?" Gee, we gave him the ice water and the smelling salts but he wasn't right even when he went out for the second round. When he got back from the third round he was worse than ever.
>
> He asked me, "What's up? Is the fight still on? What kind of fight is it?" He was gone. We all knew it. We held a consultation and decided to throw up the sponge. Willard didn't tell me to throw it up.[73]

There have been many stories about how badly Willard was beaten in the fight, how he lost six teeth, had several broken ribs, had a broken jaw and many other unpleasant injuries. Yet none of these actually occurred. Certainly he had been mauled. The right side of his face was cut and swollen. He bled a lot. He had a large lump over his left eye. But besides cuts over his eyes and cuts on his lips, he had no permanent damage. Nor did he spend any time in the hospital after the fight. Instead, he was driven home by Ray O. Archer, his business manager, and tended to by his wife. Hattie put him on a davenport, sat down by his side and applied ice cloths to his face and closed right eye. He did admit that it took him several hours to recover from the hook that Dempsey used to knock him down the first time.

"That was the blow that started me on defeat," Willard said. "I felt physically able to continue but my head wasn't clear and my eye was closed and I realized it would have been useless for me to attempt to box while half-blinded."[74]

What has not been mentioned as frequently was the fact that Dempsey himself suffered in the fight. He had commented earlier that he would not mind having light bindings on his hands since having heavy bandages would cause him to become arm weary. Nonetheless he came into the fight with heavy bandages on his hands and, by the end of the second round, his arms felt like lead weights. "By now I was feeling exhausted and my body was throbbing. I couldn't for the life of me imagine going the scheduled 12 rounds. The heat had started to get to me; I felt as though I had no air as I kept sucking it in."

By the end of round three Dempsey declared that "I was sapped both mentally and physically." The only thing that held him up was the recognition that Willard was in much worse shape. Dempsey had punched himself out in three rounds with Willard. He worried that Willard might come back for more. And Willard might have done so if his eyes had not been damaged. If Willard had been saved by the bell in round one, Dempsey was saved by Willard's eyes in round four. By the third round, Willard's right eye was closed and he had trouble seeing out of his left. He could no longer see to fight. This time Dempsey had indeed won.[75]

As soon as the towel was thrown in, Willard got up off his corner stool and walked into the ring to meet Dempsey to shake hands and offer congratulations. Technically, Willard was out. Physically he was not. But before they met, Ollie Pecord did indeed raise Dempsey's hand in the ring to demonstrate that he was the new champion. Then the new champion was raised up on the shoulders of the crowd in triumph, while Willard walked back to his dressing room saying to himself: "I have a $100,000 and a farm in Kansas; I have a $100,000 and a farm in Kansas; I have a $100,000 and a farm in Kansas."[76]

Dempsey and his supporters celebrated until late into the night. But the bout was not over yet. When Dempsey finally went to bed, he recalled being troubled by nightmares of the fight.

> In my dream, Willard had knocked me out. I woke up in a cold sweat, confused. I climbed out of bed and stumbled into the bathroom, turning on the overhead light. I peered at my face and saw some small dried patches of blood on it. I felt paralyzed. Pulling on my pants and shirt, I rushed out into the hall.... I ran outside, my heartbeat pounding in my ears. A newsboy was hollering: Extra, Extra! Read all about it !"
>
> "Ain't you Jack Dempsey?" the newsboy asked.
>
> "Yeah, Why?"
>
> I grabbed a paper. There it was, my name in big, bold headlines. I was the Heavyweight Champion of the World. All of a sudden, standing barefoot on the street with a newsboy at my side, I felt the full impact of my victory. I had the impulse to yell, Look at me! I did it! but I held myself back. I reached in my pockets to give the kid a buck but found my pockets empty. I told him to pick it up in the morning from the room clerk.
>
> "You don't owe me nothin' Champ!"[77]

The Aftermath of the Fight: Were Dempsey's Gloves Loaded?

The fight left the public in confusion. When did it end? And was Jess Willard knocked out?

Ollie Pecord ultimately decided that Willard had been knocked out and that event occurred in the third round. Warren Barbour, whom we have already established knew more about the rules than Pecord, said that the fight had actually ended in the fourth round, since the towel was thrown in after the bell to begin the round had already sounded. But Pecord's status as referee overruled Barbour as timekeeper.[78]

The conventional reporting of the outcome of the fight dwelt on the blood and gore associated with it. Otto Floto, of *The Kansas City Post*, was typical.

> Never in the history of heavyweight encounters did a principal receive such terrific punishment. No one can recall a time when a principal was practically slaughtered as they butcher

the beef in our packing industries. He spat blood by the cupful and the red fluid of life just ran in streamlets from his mouth, nose and the cuts below his eyes. His optics were completely closed, not even a slit could be discerned in his right eye. Blood from head to foot covered him and even his conqueror was finally seized with compassion and any feeling of bitter thought he may have held against Jess melted.[79]

Floto also mentions the unnatural sound of Dempsey's gloves hitting Willard.

> To have watched this enormous human being, this Kansas Leviathan, drop to the floor like beef and listen to the sickening thud of the padded gauntlet with which Dempsey executed the stunt, you'd conclude immediately that only something out of the ordinary could withstand these shell shocks and live. The noise resembled the noise made by dropping a handful of clay into a tub of water, a sort of "kerplunk."[80]

Herbert Corey, writing in *The Kansas City Star,* was more concerned with the reaction of the crowd.

> A pitiless crowd jeered at the man who had been champion as he stumbled out of the ring. He was all alone. Not even a second remained to give him a touch of the elbow on his road toward oblivion.
>
> "Yah," they screamed at him. "Coward, quitter!"
>
> Tears ran down his crushed and swollen face and mingled with his blood. One eye was closed entirely. The other so swollen he could barely see. He felt his way through the hostile crowd like some great animal seeking a friendly thicket. His mouth hung open. His lips were cut and broken. An animal odor of perspiration rose from his wet body.
>
> "Why didn't you die in the ring?" men yelled at him and shook scornful hands in his face.
>
> He reeled on, soundless, panting, unaided.[81]

T. A. Dorgan (TAD), who supported Dempsey, did not endorse the view that Willard was a quitter. Instead, Dorgan was amazingly sympathetic.

> He did quit, of course, but he quit only when he could go no further. No champion ever took a pasting such as he took.... You must remember that Willard was knocked down hard every time he took the count. He never once dropped to avoid punishment. He took everything that Dempsey had and then fought two rounds more before he quit. No one wanted to see any more of that fight.
>
> Willard quit when nature quit him. He held out just as long as he could and then caved in. No man who took the licking that he did in that first round and then came out for more in the second is a quitter.[82]

Willard proved to be gracious in defeat. "There is little to add [to] what is already known. After that first hard swing to the jaw, in the first round, Dempsey came in so fast that I never had a chance to clear my head and square away for a better offense or defense. I was fighting in a daze. This is no attempt to alibi my defeat or take the credit from Dempsey, who is a fast, clever, hard-hitting opponent, ranking with the best of the heavyweights."[83]

As W.O. McGeehan summed it up: "There is no alibi from the champion. He was no hollow shell. If he had not been in the best of condition he would have died there in the ring under the terrific punishment that Dempsey administered to him."[84]

On July 7, William Rocap, a sporting writer from Philadelphia, who had been considered as referee for the fight, contended that there had been collusion between Rickard and Willard, but that was rejected by a commission appointed to look into the allegations. The fight, as far as Toledo was concerned, was on the up and up.[85]

But was it? Many people were astonished at the power Dempsey was able to deliver in the first round. Grantland Rice summed it up by saying: "He [Willard] fell before a man who must be able to hit harder than any man who ever lived." But others were puzzled that Dempsey could no longer deliver the same power in the two succeeding rounds. Then, two days after the fight was over, Jack Doyle, a New York Commission Agent or Bookmaker, suggested that something more was involved in Willard's defeat.

> I don't want to detract from Dempsey's victory a bit, for he certainly showed his superiority over Willard and won the championship in a clean-cut and decisive manner. Nor do I want to detract from his hitting power. He showed he can land on an opponent hard enough to knock them down, from the worst to the best, but it hardly seems possible any man can hit so hard with a gloved fist as to cut up Willard in such shape as Dempsey did.

Doyle then raised the issue that has haunted Dempsey's victory since the fight. "It is possible for plaster of paris in powder form to be sprinkled within the bandages. It has been done and when they are examined in merely a superficial manner, it is impossible to detect the substance. Powdered plaster of paris gets as solid as a piece of lead when it becomes moistened."[86]

Doyle noted that the men were supposed to enter the ring bare-handed and have their bandages applied in the ring. But they both came in with bandages on their hands. Dempsey "entered the ring taped well down the wrist almost to the finger tips." Willard, "to be sure, also entered with bandages on, but they barely ran around his big hands."

Doyle's suggestion that Dempsey might have used plaster of paris was an idea with a history. It became a virtual certainty when Jack "Doc" Kearns stated in an article in *Sports Illustrated,* that he had in fact loaded Dempsey's bandages with plaster of paris. Kearns learned this trick from the early glove fighters, many of whom had historically used plaster on their bandages. When Charles "Kid" McCoy (Norman Selby) fought Tommy Ryan in 1896, the Kid had his hands bandaged with adhesive plaster. This made his hands as hard as a mallet and cut Ryan's face each time McCoy hit it. Jim Jeffries discounted the claim that Bob Fitzsimmons was going to use plaster on his bandages in their second fight, in 1902. "Let him do it," Jeffries remarked, "I'll flatten him anyway." Fitzsimmons did use plaster of paris in his gloves and cut up Jeffries so severely that those who compared the two at the end of the match swore that Jeffries must have lost. Fitzsimmons however broke both hands and Jeffries knocked him out in the eighth round. When Stanley Ketchel fought Jack Johnson in 1909 and knocked him to the canvas "the bandages on his [Ketchel's] hands were as hard as flint, and each wrist was encircled by a leather strap."[87]

The introduction of glove fighting introduced options that had not been available in the bare-knuckle era. This gave room for a great deal of creativity for managers and seconds as they prepared their fighter for the bout. As an article published in 1911 put it:

> All seconds pull away the padding over the knuckles, thus allowing their man to hit with practically a skin glove over his hands, unless he happens to have a sore or damaged fin. Then they as solicitously heap up the padding over the injured knuckle, and thus strive to protect their boy from further suffering. Manipulation of the padding, though, is understood and expected by every fighter. It's the things they put inside the gloves that must be watched for and detected.
>
> Powdered plaster of paris, dropped into the gloves, will harden and form a cast over the knuckles of the fighter who puts a wet hand into glove, but only a "boob" will let the glove out of sight while the opposing second monkeys with it.[88]

Once again, Kid McCoy was cited as a fighter who specialized in the use of plaster of paris. "Kid McCoy soaked his bandages in a solution of plaster of paris, and they looked innocent while his seconds adjusted them. Two minutes later-safe inside the glove-they solidified and became as hard as granite."[89]

Kid McCoy had asked Jess if he could serve as his manager for the Dempsey fight, but Jess turned McCoy down. He had no manager in his corner to protect him against such tricks, and when the going got tough, he had no manager who could raise objections to any actions happening in or out of the ring. Willard's greatest mistake in the Dempsey fight was not his training methods, but his lack of a manager. This was Willard's own fault. Interestingly, Dempsey was to later fall into the same trap in his fights with Tunney.

This debate over Dempsey's gloves has continued from the time that Jack Doyle first raised it on July 7, 1919. In 2004 it was analyzed by Monte Cox in an article entitled "Were Dempsey's Gloves Loaded? You Decide!"[90]

Cox does a brilliant job of dealing with the complex issues involved. He begins by posing three propositions: (1) Dempsey's hand wraps were treated with plaster of paris; or (2) Dempsey held a railroad spike/iron bolt in his glove (a possibility proposed by Joe Stone); or (3) Dempsey's gloves were not loaded. After examining all the evidence on the three propositions, Cox came to these conclusions.

(A) Plaster of paris is not feasible as it would likely have been detected before the fight. If it were not, it would break up in the glove, serving no useful purpose. If neither of these things happened, it would have been detected when the gloves were taken off.

(B) Dempsey could not have carried a railroad spike or iron bolt into the ring and used it on Willard, as there were many times when Dempsey's gloves were open during the first round and he could not have hidden the spike.

(C) Therefore, Dempsey's gloves were not loaded.

Yet questions remain.

(1) Jess Willard was a hard man to knock down. In fact, Dempsey's knockdown of Willard in Round One was the first time in Willard's ring career that he had ever hit the canvas in a fight. Nor was this a simple knockdown. When Dempsey hit Willard the first time, he hit him so hard that Willard did not recover until more than an hour and a half after the fight. Willard felt that he had been hit with a "brickbat."[91]

(2) Doc Kearns said he had used plaster of paris to load Dempsey's gloves in the Willard fight. This was not the only time Kearns claimed to have loaded Dempsey's gloves. During their vaudeville days in 1919 before the Willard fight, Kearns and Dempsey provided a $1,000 challenge to anyone who could stay three rounds with Dempsey. Kearns had hired a ringer, Max (The Goose) Kaplan, to come out of the crowd when the $1,000 announcement was made and take Dempsey on. But in Trenton, New Jersey, a fellow named "Curly" Monroe beat "Goose" Kaplan to the stage and challenged Dempsey instead. Kearns was afraid that Dempsey might lose the bet, but could not deny Monroe a chance to fight, so he delayed their fight until the next night.

"Figuring that Monroe would be on hand, I had readied Dempsey for this exhibition as if it was for the title, loading Jack's hands with heavy tin foil and wrapping them carefully in heavy black bicycle tape. I also cautioned him to fight this guy as carefully as if he was facing Willard."

This seemed to be a dress rehearsal for the Willard fight and Dempsey knocked Monroe out in the first round. Although Dempsey did not use plaster of paris in fighting Curly

Monroe, he clearly knew his gloves were loaded. And Kearns, twice in this paragraph, instructed Dempsey to fight as if he were fighting Willard for the title.[92]

(3) Kearns statement that he loaded Dempsey's gloves for the Willard fight has been generally assumed to be one final attempt to harm Dempsey. Saying that Dempsey did not win the championship in a fair fight appears to be clearly designed to damage Dempsey's reputation. But if his goal was to damage Dempsey's reputation, why did Doc state that Dempsey was not aware of this trick? What was his motive in shielding Dempsey in this way? If Kearns had wanted to protect Dempsey, he need not have raised the issue about plaster in the gloves at all. On the other hand, why would Kearns say Dempsey won the championship by having loaded gloves, but then say that Dempsey was not aware of the fraud, unless the accusation was true?[93]

(4) Who did wrap Dempsey's hands? Kearns in his article in *Sports Illustrated* said that he wrapped Dempsey's hands. Dempsey, in his rebuttal to Kearns, said that he wrapped his own hands. Billy McCarney, who claimed to be in the dressing room that day, agreed that Dempsey wrapped his own hands. But in his autobiography Dempsey said that Jimmy De Forest wrapped his hands. And Nat Fleischer, who also claimed to be in the dressing room that day, agreed that De Forest wrapped Dempsey's hands. The question of who wrapped Dempsey's hands is at the heart of the controversy.[94]

(5) John Hollis writing in *Boxing Illustrated* (May 1964) attempted to prove scientifically that plaster of paris applied to the bandages as Kearns described would not work. After putting water and then plaster on the bandages of Cleveland "The Big Cat" Williams in this experiment, he had him heat his hands by a stove for 35 minutes. Then Williams hit a heavy punching bag, not with gloved hands but with the unprotected bandages. The reason given was that the amount of plaster used on the bandages made it too tight to get ten-ounce gloves on Williams' hands. After five blows, the unprotected bandages broke up and the plaster fell apart. This supposedly proved that Dempsey, fighting with five-ounce gloves in 114-degree heat at Toledo, could not have used plaster of paris on his bandages.[95]

Plaster of paris was so named after a gypsum deposit found in Montmartre in Paris. It was used by Michelangelo in making frescoes and by women in the 1700s for beauty spots. There are a number of types of plaster of paris, therefore we cannot be sure that the plaster of paris used in this experiment is the same type of plaster of paris used by Kearns. In addition Dempsey had gloves on his hands when he hit Willard. We cannot tell what condition the bandages were in after that first round. We do know two things: (1) At the end of round one, Kearns told Dempsey to leave the ring as soon as the first round was over even though Dempsey had not a scratch on him. This was contrary to normal circumstances where the winner stays in the ring to accept the plaudits of the fans and (2) when called back to the ring for rounds two and three, Dempsey could not knock Willard down or out, despite Willard's weakened condition. This allows us to question whether *Boxing Illustrated* used the same plaster in the same way that the early boxers, such as Kid McCoy would have done or that Kearns might have done on Dempsey's hands.

(6) According to Monte Cox, "Historian J.J. Johnston puts the nail in the coffin of the plaster of paris theory with the following observation, 'The films show Willard upon entering the ring walking over to Dempsey and examining his hands. That should end any possibility of plaster of paris or any other substance on his hands.'" I do not see this in my copy of the Frank G. Hall films. Instead, I see Willard walking over to briefly shake Dempsey's hand and then promptly returning to his corner. This seems to take less than

a minute. I do not see him examining Dempsey's hands before the gloves go on. Unless Johnston had access to some type of film not commonly seen, this can hardly be conclusive proof that Dempsey did not use plaster of paris as Kearns said he did.[96]

(7) In the *Sports Illustrated* article, Kearns said that he had removed the bandages from Dempsey's hands. Contrary to that "Teddy Hayes, one of Dempsey's seconds, said he was the one who cut off Dempsey's gloves, not Kearns. 'I snipped it right in front of a whole milling crowd in the dressing room. Don't you think if there was plaster of paris, Kearns would have been there, standing guard? And you can't cut off plaster of paris with a pair of scissors. I would have to have had a hacksaw.'" It is difficult to analyze the veracity of Hayes' statement for a few reasons: (1) There was chaos and confusion in the dressing room at that time. It would have been hard to tell what actually happened and what people saw; (2) The goal Dempsey's camp had been working for years had been achieved. What incentive would Hayes or anybody there have had to spoil it?; (3) If the idea of the plaster breaking up under the conditions of the fight had any validity, it may not have been intact after three rounds. If so, there may have been no need for a hacksaw to cut his bandages off. This may also explain why Dempsey could not knock Willard out or even put him on the floor in the last two rounds. Frank Menke wrote that Dempsey hit Willard only 19 times in round one, but he hit Willard 31 times in round two and 26 times in round three. Despite having Willard nearly defenseless in rounds two and three, and being able to hit him many more times, Dempsey did not show the same power in those last two rounds that he showed in the first round. If Dempsey had used something in his gloves to get more power in his blows in the first round, by the beginning of the second round it was clearly not working. If plaster was used, had it broken up by that time?[97]

(8) Doc Kearns was dying when he wrote this article. Might it not be seen as a deathbed confession? And if so, might it be the ultimate con? Red Smith quoted Joe H. Palmer as saying: "The next best thing to a lie is a true story that nobody will believe." Could this be Kearns' legacy to us? Was Doc Kearns telling us a true story that nobody would believe?[98]

(9) Finally, Pete Herman, an old-time world champion bantamweight, claimed that he possessed Dempsey's gloves from the Willard fight and that they showed no traces of plaster of paris in them. Unfortunately this cannot be authenticated. Herman, who had been blind since he was 25, did not get the gloves from Dempsey. Instead he says: "A seaman, I can't even remember his name now, gave me the gloves 20 or 25 years ago. He knew how close Jack and I were so he promised them to me. I had to wait a long time to get them even after this guy promised them to me, but he finally came across with them." Regretfully, there is nothing in this story which can help us unravel this puzzle.[99]

Putting aside this controversy of the loaded gloves, we still have ample evidence on other grounds that the fight was fraudulently managed. Willard was robbed of the decision. Willard should not have lost the Dempsey fight, but he did. It is interesting to analyze this fight, but we cannot alter the decision.

> The moving finger writes; and, having writ,
> Moves on: nor all thy piety nor wit
> Shall lure it back to cancel half a line,
> Nor all thy tears wash out a word of it.[100]

The Lesson of the Willard-Dempsey Fight

Willard was robbed of his title in the Dempsey fight. That is established. But was that bad? Willard had become a wealthy man through boxing, but he had never liked it. He was not unhappy to leave the ring at that time to return to his farm in Kansas. Nor was his wife, nor were his children upset. Hattie said that she was sorry that Jess was beaten, "but I can truly say I am happy that he's no longer champion. It means that we shall be able to live in peace. Jess will become a private citizen again." And, when interviewed in Lawrence after the fight, 11-year-old Zella, speaking for the children, responded: "Dempsey champion? Huh-we should worry!"[101]

Dempsey, on the other hand, was delighted to win the title. He promised to be a fighting champion. Certainly he brought excitement to a sport which had been languishing under Willard's regime. Dempsey was young and charismatic. People were willing to forgive him, even if he cheated, because he was so dynamic.

But there was more to it than that. The world had just passed through a long and bloody war. Those who survived were more ruthless, more hardened, more on edge than the previous generation had been. Dempsey embodied the Jazz Age. The new music of Jazz was livelier, had a harsher tone, and more violent rhythms than previous times. Willard was a man of the pre-war era. He liked the music of John Phillip Sousa. Dempsey delighted in butchering his opponents; Willard was repelled by this. As he was to say of himself after the fight:

> My heart was never in the fighting game. I was made a fighter. I have never had the fighting instinct nor the fighting temperament. I was only roused to a fighting pitch by previous fights after I had been hurt, and today I was virtually knocked out before I had fairly started. I will probably go to my home in Chicago for a few days and later to my farm in Lawrence, Kas. After this in all probability I will be plain Jess Willard, citizen.[102]

Jess Willard was a man of an earlier age. He did not want to be in the limelight. He was more comfortable among his family than visiting night clubs and enjoying the company of reporters and movie stars. He did little to stimulate news stories. He could no longer bring excitement to boxing. Jack Dempsey could and did. And that was good for boxing.

The lesson of the Willard-Dempsey fight seems to be that everyone benefited. Willard got his $100,000. He was defeated, but not seriously hurt, and he was able to get out of the limelight, which he detested. Dempsey got the title and the opportunity to get into the limelight which he sought. He lost Kearns' bet of $10,000 but he would have many more paydays ahead. And he did not have a mark on him. Boxing itself benefited by having a new champion who fit the times and who made it exciting again. Dempsey's style of fighting and his charisma did a great deal to make boxing popular all over the United States. Because of Dempsey's popularity, boxing matches gradually became legal and became one of the great spectator sports.[103]

Willard, Dempsey and Boxing all benefited. It was an amazing result for a fraudulent fight.

10

Jess Willard Returns

Living in Lawrence and Farming in Kansas

Jess Willard came home from Toledo in a chauffeur-driven seven-passenger car with his wife and two friends. He was no longer the World Champion; he was just Jess Willard, a wealthy businessman. But he was not as wealthy as he might have liked. The Progressive Income Tax had been adopted in 1913 and a war surtax added in 1917. Willard's share of the $100,000 purse had dwindled to $68,530 by the time the tax man turned it over to him. Dempsey, on the other hand, received $23,970 out of his purse of $27,500. But Dempsey also owed $10,000, due to Doc Kearns' 10 to 1 bet that he would knock Willard out in the first round. Neither man made as much out of the fight as they had imagined.[1]

Willard's first stop on his way home was in Chicago on July 10, where he and Hattie stayed at the Blackwood Hotel on the North Side. He was met there by a reporter:

> The right side of his face was somewhat swollen and there were discolorations, especially under the right eye. There were also contusions about the lower lip, which was garnished with a strip of cornplaster. His slow smile revealed somewhat irregular but apparently sound teeth.
>
> "Hello, Jess," said the reporter. "How do you feel?"
>
> "Hello," said Willard, "I'm feeling great. Would you like to spar a few rounds?"[2]

Contrary to earlier comments, Willard was not badly hurt by the Dempsey fight.

From Chicago, they went to Hannibal, Missouri, where they arrived on July 12. In Hannibal, the chauffeur got lost and took a wrong turn. Immediately the big car attracted a crowd which grew when it was recognized that it contained Jess Willard. The crowd was friendly and it took a while before they would let Willard and his party drive away.

When he got to Bucklin, a town of about 800 residents, his car got stuck in the muddy roads due to the heavy rainstorm which had occurred that morning. Willard was forced to put the car on a freight train and for the party to board the Burlington passenger train for Kansas City. At the depot, Willard again drew a crowd. He leaned out of the train window and said: "Boys, I am out of the fight game and am now a plain business man. I am going home to vote for hard surface roads. On this trip I have seen the need for them."[3]

Jess and Hattie arrived in Kansas City at Union Station by themselves, their two friends having parted company with them earlier. From Kansas City, Jess and his wife took the 7:30 p.m. Kaw Valley Interurban train from the Tenth and Main station to Lawrence and arrived there at 9:30 p.m. But there were no joyous crowds to meet him. Silence greeted his return. No newspaper reporters attended his arrival. Willard and Hattie drove to their house at 1700 West 9th Street (what is now 9th and Iowa streets), noticed only by a few "loafers" who hung around the interurban station.[4]

As champion Willard had always felt uncomfortable around crowds. He was not a great people-person. He did not delight in the adulation of his fans and indeed tried to avoid it as much as he could. Now that he was ex-champion, the people began to pay him back: they ignored him. But Lawrence had a special reason to ignore Willard. Many of the town's people had lost money on the sure thing of his victory over Dempsey. W.G. "Billy" Hutson, owner of the largest hotel in Lawrence, was particularly bitter. He had been one of the group of Lawrencians who passed out money touting Jess in Toledo, and who may have bet $1,000 on a Willard victory. Jess' loss hit him hard.

The fickleness of Lawrence residents was a disappointment to Willard and his family. Willard's confidence that he would easily dispose of Dempsey had led many of his friends to bet on his victory. But Willard had not forced anybody to bet on him. That was their choice. He had taken the beating, but they felt they were the ones harmed. In addition, Wilford C. "Cully" Simons, publisher of *The Lawrence Daily Journal-World*, was opposed to boxing and Jess found little support in his paper. Simons spent nearly as much space publicizing the wreck that Hattie Willard had as he did on the fight itself.[5]

Before the fight, on June 21, *The Journal-World* did carry a positive story, which was reprinted in the *Topeka Daily Capital*, showing Willard's home, his children and his wife working in her victory garden.

"Jess Willard is a home body and so is his wife. They want to rear their children in happy out-door surroundings and when they have finished with the public schools they're going to the nearby center of culture-the University of Kansas."[6]

At that time, the Willards had three cars, a large brown Fiat, a seven passenger Kissel Kar, and a farm touring car. There were five children now, Zella, the eldest, age 11, Francis, nine, Jess Jr., six, Enid, four, and Alan, three. When the reporter from the paper arrived to take pictures, Zella refused to have her picture taken, while Jess Jr. was busy cleaning off decorations he had added to the garage doors. He was employed with a bucket of water and a kiyi (a small brush used by the military). "In this case, Mrs. Willard acted as the officer in command and used a small hand-carved paddle to enforce orders." When Jess, Jr., was finished, he too fled from the photographer. He only came out when they asked if they could take a picture of his muscles.[7]

Jess's face after the Dempsey fight, swollen but not broken, 1919.

The home had a small gymnasium where the children could play when it was not possible to go outside. Otherwise, there were three dogs, swings and tricycles and a Shetland pony and buggy to ride. Mrs. Willard had a big bay horse which she liked to ride every day, in addition to working in her victory garden. When the reporter visited, only Enid was happy to pose for a picture, standing by her own special swing.[8]

On July 5, *The Journal-World* carried a front page article of Willard's defeat next to an article noting that "Homecoming Picnic Was Great Success." The article noted that the whole population of Lawrence had gone to Woodland Park to celebrate the Fourth of July and hear the results of Willard's fight. The fight was to be a blow by blow account, but the telegraph reports were scrambled and the first announcement anyone heard was that Willard had lost. This placed a damper on the afternoon which was capped off by a heavy downpour which forced people to flee back to town. Despite the headline that the afternoon was a great success, few people who were there, and even fewer who bet on Willard would have agreed.[9]

On July 7, in an editorial in the *Journal-World*, W.C. Simons ridiculed Willard when he wrote that Willard's defeat was a blow to literature. He noted that "Lawrence is not a 'fight' town. Its chief interests are outside of the fistic arena. It cares little who may be the champion bruiser. It has fallen into a way of considering a man from the neck up rather than down." As a result, Simons professed to be more concerned about the loss to literature with the cancellation of the series of articles that Willard had been writing for the press detailing his health habits and callisthenic exercises. Lawrence, "though it knew little of the technique of the prize ring, it could not help being interested when Mr. Willard began writing signed articles for the press, even though he discussed chiefly his arteries and his diet."[10]

After making fun of Willard's literary pretensions, Simons suddenly reversed course in a second editorial on July 9 and proved to be very solicitous of Willard. He may have been converted by Herbert Corey's article in *The Kansas City Star* of July 5 entitled "But Willard never Quit." Corey had been at the fight and noted that the crowd that had formerly praised Willard now belittled him. In addition, *The Journal-World* carried a front page article that some rumors had been floated that Willard had died in Toledo. This was too much for Simons. Although he had not been in Toledo, he now adopted a sympathetic attitude to his fellow townsman. In an editorial entitled "The Pug's Following," Simons noted:

> As Jess Willard, beaten, dazed and bleeding, stumbled from the ring and groped his way from the scene of his defeat the crowd rose to its feet and jeered him. They called him "yellow" and "quitter" and about all the other unkindly epithets that one man can cast at another. And most of the men who joined in this chorus were men who, face to face with Jess Willard alone, would have crawled before him.
>
> These are the red-blooded men of the "fight" world who now follow the banner of young Dempsey. Whatever pride there may be in reigning over such subjects now belongs to the new pugilistic king. And some day, when his wind is shorter and his waist measure longer, he many expect to hear the same jeers showered upon him.

Simons then arrived at the same conclusion that Jess and Hattie had already gotten to: "After all, the big fellow is well quit of his championship."[11]

A few days after they returned to Kansas, Jess and Hattie drove to see Marion Willard, Jess' brother, in Topeka. While there he told the reporters that none of Dempsey's body blows bothered him: "But that story about a body blow is all wrong. There may have been a few landed after I was dazed by the first left hook to my jaw, but they didn't affect me any. That left hook landed clean on the point of my jaw. From that time on I didn't know whether I was in the ring or in a corn field."[12]

Willard did add one important thought, however: "I believe that if the referee had kept him towards his corner while I was getting up so that I could have gotten clear on to my feet I would have had better luck. But I'm not crabbing. Dempsey is entitled to his championship and I'm willing to let him have it."

On the other hand, when asked if he would fight Dempsey again, Jess replied: "I'd be willing to meet him again just to see how it would come out, but it certainly wouldn't be worth while for me and it certainly wouldn't be the thing for Dempsey to do. There is every chance in the world that my luck would be different if we fought again. But I did pretty well on the last fight and that's going to be the end of the boxing game for me. I'm going to be too busy farming from now on to be bothered."[13]

Shortly after the Willards had moved to Lawrence, Jess began to deal in land. On April 14, 1917, Jess agreed to provide mortgages to two farming couples, Maude B. Tipps and her husband and Fred Q. Blossom and his wife, on land that they owned in Jackson County near Topeka. Then on April 21, He purchased two farms, one containing 82 and 69 hundredths acres from S.E. Cathcart and his wife, and another containing 80 acres from George W. Mat-sap-te. Both of these were in Jackson County as well.

The first of these farms cost him $3,800 while the second cost $3,200. These prices of between $40 and $45 per acre seemed to be in line with current values in the region.[14]

Then following his loss to Dempsey, Willard decided to buy a much larger spread across the river from Lawrence in Jefferson County. On March 4, 1920, Willard bought 674 acres of bottom land from Ida A. Thompson and her husband. The price he paid for this was extraordinary: $168,500.00 or $250 per acre. Although bottom land near the river was normally more valuable than land further away, this was still $100,000 more than Willard had earned from his fight with Dempsey. Despite his earnings from the circuses, it left him with a debt of $67,400.00 which he covered with a mortgage from the Commerce Trust Company of Kansas City, Missouri.[15]

Unlike western cattle ranches, which might sprawl over several thousands of acres, eastern Kansas ranches were more properly called "farms" and would consist of a few hundred acres having a variety of land forms. The land where his home was located outside of Lawrence consisted of rolling hills situated above the Kansas River (the Kaw). Other land, such as that he had purchased from Ida Thompson, consisted of bottom land in the river valley. Such farms were best designed for mixed use with some wheat grown on the drier uplands, as well as alfalfa for cattle feed. The best bottom land was reserved for potatoes or corn. During the war, Kansas had faced a crisis of farm labor. Getting the crops harvested took a massive effort with shopkeepers, newspaper reporters, high school students and any able-bodied men having to pitch in. It was hard, dirty work, but it had to be brought in within a week or two of the harvest date. Everybody was essentially drafted to help bring in the harvest.

This labor shortage stimulated the automation of the Kansas farm. Good prices for farm products permitted farmers to buy farm machinery to automate the work and replace the horse and plow. Many farmers were able to buy their own tractor to handle the plowing, but relatively few could afford a combine (harvester-thresher) to handle the wheat harvest. Willard was one of those few fortunate ones who had the money to buy his own combine. And when he was not using it for his own farms, he was able to rent it out to others for use on their land. In his Emmett days, before boxing, Willard had become well-known for renting out his horse teams for harvesting. He found it easy to revert to his earlier activities once he was back on the farm. Once again he was becoming an entrepreneur. As he told reporters who questioned him about getting back in the ring, "I am too busy to fight."[16]

As part of his effort to return to the farm, Willard contracted to sell wood from his farm north of the Kaw River, to Topeka for firewood. Illustrating the axiom that no good deed goes unpunished, Willard was brought up on charges that he gained excessive profits from selling his wood. A trial was held in Kansas City, Kansas, on January 2, 1920, where it was determined that (1) no actual price had been fixed by the Citizens Fuel Committee of Topeka for the wood; (2) Willard had not been paid for the wood which had already been delivered; (3) Willard had agreed to accept whatever price the Committee set; and (4) he had specified that if poor families were suffering from the cold that they should get the wood free. Willard was represented by his friend and neighbor, Edward T. Riling. Although the news of the charge against him was spread across the country, the fact that the court completely exonerated him from any hint of profiteering did not get as much publicity. Willard learned that it was easier for people to tear down his reputation than for him to build it up.[17]

In addition to selling cord wood to Topeka, that fall after the Dempsey fight also found Willard working to benefit his hometown. The "Fort to Fort" military highway (now called 40 Highway) went through Lawrence just north of Willard's home. As the road entered Lawrence it became Seventh Street. As it passed his property, it had to ascend a steep slope to reach a plateau where the Oregon Trail (now Iowa Street) went north to the Kaw River. This plateau extended west to Topeka, and made travel from Lawrence very difficult. In the spring and fall the hill was impassible with mud, and in the winter it was covered with ice. Horses and teams could not climb it and even automobiles had difficulty. Effectively this plateau served as a wall blockading Lawrence from travel to the state capital in Topeka.

From his days in Emmett, Willard had developed an interest in better roads. He decided before he left for Toledo to do what he could to level out the Fort to Fort road so that there was at least one relatively flat and level highway going to Topeka. In May 1919, he donated the right of way to the Board of County Commissioners, and began to cut away the limestone hill that separated Lawrence from Topeka. This became known as "The Willard Cut." It served as the only easy route to Topeka south of the Kaw River for 30 years. It was replaced by the city in the 1950s when Sixth Street was widened and made a four lane road, going east and west. Like Willard himself, this road building effort has been forgotten, but at the time, "Willard's Cut" was one of the most important private gifts to the city.[18]

During the spring and summer of 1920, Jess had expanded his farming operations. In addition to his Lawrence ranch of 56 acres, he had 250 acres of wheat in Grantville and 300 acres of wheat in Mayetta. As we have seen, Grantville was across the Kansas River from Lawrence on Highway 24 in Jefferson County. Mayetta was in Jackson County, north of Topeka and near the Pottawatomie Indian Reservation, where Jess grew up. In addition to the wheat that Willard was growing at Grantville, he had 110 acres in potatoes, 100 acres of river bottom land in corn and another 110 acres in alfalfa. Willard set the standard for modern capital-intensive farming. His tractor was a 25-50 Avery and could plow nine furrows in one pass. His combination harvester-thresher cut a nine foot swath through the wheat and then threshed the grain and dumped it into trucks which followed along. He was able to deliver the grain to the elevators in Grantville at the rate of one truckload every two hours. He himself supervised the work. "Farming has fighting beat a mile," he told a reporter.[19]

By 1920, Willard was settling down into a comfortable rut in Kansas and then one of those strange twists of fate interrupted his life. He was driving his car down a narrow road and was held up by a horse and wagon which would not let him pass. Willard lost his temper, tried to drive around the wagon, which was driven by a black man, and when he finally got in front, he called the fellow names and challenged him to fight. Unfortunately for Willard, the black man was Fred Logan, a local policeman. Logan refused the challenge to fight and had a warrant issued for Willard's arrest. He charged Willard with disturbing the peace. Willard pleaded not guilty. He went to trial where he lost his case and was fined $1 and court costs for challenging the policeman to a fist fight. It was a little thing, but like the Houdini incident in California, and the warrant issued on behalf of "Tex" Dowd in Chicago, it infected Willard with unhappiness. Suddenly his wonderful Kansas home did not seem so perfect any more. Like the princess with the pea, Willard could not comfortably sleep in Kansas any more. Then in the beginning of December, three of Willard's children came down with diphtheria and the house had to be quarantined. This was the final straw. In January 1921 Willard announced that the family was moving back to California.[20]

Although Willard had repeatedly said that he was not interested in getting back into boxing, the changing circumstances in Lawrence caused him to reconsider. It is hard to understand why seemingly small disturbances could have such significant effects in Willard's life. For a big man he was surprisingly sensitive. Hattie, his wife, was made of sterner stuff and could take life's disasters in stride. The family tells a series of stories of Hattie managing the house and the home through many difficulties without batting an eye. One Thanksgiving, for example, she had set the table and was getting the family together for dinner, when some one noticed that the turkey had vanished. When no one could find it, Hattie's response was "Did you gut the dog?" She then went on to provide an alternative dinner. When the family finances were at their lowest during World War II, Hattie went to work in an aircraft factory to bring in money for support. Hattie never lost her farm background. She lived up to the Kansas code: "Make do or do without."

Jess, on the other hand, was gravely disturbed by events which most men might not like but would certainly take in stride. When he returned to Oklahoma City after winning the heavyweight championship, he locked himself in the bathroom of his Pullman car rather than accept service of a warrant by his former manager, A.W. Phillips. When he fought Joe Cox in Springfield, Missouri, in 1911, he gave up in the middle of the fight and fled town being unable to face police threats to arrest him on the charge of prizefighting should he win. When he was fighting Frank Lyon in Elk City, Oklahoma, in 1911, he was afraid to box when he saw a Sheriff standing in the crowd. And he slipped out the back door of the theatre where he was supposed to box in Shawnee, Oklahoma, and took the train back to Oklahoma City, because he felt the fight would not allow him to show his talents. Little things meant a lot to Jess Willard.

Thoughts of Getting Back into the Ring

Despite having said that he was happy farming and did not want to return to the ring Willard began to change his mind in early 1920. In May, two months after his encounter with Fred Logan, Willard met Tex Rickard and they discussed a potential rematch with Dempsey. New York had outlawed boxing in 1917, but the Walker Bill was working its way through the legislature which would allow boxing in 1921. Willard discussed the possibility of a rematch should that occur. However, at that time, Dempsey was on trial for draft-dodging during the war, and it was not clear when he would be free to fight. Despite the fact that, like Willard, he had promised to be a fighting champion, Dempsey would not return to the ring for more than a year after his victory in Toledo.[21]

By December 1, 1920, the massive debt that Willard had incurred on his farm made him realize that he might need to get back in the ring to get another payday. Although Jess denied he needed the money, he was like the farmer who, when asked what he would do if given a million dollars, responded: "I'll just keep farming until it is all used up."

Jess did not have a million dollars, but what he did have was getting used up. When Jess and Hattie decided to move the family back to California, that meant that farming was out and boxing was the way forward. Everything now depended upon Tex Rickard and Jack Dempsey. Dempsey, when asked if he would be willing to give Willard a return match, agreed: "I see no reason why Willard should not get a return bout. I think he is entitled to it, if he wants it. I think that if I were beaten, I would ask for a return match. I am perfectly willing to meet him again."[22]

Dempsey was signed to fight Bill Brennan for Tex Rickard in Madison Square Garden on December 15. Before that fight Rickard had signed Willard to a contract to fight the winner of the Dempsey-Brennan fight in March of 1921. This fight however was going to be different than that in Toledo where both fighters had been guaranteed their purse. Rickard and his backer, Frank Flournoy, may have lost money on the Toledo fight. As a result, the return match in March was to be done on a percentage basis. Nonetheless, Willard was confident both of the fight and his condition. "I am feeling fine; I am in good condition and expect to give my opponent a run for his money whether he be Dempsey or Brennan," said Willard.[23]

Nothing is certain in boxing. Banking on the fact that he had a contract to fight the winner of the Jack Dempsey v. Bill Brennan fight, Willard had actually gone into training in the fall of 1920. According to Ray Archer, Willard "is now in better shape than he was at Toledo." Before leaving for New York, Jess took several pairs of pants into a tailor in Lawrence to have two and one half inches taken out of the waist. Jess was getting back into shape. When Dempsey defeated Brennan, Willard believed that he was next in line to fight Dempsey in New York City in Madison Square Garden on March 17, 1921. Tex Rickard had purchased Madison Square Garden, which was the largest indoor arena in New York, and had held the Dempsey-Brennan fight there. But in January 1921, the New York Boxing Commission made a ruling that $15 was the highest price that could be charged for a ticket to a boxing match. This made it impossible to hold a championship fight in the Garden, since the Garden was not large enough to hold a crowd that could support a championship bout at the $15 price per seat. The ruling was then adopted by the National Boxing Association, which had just come into existence, and through that organization it was soon adopted by other states. This meant that only the very largest arenas could be used for future championship bouts.[24]

There had also been a question of whether a return match between Willard and Dempsey would be popular. This was answered when Willard visited Madison Square Garden to see a fight scheduled there for January 27. When the audience realized he was present he was met by an outpouring of enthusiasm from the fans. The crowd forced Joe Humphreys, the announcer, to halt his introduction of the fighters themselves, to introduce Willard who was sitting in the back of the arena.

"As Willard's towering form came into view the crowd arose as one man and cheered him as though he were a conquering hero instead of a defeated man. For some reason Jess is more popular now that he is a former champion than when he held the title. There is no question that he will be the sentimental favorite in the coming battle."[25]

In a follow-up article, *The Washington Post* complimented Tex Rickard on signing Willard to a return bout with Dempsey. "That Promoter Tex Rickard made a popular move when he matched Jess Willard with Jack Dempsey, there can be no further room for doubt, if there ever was any. At the moderate scale of prices now permitted, the demand for tickets will be twice as great as the supply."[26]

Then, just at the moment when Jack Kearns arrived in New York to finalize Willard's bout with Dempsey, Jess disappeared. He left New York and returned home to Lawrence without telling anybody that he had gone. Consequently the proposed Willard-Dempsey rematch was at a standstill. The next day Dempsey, who was in Los Angeles, announced that he had received a telegram from Jack Kearns saying that the fight scheduled for March 17 was off. No reason was given for the cancellation but Dempsey hinted that the delay as due to the new ruling on the $15 ticket price. According to Dempsey, a new fight date had been scheduled for Labor Day.[27]

Tex Rickard soon confirmed that both parties had agreed to postpone the fight from March 17 to September 5, Labor Day. "While both Dempsey and Willard are willing and eager to observe the original contract and meet in Madison Square Garden, March 17, I have decided that the contest had better be staged in the open, following the Dempsey-Carpentier match of July 2."[28]

The following day, Willard sent a telegram to Rickard from Lawrence saying that he was prepared to meet Dempsey on Labor Day. He also asked for 15 percent of the gross receipts, and said he was willing to put up a $15,000 forfeit in a New York bank.[29]

All that remained was for Dempsey to defeat Carpentier and Willard would get his second shot at Dempsey. But then things became complicated. Doc Kearns, who had been willing to agree to a rematch, began to have second thoughts. Willard now appeared to be a genuine threat to Dempsey. As a result, working through various sportswriters, Kearns got them to suggest that Willard needed to fight a series of preliminary fights prior to meeting Dempsey. Willard took this as an insult: "The public did not ask Jeffries or Corbett or Fitzsimmons to go out and make a reputation when they wanted return fights." Harvey T. Woodruff, sports editor of *The Chicago Daily Tribune*, in his column supported Willard. "It is an unwritten law of sport that a defeated champion be given an opportunity by his conqueror to regain his title. This dictum is a tribute to the American idea of fair play."[30]

After Willard's protest that Dempsey was trying to avoid him had been made public, Jack Kearns responded in print. He argued that (1) Dempsey would put up $50,000 to bind the contract and Willard need only put up $25,000; (2) Dempsey was not afraid of Willard and would meet him any time between the first of March and the first of May of 1921; and (3) despite Dempsey's willingness to meet Willard, it was unlikely the fight would ever take place. The reason was that the new laws restricting the amount that could be charged for a seat at a boxing match had made big-purse matches impossible "and therefore, such an important match as a Dempsey-Willard battle is out of the question."[31]

Kearns, who never allowed his opponents to see his cards, had hidden his hand cleverly. First, instead of the $15,000 guarantee Willard had offered, Kearns wanted him to put up $25,000 to Dempsey's $50,000. This was designed to make Dempsey appear to be generous. But Kearns, who himself had not been able to raise $50,000 for the Carpentier fight, felt certain that Willard would not be able to raise $25,000. This would prevent the fight from occurring. Secondly, instead of confirming the Labor Day fight, to which he had agreed, he now wanted them to meet that spring. This meant Tex Rickard would have to hold the fight outdoors, either in a specially built stadium or in a ball park. The deadline Kearns gave Willard would not allow Rickard time enough to line up the stadium, nor would it ensure that the fight could be held in good weather. Rickard had lost money on the fight in Toledo in part due to the extremely hot weather, and he had wanted to have optimal weather for the return match. That would occur either in the summer or the fall. By setting the dates for the fight between March 1 (only two weeks away) and May 1, Kearns was attempting to ensure that the fight would never take place.

Ignoring Willard's newfound popularity, Kearns also argued that there was no popular demand for the fight. Using his friends in the press, Kearns sought to play down any enthusiasm for the fight and suggested to the local authorities that Dempsey would beat Willard even worse than he had in Toledo. He hinted that any locality which allowed the return match would be embarrassed to have such a "crimson orgy" take place in their town. Once again, Willard was out-witted by Kearns. Once again Willard was harmed by not having a manager who could speak for him in the press. Once again Willard was reduced to helplessness when trying to debate with Doc Kearns.[32]

By the beginning of May, the only heavyweight bout that was being discussed was the Dempsey-Carpentier fight which was to take place July 2 in Jersey City, New Jersey. Tex Rickard was forced to build a new stadium at Boyle's Thirty Acres to accommodate the crowd. Jess Willard was invited to be at the fight as one of the former champions. He was considered not as a challenger, but was rather relegated to the ranks of the has-beens, such as Tommy Burns, Jim Jeffries and Jim Corbett. Irritated by this, when asked if he would be at the fight and who he thought would win, Willard announced that he had no favorite and that he was too busy to attend the fight.[33]

Leaving Lawrence and Moving to Los Angeles

In January 1921, Jess had told reporters in Kansas City that he was planning to move from Lawrence to Hollywood, California. At the beginning of February he had announced: "I'm through with farming. From now on I am an oil man and a prize fighter. I am going to California to train." Willard was stimulated to get out of farming due to the agricultural depression which occurred at this time in the United States. Although his farm in Jefferson County was rich bottom land, and he was using the most progressive farming techniques, the prices offered for crops simply did not pay to produce them. As Ray Archer, his business manager explained in 1923: "Jess, although it is not known out here [in Los Angeles], is the potato king of the fertile Kaw Valley. That part of the game wasn't profitable last year when he was forced to let 70,000 bushels of spuds rot because of the lack of market. He is making money on his corn and wheat."[34]

In retrospect, it was a good decision on Willard's part to get out of farming. The farm labor shortage during the war had led to the mechanization of the farm. Farmers could now increase production with less labor. This brought prosperity to farms all across the country. Between 1916 and 1920 farm prices had risen to the highest levels ever. But trouble lay just around the corner. Europe, America's best customer for food stuffs, was bankrupted by the war. The bankruptcy of Europe soon led to the bankruptcy of the American farmer. In 1919 a banker in western Kansas noted that although the farmers in his county had earned $12 million for their crops, they were still $9 million in debt. The first depression in the 1920s was the decline in food prices caused by over-production. As food prices declined, farmers like Jess found that they could not make a profit. This led to a second depression when farmers found that they could not support the debt they had taken in mechanizing their farms. To pay off their debt they began to sell the land they owned. This led to a crash in land prices. Between January 1920 and March 1923 ten percent of the farmers in Kansas lost their farms, while another 17 percent retained their farms due solely to the leniency of their lenders. But these lenders also had their problems. Many banks in small rural towns failed when farmers could not pay off their loans. The extended agricultural depression of the early 1920s was a foretaste of the Great Depression of the 1930s.[35]

Willard was one of the first people who tried to move out of farming and to sell off his land. Nonetheless, he was too late. It took him several years to get rid of his lands. On October 29, 1924, the Jefferson County farm was finally sold at auction to R. F. Hodgins of Topeka for $151,650 or $225 per acre of which $84,250 was cash and $67,400 was the mortgage which Jess had placed on the farm. This meant that Jess took a loss of $25 per acre or $16,850 in five years.[36]

Although he had planned to move from Lawrence in January it took him until December to sell his home. In typical Willard fashion, he sold the entire spread, land, buildings, livestock, equipment and even the household furnishings to Sherwin Kelly, an aviator and geologist, and his wife Alice. They were able to move in immediately since Hattie and the children had already moved to California. The sale was completed on December 6, 1921, and the newspaper reported the price to be $27,000. Since Willard had paid $15,000 plus his home in Hollywood for the property in 1917, it seems likely that he sold his home in Lawrence at a loss as well.[37]

In January 1921, Willard had purchased a $40,000 home in Hollywood. He also claimed that he had made $750,000 in oil in 1919–1920. He claimed, in fact, that he would be willing to fight Dempsey "for nothing if necessary." "What do I care about the gate receipts? Nothing! It's the crown I lost I want back, and I won't be happy without it."[38]

We have no way of confirming Jess' statements about his financial condition, but the reporters at the time viewed this with skepticism. Certainly Willard had a great deal of money pass through his hands, but it does not seem that much actually stuck to his fingers.

On July 2, 1921, Jack Dempsey defeated Georges Carpentier at Boyle's Thirty Acres, New Jersey. Carpentier put up a game but losing battle. Dempsey's victory appeared to *The Washington Post* to be a sign that God was in his Heaven, and all was right with the world. Willard, on the other hand, spent the day supervising 50 men who were digging 225 acres of potatoes on his Jefferson County farm. The day after the fight, Jack Kearns announced that Dempsey was ready to meet Willard as soon as the fight could be arranged. Having said that, Dempsey embarked on a month vacation with his family in Utah. The date for the Willard-Dempsey rematch kept getting pushed further and further away. Willard, interviewed on his Lawrence farm, said, "I've led the simple life. I'm in splendid shape today." Still, "I would need four months for training and conditioning, then I would be ready for Jack Dempsey." This meant that from Willard's standpoint, the Labor Day match was off and the fight could not occur sooner than November. That would not be an ideal time for a fight in an open air arena.[39]

While Rickard and Willard were negotiating fight dates, a new problem arose. William Muldoon, the new head of the New York State Athletic Commission, announced that he would not license any fighter over 38 years old to fight in New York. This effectively ruled out allowing either Jack Johnson, who had just gotten out of prison, or Jess Willard to fight in New York. Rickard responded that if Willard could get into shape, he would merely move the fight to New Jersey. This meant that the fight could come off as early as January. But since Rickard needed to have the fight out in the open in order to draw a large enough crowd to pay for the expenses, this actually meant that the meeting had been postponed until the summer of 1922.[40]

In the meantime, Willard had agreed to referee a fight in Wichita, Kansas, between Mike Gibbons and Mike O'Dowd, a couple of middleweight boxers. As Willard well knew, boxing was banned in Kansas, so why he got involved is difficult to say. Predictably, the fight, which was scheduled for October 18, was banned. Then it was announced that it would be transferred to Tulsa for October 25. The promoters were clearly unaware of their prizefight law. Despite the fact that the fight was to be in Oklahoma, the fighters were promptly arrested in Kansas for training and preparing for a match for which compensation was to be received and admission charged. Willard himself, along with the promoters and other officials were arrested for "aiding and abetting the preparations for the match."[41]

When Willard recovered from his trouble in Kansas he announced that his defeat by Jack Dempsey was an "accident" which would not be repeated in their return bout. Jack Kearns recognized the same thing, but could not admit it. Instead, he engaged in a variety of activities designed to keep Willard from meeting Dempsey again. While Willard now was eager to sign another contract to fight Dempsey, Kearns was not. In September, Rickard proposed to have Dempsey and Willard meet in the outdoor stadium he had built in Jersey City for the Carpentier bout. The new proposed date was to be July 1, 1922. This gave everybody ample time to train and to promote the fight. Jack Kearns refused to sign a contract in Dempsey's name. Instead he argued that Willard needed to engage in several bouts with other challengers before fighting Dempsey. Rickard said that this was unnecessary and that Willard might refuse. This was what Kearns hoped. To strengthen his hand, Kearns suggested to various newspaper reporters that they urge Willard to get back in the ring with other men before facing Dempsey. Among these reporters was Robert Edgren who began his column of October 10 with the following words:

> If Jess Willard is going to fight Jack Dempsey again, Jess ought to go out first and beat one or two good heavyweights to show that he's still in the championship class. I have mentioned this before, but it might as well be mentioned again.
>
> If Willard is put on with Dempsey again without first proving that he has a fair chance to win, the match will not deserve public support.[42]

Kearns could not have been happier had he written the column himself. Still, the next week Kearns supposedly relented and announced that "I accepted Mr. Rickard's offer and notified him that I am willing to sign for Dempsey at any time." But, as Rickard well knew, this was not the same thing as actually signing a contract. In fact, rather than signing with Rickard, Kearns signed Dempsey to a 20-week theatrical tour. As Kearns told Dempsey privately: "Remember, Jack, as long as I keep you on the stage, there ain't no way you're going to lose your championship."[43]

Rickard felt certain that Dempsey and Willard would meet again on July 1, 1922. He announced that the fight would be fought for a percentage of the gross, with Dempsey getting 35 percent and Willard getting 20 percent. It would be a 12-round bout with the referee rendering a decision in the ring. Rickard further announced that both Willard and Dempsey had verbally agreed to the terms. According to *The New York Times* that meant that "the signing of contracts, therefore, remains a mere formality." But nothing is ever a "mere formality" in boxing.[44]

Striking Oil in Kansas

Before the contracts were signed, on October 30 it was announced that Willard's oil holdings near Eureka, Kansas, had suddenly produced a gusher. Willard had oil leases on 9,000 acres in southern Kansas. This discovery was right in the center of his land. If the reports were true, this made Willard's property there worth $2,000,000. This suddenly changed Willard's commitment to meeting Dempsey in the ring. "In justice to my oil interests I cannot at this time give any attention to the consideration of sports," said Jess.[45]

Willard had begun drilling for oil in the Eureka area in May. He had joined forces with Guy Scott, a geologist, and had taken a number of leases on the Hanson, Grundy and Essick farms. On October 13, *The Eureka Herald* announced that a well had come in on land formerly owned by Willard which was producing 300 barrels a day. Although Willard no longer owned this particular well, he had leases on a large acreage around this well, which led to his extravagant claims of wealth. The paper backed up his claim: "No more important oil strike than the Essick well was ever made in Greenwood county."[46]

Robert Edgren took the news of Willard's oil well in stride. He speculated that the only reason Willard had been ready to consider a second fight with Jack Dempsey was his need for money. If he did strike oil, Edgren thought, it would only go to pay off his mortgages on farmland and oil leases. "Jess never cared for fighting as fighting-the way Dempsey does. It was just a way to avoid poverty with Jess—an easy way because of his great bulk and strength."[47]

Edgren proved to be correct in his analysis. Willard immediately abandoned fighting when his oil wells came in. But gushers in Kansas soon fade out and turn into stripper wells generating only a few barrels a day. The cost of maintaining such wells just about equals the value of the oil produced. As Ray Archer, his business manager, said a couple of years later: "Willard made no money in oil, and neither has he lost any. In that section, after a month or so a well drops down to about 30 barrels a day. The way the price was for a time I figured that he was making no money out of his wells. Then they took to grading oil there, and under the system our class of oil increased to 60 cents a barrel in price. So we started another well, which is now under way. We have four already on the pump."[48]

Tex Rickard seemed to be of the same opinion as Robert Edgren. When he heard the news, he called off the fight with Dempsey. Rickard, who was an oil man himself, knew a good deal about the vagaries of wild-catting (drilling speculative oil wells). He simply laughed when he heard that Willard had struck a gusher in his southern Kansas lands. Rickard felt it was more likely that Willard had made a small hit in an oil field, and had gotten enough money to make him comfortable and was no longer willing to go through the effort to train for Dempsey. "'I've passed up the Dempsey-Willard bout, because I can't do business with Willard. I can't get any kind of answer from him. He has the contract I sent him and I guess he's forgotten it,' Rickard said today."[49]

Willard ceased to occupy Tex Rickard's thoughts after January 21, 1922, when two adolescent girls ran into Bellevue Hospital in New York City with a story that they had been molested. Although their story had many flaws, they eventually named Tex Rickard as their molester. This set off a chain of events which led to a trial in March 1922. This ultimately cleared Rickard of any crime, but marked him for life.[50]

By the time Rickard had recovered from his legal ordeal, Dempsey and Kearns had gone to Europe for a cultural vacation. They sailed on April 11, 1922, one month after Rickard's trial. They returned in the middle of May, broke, out of shape and in need of a fight.[51]

Jack Kearns and the Harry Wills Problem

Dempsey had defeated all of the logical white contenders following his victories over Willard, Brennan and Carpentier. This left only Tommy Gibbons, a light-heavyweight (and brother to Mike Gibbons, the middleweight), and Harry Wills, the best black heavyweight of the era, to challenge Dempsey.

On March 13, 1922, 500 newspapers across the country asked their readers which fighter they thought would be the best challenger for Jack Dempsey's crown. It was expected that they would choose Tommy Gibbons as the best candidate. But just before the survey was taken, Gibbons' manager declared that Gibbons was not ready for Dempsey. As a result, the majority or 131,073 voters declared Harry Wills was the most desirable challenger to fight Dempsey next.[52]

At the same time, in February, Nat Fleischer began publishing *The Ring* magazine. One of Fleischer's goals was to eliminate the color bar in boxing. In keeping with this, he began to run articles promoting the cause of Harry Wills. In the April issue of the magazine, he ran an article by Francis Albertani entitled "Harry Wills, Most Logical Opponent for Jack Dempsey."[53]

The public's interest in a Dempsey-Wills fight was troubling to Rickard, Dempsey and Kearns.

Rickard had put on the famous fight between Jack Johnson and Jim Jeffries in Reno in 1910 and been appalled by the nationwide race riots that followed. Rickard swore he would never again put on a fight between a black and a white champion, and had left the country to take up ranching in Latin America. Then in 1919, after he had returned, there were again race riots in various cities between blacks and whites. The trigger for these riots had been the fact that many southern blacks had migrated north during the war to fill jobs in manufacturing left by the white soldiers who went overseas. When the white soldiers returned, tension and riots developed as they contested with the blacks for jobs.

This situation strengthened Rickard's resolve to avoid another biracial championship fight.[54]

Dempsey was too young to be aware of most of this history. He was not particularly worried about beating Wills. However, the success of D.W. Griffith's movie *Birth of a Nation* in 1915 had led to the revival of the Ku Klux Klan throughout the Midwest. The revival of the Klan and the fact that Dempsey was a Mormon, a church which placed restrictions on blacks, created a problem for him. Further, Dempsey had agreed to the color bar when he became champion. He was concerned about going back on his word and being only the second white champion to break the color bar established by John L. Sullivan.

Doc Kearns was specifically concerned about the possibility that Dempsey might lose to Wills. He did not want Dempsey to be made to look ridiculous as Tommy Burns had been in losing to Jack Johnson. To avoid having to deal with this problem, Kearns had taken Dempsey to Europe. In the meantime, he set in motion a secondary strategy to keep Wills at bay. Kearns reversed his previous position and began to develop a plan to get Willard back into the ring with Dempsey. Using his press contacts Kearns began to plant articles supposedly coming from Willard, demanding a return bout. These articles began to appear in papers, particularly in *The New York Times* and *The Washington Post* at the beginning of May, while Kearns was still in Europe. This ensured that his fingerprints were not on them, but then neither were Willard's. According to these articles, Willard had gone to Los Angeles where he was aggressively training for a second Dempsey-Willard fight which was to occur on Labor Day.[55]

Robert Edgren, the great sports columnist of *The Chicago Daily Tribune*, began to get curious about how anxious Willard was for another Dempsey fight. It seemed very odd for Willard to go into training without letting the world know. Edgren had argued that Willard needed to fight some other men before meeting Dempsey again. The fact that Willard was training in private to meet Dempsey made no sense. "Willard has been out of sight since Toledo. No fighter can stay out of the ring for years and come back as good as ever.... There's only one way the giant might show that he's still anything more than a colossal punching bag. If he could beat a couple of men like Brennan and Wills, for instance, nobody would doubt his right to make the public pay championship prices to see him in the ring with Dempsey again."[56]

Edgren and Kearns appeared to be on the same page. These were exactly the arguments that Kearns had made in 1921. But then Edgren drove a dagger into Kearns' heart when he came to the ultimate conclusion: "Dempsey, being without any one to give him battle in this country, possibly excepting Harry Wills, is practically out of a job."[57]

In order to make sense out of Willard's supposed challenge of Dempsey, Robert Edgren decided to go to Los Angeles, locate Willard's training camp and see what was going on.

The result was a full page spread in *The Chicago Daily Tribune*, enlivened by Edgren's own cartoons. Entitled "The Jess Willard of Today" Edgren described his visit to Los Angeles to see Willard's training establishment:

> I expected to find Jess Willard surrounded by a training staff and ready to shoot out a lot of information about what he expects to do to Jack Dempsey along in September. Arriving in Los Angeles early in the morning, I found that no one in town knew Willard was there. He hadn't visited the newspaper offices. There was a rumor that someone had seen him on the

street, but that was generally discredited. It took four hours of trailing to locate him on the outskirts of town in the newest part of the Wilshire district. I rang the bell. The front door opened and there stood Jess filling the doorway from side to side and nearly bumping his head on the lintel.

Jess looked good.

He wasn't fat, but he was at least plump, and his face was round and smiling. As I stepped in there was none of the familiar training camp smell about the place, no mixture of arnica and witch-hazel, and acrid odor of sweaty woolens and sodden gloves. There was no punching bag lying in the corner. No photos of Jess in fighting trunks decorated the mantel piece. Instead of the usual coterie of young huskies with bent noses and overhanging brows, I found only Mrs. Willard and the five little Willards-or at least those who weren't in school.

"Don't look as if you've been training very hard, Jess," I suggested.

"Training?" said Willard. "What for?"

"Why that fight with Dempsey in September. I see you have been challenging him." Jess leaned back in his chair and laughed comfortably.

"Have I?" he chuckled. "Well, that's news to me. There's been a little talk about making a match with Dempsey, but I'm not thinking seriously of fighting him again. Tex Rickard has a notion that I can beat Dempsey any time I'll train, and he wants me to do it. But I don't know whether I want to box Jack again or not. It would mean a lot of hard work."

"I'm so out of touch with sport that I hardly know what's going on in the ring nowadays. I don't say I won't meet Dempsey again, but I'm not considering the possibility of it seriously at all."

"I don't know that I'd care to go back to the ring even if I was sure of beating Dempsey. I'm in a much bigger game now. I have some pretty good oil fields developing back in Kansas-haven't put down a dry well yet."

"Then you haven't challenged him and haven't any intention of going after another match? And the story that you have been secretly training for six months is the bunk?" I asked.

Willard laughed.

"Haven't had a glove on," he said.

"Only thing on my mind just now, besides fixing up a new home for my family and keeping track of the oil business is that I want to run over and see my old friend Jim Jeffries. How is Jim, anyway? Fine?"[58]

Edgren's interview with Willard was meant to end the discussion of another Willard and Dempsey fight. Unfortunately, it did not. Kearns could not allow it.

Kearns and Dempsey returned to the United States in the middle of May. They were promptly faced with a challenge from Harry Wills. On June 13, Paddy Mullins, Harry Wills' manager, posted a $2,500 forfeit with the New York Boxing Commission, challenging Dempsey to fight Wills. Although the money was nothing compared to the forfeits placed in the Carpentier fight, it nonetheless forced Jack Kearns' hand. Unless he could show that there were other fighters in line to face Dempsey, he might be forced to accept Wills' challenge. He had to keep up the charade that somebody else was anxious to fight Dempsey again. And in this case that meant Willard.[59]

The same week that Mullins posted the forfeit in New York, *The Washington Post* reported that Willard was planning to go back east to meet with Tex Rickard at the end of the summer to discuss another fight with Dempsey. Then, in an article in *The Los Angeles Evening Express* Willard was quoted as saying that he felt Doc Kearns was "dodging" him and was attempting to keep Dempsey from getting into the ring with him again.[60]

The contrast between Edgren's article and the article in *The Los Angeles Evening*

Express as quoted by *The Washington Post,* is like day and night. The headline in the *Post* saying that Willard and Dempsey might meet on Labor Day was patently absurd. There was no way that Willard planned to meet Dempsey on Labor Day. This called into question the whole article and makes us wonder who thought to benefit from such ridiculous copy. All of this promotional material emanated from Los Angeles where both Kearns and Willard happened to be at the time. The fact that Willard denied that he had challenged Dempsey when questioned by Robert Edgren shows that he was not the source of the stories. Then *The New York Times* picked up a story from Kearns himself which confirmed that Kearns, not Willard, was manipulating the press. The article was interesting for the way it attempted to manage Willard.

> I saw Jess several days ago and he is already in pretty fair shape. He will no doubt work hard from now on so as to be in the pink of condition.
>
> Willard is not going to take on Dempsey for the purpose of making any money, because he has made plenty in the oil business during the past year or so. He is simply going into the match to prove that he is the better man than Dempsey and absolutely thinks he is Jack's master. Of course, I think Jack will lick him again, but I really believe that the Kansan will make a better showing this time.

Asked when the match would be held, Kearns replied that he felt "certain the match would be pulled off next September."[61]

Several points can be made here. (1) It is doubtful that Kearns ever saw Willard at this time. It had taken Edgren four hours of searching to locate Willard. And Kearns could not simply call Willard up and arrange an appointment, since Willard and Kearns disliked each other. (2) Willard had told Edgren that he had no plans to fight Dempsey at that time, and he was not in training. But for Kearns' purpose Willard had to be in training to fight Dempsey. So he simply made up the story that Willard was going to be working hard from now on. (3) Willard had told Edgren that if he were to go into training for another fight with Dempsey, he would need time: "Winning in the ring depends a lot on the state of mind. I would expect to win, and if I fought him again I'd have seven or eight months of hard work behind and I'd feel fit." But this would not work for Kearns. Therefore Doc assured the paper that the Dempsey-Willard fight would occur in September or in three months time. The idea of a September bout was important to Kearns' strategy and had nothing to do with Willard's position at all. Although *The Washington Post* confirmed Edgren's story with a small note on June 4 saying that Willard was not interested in fighting Dempsey, this was drowned out by a flood of stories probably inspired by Kearns saying that he was and that such a bout would occur in the fall.[62]

On June 18 *The New York Times* published an article which seemed to summarize Doc Kearns' efforts to ward off a Wills challenge. In the article, Kearns announced that Dempsey was considering fighting not just Willard in September, but Bill Brennan and Harry Greb as well. It was, he declared, likely to be "one of the busiest Fall campaigns ever participated in by a heavyweight titleholder." Kearns expected to have Dempsey fight Brennan in Michigan City, Indiana, on Labor Day, Willard in New York, Jersey City or Montreal at the end of September, and Harry Greb a few days later in a six round bout in Philadelphia. Kearns was trying to flood the boxing world with bouts so as to distract attention from Harry Wills.[63]

Of course, none of these bouts actually occurred. But they did serve a purpose. Kearns had been given a deadline to accept or decline Wills' challenge by July 10 by the

New York State Athletic Commission. To decline could mean that Dempsey would be barred from fighting in New York until he accepted the challenge. Further, he might be forced to forfeit his title. But the flurry of activity and the promises that Kearns made were designed to show the Athletic Commission that not just Wills but many other fighters wanted to get a crack at Dempsey's crown, and that Dempsey was willing to give them all a chance. Wills was just one of many fighters to be considered and he must take his place in line. "I have been notified by the State Athletic Commission that Dempsey must either accept or decline Wills' challenge by July 10, and I am trying to abide by that ruling. The agreement here is simply legal acceptance by Dempsey of Will's [sic] challenge, in accordance with the wishes and demand of the State Athletic Commission. It is the champion's answer to the commission, to the press and to the public."

"By no stretch of the imagination can the agreement be regarded in the light of a bout contract. That will come when the promoter comes forth with a proposition which appeals to us. To date, however, no offer has been made for a bout. Dempsey is ready. I have signed an agreement officially accepting Wills' challenge. When and where the bout will be held are details which the future will decide."[64]

No one could say that Dempsey had refused to fight Wills. Dempsey was willing. It was just a question of where and when. And with so many other bouts on the schedule, there was no question in Doc Kearns' mind that "when" might be some far distance in the future.

From this we can draw the conclusion that all the promotional material about Willard appearing in the newspapers in May and early June 1922, especially that criticizing Kearns and telling the public that Willard was ready to fight, came from Kearns and his friends. Kearns was keeping the Willard-Dempsey fight alive in the press for his own purpose and most of the articles had nothing to do with Willard at all.[65]

Back in the Ring

Then a strange thing happened. After being badgered by the press for several months, and listening to Kearns criticize himself, Jess Willard began to think that perhaps he should get back into the ring with Dempsey again. On June 21 a small note appeared in *The New York Times* saying that Willard had announced that he would start training for a return match with Jack Dempsey and that he planned to do so in the gymnasium of the Hollywood Post of the American Legion. This was confirmed as legitimate by an article in *The Los Angeles Times* on June 28. Doc Kearns had awakened the sleeping giant.[66]

When he first began to train Willard said that he weighed 260 and expected to be in fighting trim by September. Tex Rickard wanted to have Willard meet Dempsey on September 22 in either New York or New Jersey. But then Rickard sent him a contract for a fight in the open on October 6, while Jess argued for the date of October 31. At the end of August, with nothing signed, Willard quit his training and agreed to several weeks of vaudeville exhibition bouts. This astonished many, but Harry Williams, in his column of September 26, explained that Jess had realized that a bout with Dempsey was not likely to occur in 1922 and that the earliest it might occur was in the spring of 1923. This led him to discontinue training and take on exhibitions.[67]

After two weeks of vaudeville exhibitions, Willard and his new manager, Gene Doyle, began to express the same complaints that Jack Kearns had put into Willard's mouth in May and June. When Kearns was concerned about Dempsey having to fight Wills, he could not wait to sign Willard and others to a contract. Now that the issue with Wills seemed to be dealt with, Kearns refused to sign a contract for Dempsey to fight Willard. Kearns and Dempsey were "dodging" Willard.[68]

Willard, for his part, tried hard to convince the public that this time he meant to fight Dempsey and take the title from him. "When I go into training for Dempsey this time, I will have a camp full of the toughest sparring partners I can pick in the country. Also, I will be attended by a world's famous trainer."[69]

While Willard undoubtedly meant this when he spoke to the newspaper reporters, it is not certain that he really believed it himself. Instead, during the fall he mainly engaged in exhibitions in vaudeville and in entertainments for groups of World War I veterans, to which he donated his services.[70]

This activity did not impress Robert Edgren who continued to demand that before Willard got back into the ring with Dempsey, he try on several other fighters first. "Otherwise it would be a joke to match him with Dempsey. The public would laugh at such a match and stay away, save the ticket money and buy the morning paper next day to see what happened."[71]

Willard began to recognize the logic of Edgren's arguments. At the end of November he sent a telegram to Charles Murray, promoter of the Queensberry Athletic Club of Buffalo, where Jess had fought several times in the past, and announced that if he could not get a fight with Dempsey, he would be willing to fight Floyd Johnson as a warm up fight. "Am in great shape and will surprise a lot of wise guys when I start," said Willard.[72]

No sooner had Willard agreed to the possibility of fighting Floyd Johnson, an Iowa farmer, than publicity began to move against Dempsey. Harry Williams, the Los Angeles sports columnist, began to berate Dempsey and Kearns for not signing to fight Willard. He blamed Kearns for using the same tactics to delay the fight with Willard as he had to delay the fight with Wills.

"When the Wills matter was up we gave Dempsey the benefit of the doubt attributing his backwardness to fidelity to the color line. Willard is white all the way through. Where is the difficulty here? Friends of Dempsey aver there is not the slightest doubt that he can whip Willard. This being the case, why does not the champion rush to pick up the money?"[73]

Then Kearns met with Ray Archer and Gene Doyle in Los Angeles. And just as Harry Williams predicted, Kearns tried to delay the fight with the same tactic he had used against Wills: "Kearns told Archer and me," said Doyle, "that Willard could have a bout with Dempsey providing that a legitimate promoter would handle it." This tactic then backfired on Kearns when the next day Tom O'Rourke, a New York promoter announced that he was sending a registered letter to Willard offering to stage the bout between Willard and Dempsey in the Polo Grounds in New York in May 1923.[74]

The fact that O'Rourke was willing to put on the bout in New York City, did not mean that it would actually occur. In 1921, William Muldoon, chairman of the New York State Athletic Commission, had announced that he would not approve any boxing bout that featured a man 38 years old. Although this was designed to prevent Jack Johnson and Jess Willard, both of whom were now older than 38, from boxing in New York rings, Muldoon's edict also entrapped Johnny Kilbane, the world's featherweight champion, and Johnny Wilson, the world's middleweight champion. Designed to make boxing more civilized, such bureaucratic decisions caused much mischief to the sport.[75]

Taking advantage of this situation, W. H. Klepper, owner of the Portland Pacific Coast baseball team, offered $330,000 for the Willard-Dempsey fight if it were fought in Portland, Oregon, on July 4, 1923. Klepper and others believed that the solution to any dispute in boxing was to let the men fight it out in the ring. Any man who can stand up is welcome in the ring. He may not get far, but, as Arthur Mercante, the famous referee, has pointed out, "all that is required to become a professional boxer is a clean bill of health."[76]

By January 1923, it had become evident that Robert Edgren's suggestion had gained traction. Tex Rickard, who now was the pre-eminent promoter, had also come to the decision that in order to make a good match, Willard needed to prove himself of championship caliber by defeating some other fighters. One possible candidate, in addition to Floyd Johnson, was the Argentinean fighter, Luis Angel Firpo. Still, Rickard and Willard both had a second Dempsey bout in mind as their main objective. Tex said, "I know that Willard wants another chance at Dempsey. He's not trying to kid me or anybody else when he talks Dempsey. Jess will never understand how it came that he was licked by Jack, and he really felt sorry for the latter when the match was made. As a matter of fact, I also felt that the little Dempsey was in for a sound pasting when we signed him up."[77]

At the beginning of January Willard went to New York to meet with Tex Rickard. Jack Kearns also agreed to join them there. Not only was Rickard willing to put on a Dempsey-Willard rematch, but Tom O'Rourke, matchmaker of the Republic Athletic Club, who had rights to bouts in the Polo Grounds, also was competing for the bout. But he too now wanted Willard to have a preliminary bout with some good white heavyweight before getting back into the ring with Dempsey. At the same time, William Muldoon, chairman of the New York State Athletic Commission, reiterated his opposition to having Willard fight in New York. "Willard's talk of returning to the ring to box Dempsey or anybody else is ridiculous," said Muldoon. To prevent this, Muldoon was attempting to develop an agreement with other state athletic commissions so that Willard would be prevented from boxing in any state which had a commission form of government. This decision, which was based upon Willard's age, was, in the eyes of Tom O'Rourke, unconstitutional. Willard now claimed to be 36 years old. Muldoon had established an outer limit of 38 years for a boxer to have a license in New York, and he claimed Willard was actually 40 years old. In point of fact, Willard's birthday was December 29 and as a result, he was now 41 years old, but he would not admit it. There did seem to be a few impediments to having a second Dempsey-Willard match in New York at this time.[78]

Willard finally agreed with the newspaper men that he would fight his way back to a match with Dempsey. "I want to fight Dempsey first, and I think I've proved my right to another chance at the title, but if necessary, I'll go out and fight any other contenders," he added, mentioning Bill Brennan, Floyd Johnson and Luis Firpo as possibilities. The former title holder, however, had drawn the color line, so that Harry Wills is not included in the list.[79]

Donning his boxing togs, Willard put on a training exhibition for the newspaper men in New York while waiting for Jack Kearns to arrive. At the end of the workout, Tex Rickard announced that he thought "Willard is the best man available today as an opponent for Dempsey." Tom O'Rourke, manager of the Polo Grounds, announced that he was prepared to offer Willard $50,000 and a percentage of the gate if he fought Dempsey there.[80]

Willard was able to convince the newspaper reporters that he deserved to be back in the ring. At that point William Muldoon began to change his tune as well. Muldoon now announced, "No prejudice is held against Jess Willard by the State athletic commission." All that is required is that he provides proof of his age, and if proof is not possible, his word will be accepted. "Having complied with that condition, Willard, before getting into the ring with Dempsey, will be required to meet at least two heavyweights of good repute with purpose of proving whether he is in condition to do battle."[81]

Things began to look more favorable to Willard. He was buoyed up by his visit to the bout between Floyd Johnson and Bill Brennan. Just before the fight, Harry Wills was introduced to the crowd to a smattering of applause, he was followed by Tommy Gibbons who was also applauded, but they were all drowned out by a standing ovation given to Willard when he was introduced. As *The New York Times* was to say, "The former champion is right now riding high on a wave of popularity greater than he knew in his days as champion. Such popularity is likely to sway public opinion in favor of another Dempsey-Willard bout."[82]

Now that Willard had become the favorite of the crowds, and the barriers to fighting Dempsey had begun to ease, Jack Kearns once again began to back-peddle.

As Tex Rickard had said, Willard was the best of all of the contenders. This worried Kearns. If Willard was given another chance to fight Dempsey, he might in fact defeat him and take back the crown. This would not suit Kearns. But Muldoon's demands that Willard fight two recognized heavyweights before he could fight Dempsey in New York proved to be Kearns' ace in the hole. What was working against that was Tex Rickard's desire to sign Dempsey to a blank contract in which Rickard, not Kearns, was to pick the opponent for Dempsey to fight.[83]

The Trials of William Muldoon

During January and February of 1923, the papers were full of gossip about who would fight Dempsey. Kearns now said that he thought that the public wanted Dempsey to fight Willard and Wills and that all of the rest of the challengers were either too small (Tommy Gibbons), too young (Floyd Johnson), too old (Bill Brennan) or too inexperienced (Luis Angel Firpo). Only Willard and Wills were of the proper caliber to fight Dempsey. In the strange world managed by Jack Kearns, that really meant that Willard and Wills, of all the above fighters, would never get into the ring with Jack Dempsey.[84]

Hugh Fullerton of *The Chicago Daily Tribune* analyzed the situation as laid out by Kearns and pointed out that Willard and Wills were the only genuine threats to Dempsey's crown and "it is 50 to 1 Wills never gets a chance." He might as well have given the same odds on Willard, for William Muldoon had stated that Willard would never get a chance to fight Dempsey in New York as long as he was alive. And Louis Massano, the New Jersey State Athletic Commissioner, announced on January 31, that New Jersey was going to bar the Dempsey-Willard fight in that state as well. This appeared to have closed down the two most lucrative markets in the country for a Dempsey-Willard rematch.[85]

Robert Edgren now chided Muldoon for preventing Willard from fighting in New

York. "Name one heavyweight in the world who can beat Willard except Dempsey," Edgren wrote. "If Jess isn't able to take care of himself in the ring, all the rest of the bunch ought to have guardians. This includes Harry Wills."[86]

Two days later, Muldoon played right into Jack Kearns' hands by banning a fight between Dempsey and Wills in New York. His reasoning was not that a bi-racial fight might provoke riots but that the fight was likely to be too popular with the public.

The commercialized conditions surrounding a bout of such importance, Chairman Muldoon said, would produce an element which would jeopardize professional boxing if permitted to go unnoticed.[87]

This was curious logic, especially since Muldoon had forced Dempsey to accept Wills' challenge in the first place. He explained this all in a rather complicated way.

> When the commission decided to accept Wills challenge that was done for a purpose. That purpose has been fulfilled. The opinion prevailed in many quarters that Dempsey was afraid of his challengers and of Wills particularly. The commission demanded that he either refuse or accept Wills challenge. In this Dempsey was amenable to the boxing law, just as every champion is.
>
> It is part of the law that any champion must defend his title against a legitimate challenger when a challenge is filed accompanied by a forfeit. If the champion does not accept or reject the challenge in six months the title is declared vacated, and the first challenger stands as the man who must accept the next challenge in a bout to determine the successor to the disqualified champion.
>
> When Dempsey accepted Wills' challenge he proved his willingness to defend his title. Only the money demands of the champion prevented the bout, and for this Dempsey was not to blame.... It is no fault of Dempsey's that no promoter could be found who could promote a bout between the champion and Wills.[88]

By establishing conditions that no promoter cared to meet, Kearns prevented Dempsey from having to fight Wills at this time. In fact, Dempsey never did fight Wills. He was given a free pass because Kearns was smarter than both Muldoon and the athletic commission.

As for Willard, he recognized that his chances to fight Dempsey a second time were only marginally better than Wills. As a result, he engaged in a feat of political gymnastics similar to that performed by Jack Kearns. Willard found that if he accepted a fight for the Milk Fund with Floyd Johnson, the Iowa Farmer, he could fight in New York City with the blessing of William Muldoon. This reversal of fortune was due to the fact that Mrs. William Randolph Hearst had decided that boxing bouts were a good way to get the public to support her crusade to provide milk for the poor children of New York. Working with Tex Rickard, she provided the charitable basis for the bout. She and Rickard were also able to get the new Yankee Stadium donated for free for the day. Presented with this formidable array of good will, Muldoon was forced to suspend his rule that said Willard was too old to fight in New York, and instead give the fight his blessing.[89]

This was one of the few times Willard found things working for him in New York. While Willard and Johnson were only scheduled to receive $25,000 each, the fight itself was of much greater benefit to them than the money. Johnson was trying to make a name for himself in the ring. If he were to defeat Willard, he would have placed himself on the same level as Dempsey. He would immediately become the number one challenger. For Willard too the fight was a Godsend. There was no other way he was going to get a fight in either New York or New Jersey given Muldoon's ruling that he was too old to get back into the ring. But Mrs. Hearst's charity trumped Muldoon's bias. Muldoon could not afford to stand in the way of the poor children of New York. The barriers were broken and Willard was allowed to fight Johnson in Yankee Stadium on May 12, 1923.[90]

At the same time, Jack Kearns announced that Dempsey had been offered $200,000 to fight Tommy Gibbons in Shelby, Montana. One might say that this fight literally dropped into Kearns' lap, were it not for the fact that he already had a New York showgirl in his lap when he got the phone call. Although the blonde pouted at the interruption, the caller promised big money to Kearns. And money always trumped sex in Kearns' world. This then was the beginning of what became known as "the Rape of Shelby." Kearns and Dempsey bankrupted the entire town and a good part of the state of Montana while defeating Gibbons and leaving him without a dime.[91]

Meanwhile, back in New York City, William Muldoon watched as his bureaucratic control of boxing was dismantled. He had sworn that Willard would not fight in a New York ring because he considered Willard too old. He had been forced to give up that ruling under pressure from Mrs. Hearst. In addition it was also announced that Luis Firpo and Jack McAuliffe II would fight on the same card with Willard and Johnson. The Milk Fund battles were to become a boxing extravaganza. Then, at the beginning of April, Muldoon was forced to announce that he would allow higher prices for seats for the Willard-Johnson bout in Yankee Stadium. He had unilaterally set a top price of $15 for ringside seats to stifle the commercialism which he saw as a threat to boxing. Now, under pressure from the charity, he agreed that ringside seats might sell for $20. Muldoon, who had been so vigorous in his defense of the rules of the athletic commission, had entirely collapsed in the face of the determined power of Mrs. William Randolph Hearst and the society women of New York. In an attempt to retrieve some of his prestige, Muldoon did demand that the fighters move their camps to New York three weeks before the May 12 date, and that they not engage in any other fights before that date. But he had given away so much of his power that he had a hard time in getting it back.[92]

Almost immediately, Muldoon's rulings backfired on him. Floyd Johnson had an agreement to fight Fred Fulton on April 16 in Boston. Muldoon's ruling forced Johnson to cancel this contract. In canceling the contract and attempting to place the fight later in the year, the managers of the two fighters found they got a considerably better offer from Jersey City, New Jersey, than they had from Boston. At that point the Massachusetts commission stepped in and said that they would suspend Johnson indefinitely, and thus prevent him from fighting Willard, unless he agreed to fight Fulton in Boston at the time agreed. By seeking to regain control of the situation, Muldoon had made things worse.[93]

Charley Cook, Floyd Johnson's manager, was naïve but not stupid. He had booked Johnson to fight several men before the Willard bout because "Johnson, being a young boxer, needed experience before engaging a veteran like Willard.... In my opinion, a ten-round bout is worth fifty rounds of sparring to prepare a man for a battle with an opponent like Willard." He went on to say that if Johnson could not defeat a fighter like Fulton, he did not belong in the ring with Willard. Clearly, Charley Cook did not share Muldoon's opinion that Willard was a has-been and too old for championship fights. Muldoon's heavy-handed attempts at controlling boxing in New York were making him look like a fool.[94]

Muldoon then tried to regroup by saying that he would agree to a Johnson-Fulton bout if it were held after the May 12 fight with Willard. But this was rejected by the New

Jersey State Athletic Commission. The best they would agree to was a one-week delay until April 23.[95]

Finally, Muldoon was forced to retreat entirely. He agreed that Johnson was able to meet Fulton in Jersey City on April 23. That fight, following the suggestion of Charley Cook, now became an elimination battle to determine whether Floyd Johnson or Fred Fulton would meet Willard for the Milk Fund. Muldoon then apologized effusively in print to the Milk Fund ladies and to the sport of boxing in general. The ladies had informed him that they felt the Johnson-Fulton fight would not affect the Milk Fund battle. He now agreed with them. Then he apologized to boxing by saying that he thought there was only a verbal agreement between Johnson and Fulton.

> As a matter of fact, I thought that the match was arranged only on a verbal agreement and not through a signed contract. When I discovered the match had been signed, I realized that it had to go through. Nobody can make a person violate the law by compelling him to break a signed contract, whereas if the match was arranged on a verbal agreement only, it would have been possible to adjust the matter without involving a violation of the law.[96]

Finally, by agreeing to allow Johnson and Fulton to fight in New Jersey, Muldoon prevented a break between New York and New Jersey over boxing rules which threatened to place the two state commissions in opposition to each other. The more bureaucratic the sport became, the more problems seemed to arise. As *The New York Times* said: "The solution of the confused situation which has existed since the State Athletic Commission declined to sanction the Johnson-Fulton bout originally scheduled for last Monday night relieves the strained situation between the boxing authorities of this State and New Jersey."[97]

The only problem now was that Massachusetts had suspended Floyd Johnson and his manager, and Fred Fulton and his manager, Jimmy Johnston (the "Boy Bandit"), until they agreed to fight in Boston. Further, Massachusetts decided to seize Johnson's purse from the Milk Fund bout. However, the New Jersey commission and the New York commission decided to ignore the Massachusetts protest.[98]

Willard and Floyd Johnson

Willard, who had been training in Excelsior Springs, Missouri, while all of this had been going on, now turned up in Yonkers where he went into training in Jack Skelly's gym at the Columbus Sporting Club. By the time he got back to the East Coast, he was down to 241, only three pounds more than he had weighed when he fought Jack Johnson. Harry Newman worried that he looked as if he had over trained. He seemed slow on his feet and not able to get up on his toes.

"It may be that Willard will beat the inexperienced Johnson, but we rather think that he will never tackle Dempsey. At least he had better not."[99]

The New York Times, while just as impressed as Harry Newman was by Willard's weight and physical presence, also noted that Willard had slowed down.

"In action this comparatively aged athlete suffers in comparison to the present-day crop of heavyweights, and, to a certain extent, when compared to the Willard of seven years ago. Always slow and cumbersome, Willard now appears even slower than before and just as awkward."[100]

Both Newman and *The New York Times* writer noticed that Willard boxed flat-footed and that his timing was off. Still, Willard was confident that he would do well in the bout May 12, whomever they put into the ring with him.

On the night of April 23, Floyd Johnson, the Iowa farmer, defeated Fred Fulton, the Minnesota plasterer. It was a newspaper decision, meaning that no decision was rendered in the ring, and the fighters were forced to read the morning papers to see which of them won. But the verdict by *The New York Times* was clear: Johnson won ten out of the 12 rounds, with Fulton winning only the eighth and 12th rounds. Johnson won by being continually aggressive, pounding away at Fulton until he eventually wore both himself and Fulton out. In his actions, Johnson used Dempsey's tactics of rushing his opponent throughout the fight. He nearly succeeded in matching Dempsey's first round knock-out of Fulton by sending him to the canvas with a right and then a left to the jaw. But Johnson lacked the power of Dempsey, and Fulton was up before the referee could begin the count. Johnson had taken a big risk, but now he got his chance to fight Jess Willard. If he could defeat Willard, he would get a chance to fight Dempsey for the title.

Despite the fact that the newspaper reporters agreed that Johnson won the match, he did not win in a convincing enough manner to cause many to believe he had much of a chance against Willard. Johnson had stood up against the bigger and taller Fulton, but had clearly worn himself out by the last round. Further, he lacked the punching power they believed he needed to beat Willard, let alone to beat Dempsey, should he get that far. Johnson had rained numerous blows on Fulton's jaw, which Dempsey had proved to be Fulton's weak spot. Nonetheless, Fulton had not shown any signs of weakening under Johnson's blows. Fred Fulton had a cut lip for his troubles in the 12th-round bout, but otherwise he was unmarked. His opponent seemed much worse for wear. "Johnson's eyes were discolored, his nose was bruised, his lips were cut and his body was sore and weary from the wicked smashes of Fulton, but his spirits were singularly high.

Youth had its advantages and Johnson showed two of them: Good recuperative powers and naiveté. Johnson looked forward to meeting Willard, while Fulton talked of retiring from the ring."[101]

Not only did Johnson suffer a loss of prestige, the Milk Fund suffered as well. Johnson's poor showing, even in winning, reduced the enthusiasm of the public for the Willard bout. Few people now thought he had much chance against Willard. Despite the fact that there was also a 15-round bout scheduled between Luis Angel Firpo and Jack McAuliffe II, *The New York Times*, at least, feared that the revenues for the Milk Fund would suffer. Be that as it may, Willard was content. He had no fear of either Fulton or Johnson and was pleased to get the chance to get back in the ring and demonstrate that he deserved another shot at Dempsey.[102]

While all of this was going on, Jack Kearns decided that the offer for Dempsey to fight Tommy Gibbons in Shelby, Montana, was too good to pass up. Kearns had arranged it so that all the money was to be paid upfront. He insisted that as a measure of good faith, Shelby pay Dempsey $100,000 on signing of the contract. That money was not to be refundable even if the fight should not go through. Then he insisted that the original offer of $200,000 be paid prior to Dempsey stepping into the ring. In this way, he increased Dempsey's purse from $200,000 to $300,000, all paid before Dempsey got into the ring. Thinking to squeeze more blood from this turnip, Kearns submitted the same terms to Tex Rickard in hopes that Rickard would agree to hold the bout in New York.

Rickard rejected this offer out of hand. Instead, Rickard challenged Kearns to sign instead a contact for Dempsey to fight Willard in New York or New Jersey on Labor Day. But this idea did not suit Kearns. There was too much risk getting back into the ring with Willard, whereas he saw no risk at all in fighting the light heavyweight, Tommy Gibbons, especially since Doc got his own choice of referee, Jimmy Daugherty, to manage the fight. The ineffable peace of a confidence trick well played was settling in around Doc Kearns.[103]

Returning our attention to New York City, despite early fears the battles for the Milk Fund proved very successful. As *The New York Times* reported:

> In a setting that could scarcely have been more picturesque had it been painted by a master's brush, 63,000 persons paid $390,000 to see ten of the leading heavyweight boxers of the world fight for the benefit of the Mayor's Milk Fund at Yankee Stadium yesterday afternoon. Between rainfall, sunshine and overcast skies the men battled—not only for charity but for the chance to meet Jack Dempsey in a bout for the world's heavyweight championship. Possibly no greater collection of prominent pugilists was ever assembled in one ring.... And the charity benefited to the extent of $260,000.[104]

Willard won his bout with Floyd Johnson as he expected to do. "I proved that I have come back. I am ready to meet any one selected for me and I am confident that I can go as far in the ring as I did before." He was pleased with his showing. Although he was 41 years old, he was able to absorb all of the punishment dished out by the younger man. Johnson fought in the frenetic style of Dempsey, boring in and being impervious to Willard's blows at the beginning. But as the fight continued, Willard gradually took control and by the seventh round, he was laughing with his corner men. "Time and again Willard rammed [Johnson's] head back with long, ponderous lefts. Toward the middle of the bout Willard twice sank his right hand above Johnson's heart, and the legs of he younger man gave way beneath him." Then, "just as the bell rang for the eleventh round of the bout ... the older gladiator dropped the youngster with a right hook flush to the jaw. Johnson, who had been worrying Willard as a vigorous young terrier would worry an old mastiff, dropped face downward, inert and unconscious. That ended it."[105]

Willard's victory, however, was not clean enough to place him in contention for the next fight with Dempsey. Not only were Dempsey and Kearns fully occupied with the fight in Shelby, but Tex Rickard had decided, after the Milk Fund fights, that there was one more battle to be put on before he had the challenger he wanted for Dempsey. Willard had knocked out Floyd Johnson in the 11th round of their fight and Luis Firpo had knocked out Jack McAuliffe II in the third round of their fight. Rickard saw that a fight between these two giants was a natural. Thus he announced at the end of the boxing extravaganza that he wanted to pair them together for a bout on June 30 in either the new Yankee Stadium or in Boyle's Thirty Acres.[106]

Robert Edgren had been saying for months that Willard needed to fight at least two good heavyweights before getting back into the ring with Dempsey. It looked like he was going to get his wish. William Muldoon, on the other hand, was now trapped. He had allowed Willard to fight in New York even though he was over the age limit. Furthermore, Willard had been pronounced healthy both before and after the bout by the athletic commission doctor. The public had now seen both Willard and Firpo in action and clearly wanted to see them in a bout together. But this would be the very type of bout Muldoon had dreaded: a commercial bout capable of drawing large crowds and generating large cash purses. It promised to be the kind of commercial exploitation which had led Muldoon to cancel the Dempsey-Wills bout: it would be simply too popular with the public.[107]

But Muldoon had one last trick in his bag: He had ruled that fighters could no longer have guarantees for fights in New York. They had to fight for a percentage of the gate.

And further, the fighters in any main bout could not receive more than 50 percent of the gate. The division of the gate was up to the fighters themselves.

Rickard did not anticipate any problems in getting Willard and Firpo together on these terms. Both were anxious to get a chance to fight Dempsey, and if the elimination bout would lead to a bout with Dempsey, Rickard felt assured that both would agree. Furthermore, once Dempsey had settled with Tommy Gibbons at Shelby, he would most likely be happy to fight either Willard or Firpo rather than face Harry Wills. A public which demanded a fight with the winner of this elimination bout would clearly sidetrack any enthusiasm for a Dempsey-Wills bout for some time.[108]

Firpo had impressed people at the Milk Fund boxing matches. He had demonstrated raw power by knocking out Jack McAuliffe in the third round. He possessed a powerful right hand, nearly as powerful as Dempsey, and he knew how to hit. He was not sophisticated and needed schooling, but if he could stand up to Willard, he might prove a true challenger for Dempsey.

Willard had demonstrated that he could go 11 fast-paced rounds and knock his opponent out. But he was seen to be slower and less agile than he had been in the past. Johnson had no trouble hitting Willard in their bout. But Johnson did not have enough power to damage Willard. The question was: Could Willard stand up to Firpo's punches which were much more like those of Dempsey? If he could, the sportswriters would bless his return to defeat Dempsey. But if he could not, then he should leave Dempsey alone.

The fight between Firpo and Willard was viewed as a test match. The winner of this match would fight Jack Dempsey for the title.[109]

On May 16, Jess Willard signed with Tex Rickard to fight Luis Angel Firpo for the right to meet Jack Dempsey again for the championship. Firpo signed the following week, and then went on a short trip to Cuba where he planned to put on several exhibitions. Willard traveled to California to see his family prior to going back into training for the Firpo fight.[110]

As yet, Rickard had not announced where or when the fight would take place. On May 19, William Muldoon declared that both Willard and Firpo were barred from fighting again in New York City, despite the fact that he had suggested just such a bout only two weeks before. However, the next week, the New Jersey Athletic Commission announced that they would have no objection to Willard fighting Firpo at Boyle's Thirty Acres if he could pass a physical. And it was stated that the fight might occur on July 7.[111]

In the meantime, Dempsey was having his own problems. Loy J. Molumby, Commander of the Montana American Legion, had been the driving force behind the strategy of holding Dempsey's title fight in Shelby, Montana. However, the national Commander of the American Legion refused to allow the Legion's name to be used in connection with the bout. They could not forget that Dempsey was a slacker in World War I and that he sat out the war while many brave men died in Europe.[112]

At the beginning of June, Willard left his family in Los Angeles and took the train back to New York. On the way, he stopped off in Ponca City, Oklahoma, to see his friends at the 101 Ranch. While there a flash flood caused the Chickasha River to flood its banks, marooning a large number of the employees of the ranch in their homes. Willard became a local hero by wading through the flood waters to rescue women and children from their homes: "Children of the employees of the 101 ranch were carried to safety on the broad back of the pugilist when the waters first became menacing. Then as the torrent came the ex-champion waded waist deep through the swirl to save women stranded in their homes."[113]

This was great publicity and helped to make Willard the universal favorite in his fight with Firpo.

While Willard was definitely the crowd favorite, Robert Edgren began to suggest that Willard might lose. The keys, Edgren thought, to their battle were two. (1) Firpo usually came out swinging. He began to fight in the first round. Further, he had a devastating right hand and was learning to use his left hand under the direction of Jimmy De Forest, Dempsey's former trainer. (2) Willard had a devastating uppercut, but he scarcely used it unless he was hurt. Further, Willard never went to work until the third or fourth round of a fight. This left Firpo free to take risks without fear early in the fight, as Dempsey had demonstrated.

"This is where Firpo figures as a likely winner over Willard and Jack Dempsey's most dangerous opponent in a few months. Firpo has just what Dempsey has-an intense desire to win in the shortest possible time. It is dangerous to lead at Firpo. He counters every time and throws everything into the punch."[114]

Originally Rickard planned to have the fight on July 7, but later changed it to July 12 to allow those sportswriters who planned to be present in Shelby, Montana, on July 4, time to return to New York to attend the Willard-Firpo fight. This was important. If the fight went the full 12 rounds it would have to be decided by the newspaper men, since no decision could be given in the ring. Thus, the more newspaper men present the better.[115]

At the end of June a new problem arose. Newton A.K. Bugbee, Director of the New Jersey Boxing Commission, suddenly decided that Willard needed to be examined by a physician to show that he was in good physical condition to fight. Despite the fact that Willard had fought 11 rounds the previous month with Floyd Johnson, and had been training aggressively in Yonkers for the Firpo fight, Bugbee had concerns: "I have no objection to Willard fighting in New Jersey; in fact I regard him as a particularly high type, both as a fighter and as a man. But so much has been said about his age and physical fitness that I feel he should undergo this examination before meeting a fighter of such recognized strength as Firpo."

Clearly Bugbee was influenced by Muldoon.[116]

On June 25 Willard was examined by three physicians appointed by the New Jersey Boxing Commission and pronounced "free from any physical defects." Willard responded to the verdict by saying: "The examination shows that I am not bluffing and that I am ready."[117]

Being a promoter of boxing matches was not an easy life. When the fight was good, and the crowds came, there could be great rewards. But getting to that point was very difficult. Tex Rickard knew that better than most. So far, he had overcome all the difficulties placed in his way by William Muldoon in New York. When Muldoon sought to make indoor championship boxing impractical in New York by restricting ticket prices to no more than $15 per seat, Rickard moved his bouts outdoors into the baseball stadiums. When Muldoon then determined that no man over 38 years old could box professionally in New York, Rickard took his bouts to New Jersey. When no stadium was large enough in New Jersey to hold his fights, he built one. When rumors flew that Willard was not physically fit to box, Rickard had him examined first by his own doctors and then by state doctors. Then on July 2, the New Jersey building inspectors declared that Rickard's stadium in Boyle's Thirty Acres was unsafe and could not be used for the fight on July 12. Once again Rickard sprang into action.

Promising cooperation with the New Jersey officials, Rickard said he would do whatever was needed to repair the stadium to the satisfaction of John Saul, the Commissioner of the Jersey City Building Department. "You can say for me that I always insist upon inspections and that I have great confidence in Commissioner Saul. He is a sincere, honest, conscientious man and I will abide by any decision he makes. I will comply with every requirement of the building laws and will take every precaution to safeguard those who will attend the fight."[118]

The next day, Commissioner Saul stated that his investigation had not revealed any unsafe conditions with the stadium, while Rickard said that he had authorized any repairs that were necessary to make the stadium safe. This seemed to solve this problem.[119]

The next issue Rickard faced was choosing a referee. He hoped to have Jim Jeffries referee the bout. This would bring additional publicity and solve any issues about having someone in the ring who could keep order with the big men. Although Jeffries had not been on the East coast since 1909 when he signed the contact to box Jack Johnson, and had refereed only the four-round bouts in California, he was deemed to be ideal for this bout. "Platt Adams, chief boxing inspector in New Jersey, has assured Rickard that Big Jim will have no trouble obtaining a referee's license."[120]

Having been assured that there would be no trouble getting Jeffries a license to referee, on July 6, Rickard was informed that under no circumstances could Jim Jeffries be allowed to referee in New Jersey. "The State laws of New Jersey provided that an applicant for a referee's license must have been a resident of that State for at least three years and that the law was not elastic enough to be stretched about the corpulent form of Big Jim." As a result, Harry Lewis of Newark became the referee. The same day, Willard completed his training and announced that his weight was 238, the same weight he entered the ring in Havana in 1915. Something, at least, was going right.[121]

In the meantime Jack Dempsey had defeated Tommy Gibbons in Shelby. But it took him 15 rounds of vigorous fighting to do so. The boxing world was astonished. No one had expected Gibbons to survive the first few rounds, but he had lasted 15 and had not even been knocked down. The news reports called it one of the greatest heavyweight battles in history. Dempsey found out that he was facing not a great puncher, for Tommy Gibbons could not knock Dempsey down, but one of the best boxers of all time, for Dempsey could not knock Gibbons down either. Using his shoulders and elbows, his quick reflexes to dodge Dempsey's blows, while holding on to Dempsey's left arm with a death-like grip, Gibbons made Dempsey look slow and ineffective. Dempsey, who was considered a master of time and distance, continually missed with his swings, sometimes by a foot or more. Although Dempsey won on points, ten rounds to three with two rounds even, he lost in the field of public opinion. Gibbons was the hero of the day, while Willard and Firpo each believed that they could now defeat Dempsey at his own game.[122]

While Dempsey was losing prestige in Shelby, Willard and Firpo were gaining prestige in preparation for their battle. Willard had trained down to the weight he had entered the ring in Havana. There was no flab visible, and his reflexes were quick and precise. Firpo was supremely confident, not only that he would knock out Willard, but that he would knock out Dempsey as well. The Willard-Firpo fight had taken on the excitement of a championship bout: Whoever won had a good chance to become heavyweight champion of the world.[123]

The fight was a sell-out with nearly 100,000 people showing up in Jersey City. In Argentina people were wild with excitement. The betting odds there were 2 to 1 in favor of Firpo, while they were 8 to 5 in New York. The fight was scheduled for 12 rounds, but there was to be no decision given in the ring. This meant that unless there was a knockout, the newspapers were to make the decision of who won. However, should that happen, the real winner would be Jack Dempsey. Unless one of the two giants knocked the other out, the public would not believe them ready to fight Dempsey. But if there was a knockout, the winner would be not only guaranteed a fight for the championship, but might even be favored to win after Dempsey's poor showing with Tom Gibbons.[124]

Despite the odds, Harry Wills picked Willard to win, as did W. O. McGeehan. Harry Newman of *The Chicago Daily Tribune* thought they were both losers: "Right now Dempsey,

Jess in the ring at Boyle's Thirty Acres, New Jersey, with Luis Angel Firpo, July 12, 1923. Harry Lewis, the referee, stands between them.

in our opinion, could beat that pair in the same ring without getting up a sweat. Firpo ought to beat the venerable Mr. Willard, but he is far from being ready to tackle a man like Dempsey."

Newman proved to be prescient in his analysis. Firpo, as the younger man, had everything in his favor save experience. He seemed as strong as Willard, if not stronger. "As to skill in boxing it is just about a tossup. Just a pair of plunging giants trying to get home the old smack for the count. That is probably what the whole thing will amount to when they get to shooting in Rickard's big park Thursday night." The real question was who would be able to connect with the winning blow first. Newman predicted Firpo would knock Willard out in six rounds and then would be defeated by Dempsey. He was nearly right.[125]

The crowd at Boyle's Thirty Acres near Jersey City proved to be the largest ever to attend a boxing match. It drew more than 100,000 people; at least 10,000 more than attended the Dempsey-Carpentier battle. The revenue, however, was much lower since the prices charged for the former fight ranged from $50 down to $5 per seat, whereas at the Willard-Firpo battle, the ticket prices ranged from $15 down to $1. Nonetheless, Rickard predicted that the gate would top $600,000. Rickard claimed it was the "second battle of the century," having named the Dempsey-Carpentier fight "the first battle of the century." But neither of these titles lasted. What did prove lasting was the fact that once again Rickard had attracted the cream of society and more than 2,000 women were in attendance. Tex Rickard's greatest achievement was to so popularize boxing that it became a mainstream sport. He took an outlaw sport and turned it into an activity that society women might watch without embarrassment. Under Rickard's guidance, boxing became legitimate theatre.[126]

Unlike the Milk Fund fight, where the fighters got a modest payout and the rest went to charity, here the fighters were given a percentage of the gate. Willard was to get 35 percent of the gate and Firpo 20 percent. This meant that Willard was to receive approximately $210,000 less taxes, while Firpo was to receive approximately $120,000.

This was by far the largest payout either had ever received from a boxing match.[127]

Just before the men entered the ring, the betting odds shifted to even for the fight. Mostly the bets were small ones. The major betters withdrew feeling that the fight was so even as to be a tossup. "If any wagers of size were made they were placed so quietly that the rustle of the big bills was inaudible," wrote *The New York Times*. It was estimated that $125,000 had been bet on the fight. This was typical of most Willard fights: His ability and behavior were too difficult to predict.[128]

The available fight films of the Willard-Firpo fight are disappointing. They show only one round, the eighth, and in that round they show only the preliminary action. As the newspaper reports state, the fight had basically been uneventful up to the eighth round, although it was generally acknowledged that Firpo had the better of the brawl. Living up to his nickname "the Wild Bull of the Pampas," Firpo threw himself on Willard with a variety of swings and blows, many of which missed their mark. Willard was able to check Firpo's onrush in the first rounds, but Firpo drew first blood by cutting Willard's ear in round one. Willard came back in the second round and drove Firpo to the ropes and it appeared that the fight would be a balanced one. But after round two, Willard stopped his attack and remained on the defensive.[129]

In round seven, Firpo resumed his attack and battered Willard about the head and the body. Round eight began slowly, with both men sparring across the ring from what we can see in the film. Then suddenly Firpo began a wild attack which drove Willard to the left edge of the ring and out of the range of the camera. By the time the camera was adjusted, Willard was on the floor, holding on to the ropes with one arm, and the referee, Harry Lewis, was counting over him. Willard tried to get up but ultimately failed and the fight was over. Firpo won by a knockout in round eight. As *The New York Times* put it: "Luis Angel Firpo, the man from Argentina, knocked Jess Willard back into pugilistic obscurity in the eighth round of their bout last night at the arena in Jersey City before 100,000 people, the greatest crowd that ever saw a boxing match."[130]

This victory spelled the end to Jess Willard's boxing career. He was, as *The New York Times* said, sent back into "pugilistic obscurity." He never again was able to command public attention or to enter the ring as a boxer of accomplishment. The journey which began in Oklahoma City on December 21, 1910, ended in Boyle's Thirty Acres, New Jersey, on July 12, 1923. The mighty had fallen.

Yet he went out with some style. As W.O. McGeehan noted:

> Ten years ago Willard would have knocked Luis Angel Firpo through the ropes. But tonight he was just an old gentleman.
>
> He was a gallant old gentleman though, he laughed when he was jolted by ponderous rights to the jaw; he laughed when the young man they call the Wild Bull of the Pampas jolted him in the ribs. To the last he seemed to carry the delusion that he had in Toledo that nobody could knock him out.
>
> In the fifth round Willard seemed to have the younger man baffled. From the top rim of the huge wooden saucer there came a cry of "come on, Jess." Gentlemen of forty or over took up the shout until it sounded like a college yell, the war cry of the old gentleman.

But as the famous ring announcer Joe Humphries had noticed, by the end of the seventh round his legs were gone.

> The bell rang again [for the eighth round] and the old gentleman walked out to face the inevitable. He came with a face that was ashen gray and with eyes that stared. Firpo met him with the killer instinct that tells when the prey is weakening and ready for the spring. He drove Willard into his corner, and there battered him down.
>
> As Willard sank to that moldy bit of canvas there was a cry close to the ringside of "He's quitting." Willard did not quit. He was knocked out by something more deadly than the punches. He was just an old gentleman in the act of realizing that he was an old gentleman. This probably caused him to end his ring career in an attitude of prayer.[131]

11

Final Thoughts

Jess Willard ended his boxing career when he was knocked out before 100,000 people by Luis Firpo, the Wild Bull of the Pampas. Willard had ruled for four years as the heavyweight champion. It was assumed at the time that he would never be beaten. Then, when he was beaten by Jack Dempsey, a new view was taken of Willard and he was considered a clumsy giant who did not deserve to have ever been champion. Willard fought against this new view of his abilities and came back with the idea of proving that Dempsey's victory had been an accident. But when he was beaten by Firpo, more than just his body was beaten. His reputation was destroyed as well. Now, at 41 years of age, he was just an old man. His reputation was gone. His strength was gone. He no longer had any place in boxing, save in people's memories.

Willard left Boyle's Acres, New Jersey, and returned home to Los Angeles and to his wife Hattie and his children, Zella, Frances, Jess Jr., Enid and Alan. The children were growing up. Although Jess himself had been on the road a great deal of the time, the children were not neglected. Their mother, Harriet Bailey Evans Willard, known as Hattie B., was a woman who ran the home with an iron will. She insisted that each of the children began the day with various chores which Hattie supervised. And though neither she nor Jess had graduated from high school, she insisted that the children would be good students and planned for them to graduate from college as well. All of the children attended Glendale High School, although Zella transferred out in her senior year (1926) to attend a private girls' school in Laguna.

After high school, Zella spent three years (1928–1930) at the University of Southern California, the first in her family to attend college. After USC, Zella spent nearly ten years working for the American government in Japan. It is not clear what she did there, but when World War II began, Zella was transferred back to Hawaii for the duration of the war. Following the war, on February 20, 1953, she married Lou Walthour, but had no children. Zella died in 1980.

Frances, the second child, graduated from Glendale High in 1929 and then attended UCLA, after which she became a school teacher. She married Roy Jeremiah Reding on November 23, 1938, and adopted one child, Roger, who was born in 1944. Roy Reding was a ranch manager on a large citrus ranch in the San Fernando Valley. Frances died on September 26, 2004.

Jess Jr. graduated from Glendale High in 1931 and attended Washington State University. Although he found it difficult to be named for a famous boxer, he served as an end on the football team and starred as a hurdler on the track team. Track was his main sport, although he did take up boxing while in college and continued it after college. In

Enid Willard Mace and her elder sister, Zella, in 1934.

1936 he was hired as a halfback coach for the Washington State football team. In 1941 and 1942 Jess was in the military and assigned to the 32nd infantry regiment at Fort Ord. Later he was transferred to the Army Air Force at Amarillo, Texas, where he was put in charge of physical training for the Air Force mechanics until 1945. He was then transferred to Sheppard Field at Wichita Falls, Texas, until he was mustered out at the end of the war. Jess was married in 1942 and became the father of three children: Eileen, Verda and Alan. He moved his family to West Point in the mountains of Northern California where he worked as a lumberjack until he lost a hand in a logging accident in the 1970s. He and his daughter Eileen traveled back to Kansas and visited St. Clere in the 1980s to see where his father and mother were raised. He lived until he was 101 years old and died in 2015.

Enid, the fourth of Hattie and Jess' children, was the first to get married and the first to have children. She graduated from Glendale High in 1932 and attended Glendale Junior College until she married James Mace in 1937. She had a daughter, Mary Ann, born November 5, 1938, and a son, James Willard Mace, who was born July 3, 1943. James Mace died on January 5, 1986, and his wife, Enid Adlaide, died on August 10, 2007.

Alan Willard, the youngest child, left high school early during the war and enlisted in the 10th Mountain Division at Leadville, Colorado. This was the ski division devoted to mountain warfare. Alan married in 1941 and had one son in 1947, Scott. Alan Willard died in April 2000.[1]

The success of their children was considered a great accomplishment by Hattie and Jess. Getting their children a university education had been one of their main goals when they moved to Lawrence and it remained their goal when they returned to California.

When Jess retired from the ring in 1923, he had already weathered the agricultural depression of the early 1920s. In 1924 Jess sold the last of his farm land in Kansas and invested in California real estate. In his column of December 13, 1927, Les Shippey, "The Lee Side O'LA," could describe Jess as a well-to-do real estate investor:

> Sport history is full of stories of champion pugilists who won fortunes in their heyday, squandered them and died in poverty. So if you are one of the many who have lost track of Jess Willard, you may be a little surprised to hear that Jess is now living in the Verdugo Hills, near

> Glendale. He is engaged in the real-estate business in Hollywood, and believes he is worth about $1,000,000 and expects to have still more than that to give to his five children.[2]
>
> Jess estimated that his holdings in Los Angeles County are worth about $750,000. He has lived here fourteen years and began buying property as soon as he arrived.... Willard said, "Los Angeles real estate is the safest thing I know. It's, well, it's a knockout!"[3]

Jess and Hattie were very frugal people. Instead of spending their money on parties and lavish living, they invested it in real estate. Nonetheless the Depression of 1929–1938 had a terrible effect on their investments. As he had in both his farming activities in Kansas and his oil adventures, Jess made heavy use of borrowed money in his California investments. Willard had the misfortune of being caught up in some of the most tumultuous economic times in our nation's history. He had seen farming in the period from 1915 to 1919 develop into a cornucopia of riches, only to have it vanish just as soon as he had invested heavily in land and machinery. He had invested heavily in oil lands and had struck it rich, only to see the oil boom dry up in the early 1920s. Then he had moved to California and been in the center of the great real estate boom there in Los Angeles County prior to 1929. Jess appeared to have avoided the initial disaster, when the stock market crashed in October 1929. But the crash slowly engulfed him as banks began to foreclose on all types of loans.

James Willard Mace and his wife Marilee on the dock at Lake Tahoe, 1994.

Jess had mortgaged his house at 1616 Wabasso Way in Verdugo Woodlands to build one of the first supermarkets in Southern California in 1930, near Hollywood and Vine. It was called Jess Willard's Food Department Store. It had 16,800 square feet at a time when most grocery stores were small local Mom and Pop operations. It had a large parking lot in the rear of the store of 50 × 140 feet and was scheduled to stay open day and night. The investment at the time was $330,000. As with many department stores, each of the food sections were leased out to individual proprietors who paid a percentage of their sales to Jess. The store opened on August 15, 1930, with the celebration of a Spanish fiesta. There were two

Jess standing in front of his new supermarket on the corner of Hollywood and Vine, 1930.

orchestras and vaudeville acts to attract people to the new store. All went well for about seven months until Jess got into an argument with one of his tenants, Max Bercowitz, the delicatessen dealer, and Louis Kahn, Max's partner. As a result of the argument, Willard had attempted to throw them out of the store. They sued Willard and Willard lost. The supermarket failed shortly afterward and Willard lost his house on Wabasso Way due to foreclosure.[4]

This event was typical Willard behavior. We have seen how Jess often became entangled with various lawsuits and how they seemed to have major effects on him and his family. Jess Willard was basically an honest man, but, as Joe Stone, a personal friend commented: "I believe Jess was a square dealer, but I don't believe he thought anybody else was-and that made him a tough person to do business with."[5]

Typically this attitude embroiled him in a variety of minor lawsuits. In December 1927 he got into a fight with one George Price at his real estate office which ended with Price in the hospital. On February 26, 1929, he was sued for payment of a note on which $2,232.10 was still due. In February 1932 he was in municipal court for non-payment of a check for $120. By that time Willard had to plead poverty. He said he had no property, no bank account, no stocks or bonds, no diamonds, no automobile and no radio. Further, he owed Hattie's sister, Delnah Schulman, $6000 on a loan. It was then reported that Jess was working as a bouncer in a meat market for $15 per week. He was 51 years old.[6]

At this low spot in Willard's life Hollywood cast him a lifeline. He got a bit part in a movie *The Prizefighter and the Lady* staring Myrna Loy and Max Baer. The movie

Jess with Myrna Loy and Max Baer on set of *The Prizefighter and the Lady* (1933).

focused on Max Baer who played Steve, a saloon bouncer, who rose to become a heavyweight contender. Although Primo Carnera, the giant Italian fighter, had just won the title from Jack Sharkey, the script had Baer winning the title from the champion. This was not acceptable to Carnera, nor to the Italian population which was just regaining their dreams of empire under Mussolini. As a result the script had to be rewritten to create a draw between Carnera and Baer. Jack Dempsey played himself as referee, while Willard and many other boxers filled out the cast and advised on the fight scenes, which were the most realistic up to that time. The movie was released to popular acclaim on November 10, 1933.

While Willard was not happy having to deal with Jack Dempsey again, still the fight crowd contained old friends and the movie proved a great box office success. The film was significant as well for both Carnera and Baer who were destined to meet in the ring on June 14, 1934, at Madison Square Garden and fight for the real title. Baer had taken great advantage from the many hours spent practicing in the ring with Carnera, and had learned how to fight him. As a result he was able to win an upset victory over Carnera in 11 rounds.[7]

We lose track of Willard after this event but by late September 1934 he appears as a referee in wrestling matches in Camden, New Jersey. Once back on the road, Willard had a string of jobs as a referee during 1934 and 1935. By late 1935 he had also taken up refereeing boxing matches. In Memphis he was interviewed about the current heavyweight situation: "[Joe] Louis is a cinch to beat Jimmy Braddock when they meet next summer.

He is going to give Louis a better fight than Max Baer did, but that won't be hard to do. I've seen Baer and Louis, and Louis is bound to be the greater fighter."[8]

Willard was correct in his assessment. Jimmy Braddock, the "Cinderella Man," defeated Max Baer and then lost the title to Joe Louis who held it until after World War II.

In 1939 Willard made an appearance at the All American Air Maneuvers in Miami Beach, Florida, and then at the World's Fair in Flushing Meadows, New York, where he recounted his fight with Dempsey for the crowds. While in Miami Beach on January 17, 1939, the newspapers reported that Willard had taken a job working for Jack Dempsey. In his book *Dempsey*, Jack says that Willard had approached him for a job, since he was down and out. Jack gave him a job as a liquor salesman promoting Jack Dempsey's Special Label whisky, "the whisky with a punch.

> When word got around that Willard was going to launch the whisky in an advertising campaign, the press, along with their cameras, jammed themselves into the restaurant.
>
> The ad called for Jess to walk over to the bar where the barman would say, 'Well, well, if it isn't Jess Willard! What'll you have, Jess?'
>
> 'A Jack Dempsey Special Label on the rocks, please."'
>
> We went through it several times until it sounded natural. Then came lights and action as the lenses zoomed in on Willard.
>
> "Well, well, if it isn't Jess Willard! What'll you have, Jess?"
>
> 'I'll have a Johnnie Walker Black Label on the rocks,' said Jess.[9]

As Dempsey recalled, "Jess wasn't with me for long the first time, nor was he with me long this time. But I'll say one thing for Willard-in his own unique way, he tried."[10]

Jess, like Dempsey, kept the wolf away from the door by refereeing wrestling and boxing matches. He also worked in a small circus for a time. Then during the war years he volunteered to perform in the United Services Organization (USO) and traveled some 30,000 miles giving talks and refereeing bouts for the troops in Europe and Africa. When the war ended, he returned to California. Now approaching 70 years of age, Jess took a job as a security guard in San Pedro and in Long Beach. While he had been traveling with the USO, Hattie had taken in borders at their home and then taken a job working for the Lockheed Aircraft Company in Burbank. Having been among the wealthiest Americans in his prime, Jess and Hattie nonetheless retained the virtues of their Kansas upbringing all of their lives. They exemplified the Kansas saying that "it was better to wear out than to rust out."

They now lived at 3736 Anderson Avenue in La Crescenta. Their children were all grown and had families of their own. By 1953 they had seven grandchildren who came to dinner occasionally and at Christmas. But even when surrounded by his family Jess could be a difficult person. His grandson, James Willard Mace, recalls that it was not unusual for the grandchildren to visit and to be ignored by old Jess sitting in his chair, listening intently to a muffled radio broadcasting some incomprehensible message, or reading his newspaper hour after hour, without uttering a word to the people about. At the same time, the grandchildren often found Hattie scolding Jess for one thing or another while Jess took his scolding as a young boy. Sometimes it was simply for not putting his napkin in his lap or for eating too fast. But there were two events which caused Hattie to be particularly upset with Jess.

The first was when he burned up their car. Jess was accustomed to cover the engine of the car with a blanket on cold nights. One day, he drove the car out without removing the blanket and within a short time the engine caught fire. Jess was embarrassed and Hattie was furious at him. The second was when Jess decided to rebuild the septic system at the house. It seemed that the septic system had been poorly designed and malfunctioned each year. After several years of hiring plumbers to fix it, Jess decided to dig a new system. He began digging and digging. The yard was soon a mess and, as Hattie said, he "dug a hole big enough to bury an elephant." Unfortunately, he still could not fix the septic system and had to rehire the plumbers to put it right. Eventually Hattie forgave him. Still, as their grandson, Jim Mace, said, "One could not have left the company of Jess and Hattie Willard without having appreciated their true love and togetherness."[11]

In his later years Jess was awarded many honors. He was given an award from the City of Glendale in 1951. He was made a member of the charter class of the Kansas Athletic Hall of Fame in 1961. In 1964, shortly before he died, his friend Joe Stone made a documentary film about him entitled *The Chapter on Willard.* In 2003 he was posthumously inducted into the International Boxing Hall of Fame in Canastota, New York. But there were two special events which occurred in the 1960s which brightened Willard's last years.

Willard had always wanted to obtain a copy of the film of the Jack Johnson fight which would show his knockout of Johnson. The film had been banned from the United States in 1915 and Johnson himself had difficulty getting a copy to show outside of the United States. Eventually Jimmy Jacobs, head of an organization called Turn of the Cen-

Jack Johnson and Jess Willard, circa 1944.

tury Fights obtained a copy and on March 11 and April 3, 1962, broadcast the film over CBS. Instead of being delighted that the film had finally turned up, in typical fashion, Willard filed two lawsuits totaling $1,850,000 in the Los Angeles Superior Court claiming that his rights to the film had been violated. The case dragged on for five years. On August 8, 1967, Judge Robert S. Thompson dismissed the case, and once again Willard found the courts failed him. But the recovery of the Johnson fight films demonstrated that Willard had indeed knocked Johnson out fairly and deserved his title of "the Great White Hope."

Then, in 1964, Willard unexpectedly received perhaps the greatest gift in his life. This was when Doc Kearns admitted in an article in *Sports Illustrated* that he had indeed put plaster on Dempsey's bandages before their fight in Toledo. Although Dempsey sued *Sports Illustrated,* the damage was done and Willard felt vindicated. As Joe Stone was to later say: "I'll tell you, Jess Willard was a remarkable, wonderful man. But the whole thing with Dempsey was a shadow over his life." But having Doc Kearns admit that he loaded Dempsey's gloves before the fight was a wonderful gift to Willard in the last years of his life.[12]

It is Jim Mace's belief that *The Chapter on Willard,* which Joe Stone made in 1964, was the finest film tribute to his grandfather as a boxer. Jess realized by showing the film to the newspaper men it could make them change their opinion of him. Instead of thinking him to be simply a large clumsy man, as Damon Runyon had written, they now began to realize that he was a clever and skilled boxer. Joe Stone summed it up in his advice to Jess: "What you should have had was Jack Kearns for your manager. You'd still be heavyweight champion of the world."[13] But this would not have been correct. Kearns was a con man and Jess could not abide being around such people. He had grown up with them. His first manager, John David Brock, was a con man as was his second manager, A.W. Phillips. Both of them ended up in prison. Jess refused to take on Kid McCoy as his manager in Toledo because, as he told Stone, "he couldn't be trusted."[14] But even crooks and con men have a place in this wicked world, and Jess was too honest to understand that sometimes it takes a crook to defeat a crook. There is no question that Kid McCoy might have proved to be an ideal foil to Jack Kearns

Jess and Hattie Willard on Jess' 85th birthday in 1966.

and he could have helped Jess at Toledo, but their relationship would not have lasted long.

In 1968 Jess was 86 years old and was listed in the Guinness Book of World Records as the oldest living prizefighter. Most of those he had known were now gone. Ray Archer, whom he had grown up with in Emmett, Kansas, was dead, as was Walter Monahan, his sparring partner. George "Tex" Rickard had died of complications of appendicitis in 1929. Jack Johnson had died in a car wreck in 1946. "Professor" Billy McCarney, who had managed Willard in Springfield, Missouri, during the infamous Joe Cox fight, died in 1948. George "Boer" Rodel, the "Hero of Ladysmith," had died in 1955. Luis Firpo, the "Wild Bull of the Pampas," died in Argentina in 1960 at age 67. Jack "Doc" Kearns died one month shy of his 81st birthday in 1963. Frank Moran, who had lost in his bids for the title with both Jack Johnson and Jess Willard, died in Los Angeles in 1967.

In addition to his old compatriots, Jess also outlived his own brothers. Robert who was closest to Jess in age, worked as a grocer and later as a fireman, and died in 1954. John, the next eldest, who had become a cotton farmer in Oklahoma, died in 1959. Marion, the eldest, worked in the post office in Topeka, and died in 1962. By early summer 1968, Jess began to show traces of senility. He began to see people who were not there and he failed to recognize people who were there. He had suffered a stroke on May 31, 1968, but he hung on until December 15, 1968, when he died of a congenital heart condition. He was buried in Forest Lawn Memorial Park in Glendale, California.

Hattie survived her husband of 60 years, but she too suffered a stroke on June 15, 1969. She required constant care until she died at 2 a.m. on the morning of November 25, 1970. She too was buried in Forest Lawn Memorial Park in Glendale, California.

Jess and Hattie Willard were sturdy folk. They grew up on the farm and weathered life together through some of the most difficult times in American history. They were childhood sweethearts who were married for nearly 61 years. They survived World War I, the influenza epidemic of 1917–1919, the agricultural depression following World War I, the Great Depression of 1929–1938 and World War II. They raised a family and sent all of their children, who wished to go to high school and college. Jess became the most famous man in America and heavyweight champion of the world. And, as he said, when some people tried to criticize Cassius Clay (Muhammad Ali) in his presence: "If a man's heavyweight champion, ain't that high as a man can get?"

But in many ways, he never left the farm. In one of his last conversations with Hattie before he died, he asked, "Do you think it's time to curry the horses now?"

Jess and Hattie Willard lived all-American lives. Theirs was an American success story. Like all success stories it had its ups and downs, but they were people of whom one could be proud. It has been a pleasure to share their lives and experiences.

Chapter Notes

Chapter 1

1. It is not my intention to recapitulate the vast amount of scholarship which has been devoted to the issues of slavery, segregation and the integration of the American Negro into American Society. I merely wish to draw attention to the fact that during the nineteenth century following the end of the Civil War, first during Reconstruction (1867–1877) and then through the beginning period of segregation (1877–1910), a significant change developed in the white attitude toward the Negro presence in the United States.

2. Leon F. Litwack, *North of Slavery: The Negro in the Free States, 1790–1860* (Chicago: University of Chicago Press, 1961) p. 71.

3. Alexis De Tocqueville, *Democracy in America*, ed. Harvey C. Mansfield and Delba Winthrop (Chicago: University of Chicago Press, 2000 [1835]) v. 1, p. 330.

4. Frederick Douglass, writing in the 1850s, spoke about the problem the Negro in the cities faced in competing with European migration: "Every hour sees the black man elbowed out of employment by some newly arrived emigrant whose hunger and whose color are thought to give him a better title to the place." Quoted in August Meier and Elliott Rudwick, *From Plantation to Ghetto* (New York: Hill and Wang, 1976 [1966]), p. 116.

5. After the Civil War a number of other sports initially allowed Negroes to participate. But gradually they were eliminated. Track and field competitions excluded blacks after 1879. Baseball banned black and white competition after 1890. Bicycle racing banned Negroes from competition after 1894, although it made a special exception for Marshall "Major" Taylor who won the American long-distance races in 1898, 1899 and 1900. Horse racing, which had always had Negro jockeys, banned new black riders in 1894, but allowed those already established to continue to ride. In 1875, 14 out of the 15 riders in the Kentucky Derby were blacks. After 1911, blacks were no longer allowed to ride in the Kentucky Derby. Boxing remained the sole sport in which blacks and whites could compete in public. "The period after the 1880s, when blacks were often legally and socially segregated in sport as in society, lends credence to the belief that this was the nadir of blacks in sport." John A. Lucas and Ronald A. Smith, *Saga of American Sport* (Philadelphia: Lee & Febiger, 1978), p. 267. See also *Out of the Shadows*, ed. David K. Wiggins (Fayetteville: University of Arkansas Press, 2006) and Arly Allen, "Seeking 'The Great White Hope': Heavyweight Boxing in Springfield, 1910–1912," Part I, *Missouri Historical Review*, v. 100, no. 3 (April 2006), 159–173. See also "Negroes in the World of Sport," *The Duluth Herald*, July 1, 1911, p. 11 where the author contends that "the blacks have no cause to kick on their treatment in racing and boxing. They always get a fair break and rise according to their ability." While this remained true in boxing, blacks were being phased out of horse racing at the very time this was written.

6. The Cribb-Molineaux fights were described in *The Times* of London. After the first battle, *The Times* praised Molineaux as "certainly one of the most promising pugilists that has appeared" (December 19, 1810, p. 3). After the second bout, *The Times* noted that "the Black's prowess was regarded by Crib's [sic] friends with a jealousy which excited considerable national prejudice against him ... inasmuch as the laurels of the British Champion were in danger of being wrested from him by a Baltimore man of colour" (September 30, 1811, p. 3). And quoting a Lincolnshire paper account of the second battle, *The Times* noted, "No one can say, that in this battle Molineaux had not fair play shewn him" (October 7, 1811, p. 3).

Questions have been raised about whether the first fight was a fair one. After reviewing five contemporary reports of the fight, Carl B. Cone sums up his findings: "My judgment is that Molineaux fought under unavoidable disadvantages but he 'wuz not robbed' and by a narrow margin Cribb properly retained his championship" (p. 90). Carl B. Cone, "The Molineaux-Cribb Fight, 1810: Wuz Tom Molineaux Robbed?" *Journal of Sport History* (Winter 1982), pp. 83–91.

Others have argued differently, but without citing all of the sources Cone used. Peter Radford, *The Celebrated Captain Barclay* (London: Headline Book Publishing, 2001), p. 161 even considered the fight "one of the darkest chapters in the history of British sport."

I would argue that this was far from the case. Pierce Egan, the most well-known sportswriter of the time, made a distinction between the fights in the ring and the behavior of the population outside the ring. Egan noted: "It is not meant to be urged that Molineaux had not fair play throughout the fight *in the ring*—it is well-known that he had—but the *Black* had to contend with a prejudiced multitude; the pugilistic honour of the country was at stake, and the attempts of Molineaux were viewed with jealousy, envy and disgust" (Pierce Egan, *Boxiana: Or Sketches of Ancient and Modern Pugilism from the Days of the Renowned Broughton and Slack to the Championship of Cribb* [Brighton, MA: Elibron Classics, 2006] which is reprinted from the 1830 edition. Original publication date 1812, vol. 1, p. 367). The events which occurred during the first fight, while not strictly legal, were common enough in many fights. They were not resorted to because Molineaux was either black or an American. Instead, they were part and parcel of the sport of bareknuckle fighting. What was unique was that the fair-play rules of boxing were extended to protect a black American at a time when both his color and his nationality stood against him. He was twice given a chance to challenge for the championship when it might have been very easy to have denied him that right. Instead, he was granted fair-play by boxing in a way that would not have happened in any other country or in any other environment at that time.

7. John Lardner, *White Hopes and Other Tigers* (Philadelphia: J.B. Lippincott, 1951), p. 20. For black champions in other classes save the heavyweight, see the biographies of George "Little Chocolate" Dixon (pp. 48–59), Joe Gans (pp. 79–101), "Barbados" Joe Walcott (pp. 109–128) and Aaron Brown "The Dixie Kid" (pp. 129–143) in Colleen Aycock and

Mark Scott, *The First Black Champions: Essays on Fighters of the 1800s to the 1920s* (Jefferson, NC: McFarland, 2011).

8. Michael T. Isenberg, *John L. Sullivan and His America* (Urbana: University of Illinois Press, 1994 [1988]), p. 13 and following. Tony Gee, *John L. Sullivan: Cradle to Grave* (Romford, Essex: Sporting Profiles, 1998) argues that Sullivan became the transformative figure in boxing due both to his compelling personality and to his decision to embrace the use of the Marquess of Queensberry Rules rather than the London Prize Ring Rules in fights. Gee notes that "his [Sullivan's] rushing tactics were infinitely more effective when an opponent was neither able to drop without a blow being struck nor wrestle for a throw.... Hence it was purely for his own benefit that Sullivan eschewed the traditional approach in order to box with padded fists" (p. 3). Gee further points out that "although dropping without a blow being struck was not permitted by the 'New Rules 'of 1838, nevertheless it continued to be prevalent in bareknuckle fights. However, it was much more difficult to use that strategy in a glove contest without considerably increasing the risk of disqualification" (personal correspondence, 2016).

Gee also points out that the correct spelling of the Marquess of Queensberry Rules is as above. He has not only checked this in various peerage books but also with the Marquess himself (personal correspondence, 2015).

9. Isenberg, *John L. Sullivan*, p. 27; Leslie M. Harris, *In the Shadow of Slavery: African Americans in New York City, 1626–1863* (Chicago: University of Chicago, 2003), pp. 279–288. Litwack, *North of Slavery*, pp. 162–166.

10. Isenberg, *John L. Sullivan*, p. 293.

11. Kelly Richard Nicholson, *A Man among Men* (Draper, UT: Homeward Bound Publishing, 2002), p. 109, n. 14; Adam J. Pollack, *In the Ring with James J. Jeffries* (Iowa City: Win by KO Publications, 2009), pp. 99–110; David K. Wiggins, "Peter Jackson and the Elusive Heavyweight Championship: A Black Athlete's Struggle against the Late Nineteenth Century Color-Line," *Journal of Sport History*, v. 12, no. 2 (Summer 1985), 143–168.

12. At the time the Root-Hart fight occurred on July 3, 1905, neither fighter held any world title. Marvin Hart won the vacated heavyweight title in the fight with Root. Hart then lost the title on February 23, 1906, to Tommy Burns. Dan McCaffery, *Tommy Burns: Canada's Unknown World Heavyweight Champion* (Toronto: James Lorimer & Company Ltd., 2000).

13. For the Burns-Johnson fight see Jeff Wells, *Boxing Day: The Fight That Changed the World* (Sydney: HarperSports, 1998).

14. Jack London, "Jack London Says Johnson Made a Noise like a Lullaby with His Fists as He Tucked Burns in His Little Crib in Sleepy Hollow," *New York Herald*, December 27, 1908, Section 2, p. 3 reprinted in *Jack London Reports: War Correspondence, Sports Articles, and Miscellaneous Writings* ed. King Hendricks and Irving Shepard (Garden City, NY: Doubleday, 1970), "Burns-Johnson Fight," pp. 258–264.

15. *Boxing*, October 23, 1909, quoted in Geoffrey C. Ward, *Unforgivable Blackness: The Rise and Fall of Jack Johnson* (New York: Alfred K. Knopf, 2004), pp. 164–165.

16. In his book *Jack Johnson vs. James Jeffries: The Prize Fight of the Century: Reno, Nevada, July 4, 1910* (Reno: Jack Bacon & Company, 2004), pp. 35–41, Robert Greenwood discusses the validity of Johnson's title and the issues that led Jeffries to fight Johnson.

17. "Johnson is looked on by the colored people as the pugilistic Moses." "The Great Combat," *The Indianapolis Freeman*, July 2, 1910, p. 2. Johnson was not uncomfortable in being seen as the champion of his race. "I have a romantic temperament and the idea of being the champion of an entire race would have had quite an effect on me." Jack Johnson, *My Life and Battles*, ed. and trans. Christopher Rivers (Westport, CT: Praeger, 2007), p. 93. Muhammad Ali (Cassius Clay) said that Jack Johnson was the greatest influence in his life before he discovered Islam. "He came along at a time when black people felt they had nothing to be proud of, and he made them proud," quoted in Jeff Wells, *Boxing Day: The Fight That Changed the World*, p. 232. Emily Dickinson, "Success is Counted Sweetest," *Selected Poems and Letters of Emily Dickinson*, ed. Robert N. Linscott (New York: Doubleday Anchor Books, 1959).

18. "The Prizefight," *The New York Times*, July 5, 1910, p. 12.

19. "Punch on!" *The Chicago Daily Tribune*, July 4, 1910, p. 4.

Longfellow's lines were: "Thou too, sail on, O Ship of State! / Sail on, O UNION, strong and great! / Humanity with all its fears, / With all the hopes of future years, / Is hanging breathless on thy fate!"

"For Longfellow, 'The Building of the Ship' was not merely a literal description of what he had so often observed in the shipyards of his native Portland; but it was also for him an allegory of the growth of the Union." Henry Wadsworth Longfellow Dana, "'Sail on, O Ship of State!' How Longfellow Came to Write These Lines 100 Years Ago," *Colby Library Quarterly*, series 2, no. 13 (February 1950), pp. 209–214, p. 210. These lines of the Ship of State were quoted by Abraham Lincoln and Franklin D. Roosevelt in the midst of their wars and expressed their concerns about the fate of the Union as well.

Prayers were widely offered in the Negro churches for the victory of Jack Johnson. "Prayer, silent, fervent, reiterated prayer, flowed from the lips of holy men, not that the fight might be stopped, but that Johnson might win.... [S]cores of Negro ministers through out the country, have confessed that they asked this favorable disposition of the affray at the hands of the Almighty." "Prayer in the Prize Fight," *The Colorado Statesman*, July 23, 1910, p. 4.

20. "A Word to the Black Man," *The Los Angeles Times*, July 6, 1910, quoted in Ward, *Unforgivable Blackness*, p. 216.

21. Allen, "Seeking 'The Great White Hope,'" Part 1, p. 163.

22. Lardner, *White Hopes*, p. 27; Allen, "Seeking 'The Great White Hope,'" Part 1, p. 163.

23. Billy McCarney, "Phrase 'White Hope' A Money Enchanter," *The Springfield [MO] Republican*, February 18, 1912, pt. 2, p. 1; "Carl Morris, White Man's Hope, is Boy," *The Springfield [MO] Republican*, January 15, 1911, p. 9 [Sports Section, p. 1]

24. For the Great White Fleet, see Frank Uhlig, Jr., "The Great White Fleet," *American Heritage*, v. XV, no. 2 (February 1964), pp. 31–34, 103–106.

25. Lardner, *White Hopes*, pp. 41–42.

26. "Indian from Arizona wants to be 'Hope,'" *The Winnipeg Tribune*, September 14, 1912, p. 19; Eddie Robinson, "Boxing Game due to be Elevated," *The Daily Oklahoman*, January 8, 1911, p. 8, also *Springfield [MO] Republican*, January 15, 1911, p. 9 [Sports Section, p. 1]: "Setting aside Johnson's color, while his physical and intellectual qualifications might be sufficient to fill all the requirements, his mode of living would bar him from the society."

27. "Johnson to fight Willard in Mexico," *The New York Times*, January 9, 1915, p. 9; Jack Curley, "The Promoter's Own Story: Curley Tells of His Work," *The Kansas City Post*, April 25, 1915, p. 7A.

28. Robert Edgren, "Willard Told Promoters He'd Fight Jack Johnson for a Hat, "No. 8—"Willard's Rise to the Championship," *The St. Louis Post-Dispatch*, April 26, 1915, p. 11; Jack Curley's own story is slightly different. According to him, Frazee had contacted him to see if he knew of anyone who could beat Johnson, and Curley recommended Willard. Jack Curley, "Promoter's own Story: Curley Tells of His work," *The Kansas City Post*, April 25, 1915, p. 7A.

29. Robert Edgren, "Willard Told Promoters He'd Fight Jack Johnson for a Hat, " No. 8-"Willard's Rise to the Championship," *The St. Louis Post-Dispatch*, April 26, 1915, p. 11; This contract was signed on September 15, 1914. See *Jess Willard, et al. vs Charles F. Knoblauch*, 8th Circuit Court of

Appeals, Case No. 6061, Court of Civil Appeals, El Paso, Texas, p. 11 (this case is part of case No. 890 Civil Court of Appeals, Filed April 2, 1918). Case no. 890 is found in Box No. H45 in the C.L. Sonnichsen Special Collections Department of the University of Texas at El Paso Library. Apparently the basic agreement with Johnson was for $30,000 win, lose, or draw, the same terms Tommy Burns got in Australia. In addition, Johnson was to get $2,000 in travel and training expenses and 50 percent of the fight film revenue. The syndicate however did not wish to pay Johnson all the money before the fight, so they advanced Johnson travel and training money, with the balance, in this case $29,000, to be paid when he actually got into the ring with Willard. There is always a question of trust in most boxing agreements. Curley's biggest concern was that Johnson might not show up. Johnson's biggest concern was that the promoters would cheat him Both parties reserved what trust they had until they actually had cash in hand. Jack Curley, "Promoter's own Story: Curley Tells of His work," *The Kansas City Post*, April 25, 1915, p. 7A.

30. Jess Willard entered the original contract with Johnson into evidence in the trial with Charles Knoblauch over rent. See *Jess Willard, et al. vs Charles F. Knoblauch*, 8th Circuit Court of Appeals, Case No. 6061, Court of Civil Appeals, El Paso, Texas, p. 11 (part of papers on case No. 890) filed April 2, 1918; Robert Ripley, "Jack Curley: From a Shoestring Up," *Omaha World-Herald*, April 11, 1915, p. 2.

31. Ed W. Smith, "Jess unexpectedly meets Jack Johnson," *The Marion [OH] Daily Star*, April 17, 1915, p. 8.

32. I.G. Edmonds, *The Big U: Universal in the Age of Silent Films* (South Brunswick, NJ: A. S. Barnes and Co., 1977) p. 61–62; Independent Film Stories, Imp, "The Heart Punch," *The Moving Picture World*, February 6, 1915, p. 884; "Jess Willard Makes His Debut in Motion Pictures," *The Universal Weekly*, p. 16.

33. "Willard showed his wares," *The Kansas City Times*, January 22, 1915, p. 10. Jess apparently made a short trip to Topeka at this time to see his attorney, A.E. Crane. He presented Crane with the documents concerning *The Heart Punch* and asked him to handle the financial details ("Willard Has Quiet Day with Kin," *The Topeka Daily Capital*, May 3, 1915, p. 2).

34. While in Buenos Aires, Argentina, Jack met with George "Tex" Rickard who had promoted the Reno fight with Jim Jeffries on July 4, 1910. Rickard had retired from the prizefight racket and was running one of the largest cattle ranches in the world in Paraguay, just up the river from Buenos Aires. He returned to the United States on April 9 to discover that Jack had lost the title in the bout at Havana. "'Tex' Rickard Lord over 50,000 Cattle," *The New York Times*, April 10, 1915, p. 7; Colleen Aycock and Mark Scott, *Tex Rickard: Boxing's Greatest Promoter* (Jefferson, NC: McFarland, 2012), pp. 104–115; Charles Samuels, *The Magnificent Rube: The Life and Gaudy Times of Tex Rickard* (New York: McGraw-Hill, 1957), pp. 176–179; "Would bar Jack Johnson," *The New York Times*, January 14, 1915, p. 1; "Carranza Edict to bar Johnson out of Mexico," *The Chicago Daily Tribune*, January 14, 1915, p. 9; "Carranza Will Arrest Johnson if Pugilist Gets within Reach," *The Washington Post*, February 25, 1915, p. 8; "Army Fights for Jack Johnson; Gen. Villa's Attack on Tampico," *The Washington Post*, January 27, 1915, p. 8; "Villa Aids Jack Johnson," *The Washington Post*, February 8, 1915, p. 3.

35. "Insurance for Fans Who Go to Mexico," *The Chicago Daily Tribune*, January 16, 1915, p. 9; "Villa Promises Protection to Fight Patrons," *The Chicago Daily Tribune*, January 28, 1915, p. 11).

36. "Jess Willard hires 4 trainers for big fight," *The Topeka Daily Capital*, January 24, 1915, p. 2B; "Willard at El Paso," *The Daily Oklahoman*, January 26, 1915, p. 10.

37. "Jack Johnson's Pleasant Visit to Barbados," *The Chicago Defender*, March 13, 1915, p. 4; "Jack Johnson scores Victory in Barbados," *The Chicago Defender*, March 20, 1915, p. 5; "Johnson to ride into Mexico in Aeroplane," *The Topeka Daily Capital* February 10, 1915, p. 2; "Johnson lands on Mexican Soil to Fight Willard," *The Chicago Daily Tribune*, February 19, 1915, p. 9.

38. "Jack Johnson is in Havana," *The Havana Daily Post*, February 22, 1915, p. 1; Floyd Gibbons, "Johnson found; Cuba this time." *The Chicago Daily Tribune*, February 22, 1915, p. 14; Floyd Gibbons, "Jack Johnson-Willard Battle must be postponed," *The Chicago Daily Tribune*, February 23, 1915, p. 9; "Jack Johnson appears and then he disappears," *The Los Angeles Times*, February 23, 1915, pt. III, p. 3; "Jack Johnson to Stay Here," *The Havana Daily Post*, February 24, 1915, p. 1.

39. Robert Edgren, "Johnson feared Shake-Down by Villa, if He fought at Juarez," No. 9 "Willard's Rise to the Championship," *The St Louis Post-Dispatch*. April 27, 1915, p. 17.

40. "Willard and Jones at outs," *The Los Angeles Times*, February 24, 1915, pt. 111, p. 1; "Jess Willard breaks training," *The New York Times*, February 25, 1915, p. 10.

41. *The National Police Gazette* described the Frank Moran fight as "one of the most disgraceful episodes of Johnson's career.... It was openly asserted at the time by those who were close to both principals that the results were prearranged and that Moran would have refused to go into the ring unless he had been assured and backed up by an agreement which involved the forfeiture of $30,000 that Johnson would not knock him out." "Jack Johnson's Record," *The National Police Gazette*, April 17, 1915, p. 3; "Some Facts and Comment from Realm of Sportdom," *The Washington Post*, February 9, 1915, p. 8; Grantland Rice, "The Sportlight," *The Kansas City Star*, April 1, 1915, p. 12.

42. "Stray Items of Sport Gleaned from Various Sources," *The Washington Post*, January 24, 1915, Sporting Section, p. 1; "Johnson not in Training," *The Kansas City Star*, February 20, 1915, p. 7; "Little Interest in the Fight," *The Evening Star*, Independence, Kansas, March 30, 1915, p. 2; Frank G. Menke, "Willard-Johnson to draw a Poor House," *The Milwaukee Free Press*, January 22, 1915; William Rocap, "Jack Johnson in No Condition for Grueling Battle in Ring," *The Chicago Daily Tribune*, April 1, 1915, p. 13.

43. "Curley Comes to Cuba Now," *The Havana Daily Post*, February 25, 1915, p. 1; "Juarez Fight is Now Off," *The Havana Daily Post*, February 26. 1915, p. 1; "Jack Curley is on the Ground," *The Havana Daily Post*, March, 3, 1915, p. 1; "Fight Likely in Havana," *The New York Times*, March 4, 1915, p. 10; "Fight Muddle gets Thicker Each Day," *The New York Times*, March 5, 1915, p. 10; "Boxing Camp Broken Up," *The New York Times*, March 6, 1915, p. 9; "Jess Willard is Coming Here," *The Los Angeles Times*, March 6, 1915, p. 16.

44. "Fight in Havana early in April," *The Chicago Daily Tribune*, March 7, 1915, p. B1; Jess Willard, *Here's My Story* (1967) p. 10. This is an unpublished typescript dictated by Jess Willard to John Patrick prior to Willard's death and provided to me by his grandson, James Willard Mace; "Willard off for Havana," *The New York Times*, March 12, 1915, p. 12.

45. "Untitled Article," *Illustrated Record*, March 1, 1915; "Puts Ban on Title Scrap," *The Chicago Daily Tribune*, February 28, 1915, p. B4. For the comments of Captain Cushman Albert Rice and his attitude to the race issues in Cuba, see Theresa Runstedtler, *Jack Johnson, Rebel Sojourner* (Berkeley: University of California Press, 2012), pp. 212–213; Jack Curley had concerns about Cuba as a place for the fight. He had gotten a telegram from a trusted source telling him that if Johnson went to Cuba he would be interned and sent back to the United States. This did not happen but there was some logic to it as Menocal owed his position as president to the support of the United States. Jack Curley, "Why Jack Stayed in Cuba," *The Kansas City Post*, April 27, 1915, p. 6.

46. "Cuba in Throes of Black Revolt," *The Chicago Daily Tribune*, May 23, 1912, p. 1. "Johnson barred at Havana Hotel," *The Chicago Daily Tribune*, February 25, 1915, p. 9; "Jack Johnson's Wife and White Manicure Fight," *The St. Louis Globe-Democrat*, March 26, 1915, p. 4; "Fear is felt that race trouble

may arise," *The Colorado Statesman*, April 10, 1915, p. 1; Walter St. Denis, "Jack Johnson Weighs nearly 240 and his Training Smacks of a Joke," *The St. Louis Globe-Democrat*, April 1, 1915, p. 12; "While the Cuban authorities readily granted permission for the fight [between Johnson and Willard] they will not, it is announced, sanction fights between local white and black men in the future. They say they are not concerned with foreign race problems, but they have their own to deal with." "Big Heavyweights in Cuba sized up," *The New York Times*, April 4, 1915, S. 4, p. 1.

47. "Famous Boxing Masters Here," *The Havana Daily Post*, February 2, 1915, p. 2; "Interest in Boxing Grows," *The Havana Daily Post*, February 8, 1915, p. 1; "Stadium Ready February 6th," *The Havana Daily Post*, January 16, 1915, p. 2; "President Gives Park for Stadium's Site," *The Havana Daily Post*, January 28, 1915, p. 2; "Boxing Men Leave to Bring Fine Talent to Meet in Havana Stadium," *The Havana Daily Post*, January 19, 1915, p. 2; See ad for the opening night of the Stadium on February 13, 1915, *The Havana Daily Post*, February 10, 1915, p. 2; See advertisement for a boxing carnival March 29, 30, 31, and April 1, 2, 3 in Havana Stadium, *The Havana Daily Post*, March 28,1915, p. 3.

For the early history of boxing in Cuba, see Theresa Runstedtler, *Jack Johnson, Rebel Sojourner*, pp. 203–205, 217–218; Once the Cubans became accustomed to boxing they developed a taste for it which ultimately led to state-sponsored boxing schools.

48. "Pugilists Continue to Train for Coming Bout," *The Florida Times-Union*, March 29, 1915, p. 8; same story in *New York Times*, March 30, 1915, p. 12 and *The Los Angeles Times*, March 30, 1915, p. III 2.

49. Mike Sowell mistakenly gives credit to Nellie Bly as being the first female to cover a championship bout. See Mike Sowell, "Nellie Bly's Forgotten Stunt: As the First Woman to Cover a Championship Prize Fight, She Claimed to Have Gained Rare Access to Jack Dempsey," *American Journalism*, v. 21, no. 3, pp. 55–76. For Cecilia Wright see *The Havana Daily Post*, March 9, 1915, p. 1; "Fair Woman on Manly Boxing," *The Havana Daily Post*, March 9, 1915, p. 2; "Ladies' Don'ts at the Fight," *The Havana Daily Post*, March 10, 1915, p. 1; Miss Cecilia Wright, "'Kid' Lewis Clearly Outpoints Mack in Twenty Fast Rounds," *The Havana Daily Post*, March 11, 1915, p. 2; "Miss Wright Tells of Cuba," *The Havana Daily Post*, March 14, 1915, p. 2; "Miss Wright is to See Fight," *The Havana Daily Post*, March 20, 1915, p. 2; Miss Cecilia Wright, "'Knockout' Sweeney wins over Gilbert," *The Havana Daily Post*, March 21, 1915, p. 1; G.W. Krick, "Stadium Stabs," *The Havana Daily Post*, March 26, 1915, p. 5.

50. "Johnson Doomed by Fight 'Dope,'" *The Washington Post*, March 14, 1915, p. S2; "J. Willard is 33 Years Old, Not 28, Says His Stepfather," *The Joplin News Herald*, April 7, 1915, p. 6; "Tells Willard He Should Beat Negro Champion," *The Chicago Daily Tribune*, March 14, 1915, p. B3.

51. "'Cowboy' Jess Now in Havana," *The Havana Daily Post*, March 17, 1915, p. 2; "Welcome given Willard in Cuba," *The Chicago Daily Tribune*, March 17, 1915, p. 11; "Women flock to Willard's Camp," *The New York Times*, March 25, 1915, p. 9; "Johnson and Willard draw big crowds at Havana," *The Chicago Daily Tribune*, March 25, 1915, p. 10; "Many Women Witnessed Heavyweight Workout at Havana yesterday," *The Florida Times-Union*, March 27, 1915, p. 8; "Willard in Cuba; Heralded Winner," *The Daily Oklahoman*, March 18, 1915, p. 10; "Curley Tells Why He Picks Willard to Win," *The St. Louis Globe-Democrat*, March 21, 1915, Sport Section, p. 1.

52. "Willard-Johnson fight is now set for Easter Morn," *The Springfield [MO] Republican*, March 11, 1915, p. 7; "Title Fight Postponed; Scheduled for April 5," The *Washington Post*, March 28, 1915, p. E1; "Havana's Fight Holiday," *The New York Times*, March 28, 1915, p. 11; See the letter from William E. Gonzales, the American ambassador, asking for the fight to be postponed to Monday, April 5, in *The Havana Daily Post*, March 28, 1915, p. 1.

53. "Advance Seat Sale at Havana $50,000," *The Miami Herald*, March 28, 1915, p. 10; "Jack Welsh chosen as Havana Referee," *The Chicago Daily Tribune*, March 26, 1915, p. 19.

54. "Fear of Defeat Urges Johnson to Real Labor," *The Chicago Daily Tribune*, March 21, 1915, p. B2; "Big Fighters Active in Havana Camps," *The Milwaukee Free Press*, March 27, 1915, p. 7; Ray Pearson, "Johnson Ready? That's the Question of Big Battle," *The Chicago Daily Tribune*, March 28, 1915, p. B1; "Willard has advantages over Johnson; Can he match Champion's Cleverness?" *The Washington Post*, March 28, 1915, p. E2; "Jess Willard, Surviving Hope of the White Race, Will Battle Johnson," *The Milwaukee Free Press*, March 28, 1915; "Newspaper Men here for bout," *The Havana Daily Post*, April 1, 1915, p. 2.

55. "Watch Fighters do their Stunts," *The Washington Post*, March 29, 1915, p. 8; Damon Runyon, "American Opinion Almost Stampeded to Jess Willard," *The Florida Metropolis*, April 4, 1915, p. 3D.

56. "Will not Rush Johnson, is Willard's Assertion," *The Washington Post*, March 30, 1915, p. 8; Jess Willard, *Here's My Story* (1967), p. 10. "The Contracts for the fight gave Curley the privilege of scheduling the fight for 20 rounds to 45 rounds and he set the fight at the latter number of rounds."

57. "Will not Rush Johnson, is Willard's Assertion," *The Washington Post*, March 30, 1915, p. 8.

58. I am grateful to Tony Gee, the British prize-ring historian (personal correspondence) for insisting that I pay attention to the fact that the fight was scheduled for 45 rounds as one of the key reasons Johnson lost. Although the fight did not last 45 rounds, once Johnson found that he could not defeat Willard in the shorter distance and that he had seriously under estimated Willard's staying power, he lost all hope of winning. Had the fight been for 20 rounds Johnson would have won on points according to the referee, Jack Welsh.

59. "Will not Rush Johnson, is Willard's Assertion," *The Washington Post*, March 30, 1915, p. 8.

60. "Johnson wrestles bull to celebrate his birthday," *The Topeka Daily Capital*, April 1, 1915, p. 2; "Willard wins supporters in training for fight," *The Chicago Daily Tribune*, April 2, 1915, p. 21; "Furious Snow Gale Sweeps Atlantic Coast; Halts Traffic, Causes Death and Injury," *The New York Herald*, April 4, 1915, p. 3; "Easter of Snow and Chilling Gale Blights Fashion Show; Relief To-day," *The New York Tribune*, April 4, 1915, p. 1; "Liners Race to aid Stricken Steamer," *The New York Tribune*, April 4, 1915, p. 1; "Death Toll in Atlantic Gale is probably 100, Dozen or More Vessels are Reported Wrecked," *The New York Herald*, April 5, 1915, p. 3; April 1915 Snowstorm (http://wintercenter.homstead.com/photo1915.html).

61. A British soldier compared the war to the Johnson-Willard fight.

"We're out of our old trenches and into the new ones in Neuve Chapelle. It's just like that cowboy and Jack Johnson fight." I asked him how the two were alike.

"Well, we were like the cowboy in the first part of the war and Germany was like Jack Johnson. Germany knew that if she licked us she would have to do it in the early rounds, she couldn't make a long night of it."

"Well, last winter's fighting was just like the early rounds in the cowboy- Johnson fight. Can you imagine how worried that cowboy was until he saw that Johnson was beginning to get tired? And can you imagine how happy he felt when he found out that all his blows were beginning to worry the big black fellow? Well, that was us at Neuve Chapelle. And all of us fellows who were in that fight felt like Willard must have felt about the sixteenth round."

William G. Shepherd, "'Tommy' likens War to Jess Willard's Battle at Havana," *The Oklahoma News*, April 27, 1915, p. 6.

62. Grantland Rice, "The Sportlight: The Big Fight," *The New York Tribune*, April 6, 1915, p. 12; See also *The Kansas City Star*, April 7, 1915, p. 11.

63. Jackson J. Stovall, "Can Willard return the Pugilistic Scepter to the Caucasian Race," *The Chicago Defender*, April 3, 1915, p. 7.

64. "Johnson fights M'Vey Saturday," *The Havana Daily Post*, April 2, 1915, p. 1; Jack Johnson to Box with M'Vey," *The Havana Daily Post*, April 3, 1915, p. 3; Frank Menke, "Johnson and S. M'Vey Fight a Burlesque," *The Florida Metropolis*, April 4, 1915, 3D; "Johnson-M'Vey six round bout a farce marked by clinches," *The Pueblo [CO] Chieftain*, April 4, 1915, p. 20.

65. Barry Faris, "The M'Vey Bout a Joke," *The Kansas City Star*, April 4, 1915, p. 12A

66. "The Fight in Havana," *The New York Times*, April 4, 1915, S.4, p. 1.

67. Cecilia Wright Keith, "Johnson's Wife Hit hardest by Blow that beat Husband," *The St. Louis Times*, April 7, 1915, p. 4.

68. "Jess Jr. Pulling for Dad to Win," *The Chicago Daily Tribune*, April 4, 1915, p. B1.

69. William H. Rocap, "Jack Johnson in No Condition for Grueling Battle in Ring," *The Chicago Daily Tribune*, April 1, 1915, p. 13; Willard expressed the same view to Ed W. Smith: "This is a fortune for the kids, if I can pull it off and I mean to do it. I simply can't lose and go home to them. I would almost rather die first." Ed W. Smith, "Will Fight for My Kids," *The Kansas City Post*, March 31, 1915, p. 6.

70. There is some confusion about the weather at the fight. Jess Willard remembered it was hot in the ring and said when the fight was over he wanted to get out of the sun and back in the shade. Johnson supposedly raised his arms to block out the sun while he lay on his back in the ring. On the other hand, the sportswriter for the *The National Police Gazette* reported that at the beginning of the fight "the sky was overcast, but the sun broke through at times. There was a chilly wind and overcoats were in evidence." "Willard Knocks Johnson Out," *The National Police Gazette*, April 17, 1915, p. 7. Frank G. Menke also noted, "Four hours before the men entered the ring to battle for the title the weather was partly cloudy and cool with every prospect of it being clear by 12:30 p.m. when the gong is scheduled to ring and send the men off on the first round of their fight." Frank G. Menke, "Troops to Keep Down Riots," *The Kansas City Post*, April 5, 1915, p. 5. The fight films do not show overcoats, but they do show most men wearing suitcoats and jackets as well as straw hats. According to the *Havana Daily Post*, the high temperature on April 5 was 70.7 degrees Fahrenheit and 21.5 Centigrade while the low temperature was 59 F and 15 C. There was a strong north wind of 20 miles per hour. Under these weather conditions it is hard to imagine heat or brilliant sunshine being a problem to either man. "Weather Conditions," *The Havana Daily Post*, April 6, 1915, p. 4.

71. "The Fight in Havana," *The New York Times*, April 4, 1915, S.4, p. 1; G.W. Krick, "Stadium Stabs," *The Havana Daily Post*, April 7, 1915, p. 3; "Sidelights on the Big Fight," *The St. Louis Post Dispatch*, April 5, 1915, p. 1.

72. "Willard Ascends to Top of Pugilistic Ladder by Knocking Out Johnson," *The New York Herald*, April 6, 1915, p. 3. What follows is a distillation of the many reports of the fight, including analysis based upon the fragmentary fight films.

73. "Willard Ascends to Top of Pugilistic Ladder by Knocking Out Johnson," *The New York Herald*, April 6, 1915, p. 3.

74. Willard, *Here's My Story* (1967), p. 11; "Says Willard Could have Won in Eighth," *The Omaha World-Herald*, April 14, 915, p. 9; "Kansas Cowboy Wins by Knock-out in Twenty-Sixth," *The Lawrence [KS] Daily Journal-World*, April 5, 1915, p. 1.

75. Willard, *Here's My Story* (1967), p. 11.

76. Willard, *Here's My Story* (1967), p. 11.

77. Robert Edgren, "Johnson offered to Wager $10,000 He'd Beat Willard," No. 11—"Willard's Rise to the Championship," *The St. Louis Post Dispatch*, April 30, 1915, p. 18.

78. Willard, *Here's My Story* (1967), p. 11.

79. Cecilia Wright Keith, " Johnson's Wife Hit Hardest by Blow that beat her Husband," *The St. Louis Times*, April 7, 1915, p. 4; According to *The New York Herald* reporter, in round 24, Johnson asked Tom Flanagan, his trainer, to have someone get his wife away from the ring. Flanagan asked Jack Curley who arrived just at the time Johnson was knocked out. "Willard Ascends to Top of Pugilistic Ladder by Knocking Out Johnson," *The New York Herald*, April 6, 1915, p. 4.

80. Willard, *Here's My Story* (1967), p. 11.

81. "Willard Ascends to Top of Pugilistic Ladder by Knocking Out Johnson," *The New York Herald*, April 6, 1915, p. 3.

82. Willard, *Here's My Story* (1967), p. 11.

83. Willard, *Here's My Story* (1967), p. 11–12.

84. Robert Edgren, "Cry of 'Fake' is Unfair to Negro, Edgren Declares," *The St. Louis Post-Dispatch*, April 11, 1915, p. 1S.

85. "Willard Knocks Johnson Out," *The National Police Gazette*, April 17, 1915, p. 7.

86. Robert Edgren, "Johnson offered to Wager $10,000 He'd Beat Willard," No. 11—"Willard's Rise to the Championship," *The St. Louis Post Dispatch*, April 30, 1915, p. 18.

87. Robert Edgren, "Johnson offered to Wager $10,000 He'd Beat Willard," No. 11—"Willard's Rise to the Championship," *The St. Louis Post Dispatch*, April 30, 1915, p. 18.

88. "*So passes worldly fame*." William H. Rocap, "Right to Jaw Gives Kansan Title Victory," *The Chicago Daily Tribune*, April 5, 1915, p. 11; "Cowboy Wins Battle when Jack Weakens," *The Chicago Daily Tribune*, April 6, 1915, p. 12; "Images of the Willard-Johnson Battle, from Opening Round," *The St. Louis Post Dispatch*, April 10, 1915, p. 3.

89. "Cowboy Wins Battle when Jack Weakens," *The Chicago Daily Tribune*, April 6, 1915, p. 12.

90. "Cowboy Wins Battle when Jack Weakens," *The Chicago Daily Tribune*, April 6, 1915, p. 12.

91. Robert Edgren, "Cuba Talks Only Fight," *The Kansas City Star*, April 4, 1915, p. 12A; "Cowboy Wins Battle when Jack Weakens," *The Chicago Daily Tribune*, April 6, 1915, p. 12; Roy Stockton, "Willard Deserved His Victory; No Indications that the Fight Was a Fake, Says Fistic Expert," *The St. Louis Globe-Democrat*, April 6, 1915, p. 11. Johnson had said the same thing to the *Washington Post* reporter on March 30. "I'm going to win this fight," said Johnson. " And then I'll never fight anybody again.... Nothing on earth could buy that title from me, but if Willard can beat me I'll congratulate him and be a sportsman. I won't begrudge him anything he can take from me, but he'll have to take it, and I don't think it's possible for him to do it." He then went on to explain why he would not fight other blacks for the title: "Defeat always come to a champion some time. That's why I won't fight McVey or Langford or any one after this battle with Willard is over." "Will not Rush Johnson, is Willard's assertion," *The Washington Post*, March 30, 1915, p. 8.

92. Herbert B. Swope, "Joy-Riot Follows Willard Victory; Negro Outfought," *The St. Louis Post-Dispatch*, April 6, 1915, p. 15; "Willard Ascends to Top of Pugilistic Ladder by Knocking Out Johnson," *The New York Herald*, April 6, 1915, p. 3.

93. "Johnson Wishes Jess Good Luck," *The Daily Oklahoman*, April 8, 1915, p. 8; Willard always had respect for Jack Johnson. As he said after the fight: "I want to say for Johnson that I have never fought a cleaner man. Not once did he resort to foul tactics, but on the contrary he tried always to make it a good, clean fight. He has been the most criticized champion that ever lived, but I certainly found him a 'white man' in the ring." "Right Smash to Jaw Put Johnson Out," *The Washington Post*, April 6, 1915, p. 1; Johnson, as the above example testifies, had respect and admiration for Willard as well. According to Otto Floto, "The big negro likes Willard and is always a booster for him. He regards Jess as an ideal American type of manhood." Otto Floto, "Jack's Funeral Oration," *The Kansas City Post*, April 7, 1915, p. 6; Hype Igoe, writing before the fight, quoted a veteran fighter: "Johnson's title is priceless, and if you think he isn't smart enough to know it you are sadly mistaken.... As long as he lives money will come to him every time he lifts his hands. I believe John-

son when he says he would rather die than lose the title." Igoe, "Johnson Victor, Predicts Critic," *The Chicago Daily Tribune*, April 5, 1915, p. 13; It is clear that in later life Johnson made a number of comments that he either agreed to throw the fight in order to get back in the United States, or threw the fight to get money. These comments carry no weight when compared to the comments made immediately after the fight itself. Both Johnson, and Willard after him, told the truth about their fight when interviewed shortly afterward. The further their statements are from the fight itself, the less reliable they are.

94. Grantland Rice, "The Finish," *The New York Tribune*, April 9, 1915, p. 15.

95. William H. Rocap, "Right to Jaw Gives Kansan Title Victory," *The Chicago Daily Tribune*, April 5, 1915, p. 11; Herbert B. Swope, "Joy-Riot Follows Willard Victory; Negro Outfought," *The St. Louis Post Dispatch*, April 6, 1915, p. 15; "The vast crowd that witnessed the event was insignificant when compared to the multitudes that gathered before bulletin windows all over the United States. No national election returns displayed at night ever drew such crowds as the fight bulletins did in the daytime." "White Race is Saved," *The St. Louis Globe-Democrat*, April 6, 1915, p. 8.

96. Sid C. Keener, "Thousands on streets cheer when knockout decision is received," *The St. Louis Times*, April 5, 1915, p. 3.

97. "City Joyful at News of White Hope Victory," *The New York Tribune*, April 6, 1915, p. 1.

98. "Brother Rejoices," *The Daily Oklahoman*, April 7, 1915, p. 12.

99. "Johnson Wishes Jess Good Luck," *The Daily Oklahoman*, April 8, 1915, p. 8; Robert Edgren, "Defeated Champ Says Good-by to Jess Willard," *The Los Angeles Times*, April 8, 1915, p. III1.

100. "Shatter Fences at Key West in Mad Rush to Greet Willard," *The Chicago Daily Tribune*, April 8, 1915, p. 10; Robert Edgren, "Key West Crowd First to Greet White Ring Hero," *The St. Louis Post-Dispatch*, Apr. 8, 1915, p. 14.

101. Robert Edgren, "Willard Wearied of Hand-Shaking, still Amiable," *The St. Louis Post-Dispatch*, April 9, 1915, p. 10; Edgren also reports that "at Key West a man came up to me as I stood near Jess and said: 'You fellows ought to have been there Monday, if you wanted to see a sight. Half a minute after the flash that Willard had won every nigger in town was streaking for the woods. They all expected trouble, but we only laughed at them."

102. "Willard is Hero Throughout Land," *The Daily Oklahoman*, April 9, 1915, p. 12.

103. Robert Edgren, "Will not rush Johnson is Willard's assertion," *The Washington Post*, March 30, 1915, p. 8.

104. Johnson had reason to stay in Cuba if he wished. Once he had arrived in Havana, a prominent politician urged him to become a citizen and go into Cuban politics. "He declared that by becoming a citizen Johnson would be eligible for any office in Cuba except that of senator or president and his popularity would be such that he could command the entire colored vote in any part of Cuba and would soon put such colored leaders as Congressman Campos Marquetti and Escoto Carrion into the shade." "Curley Comes to Cuba Now," *The Havana Daily Post*, February 25, 1915, p. 1; "Johnson threatens to stay in Havana," *The Daily Oklahoman*, March 19, 1915, p. 13.

105. "Jess Willard Tires of Cheering Throngs," *The Chicago Daily Tribune*, April 9, 1915, p. 15.

106. "Big Offers for Willard," *The New York Times*, April 6, 1915, p. 8; "Willard on Local Stage," *The New York Times*, April 7, 1915, p. 11.

107. "Paris Paper disputes Jess Willard's Title," *The Chicago Daily Tribune*, April 10, 1915, p. 8; Clay Moyle, *Sam Langford*, p. 289.

108. "Will Challenge Willard," *The Florida Times-Union*, April 6,1915, p. 8; "Jacksonville Policeman will Challenge Willard," *The Miami Metropolis*, April 8,1915.

109. "Willard Changes Name?" *The Chicago Daily Tribune*, April 8, 1915, p. 10.

110. "Ex-Cowboys Honor Willard," *The Washington Post*, April 6, 1915, p. 2.

111. "For Cattle Inspector," *The Daily Oklahoman*, April 7, 1915, p. 12; "Jess Willard Offered Job," *The Chicago Daily Tribune*, April 8, 1915, p. 10.

Chapter 2

1. "Champion Jess is Emmett's Hero," *The Topeka Daily Capital*, April 11, 1915, p. 2; "Myron B. Willard," 1850, 1870, 1880 Census records, in Ancestry.com; James Willard Mace, *Unpublished Life of Jess Willard*, given to me by James Willard Mace, 2003, chapter I, pp. 1–3.

2. Lynette Abitiz, "*A History of St. Clere*," A 4-H Self-Determined Project, August 2, 1991. This unpublished document is not accurate for much of the material on Jess Willard and his family, but is useful for the later history of St. Clere up to 1991. I am grateful to James Willard Mace for providing me with a copy of this paper.

3. Robert W. Baughman, *Kansas in Maps* (Topeka: Kansas State Historical Society, 1961), pp. 24–27; See also the document of the General Land Office dated August 13, 1869, in the *Half-Breed Survey*, pp. 6–8 found in the records of the Register of Deeds, Oskaloosa, Jefferson County, Kansas.

4. Rev. James M. Burke, S.J., "Early Years at St. Mary's (sic) Pottawatomie Mission," *Kansas Historical Quarterly*, v. XX, no. 7 (August 1953), pp. 501–529; Thomas P. Barr, "The Pottawatomie Baptist Manual Labor Training School," *Kansas Historical Quarterly*, v. XLIII, no. 4 (Winter 1977), pp. 377–431; Doc Maskil, "The Early History of Pottawatomie County," reprinted from *The Westmorland Recorder*, June 3, 1954; Frank W. Blackmar, "Pottawatomie County," in *Kansas: a Cyclopedia of State History* (1912), pp. 490–492; For a description of the Federal Government Pay-Day at St. Marys, see "Pottawatomie Pay-Day," *The St. Louis Daily Globe*, January 6, 1874, p. 2. Although the Pottawatomie were originally a forest tribe, after 150 years they have acclimatized and now call themselves the Prairie Band.

5. Warranty Deed No. 53, Register of Deeds Office, Pottawatomie County, Westmoreland, Kansas.

6. 4 in Block 1 in Section 10, Township 8, Range 12 in St. Clere, Warranty Deed No.373, Register of Deeds Office, Pottawatomie County, Westmoreland, Kansas.

7. Book V, page 84, October 25, 1880, Register of Deeds Office, Pottawatomie County, Westmoreland, Kansas and Book V, page 324, January 29, 1881, Register of Deeds office, Westmoreland, Kansas.

8. Myron Willard in 1880 United States Census found on Ancestry.com; Petition for Letters of Administration, 9 November 1881, Probate Court, Pottawatomie County, Westmoreland, Kansas W-78; Administrator's' Bond, Estate of M.B. Willard deceased, 9 November 1818, Probate Court, Pottawatomie County, Westmoreland, Kansas W-78; Inventory and Appraisement of the Estate of M.B. Willard in Probate Court, Pottawatomie County, 24 November 1881, Westmoreland, Kansas W-78.

9. 1900 Census of Elisha Leonard Stalker from Ancestry.com; "Wife Tells Jess' History," *The Los Angeles Times*, April 12, 1915, p. III1; Jess Willard, "*Here's My Story*" (1967), unpublished typescript supplied by James Willard Mace, pp. 1–2; "Jess was Champ Playing 'Hooky' Stepfather says," *The Topeka Daily Capital*, April 6, 1915, p. 1 and p. 3; "Jess a Handsome Giant," *The Kansas City Times*, April 7, 1915, p. 10 for Stalker's comments.

10. "Jess was Champ at Playing 'Hooky' Stepfather says," *The Topeka Daily Capital*, April 6, 1915, p. 1.

11. Jess Willard, "*Here's My Story*" [1967], p. 2; "Letter to T.J. Ryan from A.L. Bell," *The St. Marys Star*, April 22, 1915, p. 6; According to the article " County Records in Kansas Prove Age of Big Jess to be 41," *The Chicago Daily*

Tribune, January 24, 1923, p. 21, Jess was in school at least until he was 14. He attended District County School No. 45 at Aidan Township and was a student there according to a document at Holton, Kansas signed by his step father, E.L. Stalker, as clerk of the School Board on July 30, 1896.

12. "The Kansan who is Champ," *The Kansas City Times*, April 6, 1915, p. 1; On January 23, 1901, Jess' mother, then Maggie Stalker, sold 50 acres of land to John P. Speckelmire for $1,600 in order to get Jesse his inheritance so that he could buy horses. $1,600 was more than Willard's inheritance, but according to the "Guardian's petition to sell real estate," the plot of land "can not be divided without depreciating the value thereof." At the same time, since he was 19 and still a minor, Robert, his older brother, was appointed his guardian. Documents filed under W-124 in Westmoreland County Court House, Westmoreland, Kansas.

13. The pony appears in the Administrator's Bond of the Estate of M. B. Willard, dated November 4, 1881, where it is noted that "Pony called Dyke, saddle and bridle given to Marion by his father" was worth $35. It is possible that this same pony had been handed down to Jess who sold it when he was 12 years old in 1893. Administrator's Bond W-78, Westmoreland Court House, Westmoreland, Kansas. Willard, "*Here's My Story*" (1967), p. 2; "Willard Makes First Speech," *The New York Times*, April 8, 1915, p. 8; "J. Willard is 33 Years Old, Not 28, Says His Stepfather," *The Joplin News Herald*, April 7, 1915, p. 6; "Jess was Champ Playing 'Hooky' Stepfather Says," *The Topeka Daily Capital*; April 6, 1915, p. 1–2; "Emmett, Kansas, Backing Willard 'To the Limit,'" *The Topeka Daily State Journal*, June 28, 1919, p. 5; Quote in "Back to Kansas," *The St. Marys [Kansas] Star*, April 15, 1915, p. 4.

14. Ed W. Smith, "Jess has first scrap with gang of rowdies," in "How I won the title, as told by Jess Willard," No. 2, *The Marion [Ohio] Daily Star*, April 14, 1915, p. 14. The world record for the 100-yard dash in 1906 was 9.6 seconds. In the national AAU championship of 1907, P.C. Gehard won the Junior 100-yard dash in 10.4 seconds while H.J. Huff won the Senior 100-yard dash in 10.2 seconds (*The World Almanac and Encyclopedia, 1908* [New York: Press Publishing Co. New York World, 1907]). An untrained runner doing the dash in 11 seconds was extraordinary. As Jess was being timed by men with stop watches used to time horse races, it is clear that he was fast on his feet. According to one story, Willard had a standing offer of $25 to anyone who could beat him in the hundred yard dash, and this money was never claimed. "In Willard's Home Town," *The Kansas City Star*, April 6, 1915, p. 2.

15. "In Willard's Home Town," *The Kansas City Star*, April 6, 1915, p. 2.

16. "In Willard's Home Town," *The Kansas City Star*, April 6, 1915, p. 2.

17. "Champion Jess is Emmett's Hero," *The Topeka Daily Capital*, April 11, 1915, p. 2; "Wife Tells Jess' History," *The Los Angeles Times*, April 12, 1915, p. III 1;

18. "In Willard's Home Town," *The Kansas City Star*, April 6, 1915, p. 2; Kate Thomen, "Boost Jess in Emmett or Hurry Out of Town," *The Topeka Daily Capital*, June 29, 1919, p. 9B.

19. Ed W. Smith, "Jess has first scrap with gang of rowdies," in "How I won the title, as told by Jess Willard," *The Marion [Ohio] Daily Star*, April 14, 1915, p. 14; "Champion Jess is Emmett's Hero," *The Topeka Daily Capital*, April 11, 1915, p. 2; "In Willard's Home Town," *The Kansas City Star*, April 6, 1915, p. 2.

20. As mentioned above (note 12), when he was still a minor, Jess traveled to Montana, Idaho and Wyoming to buy mustangs to break for farm animals. In order to gain the funds to do this, his older brother, Robert, had to serve as his guardian and his mother had to sell fifty acres of land in order to provide Jess his inheritance from his father. See file W-124 in the Westmoreland County Court Office, Westmorland, Kansas; "J.M. Willard has a force of men busy baling hay for the market," *The Emmett Citizen* September 11, 1907; "Willard Native Jayhawker," *The Manhattan Daily Nationalist*, April 6, 1915; Kate Thomen, "Boost Jess in Emmett or Hurry Out of Town," *The Topeka Daily Capital*, June 29, 1919, p. 9B.

21. "Obituary," *The Topeka Daily Capital*, February 11, 1908, p. 8; "Deaths and Funerals," *The Topeka State Journal*, February 11, 1908, p. 5; *The Emmett Citizen*, v. 1, #41 (February 20, 1908) p. 1; "Willard-Evans"—"Jess M. Willard of Emmett and Miss Hattie B. Evans of St. Clere were married in Leavenworth, Kansas Friday March 13th. The couple have a host of friends here who wish them a long happy and prosperous life." *The Emmett Citizen* no. 45 (March 19, 1908), p. 3; Jess Willard, "*Here's My Story*" (1967), p. 3.

22. Kate Thomen, "Boost Jess in Emmett or Hurry Out of Town," *The Topeka Daily Capital*, June 29, 1919, p. 9B. In an interview after the fight in Havana, Willard remarked: "I knew Hattie Evans all my life and it seemed perfectly natural that we should become engaged when we were about 20. I was working on the same farm where she lived in Kansas. We were engaged for two years and married on March 3, 1907, at Leavenworth. That's what I call a safe, comfortable sort of romance. No other sort of romance counts." Ruth M. Byers, "Jess Willard Tells Story of Start on Road to Championship," *The Milwaukee Free Press*, April 18, 1915, Sport Section, p. 3. Jess' memory is faulty on a number of points. (1) If they were engaged for two years, they kept it to themselves. Certainly, Hattie's parents were not aware of the engagement; (2) It is unlikely that Jess worked for Barney Evans on his farm, since Evans barred him from his property, and since Evans did not think much of Jess as a workman; (3) Their marriage took place on March 13, 1908, not March 3, 1907; and (4) Jess was 26 years old and Hattie was 21 when they were married.

23. "Champion Jess is Emmett's Hero," *The Topeka Daily Capital*, April 11, 1915, p. 2; "'Jess was generally broke,' says Jim Donovan." Kate Thomen, "Boost Jess in Emmett or Hurry Out of Town," *The Topeka Daily Capital*, June 29, 1919, p. 9B; "Wife Tells Jess' History," *The Los Angeles Times*, April 12, 1915, p. III1.

24. "Neighbors 'Tell On' Jess," *The Kansas City Star*, April 7, 1915, p. 3.

25. A copy of Zella's birth certificate was provided to me by Gail Denn, County Clerk of Matagorda County, Bay City, Texas, on October 15, 2003. Interestingly, *The Emmett Citizen* noted that Jess had returned to Emmett on April 6 and visited St. Clere the following week on business. We certainly hope that he was back in Palacios in time for Zella's birth. *The Emmett Citizen*, v. 1, no. 49, p. 1 and v. 1, no. 50, p. 4 under *St. Clere News*.

26. Colleen Clayborn, *Historic Matagorda County*, v. 1 (Houston: D. Armstrong Co., 1986), pp. 367–384; "Heavyweight Champion Once Resided in Matagorda County," *The Matagorda County Tribune*, April 9, 1915, p. 8. There was a story, reported in *The Kansas City Times*, that after a brief stay in Texas, Jess returned to Topeka and applied to become a policeman. This may have occurred around April 6, as noted above in note 25. He told them that, though he had been selling land in Texas, he actually lived on a farm in Emmett. He was turned down by the police chief who said that he had to live six months in Topeka before being hired, and besides, "we are full anyway." So Willard returned to Texas. "Jess Wanted to be a Cop," *The Kansas City Times*, April 7, 1915, p. 10.

27. "Heavyweight Champion Once Resided in Matagorda County," *The Matagorda County Tribune*, April 9, 1915, p. 8.

28. Jess Willard, "*Here's My Story*," p. 3; "Can Oklahoma 'Hopes' beat J. Johnson?" *The Daily Oklahoman*, December 25, 1910, p. 8. Speaking of the cotton bale incident much later: "It's not too hard if you know how," he explained quite seriously. "You use a hand-hook" (Dave Anderson, "Jess Willard, nearing 85, is Bitter-Sweet," *The New York Times*, December 23, 1966, p. 31).

29. "Celebration Visitors Will See Willard in Pageant Every Night," *The Elk City Daily News*, April 21, 1951, p. 1.

30. Herbert B. Swope, "Dangerous for Whites Fight Ne-

groes—Willard," *The Los Angeles Times*, April 7, 1915, p. III1; "Wife Tells Jess' History," *The Los Angeles Times*, April 12, 1915, p. III1; Charles Samuels, *The Magnificent Rube: The Life and Gaudy Times of Tex Rickard* (New York: McGraw-Hill, 1957), p. 179.

31. Ed W. Smith, "The Reno fight inspires Jess to be champion," in "How I won the title," by Jess Willard as told to Ed W. Smith, *The Marion [Ohio] Daily Star*, April 15, 1915, p. 8. It is interesting to compare this comment with Jess' later statement that he had always hated boxing and that he only got into it because of the money. It seems clear from his many statements that he did not like punishing his opponents and that he did not have the "killer instinct" of some great fighters. On the other hand, he seemed to enjoy getting into the ring with men he considered his equal in size and strength. He did not enjoy fighting smaller men and indeed let them either win or let them punish him without retaliation. But he did enjoy the idea of fighting Jack Johnson and Carl Morris and others whom he felt either were his equals or deserved to be beaten. (See note 56 below.)

32. "Brock Resigns Insurance Job," *The Daily Oklahoman*, November 26, 1910, p. 8; "Union A.C. takes C.A.C. Quarters," *The Daily Oklahoman*, November 30, 1910, p. 8.

33. Willard, *"Here's My Story,"* p. 3; Ruth M. Byers, "Jess Willard Tells Story of Start on Road to Championship," *The Milwaukee Free Press*, April 18, 1915, Sport Section, p. 3.

34. Willard, *"Here's My Story,"* p. 3; Frederick E. Tarman, "Brill and Brock, Willard Finders," *The Daily Oklahoman*, April 6, 1915, pp. 1–2.

35. "Memsic to Train New Heavyweight," *The Daily Oklahoman*, December 23, 1910, p. 8.

36. Frederick E. Tarman, "Brill and Brock Willard Finders," *The Daily Oklahoman*, April 6, 1915, p. 1,13.

37. Ed W. Smith, "Reno fight inspires Jess to be a champion," in "How I won the title," by Jess Willard as told to Ed. W. Smith, *The Marion [Ohio] Daily Star*, April 15, 1915, p. 8.

38. "All's Well in Oklahoma Ring," *The Daily Oklahoman*, December 24, 1909, p. 8; Arly Allen, "Jess Willard and Carl Morris: Heavyweight Boxing in Oklahoma," *The Chronicles of Oklahoma*, v. 83, no. 4 (Winter 2005–2006), pp. 432–451; "Blue Laws for Oklahoma City," *The Daily Oklahoman*, January 13, 1911, p. 10.

39. Frank Mayo was a wrestler working out of Oklahoma City before he became Brock's trainer. "Greek Throws Mayo," *The Oklahoma City Times*, August 19, 1910, p. 8. Frank shifted to boxing by August 31. "175 pounders to Box: Entire Card made up," *The Oklahoma City Times*, August 31, 1910, p. 6.

40. Jesse McKeever, "Sport News," *The Sapulpa Evening Light*, February 15, 1911, p. 1. "Although Finke sent Willard's head back in nearly every round the blows seemed to have no telling effect and Willard was never dazed." "Willard Loses His First Bout," *The Daily Oklahoman*, February 16, 1911, p. 8; For Fink as trainer of Gene Tunney see "Officials Outline Rules for Battle," *The New York Times*, September 11, 1926, p. 11.

41. "Hope Upended in Flying Ring Time," *The Sapulpa Evening Light*, February 16, 1911, p. 1; "Willard Loses His First Bout," *The Daily Oklahoman*, February 16, 1911, p. 8.

42. "Willard Back in Harness Again," *The Daily Oklahoman*, February 19, 1911, p. 10.

43. Arly Allen, "The Early Boxing Career of Jess Willard (1910–1911)," *The Journal of the International Boxing Research Organization (IBRO)*, December 20, 2004, pp. 39–46; "Willard Meets Cavanaugh Next," *The Daily Oklahoman*, February 17, 1911, p. 8; "Willard is Back in Harness Again," *The Daily Oklahoman*, February 19, 1911, p. 10; "Sapulpans Will Support Fink," *The Daily Oklahoman*, February 21, 1911, p. 8; "Finke's Backers are in a Hurry," *The Daily Oklahoman*, February 22, 1911,p. 8.

44. Robert Ripley, "Jim Flynn's Hardest Battle," *The Buffalo Evening News*, December 11, 1913, p. 25; "Morris will take Jim Flynn Next," *The Daily Oklahoman*, December 29, 1910, p. 8; "Oklahoma City to get Big Bout," *The Daily Oklahoman*, January 5, 1911, p. 10; "Three Oklahomans in 'Hope' Class," *The Daily Oklahoman*, January 29, 1911, p. 8; "Twenty-five Thousand Dollars is paid for Control of Morris," *The Daily Oklahoman*, January 29, 1911, p. 8; "Jim Flynn Here; Expected Bout," *The Daily Oklahoman*, February 15, 1911, p. 8; "Flynn Enters His Challenge," *The Los Angeles Times*, February 16, 1911, p. III2; "Flynn Camps on Trail of Morris," *The Daily Oklahoman*, February 18, 1911, p. 8; "Flynn to Spar at U.A.C. Gymnasium," *The Daily Oklahoman*, February 19, 1911, p. 11; "Ufer is Playing for High Stakes," *The Daily Oklahoman*, April 1, 1911, p. 8; "Flynn Demands Consideration," *The Daily Oklahoman*, April 2, 1911, p. 9; Jim Flynn, "Morris no Hope says Jim Flynn," *The Daily Oklahoman*, April 6, 1911, p. 9.

45. "Fireman Jim Flynn Whips Carl Morris: Oklahoma Giant and 'White Hope' Shows No Class in Garden Fight," *The New York Times*, September 16, 1911, p. 8; "Flynn Whips Carl Morris in 10th Round," *The Evening News*, Ada, Oklahoma, September 16, 1911, p. 1.

46. "Flynn Camps on Trail of Morris," *The Daily Oklahoman*, February 18, 1911, p. 8; "Jim Flynn May Meet Willard; Once Beat Him," *The Pueblo (Colorado) Star-Journal*, April 5, 1915, p. 8; "Willard Meets Burke Tonight," *The Daily Oklahoman*, March 7, 1911, p. 8.

47. "Willard Defeats Burke in Third," *The Daily Oklahoman*, March 8, 1911, p. 8.

48. "Willard Defeats Burke in Third," *The Daily Oklahoman*, March 8, 1911, p. 8.

49. I am grateful to Tracy Callis of Cyberboxingzone.com for calling my attention to the fact that there were several men from Galveston who had the nickname "Big Six." "Big Six" Warner appears to have been a different person from "Big Six," the Negro politician, whom Jack Johnson encountered in his early career. Jack Johnson, *My Life and Battles* ed. and trans. Christopher Rivers (Westport, CT: Praeger, 2007), pp. 25–28.

50. "Willard Ducked the Big Texan," *The Shawnee Daily News*, March 14, 1911, p. 6; "Jess Willard's Feet Got Cold Last Night," *The Shawnee Daily Herald*, March 14, 1911, p. 3.

51. "Only Members to Witness Bouts," *The Daily Oklahoman*, January 17, 1911, p. 8; "Charter Granted Athletic Club," *The Daily Oklahoman*, January 25, 1911, p. 8; "Heavyweights Clash Tonight," *The Daily Oklahoman*, March 24,1911, p. 8 The legal status of boxing and prizefighting had been confused for many years. During the nineteenth century, "prize fighting" had been outlawed in the majority of the United States. In the United States "prize fighting" meant a public boxing match in which the winner (and perhaps the loser) received a prize of money. After 1750, such matches were bare-knuckle bouts fought outside "on the turf" under the London Prize Ring rules of 1838 and 1853. These rules called for "fights to the finish," that is, until one of the fighters could no longer "come up to scratch." Scratch was a line marked on the turf in the center of the ring where the fighters met at the beginning of each "round." A round ended when one or both of the fighters fell to the ground. A new round began when 30 seconds later the two fighters "came up to scratch" again. These "prize fights" were often interrupted by violence on the part of the crowd, depending on how their man was doing. Such fights could turn into riots and the fighters might be seriously injured or killed in the ring.

In contrast to such "prize fights," boxing and sparring exhibitions were generally fought with gloves and in arenas. Although they too might follow the London Prize Ring rules, by the end of the century and into the early twentieth century, most were fought under the Marquess of Queensberry rules. These rules provided for a set number of rounds with each round lasting three minutes and a one minute break between rounds. Since boxing and sparring matches were "stage fights" in arenas and often inside, they had fewer cases of crowd riots. Also, they tended to be less bloody and dangerous to the fighters. But, like "prize fights," they were both public and professional bouts with the fans paying admission and the fighters getting a reward for the fight.

52. "All's well in Oklahoma Ring," *The Daily Oklahoman*, December 24, 1909, p. 8.

53. It was easier to argue that the bouts of lightweights were "exhibitions of cleverness" than were the bouts of the heavyweights. As a result, in Oklahoma and many other states, matches between the lighter weight fighters were allowed and only heavyweight bouts were banned. As *The Daily Oklahoman* put it in an article of January 11, 1911: "The history of cities where fighting is under a ban is that boxing exhibitions between men from paper to middleweight are classed strictly as scientific boxing exhibitions, and as long as the game is clean, no opposition is made to such bouts. But it is hard to make the authorities believe that a heavyweight scrap is a scientific boxing exhibition, and these heavies have queered the game in too many towns before." "Camp Notes," *The Daily Oklahoman*, January 11, 1911, p. 8.

54. Beginning in the late 1850s in England, urban reformers recognized that young men needed some athletic outlets for their energy or else they might turn to crime. Boxing and gymnastics seemed suitable indoor urban activities into which to channel this energy. Younger members of the clergy also found that they could make converts among urban males by divesting Christianity of its soft, feminine trappings and preaching a vigorous, manly Jesus. Muscular Christianity preached that you might turn the other cheek once, but if you were hit a second time you should knock your opponent down. Thus many ministers took up boxing and encouraged boxing in gyms and chapels.

Boxing was also taken up by the members of the YMCA movement in the United States and then by athletic clubs in big cities. Beginning in 1890, first in New Orleans and then in New York, private athletic clubs were allowed to hold legal boxing bouts and exhibitions for their members, even while prizefights, which were open to the public, remained illegal. During the period from 1909 to 1911, Oklahoma had a vigorous athletic club environment with clubs in many towns such as Tulsa, Bartlesville, Muskogee and Shawnee as well as Oklahoma City. Prior to 1959 when Oklahoma finally legalized public prizefighting, these clubs provided the only outlet for boxing. However, following the election of Governor Lee Cruce in 1910, the athletic club movement went into a decline, not just in Oklahoma City, but throughout the entire state. Private athletic clubs were periodically revived, but they always led an uncertain existence. Orben J. Casey, "Governor Lee Cruce and Law Enforcement, 1911–1915," *Chronicles of Oklahoma*, v. 54, no. 4 (Winter 1976–1977), pp. 435–460.

55. "Willard Wins in Third Round," *The Daily Oklahoman*, March 25, 1911, p. 8.

56. Samuels, *The Magnificent Rube*, p. 179. As noted above (note 31) Willard was not a born fighter with a killer instinct. Still, one does not get to be world champion without some love of the sport.

57. "Willard makes full surrender," *The Daily Oklahoman*, March 28, 1911, p. 8; Oklahoma County Common Pleas Book, Docket # 2491, March 25, 1911, Book 5, p. 187.

58. "Carl Morris the Victor," *The Evening News*, Ada Oklahoma, March 29, 1911, p. 1; "Willard Really Desires Morris," *The Daily Oklahoman*, March 31, 1911, p. 8.

59. Arly Allen, "Jess Willard and Carl Morris: Heavyweight Boxing in Oklahoma," *Chronicles of Oklahoma*, v. 3, no. 4 (Winter 2005–2006), pp. 432–451, especially p. 442; In the absence of Britt, Willard was forced to spar with his former trainer, Frank Mayo, his new trainer, Patsy Corrigan, and a restaurant owner, E. A. Cruse. "Willard Leaves to Oppose Britt," *The Daily Oklahoman*, April 10, 1911, p. 3; Mandino Arrives Today for Bout," *The Daily Oklahoman*, April 13, 1911, p. 8.

60. "Willard Knocks Out Al Mandino," *The Daily Oklahoman*, April 15, 1911, p. 8. It was later reported that shortly after this fight, Mandino moved to Cleveland and changed his name to Al Williams. "Jess Willard is found by Cutler," *The Daily Oklahoman*, February 12, 1912, p. 3; "Won on the level," Edw. W. Cochrane's Column, *The Kansas City Journal*, February 15, 1913, p. 8.

61. "Warrants out for Prize Fighters," *The Daily Oklahoman*, April 16, 1911, p. 8.

62. "Referee Beats Jess Out of First Fight," "How I won the title," as told by Jess Willard to Ed. W. Smith, *The Marion [OH] Daily Star*, April 16, 1915, p. 6; John Mooney, sports editor of *The Salt Lake Tribune*, in his column "Sports Mirror" comments: "Charley Cavanaugh, who died Friday [February 10, 1950] in Ogden [Utah] fought Jess Willard in 1911 ... in recent years he had been scouting for the St. Louis Cards." John Mooney, "Sports Mirror," *The Salt Lake Tribune*, February 13, 1950, p. 14.

63. "Willard 'Wins' in Fourth Round," *The Daily Oklahoman*, May 16, 1911, p. 8.

64. Ed W. Smith, "How I won the Title," by Jess Willard, No. 9, "Good Fortune with Jess in his Fists," *The Marion [OH] Daily Star*, April 22, 1915, p. 9.

65. "Morris Finally Accepts Willard," *The Daily Oklahoman*, May 10, 1911, p. 10.

66. "Brock Leaving The Boxing Game," *The Daily Oklahoman*, May 29, 1911, p. 3; "Jury Knocks Out Boxing Contests," *The Daily Oklahoman*, June 1, 1911, p. 8; "Willard Traded for Real Estate," *The Daily Oklahoman*, June 7, 1911, p. 8. Following the trial of Jess Willard, Patsy Corrigan was put in charge of the Benevolent Athletic Association, but by the end of 1911, that club had folded. Corrigan then founded the Pastime Athletic Club which lasted until 1913. It was succeeded by the Business Men's Athletic Association in 1916. Finally, in 1919 *The Daily Oklahoman* was again calling for the creation of athletic clubs as a place where boys and men could engage in boxing and gymnastics. "Athletic Club is Needed to Boost Sports in City," *The Daily Oklahoman*, November 19, 1919, p. 12.

67. "Fistic Artists Face Indictments," *The Daily Oklahoman*, April 14, 1911, p. 8; "Fort Smith gets real Prize Fight," *The Daily Oklahoman*, August 6, 1911, p. 9.

68. "Prize Fight Will be Pulled Off Elsewhere," *The Evening News*, Ada, Oklahoma, June 21, 1911, p. 4; Orben J. Casey, "Governor Lee Cruce and Law Enforcement, 1911–1915," *Chronicles of Oklahoma*, v. 54, no. 4 (Winter 1976–1977), 435–460, especially pp. 450–451; Arly Allen, "Jess Willard and Carl Morris: Heavyweight Boxing in Oklahoma," *Chronicles of Oklahoma*, v. 3, no. 4 (Winter 2005–2006), 432–451, especially p. 445.

69. William H. Manz, "Benjamin Cardozo Meets Gunslinger Bat Masterson," *New York State Bar Association Journal* (July-August 2004), 10–17; "Fireman Jim Flynn Whips Carl Morris; Oklahoma Giant and 'White Hope' Shows no Class," *The New York Times*, September 16, 1911, p. 8.

70. "Jury Knocks Out Boxing Contests," *The Daily Oklahoman*, June 1, 1911, p. 8; Arly Allen, "Jess Willard and Carl Morris: Heavyweight Boxing in Oklahoma," *Chronicles of Oklahoma*, v. 3, no. 4 (Winter 2005–2006), 432–451, especially p. 445. Although it is easy to see that Brock was a victim as well, Willard did not see things this way. "Willard believes that J. D. Brock, at that time his manager, was responsible for his arrest; and so strongly does he believe it that he refused the invitation of the warden of the federal penitentiary at Leavenworth and a pleading letter from a representative of the prisoners to visit simply because J.D. Brock was an inmate." Brock was inmate # 9063 at the Federal Penitentiary in Leavenworth. Kansas from June 1914 until June 1924. His crime was mail fraud. "Friends may get Willard Pardon," *The Daily Oklahoman*, April 28, 1915, p. 11.

71. "Willard gets off Easy," *The Daily Oklahoman*, June 18, 1911, p. 2; "Wife Tells Jess' History," *The Los Angeles Times*, April 12, 1915, p. III1; "Locals," *The Elk City Record*, June 21, 1911, p. 6. "Intent to Develop Willard into a Champion held Ground for Dismissing $40,500 Suit," *The Daily Oklahoman*, November 19, 1915, p. 10; "Mrs. Jess Willard of Oklahoma is visiting this week with her parents, Mr. and Mrs. B. B. Evans." *The Emmett Citizen*, August 24, 1911, p. 1.

72. "'Big Lazy Jess' Willard had pronounced aversion for work in his less prosperous days," *The Trenton* [New Jersey] *Evening Times*, May 23, 1915, p. 26; This account is inaccurate in at least one area: Willard had two children at that time, Zella and Frances. Whether it is accurate in the rest of the details is unknown. According to A. Porter Hamlin of Sayre, Hattie had to testify in court in Sayre in 1911. Although the account is confused, it is possible that Hattie did make money from taking in laundry. Terry Callahan Ford, "World Champ gets boxing start in Sayre and Elk City," *The Sayre Record*, January 17, 1990, p. 8. This reference is courtesy of Bob Steere of Joplin, Missouri.

73. Ed W. Smith, "How I won the title as told by Jess Willard," no. 4, "Referee Beats Jess out of First Fight," *The Marion [OH] Daily Star*, April 16, 1915, p. 6; "Willard is Given Popular Decision," *The Daily Oklahoman*, July 5, 1911, p. 9; It seems likely that Lyon and his manager, Charles Leonhardt, came to Oklahoma as so many others did to get a fight with Carl Morris. When they were not successful, they may have gone to Oklahoma City and met with A.W. Phillips to see about a fight with Jess. Phillips apparently arranged the July 4 fight in Elk City, since Jess mentioned that Phillips had a role in doling out the finances after that fight. *The Daily Oklahoman*, July 5, 1911, p. 10. It may also be true that the sheriff was watching the fight. This would explain why Willard was so tentative in the fight. He often argued that he wanted to fight fellows his size who could give him a good battle. The fact that he did not do that in the fight with Lyon suggests that he may have been afraid of being arrested again by the sheriff. After his time as a "White Hope" Frank Lyon returned to Jacksonville and became a policeman. "Will Challenge Willard," *The Jacksonville Florida Times-Union*, April 6,1915, p. 8; "Jacksonville Policeman will Challenge Willard," *Miami Metropolis*, April 8, 1915, p. 1.

74. "Banker Might have Become a Pugilist," *The Daily Oklahoman*, April 20, 1919, p. 26.

75. In Willard's life story by Ed W. Smith, "How I won the title," Willard said that "two weeks later [after the Frank Lyon bout] I also scored a victory over Mike Comiskey in Hammon, Oklahoma, also in ten rounds." "Referee Beats Jess Out of First Fight," *The Marion [OH] Daily Star*, April 16, 1915, p. 6.

76. "A Great Success," *The Hammon News*, August 10,1911, p. 1; An advertisement for a "Sparring Exhibition between Jess Willard and Mike McKimminsky" appeared in *The Hammon News* on August 3, 1911, p. 4 Con Comiskey was a baggage handler at the Santa Fe Station on Polk Street in Chicago who weighed about 210 pounds. His manager, Larney Lichtenstein, a Chicago sportswriter, agreed to a contract with J. D. Brock for Comiskey to fight Carl Morris on December 30, 1910. But, Morris had already left Oklahoma City and Brock's management by that time. Morris was now under the management of Eddie Robinson and fought Marvin Hart instead. Brock appears to have had some further interest in matching Comiskey with Morris, but failed as others had done. Eddie Robinson then picked Comiskey up and arranged a bout with Jack Burns in Muskogee on February 28, 1911, which Comiskey won. He was back in Oklahoma in 1912 when he finally got his bout with Morris on July 11. That fight was stopped in the first round when Comiskey was knocked down and out by Morris and the Adjutant General of the Oklahoma Militia, Frank Canton, stepped in.

77. An article "Promoter now after Willard," *The Daily Oklahoman*, August 6, 1911, p. 9 gives O.H. Stacy's name and describes him as from the Knickerbocker Athletic Club of New York. A list of the licensed Athletic Clubs in New York State in 1912 shows a Knickerbocker Athletic Club at 22 Green Street, Albany but no Knickerbocker Club in New York City. *Second Annual Report of the State Athletic Commission* (Albany, NY: J. B. Lyon Company, Printers, 1912) reprinted in the *Journal of the International Boxing Research Organization (IBRO)*, #97 (March 12, 2008), pp. 71–72.

78. "Mrs. Jess Willard of Oklahoma is visiting this week with her parents Mr. and Mrs. B.B. Evans," *The Emmett Citizen*, August 24, 1911, p. 1; "Big Jess Willard worked as Farm Hand near Pueblo," *The Pueblo Chieftain*, April 6, 1915, p. 3, also same story in *The Colorado Chieftain*, April 8, 1915, p. 5; "From Dollar a Day to Chance at a Million," *The New York Herald*, April 7, 1915, p. 13.

Chapter 3

1. "Wants Fight With Cox," *The Joplin Globe*, September 23, 1911, p. 8.

2. "Launching a New Oklahoma Heavyweight," *The Daily Oklahoman*, February 19, 1911, p. 9; Arly Allen, "The Early Boxing Record of Joe Cox, the Missouri White Hope (1911)" *The Journal of the International Boxing Research Organization (IBRO)*, no. 84 (December 20, 2004), pp. 52–55.

3. "Joe Cox may be Champion of the World Some Day," *The Joplin Globe*, March 12, 1911, p. 6.

4. "Cox Fights Tonight with Oklahoman," *The Springfield Missouri Republican*, March 16, 1911, p. 5; "Joe Cox Whips Willard, Fight for 14 Rounds," *The Springfield Missouri Republican*, March 17, 1911, p. 3.

5. "Flynn Consents to take Cox as a Boxing Partner," *The Joplin Globe*, April 9, 1911, p. 4; "Joe Cox Puts Tim Hurley Out in 3 Rounds," *The Springfield Republican*, April 19, 1911, p. 7.

6. Allen, "Early Boxing Record of Joe Cox," pp. 52–55.

7. "Queen City May Produce Conqueror of Jack Johnson—Never Knocked Out," *The Cincinnati Post*, July 30, 1910, p. 6; Queen City Boy is Being Groomed to Meet Top-Notchers of his Class," *The Cincinnati Post*, August 5, 1910, p. 6.

8. John Lardner, *White Hopes and other Tigers* (Philadelphia: J.B. Lippincott, 1951), p. 41; "Joe Cox Lasted Fourteen Rounds," *The Tulsa Democrat*, May 30, 1911, p. 3.

9. Arly Allen, "Seeking 'The Great White Hope': Heavyweight Boxing in Springfield, 1910–1912," Pt. 1, *Missouri Historical Review*, no. 3 (April 2006), 159–173.

10. Billy McCarney, "Cox is Getting Known in East," *The Springfield Daily Leader*, August 30, 1911, p. 2.

11. Allen, "Seeking 'The Great White Hope,'" Pt. 1, p. 168.

12. "Wants Fight with Cox," *The Joplin Globe*, September 23, 1911, p. 8; "Title Willard's Only Reward in Havana Battle; Jess Says Phillips Destroyed Contract," *The Daily Oklahoman*, November 18, 1915, p. 12.

13. "Oklahoma Boxer in Springfield," *The Springfield Daily Leader*, September 23, 1911, p. 2; "Scraps about Scrappers," *The Springfield Missouri Republican*, September 26, 1911, p. 4.

14. "Heavyweights to Appear Thursday," *The Springfield Daily Leader*, September 25, 1911, p. 2.

15. "Fast Tryout at the Athletic Rooms," *The Springfield Daily Leader*, September 26, 1911, p. 2.

16. After he destroyed Carl Morris, Jim Flynn, the "white hope crusher" may have ended McLaglen's boxing hopes as well. "Another 'White Hope' Fades. Jim Flynn Disposes of Victor MacLachlan's Aspirations in Three Rounds in Milwaukee," *The Chicago Daily Tribune*, February 24, 1912, p. 8.

17. Arly Allen, "Seeking 'The Great White Hope'; Heavyweight Boxing in Springfield, 1910–1912," Pt. 2, *Missouri Historical Review*, no. 4 (July 2006), 212–223.

18. "Willard Admits He Quit in Fight with Cox, but says He was forced to—Comment," Edw. W. Cochrane's Column, *The Kansas City Journal*, February 15, 1913, p. 8; "Faked Once," *The Fort Wayne Daily News*, February 15, 1913, p. 12; "Jess Willard is in Town," *The Los Angeles Times*, March 29, 1913, p. III3; "Oklahoma Officer Here with Papers for Boxer," *The Springfield Daily Leader*, September 30, 1911, p. 8; "Pugilist Held to Pay Heavy Fine and Costs," *The Springfield Missouri Republican*, October 1, 1911, p. 2.

19. "Cox Matched with Willard for Next Bout," *The Springfield Missouri Republican*, October 1, 1911, p. 6.

20. "Willard Has Informal Bout with Unknown," *The Springfield Missouri Republican*, October 5, 1911, p. 2.

21. "Few Willing to Serve as Punching Bag," *The Springfield Missouri Republican*, October 6, 1911, p. 5; Allen, "Seeking 'The Great White Hope,'" Pt. 2, *Missouri Historical Review*, v. 100, no. 4 (July 2006), 212–223.

22. John D. McCallum, *The World Heavyweight Boxing Championship: A History* (Radnor, PA: Chilton Books, 1974), pp. 81–83.

23. "Willard Quits End of Fifth with Joe Cox," *The Springfield Missouri Republican*, October 10, 1911, p. 3; "Willard easily defeated by Cox," *The Springfield Daily Leader*, October 10, 1911, quoted by Robert Ripley, "The Man who Stopped Willard," *The Buffalo Evening News*, July 15, 1915, p. 19. In *The Springfield Daily Leader* article, Willard complained that he broke his hand in the fight: "I broke my hand because I could not use any tape. The gloves were too small and I couldn't get them on with tape on my hands. I could not fight with only one hand. Perhaps I could, but what's the use?"

24. Ed W. Smith, "Referee Beats Jess Out of First Fight," *The Marion [OH] Daily Star*, April 16, 1915, p. 6; Edw. W. Cochrane, "Willard Admits He Quit in Fight with Cox, but Says he was Forced to—Comment," *The Kansas City Journal*, February, 15, 1913, p. 8; "Willard Once U.S. Marshal," *The St. Louis Globe-Democrat*, April 6, 1915, p. 11; "Willard Made Many Friends as Marshal for the Government," *The St. Louis Globe-Democrat*, April 7, 1915, p. 10; Knockout, "Papke's Fight with Mantell will be of the Tryout Variety," *The Chicago Daily Tribune*, Feb. 7, 1912, p. 8; "Jess Willard is Found by Cutler," *The Daily Oklahoman*, Feb 12, 1912, p. 3; "Kansas Giant Found by Charley Cutler Said to Be Fighter of Rare Promise," *The Chicago Evening American*, February 13, 1912, p. 6.

25. "M'Farland Sure to Fight Murphy," *The Chicago Daily Tribune*, February 9, 1912, p. 12; "Packey's Manager to Hold his Job," *The Chicago Daily Tribune*, February 10, 1912, p. 10.

26. "Pederson Beats Cutler; Latter Hurt, Can't Go On," *The Chicago Evening American*, February 8, 1912, p. 9.

27. "Kansas Giant Found by Charley Cutler Said to Be Fighter of Rare Promise," *The Chicago Evening American*, February 13, 1912, p. 6.

28. TAD, "Al Palzer Now the Real 'White Hope'; Loves to Box," *The Chicago Evening American*, January 3, 1912, p. 6; "Al Palzer is Restless," *The Kansas City Star*, February. 7, 1912, p. 10.

29. "Johnson-Flynn Bout Regarded as a Joke," *The New York Times*, June 23, 1912, p. 9; "Little Interest in Champ Mills," *The Daily Oklahoman*, June 30, 1912, p. 8; "Extravagance of Mayor Depletes Funds," *The Las Vegas [NM] Daily Optic*, July 11, 1912, p. 4.

30. "Johnson Considers Willard Real 'Hope,'" *The Daily Oklahoman*, March 15, 1912, p. 8; "Condon's Con," *The Tulsa Daily World*, March 16, 1912, p. 6; "Johnson Once Said Jess Would be Champ," *The Springfield [Missouri] Daily* Leader, April 9, 1915, p. 6; Johnson also had praise for Flynn as the best of the white heavyweights, while Carl Morris and Al Palzer were given praise as well. "McGoorty Refuses to Box Champion Jack Johnson," *The Indianapolis Star*, March 16, 1912, p. 11.

31. "Jess unexpectedly meets Jack Johnson," "How I won the title," by Jess Willard as told to Ed W. Smith in *The Marion [OH] Daily Star*, April 17, 1915, p. 8; "Boxing Gossip," *The Chicago Evening American*, March 16, 1912, p. 7; "Condon's Con," *The Tulsa Daily World*, March 16, 1912, p. 6.

32. "News of the Ring," *The Chicago Evening American*, March 27, 1912, p. 6; "Sporting News Notes," *The Chicago Daily Tribune*, April 4, 1912, p. 10.

33. Ed W. Smith, "Jess unexpectedly meets Jack Johnson," *The Marion [OH] Daily Star*, April 17, 1915, p. 8.

34. Spike, "East Chicago will have another try," *The Lake County [IN] Times*, May 1, 1912, p. 3; "Police and Promoter at Loggerheads," *The Lake County Times*, May 2, 1912, p. 1; "Fight Law to get New Court Test," *The Lake County Times*, may 7, 1912, p. 3; "Fights Are Postponed," *The Lake County Times*, May 9, 1912, p. 1; "Indiana Promoter and Police Chief at War," *The Chicago Evening American*, May 9, 1912, p. 12; Spike, "East Chicago to Have Bouts Saturday," *The Lake County Times*, May 17, 1912, p. 1; Fight Lids Jammed Tightly," *The Lake County Times*, May 18, 1912,p. 1; "No Fights Saturday," *The Lake County Times*, May 20, 1912, p. 8.

35. HEK, "In the Wake of the News," *The Chicago Tribune*, October 31, 1912, p. 11; Ed W. Smith, "Get a White Hope and Be in Style, Ed Smith's Advice," *The Chicago Evening American*, May 12, 1912, p. 11; Ed W. Smith, "Human Battleships to Clash in Reinforced Indiana Ring," *The Chicago Evening American*, May 21, 1912, p. 5.

36. "Fight World is Watching Young," *The Fort Wayne News Sentinel*, May 21, 1912, p. 8; "Young is Ready for the Battle," *The Fort Wayne News Sentinel*, May 22, 1912, p. 8; "All is in Readiness for To-Night's Boxing Show; Chicago Fans Coming," *The Fort Wayne Journal Gazette*, May 22, 1912, p. 6;" Arly Allen, "The Thirteen Party and the Boxing Deaths of Luther McCarty and John "Bull" Young (May to August 1913), *The Journal of the International Boxing Research Organization (IBRO)* no. 99 (September 2008), pp. 7–15.

37. "Willard Knocks Out Young in Sixth Round; Floored Three Times; Hirsch and Mason Draw," *The Fort Wayne Journal Gazette*, May 23, 1912, p. 7.

38. "Young Will Not Give up Hoping," *The Fort Wayne News Sentinel*, May 23, 1912, p. 8.

39. There is some confusion about the spelling of Bower's last name and also his nationality. *The Chicago Record-Herald* describes him as Frank Bauer, a St. Charles, Illinois milkman, while *The Fort Wayne Journal Gazette* says Frank Bowers was a Canadian from St. Charles, Ontario. It seems clear that both papers are talking about the same man. *The Chicago Record-Herald* specifically notes that Willard and Bowers met first in St. Charles, Illinois when Willard beat Bowers in three rounds before the police intervened to stop the fight. "Gilmores Think Well of Boxer," *The Fort Wayne Sentinel*, January 22, 1913, p. 8; *The Chicago Record-Herald*, January 22, 1913, p. 13; "Packey to Leave City Today," *The Chicago Daily Tribune*, May 27, 1912, p. 7; "Pugilistic Pointers," *The Chicago Daily Tribune*, May 31, 1912, p. 9. Willard himself calls him Frank Bowers, but says their fight was on June 1, 1912, in St. Charles, Illinois. Willard, *Here's My Story* p. 5 .

40. "Willard Whips Young Again," *The Chicago Evening American*, July 3, 1912, p. 7; Prizefights had been outlawed in Chicago following a fixed fight between Joe Gans and "Terrible" Terry McGovern which had occurred at Tattersall's Gym on December 13, 1900. "They Call it a Fake," *The Chicago Daily News*, December 14, 1900, p. 6; "Tells of Fake Pact, "*The Chicago Daily News*, December 15, 1900, p. 6; "Fighting Must Stop," *The Chicago Daily News*, December 19, 1900, p. 1.

41. "White Hopes, Beware," *The Wilkes-Barre Times*, July 13, 1912, p. 11; "Willard Gets New York Trial To-Night," *The Chicago Evening American*, July 29, 1912, p. 7; "Willard has Good Record," *The Buffalo Sunday Times*, December 1, 1912, p. 79; "Real Champion is Jess Willard," *The Daily Oklahoman*, December 5, 1912, p. 8;

42. Willard, "*Here's My Story*" (1967), p. 5; Robert Edgren, "Willard First Showed Title Class in Bout with McCarty," no. 4 of "Willard's Rise to the Championship," *The St. Louis Post-Dispatch*, April 19, 1915, p. 9.

43. Robert Edgren, "Willard First Showed Title Class in Bout with McCarty," no. 4 of "Willard's Rise to the Championship," *The St. Louis Post-Dispatch*, April 19, 1915, p. 9.

44. "Spirited Bouts at Garden," *The New York Tribune*, July 30, 1912, p. 11; "Western Hope Fight Winner," *The Washington Post*, July 30, 1912, p. 8; "Jess Willard Bests Pelkey; Battle Goes Ten Rounds," *The Chicago Daily Tribune*, July 30, 1912, p. 12; Willard, "*Here's My Story*," pp. 5–6.

45. The Frawley act was named for State Senator James, J. Frawley of New York who first introduced the idea of a state athletic commission to oversee the sport of boxing. The rule about no decisions did not meet with unanimous support among the boxing community. See Ed W. Smith " No Decision Bouts Hurt Boxing Game," *The Chicago Evening*

American, September 28, 1912, p. 7; Ed W. Smith, "No-Decision Contests Tangle Up the Boxing Fans; But Few Chances Now for Titles to Shift," *The Chicago Evening American*, October 11, 1912, p. 8; "J.J. Corbett Dislikes Decisionless Bouts," *The Buffalo Evening News*, December 14, 1912, p. 10. Occasionally nobody knew who won the bout since the newspapers gave conflicting results. Mike Glover fought Jack Britton in a ten round bout at the Irving A.C. in Brooklyn on November 27, 1913. Three papers named Glover as the winner, three named Britton as the winner and the seventh declared it a draw. ("Pretty Hard to decide this Fight," *The Buffalo Evening News*, November 28, 1913, p. 18.)

46. "Fight Referee Gives Decision in a Bout," *The New York Times*, May 10, 1912, p. 12; "National Sporting Club on the Rack," *The New York Times*, May 16, 1912, p. 12; " National Club and Haley Lose License," *The New York Times*, May 18, 1912, p. 11; "Boxing Commission Sustained by Court," *The New York Times*, May 25, 1912, p. 14; "Boxing Commission Reinstates a Referee," *The Chicago Evening American*, June 6, 1912, 9.

47. "Biggest Boxers in Business to Battle," *The Chicago Evening American*, August 15, 1912, p. 6; "McCarthy Going to Take on Willard This Week," *The Duluth News-Tribune*, August 18, 1912, p. 2; *The New York Times*, August 19, 1912, p. 7 in an article entitled "All-Star Boxing Shows," incorrectly describes this as a bout between McCarty and Arthur Pelkey.

48. "Willard is to Meet M'Carty," *The Daily Oklahoman*, August 19, 1912, p. 3; Ed W. Smith, "N.Y. Thinks M'Carthy [sic] is a Game Man," *The Chicago Evening American*, August 19, 1912, p. 6; Later, in 1915, a myth developed that Frank Lyon (whom Willard fought in Elk City in 1911) was in actuality the boxer Luther McCarty. According to this myth, McCarty tore into Willard at the opening of the bout and Willard refused to fight back. By the close of the third round, A.W. Phillips, who was at ringside, told Willard that he would have to fight or he would "be filled full of holes about the size of a .45 caliber Colts." Willard said that he didn't want to fight because he was afraid that the sheriff, who was standing nearby, would arrest him. Phillips assured him that the sheriff would not and that he should tear into McCarty. This he did, and knocked his opponent through the ropes twice in the fourth round. From then on it was Willard's fight. As attractive as this story is, it is a myth. The newspaper articles from Florida, from 1915, prove that Frank Laznicka, fighting under the name of Lyon, was the man Willard fought in Elk City. Further, McCarty was boxing in Fargo, North Dakota on July 4, 1911.

49. "Few Regrets over Johnson's Defeat," *The New York Herald*, April 7, 1915, p. 13.

50. Robert Edgren, "Willard First Showed Title Class in Bout with McCarty," no. 4 of "Willard's Rise to the Championship," *The St. Louis Post-Dispatch*, April 19, 1915, p. 9. Edgren himself was personally at the Willard-McCarty fight.

51. "Willard Winner of Garden Bout," *The New York Times*, August 20, 1912, p. 7; "Madden an Easy Victim," *The New York Tribune*, August 20, 1912, p. 10; "Willard Stood Off Luther M'Carty," *The Trenton Evening Times*, August 20, 1912, p. 13; "Jeannette Wins in Second; Willard Bests McCarty," *The Chicago Evening American*, Aug. 21, 1912, p. 6; "Willard Whips Morris' Jinks," *The Daily Oklahoman*, August 21, 1912, p. 6; "M'Carty Battles Willard to Draw," *The Chicago Daily Tribune*, August 20, 1912, p. 13.

52. "Palzer may meet Willard," *The Washington Post*, September 1, 1912, p. S3; "Palzer Again with O'Rouke," *The Washington Post*, October 22, 1915, p. 8; "'Al' Palzer sues State Boxing Head," *The New York Times*, October 25, 1912, p. 20; "Palzer to Box Flynn or McCarty," *The New York Times*, November 27, 1912, p. 11.

53. "Today's Sporting Events," *The Chicago Tribune*, September 2, 1912, p. 12; "Bouts This Week," *The Duluth News-Tribune*, October 27, 1912, p. 10; Ed W. Smith, "Tough Sledding for Willard in New York," *The Marion [OH] Daily Star*, April 19, 1915,p. 8.

54. "Johnson-Flynn Bout Regarded as a Joke," *The New York Times*, June 23, 1912, p. C9; London Prize Ring Rules of 1838, no. 13: "That butting with the head shall be deemed foul, and the party resorting to this practice shall be deemed to have lost the battle." From Cyberboxingzone.com. For a video of this fight, see YouTube. For the Las Vegas fight see David Kammer, "TKO in Las Vegas: Boosterism and the Johnson-Flynn Fight," *The New Mexico Historical Review* 1986 61(4): 301–318 and Raymond Wilson," Another White Hope Bites the Dust: The Jack Johnson-Jim Flynn Heavyweight Fight in 1912," *Montana: The Magazine of Western History* 1979 29 (1): 30–39.

55. "Johnson's Actions Become Tiresome," *The New York Times*, February 11, 1912, p. C2; "Big Fights To Be Held in the Garden," *The New York Times*, April 11, 1912, p. 8 "Masons Reject Johnson," *The New York Times*, April 10, 1912, p. 4; "Masons Discipline Lodge," *The New York Times*, April 12, 1912, p. C4; " Jack Johnson Indicted," *The New York Times*, June 22, 1912, p. 10.

56. Although Johnson's liaisons with local girls was kept out of *The Las Vegas Optic* at the time, Manuel Alcon describes how Enriques Sosa, a local photographer, made quite a bit of money selling photographs of Johnson with various local white girls. "After the fight Mr. Sosa kept on making money with his negatives which at this time were printed on glass. He sold a copy to one of the girl's brother for $5 and the boy thought it was the only negative left, so he gladly paid the $5 and left. The first rock he encountered he used as a tool to break the negative to pieces. But Mr. Sosa, a good businessman, had kept copies of them. The idea of getting rid of the negatives was to save embarrassment to the girl's families." For a picture of Johnson in the middle of a crowd with his arms around two white girls in front of the Butler Hotel in Mora, New Mexico see Manuel Alcon, Lo de Mora (Victoria, BC, Canada: Trafford Publishing, 2005), p. 27.

57. "Deep down, it appears, the best boxer in history wanted to be white, yet he hated the white world." Joseph Dorinson, "Black Heroes in Sport: From Jack Johnson to Muhammad Ali," *Journal of Popular Culture*, v. 31, no. 3 (Winter 1997), pp. 115–135, on p. 118. Dorinson's analysis is inexact. Johnson did not hate the white world. He envied it. This is why he did everything he could to become a part of it. What he hated was the fact that despite his best efforts, white society rejected him. The feeling that by winning the heavyweight championship and the money that went with it, a black fighter might become white was not unique to Johnson. As Larry Holmes, heavyweight champion (1978–1985) was to say, "It's hard being black. You ever been black? I was black once—when I was poor." Quoted by Joyce Carol Oates, "On Boxing," *The New York Times Magazine*, June 16, 1985, p. 31.

As indicative of Johnson's desire to achieve acceptance in white society he tied to model himself on Philadelphia Jack O'Brien (Joseph Francis Aloysius Hagan) whom Jack described as "a born gentleman." O'Brien was no more a "born gentleman" than Jack, having come up from poverty just like Jack. But O'Brien had made good in the center of Philadelphia society. It seems clear from his French memoir, that Johnson not only envied O'Brien but sought to replicate his success. And just like Larry Holmes, Johnson seemed to feel that money was the key to being accepted into society. (See "The Boxer as Man of the World" in Jack Johnson, *My Life and Battles*, ed. and trans. Christopher Rivers [Westport, CT: Praeger Publishers, 2007], pp. 79–83).

58. "Wife of Champion a Suicide," *The Chicago Evening American*, September 12, 1912, p. 1; Harold C. McGrath, "In the World of Sport," *The [Indianapolis] Freeman*, September 21, 1912, p. 7.

59. Geoffrey C. Ward, *Unforgivable Blackness: The Rise and Fall of Jack Johnson* (New York: Alfred A. Knopf, 2004), p. 287.

60. "Pugilist Weeps at Inquest," *The Chicago Evening American*, September 12, 1912, p. 1; "Mrs. Etta Duryea-Johnson Laid

to rest in Graceland Cemetery"; *The [Chicago] Broadax*, September 21, 1912, p. 1; "If My Daughter's Suicide Would Only Warn Other White Girls," Says Mother of Johnson's Dead Wife," *The Buffalo Evening News*, October 24, 1912, p. 19.

61. Cary B. Lewis, "Jack Johnson in Bad!" *The [Indianapolis] Freeman*," October 26, 1912, pp. 1 and 4; "Kidnapping Warrant for Jack Johnson," *The Chicago Evening American*, October 18, 1912, p. 1; "Jack Johnson Attacked; Heavy Bottle Thrown," *The Chicago Evening American*, October 19, 1912, p. 1; "J. Johnson Hides; New Arrests," *The Chicago Evening American*, October 21, 1912, p. 1; "J. Johnson's Café Raided by the U.S.," *The Chicago Evening American*, October 21, 1912, p. 1 [Night Extra Editon]; "Negroes Call on Johnson to Quit Chicago," *The Chicago Evening American*, October 22, 1912, p. 1 [Afternoon Edition]; "Johnson Denies Gilt [sic]," *The [Indianapolis] Freeman*, November 2, 1912,p. 1; "Negro Was Shot in Leg say U.S. Men," *The Chicago Evening American*, October 22, 1912, p. 1 [3rd One O'Clock Edition]; " 'I Never Shot Jack Johnson, Daily Papers Lied on Me.' Says Mrs. Ada Banks-Davis," *The Chicago Defender*, November 2, 1912, p. 1; "Closed Doors for Johnson," *The Chicago Evening American*, October 23, 1912, p. 6; "British Hostility to Jack Johnson," *The Buffalo Evening News*, October 24, 1912, p. 18; "Champion's Brother helps U.S. in War on Black Fighter, "*The Chicago Evening American*, October 23, 1912, p. 1 [10th Edition]; "Pugilist is Sued as Love Pirate," *The Chicago Evening American*, October 23, 1912, p. 1 [Late Night Special]; "Johnson Arrested as White Slaver," *The Chicago Evening American*, November 8, 1912, p. 1 [Home Edition]

62. Harry Carr, "No Black Man May Fight for Heavyweight Belt," *The Los Angeles Times*, January 1, 1913, pt. III, p. 3; Ward, *Unforgivable Blackness*, pp. 299–311.

63. Ray C. Pearson, "White Champion Promoters' Hope," *The Chicago Tribune*, December 19, 1912, p. C1; the same view was also found in the Negro newspapers. See "The Passing of Champ Johnson," *The [Indianapolis] Freeman*, November 9, 1912, p. 7.

64. According to *The Washington Post*, Billy McCarney had been quoted in a San Francisco paper as telling McCarey "I consider Smith a much tougher proposition than Palzer, and I do not care to send Luther against him just at this time, but if you can get Palzer for us we will take him on and then if we whip him why McCarty will be ready to meet Smith within two weeks thereafter. I have a reason for not wishing to box Smith just at this time." "'White Hopes' Fight," *The Washington Post*, December 22, 1912, p. S3; "Willard looks Best of All Heavyweights," *The Daily Oklahoman*, December 29, 1912, p. 8. This article selects four heavyweights for the possible title: Luther McCarty, Al Palzer, Jess Willard and Edward "Gunboat" Smith. It also gives a nod to Carl Morris, although noting that Morris had lost to both Flynn and McCarty.

65. "Cutler Again After Mat Stars," *The Chicago Evening American*, August 27, 1912, p. 7; "Cutler May Work in Mat Show set for Monday," *The Chicago Evening American*, September 26, 1912, p. 6; "All Star Card at Globe; Cutler Takes on Vincent," *The Chicago Evening American*, November 15, 1912, p. 6; "Wrestler Cutler Downed Managoff," *The Buffalo Evening News*, Nov. 21, 1912, p. 19; "Cutler Predicts Two Falls in Sixty Minutes," *The Chicago Evening American*, December 9, 1912, p. 6; "Ad Wolgast Wants to Try a Ring Comeback," *The Los Angeles Times*, May 5, 1918, pt. VII, p. 2. Willard was not the only heavyweight to suffer a drought at this time. Al Plazer also had troubles with his manager, Tom O'Rourke, and was so discouraged with the lack of bouts that he planned to retire to Iowa. "Palzer will quit the Ring," *The Chicago Evening American*, October 3, 1912, p. 7.

66. "Sailor White Forgot to Bring his Sea Legs," *The Buffalo Evening Times*, December 3, 1912, p. 12.

67. "Real Champion is Jess Willard," *The Daily Oklahoman*, December 5, 1912, p. 8; "Man who beat Luther M'Carthy is here in Buffalo," *The Buffalo Evening Times*, December 11, 1912, p. 16; "Trying to Match Willard and O.R. Davis," *The Buffalo Evening Times*, December. 13, 1912,p. 18; Knockout, "J. Willard Seeks Pugilistic Title," *The Chicago Tribune*, December 19,1912, p. 16; Knockout, "Willard Shows Good Form in Bout with Marty Cutler," *The Chicago Tribune*, December 20, 1912, p. 18; "Jess Willard Still Ranks High Among Promising List of 'Hopes,'" *The Boston Journal*, December 20, 1912, p. 9; "Soldier Kearns Out in the Eighth Round," *The New York Times*, December 28, 1912, p. 8; "See Champ in Willard; Stops Kearns in Eighth," *The Chicago Evening American*, December 30, 1912, p. 7.

68. "Willard Puts Kearns Away," *The Washington Post*, December 28, 1912,p. 8; "Willard Puts Kearns Away," *The Los Angeles Times*, December 28, 1912, pt. II p. 10; see also Robert Edgren, "Willard Forced to Box for Starvation Purses at Start," no. 5, "Willard's Rise to the Championship," *The St. Louis Post-Dispatch*, April 20, 1915, p. 17.

69. "Soldier Kearns Out in the Eighth Round," *The New York Times*, December 28, 1912, p. 8.

70. "Chicago Surprised at Jess Willard," *The Daily Oklahoman*, December 12, 1912, p. 13.

71. "Bob Fitzsimmons Picks Willard as Next Champ," *The Chicago Evening American*, January 17, 1913, p. 7.

72. "Daily is given sound thrashing by O.R. Davis," *The Buffalo Evening Times*, January 2, 1913, p. 12.

Chapter 4

1. Ray C. Pearson, "Pugilistic World Hails L. McCarty as Real Champion," *The Chicago Daily Tribune*, Jan. 5, 1913, p. C1. As *The Kansas City Star* was to say: "It looks as though all authorities are willing to allow Luther McCarty to call himself the champion of the world and let it go at that. They are all trying to forget Jack Johnson and it looks like they are forgetting with a vengeance." Sporting Comment, *The Kansas City Star*, January 11, 1913, p. 7.

2. Sporting Comment, *The Kansas City Star*, January 11, 1913, p. 7.

3. "Color Line is Drawn by 'Heavy' Champion," *The Chicago Record-Herald*, January 3, 1913, p. 10. Jess Willard was sympathetic: "McCarty is right in drawing the color line, and I would do the same thing if I were in his position. A white man has no right battling a negro. There are enough black fighters in the business to keep them busy among themselves, and the crop of good white boxers is large enough to accommodate all the promoters." Walter H. Eckersall, "Willard Refuses Offer for Match," *The Chicago Daily Tribune*, January 6, 1913, p. 16.

4. "Hiss Johnson and White Wife," *The Chicago Evening American*, January 3, 1913, p. 3; "Even the Darkies Cannot See Jack Johnson these Days," *The Buffalo Evening Times*, January 4, 1913; Geoffrey Ward, *Unforgivable Blackness*, p. 325.

5. Walter H. Eckersall, "Big Crowd Sees Athletes Train," *The Chicago Daily Tribune*, January 9, 1913, p. 13; Walter H. Eckersall, "Johnson Ordered Away from Gym," *The Chicago Daily Tribune*, January 10, 1913, p. 10; "Jack Johnson Barred from Chicago Gym," *The Chicago Evening American*, January 11, 1913, p. 8.

6. "New Ban on Jack Johnson," *The New York Times*, January 10, 1913, p. 12.

7. "Johnson Jumps Bail; Caught," *The Chicago Evening American*, [Third One o'clock Edition: Extra], January 14, 1913, p. 1; Ward, *Unforgivable Blackness*, pp. 314–325.

8. "M'Carty Willing to Meet 'Em All," *The Philadelphia Inquirer*, January 3, 1913, p. 10; "Willard Will Have to Wait," *The Kansas City Star*, January 5, 1913, p. 13A

9. Walter H. Eckersall, "Willard Refuses Offer for Match," *The Chicago Daily Tribune*, January 6, 1913, p. 16.

10. "Kid Williams wants Coulon," *The Los Angeles Times*, January 16, 1913, pt. III, p. 1.

11. Walter H. Eckersall, "Willard Refuses Offer for Match," *The Chicago Daily Tribune*, January 6, 1913, p. 16; "Willard

his "Meal Ticket," Charles Cutler Declares," *The Chicago Daily Tribune*, January 5, 1913, p. C1; "Willard for a New Manager," *The Daily Oklahoman*, January 7, 1913, p. 6; "Up to Benefactor Declares Willard," *The Daily Oklahoman*, January 9, 1913, p. 6; "Cutler out to Win Title," *The Chicago Evening American*, January 8, 1913, p. 7; "Cutler no Match for Zbysco; He Admits It," *The Chicago Evening American*, January 15, 1913, p. 6; Ed W. Smith, "Tough Sledding for Willard in New York," *The Marion [OH] Daily Star*, April 19, 1915, p. 8.

12. "Tom Jones Takes New Protégé Under Wing," *The Los Angeles Record*, January 7, 1913, p. 7; "Jones Now Manager of Jess Willard," *The Los Angeles Times*, January 7, 1913, pt. III, p. 1 "Ad Wolgast Wants to Try a Ring Comeback," *The Los Angeles Times*, May 5, 1918, p. VI 12; "Willard Sticks to Big Wrestler," *The Daily Oklahoman*, January 18, 1913, p. 8; Walter H. Eckersall, "Holds Jess as Meal Ticket," *The Chicago Daily Tribune*, January 15, 1913, p. 6; "Cutler Turns Down $2,500 Offer," *The Kansas City Star* January 15, 1913, p. 10.

13. "England Offers Willard Purses," *The Fort Wayne Sentinel*, January 7, 1913, p. 8; "Will Not Box The 'Hopes,' " *The Kansas City Star*, January 10, 1913, p. 3B; "Big Crowd Sees Athletes Train," *The Chicago Daily Tribune*, January 9, 1913, p. 13; "Promoters Look To Jess Willard," *The Duluth News Tribune*, January 11, 1913, p. 11; "'Sunny Jim' got his name due to his good luck in staging outdoor fights. It might rain for days before one of his fights, but the day of the fight the sun would come out and all would be well." Paul Lowry "Good Fortune Gave Coffroth His Knickname," *The Los Angeles Times*, February 7, 1943, p. 15.

14. "Willard Signs for a Battle," *The Buffalo Evening Times*, December 21, 1912, p. 8; "Biemer Lands Willard Go," *The Fort Wayne Daily News*, January 10, 1913, p. 3; "Willard Gets Ft. Wayne Go," *The Chicago Evening American*, January 13, 1913, p. 7.

15. " Bowers is a Rugged Scrapper," *The Fort Wayne Daily News*, January 14, 1913, p. 3; "Gilmores Think Well of Boxer," *The Fort Wayne Sentinel*, January 22, 1913, p. 8; Knockout, "Test for Willard in Bout Tonight," *The Chicago Daily Tribune*, January 22, 1913,p. 14.

16. I have never seen the film of Willard breaking this horse, if in fact it was created. "White Hope Willard is Not Seeking Long Bouts," *The Los Angeles Times*, January 17, 1913, pt III, p. 12; "Jess Willard to Show," *The St. Paul Pioneer Press*, January 19, 1913, p. 41; "Jess Willard is in St. Paul Today," *The St. Paul Pioneer Press*, January 20, 1913, p. 6; "Holds Jess as Meal Ticket," *The Chicago Daily Tribune*, January 15, 1913, p. 6; "Cutler Will Quit Mat Game," *The Chicago Tribune*, January 15, 1913, p. 6; "Willard Sticks to Big Wrestler," *The Daily Oklahoman*, January 18, 1913, p. 8.

17. "Willard Beat the Police," *The Fort Wayne Daily News*, January 23, 1913, p. 3; "Great Willard Scores Knockout Over Bowers in the Fifth Round before a Large Crowd," *The Fort Wayne Journal Gazette*, January 23, 1913, p. 6; Walter H. Eckersall, "Willard Floors Bauer in Fifth," *The Chicago Daily Tribune*, January 23, 1913, p. 6; "Jess Willard Stopped Bauer," *The Los Angeles Times*, January 23, 1913, pt. III, p. 1; "Willard Breaks His Hand," *The Washington Post*, January 24, 1913, p. 8.

18. Ray C. Pearson, "Willard Needs More Work," *The Chicago Daily Tribune*, January 26, 1913, p. C3; See also Walter H. Eckersall, "Willard's Boxing Not Impressive," *The Chicago Daily Tribune*, January 24, 1913, p. 10.

19. "Santry Strong for Willard," *The Fort Wayne Daily News*, January 24, 1913, p. 3.

20. Robert Ripley, "This is the Tallest 'Hope'" *The Kansas City Star*, January 20, 1913, p. 9.

21. "Jess Willard Uses Fitz Tactics in Ring Battles," *The Chicago Evening American*, December 27, 1912, p. 6. On April 3, 1915, when Fitzsimmons was interviewed about the upcoming Johnson-Willard fight in Havana, he predicted that "Johnson will beat Jess Willard in four rounds." Fitzsimmons did admit however that he had offered to train Willard when he was in Chicago. "Some time ago I wanted to teach him a few things. He said he would come out to my place, but never did." Later, after Willard won the championship, on April 10, 1915, Willard and Fitzsimmons met in the Washington, D.C., train station for what was billed as the first time they had ever met. In addition to predicting Johnson would win, Fitzsimmons supposedly told the press that he himself could beat Willard in four rounds, to which Willard replied, "That's sad, but I won't bother with old fogies." These comments do not suggest that the two had a mentor-pupil relationship. It suggests instead that the report of 1912 may have been inaccurate. Still, Willard did adopt the strategy of the short, sharp blows which made Fitzsimmons so powerful in the ring, as well as the strategy of letting the other fighter come to him. "Johnson will win in 4 Rounds," *The St. Louis Post-Dispatch*, April 4, 1915, p. 18; Alfred L. Stern, "Champion and 'Fitz' Meet for First Time," *The Washington Post*, April 10, 1915, p. 8.

22. "Big Jess Willard Hits Fort Wayne and is out for Decisive Winning To-Night; Club Expects Big Crowd," *The Fort Wayne Journal Gazette*, January 22, 1913, p. 6; "Willard is Ambitious," *The Kansas City Times*, February 10, 1913, p. 8.

23. "Jones Seeks another Champ," *The Los Angeles Times*, February 1, 1913, pt. II, p. 10.

24. "Willard is Ambitious," *The Kansas City Times*, February 10, 1913, p. 8.

25. "Jack Johnson will box Jess Willard at Century," *The Kansas City Journal*, February 11, 1913, p. 9; Edw. W. Cochrane's Column, "Willard Admits he Quit in Fight with Cox, but says He was Forced to—Comment," *The Kansas City Journal*, February 15, 1913, p. 8.

26. "Ferns and Howell Here," *The Kansas City Star*, February 9, 1913, p. 12A; "Willard now in Hands of Ferns," *The Daily Oklahoman*, December 24, 1910, p. 24; "Camp Notes," *The Daily Oklahoman*, December 28, 1910, p. 8; "Willard Challenges Ferns for Stage Bout," *The Kansas City Journal*, February 11, 1913, p. 9; "Truly, Willard is Brave," *The Kansas City Star*, February 11, 1913, p. 9.

27. "Edward W. Cochrane's Column," *The Kansas City Journal*, February 11, 1913, p. 9; "Wolgast and Jones Quit," *The Kansas City Journal*, February 13, 1913, p. 8; W.W. Naughton, "Fall of Wolgast due to Operation," *The Daily Oklahoman*, May 4, 1913, p. 12.

28. "Edward W. Cochrane's Column," "Willard Admits he Quit in Fight with Cox, but says He was Forced to—Comment," *The Kansas City Journal*, February 15, 1913, p. 8.; "Jess Willard Confesses Fake," *The Los Angeles Times*, February 17, 1913, pt. III, p. 1; "Jess Willard Wonders Why He Is Out of Work," *The Los Angeles Times*, March 29, 1913, pt. III, p. 3.

29. "McCarty will never become popular in this locality until he consents to box Willard again." James J. Corbett, "Boxing Gossip," *The St. Paul Pioneer Press*, January 19, 1913, p. 42; W.W. Naughton, "M'Carty Must Come Clean with Willard," *The Daily Oklahoman*, January 19, 1913, p. 10.

30. Walter H. Eckersall, "M'Carty and Willard Meet," *The Chicago Daily Tribune*, February 23, 1913, p. C3; "McCarty Quotes Terms to Willard," *The Washington Post*, February 23, 1913, Sporting section, p. 1; "Willard Starts Training," *The Fort Wayne News*, February 21, 1913, p. 3.

31. "Police Watch at Mat Bout," *The Chicago Daily Tribune*, January 30, 1910, p. C1; "Dunning dies after Fight," *The Chicago Daily Tribune*, November 26, 1910, p. 11; "Leon is not held responsible for death," *The Chicago Daily Tribune*, April 14, 1911, p. 22; Cutler also seems to have signed a contract for Jess to fight Jack Heinen, another Chicago heavyweight, but nothing seems to have come of this fight. "Willard to Take on Jack Heinen," *The St. Paul Pioneer Press*, February 6, 1913, p. 7; See also "Heinen Hunting Scrap with Jess," *The Daily Oklahoman*, February 23, 1913, p. 10. However, Jack Heinen would become one of Willard's sparring partners prior to the Dempsey fight in 1919.

32. "Willard Must Extend Self," *The Fort Wayne Daily News*, March 5, 1913, p. 3; "Jess Willard Puts Jack Leon Away

with Right Uppercut in 4th Round; Russian is Hopelessly Outclassed," *The Fort Wayne Journal Gazette*, March 6, 1913, p. 6; "Did He Knock Me Out?" *The Fort Wayne Daily News*, March 6, 1913, p. 3; "Leon Hoped For at Least a Draw," *The Fort Wayne Sentinel*, March 6, 1913, p. 8; "Willard Knocks Out Jack Leon," *The Daily Oklahoman*, March 6, 1913, p. 10; "Willard Floors Leon in Fourth," *The Chicago Daily Tribune*, March 6, 1913, p. 10.

33. "Sporting Notes," *The Fort Wayne Daily News*, March 6, 1913, p. 9.

34. "New York Ban is on Willard," *The Washington Post*, February 5, 1913, p. 5; "Jess Willard is in Town," *The Los Angeles Times*, March 29, 1913, pt. III, p. 3; Willard moved his family from Kansas at this time and purchased a bungalow at 5838 Gregory Avenue in Hollywood. Hattie and the children stayed here until December 1915 when Willard moved them to Rogers Park in Chicago.

35. W.W. Naughton, "America Corners Market on Pugs," *The Daily Oklahoman*, March 30, 1913, p. 11.

36. "M'Carty in Four Rounds," *The Kansas City Star*, January 12, 1913, p. 12A; http://cyberboxingzone.com/boxing/mccarthy.htm. "Skill of McCarty Beats Jim Flynn," *The Chicago Daily Tribune*, April 17, 1913, p. 14; "Luther M'Carty to box Frank Moran," *The New York Times*, April 28, 1913, p. 9; "M'Carty Totters Moran at the End," *The New York Times*, May 1, 1913, p. 9; http://cyberboxingzone.com/boxing/mccarthy.htm.

37. Arly Allen, "The Thirteen Party and the Boxing Deaths of Luther McCarty and John "Bull" Young (May to August 1913)," Part I: "The boxing Death of Luther McCarty (May 24, 1913)," *The Journal of the International Boxing Research Organization [IBRO]*, No. 98 (June 15, 2008), pp. 6–19.

38. Joe Price, "Story of McCarty's Last Fight by the Sporting Editor of the Albertan," *The Morning Albertan*, May 26, 1913, p. 1.

39. Joe Price, "Story of McCarty's Last Fight by the Sporting Editor of the Albertan," *The Morning Albertan*, May 26, 1913, p. 1.

40. H. M. Walker, "Pelkey and Miller to Meet," *The Los Angeles Examiner*, August 5, 1913, p. 11.

41. "Spark-Plug M'Closky," *The Los Angeles Times*, August 16, 1913, pt. IV, p. 3.

42. "Wolgast's Manager would like to Land Jess Willard also," *The Salt Lake Telegram*, January 10, 1913, p. 14; Walter H. Eckersall, "Willard 'Throws' Manager Cutler," *The Chicago Daily Tribune*, March 27, 1913, p. 17; Knockout, "Willard Offers Balm to Cutler," *The Chicago Daily Tribune*, April 5, 1913, p. 10; "Willard will be better Fighter after Operation: On Coast Looking for Trouble; Prefers McCarty," *The Daily Oklahoman*, April 6, 1913, p. 12.

43. "Willard to Meet 'Gunboat' Smith," *The Chicago Daily Tribune*, April 21, 1913, p. 10; "Heavy-Weights Smith and Willard will be Next Local Attraction," *The San Francisco Chronicle*, May 4, 1913, p. 62; "Gunboat Smith and Jess Willard Arrive for Bout on Saturday, May 17," *The San Francisco Chronicle*, May 6, 1913, p. 13.

44. "Willard Beaten in Coast Fight," *The Chicago Daily Tribune*, May 21, 1913, p. 10; "Gunboat Smith Wins From Jess Willard," *The New York Times*, May 21, 1913, p. 9; George D. Pardy, "Willard Beaten, But Not Out of Fighting Game," *The Chicago Inter-Ocean*, May 25, 1913, p. 1.

45. Harry B. Smith, "Gunboat Smith Wins Shade Decision Over Jess Willard in 20 Rounds," *The San Francisco Chronicle*, May 21, 1913, p. 9; W. W. Naughton, "Gunboat," *The Cincinnati Enquirer*, May 21, 1913, p. 14.

46. Harry B. Smith, "Gunboat Smith Wins Shade Decision over Jess Willard in 20 Rounds," *The San Francisco Chronicle*, May 21, 1913, p. 9.

47. "Willard Satisfied," *The Cincinnati Enquirer*, May 22, 1913, p. 9; "Knock Jones for Willard Defeat," *The Fargo Daily Courier-News*, May 24, 1913, p. 6.

48. Harry B. Smith, "Gunboat Smith Wins Shade Decision over Jess Willard in 20 Rounds," *The San Francisco Chronicle*, May 21, 1913, p. 9; Robert Edgren, "Willard's Knockout Blow Did Not Cause Bull Young's Death," No. VI "Willard's Rise to the Championship," *The St. Louis Post-Dispatch*, April 22, 1915, p. 23; W.W. Naughton, "Naughton Says Jess Willard Has Plenty of Courage if Nothing Else," *The Cincinnati Enquirer*, June 1, 1913, s. 3, p. 4.

49. "Two Extremes of Fighters in Limelight This Week," *The Washington Post*, June 22, 1913, p. 2; "New Hope to Seek Battles," *The Chicago Evening American*, August 1, 1912, p. 6; W. W. Naughton, "Flynn Stops Miller; Latter Has Ribs Broken," *The Chicago Evening American*, September 3, 1912, p. 7.

50. Edward W. Smith, "Jess Learns a Lesson in Bout with Miller," The *Marion [OH] Daily Star*, April 21, 1915, p. 8;

51. "Two More White Hopes Eliminated," *The New York Times*, December 7, 1913, p. S3.

52. "Jess Willard is found by Cutler," *The Daily Oklahoman*, February 12, 1912, p. 3; "Williams Outclassed, Hammered Helpless by Big Jess Willard," *The Nevada State Journal*, July 5, 1913, p. 5.

53. R. W. Lardner, "In the Wake of the News," *The Chicago Daily Tribune*, July 23, 1913, p. 13; H.M. Walker, "Sam Langford Home, Willing to Box Anyone," *The Los Angeles Examiner*, July 19,1913, p. 11; "Fighters Draw Color Line," *The Washington Post* , July 20, 1913, p. 4; "Bars Up To Sam Langford," *The Chicago Daily Tribune*, July 22, 1913, p. 14; Ed. W. Smith, "Promoters All Draw Color Line," *The Los Angeles Examiner*, August 10, 1913, pt. V, p. 4.

54. H. W. Walker, "Many Boxers Contract to Appear Here," *The Los Angeles Examiner*, August 10, 1913, pt. V, p. 2.

55. Tracy Callis and Chuck Johnston, *Boxing in the Los Angeles Area: 1880–2005* (Victoria, B.C., Canada: Trafford Publishing, 2009); James Kilty, *Leonis of Vernon* (New York, NY; Carlton Press, 1963.)

56. H.M. Walker, "470 Pounds in Ring Tonight: Young and Willard to Meet," *The Los Angeles Examiner*, August 22, 1913, p. 10; "Measurements of Bull Young," *The Los Angeles Times*, August 24, 1913, pt. VII, p. 8; DeWitt Van Court, "Beef Against Beef Tonight," *The Los Angeles Times*, August 22, 1913, pt. IV, p. 1; Arly Allen, "The Thirteen Party and the Boxing Deaths of Luther McCarty and John "Bull" Young (May to August 1913)," Pt. II: "The Boxing Death of Bull Young (August 23, 1913)" *The Journal of the International Boxing Research Organization [IBRO]*, No. 99 (September 2008), pp. 7–15.

57. "Jess Willard to Meet Young," *The Los Angeles Times*, July 25, 1913, pt. IV, p. 3;
"Defendant's Statement Given by Earl Rogers," *The Los Angeles Times*, August 24, 1913, pt. VII, p. 1;

58. "Willard Blow Floors Young; Death Hovers," *The Los Angeles Examiner*, August 23, 1913,p. 1; "Willard Knocks Out Young," *The Los Angeles Examiner*, August 23, 1913, p. 10; De Witt Van Court, "How Young was Knocked Out," *The Los Angeles Times*, August 23, 1913, pt III, p. 1.

59. "The Right Upper Cut that Finished Young," *The Los Angeles Times*, August 23, 1913, pt. III, p. 1.

60. Earl Andrus Rogers (1869–1922) was one of the finest defense lawyers in the United States in his time. His distinctly colorful life has been told in a number of books, most notably that of his daughter, Adela Rogers St. Johns, *Final Verdict* (Garden City, NY; Doubleday & Co. 1962). The trial of Jess Willard for the death of Bull Young is briefly described in Michael Lance Trope, *Once Upon a Time in Los Angeles: The Trials of Earl Rogers* (Spokane, WA: Arthur H. Clark Co., 2001), pp. 211–215.

61. Addison Hughes, "Bull Young near Death from Battle in Ring," *The Los Angeles Times*, August 23, 1913, pt. III, p. 1.

62. Addison Hughes, "Bull Young near Death from Battle in Ring," *The Los Angeles Times*, August 23, 1913, pt. III, p. 1.

63. "Criminal Prosecutions to Follow Death of 'Bull' Young," *The Los Angeles Times*, August 24, 1913, pt. VII, p. 1.

64. In the Justice's Court of Los Angeles City, Case No. 5808, *The people of the state of California, Plaintiff vs. Jess*

Willard, et al, Defendants, Complaint: Criminal (August 23, 1913); "Criminal Prosecutions To Follow Death of 'Bull' Young," *The Los Angeles Times,* August 24, 1913, pt. VII, p. 1; "Death Follows Ring Knockout," *The Chicago Daily Tribune,* August 24, 1913, pt. C, p. 1.

65. "Report All Greek to Young Inquest Jurors," *The Los Angeles Times,* August 27, 1913, pt. II, p. 1.

66. "Second-Degree Murder Charge," *The Los Angeles Times,* August 30, 1913, pt. II, p. 2; " Willard Held for Trial in Higher Court," *The Los Angeles Examiner,* September 9, 1913, p. 5; "Twelve Men Held for 'Bull' Young's Death," *The Los Angeles Times,* September 9, 1913, pt. II, p. 1; In the Justice's Court of Los Angeles City, Case No. 5808, *The people of the state of California, Plaintiff vs. Jess Willard, et al, Defendants,* Complaint: Criminal (September 8, 1913.)

67. Earl of Halsbury, *The Laws of England* (London: Butterworth, 1909), 9: 582.

68. "An Act concerning Crimes and Punishments (April 16, 1850)," *The Statutes of California passed at the First Session of the Legislature* (San Jose: J. Winchester, State Printer, 1850), Chapter 99, sec. 44, p. 233.

69. Harry B. Smith, "Gunboat Smith and Jess Willard," *The San Francisco Chronicle,* May 11, 1913, p. 62; "Manslaughter is to be the Charge in Young Case," *The Los Angeles Examiner,* August 24, 1913, pt. 1, p. 2; "Fighters and Officials under Arrest on Charge of Conducting Prize Fight," *The Los Angeles Times,* March 18, 1911, pt. II, p. 1; "Judge Willis Grants Writ," *The Los Angeles Times,* May 9, 1911, pt. III, p. 1; "Second-Degree Murder Charge," *The Los Angeles Times,* August 30, 1913, pt. II, p. 2; "Could Young Have Lived?" *The Los Angeles Times,* September 6, 1913, pt. II, p. 2; "Jess Willard Will Be Held," *The Los Angeles Times,* September 6, 1913, pt. II, p. 2.

70. "Jess Willard Murder Case Now Dropped," *The Los Angeles Examiner,* October 4, 1913, p. 5; "Definite Test of Fight law," *The Los Angeles Times,* October 4, 1913, pt. III, p. 4; Superior Court ,County of Los Angeles, *The People of the State of California against Jess Willard , et al.* Case No. 8740 (October 13, 1913.)

71. "Spark-Plug M'Closky," *The Los Angeles Times,* January 19, 1913, pt. VII, p. 7.

72. " 'Bar Prize Fights'—Brown: Senator will Push Initiative," *The Los Angeles Examiner,* August 25, 1913, p. 1; "The Boxing Game Now on Trial for Its Life: Best Friend—Bitterest Foe State the Case," *The Los Angeles Times,* August 26, 1913, pt. III, p. 1; "Start of War on Boxing," *The Washington Post,* August 26, 1913, p. 7; "Boost Anti-Boxing Crusade," *The Chicago Daily Tribune,* August 28, 1913, p. 16; "Need 50,000 Anti-Fight Names: Men and Women Unite Work," *The Los Angeles Examiner,* September 11, 1913, p. 7; "Rev Talbott Leads Move on Prizefights," *The Los Angeles Examiner,* September 12, 1913, p. 5; " 'No Prize Fights,' Say Clergy," *The Los Angeles Examiner,* September 15, 1913, p. 7.

73. "Tom M'Carey Calls off All Fights at Vernon as Result of Young's Death," *The Los Angeles Examiner,* August 23, 1913, p. 1; "Both County and City Fight the Fight Game," *The Los Angeles Times,* August 27, 1913, pt. II, p. 1; "Trustees Stop Venice Boxing," *The Los Angeles Times,* August 26, 1913, pt. III, p. 3; "Fifty-Six Slain for Entertainment," *The Los Angles Examiner,* August 27, 1913, p. 28 "Help the Church Federation ! Stamp Out Prize Fighting!," *The Los Angeles Examiner,* September 15, 1913, p. 16; "Californians Want State Boxing Law," *The Washington Post,* August 30, 1913, p. 6; "Riverside Council Firm for Anti-Fight Laws," *The Los Angeles Examiner,* September 12, 1913, p. 5; "'Bout' for Vernon Rouses Pastors," *The Los Angeles Examiner,* September 17, 1913, p. 4; "McCarey Collapses; Prize Fight Hearing Will be Postponed," *The Los Angeles Examiner,* September 18, 1913, p. 17";Worry and Criticism Too Much for M'Carey," *The Los Angeles Times,* September 18, 1913, pt. III, p. 1; "Legal Steps Proposed to Stop Fights," *The Los Angeles Examiner,* September 25, 1913, p. 3; "Ford May Prevent Bouts at Vernon," *The Los Angeles Examiner,* September 26, 1913, p. 3; "McCarey Is Flayed for Inviting L.A. Pastors to Bouts," *The Los Angeles Examiner,* September 28, 1913, pt. I, p. 6; "Opponents of Squared Circle," *The Los Angeles Times,* October 14, 1913, pt. II, p. 8; "Counted Out at the Beach," *The Los Angeles Times,* November 6, 1913, pt. II, p. 10.

74. "Witnesses State Bout Was Not a Prize Fight," *The Los Angeles Times,* March 21, 1911, pt. III, p. 1.

75. Superior Court, County of Los Angeles, *The People of the State of California against Jess Willard, et al.* Case No. 8740, Demurrer October 14, 1913.

76. Superior Court, County of Los Angeles, *The People of the State of California against Jess Willard, et al.* Case No. 8740, Opinion of the Court, October 21, 1913; "New View of Prize Fights," *The Los Angeles Times,* October 22, 1913, pt. III, p. 4.

77. Superior Court, County of Los Angeles, *The People of the State of California against Jess Willard , et al.* Case No. 8740, Opinion of the Court, Oct. 21, 1913, pp. 3–4. Following page citations are to Judge Craig's opinion.

78. For a discussion of the ideas of the reformers, see "Need 50,000 Anti-Fight Names," *The Los Angeles Examiner,* September 11, 1913, p. 7.

79. Superior Court, County of Los Angeles, *The People of the State of California against Jess Willard , et al.* Case No. 8740, Opinion of the Court, October 21, 1913, p. 11; "The Killing of Young," *The Los Angeles Times,* August 25, 1913, pt. II, p. 4.

80. R.W. Lardner, "In the Wake of the News," *The Chicago Daily Tribune,* August 27, 1913, p. 11;

81. "Jess Willard Will Go Back to His Boxing," *The Los Angeles Times,* October 22, 1913, pt. III, p. 3.

82. "Wolgast gets $10,000 from Jones-Willard Co.," *The Cadillac [Michigan] Evening News,* November 16, 1915. This reference was sent to me courtesy of John Bunny.

83. "Van Court says Chavez is a Dangerous Boxer," *The Los Angeles Times,* November 1, 1913, pt. III, p. 1; "Willard Cannot Box Morris Here," *The New York Times,* November 12, 1913, p. 10.

84. Jack Singer, "Jimmy Johnston Here, Tells of Past, Present and Future," *The Los Angeles Times,* April 28, 1938, p. A9.

85. John Lardner, *White Hopes and Other Tigers,*, p. 39; Knockout, "Willard Meets Rodel Tonight," *The Chicago Daily Tribune,* November 17, 1913, p. 17; "Earth Will Shake When Hopes Arrive," *The Milwaukee Free Press,* November 13, 1913, p. 7; "Willard and Rodel To Clash in Battle," *The Milwaukee Free Press,* November 17, 1913, p. 7; Billy Evans, "SportLaffs," *The Beloit Daily News,* November 24, 1938; J. A. Ermatinger, "Willard Beaten by Rodel in Burlesque," *The Milwaukee Free Press,* November 18, 1913, p. 7; "Jess Willard Lucky to get a Draw with Rodel," *The Los Angeles Times,* November 18, 1913, pt. III, p. 1; Ed W. Smith, "Good Fortune With Jess in his Fights," *The Marion [Ohio] Daily Star,* April 22, 1915, p. 8.

86. J. A. Ermatinger, "Willard Beaten by Rodel in Burlesque," *The Milwaukee Free Press,* November 18, 1913, p. 7.

87. "Jess Willard Lucky to get a Draw with Rodel," *The Los Angeles Times,* November 18, 1913, pt. III, p. 1.

88. Jack Singer, "Jimmy Johnston Here, Tells of Past, Present and Future," *The Los Angeles Times,* April 28, 1938, p. A9.

89. Knockout, "Cutler, with blow on Tom Jones' Jaw, Squares 'Account,'" *The Chicago Daily Tribune,* November 8, 1913, p. 13; Knockout, "Act II of 'Cutler's Revenge,'" *The Chicago Daily Tribune,* November 11, 1913, p. 16; "Tom Jones Hit by Charles Cutler; Gotch Present," *The Milwaukee Free Press,* November 8, 1913, p. 8.

90. Walter H. Eckersall, "Willard loses Morris Bout; George Rodel Substituted," *The Chicago Daily Tribune,* November 19, 1913, p. 16; "Jess Willard to Fight Reed," *The Chicago Daily Tribune,* November 24, 1913, p. 17; " Big Reed Has Good Record," *The Fort Wayne Journal-Gazette,* November 23, 1913, p. 25.

91. "Rubber Took up Real Hard Work," *The Fort Wayne Sentinel,* November 22, 1913, p. 8; "Jones Respects Willard's Toledo Opponent; Another Trainer Coming," *The Fort*

Wayne Journal-Courier, November 22, 1913, p. 10; "Jack Reid Here for Willard Go," *The Fort Wayne Sentinel*, November 24, 1913, p. 8; "All in Readiness for To-Night's Boxing Show; Great Matches Expected," *The Fort Wayne Journal-Gazette*, November 24, 1913, p. 6; "Reed Takes Fright and Quits in the Second," *The Fort Wayne Journal-Gazette*, November 25, 1913, p. 14; "Reid Lands One Blow in Battle," *The Fort Wayne Sentinel*, November 25, 1913, p. 6.

92. "Willard Allowed to Box Carl Morris," *The New York Times*, December 1, 1913, p. 7.

93. Ed W. Smith, "Jess takes Delight in Beating Morris," *The Marion [OH] Daily Star*, April 20, 1915, p. 8.

94. Damon Runyon, "Willard Better than Morris but Both Poor: Only Referee William Joh in Peril when Heavy Aspirants Mix," *The Milwaukee Free Press*, December 4, 1913, p. 7; Jack Curley, whose memory of events was not always to be trusted, added a comment about this fight in his "Memoirs of a Promoter, as told to Frank Graham," part sixteen, *Ring Magazine* (April 1931), p. 35. Curley was trying to persuade L. Lawrence Weber to back Willard for the fight with Jack Johnson. Weber had seen Willard fight against Carl Morris, and was not impressed. Curley responded: "Willard, I thought, had made a good one in the circumstances, since on the morning of the fight he had caught his heel in a torn spot in the carpet on the stairs at Dal Hawkin's road house, where he had trained for the fight, and had fallen eight or ten stairs on his face; that his knee had been so lame he had been plucky to make the fight and that he had handled himself extremely well against Morris." Weber acknowledged that Curley knew more about these things than he did, and backed Willard to fight Johnson.

95. Damon Runyon, "Willard Better than Morris but Both Poor: Only Referee William Joh in Peril when Heavy Aspirants Mix," *The Milwaukee Free Press*, December 4, 1913, p. 7.

96. "Carl Morris Favorite over Big Jess Willard," *The Los Angeles Times*, December 3, 1913, pt. III, p. 4; "Gee! What a Rotten Fight," *The Los Angeles Times*, December 4, 1913, pt. III, p. 1.

97. "Two More White Hopes Eliminated," *The New York Times*, December 7, 1913, p. S3.

98. Ed W. Smith, "Jess Takes Delight in Beating Morris," *The Marion [Ohio] Daily Star*, April 20, 1915, p. 8; Charles Samuels, *The Magnificent Rube*, p 179. Robert Edgren spoke to Willard after the Morris fight. Willard explained that the reason that fight was so lousy was that Morris was afraid to lead and Willard could not "because every time I wanted to let a punch go I saw Bull Young there in front of me instead of Morris and I didn't dare to." Robert Edgren, "Champions I have Known," *Jess Willard [Archive]- Boxing Forum* http://www.boxingscene.com/forums/archive/index.php/t-451974.html. (Seen July 26, 2014.)

99. "Willard-Davis Bout Friday," *The Milwaukee Free Press*, December 9, 1913; "Willard Knocks Out Davis," *The New York Times*, December 13, 1913, p. 11; Robert Edgren, "Willard Couldn't and Morris Wouldn't Fight, Edgren says," No. 7 "Willard's Rise to the Championship," *The St. Louis Post-Dispatch*, April 23, 1915, p. 17.

100. "It was Fixed Right," *The Daily Oklahoman*, December 18, 1913, p. 8.

101. "Rodel Knocked Out," *The New York Times*, December 30, 1913, p. 10; "Jess Willard Knocks Out Boer George Rodel," *The Los Angeles Times*, December 30, 1913, pt. III, p. 3 "Rodel Loses to Willard By Knockout," *The Bridgeport Evening Post*, December 30, 1913, p. 10. When Willard arrived in Buffalo on December 10 before the Davis fight he appeared to a newspaper reporter "very bitter" due to the criticism which had been launched at him for not being aggressive enough in the Morris fight. "'I rather think that Buffalo and Davis and a few weeks later New Haven and Rodel will not have any ground for complaint on the aggressive lines,' said he grimly." "Big Jess Willard Arrives this Morning," *The Buffalo Evening News*, December 10, 1913, p. 14. Willard was true to his word in both fights.

Chapter 5

1. So wrote Alfred Cohn and Joe Chisholm, in a book about the court cases of Earl Rogers, *"Take the Witness!"* (Garden City, NY: Garden City Publishing Co., Inc., 1934), pp. 240–241; Superior Court, Los Angeles County, California, *People vs. Jess Willard*, Case No. 8740 [January 7–13, 1914]; Michael Lance Trope, *Once Upon a Time in Los Angeles: The Trials of Earl Rogers* (Spokane, WA: The Arthur Clark Co., 2001), pp. 211–215.

2. De Witt Van Court, "Packey M'Farland's Record is Punctured," *The Los Angeles Times*, January 9,1914, Pt. III, p. 1; "Invented Knockouts," *The New York Times*, January 9, 1914, p. 12; "Making a Night of Boxing Case," *The Los Angeles Times*, January 13, 1914, pt. II, p. 6.

3. "Willard Testifies at Trial," *The Chicago Daily Tribune*, January 10, 1914, p. 14.

4. Superior Court, Los Angeles County, California, *People vs. Jess Willard*, Case No. 8740 [January 7–13, 1914], Instructions to the jury by Judge Gavin W. Craig. Jr.

5. *Ibid.*, Instructions given to the jury by Judge Gavin W. Craig, Jr.

6. "Jess Willard is Acquitted," *The Los Angeles Times*, January 14, 1914, pt. III, p. 2; "Acquittal for Jess Willard," *The Chicago Daily Tribune*, January 14, 1914, p. 8; "Boxer Willard Acquitted," *The New York Times*, January 14, 1914, p. 9; Ray C. Pearson, "What is Boxing? What Prize Fighting?" *The Chicago Daily Tribune*, January 18, 1914, p. B4; Superior Court, Los Angeles County, California, *People vs. Jess Willard*, Case No. 8740, Decision (January 13, 1914).

7. "'Gunboat' Smith Wins in Fifteenth," *The New York Times*, January 2, 1914, p. 10; "Smith's Claim to Title Now Clear," *The New York Times*, January 4, 1914, p. S2.

8. "Gunboat Smith Meets Willard July Fourth," *The Los Angeles Times*, January 19, 1914, pt. III, p. 1; "Smith Not of Title Class say Coast Boxing Critics," *The Chicago Daily Tribune*, January 3, 1914, p. 14; "Jack Johnson is Their Goal," *The Washington Post*, January 12, 1914, p. 8.

9. "Naughton Terms Willard a Joke," *The Daily Oklahoman*, February 1, 1914, p. 10; De Witt Van Court, "Jess Willard Will be the Next World Champ," *The Los Angeles Times*, January 31, 1914, pt. III, p. 3.

10. Walter H. Eckersall, "Smith's Ambition to Fight Johnson," *The Chicago Daily Tribune*, January 19, 1914, p. 12.

11. "Cutler Sues Jess Willard," *The Chicago Daily Tribune*, March 27, 1914, p. 12. This lawsuit was settled in April 1915 after Willard had won the title. Willard met with Cutler in Chicago on April 21, 1915, and they compromised on the amount, with Willard giving Cutler a check for $1,250. "Jess Willard got $13, 000," *The New York Times*, April 23, 1915, p. 11.

12. John Lardner, *White Hopes*, p. 27, 49; "Battler Ill After Defeat by Bob Moha," *The Youngstown Daily Vindicator* , March 24, 1914, p. 19; "Willard is Opponent of Tom M'Mahon," *The Youngstown Daily Vindicator*, March 26, 1914, p. 19; "Big Jess Willard takes Bat's Task," *The Youngstown Telegram*, March 26, 1914, p. 17.

13. C. Hugh Blair, "Tom M'Mahon Wallops Big Jess Willard In Twelve Rounds," *The New Castle News*, March 28, 1914, p. 11; John Lardner, *White Hopes*, p. 49; "David M'Mahon vs Goliath Willard," *The Youngstown Telegram*, March 28, 1914, p. 15; "Bearcat Beats Willard Although Outweighed," *The Youngstown Daily Vindicator*, March 28, 1914, p. 8; "McMahon Outpoints Willard," *The New York Times*, March 28, 1914, p. 11.

14. Charles Samuels, *The Magnificent Rube*, p. 179; The same comments are found in Ed W. Smith, "Jess takes delight in beating Morris," in "How I won the title," by Jess Willard as told to Ed W. Smith, *The Marion [OH] Daily Star*, April 20, 1915, p. 8.

15. "Pugilistic Pointers," *The Chicago Daily Tribune*, March 8, 1914, p. B4; "Willard Knocks Out Dan Daly," *The New York Times*, April 14, 1914, p. 8; "Jinx Pursuing Our Own

Little Jimmy Dime," *The New Castle News,* April 14, 1914, p. 11.

16. "Jess Willard Stops Rodel: Oklahoma Boxer Wins Victory from Australian Champion in Sixth Round," *The Milwaukee Free Press,* April 29, 1914, p. 9; "Good Boxing Card On For Tuesday," *The Atlanta Constitution* April 24, 1914, p. 10.

17. "Rodel and Willard are Confident of Outcome in Tuesday's Big Bout," *The Atlanta Constitution,* April 26, p. 6B; "Willard and Rodel Meet at Orpheum Tonight; Winner Fights "Gunner," *The Atlanta Constitution,* April 28, 1914, p. 12.

18. "Willard Stops Boer Rodel; Boer Was Game, That's All," *The Atlanta Constitution,* April 29, 1912, p. 10.

19. "It would undoubtedly be considered a breach of etiquet [sic] to accuse a fighter of modesty, but Willard has time and again shown evidence of an inborn dislike for notoriety." "Tex" O'Rourke, "Willard thoroughly enjoys life while training for mill," *The Daily Oklahoman,* February 17, 1915, p. 10.

20. "Gunboat Smith v. Carpentier: Prospects of a Match," *The London Times,* April 15, 1914, p. 12; "Carpentier v. Gunboat Smith: Articles Signed Yesterday," *The London Times,* April 21, 1914, p. 13; "Arrival of Gunboat Smith," *The London Times,* June 1, 1914, p. 15. Eugene Corri, the referee of the Smith-Carpentier fight, describes this fight in his book *Refereeing 1000 Fights: Reminiscences of Boxing* (London: C. Arthur Pearson, Ltd., 1919), pp. 23–44.

21. Timothee Jobert, "Paris et la Revanche de l'Homme 'Blanc' (1908-1915)," *Stadion,* v. 28, no. 2 (2002), pp. 195–213 quote on p. 208.

22. C. F. Bertelli, "Johnson Defeats Moran, Mauling Him at Will; Fight is Merest Farce," *The Milwaukee Free Press,* June 28, 1914, Sports Section, p. 1. Jack Adams, a Johnson backer, declared the day after it occurred that the fight was fixed. According to him, Johnson could easily have knocked Moran out but did not do so in order to promote the movies of the fight and to set up a real fight later in the United States. "Johnson's Trainer Calls Fight Fake," *The Milwaukee Free Press,* June 29, 1914, p. 7.

23. John Lardner, *White Hopes,* pp. 40–48; Frank C. Menke, "To Hold Crown," *The Washington Post,* July 1, 1914, p. 9; Ward, *Unforgivable Blackness,* pp. 357–363.

24. Timothee Jobert, "Paris et la Revanche de l'Homme 'Blanc' (1908-1915)," *Stadion,* v. 28, no. 2 (2002), pp. 195–213.

25. "Willard Next White Hope," *The Milwaukee Free Press,* June 29, 1914, p. 7; "Match Me and Jess Willard," *The Los Angeles Times,* July 15, 1914, pt. III, p. 1; Ringside, "Willard appears to be best white hope," *The Milwaukee Free Press,* August 2, 1914, Sport Section, p. 2.

26. "New Trial Granted to Jack Johnson," *The Milwaukee Free Press,* April 15, 1914, p. 9 "Retrial of Jack Johnson," *The London Times,* April 16, 1914, p. 7.

27. Ward, *Unforgivable Blackness,* p. 357.

28. De Witt van Court, "Jeffries will Second Willard against Johnson," *The Los Angeles Times,* July 16, 1914, pt. III, p. 1; "Some Facts and Comment from the Realm of Sportdom," *The Washington Post,* August 5, 1914, p. 8.

29. De Witt Van Court, "Jeffries will Second Willard against Johnson," *The Los Angeles Times,* July 16, 1914, pt. III, p. 1.

30. Knockout, "Morris Scorns Offer of $4, 000," *The Chicago Daily Tribune,* August 3, 1914, p. 16; "Morris Beats Flynn," *The Daily Oklahoman,* October 30, 1914, p. 10.

31. "Curley to Manage Willard," *The Milwaukee Free Press,* August 26, 1914, p. 6; Knockout, "Groom Willard for Title Bout," *The Chicago Daily Tribune,* August 26, 1914, p. 14; "Syndicate backs Willard," *The New York Times,* September 14, 1914, p. 7.

32. Ward, *Unforgivable Blackness,* p. 363.

33. Ward, *Unforgivable Blackness,* pp. 364–365; According to Johnny Schiff, a Los Angeles boxer, by September 24, it was well known in London that Johnson had signed to fight Willard. "Johnny Schiff's Fight Letter [dated Sept. 24]," *The Los Angeles Times,* October 21, 1914, pt. III, p. 1. This was confirmed by Tom Jones in Chicago on October 15: "Willard-Johnson Bout On," *The Milwaukee Free Press,* October 16, 1914, p. 5. Jones' comments may have been wishful thinking, since Johnson's signature was not on any contract. Curley did not leave New York until November 3, and the contract was not signed until a day after he arrived in London. According to *The Chicago Daily Tribune,* Tom Jones was to have been sent to London but once the syndicate bought Tom Jones out, Jack Curley took over the fight negotiations. It is well that he did, as Jones had no entrée to Johnson and might not have succeeded in these negotiations. "Jones to go to England to Clinch Johnson Bout," *The Chicago Daily Tribune,* October 19, 1914, p. 14; Ed Curley, "Willard and Johnson are near to a Match," *The Milwaukee Free Press,* October 30, 1914, p. 7.

34. Ward, *Unforgivable Blackness,* pp. 26–29; "Where did Jack [Curley] Get Fynn's Wages," *The Las Vegas [NM] Optic,* July 10, 1912, p. 5; "Extravagance of Mayor Depletes Funds," *The Las Vegas Optic,* July 11, 1912, p. 4.

35. "Willard-Johnson Bout On," *The Milwaukee Free Press,* October 16, 1914, p. 5; Ed Curley, "Willard and Johnson Are near a Match," *The Milwaukee Free Press,* October 30, 1914, p. 7.

36. Johnson was indicted on April 30, 1913, for violation of section 2 of the White Slave Traffic Act with "a certain girl, to wit, Belle Schreiber, otherwise known as Mrs. J. Johnson, for the purpose of prostitution." *The United States of America vs. John Arthur Johnson, otherwise known as Jack Johnson,* United States District Court, Northern District of Illinois, Case No. 5166, April 30, 1913. He fled the country going to Canada first and then to Europe on June 24, 1913.

37. Knockout, "Vote on Coast Indicates Boxing will be killed." *The Chicago Daily Tribune,* November 5, 1914, p. 16.

38. "Fate of California Boxing Hangs On Thread," *The Los Angeles Times,* Nov. 5, 1914, pt. III, p. 1; "'Dry' Carries In the South, But California is 'Wet'" *The Los Angeles Times,* November 6, 1914, pt. II, p. 1.

39. "Poolrooms Raided [in San Francisco]," *The Atlanta Constitution,* January 5, 1913, p. 7; "Is Pool Room Crime School?" *The Los Angeles Record,* February 7, 1913, p. 13; "Says Drug Ring Ruins Thousands," *The Los Angeles Record,* February 7, 1913, p. 13; "Dancers Flee From Fire as Pastor Scores Halls," *The Los Angeles Record,* January 6, 1913, p. 7; "All Policemen on Duty Must Go Dry," *The Los Angles Examiner,* December 12, 1912, p. 1; "Church Takes Steps to Stop Marriage of the Unhealthy," *The Los Angles Examiner,* December 9, 1912, p. 1; Marriage of Healthy Ones to Result in Strong Race," *The Los Angeles Examiner,* December 8, 1912, p. 1; " 'Turkey Trot' Dance Doomed by Committee," *The Los Angeles Examiner,* December 4, 1912, p. 3; "Free Saloon Lunch Scored by Minister," *The Los Angeles Examiner,* December 2, 1912, p. 10; "Evil of Salome Is Set Forth by Dr. Brougher," *The Los Angeles Examiner,* November 18, 1912, p. 14; "Purists Peeped, They Did, At Salome, Then Protested," *The Los Angeles Record,* November 2, 1912, p. 1; " Begin Fight Against Race Track Measure," *The Los Angeles Record* , October 8, 1912, p. 2; Racing Bill is Denounced by Labor Leader," *The Los Angeles Record,* October 11, 1912, p. 10; "Author Laughs at Cigarette Protest," *The Los Angeles Examiner,* October 3, 1912, p. 1; "I'll Never Smoke in Public Again, says Gertrude Atherton," *The Los Angeles Examiner,* October 5, 1912, p. 1; "Citizens Say Let Smokers use Tobacco on End of Car," *The Los Angeles Examiner,* November 11, 1912, p. 13.

40. There was more to this story than boxing, however. Charles Eyton (1871–1941), the referee at Tom McCarey's boxing emporium became famous as the head of Paramount Studios in the 1920s and 1930s. Thomas Leo McCarey, Tom's son became famous as a movie producer, most notably of such films as *Going My Way* (1944) and *The Bells of St. Mary's* (1945) staring Bing Crosby and Barry Fitzgerald as well as *An Affair to Remember* (1957) starring Cary Grant and Deb-

orah Kerr. Sunny Jim Coffroth moved to San Diego and took over the Tijuana Race track in 1916 and made horse racing a very popular sport there. Tracy Callis and Chuck Johnston, *Boxing in the Los Angeles Area, 1880–2005* (Victoria, BC, Canada: Trafford Publishing, 2009) and F. Daniel Somrack, *Boxing in San Francisco* (Charleston, SC: Arcadia Publishing, 2005).

41. Ringside, "Willard Appears to be Best White Hope," *The Daily Oklahoman*, August 2, 1914, p. 15.

42. Otto Floto, "Otto Floto Thinks Willard is the only Hope of the White Race," *The Daily Oklahoman*, November 14, 1914, p. 5.

43. Knockout, "Groom Willard for Title Bout," *The Chicago Daily Tribune*, August 26, 1914, p. 14; "Syndicate Backs Willard," *The New York Times*, September 14, 1914, p. 7.

44. Ed Curley, "Willard and Johnson Are Near to a Match," *The Milwaukee Free Press*, October 30, 1914, p. 7; "Johnson signs for Willard Go," *The Chicago Daily Tribune*, November 18, 1914, p. 11.

45. De Witt Van Court, "Willard-Johnson Match Would Be Pretty Rotten," *The Los Angeles Times*, October 18, 1914, pt. VII, p. 5.

46. "Sport of Fists One of Defense, Not Aggression," *The Chicago Daily Tribune*, Dec. 20, 1914, p. B3. Jack Skelly's description of boxing is perhaps what Judge Gavin W. Craig was attempting to describe in his instructions to the jurors in Jess Willard's trial in Los Angeles. Due to his ignorance of the sport, the judge could not make his point.

47. Ringside, "Johnson Can Win by Being Beaten," *The Daily Oklahoman*, November 22, 1914, p. 10.

48. "Boxers Put up Forfeits for Bout," *The New York Times*, December 1, 1914, p. 11.

49. Ringside, "Jack Johnson Will be Busy Boxer in Spring," *The Milwaukee Free Press*, December 6, 1914, Sporting Section, p. 3; "Willard Willing to Defend Claim," *The Daily Oklahoman* December 6, 1914, p. 17; "McVea Boxes Lightweight," *The New York Times*, December 8, 1914, p. 8; "Willard is Afraid of Levinsky, says Morgan," *The Milwaukee Free Press*, December 11, 1914, p. 7; "Willard Willing to Fight," *The Washington Post*, December 13, 1914, p. 16.

50. "Smith and Coffey Fit," *The New York Times*, December 15, 1914, p. 11; "Bantam Problem Growing Complex," *The Daily Oklahoman*, December 17, 1914, p. 12; "Morris Must Whip Coffey, Says Jess," *The Daily Oklahoman*, December 18, 1914, p. 12.

51. "Fight-a-Night is Willard's Offer," *The Daily Oklahoman*, December 24, 1914, p. 10.

52. "Fight-a-night is Willard's Offer," *The Daily Oklahoman*, December 24, 1914, p. 10.

Chapter 6

1. "No Share for Willard," *The New York Times*, April 7, 1915, p. 11; Oklahoma Law Suit against A.J. Phillips (November 1915).

2. Jones and Willard went to Havana leaving their rent to Charles F. Knoblauch of Ysleta, Texas unpaid. Knoblauch sued them for $250 for rent for the house and grounds where the training exercises were undertaken. It took two trials and three years for Knoblauch to collect from Willard. El Paso County Court at Law, case No. 6061 filed 23 February 1918. Court of Civil Appeals, Eighth Supreme Judicial District of Texas, case No. 890 filed November 21, 1918. (Box no. H45 in the C. L. Sonnichsen Special Collections Department of the University of Texas at El Paso); Willard, *Here's My Story*, p. 6.

3. Jack Curley, "Curley Makes a Statement," *The Havana Daily Post*, April 6, 1915, p. 4; This statement is basically a lie. Curley was not able to come to Johnson's corner until the end of the fight because he was counting the receipts for the fight. His dislike of George Bradt was still visible in his Memoirs published in 1931. And he tried to get out of Havana as quickly as he could, leaving his creditors crying behind him.

4. "Citizens Honor Champ Willard," *The Havana Daily Post*, April 7, 1915, p. 2.

5. "Police arrest 'Jack' Curley," *Havana Daily Post*, Apr. 7, 1915, p. 2.

6. "Police arrest 'Jack' Curley," *The Havana Daily Post*, April 7, 1915, p. 2. The financial figures associated with prizefights are suspect in the best of cases. Jack Johnson, being wise to the ways of promoters, insisted that he have his cash in hand before the fight began. This was smart, because just as soon as Harry Frazee returned to the United States, his office was invaded by a Deputy Sheriff seeking to impound Johnson's money. Frazee could tell him that he no longer had any of Johnson's money. ("No Johnson Money Here," *The New York Tribune*, April 13, 1915, p. 15). Jess Willard, anxious to have a chance to gain the title, was willing, as he said, to fight for a straw hat or a glass of water. The newspapers suggested that daily living expenses were met by the fees charged for watching the fighters train at the Stadium (Johnson) or at the Miramar Hotel (Willard), but obviously a large number of other bills went unpaid. "$150,000 Expected Gross of Johnson-Willard Co.," *Variety*, February 12, 1915, p. 1; "32,000 at Fight; Receipts $110, 000," *New York Times* April 7, 1915, p. 11; "No Share for Willard?" *New York Times*, April 7, 1915, p. 11; "Map out Tour as Willard Makes $4,000 Vaudeville Debut," *Variety*, April 9, 1915, p. 4.

7. "Curley Jumps Many Accounts," *The Havana Daily Post*, April 8, 1915, p. 2; G.W. Krick, "Stadium Stabs," *The Havana Daily Post*, April 8, 1915, p. 3; "Curley Leaves Debts Behind," *The New York Times*, April 8, 1915, p. 11; At the time Curley claimed he was the victim of his creditors. "Curley said he has been the victim of various cheap hold-up games and was charged $25 for an automobile ride he never took. Another charged $8 for splicing the ring ropes, and so it went." "Curley Comes to Town Ahead of Jess Willard," *The New York Tribune*, April 10, 1915, p. 13. In his "Memoirs," Curley disputes this. He said that "Within a week or so we had cleaned up all the remaining details and turned our faces for home. I left Havana with the sense of a job well done and with my debt to Weber paid, approximately $1,500 in my pocket." Jack Curley, "Memoirs of a Promoter as told to Frank Graham," part seventeen, *Ring Magazine* (September 1931), p. 44; He repeated this in part eighteen of his "Memoirs" where he says: "We had settled our affairs in Havana—and paid all our bills, contrary to the stories circulated at the time by persons who did not precisely wish us well—and were ready to depart this country." *Ring Magazine* (October 1931), p. 36. Since Curley left Havana on the first boat out the day after the fight, it seems clear that his memory of the events was playing tricks on him.

8. "A Sermon in Black and White," *The Havana Daily Post*, April 14, 1915, p. 4.

9. "Johnson Races for his Films," *The Havana Daily Post*, April 9, 1915, p. 8; "A 'Movie Sniper' Worries Johnson," *The New York Tribune*, April 9, 1915, p. 15.

10. "Johnson is a Manana Victim," *The Havana Daily Post*, April 10, 1915, p. 10.

11. "Pirate Films of the Fight," *New York Times*, April 9, 1915, p. 12; "Johnson put off Again," *New York Times*, April 10, 1915, p. 9; Ward, *Unforgivable Blackness*, pp. 385; Dan Streible, *Fight Pictures: A History of Boxing and Early Cinema* (Berkeley: University of California Press, 2008), p. 252, 259; "Johnson's Song and Dance," *Variety*, May 28, 1915, p. 4; Ad for the Willard-Johnson fight film in *Variety*, May 7, 1915, p. 21.

12. Herbert Bayard Swope, "Willard Leaves Cuba Today to Tour the States," *The Chicago Daily Tribune*, April 7, 1915, p. 1; "Jess Willard Tires of Cheering Throngs," *The Chicago Daily Tribune*, April 9, 1915, p. 15; Damon Runyon, "American Opinion Almost Stampeded to Jess Willard," *The* [Jacksonville]*Florida Metropolis*, April 4, 1915, 3D; "Prize Fight Pictures will not be Shown in U.S., Against the Law," *The*

Miami Metropolis, April 7, 1915, p. 1; "Fight Pictures Barred," *The New York Times*, April 8, 1915, p. 11; "Havana Fight Films Barred from U.S." *The New York Times*, April 16, 1915, p. 8; "Fight Films Case Lost," *The New York Times*, May 6, 1915, p. 11.

13. See ad in *The Kansas City Post*, April 25, 1915, p. 3B.

14. *Mutual Film Corporation, Appt., v. Industrial Commission of Ohio et al. The Supreme Court Reporter* v. 35 (October Term, 1914) (December 1914–August 1915) (St. Paul: West Publishing Co., 1915), pp. 387–396.

15. *L. Lawrence Weber, Appt. v. Frederick S. Freed, Deputy Collector of United States Customs in Charge of the Port of Newark, N.J., Supreme Court of the United States, October term, 1915*, 239,240,241, U.S. Book 60 (Rochester, NY, Lawyers Cooperative Publishing Company, 1916), pp. 308–310; See also, *The Supreme Court Reporter*, v. 36 (October Term, 1915) (December 1915- July 1916) (St. Paul: West Publishing Co. 1916), pp. 131–132.

I want to thank my friend, the Honorable John Lungstrum, Senior United States District Judge, for kindly looking over my analysis of this decision. Naturally all of the mistakes in this analysis are my own.

"Edward Douglass White," *Wikipedia, the Free Encyclopedia*, seen June 13,2014; Judith A. Baer, "Edward Douglass White," *The Supreme Court justices: A Biographical Dictionary* ed. Melvin I. Urofsky (New York: Garland, 1994), pp. 525–531; Clare Cushman, "Edward Douglass White, 1894–1910, 1910–1921" *The Supreme Court Justices: Illustrated Biographies*, 1789–1993, ed. Clare Cushman (Washington, D.C. Congressional Quarterly, 1993).

16. "Willard on Local Stage," *The New York Times*, April 7, 1915, p. 11; "Map Out Tour as Willard Makes $4,000 Vaudeville Debut," *Variety*, April 9, 1915, p. 4; As a further comparison, Nellie Melba earned $4,000 per week, Eva Tanguay and Ethel Barrymore both earned $3,000 per week, Irene and Vernon Castle earned $2,000, per week, while, Mary Pickford earned $2,000 and Charles Chaplin $1,500 per week. ("Vaudeville may pay Melba $4,000 in Weekly Salary," *Variety*, February 20, 1915, p. 1 and throughout.) Prices for Ford cars were advertised in 1915 as $400 for a Touring Car, $440 for a Runabout, $500 for a Town Car, $750 for a Coupelet, and $975 for a Sedan, all f.o.b. Detroit. *The Kansas City Journal*, April 25, 1915, p. 8A. A survey made of the garment industry in New York City by the Department of Labor found that "cutters" in the cloak, suit and skirt industry earned $8.00 per week. "$8 Average Wage of Suit Cutters," *The New York Tribune*, April 5, 1915, p. 15.

17. "Willard Runs into a Frost," *The New York Herald*, April 10, 1915, Sect. I, p. 6; "Willard Reception Here," *The New York Times*, April 9, 1915, p. 12; "Only Faithful Few Pay to Greet New Champion," *The New York Herald*, April 11, 1915, Sect I, Pt. 1, p. 13; "Two Vaudeville Headliners Furnish Peculiar Contrast," *Variety*, April 16, 1915, p. 6.

18. "Sunday Laws Stop Bout for Willard," *The New York Times*, April 12, 1915, p. 7; Billy Sunday, the evangelist, had trouble drawing crowds at the same time. "'Billy' Sunday's Tabernacle not yet Overcrowded," *The New York Herald*, April 11, 1915, First Section, Pt. II, p. 4.

19. "Johnson's Song and Dance," *Variety*, Mary 28, 1915, p. 4; "Ritchie can Act as well as Fight," *Variety*. February 20, 1915, p. 33; "Ritchie on Big Time," *Variety*, March 19, 1915, p. 5; "Willard Makes his First Speech," *The New York Times*, April 13, 1915, p. 8.

20. "The crowd sat through two or three preliminaries, but took little interest in them. When the announcement was made that Willard had refused to go on, the 'sports' became furious and demanded their money back, which they did not get. Finally, one by one they left the building, expressing anything but complimentary things of the world's champion." "Waited to See Willard," *The New York Times*, April 17, 1915, p. 13.

21. "Willard Makes His First Speech," *The New York Times*, April 13, 1915, p. 8.

22. "Willard Makes His First Speech," *The New York Times*, April 13, 1915, p. 8.

23. "Crowds Cheer 'Jess' Willard in Vaudeville," *The New York Herald*, April 13, 1915, p. 16; "Jess Willard. Athletic. 13 minutes, Full Stage (Exterior.)

Hammerstein's," *Variety*, April 16, 1915, p. 14; "Willard Fails to Draw in New York, Closes," *The Los Angeles Times*, April 19, 1915, sect III, p. 1.

24. "Willard Fails to Draw in New York, Closes," *The Los Angeles Times*, April 19, 1915, sect. III p. 1; "Willard Pines for Kansas Home," *The New York Tribune*, April 11, 1915, p. 13.

25. "Two Vaudeville Headliners Furnish Peculiar Contrast," *Variety*, April 16, 1915, p. 6.

26. "Champ and Ex-Champ to Meet here on the 19th," *The Boston Herald*, April 17,1915, p. 9; "Over the Roofs with Willard," and "Jess Willard Balks at Stage Spotlights," *The Boston Herald*, April 19,1915, p. 7; Walter E. Hapgood, "Along the Sport Trail," *The Boston Herald*, April 19, 1915, p. 6; "Small Crowd Turns Out to see Willard," *The Boston Herald*, April 20, 1915, p. 10.

27. "Willard Dislikes Tours," *The Kansas City Star*, April 20, 1915,p. 11; "Not a Loquacious Champ," *The Kansas City Times*, April 22, 1915, p. 1; Otto Floto, "Welcome to Our City, Jess," *The Kansas City Post*, April 22, 1915, p. 6.

28. Otto Floto, "Welcome to Our City, Jess," *The Kansas City Post*, April 22, 1915, p. 6.

29. "Willard Coming Soon; Is on Way," *The Daily Oklahoman*, April 22, 1915, p. 11.

30. "Jess Willard got $13,000" *The New York Times*, April 23, 1915, p. 11.

31. "Not a Loquacious Champ," *The Kansas City Times*, April 22, 1915, p. 1.

32. Boxing matches in Missouri theaters were popular and common in the 1860s and 1870s. However they were outlawed by the Missouri Prizefight Law of 1874. Nonetheless, they were reinstated by 1911 and Governor Herbert Spencer Hadley allowed boxing matches in theatres as well as athletic clubs. Arly Allen, "The Boxer and the Duelist: The Origins of the Missouri Prizefight Law of 1874," *Missouri Historical Review*, v. 104, no. 4 (July 2010) pp. 213–232 on p. 225–226; Arly Allen, "Seeking 'The Great White Hope,'" pt. 2, *Missouri Historical Review*, v. 100. no. 4 (July 2006), pp. 212–223, on p. 217; "Willard on Border of Native State," *The Daily Oklahoman*, April 22, 1915, p. 2, "Jess to be here May 3; Is Signed," *The Daily Oklahoman*, April 25, 1915, p. 13; "$1,000 a day for Jess Willard is what 101 Ranch will pay," *Variety*, April 30, 1915, p. 4.

33. Edward W. Cochrane, "Willard Impresses K.C. Business Men," *The Kansas City Journal*, April 23, 1915, p. 8.

34. J. A. Boyle, "Be your Boy's Chum, Teach him the Ways of the World, Willard's Advice to Fathers," *The Kansas City Post*, April 23, 1915, p. 1.

35. "Willard to be in Omaha Soon," *The Omaha World-Herald*, April 18, 1915, p. 1 Sports; "Jess Willard's Coming is Much Discussed," April 18, 1915, p. 3 Sports; "Willard's Ovation Like Jim Corbett's," *The Omaha World-Herald*, April 25, 1915, p. 3 Sports; "Giant Kansan Bigger Fighter than John L., "*The Omaha World-Herald*, April 26, 1915, p. 5.

36. "Willard Coming Soon; Is on Way," *The Daily Oklahoman*, April 23, 1915, p. 11.

37. "Willard Dodges Crowd to Visit 'Grandma Wade.'" *The Topeka Daily Capital*, May 2, 1915, p. 1 on p. 8B.

38. "Willard dodges Crowd to visit 'Grandma Wade'" *The Topeka Daily Capital*, May 2, 1915, p. 1; "Willard Has Quiet Sunday with Kin," *The Topeka Daily Capital*, May 3, 1915, p. 2; "Company beats Willard to City," *The Daily Oklahoman*, May 2, 1915, p. 5.

39. "Willard has Quiet Sunday with Kin," *The Topeka Daily Capital*, May 3, 1915, p. 2.

40. When Willard appeared in New York City, Tom Jones prevented Jess from being seen in public. Since Hammerstein was paying Willard to appear at his theatre, he did not want Willard exposed to the public. "Tom Jones, the Barber, finds

Stanch Defender," *The New York Tribune*, April 15, 1915, p. 14 The same thing occurred in Kansas. When Willard was visiting with his friends and acquaintances in Topeka, Tom Jones ordered him into a car and told the driver to take him out into the country. "We got sixty thousand dollars for the photographic rights to Willard and we can't just let people take snapshots of the new champion," said Tom Jones to a newspaper man who was trying to get a photograph of Jess Willard for use in *The Daily Capital*. "Willard Dodges Crowd to Visit with Grandma Wade," *The Topeka Daily Capital*, May 2, 1915, p 1.

41. "Fate of 'Heart Punch' still in the Balance," *The Topeka Daily Capital*, May 2, 1915, p. 14B; "Willard Pictures Under Kansas Ban," *The Daily Oklahoman*, May 4, 1915, p. 11; "Jess Willard!! Champion of the World," *The Topeka Daily Capital*, April 11, 1915, p. 9A .

42. "Jess to be here May 3, Is Signed," *The Daily Oklahoman*, April 25, 1915, p. 13 and ad in paper *The Daily Oklahoman*, April 27, 1915, p. 8.

43. "Champion Jess Returns Tonight," *The Daily Oklahoman*, May 2, 1915, p. A-13; " Company Beats Willard to City," *The Daily Oklahoman*, May 3, 1915, p. 5; "Big Champ Given Great Reception," *The Daily Oklahoman*, May 4, 1915, p. 11; "No Umpiring Goes with Champ Jess," *The Oklahoma News*, May 1, 1915, p. 4.

44. "Jess Willard World's Heavyweight Champion," *The Daily Oklahoman*, May 2, 1915, p. 15; "Tom Jones will Boost Local Lad," *The Daily Oklahoman*, May 6, 1915, p. 11.

45. "Willard's Trouble May be Banished," *The Daily Oklahoman*, April 6, 1915, p. 8; "Big Champ Given Great Reception," *The Daily Oklahoman*, May 4, 1915, p. 11; "Willard's Fine not Lawful," *The Daily Oklahoman*, May 3, 1915, p. 8 "Jess Must pay Fine," *The Wichita Eagle*, May 4, 1915, p. 10; "Willard Pays Old Fine in Oklahoma," *The Springfield Daily Leader*, May 5, 1915, p. 10.

46. "Willard Defendant in $20,500 Action," *The Daily Oklahoman*, May 5, 1915, p. 14; "Phillips is Bound to Federal Jurors," *The Daily Oklahoman*, May 6, 1915, p. 4.

47. "Willard Defendant in $20,500 Action," *The Daily Oklahoman*, May 5, 1915, p. 14) "Oklahoma Men Sue Jess Willard for $20,000," *The Topeka Daily Capital*, May 5, 1915, p. 9; "Legal Papers are served on Willard," *The Wichita Eagle*, May 5, 1915, p. 7 "Willard Loses Bout; Deputy Sheriff Wins," *The Milwaukee Free Press*, May 5, 1915.

48. "Won't let Willard Box Here," *The Wichita Eagle*, May 4, 1915, p. 5; "Jess Willard Here Tonight," *The Wichita Eagle*, May 4, 1915, p. 10"; Packed Station to say Howdy to J. Willard," *The Wichita Beacon*, May 4, 1915, p. 6; "J. Willard Show Lacked the Punch," *The Wichita Beacon*, May 5, 1915, p. 8.

49. Barbara Williams Rush, "The 101 Ranch Wild West Show, 1904–1932," *Chronicles of Oklahoma*, v. 43, no. 4 (Winter 1965–1966), pp. 416–431 on p. 422; "$1,000 a day for Jess Willard is what 101 Ranch will Pay," *Variety*, April 30, 1915, p. 4.

50. Ellsworth Collings and Alma Miller England, *The 101 Ranch* (Norman and London: University of Oklahoma Press, 1971 [1937]), p. xiii; Michael Wallis, *The Real Wild West: The 101 Ranch and the Creation of the American West* (New York: St. Martin's Press, 1999), pp. 431–433.

51. "$1,000 a day for Jess Willard is what 101 Ranch will pay," *Variety*, April 30, 1915, p. 4; "Willard is Making $1,000 per day with Wild West Show," *The Fort Worth Star-Telegram*, May 23, 1915, p. 17; E.W. Dickerson, "Success has not spoiled Champion Jess Willard," *The Grand Rapids Press*, June 3, 1915, p. 14. Hattie shows up in the pictures of the 101 Ranch show, but the children do not. Possibly they were taken care of by Hattie's parents and her sister, Delna, who lived on the farm near St. Clere, Kansas.

52. "Wife tells Jess' History," *Los Angeles Times*, April 12, 1915, p. III, 1 and James Willard Mace personal information.

53. E.W. Dickerson, "Success has not Spoiled Champion Jess Willard," *The Grand Rapids Press*, June 3, 1915, p. 14; "Picture Rosy for his Family," *The Kansas City Star*, April 6, 1915, p. 2; "Title means big Ranch Home for Mrs. Willard and the Babes," *The Daily Oklahoman*, April 6, 1915, p. 13.

54. "Here's What Inspired Jess," *The Daily Oklahoman*, April 25, 1915, p. 13.

55. "Jess Willard to Appear in Cowboy Attire Here Oct. 4," *Daily Oklahoman*, Oct. 2, 1915, p. 9; Wallis, *The Real Wild West*, p. 432.

56. "Jess's Trainer is Interviewed," *The (Rochester, MN) Daily Post and Record*, May 14, 1915, p. 5; "As We Heard It," *The Daily Post and Record*, May 15, 1915, p. 8; "Victory is Expected," *The Daily Post and Record*, June 2, 1915, p. 2; Anne Beiser Allen, "Fred Fulton, the Rochester Plasterer," *Minnesota History* (Summer, 2004), pp. 74–87.

57. "Mrs. Jess Willard Dying," *The Washington Post*, June 28, 1915, p. 3. In an interview in Oklahoma City in October, Willard explained: "Say," he said, "Did you folks down here believe that 'T.B.' stuff? Let me tell you how that story got out. Up in Chicago one day while Mrs. Willard was visiting us, a newspaper reporter came into camp and wanted to see me. If I have anything worthwhile I don't mind giving it out, but I don't like all this gush and they generally have to wrestle with Tom Jones before they get to where I am. This fellow was rather peevish and you know you can't get anywhere with Tom Jones if you're that kind of guy. So Jones told him I was with Mrs. Willard who was ill and couldn't be bothered. Mrs. Willard had a bad cough, Jones said, which was true, for she had taken cold. Well that reporter walked off, and the next thing we knew, the papers everywhere were printing a story to the effect that Mrs. Willard was dying of consumption. Can you believe it? As a matter of fact she is in excellent health, and so are the babies. Just the other day I sent them an automobile and I guess they are enjoying themselves out there on the coast. "Jess Willard's Back Home Again," *The Daily Oklahoman*, October 4, 1915, p. 8.

58. "Willard Will Stick," *Variety*, Aug. 27, 1915, p. 4.

59. "Sue Willard for $27, 333," *New York Times*, June 12, 1915, p. 8.

60. Frank G. Menke, "Troops to Keep Down Riots," *The Kansas City Post*, April 5, 1915, p. 5; E.W. Dickerson, "Success had not spoiled Champion Jess Willard," *The Grand Rapids Press*, June 3, 1915, p. 14; "Jess Willard buys 7-Passenger Auto," *The Daily Oklahoman*, June 13, 1915, p. 22.

61. *The St. Marys Star* of August 19, 1915, p. 4 noted that "Mrs. Jess Willard is visiting her parents Mr. and Mrs. B.B. Evens (sic)." The paper noted as well, "B.B. Evens (sic) and wife and daughters, Mrs. Jess Willard, and Delna, went down to St. Marys one day last week." Hattie and the children were back in California in September. "Jess Willard sends Cole Eight to Wife," *The Los Angeles Times*, September 26, 1915, p. V 14.

62. "Jess Willard Sends Cole Eight to Wife," *The Los Angeles Times*, Sept. 26, 1915, p. V14.

63. "The Sport Budget," by Frank Menke, *The Milwaukee Free Press*, November 21, 1915, p. 7.

64. Wallis, *The Real Wild West*, p. 433.

65. Collings and England, *The 101 Ranch*, p. xiii; Wallis, *The Real Wild West*, pp. 455, 423–426, 431; "Huge Payment for War Horses Held up; Return to '101' Ranch probable," *The Daily Oklahoman*, April 17, 1915, p. 6.

66. H.M. Walker, "An Ear to the Ground," *Los Angeles Examiner*, November 21, 1915, Sect. VI, p. 4.

67. "Willard Driven From Theatre by Audience Hoots and Calls," *Variety*, December 3, 1915, p. 3.

68. H. M. Walker, "An Ear to the Ground," *Los Angeles Examiner*, December 1, 1915, Sect. II, p. 3.

69. Kenneth Silverman, *Houdini!!! The Career of Ehrich Weiss* (New York: Harper Collins Publishers, Inc. 1996) pp. 199–201; "The Culliton Papers: Willard's Side," http://www.wildabouthoudini.com/ 2001/08/culliton-papers-willards-side.html); "Houdini Unchained," http://www.boxing.com/houdini_unchained.html).

70. "Willard Tells His Side of Row with Vaudeville Star," *Los Angeles Examiner*, December 3, 1915, Sect. II, p. 3.

71. "Willard and Gotch, Extra," *Variety,* January 21, 1916, p. 3; "Tammen to Pay $1,200 per day to Jess Willard & Frank Gotch," *The Billboard,* January 24, 1916, p. 1.

72. Bob Tabor, "Jess Willard: Prize Fighter, Wild West Attraction, Circus Owner," *The White Tops, Worlds foremost publication devoted exclusively to the Circus,* v. 38, no. 2 (March–April 1965), pp. 3–8; Nancy M. Peterson. "Buffalo Bill's Legacy," *American History v 38, no. 4.* (October 2003), pp. 51–56, 80.

73. "Another 'White Hope' in the Willard Family," *The Washington Post,* April 15, 1916, p. 9; "Sells-Floto Circus Came this Morning," *The Wichita Beacon,* April 25, 1916, p. 10; "Willard Not Likely to Box," *The Los Angeles Times,* June 22, 1916, p. III 1 Both Jess and Hattie had good memories of the Sells-Floto circus. H. H. Tammen was very diplomatic in handling his help. When a worker complained that he had been denied a second helping of ice cream at mealtime, Tammen ordered that all of the staff could have all of the ice cream they could eat. He rightly recognized that they would soon tire of ice cream. When a young lady complained that her tights had been torn by the high weeds around the site, he ordered the Circus management to buy hose by the gross for the women, so that they would never have to perform without tights. Bob Tabor, "Jess Willard: Prize Fighter, Wild West Attraction, Circus Owner," *The White Tops,* v. 38, no. 2 (March-April 1965), p. 4.

74. "Famous Promoter Pulling for Wichita," *The Wichita Eagle,* April 22, 1916, p. 7; "Famous Athletes Failed to Appear." *The Wichita Beacon,* April 26, 1916, p. 7.

75. "May Not Let Jess Show Off," *The Wichita Eagle,* April 27, 1916, p. 2; "Expects to Balk Sheriff," *The Wichita Eagle,* April 28, 1916, p. 2; "Big Show Opens up with Pep," *The Wichita Eagle,* April 30, 1916, Section C, p. 2. Sheriff Sarver was clearly concerned about his own job if he did not enforce the law. The law forbidding prizefighting and boxing in Kansas had a clause in Section 3 which said: "The failure or neglect of any sheriff, constable, marshal or other police officer to perform any duty imposed upon him by the provisions of this act shall work a forfeiture of his office, and it shall be the duty of the county attorney of such county to cause such forfeiture to be adjudged and such officer removed from his office..." Session Laws, 1901, chapter 274, section 3, *State of Kansas* (Topeka: W.Y. Morgan, State Printer, 1901), p. 501.

76. "Two Champions," *The Times-Picayune,* November 1, 1915, p. 4; The Hub ad, *The Wichita Eagle,* April 28, 1916, p. 2; "Nuxated Iron Helped Me Whip Frank Moran," *The Wichita Eagle,* April 30, 1916, Section C, p. 2; "Jess Willard Trains for Big Bouts with Nuxated Iron," *The Daily Oklahoman,* December 31, 1916, p. 6; Jess Willard, "How to have Health and Muscle like Mine," *The Los Angeles Examiner,* December 5, 1915, sect. VI, p. 6.

77. Harry Carr, "Jess Willard is a Good Judge of Live Stock When it comes to Talking about being Champ. " *The Los Angeles Times,* October 17, 1916, p. III 1; "Fine Willard for Speeding," *The Washington Post,* May 19, 1916, p. 8.

78. "Sells-Floto's Big Day," *Variety,* August 18, 1916, p. 8.

79. "Frank Gotch Breaks Leg," *The Los Angeles Times,* July 19, 1916, p. III, 1; "Frank Gotch Breaks Leg," *The New York Times,* July 19, 1916, p. 10; Bob Tabor, "Jess Willard: Prize Fighter, Wild West Attraction, Circus Owner," *The White Tops,* v. 38, no. 2 (March-April 1965), pp. 3–8; Jess Willard, et al. vs Charles F. Knoblauch, 8th Circuit Court of Appeals, case no. 890 in Box No. H45 in the C.L. Sonnichsen Special Collections Department of the University of Texas at El Paso Library; "Willard Admits Feet are Large," *The Los Angeles Times,* October 22, 1916,p. VII 10; "Jess Willard Sneaks Out of El Paso on Freight," *The Los Angeles Times,* November 2, 1916, p. III 1.

80. " Jess Willard in Class by Himself; May Retire Undefeated Champion," *The Daily Oklahoman,* November 2, 1916, p. 10; "Kansas City Bids for Title Fight," *The Daily Oklahoman,* November 7, 1916, p. 8; "Denver Angling for Title Mill," *The Daily Oklahoman,* November 21, 1916, p. 12; J. A. Ermatinger, "Promoters Bidding Spiritedly for Willard's First Contest," *The Daily Oklahoman,* November 25, 1916, p. 30.

81. "Willard Weighs 270, But Willing to Fight," *The Washington Post,* November 27, 1916, p. 6.

82. Three articles in the *New Orleans Times-Picayune* at the end of 1915 illustrate Joe Miller's concerns. "America's $40,000,000 a week Trade Balance to Grow: Europe's Indebtedness Increases Every Day," November 7, 1915, pt. 1, sect. 2, p. 1; Cartoon: "Nation's 1915 Farm Crops valued at $5,500,000,000: All Previous Records Broken," November 10, 1915, p. 1; "Frenchmen Arrive to order supplies worth $160,000,000." November 10, 1915, p. 3.

83. "Willard with Circus for Another Season," *The Washington Post,* February 23, 1917, p. 5; "Buffalo Bill's Son Killed," *Variety,* March 9, 1917, p. 8; Bob Tabor, "Jess Willard: Prize Fighter, Wild West Attraction, Circus Owner," *The White Tops,* v. 38, no. 2 (March-April 1965), p. 4.

84. "Jess Willard May Buy Property and Locate in Oklahoma City," *The Daily Oklahoman,* March 20, 1917, p. 8.

85. "Business Off All Over," and "Administration's War Tax a Bombshell to Managers," *Variety,* April 27, 1917, pp. 10–11; " Western Business Dropping, and Circuses Worrying," *Variety,* May 4, 1917, p. 3; "Conscription Sure to Draw Stage Men in Army Service," *Variety,* May 4, 1917, p. 4; "Ringlings Preparing," *Variety,* May 11, 1917, p. 3; "Bar All Circuses During War," *Variety,* May 18, 1917, p. 3; "Circus Lots Cultivated," *Variety,* June 2, 1917, p. 3; Bob Tabor, "Jess Willard: Prize Fighter, Wild West Attraction, Circus Owner," *The White Tops,* v. 38, no. 2 (March–April 1965), pp. 6–7.

86. "Record Circus Season Cheers Legitimate Managers," *Variety,* June 2, 1917, p. 11; "Buffalo Bill Show Sold," *The New York Times,* June 10, 1917, p. 4; "Willard Buys Circus," *The New York Times,* June 12, 1917, p. 10; "Willard's Show Now," *Variety,* June 15, 1917, p. 8.

87. "Circuses Routed Together," *Variety,* July 13, 1917, p. 3; "Circus Clash," *Variety,* July 20, 1917, p. 17.

88. "Circus Clash," *Variety,* July 20, 1917, p. 17.

89. "Willard Show out Late," *Variety,* August 10, 1917, p. 8.

90. "Jess Willard is an unfortunate individual," *The Milwaukee Free Press,* November 9, 1917, p. 7; Bob Tabor, "Jess Willard: Prize Fighter, Wild West Attraction, Circus Owner," *The White Tops,* v. 38, no. 2 (March–April 1965), p. 7.

Chapter 7

1. "Fighters Prepare to Leave Havana," *The Washington Post,* April 7, 1915, p. 8; "Willard Makes his First Speech," *The New York Times,* April 13, 1915, p. 8.

2. "Big Offers for Willard," *The New York Times,* April 6, 1915, p. 8; "London Offer for Willard," *The New York Times,* April 8, 1915, p. 11; "Champion Spurns $20,000 to Box Moran in London," *The Washington Times,* April 8, 1915, p. 8.

3. "Boxing Interest Revives," *The New York Times,* April 12, 1915, p. 7; "Coffey Wins Hard Bout from Morris," *The New York Times,* April 8, 1915, p. 11; "Gunboat Smith Whipped," *The New York Times,* April 14, 1915, p. 10; "Wells Knocked Out in Tenth," *The National Police Gazette,* April 17, 1915, p. 7.

4. "Willard May Box Here," *The New York Times,* April 19, 1915, p. 10; "Public Will Not stand for Jess Willard," *The Chicago Defender,* May 8, 1915, p. 1; Hal Sheridan, "Sport Notes," *The Beloit Daily News,* May 18, 1915.

5. "Willard Ready to Box," *The New York Times,* August 28, 1915, p. 5; "Willard will fight for $30,000 Purse," *The Washington Post,* August 29, 1915, p. D1.

6. Ringside, "Willard expects Five-Year 'Term'" *The Daily Oklahoman,* April 25, 1915, p. 13; "Bring on Jim Coffey," say Willard and Jones," *The Milwaukee Free Press,* September 21, 1915; George R. Holmes, "Heavyweight Fight Near," *The Beloit Daily News,* September 21, 1915.

7. "Willard Ready to Fight," *The Washington Post,* October 4, 1915, p. 9.

8. "Big Offer is Made to Jess," *Los Angeles Times*, October 5, 1915, p. III 1. After the debacle in Calgary, Alberta in May 1913 when Luther McCarty died in the ring and his arena was burned down, Tommy Burns became a nomad. He finally turned up in New Orleans working with Dominick Tortorich.

9. "$30,000 for Willard Bout at the Garden," *The New York Times*, October 10, 1915, p. 35.

10. "Short Sports," *The Daily Oklahoman*, October 24, 1915, p. 14; John Lardner, *White Hopes and Other Tigers* (Philadelphia and New York: J. B. Lippincott Company, 1957), pp. 46–47.

11. "Right Hook to Jaw Tells; Coffey Recovers Quickly," *The Washington Post*, October 20, 1915, p. 8.

12. "Jess Willard Settles Down to Real Home Life," *The Los Angeles Times*, November 7, 1915, p. IV 7.

13. "Willard defendant in $20,500 Action," *The Daily Oklahoman*, May 5, 1915, p. 14; Phillips is Bound to Federal Jurors," *The Daily Oklahoman*, May 6, 1915, p. 4; "Intent to Develop Willard into Champion held Ground for Dismissing $40,500 Suit," *The Daily Oklahoman*, November 19, 1915, p. 10; "Willard Jury is Seven and Five," *The Daily Oklahoman*, November 20,1915, p. 8; "One-Dollar Verdict in Phillips-Cuttrell Suit against Jess Willard," *The Daily Oklahoman*, November 21, 1915, p. 15 This was not the end of A.W. Phillips' troubles. In May 1915, Phillips had been indicted for paying for a young woman to come from Arkansas to Oklahoma City for the purpose of illegal sex. Phillips was convicted of the crime of "white slavery" in February 1916 and in March he was sent to the Federal Penitentiary at Leavenworth as inmate no. 10726. There he joined Willard's first promoter, J.D. Brock, inmate no. 9063, who had been convicted of mail fraud in 1914. Willard felt he had been mistreated by these two promoters, so to have them both residing in prison while he enjoyed the fame of being world champion was very satisfying to him. "Phillips Convicted of Slavery Charge," *The Daily Oklahoman*, February 12, 1916, p. 14.

14. "Willard Signs to Meet Pick of Heavyweights," *The [New Orleans] Times-Picayune*, November 3, 1915, p. 11.

15. "Jess Willard to Defend Title in New Orleans," *The Los Angeles Times*, November 1, 1915, p. III 3.

16. "Another White Hope on Willard's Trail," *The Washington Post*, October 26, 1915, p. 8; "Here's Man Who'll Likely Tackle Jess; Has Longest Reach in the Ring," *The Oklahoma News*, November 17, 1915, p. 5; "As We Heard It" (Rochester, Minnesota) *The Daily Post and Record*, May 18, 1915, p. 8; "Victory is Expected," (Rochester, Minnesota) *The Daily Post and Record*, June 2, 1915, p. 2.

17. George R. Holmes, "Jess to Fight but Opponent is not Found," *Beloit Daily News*, November 6, 1915; "Seven Contend for Heavyweight Title," *The Oklahoma News*, November 16, 1915, p. 5.

18. Sam C. Austin, "Willard's Title Disputed by a Bad Lot of Fighters," *The National Police Gazette*, November 27, 1915, p. 10.

19. "Willard Is offered $50,000 to Battle Langford in Boston," *The Los Angeles Examiner*, November 30, 1915, Sect. II, p. 3; H.M. Walker, "An Ear to the Ground," *The Los Angeles Examiner*, December 2, 1915, Sect. II, p. 3; Clay Moyle, *Sam Langford: Boxing's Greatest Uncrowned Champion* (Seattle, WA: Bennett and Hastings Publishing, 2006), p. 293.

20. De Witt Van Court, "Willard a Wonderfully Improved Boxer—Will Keep Title a While," *The Los Angeles Times*, December 1, 1915, p. III 3.

21. "Fred Fulton is Matched to Meet Willard Here March 4," *The [New Orleans] Times-Picayune*, December 3, 1915, p. 11.

22. "Frank Moran Must Defeat Fulton to get Big Match," *The Times-Picayune*, November 21, 1915, p. B-11.

23. "Tortorich Out of Boxing Game—Sells to W.F. Steele," *The Times-Picayune*, December 10, 1915, p. 13.

24. "Managers Meet Sans Articles," *The Los Angeles Times*, December 14, 1915, p. III 2; "Principals Sign for Big Bout," *The Times-Picayune*, December 16, 1915, p. 15; "Willard and Fulton Sign," *The New York Times*, December 16, 1915, p. 12; "Tortorich Matches Herman and Williams—To Build New Arena," *The Times-Picayune*, December 19, 1915, p. 11-B

25. "Willard to Spend Holidays in East," *Los Angeles Examiner*, December 21, 1915, sect. II, p. 2; "Champ Desires To Have Family Nearer to Him," *Los Angeles Examiner*, December 23, 1915, sect. II, p. 2; H. M. Walker, "An Ear to the Ground," *Los Angeles Examiner*, December 17, 1915, sect. II, p. 2.

26. "Willard to Make Home in Chicago," *The Times-Picayune*, December 23, 1915, p. 11";Promoters Discard Fulton; Want Moran to Meet Jess," *The Times-Picayune*, December 25, 1915, p. 11; "Championship Bout Wabbling; Result of Proposed Switch," *The Times-Picayune*, December 27, 1915, p. 10.

27. "Moran is signed for Coffey Bout," The Times-Picayune, December 21, 1915, p. 12; "May Sign Moran for Willard Go," *The Washington Post*, December 25, 1915, p. 8; "Fight for the Right of Title Bout," *The Washington Post*, December 26, 1915, p. SP1.

28. "Fulton or None," *The Times-Picayune*, December 27, 1915, p. 10; "First Chance for Fulton, Jones is Stirred to Wrath," *Los Angeles Examiner*, December 27, 1915, sect. II, p. 2; "Jones determined in his Stand," *The Times-Picayune*, December 28, 1915, p. 11; "Tortorich Retires and Burns Will Promote Original Match," *The Times-Picayune*, December 28, 1915, p. 11.

29. "Jones and Andrews Come Today to Settle Argument," *The Times-Picayune*, December 29, 1915, p. 11.

30. "Willard-Fulton Bout off Here; Will Take Place in Milwaukee," *The Times-Picayune*, December 30, 1915, p. 11; "Promoter of Fight Balks at Fulton," *The New York Times*, December 30, 1915, p. 11; "Willard-Fulton Fight Off As Regards New Orleans," *The Washington Post*, December 30, 1915, p. 8.

31. "Andrews to Meet Champion," *The Times-Picayune*, December 31, 1915, p. 11; "Andrews to Make Offer, "*The New York Times*, December 31, 1915, p. 10; "Willard to Fight Fulton 10 Rounds," *The Washington Post*, December 31, 1915, p. 8.

32. "Willard to Fight Fulton 10 Rounds," *The Washington Post*, December 31, 1915, p. 8; "Call Off Willard-Fulton Bout," *The Washington Post*, January 2, 1916, p. S3; "Bout is Off" and "Fulton vs. Porky Flynn," *The Times-Picayune*, January 3, 1916, p. 11; "Fulton is Matched for Go with Flynn," *The Washington Post*, January 4, 1916, p. 8.

33. "Willard will fight Moran if present plans carry," *The Washington Post*, January 13, 1916, p. 8; "$45,000 for Willard Bout with Moran," *The New York Times*, January 13, 1916,p. 13; "Willard and Moran are to Clash at New York," *The Los Angeles Times*, January 13,1916, p. III 1; "Career of Rickard Vivid and Colorful," *The New York Times*, January 7, 1929, p. 34; Charles Samuels, *The Magnificent Rube: The Life and Gaudy Times of Tex Rickard* (New York, Toronto and London: McGraw-Hill Book Company, Inc., 1957); Colleen Aycock and Mark Scott, *Tex Rickard: Boxing's Greatest Promoter* (Jefferson, NC: McFarland, 2012).

34. Harry A. Williams, "Tex Rickard Cunning and Crafty Promoter," *The Los Angeles Times*, January 14, 1916, p. III 3.

35. Harry A. Williams, "Tex Rickard Cunning and Crafty Promoter," *The Los Angeles Times*, January 14, 1916, p. III 3; Frank Moran, "Says He Will Stop Willard, and Wishes Foe was Bigger," *The Washington Post*, January 16, 1916, p. S1.

36. Johnston Offers $55,000 for Fight," *The New York Times*, January 22, 1916, p. 11.

37. Samuels, *The Magnificent Rube*, p. 113.

38. "Offer 2 Fat Purses for Heavyweight Go," *The Washington Post*, January 22, 1916, p. 8.

39. "O'Brien's Bid Rejected," *The New York Times*. January 21, 1916, p. 7; "Willard gets Offer to Box Jim Coffey," *The New York Times*, January 25, 1916, p. 7; "Jess Willard is in Demand," *The Los Angeles Times*, January 17, 1916,p. III 3.

40. "Jess Willard has signed with Jack Curley to box Frank Moran Ten Rounds," *The Los Angeles Times*, January 18, 1916,

p. III 2; "Promoters are plentiful for Willard-Moran Fight," *The Washington Post,* January 20, 1916, p. 8.

41. "Moran must Accept Curley's Terms," *The New York Times*, January 20, 1916, p 7; "Moran Must Reduce Terms for Big Bout," *The New York Times,* January 23, 1916, p. S4.

42. "Squabble Tires Rickard," *The New York Times*, January 25, 1916, p. 7.

43. "Champion Willard to begin training," *The Times-Picayune*, January 18, 1916, p. 11 "Jess Willard is now in Training," *The Los Angeles Times*, January 26, 1916, p. III 4; Willard had signed a contract with the Sells-Floto circus which would pay him $5,000 per week and last from April 1 through November 1, 1916. See "Willard Has Bank Roll; Money No Worry to Him," *The Washington Post*, March 5, 1916, p. S4.

44. "Champion Gets $32,500 for a Ten-Round Battle," *The Washington Post*, Feb. 3, 1916, p. 8; "Willard and Dillon Bout Now Planned," *The New York Times*, February 3, 1916, p. 11.

45. "Willard and Moran to Box Here on Mar. 17," *The New York Times*, February 4, 1916, p. 10; "Give Champion $47,500 for a Ten-Round Fight," *The Washington Post*, February 4, 1916, p. 8; Xerox of typed contract in my personal file.

46. "Tom Jones, Willard, Curley getting Rich," *The Los Angeles Times,* February 4, 1916, p. III 1; Interestingly, Jack Curley does not comment in his Memoirs about this bluff of Tex Rickard.

47. "Willard Bout Mar. 8 in Garden Arena," *The New York Times*, February 9, 1916, p. 8; "Big Battle March 8 in Madison Square," *The Washington Post*, February 9, 1916, p. 8.

48. "Willard Bout Mar. 8 in Garden Arena," *The New York Times*, February 9, 1916, p. 8; "Jess Willard a Grip Victim," *The Los Angeles Times*, February 10, 1916, p. III 3; "Jess Willard Ready to Begin Training," *The Washington Post*, February 11, 1916,p. 8.

49. "Champion Unable to Train, So He Decides to Withdraw," *The Washington Post*, February 15, 1916, p. 8; "Jackson Connects with Jess in Chi.," *The Daily Oklahoman*, February 15, 1916, p. 10.

50. "Fight Latter Part of March If Present Plans Hold Good," *The Washington Post*, February 16, 1916, p. 8; Robert Edgren, "Willard Needs Time to Train; May Explain Delay of Fight," *The Washington Post*, February 18, 1916, p. 9; Jess Willard, "Ash Wednesday Brings Fight Delay, Says Willard, Giving True Reason," *The Washington Post,* February 19, 1916, p. 8; Robert Edgren, "Tom Jones, Not Willard, to Decide if Fight is Postponed," *The Washington Post*, February 17, 1916, p. 8; "Think Fight Helped by 2 Weeks' Delay," *The Washington Post*, February 20, 1916, p. 8.

51. "Willard Ordered to Bed," *The New York Times*, February 21, 1916, p. 8; "Physicians Order Willard to Bed; May Not Fight Moran on March 25," *The Washington Post*, February 21, 1916, p. 9; "Champion Now in Fine Trim, According to Manager Jones," *The Washington Post*, February 22, 1916, p. 8; Robert Edgren, "Willard-Moran Bout Cannot be Postponed Again, Says Edgren," *The Washington Post*, February 22, 1916, p. 8; "Willard is Training but Only Road Work," *The Washington Post*, February 24, 1916, p. 8.

52. "Lord Lonsdale May See Willard Bout," *The New York Times*, February 24, 1916, p. 10; "Several Women see Jess Willard Train," *The New York Times*, March 1, 1916, p. 12.

53. Willard is En Route to Scene of Battle, *The Washington Post*, February 25, 1916, p. 8.

54. "Throng Greets Willard on Arrival in New York," *The Washington Post*, February 26, 1916, p. 8.

55. "Throng Greets Willard on Arrival in New York," *The Washington Post,* February 26, 1916, p. 8.

56. "Willard Pronounced 'Fit' after Physician Examines," *The Washington Post,* February 27, 1916, p. M3; "Willard Weighed After a Squabble," *The New York Times*, February 27, 1916, p. S2; Robert Edgren, "Willard's Cold Cost $10,000, But Champion Has No Regrets," *The Washington Post*, February 27, 1916, p. M7.

57. "Willard Declines to Train on Sunday," *The New York Times*, February 28, 1916, p. 10; Jess Willard, "Walking is Best Exercise in Willard's Estimation," *The Washington Post,* February 28, 1916, p. 8.

58. Nixola Greeley-Smith, "Champion Jess Believes in Preparedness (With Fists), but Big Fellow is Against Fighting," *The Washington Post*, February 27, 1916, p. A9.

59. Jess Willard, "More Fighters Sought to Spar with Willard," *The Washington Post*, March 1, 1916, p. 8; Jess Willard, "Willard Floor Monahan, Who Attempts to 'Land,'" *The Washington Post*, March 2, 1916, p. 8; "Hard for Willard to Reduce Weight," *The New York Times*, March 2, 1916, p. 8; Robert Edgren, "Willard Invites the 'Heavies' to Help Him Train for Fight," *The Washington Post*, March 3,1916, p. 8; "Willard Shy of Partners," *The Los Angeles Times,* March 3, 1916, p. III 3; "Boxers Shun Willard," *The New York Times*, March 3, 1916, p. 8; Robert Edgren, "Jim Coffey Meets Willard; Awed at Champion's Size," *The Washington Post*, March 5, 1916, p. S3.

60. "Sale of Tickets to $100,000 for Willard-Moran Contest," *The Washington Post*, March 5, 1916, p. S1; "Willard Weighed After a Squabble," *The New York Times*, February 27, 1916, p. S2.

61. Robert Edgren, "Willard's Training Quarters Are Badly Chosen, Declares Edgren," *The Washington Post,* February 25, 1916, p. 9; Robert Edgren, "Willard and Moran Differ on The Best System of Training," *The Washington Post*, March 7, 1916, p. 8.

62. "Stops Fees for Willard; Pioneer A.C. Suspended," *The Washington Post,* March 12, 1916, p. S1";Boxing Commission Stops Jess Willard," *The New York Times,* March 12, 1916, p. S2; "Willard to Stay Here, Despite Ire," *The New York Times,* March 13, 1916, p. 10.

63. "Forestall Measure to Stop Title Bout," *The Washington Post*, March 9, 1916, p. 8.

64. Robert Edgren, "Willard Is Not Too Fat, View of Men Who Know Fighters," *The Washington Post*, March 9, 1916, p. 8; "Close to Weight Asserts Willard," *The Washington Post*, March 10, 1916, p. 8; Robert Edgren, "Attacks Upon Willard-Moran Bout Sure to Prove Unpopular," *The Washington Post,* March 11, 1916, p. 8.

65. Robert Edgren, "Attacks Upon Willard-Moran Bout Sure to Prove Unpopular," *The Washington Post,* March 11, 1916, p. 8.

66. "New Stakeholder Plan is Dropped," *The New York Times*, March 14, 1916, p. 12.

67. Robert Edgren, "'Trained Down and Feel Just About Right,' Says Willard," *The Washington Post,* March 15, 1916, p. 8; "Moran to Rickard's Relief," *The New York Times*, March 11, 1916, p. 12. Wenck had told Rickard that for his own protection, he needed to turn over the revenues of the fight to the Athletic Commission who would find a stakeholder "satisfactory" to the commission. Further, he said that the boxers could only be paid on the commission's order. Rickard responded that he intended to carry on his business in his own way. He would pay the boxers according to the agreements that he had made. Rickard believed in the honesty of the boxers and that if Wenck did not, he, Rickard would pay the boxers the amount owed them directly and pay Wenck the same amount so that the "public" would be protected. Further, on his own initiative, Rickard increased the amount he was to pay Moran to $23,500 from $22,000 since he had given his word to Moran that he would pay him one half of what he paid Willard.

68. "Bar 5-ounce Gloves if Law is Observed," *The Washington Post*, March 15, 1916, p. 8; "Just before the Gong," *The Los Angeles Times,* March 26, 1916, p. VII 4; "M'Cue's Effort to Kill Bout Futile," *The New York Times*, March 15, 1916, p. 12; "Wenck Will Not Quit Job," *The New York Times,* March 15, 1916, p. 12.

69. Robert Edgren, "Willard and Moran Train Long for a Ten-Round Bout," *The Washington Post*, March 18, 1916, p. 8.

70. "Moran a Peacemaker," *The New York Times*, March 21, 1916, p. 8; John Lardner, *White Hopes and Other Tigers*, pp. 42–48.

71. "Puts O.K. on Fighters," *The Washington Post*, March 20, 1916, p. 5.

72. James J. Corbett, "Corbett expects Willard to Get Decision at end of 10 Rounds," *The Washington Post*, March 12, 1916, p. S4; James J. Jeffries, "Jeffries Says Moran has Little Chance to Win from Willard," *The Washington Post*, March 12, 1916,p. S 4; "Moran to Win if not 'Scared,'" *The Washington Post*, March 22, 1916, p. 8; Kid McCoy, "'Willard Real Champion,'—McCoy," *The Washington Post*, March 22, 1916, p. 8.

73. James J. Corbett, "Moran Has only Single Chance: That is a Knock-out, Says Corbett," *The Washington Post*, March 24, 1916, p. 9.

74. "Big Boxers Ready for Tonight's Fray," *The New York Times*, March 25, 1916, p. 10; "Total Ticket Sale is Put at $150, 000," *The New York Times*, March 26, 1916, p. 22.

75. "12 to 5 Bet on Willard," *The New York Times*, March 26, 1916, p. 22; "Views of Former Champions and other Famous Fighters on Outcome of Bout Tonight," *The Washington Post*, March 25, 1916, p. 9; TAD, "Willard Great in Training, But Moran Better in Ring," *The Washington Post*, March 25, 1916, p. 8; "Willard Defeats Moran on Points; 13,000 See Bout," *The New York Times*, March 26, 1916, p. 1.

76. "Willard Has a Fractured Hand in Addition to Broken Finger," *The Washington Post*, March 30, 1916, p. 8; "Spurns Knock-out for Sake of Sport," *The Washington Post*, March 28, 1916, p. 8.

77. Harry Carr, "This Moran Person Couldn't Even Get Willard Interested," *The Los Angeles Times*, March 26, 1916, p. VI 1.

78. Robert Fitzsimmons, "Willard Real Champion in Estimation of 'Fitz'" *The Washington Post*, March 26, 1916, p. S1.

79. "Willard Wins Easily with Knuckle Hurt," *The Washington Post*, March 26, 1916, p. 1. There was a minor event which occurred at the fight. Nate Jackson, a bantamweight from Oklahoma City, was given a chance to fight on the national stage. Tom Jones had told his backer, Sammy Samson, owner of the Oklahoma Auditorium where Willard played on May 4, 1915, that they would try to make things up to Sammy for the loss he took. Jones suggested to Samson that he send Nate Jackson back to the East Coast, where he could get far more money and exposure than he could in Oklahoma City. Jones kept his word to Samson and persuaded Tex Rickard to put Jackson in the first preliminary bout of the night. And Jackson took advantage of it and out pointed his opponent Peter Slaight from New York City "Jess Willard Easy Victor over Frank Moran," *The Daily Oklahoman*, March 26, 1916, p. 1.

80. "Wishes 'Daddy' Luck," *The Washington Post*, March 25, 1916, p. 8.

81. "Won't Let Willard Battle for $30, 000," *The New York Times*, March 29, 1916, p. 12; Robert Edgren, "Willard is to Fight Fulton Next, says New York Report," *The Washington Post*, April 1, 1916, p. 8.

82. "Willard Crown Absolutely Safe," *The Daily Oklahoman*, April 2, 1916, p. 15.

83. Rozemen Bulger, "Willard 'Wires' Blows and Shy Fighting Spirit," *The New York World*, April 1, 1916, reprinted in *The Washington Post*, April 2, 1916, p. S4.

84. Robert Edgren, "Fulton on Deck and Ready to take Scalps of Heavyweights," *The Washington Post*, April 12, 1916, p. 8; Robert Edgren "Fulton Likely to Whip Reich If First Round Passes Safely," *The Washington Post*, April 26, 1916, p. 8. There was one other alternative for Willard to fight: "the Orchid Man," little Georges Carpentier. However, there were problems with this. Carpentier was enrolled in the French Air Force and deeply involved in the war. Tex Rickard, with the active help of Anne Morgan, daughter of financier J.P. Morgan, tried to set up a fight in New York City for the benefit of the French Relief. However this fight failed to develop. Willard was left with no one to fight save Fred Fulton.

85. "Jess Willard to Fight F. Fulton," *The Los Angeles Times*, May 15, 1916, p. I 6; "Fulton to Fight Willard," *The New York Times*, May 15, 1916, p. 11; "Willard not likely to Box," *The Los Angeles Times*, June 22, 1916, p. III 1; Robert Edgren, "Offer of $45,000 for Willard to Box Fulton is Turned Down," *The Washington Post*, July 4, 1916, p. 6.

86. Robert Edgren, "Offer of $45,000 for Willard to Box Fulton is Turned Down," *The Washington Post*, July 4, 1916, p. 6.

87. Robert Edgren, "Pugilistic 'Champions' on Lookout for Easy Battles," *The Washington Post*, July 15, 1916, p. 9; "Weight Real Bother to Fighter Willard," *The Washington Post*, July 16, 1916, p. S4; "Willard Saves Coin Earned by Fighting," *The Washington Post*, July 16, 1916, p. S4; Frank G. Menke, Daily Sport Budget, *The Nevada State Journal*, August 13, 1916, p. 5.

88. Robert Edgren, "Darcy Can't Come to U.S. to Box until After Close of War," *The Washington Post*, July 12, 1916, p. 7; "Jack Curley Here, Says Willard is Really Thin," *The Los Angeles Times*, October 12, 1916, p. III 1; Harry Carr, "Jess Willard is a Good Judge of Live Stock when it comes to Talking about being Champ," *The Los Angeles Times*, October 17, 1916, p. III 1.

89. "Kansas City Bids for Title Fight," *The Daily Oklahoman*, November 7, 1916, p. 8; "Denver Angling for Title Mill," *The Daily Oklahoman*, November 21, 1916, p. 12; J. A. Ermatinger, "Promoters Bidding Spiritedly for Willard's First Contest," *The Daily Oklahoman*, November 26, p. 14A

90. "Jess Willard in Class by Himself; May retire Undefeated Champion," *The Daily Oklahoman*, November 2, 1916, p. 10; "Willard's Manager Assents, *The New York Times*, December 6, 1916, p. 10; "Jess likes Tex's Offer," *Los Angeles Times*, November 28, 1916, p. III 1; "Tex Finds Jess Hard to Sign," *Los Angeles Times*, November 30, 1916, p. III 2; "Willard Weighs 270, But Willing to fight," *The Washington Post*, November 27, 1916, p. 6.

91. "Carpentier Likely to fight in a New York Arena Soon," *The Washington Post*, December 6, 1916, p. 10; "Willard May Box Carpentier Here," *The New York Times*, December 6, 1912, p. 10; "Women Backing Bout," *The Washington Post*, December 6, 1916, p. 3; "Woman is Sponsor of Big Prizefight," *The Daily Oklahoman*, December 8, 1916, p. 3; "Prefers Flying Now to The Boxing Ring," *The Washington Post*, December 7, 1916, p. 10; "Willard Asks Too much Coin to Please Promoter Rickard," *The Washington Post*, December 8, 1916, p. 8; "Big Bout in Making but Still Unsettled," *The Washington Post*, December 13, 1916, p. 8; "T. Jones Get Cut, Willard or Darcey," *The Daily Oklahoman*, December 12, 1916, p. 12; "Carpentier likely to Box Australian," *The New York Times*, December 25, 1916, p. 6; "Les Darcy is Likely Choice to meet Georges Carpentier," *The Washington Post*, December 26, 1916, p. 8.

92. "Wenck in Fist Fight," *The New York Times*, December 6, 1916, p. 10.

Chapter 8

1. "Jess Willard May Box Carpentier Ten Round Bout in Milwaukee," *Milwaukee Free Press*, January 5, 1917, p. 7; "Fulton vs. Cowler Tonight," *The New York Times*, January 9, 1917, p. 15; "Fulton in Title Go if Weinert Beaten," *The Washington Post*, February 10, 1917, p. 8; "Fulton Easy Winner in Go with Weinert," *The Washington Post*, February 13, 1917, p. 8; For Fred Fulton, see Anne Beiser Allen, "Fred Fulton, The Rochester Plasterer," *Minnesota History* (Summer 2004), pp. 74–87.

2. "Carl Morris Wins over Fred Fulton," *The Daily Oklahoman*, April 5, 1917, p. 12; "Was Morris-Fulton Bout on Square? There are Doubts," Carl Morris vs. Fred Fulton, *Boxrec Boxing Encyclopedia*; "No Opponents for Willard and Crown," Carl Morris vs. Fred Fulton, *Boxrec Boxing Encyclopedia* (http://boxrec.com/media/index.php?title=Carl_Morris_vs._Fred_Fulton&oldid=213601); Seen 10/2/2014; "Boxing News," *The New York Times*, April 8, 1917, p. S2; "Champ Willard Lost Nice Sum when Fred Quit," *The Milwaukee Free Press*, April 29, 1917, p. 7.

3. George M. Cohan, "Over There," *Wikipedia,* seen November 8, 2014.
4. "Jess Willard to Enlist," *The New York Times,* April 6, 1917, p. 10.
5. "Champion Willard Can join U.S. A. Says an Official," *The Milwaukee Free Press,* April 15, 1917, p. 7.
6. "Jess Willard Aiding U.S.," *The Washington Post,* April 10, 1917, p. 4.
7. "Willard to Fight Before He Retires," *The Washington Post,* April 23, 1917, p. 5; "Willard Comes to Town," *The New York Times,* April 30, 1917, p. 10.
8. Barbara Tuchman, *The Zimmerman Telegram* (New York: Macmillan Company, 1958); "Kaiser's Agents Inciting Negroes," *The Daily Oklahoman,* April 5, 1917, p. 1 "Pacifists Dashed Amuck in Capital," *The Daily Oklahoman,* April 3, 1917, p. 3; "Athletics Banned in Universities," *The Daily Oklahoman,* April 7, 1917, p. 8; "Geronimo's Tribesmen to Join Army," *The Daily Oklahoman,* April 8, 1917, p. 17.
9. "Buffalo Bill Show Sold," *The New York Times,* June 10, 1917, p. 4; "Willard Buys Circus," *The New York Times,* June 12, 1917, p. 10; "Willard Breaks with Manager; Will Quit Game," *The Milwaukee Free Press,* June 24, 1917,p. 7; "Curley and Jones Notified to Quit by Jess Willard," *The Daily Oklahoman,* June 24, 1917, p. 31; "Jess Willard has not Quit," *The Los Angeles Times,* July 10, 1917, p. I 6.
10. "Would Stop Willard from Running Circus," *The Washington Post,* June 26, 1917, p. 10; "Willard's Show Released," *The Milwaukee Free Press,* June 29, 1917, p. 1; Curley Can't Keep Jess Willard out of Sight," *The Los Angeles Times,* July 17, 1917, p. I 6; "Jess to Box for Soldiers, *The Milwaukee Free Press,* August 8, 1917, p. 7.
11. Arthur Struwe, "Jess Willard to retire from Fighting Game," *The Milwaukee Free Press,* November 20, 1917, p. 7.
12. Arthur Struwe, "Willard Comes to Life Saying he will Fight," *The Milwaukee Free Press,* November 21, 1917, p. 7; "Champ Willard Will Fight if Public Demands," *The Milwaukee Free Press,* November 24, 1917, p. 7.
13. J. V. Fitzgerald, "Jess Says He'll Meet Carpentier," *The Washington Post,* November 21, 1917, p. 10; "Fred Fulton Looms up now as the Logical Man to get a chance at Willard's Title," *The Washington Post,* November 29, 1917, p. 8.
14. Jack Veiock, "Willard Must soon defend his Fistic Laurels," *The Milwaukee Free Press,* December 3, 1917, p. 7; "Tom Jones Sure Champ Willard has Quit Game," *The Milwaukee Free Press,* December 8, 1917, p. 7; "Willard Willing to Fight for Benefit of Red Cross," *The Washington Post,* December 18, 1917, p. 10; "Willard is Ready to Defend Title," *The New York Times,* December 18, 1917, p. 19.
15. "$1,000,000 for Fund in Bout Jess thinks," "Langford and Brennan Bid," "Moran wants a Chance," "Greb Would Meet Willard," *The Washington Post,* December 19, 1917, p. 10";Challenges for Willard," *The New York Times,* December 20, 1917, p. 14; "Willard Considering Challenges Already," "Willard and Fulton Certain to Meet, is belief in New York," *The Washington Post,* December 20, 1917, p. 8.
16. J. V. Fitzgerald, "Red Cross Unlikely to Accept Willard's Offer," *The Washington Post,* December 20, 1917, p. 8.
17. J.V. Fitzgerald, "The Round Up," *The Washington Post,* December 21, 1917, p. 8.
18. J. V. Fitzgerald, "The Round-Up," *The Washington Post,* January 8, 1918, p. 8; J.V. Fitzgerald, "The Round-Up," *The Washington Post,* January 21, 1918, p. 8; Arthur Struwe, "Willard Stands Alone Among Heavyweights," *The Milwaukee Free Press,* December 27, 1917, p. 7.
19. "Joe Stecker Stands Alone like Willard,—Tex Dowd," *The Omaha World-Herald,* April 26, 1915, p. 5; "Sues Jess Willard for $25,000," *The New York Times,* January 15, 1918, p. 15; "Deputies Corner Jess Willard Upstairs ," *The Daily Oklahoman,* January 19, 1918, p. 1; "Offers Willard $75,000 for 45-Round Title Bout," *The Washington Post,* January 18, 1918, p. 8; J. V. Fitzgerald "The Round-Up," *The Washington Post,* January 18, 1918, p. 8. Later Grantland Rice made the same criticism of Jack Dempsey: "His continued statements that he is keen to fight and his continued refusal to do so have put him in the attitude of kidding the public. He now ranks with Jack Johnson as being the most unpopular of heavyweight champions." Kahn, *A Flame of Pure Fire,* p. 381.
20. "Boxing Holds its place among leading Sports in the Country, Statistics Show," *The Washington Post,* January 13, 1918, p. 15; J. V. Fitzgerald, "The Round-Up," *The Washington Post,* January 8, 1918, p. 8. Boxing was the most popular sport among the soldiers during the war. In 1919 the Commission on Training Camp Activities revealed that they had purchased 52,032 pairs of boxing gloves for the troops compared to 22,500 baseball bats and 7,920 baseballs, 36,296 soccer balls, 3,000 basket balls and 1,100 pairs of basketball shoes. ("How the Yanks Kept Fit for 'Zero Hour,'" *The Denver Express,* May 20, 1919, p. 2).
21. "Jess Willard in Town," *The Lawrence [Kansas] Daily Journal-World,* February 13, 1918, p. 1; "Willard Here to Purchase a Farm," *The Lawrence Daily Journal-World,* February 14, 1918, p. 1; Douglas County Kansas, Warranty Deed Record No. 99, p. 617, February 27, 1918; "Jess Willard Will Move to Lawrence," *The Lawrence Daily Journal-World,"* February 28, 1918, p. 1; "Willard Family Coming," *The Lawrence Daily Journal-World,* March 1, 1918, p. 1; "Jess Willard now Hails from Kansas," *The Daily Oklahoman,* March 10, 1918, p. 15; "Lawrence, Kansas and Mr. Willard," *The Kansas City Star,* March 4, 1918, p. 12.
22. "Willard to Meet Dempsey, He Says," *The Washington Post,* February 13, 1918, p. 8; "Curley Says $100,000 Offer for Title Go in Cheyenne is O.K." *The Washington Post,* February 16, 1918, p. 8; "Wyoming's Big Offer to Willard is Withdrawn," in J.V. Fitzgerald, "The Round-Up," *The Washington Post,* February 23, 1918, p. 8; "Fulton Knocks Out Moran in Third Round of Bout," *The Washington Post,* February 26, 1918, p. 10; "Offers $100,000 for Willard-Fulton Go," *The Washington Post,* February 27, 1918, p. 8.
23. "Fulton Knocks Out Harper," *The Washington Post,* March 2, 1918, p. 8; "Fulton and Cowler will fight March 11," *The Washington* Post, March 2, 1918, p. 8; "Fulton Stops Cowler in Fifth Round," *The Washington Post,* March 12, 1918, p. 10; "Dempsey Has Won 9 Battles in Opening Round by Knockout," *The Washington Post,* March 10, 1918, p. 20.
24. "Signs Willard for Championship Bout," *The Washington Post,* March 12, 1918, p. 10.
25. "Willard Expects Fight Agreement," *The Daily Oklahoman,* March 14, 1918, p. 11; "Promoters Expect to Confer with Willard," *The Daily Oklahoman,* March 14, 1918, p. 11; "Fight Promoters Disagree on Terms," *The Daily Oklahoman,* March 15, 1918, p. 11; "Matched for Heavy Title," *The Los Angeles Times,* March 16, 1918, p. I, 5.
26. "Fulton Worthiest Rival of Willard," *The New York Times,* March 17, 1918, p. 10; J. V. Fitzgerald, "The Round-Up," *The Washington Post,* March 17, 1918, p. 23; "Lawrence Soon to be Fighters Mecca," *The Lawrence Daily Journal-World,* March 18, 1918, p. 1.
27. "Death of Wesley Cook," *The Junction City Daily Union,* March 16, 1918, p. 1.
28. John M. Barry, *The Great Influenza: The Epic Story of the Deadliest Plague in History* (New York: Viking, 2004) pp. 92–97.
29. Barry, *The Great Influenza,* pp. 96–97.
30. "Wisconsin to be out of it," *The Los Angeles Times,* March 21, 1918, p. I 6; "Plans for Bout Progress," *The New York Times,* March 21, 1918, p. 14; "New Orleans Club Offers $130, 000 for Willard-Fulton Go," *The Washington Post,* March 24, 1918, p. 20; "$140,000 Bid for Bout by Fort Wayne Man," *The Washington Post,* March 25, 1918, p. 10; "Signs Articles for Championship Bout," *The Washington Post,* March 25, 1918, p. 10; Ed W. Smith, "Willard and Fulton Sign Articles," *The Chicago Evening American,* March 26, 1918, p. 7; Ed W. Smith, "Willard-Fulton Title Bout Now up to Bidders," *The Chicago Evening American,* March 27, 1918, p. 6.
31. "Encourage Canning"; "Lightless Nights"; "Autos Will Solve Red Cross Problem"; all in *The Lawrence Daily Journal-*

World, March 23, 1918, p. 1; "Lawrence Quota to Leave with Honors," *The Lawrence Daily Journal-World*, March 27, 1918, p. 1; "Death of Chas. L. Wall," *The Lawrence Daily Journal-World*, March 25, 1918, p. 1.

32. "Jess in Baltimore," *The Lawrence Daily Journal-World*, March 28, 1918,p. 8; "Baltimore Police give Jess Willard no encouragement," *The Daily Oklahoman*, March 28, 1918, p. 11; "Col. Miller is Here to Place Big Bout," *The New York Times*, March 29, 1918, p. 12; "Big Bout Without a Home, *The New York Times*, March 30, 1918, p. 16.

33. "Favor Denver for Battle of Willard-Fulton," *The Beloit Daily News*, April 2, 1918; "Willard Begins Work for Go with Fulton," *The Washington Post*, April 4, 1918, p. 8; "Have Mysterious Disease," *The Lawrence Daily Journal-World*, April 2, 1918, p. 1; "One Letter Man on K.U. Team," and "Chances for Winner Gone Glimmering," *The Lawrence Daily Journal-World*, April 8, 1918, p. 8.

34. "Places Available for Bout Decrease," *The New York Times*, April14, 1918, p. E6 .

35. "Places Available for Bout Decrease," *The New York Times*, April 14, 1918, p. E6.

36. J.V. Fitzgerald, "The Round-Up," *The Washington Post*, April 15, 1918, p. 8.

37. "Minnesota to get Big Ring Battle," *The Washington Post*, April 18, 1918, p. 8; "Must Raise $10,000 to get Title Bout," *The Washington Post*, April 19, 1918, p. 8; "Plans for the Big Fight being Arranged in Twin Cities," *The Daily Oklahoman*, April 19, 1918, p. 11.

38. J.V. Fitzgerald, "Ten Rounds not Long Enough for a Big Fight," *The Washington Post*, April 21, 1918,p. 19; "Willard May Block Fight to Decision," *The New York Time*,, April 21, 1918, p. 27; "Protest Against Bout," *The New York Times*, April 20, 1918, p. 10; "Don't Let Them Pick His Pockets," *The Lawrence Daily Journal-World*, April 22, 1918, p. 1.

39. "Title Fight Talk is Tiring Public," *The New York Times*, May 5, 1918, p. 31.

40. Ray Pearson, "Willard-Fulton Fight for Title Called Off by Miller," *The Chicago Daily Tribune*, May 11, 1918, p. 8; Anne Allen, relying on the Rochester newspaper, believes that Colonel Miller called off the fight due to the opposition of the WCTU. She quotes him as saying that he could do nothing in the face of "one hundred angry women."

Allen, "Fred Fulton, The Rochester Plasterer," *Minnesota History* (Summer 2004), p. 81.

41. J. V. Fitzgerald, "The Round-Up," *The Washington Post*, May 13, 1918, p. 4; "Failure of Title Bout No Surprise," *The New York Times*, May 19, 1918, p. 31; Ray Pearson, "Jess Willard Has Quit Ring, Signs Indicate," *The Chicago Daily Tribune*, May 17, 1918, p. 12. Apparently, Willard did not sell off all his real estate in Chicago at this time. He must have kept a house in Chicago, for after the Dempsey fight in Toledo, he mentions it. However, when he returned to Chicago after the fight he and Hattie stayed in a hotel. "Fulton Will Claim Title and Willard's Forfeit," *The Chicago Daily Tribune*, May 11, 1918, p. 8.

42. "German Pastor Given a Coat of Tar," and "Another Dead One," *The Lawrence Daily Journal-World*, May 9, 1918, p. 1.

43. "Allow No Slackers is Order to Police," *The Lawrence Daily Journal-World*, May 11, 1918, p. 1; "Work or Fight Now Edict by Gen. Crowder," *The Lawrence Daily Journal-World*, May 23, 1918, p. 1.

44. "No Rest for Jess," *The Lawrence Daily Journal-World*, May 23, 1918, p. 8.

45. "Fulton will Box Dempsey July 4," *The Kansas City Journal*, May 31, 1918, p. 8.

46. "Fulton May Box Dempsey," *The New York Times*, June 2, 1918, p. 29.

47. "Heavyweight Bout Fails," *The New York Times*, July 2, 1918, p. 10.

48. Jack Dempsey and Barbara Piattelli Dempsey, *Dempsey* (New York: Harper & Row, Publishers, 1977), p. 78 [cited as Dempsey, *Dempsey* in the future]. Dempsey's comments here demonstrate the value of having a talented manager on one's side. Kearns was able to overcome barriers that would easily have stopped Willard operating on his own, and which did in fact stop Colonel Miller as well.

49. "Dempsey Knocks out Fulton in 23 Seconds," *The Washington Post*, July 28, 1918, p. 15.

50. Nat Fleisher, *Jack Dempsey: The Idol of Fistiana* (New York: Bantam Books, 1949), pp. 102–106. Fleisher's comments don't ring true at this point. It is hard to believe that Dempsey scared Fulton into losing, since Dempsey was really an unknown at the time and Fulton towered over him. Anne Allen quotes sports writer Dick Cullum who gives an alternative explanation. Cullum said that Jack Kearns met with Fulton before the bout and urged Fulton to go easy on Dempsey so that the fight might be close and they could build a better crowd for a return match. This sounds like something Kearns would do. It may lulled Fulton into a false sense of security and have set him up for a quick knockout. Anne Allen, "Fred Fulton, The Rochester Plasterer," *Minnesota History* (Summer, 2004), p. 85.

51. "Willard to be at Riley," *The Junction City Union*, June 29, 1918, p. 4; "Jess Willard the Boxing Attraction at Ft. Riley Celebration of Fourth," *The Topeka Daily Capital*, July 1, 1918, p. 2; "Saw Willard in Action," *The Junction City Union*. July 5, 1918, p. 1; "Saw Jess Fight," *The Lawrence Daily Journal-World*. July 8, 1918, p. 6; "Jess Says He'd Like to Battle Dempsey," *The Washington Post*, July 28, 1918, p. 15.

52. In preparing for his trial on Draft-Dodging in 1920, Dempsey was questioned by Gavin McNab, his attorney. Had Dempsey actually worked in a shipyard? "Not really worked in one," Dempsey said. "Sort of more like I made appearances in shipyards to encourage other guys to go into defense work." Roger Kahn, *A Flame of Pure Fire: Jack Dempsey and the Roaring 20s* (New York: Harcourt Brace & Company, 1999), p. 135.

53. "Dempsey Knocks out Fulton in 23 Seconds," *The Washington Post*, July 28, 1918, p. 15; "Dempsey Ready for Fred Again," *The Chicago Daily Tribune*, August 6, 1918, p. 15.

54. Kahn, *A Flame of Pure Fire*, p. 146; "Dempsey on stand denies charges in U.S. Slacker Trial," *The Chicago Tribune*, June 15, 1920, p. 14. As the trial showed, Dempsey did send all of them money, but each of them had additional sources of income. The issue was: Did Dempsey deserve an exemption from service on the basis of his support of his family? As John W. Preston, one of Dempsey's lawyers told the press: "You gentlemen are getting lost in detail. The draft law did not say you had to be the *entire* source of support for a dependent. You simply had to be the *main* source. Jack was the main source of income for his whole family." The jury agreed with Dempsey's lawyers and declared him not guilty of dodging the draft illegally.

55. "Champions of Ring to Battle for Salvation Army," *The Chicago Daily Tribune*, August 4, 1918, pt. 2, p. 4; "Dempsey's Task now is to get Jess into Ring," *The Chicago Daily Tribune*, August 4, 1918, pt. 2 p. 4; "Willard on way to Chicago for Bout Saturday," *The Chicago Daily Tribune*, August 7, 1918, p. 8; "Chief Alcock Forbids Bouts for War Benefit," *The Chicago Daily Tribune*, August 8, pt. 2, p. 15; "Barry Knocks out Salvation Army's Bouts," *The Chicago Daily Tribune*, August 10, 1918, p. 1; Harvey Woodruff, "Through the Editor's Specs," *The Chicago Daily Tribune*, August 11, 1918, pt. 2, p. 1.

56. Ed W. Smith, "Will Force Willard to Make Good on his Word," *The Chicago Evening American*, September 5, 1918, p. 7; "Kearns Denies Agreement with Jess," *The Chicago Evening American*, September 21, 1918, p. 5.

57. "Kearns Denies Agreement with Jess," *The Chicago Evening American*, September 21, 1918, p. 5; Ray Pearson, "Dempsey's Task Now is to Get Jess into the Ring," *Chicago Daily Tribune*, August 4, 1918, pt. 2, p. 4.

58. It was ironic that Kearns blamed Eddie Graney, a competent and trusted referee, for robbing Dempsey of the decision in the Meehan fight, while later saying nothing about Ollie Pecord's obviously incompetent decision in the Willard-

Dempsey fight. "Says Dempsey Was Robbed," *The Chicago Evening American*, September 16, 1918, p. 5.

59. J.V. Fitzgerald, "The Round-Up," *The Washington Post*, October 6, 1918, p. S1; "Willard May Box in Local Carnival," *The New York Times*, October 20, 1918, p. 31.

60. "Willard to Box for Fund," *The New York Times*, October 25, 1918, p. 10; "Dempsey to Box Willard," *The New York Times*, October 26, 1918, p. 8; "Boxing to Raise Million," *The New York Times*, October 27, 1918, p. 4.

61. "Bouts Are Banned in War Fund Drive," *The New York Times*, October 31, 1918, p. 14.

62. "Easy Pickings for Willard," *The Washington Post*, November 1, 1918, p. 10; J.V. Fitzgerald, "The Round-Up," *The Washington Post*, November 6, 1918, p. 12; "Willard is Ready to Fight Dempsey," *The Washington Post*, December 27, 1918, p. 10.

63. Barry, *The Great Influenza*, pp. 170–171.

64. Barry, *The Great Influenza*, pp. 370–371.

65. Carol R. Byerly, "The U.S. Military and the Influenza Pandemic of 1918–1919," *Public Health Report*, 2010, 125 (Suppl. 3): 82–91.

66. Barry, *The Great Influenza*, p. 362; Molly Billings, "The Influenza Pandemic of 1918," http://virus.stanford.edu/uda/).

67. Barry, *The Great Influenza*, p. 362.

Chapter 9

1. "Jess Willard's Great Luck," *The Washington Post*, December 2, 1918, p. 8; J.V. Fitzgerald, "The Round Up," *The Washington Post*, December 18, 1918, p. 10). Tracy Callis, to whom I owe so much for editing my paper, reminds me that Jim Jeffries retired undefeated before he came out of retirement in July 1910 to fight Jack Johnson. Jeffries defeat, as mentioned in Chapter 1 of this book, triggered the White Hope movement.

2. "Jess Will Box Dempsey," *The New York Times*, December 27, 1918, p. 12; "Willard Says He'll Fight," *The New York Times*, December 29, 1918, p. 26.

3. "Willard Accepts $100,000 Fight Offer," *The New York Times*, January 25, 1919, p. 8; "With the Boxers," *The Washington Post*, February 11, 1919, p. 10. I appreciate the corrections Tony Gee, the Prize-Ring Historian made to this paragraph, especially the fact that the fight between Ted "Kid" Lewis and Jack Britton was not conducted on February 24 but on March 17.

4. J. V. Fitzgerald, "The Round-Up," *The Washington Post*, January 5, 1919, p. SP2; "Willard Accepts $100,000 Fight Offer," *The New York Times*, January 25, 1919, p. 8.

5. "$100,000 Purse Lures Willard Back to Ring: Will defend his Title in July," *The Washington Post*, January 25, 1919, p. 10.

6. Charles Samuels, *The Magnificent Rube: The Life and Gaudy Times of Tex Rickard* (New York, Toronto, London: McGraw-Hill Book Company, Inc., 1957), pp. 207–208.

7. Samuels, *The Magnificent Rube*, pp. 208–209.

8. "Injury Might Cheat Dempsey of Chance," *The Washington Post*, January 31, 1919, p. 10.

9. "Dempsey is Matched to Fight Willard for the World's Heavyweight Title," *The Washington Post*, February 5, 1919, p. 10; "Dempsey to get $27,500 for Bout," *The New York Times*, February 5, 1919, p. 12; Jack Dempsey with Barbara Piattelli Dempsey, *Dempsey* (New York: Harper & Row, Publishers, 1977), pp. 90–93. (Cited as Dempsey, *Dempsey*, hereafter.)

10. "Jones Thinks Jess Peerless," *The Los Angeles Times*, February 2, 1919, p. VI 11; "Bout With Dempsey Fake, says Fulton," *The Washington Times*, February 2, 1919, p. 22.

11. "Will Knock Fred Fulton Out Again when he Sees him, Dempsey Threatens, Denying that their July bout was Prearranged." *The Washington Post*, February 4, 1919, p. 10; "Carpentier Wont Fight Jess, "*The Washington Post*, February 4, 1919, p. 10; "New Jersey Bars Fight," *The New York Times*, March 2, 1919, p. 26.

12. "Johnson Lays Claim to the Championship," *The Lawrence Daily Journal-World*, March 13, 1919, p. 1, 3.

13. "Jess Willard," *The Lawrence Daily Journal-World*, March 15, 1919, p. 4.

14. "Rickard is Oil Magnate," *The Los Angeles Times*, March 15, 1919, p. 4.

15. "Willard in Training for Dempsey Battle; Disposes of Circus," *The Washington Post*, February 15, 1919, p. 8 *The New York Herald* of June 15 also carried an ad for *The Challenge of Chance* which was to open at the Park Theatre at Columbus Circle on Wednesday, June 18. It was billed as "The Most Stupendous Drama of the Plains ever Screened." Unfortunately, *The Challenge of Chance* failed to live up to expectations. Despite the money spent on it, it was poorly edited and poorly managed. This, coupled with Willard's spectacular loss to Dempsey, killed the film and it never produced the revenue Willard and the producers hoped.

16. "Willard Seeks Manager," *The New York Times*, April 20, 1919, p. E6; Jess Willard, *Here's My Story* (unpublished typescript 1967), pp. 13–14.

17. Dempsey, *Dempsey*, p. 100.

18. "Would Help Bury Victim," *The Los Angeles Times*, April 5, 1919, p. II 7.

19. "Champion Here to Start Work," *The Los Angeles Times*, May 2, 1919, p. III 1.

20. "Toledo chosen as scene of Willard-Dempsey Heavyweight Championship bout July 4," *The New York Times*, May 6, 1919, p. 17; "Only 20,000 saw fight, Rickard Says," *The Washington Post*, July 9, 1919, p. 10; Colleen Aycock and Mark Scott, *Tex Rickard: Boxing's Greatest Promoter* (Jefferson, NC: McFarland, 2012), p. 133 say that Tex Rickard and Frank Flourney gained a profit of about $100,000. But other sources suggest that they may not have done well on this fight. After the fight, Flourney cut back on the amounts promised Ollie Pecord and Nathan Weinstern, the announcer. Pecord had a contract for $2,500 but Flourney offered him only $500 for his services. Weinstern received only $100. "Fight Official Says Title Won in Fourth," *The Lawrence Daily Journal World*, July 12, 1919, p. 1.

21. Toledo Selected as Big Bout Site," *The Washington Post*, May 6, 1919, p. 9; "Willard Must Report May 24 for Training," *The Washington Post*, May 19, 1919, p. 10; "Dempsey in Light Boxing Workout," *The Washington Post*, May 25, 1919, p. 10; Dempsey, *Dempsey*, pp. 93, 96–97.

22. "I'll be my Chief Trainer, Then if Beaten Will Blame No One Else," says Willard, *The New York Herald*, June 3, 1919, pt. 2, p. 9; "Willard Amazes Crowd over Apparent Excellent Condition," *The New York Herald*, June 4, 1919, pt. 2, p. 10.

23. "Heavyweight Starts Intensive Training by Knocking Lavan Reeling though the Ropes," *The New York Herald*, June 4, 1919, pt. 2, p. 10; "Willard has the Knockout Punch," *The New York Herald*, June 5, 1919, pt. 2, p. 12; "Willard Knocks Partners Groggy," *The New York Herald*, June 9, 1919, pt 2, p. 9.

24. J.V. Fitzgerald, "Jess Willard Hands K.O. to Monohan in Practice," *The Washington Post*, June 9, 1919, p. 8.

25. "Jess Willard is 37," *The Topeka Daily Capital*, June 27, 1919, p. 8.

26. J. V. Fitzgerald, "Willard Must Train Vigorously to fit himself for the Battle of July 4," *The Washington Post*, June 6, 1919, p. 10.This was confirmed by the sports writer from *The Los Angeles Times* who, when watching both fighters, found it difficult to choose who was the best. Still, he gave Willard the edge. "At Maumee Bay [Dempsey's camp] there is no such thing as boxing: it is fighting, and in this respect the training differs from that of the Casino [Willard's camp].Dempsey's men can and do fight him; Willard's sparring partners cannot take his punches and Jess is forced to hold back in his assaults in order to refrain from knocking out the men who are trying to help him." "Experts find it hard to decide," *The Los Angeles Times*, June 9, 1919, p. I 5.

27. "May Control the Big Fight," *The Los Angeles Times*, June 11, 1919, p. III 1.

28. "Willard is Found Fit," *The Los Angeles Times*, June 13, 1919, p. I 1; "Big Fight to be in 20 Foot Ring," *The New York Herald*, June 14, 1919, pt. 2, p. 6.

29. "Willard's Wife May See Bout," *The New York Herald*, June 15, 1919, pt 2, p. 12; Writing after the fight, Harvey Woodruff, destroyed any belief that Willard threw the fight. "Statements that Jess Willard entered the ring at Toledo solely for the $100,000 purse paid to him with no expectation of winning, carry no weight with those present on that occasion.... Neither you, nor I, nor any male person, wants to look like a boob before his wife. It's hard enough to keep the missus thinking you are a real fellow without being bumped and clouted about by a fellow fifty pounds lighter. Whether we believe it or not, we like the so-called weaker sex to think we are possessed of physical prowess. Therefore Jess Willard did not invite his wife to Toledo to see him defeated by Dempsey. Q.E.D." Harvey Woodruff, "Through the Editors' Specs," *The Chicago Daily Tribune*, July 13, 1919, p. A1. Woodruff's argument stood good for Jack Johnson as well. It is to be remembered that Johnson also had his wife at the ringside. Despite his later claims that he threw the fight with Willard, before the fight Johnson was completely confident that he would retain his title. Then when he began to sense he would lose, he wanted Lucille taken from the ring so as not to see his defeat.

30. "Eight Fast Rounds Boxed by Willard," *The New York Times*, June 16, 1919, p. 16; "Willard Punishes Sparring Mates," *The New York Herald*, June 17, 1919, pt. 2, p. 8; "Dempsey Tops 200 on Tested Scales," *The Washington Post*, June 19, 1919, p. 5.

31. "Willard Admirers Jolted When Dempsey Tips Scales at 201," *The New York Herald*, June 18, 1919, pt. 2, p. 11; "Although Dempsey's Ribs Bother him, Benny Leonard has Inside Information That is Encouraging," *The New York Herald*, June 15, 1919, pt. 2, p. 4; Kerr N. Petrie, "Dempsey in Perfect Condition Proves He Can Hit Hard Blow," *The New York Herald*, June 21, 1919, pt. 2, p. 7.

32. This color contrast between the two was due not just to the sun but to Dempsey's habit of soaking his skin in beef brine. When he first started out in boxing, his brother, Bernie, bathed his face in brine to toughen the skin. "Bernie called it pickling and said that if I ever got cut, I wouldn't bleed. Once a day I would trek to and from the butcher shop, carrying back pails of the stinking stuff. At first the brine burned like hell, but then I got used to it. Eventually my face got as tough as a saddle. Dempsey, *Dempsey*, pp. 16–17; Al Wolgast also used brine to strengthen his skin. "Wolgast Plunges His Face into Brine to Make his Skin Tough," *The Buffalo Evening Times*, January 6, 1913, p. 10.

33. Some boxers and MMA fighters have adopted the strategy of Wolff's Law, originated by Dr. Julius Wolff (1836–1902) to strengthen their hands. It is proposed that fighters can increase the bone density in their fists though repetitive efforts and make them hard as stone. See Wolff's Law in *Wikipedia*. If Dempsey used such a training strategy it could help explain his succession of one-round knock outs, and also his ability to survive fighting with his hand encased in plaster. See also Michael Blackett, "A Helping Hand," in *Jeff Mayweather: Proboxinginsider*, September 25, 2012 [http://proboxinginsider.com/a-helping-hand/]; "Pugs Protect Hands," *The Washington Post*, March 6, 1910, p. M5.

34. W. O. McGeehan, "Challenger Boxes 5 Rounds; Gov. Cox Not to Stop Bout," *The New York Tribune*, June 22, 1919, p. 3–5.

35. "Willard Objects to Tape on Hands," *The New York Herald*, June 20, 1919, pt. 2, p. 12; W. O. McGeehan, "Challenger Boxes 5 Rounds; Gov. Cox Not to Stop Bout," *The New York Tribune*, June 22, 1919, p. 3-S; Benny Leonard, "Pillow of Fat May Stand Willard in Good Stead if he has worked off Inside Layer, Writes Leonard," *The New York Herald*, June 29, 1919, pt. 2, p. 12.

36. "Decide on Rules Today," *The Kansas City Star*, July 2, 1919, p. 5; "To Enter Ring Barehanded," *The New York Times*, July 2, 1919, p. 14.

37. Jack "Doc" Kearns with Oscar Fraley, *The Million Dollar Gate* (New York: Macmillan, 1966), p. 7.

38. J.V. Fitzgerald, "Experts Divided on the Outcome of Fight," *The Washington Post*, June 29, 1919, p. 22.

39. Grantland Rice, "The Sportlight," *The New York Tribune*, June 22, 1919, pt. 2, p. 13.

40. "Take Marked Money to Toledo Battle," *The Lawrence Daily Journal-World*, June 26, 1919, p. 8; "Dollar bills given away as souvenirs by bunch of Willard's neighbors," *The Topeka Daily Capital*, June 29, 1919, p. 8B; "Lawrence Trio are getting Publicity," *The Lawrence Daily Journal-World*, July 1, 1919, p. 6; Otto Floto, "Kansas City Sportsmen Cause Stir Along Nation's Fistic Rialto," *The Kansas City Post*, July 4, 1919, p. 10; "The Kansas Delegation," *The New York Times*, July 4, 1919, p. 13 Other members of the group were: E. C. "Ed" Bricken, owner of a restaurant near the University, T. D. "Tildy" Funk, owner of Funk's Mortuary, Wallace Robinson, cashier on the Union Pacific Railroad, Jack Henly, secretary of the American Cement Plaster Co., and Jim Corbett, an oil operator from Wichita. These same sporting men completely deserted Willard when he lost.

41. John Lardner, *White Hopes and Other Tigers* (Philadelphia and New York: J.B. Lippincott Co., 1951), p. 67.

42. Grantland Rice, "Wide Contrast in the Rival Fighters Creates Keen Interest in Title Bout," *The New York Tribune*, June 29, 1919, p. 3-S

43. Dempsey, *Dempsey*, p. 102. Jack Rohan, writing in *The Chicago Daily Tribune* on July 8, quoted Theodore van Cina, a student of psychology, who described Willard as possessed of great passive courage. "Those who possess it are tolerant. They hesitate to inflict suffering. They are squeamish about striking a fellow being—fearful lest their great strength exerted to the fullest may cause death. They do not fear being struck, but to strike—it is a peculiar frame of mind but one with which psychologists are entirely familiar." Jack Dempsey was a different type altogether: "When he [Willard] met this fearless and ferocious opponent, this Dempsey, who possesses that atavic quality which delights in seeing an opponent reel under his blows, his hesitation, his reluctance to utilize his great strength immediately, ruthlessly, cost him his title." Jack Rohan, "Here's a New Version of Why Willard lost Title to Dempsey," *The Chicago Daily Tribune*, July 8, 1919, p. 16.

44. Kearns, with Fraley, *The Million Dollar Gate*, p. 9; Samuels, *The Magnificent Rube*, pp. 211–212. Tex Rickard took out a 10,000 pound insurance policy (then worth $28,690) with Lloyds of London to cover both Dempsey and Willard against death by accident, accident causing bodily injury and sickness of any kind necessitating confinement to the house. I have not found a special policy to insure Willard against killing Dempsey in the ring. "Tex Takes no Chances on Health of Boxers," *Lawrence Daily Journal-World*, May 15, 1919, p. 2. Despite the comments by Dempsey about his fear of being killed in the ring by Willard, many boxing scholars, even today, doubt Dempsey's words. Among those members of International Boxing Research Organization (IBRO) to whom I have shown this chapter, most doubt that Dempsey ever feared any man in the ring. They challenge my analysis of the events of this fight, and discount Dempsey's comments, while believing Dempsey's statements that his gloves were not loaded. Nonetheless, as one very knowledgeable critic wrote: "JD was a 'junkyard dog' and at this time would kill for a bone." I agree.

45. Jack Kearns and Oscar Fraley, "He Didn't Know the Gloves Were Loaded," *Sports Illustrated*, January 13, 1964, p. 51.

46. Dempsey, *Dempsey*, pp. 105–109.

47. Roger Kahn, *A Flame of Pure Fire: Jack Dempsey and the Roaring '20s* (New York: Harcourt Brace & Company, 1999), p. 91. Scholars from the IBRO reject such statements

by Dempsey as "hype" with no real meaning. One commented: "Mostly I see this type of talk (words) as hype, talk not to be taken seriously." Others have compared Dempsey to Muhammad Ali, who was widely known to use exaggerated speech to make his points. Dempsey, from what I have read, was much more reticent than Ali and seemingly much less prone to hyperbole. While Ali was popularly known as "The Mouth," Dempsey, for most of his career, preferred to let Jack Kearns do his talking for him. All I can do is to record what he said or, was reported to have said, and draw conclusions from his reported words.

48. "Rickard May Referee Bout," *The Denver Express*, June 24, 1923, p. 1; "Willard Practically Declines to Accept any Referee except Rickard tho (sic) Pecord is Boomed," *The Denver Express*, June 25, 1923, p. 7; "Ollie Pecord will Referee Willard-Dempsey Bout with Rickard and Biddle Judges," *The Denver Express*, June 27, 1923, p. 11.

49. "Both Champion and Challenger Go to Bat in Last Word before the Title Mill Curtain Lifts," *The Denver Express*, July 4, 1919, p. 7.

50. W. O. McGeehan, "Maj. Biddle and Rickard Named to Serve as Judges, *The New York Tribune*, June 28, 1919, p. 13; "Pecord Seriously Burned," *The New York Times*, July 5, 1921, p. 25.

51. H. C. Hamilton, "Rules of the Toledo Boxing Commission Will Govern Bout," *The Denver Express*, June 28, 1919, p. 7. I am grateful to IBRO member Bill Schutte for this reference. W.O. McGeehan, "Judges to Name Winner if Bout Lasts 12 Rounds: Two Blows to be Barred," *The New York Tribune*, June 29, 1919, p. 3-S; "Decide on Rules Today," *The Kansas City Star*, July 3, 1919, p. 5.

52. "Records will be broken by Title Bout at Toledo," *The Washington Post*, July 4, 1919, p. 9; J. V. Fitzgerald, "Jess Willard now a 10 to 8 Favorite," *The Washington Post*, July 4, 1919, p. 9; "Blows to the Jaw Won for Dempsey," *The Washington Post*, July 5, 1919, p. 8.

53. Grantland Rice, "Big Champion is Crushed in Nine Minutes," *The New York Tribune*, July 5, 1919, p. 11.

54. This description and what follows is based upon the uncut fight films prepared by Frank G. Hall on July 4, 1919. These films were kindly sent to me by Dennis Magin of Cohoes, NY. They are the same films that Jess Willard used to review the fight.

55. Dempsey, *Dempsey*, p. 110.

56. Dempsey, *Dempsey*, p. 110.

57. Samuels, *The Magnificent Rube*, pp. 214–215.

58. Damon Runyon, "Willard, Battered and Beaten, Resembled Train Wreck Victim," *The Kansas City Post*, July 5, 1919, p. 6.

59. Nellie Bly, "Nellie Bly Describes Fall of Ring Goliath," *The New York Evening Journal*, July 5, 1919, p. 3. Quoted in Mike Sowell, "Nellie Bly's Forgotten Stunt: As the First Woman to Cover a Championship Prize Fight, She Claimed to Have Gained Rare Access to Jack Dempsey," *American Journalism*, 21 (3) 55–76.

60. *London Prize Ring Rules, 1853*, no. 24 found in Cyberboxingzone.com. In Cyberboxingzone, see *Encyclopedia: Laws, Rules and Regulations*. Here the Marquess of Queensberry rules are dated 1865. I am informed by Tony Gee, the British Prize-Ring Historian, that the correct spelling is Marquess, not Marquis. Tony has checked this with the current Marquess of Queensberry himself, as well as noting the correct title is listed in a variety of peerage books. Tony also notes that the original rules were designed for amateur boxing bouts, not professional ones, and that the exact date in which the rules were first published is not known for certain. Three dates have been suggested, 1865, 1866 and 1867. Tony notes that the grandson of the Marquess associated with the rules suggests 1866, not 1865 in his book *The Sporting Queensberrys* by the 10th Marquess of Queensberry (London: Hutchinson, 1942) while Linda Stratmann, *The Marquess of Queensberry: Wilde's Nemesis* (New Haven and London: Yale University Press, 2013), pp. 67–80, suggests the date as 1867 for the first use of the rules. She agrees with Tony Gee that the rules were originally used only for amateur bouts and were not originally linked to the London Prize Fight rules of 1853 until somewhat later. I, at least, find them linked in 1892 when they were used for the Sullivan-Corbett fight of that year. See below note 63.

61. When Willard was attempting to rise from the fourth knockdown, Dempsey hit him with a kidney punch as he was getting back to his feet. This was not noted or called. Then, when he was rising back up from the sixth knockdown, it appears that Dempsey hit him with another kidney punch which was also ignored by Ollie Pecord. Interestingly these two blows occurred when Willard had only partly gotten off the floor. Eugene Corri, in his book, *Refereeing 1000 Fights: Reminiscences of Boxing* (London: C. Arthur Pearson, Ltd., 1919), pp. 40–43 describes disqualifying Ed "Gunboat" Smith for hitting Georges Carpentier when he was in the exact same situation in their bout in London in 1914. (See picture in Corri, p. 40). Had Corri been the referee in the Willard fight, Dempsey would have been disqualified and Willard would have retained his title.

62. *Marquis [Sic] of Queensberry Rules Governing contests for Endurance, 1865*, no. 4 found in Cyberboxingzone.com, my italics.

63. "Queensberry Rules: Code Under Which the Corbett-Sullivan Contest was Determined." *Wheeling [West Virginia] Sunday Register*, September 11, 1892, p. 3. It is hard at this distance to find examples of knockdowns in the pre–Dempsey era. However the fight film of Tommy Burns vs. Gunner Moir in 1907 (with Eugene Corri referee), and the film of Jack Johnson vs. Stanley Ketchel in 1908 (with Jack Welsh as referee) show Burns and Johnson both going to their corners after knocking down their opponent. They do not return to the center of the ring until signaled by the referee. Ed Graney, who served as the referee for the second Jeffries-Fitzsimmons fight (July 25, 1902), informed both men that "in the case of a knockdown, the other man must go to his corner until the man on the mat had regained his feet." Later, when Jeffries knocked Fitzsimmons down, Graney noted "When Fitz went down on his knee Jeff moved over to his own corner as provided in the rules." [Adam J. Pollack, *In the Ring with James J. Jeffries* (Iowa City, Iowa: Win by KO Publications, 2009), p. 520; 538] On the other hand, Tony Gee, the British Prize-Ring Historian, points out that Jack Johnson (with Tex Rickard as referee) did not go to his corner in his fight with Jim Jeffries in the Reno fight of 1910. Nor did I find that Tommy Burns went to his corner (when Jim Jeffries was referee) in the fight with Bill Squires in 1907, although Jeffries did hold Burns back so that he could not stand over Squires (save in the final knockdown). Nor did George "Little Chocolate" Dixon go entirely to his corner in his fight with Chester Leon in 1906. However, Dixon did back up to give Leon a chance to get back on his feet when he was knocked in down. The Dixon-Leon fight, as Tony Gee has noted, was not a full-fledged bout but was abbreviated and designed for film distribution. The rule about going to a corner after knocking down one's opponent was apparently enforced by referees who knew their business, but not enforced by referees who did not. Tex Rickard had never refereed a bout before the Johnson-Jeffries fight, and Jeffries himself was not a professional referee. Corri , Welsh and Graney on the other hand, were professional referees and knew their rules and enforced them.

Some members of IBRO have suggested that since Johnson did not go to his corner after he knocked down Jeffries in Reno in 1910 it served as "precedence as in a court ruling." However, I would suggest that ignorance of the law does not stand as a legal argument in court. The fact that Tex Rickard was refereeing his first prizefight could explain his ignorance, but it does not establish a legal precedent to ignore the law.

64. Paul Gallico, "The Golden People of a Golden Decade," *The Chicago Daily Tribune*, January 26, 1964, p. B1.

65. Damon Runyon, "Kearns Fears Champ May fail to Show Up," *The Kansas City Post*, July 1, 1919, p. 10.

66. Arthur Daley, "Sports of *The Times*," *The New York Times*, November 23, 1965, p. 55.

67. Frank Menke, "Dempsey is Hailed as 'Miracle Man'; Referee Panned," *The Kansas City Post*, July 5, 1919, p. 1; Otto Floto, "Super-Punch Triumphed over Super-Man, Declares Floto," *The Kansas City Post*, July 5, 1919, p. 6.

68. Frank Menke, "Dempsey is Hailed as 'Miracle Man'; Referee Panned," *The Kansas City Post*, July 5, 1919, p. 1; Otto Floto, "Fans Depart and Toledo Returns to Tranquility," *The Kansas City Post*, July 6, 1919, p. 12A

69. *Marquis [Sic] of Queensberry Rules Governing Contests for Endurance, 1865*, no. 5 found in Cyberboxingzone.com, [my italics.]

70. Had Pecord noticed this problem and declared a foul, the special rules established for the Toledo Fight, would have dealt with this situation: "6. In the event of the referee deciding a foul has been committed or the rules violated he shall thereupon consult the two judges and require the confirmation of one or both before disqualifying the offender." The problem was that neither Ollie Pecord, nor the judges called a foul. "Here Are the Rules of the Battle for Fistic Crown Jess Wears," *The Chicago Daily Tribune*, July 4, 1919, p. 9.

71. Jess Willard, *Here's My Story* (1967), p. 14.

72. Jess Willard, *Here's My Story*," pp. 15–16.

73. T.A. Dorgan, "Jess was only champ to quit Cold in Bout," The *Kansas City Post*, July 7, 1919, p. 6.

74. "Wife Saw Big Jess Beaten and is Glad He can Now Retire," *The Washington Post*, July 5, 1919, p. 8; It is also of interest that when Tunney defeated Dempsey in 1926, it struck the *New York Times* writer as the same type of beating that Willard had gotten. "He [Tunney] battered Dempsey to a pulp, until the beaten champion at the finish was a close resemblance to the giant Jess Willard, whom Dempsey pounded and hammered into a helpless hulk out on the shores of Maumee Bay seven years ago when he won the title." James P. Dawson, "Tunney Always Master," *The New York Times*, September 24, 1926, p. 1.

75. Some scholars from the IBRO discount Dempsey's comments about his own condition at the end of the fight. While they recognize that Willard was beaten, they do not believe Dempsey when he said that he was also exhausted. This is proof that the belief that Dempsey was a superman still has value. Dempsey, *Dempsey*, p. 111; As for Willard: "Tears ran down his big crushed and swollen face and mingled with his blood. One eye was closed completely. The other was so swollen he could barely see." Herbert Corey, "But Willard Never Quit," *The Kansas City Star*, July 5, 1919, p. 3; "Wife Saw Big Jess Beaten and is Glad He Can Now Retire," *The Washington Post*, July 5, 1919, p. 8; Damon Runyon, "Willard, Battered and Beaten, Resembled Train Wreck Victim," *The Kansas City Post*, July 5, 1919, p. 6.

76. Samuels, *The Magnificent Rube*, p. 216.

77. Dempsey, *Dempsey*, p. 113.

78. "Jack Handed K.O. to Jess in Third, is Pecord's Ruling," *The Washington Post*, July 7, 1919, p. 8; "Fight Official Says Title Won in Fourth," *The Lawrence Daily Journal-World*, July 12, 1919, p. 1.

79. Otto Floto, "Fans Depart and Toledo Returns to Tranquility," *The Kansas City Post*, July 6, 1919, p. 12A

80. Otto Floto, "Fans Depart and Toledo Returns to Tranquility," *The Kansas City Post*, July 6, 1919, p. 12A

81. Herbert Corey, "But Willard Never Quit," *The Kansas City Star*, July 5, 1919, p. 3.

82. T. A. Dorgan (TAD) "Jess was the only Champ to quit Cold in Bout," *The Kansas City Post*, July 7, 1919, p. 6.

83. "Fight Gate Receipts are likely to exceed $500,000," *The Washington Post*, July 6, 1919, p. 20.

84. W. O. McGeehan, "Dempsey Wins the Title; Willard, Severely Beaten, Quits after 3rd Round," *The New York Tribune*, July 5, 1919, p. 1.

85. "Willard Leaves for Home; Solons Uphold Rickard," *The New York Tribune*, July 8, 1919, p. 13; "Blot Out Stain on Toledo Mill," *The Denver Express*, July 6, 1919, p. 7:

"WHEREAS, The Toledo boxing Commission is of the opinion that the Willard-Dempsey boxing match was in every way regular and legitimate and in every way squarely and honorably conducted by the promoter, Tex Rickard, the participants, Jess Willard and Jack Dempsey, and all concerned."

86. J.V. Fitzgerald, "The Round Up," *The Washington Post*, July 7, 1919, p. 8.

87. Jack "Doc" Kearns with Oscar Fraley, *Sports Illustrated*, January 13, 1964, pp. 48–56. "Pugs Protect Hands," *The Washington Post*, March 6, 1910, p. M5; For information on Fitzsimmons' use of plaster of paris in his second fight with Jeffries see the discussion in Adam J. Pollack, *In the Ring with James J. Jeffries* (Iowa City, Iowa: Win by KO Publications, 2009), pp. 541–543. Although Jeffries did not initially complain about Fitzsimmons' use of plaster of paris on his bandages, the resulting damage Fitzsimmons did to his face led him to object to Jim Corbett using any bandages at all in their fight in 1903 (p. 543). It should also be noted that Jeffries and Fitzsimmons had fought using 5 ounce gloves (p. 541). This challenges the argument from *Boxing Illustrated* that bandages covered with plaster of paris would not fit into 10 ounce gloves.

88. Tony Gee, the British Prize-Ring Historian, has commented that repeated blows with the bare fist to the face [in addition to the head] is likely to damage the hand. The only safe place to land blows with a bare fist is on the body where one is not likely to encounter any hard bones. Hitting the arms of your opponent might also work, but fighters hitting blows to the shoulders or more especially the elbows could suffer an injury. (Personal communication 25–27 March 2015). See also "Gloves Hide Armor Plate," *Fargo Courier-News*, April 2, 1911, p. 6.

89. "Gloves Hide Armor Plate," *Fargo Courier-News*, April 2, 1911, p. 6.

90. Monte Cox, "Were Dempsey's Gloves Loaded? You Decide!" http://coxscorner.tripod.com/dempsey_gloves.html) December 1, 2004. In addition to the help I have received from Monte Cox, I would like to thank Tracy Callis, Frank Lotierzo and Dan Cuoco, all members of the International Boxing Research Organization (IBRO) for their special criticism of this part of my paper. All of them have challenged individual points in my analysis, and none of them agree entirely with my conclusions. But through their criticism, they have helped me improve this section of the book. Any faults that remain are not due to their attempts to guide me but are the results of my mistakes alone.

91. Jess Willard, *Here's My Story*, p. 14.

92. Kearns and Fraley, *The Million Dollar Gate*, pp. 98–102.

93. Jack "Doc" Kearns with Oscar Fraley, "He didn't know the gloves were loaded," *Sports Illustrated*, January 13, 1964, pp. 48–56.

94. Jack (Doc) Kearns with Oscar Frawley, "He Didn't Know the Gloves were Loaded," *Sports Illustrated*, January 13, 1964, p. 52. Jack Kearns: "Reaching our dressing room, I quickly wound on Dempsey's bandages under Moynahan's vigilant inspection." Dempsey: "I bandaged up my own hands," he insisted, "and nobody put anything on them. How could he put anything on without me knowing it?" (*ibid.*em p. 52); Billy McCarney: "Dempsey was a quick-thinking fellow, something of a kidder. He put the tape on himself, while Walter Monahan and Ray Archer, two of Willard's cut rate assistants, watched him" (John Lardner, *White Hopes and Other Tigers*, p. 73); "Jimmy De Forest taped my hands and then slapped me on the back to wish me luck" (Dempsey, *Dempsey*, p. 107); Nat Fleisher: "I was at the fight. I saw Jimmy Deforest, Dempsey's trainer, tape Jack's hands. I watched every move of the men in Jack's quarters" (quoted in Monte Cox, "Were Dempsey's Gloves Loaded? You Decide!" p. 5).

95. John Hollis, "Were Dempsey's Fists Loaded in Toledo?" *Boxing Illustrated* (May 1964), pp. 20–24, 66. Robert Fitzsimmons admitted he used plaster of paris on his bandages in

his second bout with James J. Jeffries in 1902 (see note 87 above and note 96 below). Both men fought with 5 ounce gloves. The *Boxing Illustrated* experiment cannot stand as authoritative and needs to be repeated.

96. In discussing the Jeffries-Fitzsimmons fight of 1902, Jeffries wrote: "After the fight Fitz admitted that he had worn plaster of Paris in his bandages." Yet Jeffries and his trainer, Billy Delaney, examined the bandages before the fight and made no objection to them. This suggests that a cursory examination might not reveal the presence of plaster of paris. Adam J. Pollack, *In the Ring with James J. Jeffries*, p. 542.

97. "Afterward, when I cracked off the bandages and ditched them, he [Dempsey] was so numb at being the heavyweight champion of the world that you could have hit him with a hammer and he wouldn't have blinked an eye." Kearns with Frawley, "He Didn't Know the Gloves were Loaded," p. 56; Frank Menke, "Dempsey is Hailed as 'Miracle Man'; Referee Panned," *The Kansas City Post*, July 5, 1919, p. 1.

98. Kearns entered a hospital in Los Angeles in March 1963, and then spent time in a hospital in Miami in April and May. He fell and broke his arm in June and died in his sleep on July 7. "Kearns Dies; Managed Champs," *The Chicago Daily Tribune*, July 8, 1963, p. C1; Red Smith, "Nothing Sacred From Debunking," *The Washington Post*, January 23, 1964, p. F5.

99. "No Sign of Plaster. Pete Herman Claims he has Dempsey Gloves," *The Washington Post*, January 11, 1964, p. B6. Eric Bottjer, "Jack Dempsey KO3 Jess Willard, July 4, 1919, Bay View Park Arena, Toledo, Ohio," *The Ring Magazine* (March 1997), pp. 32–33 notes that a Jack Robinson "who sold concessions at the fight" supposedly took charge of Dempsey's discarded hand-wrappings after the fight. When he later examined them, he could not find any trace of plaster of paris. Again, it is difficult to be sure that Robinson's judgment is correct since there is no confirmation that these were indeed Dempsey's unaltered hand wraps, and that they had not been disturbed in the years following the fight. I wish to thank Dan Cuoco of the IBRO for sending me this article.

The purpose of this analysis is not to argue that Dempsey's gloves were loaded. It is to argue that whether Dempsey's gloves were loaded or not is still an open question. We cannot settle the issue by relying on the contradictory statements of the parties involved. Kearns said the gloves were loaded, but Kearns was a notorious liar. Dempsey said they were not, but Dempsey went into ring willing to do whatever was needed to survive and to achieve the goal of a lifetime. Neither Kearns nor Dempsey can be considered trustworthy on this point. The only solution to this problem would be to find a plaster that hardens quickly on the hands and that does not break the hands nor burn them (assuming that those hands that had been hardened with brine as Dempsey's were), and test it. We would want to discover if such a fighter with brine-treated hands could fight for several rounds with plaster in 5 ounce gloves. Given the vast range of plasters available, our task would be to find what would work, rather than to find what would not work. If we could find such a plaster, we could then determine if it was possible for Dempsey's gloves to have been loaded as described. Until such a test can be developed, I believe the question remains open.

100. Omar Khayyam, *The Rubaiyat of Omar Khayyam*, rendered into English by Edward T. FitzGerald (New York: St. Martin's Press, 1983), stanza 51.

101. "Mrs. Willard is Happy," *The Kansas City Times*, July 5, 1919, p. 10; "Huh—We Should Worry," *Topeka Daily Capital*, July 5, 1919, p. 1.

102. "Jack Was My Master," *The Kansas City Times*, July 5, 1919, p. 10.

103. Benny Leonard, the lightweight champion of the world at the time, noted this shortly after the fight was over (Benny Leonard, "Stimulus Given Boxing," *The Los Angeles Times*, July 25, 1919, p. III 3).

Tony Gee, the British Prize-Ring Historian, suggests that I have overemphasized Dempsey's role in making boxing a popular and legal sport in the 1920s. He notes that boxing had a major role in training soldiers for World War I, and that this helped to make it popular after the war. Eugene Corri, one of the most famous referees in England (along with B. J. Angle), noted that the same situation prevailed there after the war. "Of all the sports during the War none lived a more lusty life than boxing; none thrived so, none ate itself more surely into the affections of the people; and now we may say with complete certainty that it has come into its kingdom. It is true that it has yet to be legalized, but it is not any hole-and-corner business. We may and do practice it with the approval and sympathy of everybody" (Corri, *Refereeing 1000 Fights*, p. 167). My point is that having a young, dynamic, heavyweight champion like Dempsey helped to make boxing both popular and legal after World War I.

Chapter 10

1. "Jess Willard Pays a Heavy Surtax," *The Los Angeles Times*, July 29, 1919, p. III 1.

2. "No 'Comeback' for Jess," *The Kansas City Star*, July 10, 1919, p. 10.

3. "The Ex-Champion in Chillicothe," *The Chillicothe Constitution*, July 12, 1919, p. 1.

4. "Willard is on Motor Trip to Lawrence Home," *The Kansas City Journal*, July 8, 1919, p. 7; "Jess Willard was Here," *The Kansas City Times*, July 12, 1919, p. 12; "Plain Jess Willard eases Quietly into his Old Home Town," *The Chicago Daily Tribune*, July 12, 1919, p. A1; "Jess Gets Back Home," *The Topeka Daily Capital*, July 13, 1919, p. 1.

5. "To Bet on Jess Again," *The Lawrence Daily Journal-World*, July 9, 1919, p. 8; "Would Bet on Willard—To Lose," *The Kansas City Times*, July 10, 1919, p. 12.

On June 9, shortly after Willard left Lawrence to go to Toledo, Hattie was driving west on Ninth Street when she met Deputy Sheriff Charles Crowder at the corner of Ninth and Tennessee as he was hurrying south to attend to a fire on a farm. The two cars were able to avoid a direct crash, but the Willard car smashed into the curb while Crowder crashed into a telephone pole. Hattie was driving with her sister, Miss Delhna Evans, in the front seat, while Mrs. E.S. Post, who served as governess to the Willard children, was in the back seat with Alan Willard, age 3. Neither Hattie nor Delhna were hurt but Mrs. Post was thrown against the front seat, while trying to protect Alan. She broke several ribs and had internal injuries. The paper reported that she was rushed to Chicago to receive expert medical advice, although it seems more likely that she was sent to the Medical School in Kansas City. "Wife of Champion had Narrow Escape," *The Lawrence Daily Journal-World*, June 9, 1919, p. 1.

6. "Keeping the Home Fires Burning," *The Lawrence Daily Journal-World*, June 21, 1919, p. 8; *The Topeka Daily Capital*, June 22, 1919, p. 10B

7. "Willard's Kiddies Never See their Big Father in Training," *The Lawrence Daily Journal-World*, June 7, 1919, p. 2.

8. "Willard's Kiddies Never See their Big Father in Training," *The Lawrence Daily Journal-World*, June 7, 1919, p. 2.

9. "Is First Title won by Thrown Sponge," and "Homecoming Picnic Was Great Success," *The Lawrence Daily Journal-World*, July 5, 1919, p. 1; "Fight News at the Park," *The Lawrence Daily Gazette*, July 3, 1919, p. 1; " Great Crowd Gathered in Woodland," *The Lawrence Daily Gazette*, July 5, 1919, p. 1.

10. "A Blow to Literature," *The Lawrence Daily Journal-World*, July 7, 1919, p. 2. Not only did Willard lose the revenue from his newspaper articles, he lost the advertising revenue which he had previously enjoyed. Nuxated Iron, which had formerly touted his strength in newspapers across the country, now ran a new ad: "How Nuxated Iron Helped Me to Whip Jess Willard and win the World's Championship by Jack Dempsey 'Tiger of the Ring.'" This appeared in *The Los Angeles Times* on July 20, 1919, p. II 5.

11. "Many Rumors at Toledo About Willard's Death," *The Lawrence Daily Journal-World*, July 7, 1919, p. 1; "The Pug's Following," *The Lawrence Daily Journal-World*, July 9, 1919, p. 4.

12. Nellie Bly was one who had promoted the idea that it was not the blow to the jaw, but the heart-punch which defeated Willard. According to Miss Bly, Jack Dempsey told her: "I was sorry for Mr. Willard, Miss Bly," he said, regretfully. "The blow we had planned—the blow over the heart, finished him. It was almost the first blow. As soon as it landed, I knew he was finished. I saw the pain in his eyes. I was sorry." Nellie Bly, "'Knew I'd Win and I'm Sorry for Willard,' Dempsey tells Nellie Bly, Joyfully Celebrating 'His Day,'" *The New York Evening Journal*, July 8, 1919, p. 17 and Mike Sowell, "Nellie Bly's Forgotten Stunt: As the First Woman to Cover a Championship Prize Fight, She Claimed to have Gained Rare Access to Jack Dempsey," *American Journalism*, 21(3), 55–76, on p. 65.

13. "Left Hook to the Jaw Settled it, Says Jess," *The Topeka Daily Capital*, July 16, 1919, p. 8.

14. Mortgage Records No. 72/309 and 72/310; Warranty Deed Records 77/568 and 77/ 569, Register of Deeds, Holton, Jackson County, Kansas.

15. Deed Record no. 133 and Mortgage Record, no. 128 in the Half-Breed Survey, No. 9 and No. 8, Register of Deeds, Oskaloosa, Jefferson County, Kansas.

16. "Jess Willard now a Tractor Farmer," *The Los Angeles Times*, December 14, 1919, p. VI 6; "Willard Won't Try to Make 'Come Back,'" *The Washington Post*, November 23, 1919, p. 19; "Will Not Re-Enter Ring," *The New York Times*, November 23, 1919, p. S4.

17. "Warrant for Jess Willard as Profiteer in Cordwood," *The New York Times*, December 13, 1919, p. 14; "Willard Arraigned on Profiteering Charge." *The Washington Post*, December 14, 1919, p. 22; "Jess No Profiteer Decision of Court," *The Lawrence Daily Journal-World*, January 5, 1920, p. 1; "Clear Jess Willard of Gouging," *The New York Times*, January 4, 1920, p. 6; "Jess Not a Profiteer, Topeka Officials Say," *The Washington Post*, January 4, 1920, p. 20.

18. "Finish Willard Hill Cut," *The Lawrence Daily Journal-World*, January 5, 1920, p. 1; "Slab Laying Near the Willard Cut," *The Lawrence Daily Journal-World*, October 20, 1921, p. 1.

19. "'Big Jess' Tastes Joy of Farm Life." *The Lawrence Daily Journal-World*, July 12, 1920, p. 1.

20. "Challenged a Cop to a Fistic Battle," *Lawrence Daily Journal-World*, March 19, 1920, p. 1; "Pleads Not Guilty," *Lawrence Daily Journal-World*, March 20, 1920, p. 1; "Willard is Fined Dollar and Costs," *Lawrence Daily Journal-World*, March 30, 1920, p. 1; "Jess Willard Arrested," *The New York Times*, March 20, 1920, p. 15; "Willard Seeks Fight and Must Face J.P.," *The Washington* Post, March 20, 1920, p. 12; "Willard's Children Ill," *The New York Times*, December 7, 1920, p. 20.

21. "Former Champion Seeking Chance to Regain Title," *The Washington Post*, May 22, 1920, p. 11.

22. "Willard Signs to Fight Next March," *The New York Times*, December 1, 1920, p. 23.

23. "Willard Signs to Fight Next March," *The New York Times*, December 1, 1920, p. 23; "Rickard Discusses Bout," *The New York Times*, December 2, 1920, p. 18; "Willard is Ready to Battle Dempsey," *The Washington Post*, December 2, 1920, p. 13.

24. For the background on Rickard's purchase of Madison Square Garden, see Colleen Aycock and Mark Scott, *Tex Rickard: Boxing's Greatest Promoter* (Jefferson, NC: McFarland, 2012), pp. 153–172; "Willard on Way East for Battle," *The Washington Post*, January 24, 1921, p. 8 "Willard Wires East for Training Quarters for Bout," *The New York Times* January 13, 1921, p. 15; "Willard Goes East to Train for Bout," *The Lawrence Daily Journal-World*, January 24, 1921, p. 4; "New York Ruling Might Cancel Title Bout," *The Washington Post*, January 14, 1921, p. 9; "Promoters Call World Title Bout for $500,000 Off," *The New York Times*, January 19, 1921, p. 1.

25. "Fans Give Willard Great Reception," *The Washington Post*, January 27, 1921, p. 10.

26. "Fans Interested in Jess' Comeback," *The Washington Post*, January 30, 1921, p. 20.

27. "Willard Awaits Kearns' Arrival," *The Washington Post*, January 27. 1921, p. 10; "Await Word from Willard," *The New York Times*, February 2, 1921,p. 18; "Willard-Dempsey Match Cancelled," *The Lawrence Daily Journal-World*, February 2, 1921, p. 1; "March 17 Bout Declared Off," *The Los Angeles Times, February* 3, 1921, p. III 1.

28. "March 17 Bout Declared Off," *The Los Angeles Times, February* 3, 1921, p. III 3; "Outdoor Arena for Big Match," *The Lawrence Daily Journal-World*, February 3, 1921, p 2.

29. "Jess Willard Agrees to Meet Champion Dempsey on Labor Day," *The Washington Post*, February 4, 1921, p. 11; "Jess Agrees to New Date," *The Los Angeles Times*, February 4, 1921, p. III 1.

30. "Willard Denies He will Fight Fulton," *The New York Times*, February 16, 1921, p. 19; "Jess Will fight Dempsey or Quit," *The Washington Post*, February 16, 1921, p. 12; Harvey T. Woodruff, "In the Wake of the News," *The Chicago Daily Tribune*, February 17, 1921, p. 11.

31. "Kearns Says Dempsey is Ready for Jess," *The Washington Post*, February 18, 1921, p. 10.

32. "Kearns Says Dempsey is Ready for Jess," *The Washington Post*, February 18, 1921, p. 10.

33. "Invites Ring Champions," *The New York Times*, May 7, 1921, p. 17; "Willard, Too Busy to Attend Fight, Will Not Pick Winner," *The New York Times*, June 24, 1921, p. 22.

34. Harry A. Williams, "Sport Shrapnel," *The Los Angeles Times*, May 31, 1923, p. II 7 "Willard on way East for Battle," *The Washington Post*, January 24, 1921, p. 8; "Willard Denies He will Fight Fulton," *The New York Times*, February 16,1921, p. 19; "Jess To Make His Home Here," *The Los Angeles Times*, February 16, 1921, p. III 1.

35. Floyd Benjamin Streeter, *The Kaw: The Heart of a Nation* (New York and Toronto: Farrar and Rinehart, 1941), pp. 275–276.

36. "R. F. Hodgins Buys Farm," *The Topeka State Journal*, October 29, 1924, p. 1; "Jess Willard's Kansas Farm Sold," *The New York Times* October 30, 1924, p. 23. The farm was sold at auction for $225 per acre. Willard declared that since his home was now in California he wanted to "wind up all outside estates." "Jess Willard, Kansas Fight Ring King, Points Out Evils of Boxing," *The Topeka State Journal*, October 22, 1924, p. 1.

37. "The Willard Home in Lawrence Sold," *The Lawrence Daily Journal World*, December 6, 1921,, p. 1; Warranty Deed Record, no. 99; Warranty Deed Record no. 111, Mortgage Record no. 60, 238, Register of Deeds, Lawrence, Douglas County, Kansas.

38. "Jess Willard Spouts Galore," *Los Angeles Times*, January 30, 1921, p. I 9.

39. "The Fight and Normalcy," *The Washington Post*, July 5, 1921, p. 6; "Jess Would box Jack Labor Day," *The Washington Post*, July 3, 1921, p. 3; "World's Champ Ready to Fight Jess Willard," *The Washington Post*, July 4, 1921, p. 6; "Willard Anxious to Meet Jack Dempsey," *The Washington Post*, July 6, 1921, p. 8; "Willard Wires Rickard Terms," *The Washington Post*, August 3, 1921, p. 10; "Dempsey Gets Restless and Wants a Bout," *The Daily Constitution*, Chillicothe, MO, August 4, 1921, p. 5.

40. "Rickard to Confer with Ray Archer," *The New York Times*, August 5, 1921, p. 16; "Willard's Manager Confers with Tex," *The New York Times*, August 6, 1921, p. 11; "Willard will battle Dempsey next Summer," *The Washington Post*, September 20, 1921, p. 13.

41. The 1901 version of the Kansas Prize-Fight law read as follows, Section 1: "Any person or persons who shall send or cause to be sent, publish or otherwise make known any challenge to fight what is commonly known as a prize-fight, or shall accept such challenge or shall engage in such fight, or shall engage in any public or private boxing or sparring

match, exhibition or contest, with or without gloves of any kind, for any prize, reward, or compensation, or at which any admission fee is charged or received, either directly or indirectly, or shall go into training preparatory to such fight, exhibition, or contest, or act as trainer for any person or persons contemplating a participation in such fight, exhibition, or contest, or shall act as aider, abetter, backer, umpire, trainer, second, surgeon, assistant, reporter or attendant at such fight, exhibition, or contest, or in any preparation for the same, and any owner or lessee of any grounds, lots, building, hall or structure of any kind permitting the same to be used for such fights, exhibitions, or contests, shall be deemed guilty of a misdemeanor, and upon conviction thereof, shall be imprisoned in the country jail not less than thirty days nor more than one year." Chapter 274: Relating to Prize-Fights, Section 1, *Session Laws, 1901* (Topeka: W.Y. Morgan, State Printer, 1901), pp. 499–500.

"Willard Will Referee Bout between Gibbons and O'Dowd," *The New York Times*, August 21, 1921, p. 72"; Fight Promoters Are All Arrested," *The Lawrence Daily Journal-World*, October 17, 1921, p. 1; "Boxers Are Arrested," *The New York Times*, October 18, 1921, p. 25.)

42. Robert Edgren, "Sports Through Edgren's Eyes," *The Chicago Daily Tribune*, October 10, 1921, p. 18; See also "Jess Willard Should Fight Second Rater," *The Washington Post*, October 27, 1921, p. 14; "Bill Brennan Wants to Meet Jess Willard," *The Washington Post*, October 29, 1921, p. 11.

43. "Willard Will Meet Dempsey This Spring," *The Washington Post*, October 17, 1921, p. 12; Roger Khan, *A Flame of Pure Fire*, p. 297.

44. Ray Pearson, "Jack-Jess Will box to Decision Rickard Says," *The Chicago Daily Tribune*, October 21, 1921, p. 18; "Dempsey Agrees to Willard Bout, Fails to Sign Articles," *The New York Times*, October 21, 1921, p. 1; "Percentage Basis for Willard Bout," *The New York Times*, October 22, 1921, p. 16.

45. "Flaudera, Ralston and association..." *The Eureka Herald*, October 13, 1921, p. 1; "Willard to Drill Offsets to Essick," *The Wichita Eagle*, October 14, 1921, p. 3; "Kansas Gusher Brings Fortune to Jess Willard," *The Chicago Daily Tribune*, October 31, 1921, p. 14; "Willard Strikes Oil, Now a Millionaire," *The Washington Post*, October 31, 1921, p. 11. These wells were much more modest that the east coast papers suggested. The wells were estimated to produce between 50 to 300 barrels a day. With oil selling at $1.00 to $2.00 per barrel at the time, this represented a decent, but not spectacular income flow. But since the Flaudera well was in the middle of Willard's lease of 9000 acres, it was assumed that he might gain substantially from the development of the field.

46. Additional wells came in on the Hanson farm in November and the Grundy and Climax farms in December. "Oil in Hanson Well," *The Eureka Herald*, November 24, 1921, p. 1; "Willard & Scott get a big well on the Grundy, Climax Pool," *The Eureka Herald*, December 8, p. 1. I am grateful to Mr. Mike Pitko of the Greenwood County Historical Society in Eureka, Kansas for providing me with these references.

47. Robert Edgren, "Is It Pride with Willard?" *The Chicago Daily Tribune*, November 20, 1921, p. A4.

48. Harry A. Williams, "Sport Shrapnel," *The Los Angeles Times*, May 31, 1923, p. II 7.

49. "New York Promoter Through with Jess," *The Washington Post*, December 3, 1921, p. 15; "Jess Willard Mystifies Rickard," *The Kansas City Star*, December 7, 1921, p. 13.

50. Aycock and Scott, *Tex Rickard*, pp. 145–147; Samuels, *The Magnificent Rube*, pp. 252–262; Randy Roberts, *Jack Dempsey: The Manassa Mauler* (New York: Grove Press, 1979), pp. 136–141.

51. "Dempsey May Fight Jess Willard Again," *The Washington Post*, May 4, 1922, p. 14; Jack Dempsey, *Dempsey*, pp. 138–139.

52. Billy Evans, "Fight Fans Pick Wills as best Bet," *The St. Petersburg Independent*, March 13, 1922, p. 7.

53. Roberts, *Jack Dempsey*, pp. 142–143.

54. For the role of Tex Rickard in the Harry Wills affair see Aycock and Scott, *Tex Rickard*, pp. 170–172; 174–76.

55. "Dempsey May Fight Jess Willard Again," *The Washington Post*, May 4, 1922, p. 14; Jack Dempsey, *Dempsey*, pp. 140–141; "Dempsey may Box Willard in Jersey," *The New York Times*, May 4, 1922, p. 27; "Will Gladly Meet Jess, Says Dempsey," *The New York Times*, May 5, 1922, p. 23; "Dempsey Receives Big Offer in Paris," *The New York Times*, May 7, 1922, p. 26; "Wills or Willard Champions' Opponent," *The Washington Post*, May 18, 1922, p. 14; "Willard Again in Training, May be after Jack's Crown," *The New York Times*, May 20, 1922, p. 19.

56. Robert Edgren, "Sports through Edgren's Eyes," *The Chicago Daily Tribune*, May 22, 1922, p. 17.

57. Robert Edgren, "Sports through Edgren's Eyes," *The Chicago Daily Tribune*, May 22, 1922, p. 17.

58. Robert Edgren, "The Jess Willard of Today," *The Chicago Daily Tribune*, June 4, 1922, p. A4.

59. "Death of Paddy Mullins, Manager of Harry Wills, Revives Old Memories," *Afro-American Weekly*, April 2, 1932, p. 2.

60. "Willard and Dempsey May Meet Labor Day," *The Washington Post*, June 16, 1922, p. 16.

61. "Kearns Says Good Word For Willard," *The New York Times*, June 17, 1922, p. 16.

62. "Willard too busy to Discuss Proposed Bout," *The Washington Post*, June 4, 1922, p. 50; "Jess Willard Wants Return Match with Jack Dempsey," *The Washington Post*, June 15, 1922,p. 14; "Willard and Dempsey May Meet Labor Day," *The Washington Post*, June 16, 1922; "Expect Fall Date for the Big Fight," *The Washington Post*, June 17, 1922, p. 13; "Willard May Get Bout With Dempsey," *The New York Times*, June 16, 1922, p. 21.

63. "Kearns on Way East to Lay Fall Plans," *The New York Times*, June 18, 1922, p. 29.

64. "Dempsey and Wills Still Unmatched," *The New York Times*, July 9, 1922, p. 24.

65. Dempsey, *Dempsey*, pp. 140–141; Further information on Wills position at this time can be found in Brian D. Bunk, "Harry Wills and the Image of the Black Boxer from Jack Johnson to Joe Louis," *Journal of Sport History*, v. 39, no. 1 (Spring 2012), pp. 63–79.

66. "To Train for Dempsey," *The New York Times*, June 21, 1922, p. 22; Leepson Bownes, "Jess Willard Holds First Public Workout since losing Crown," *The Los Angeles Times*, June 28, 1922, p. III 1.

67. Leepson Bownes, "Jess Willard Holds First Public Workout since losing Crown," *The Los Angeles Times*, June 28, 1922, p. III 1; "Plan Jack-Jess Bout for September 22, in East," *The Chicago Daily Tribune*, July 7, 1922, p. 12; "Willard Has Received Contract from Rickard," *The Washington Post*, July 30, 1922, p. 48; "Jess Willard Accepts Theatrical Engagement," *The Washington Post*, August 27, 1922, p. 45; Harry A. Williams, "Sport Shrapnel," *The Los Angeles Times*, September 26, 1922, p. III 2.

68. "Jess Willard Returns," *The Los Angeles Times*, September 19, 1922, p. III 1.

69. "Willard Determined to Regain World's Crown," *The Washington Post*, September 24, 1922, p. 53.

70. "Jess Will Spar for Veterans," *The Los Angeles Times*, September 25, 1922, p. III 1; "Upper Ten at Boxing Session," *The Los Angeles Times*, November 2, 1922, p III 3; "Ring Tilts in Benefit Arranged," *The Los Angeles Times*, November 7, 1922, p. III 1; "Former Champion to Appear at Hollywood Tonight," *The Los Angeles Times*, November 15, 1922, p. III 2.

71. Robert Edgren, "Sports through Edgren's Eyes," *The Washington Post*, November 9, 1922, p. 12.

72. "Willard Turns Down Big Offer," *The Washington Post*, November 25, 1922, p. 15; "Willard Ready to Box Johnson if Dempsey Refuses Him Bout," *The New York Times*, November 26, 1922, p. 27.

73. Harry A. Williams, "Sport Shrapnel," *The Los Angeles Times*, December 5, 1922, p. III, 2.

74. "Kearns and Archer to Discuss Bout," *The New York Times*, December 12, 1922, p. 24; "O'Rourke Offers Willard Bout with Dempsey at Polo Grounds," *The New York Times*, December 13, 1922, p. 31; "Republic Club May Land Dempsey-Willard Battle," *The Washington Post*, December 14, 1922, p. 16.
75. "Willard Barred by Boxing Board," *The New York Times*, December 21, 1922, p. 19.
76. "Offers $330,000 for Willard-Dempsey Bout," *The Washington Post*, December 20, 1922, p. 18; Arthur Mercante, *Inside the Ropes* (Ithaca, NY: McBooks Press, Inc., 2006, p. 155.
77. "Jess Willard May Fight Luis Firpo," *The Washington Post*, January 2, 1923, p. 12.
78. "Willard Barred by State Commission," *The New York Times*, January 10, 1923, p. 27; "Title Bout Awaits Arrival of Kearns," *The New York Times*, January 11, 1923, p. 27; "Willard is 40 Years Old, Kansas Authorities Agree," *The New York Times*, January 11, 1923, p. 27; "Jess No Spring Chicken," *The Topeka Daily Capital*, January 11, 1923, p. 10; "County Records in Kansas Prove Age of Big Jess to be 41," *The Chicago Daily Tribune*, January 24, 1923, p. 21.
79. "Willard to Fight For Return Match," *The Washington Post*, January 11, 1923, p. 14.
80. "Jess Willard Convinces Critics He's In Condition," *The Washington Post*, January 12, 1923, p. 14.
81. "Chairman Muldoon May Sanction Bout," *The Washington Post*, January 13, 1923, p. 19.
82. "Willard and Johnson Meet on Friendly Terms, " *Indianapolis Star*, January 14, 1923, p. 24; "Willard receives Ovation," *Indianapolis Star*, January 14, 1923, p. 26; "Boxing," *The New York Times*, January 15, 1923, p. 13.
83. "Kearns Will Come East This Week," *The New York Times*, January 15, 1923, p. 12.
84. "Kearns Insists on Wills or Willard," *The Washington Post*, January 22, 1923, p. 12; "$1,000,000 Offer Made to Dempsey," The *New York* Times, January 22, 1923, p. 22; "Dempsey-Willard Bout Still in Air," *The New York Times*, January 28, 1923, p. S1; "Jess and Luis, Tex's Choice as Catchers for Jack's Pitching," *The Chicago Daily Tribune, January* 28, 1923, p. A2; "Deny That Heavies Signed for Battle," *The Washington Post*, January 28, 1923, p. 51; Hugh Fullerton "Oracle Kearns to Speak, But Won't Say Much," *The Chicago Daily Tribune*, February 1, 1923, p. 26.
85. Hugh Fullerton "Oracle Kearns to Speak, But Won't Say Much," *The Chicago Daily Tribune*, February 1, 1923, p. 26; "New Jersey Bars Big Ring Battle," *The New York Times*, February 1, 1923, p. 14; "New Jersey Will Not permit Dempsey-Willard Bout," *The Washington Post*, February 1, 1923, p. 21.
86. Robert Edgren, "Sports through Edgren's Eyes," *The Washington Post*, January 29, 1923, p. 12.
87. "Bans Dempsey-Wills Bout in This State," *The New York Times*, February 3, 1923, p. 10.
88. "Bans Dempsey-Wills Bout in This State," *The New York Times*, February 3, 1923, p. 10.
89. "Willard is matched with Floyd Johnson," *The New York Times*, February 8, 1923, p. 22.
90. "Match Willard to Box Floyd Johnson," *The Washington Post*, February 8, 1923, p. 14.
91. "$200,000 Offered Dempsey for Bout," *The New York Times*, April 7, 1923, p. 11; Jack "Doc" Kearns and Oscar Fraley, *The Million Dollar Gate*, pp. 162–179.
92. "Boxing Prices Set for Benefit Bouts," *The New York Times*, April 7, 1923, p. 11; "Muldoon Enjoins Benefit Boxers," *The New York Times*, April 8, 1923, p. S1.
93. "Johnson's Dates Conflict," *New York Times*, April 9, 1923, p. 20; "Boxing Notes," *The Washington Post*, April 9, 1923, p. 11.
94. "Johnson's Manager Explains Situation," *The New York Times*, April 12, 1923, p. 16.
95. "New Jersey Board Postpones Action," *The New York Times*, April 14, 1923, p. 10; "Holmes Consents to Postpone Johnson Bout for One Week," *The New York Times*, April 15, 1923, p. S3.
96. "Muldoon Reverses Ruling on Johnson," *New York Times*, April 18, 1923, p. 18; "Johnson Risks Willard Bout to Fight Fulton," *The Washington Post*, April 18, 1923, p 13; "New York Boxing Commission Gets Change of Heart," *The Los Angeles Times*, April 18, 1923, p. III 3;
97. "Muldoon Reverses Ruling on Johnson," *The New York Times*, April 18, 1923, p. 18.
98. "Johnson Reinstated by New Jersey Body," *The New York Times*, April 20, 1923, p. 14.
99. Harry Newman, "'Poor Old Jess!' East Says after Lamping Kansan," *The Chicago Daily Tribune*, April 22, 1923, p. A1; "Willard to Arrive in City Tomorrow," *The New York Times*, April 20, 1923, p. 14 "Willard is Due to Arrive Today," *The New York Times*, April 21, 1923, p. 8.
100. "Willard Training at Yonkers Camp," *The New York Times*, April 22, 1923, p. S1; It should be noted that these comments about Willard being slow and clumsy contrast sharply with the descriptions of the early Willard who was repeatedly described as very quick and agile for a man his size.
101. "Johnson Suffers Loss of Prestige," *The New York Times*, April 25, 1923, p. 18.
102. "Comment on Current Events in Sports: Boxing," *The New York Times*, April 30, 1923, p. 13.
103. "Dempsey Will meet Gibbons on July 4," *The New York Times*, May 1, 1923, p. 17; "Kearns Says He Will Sign Today," *The New York Times*, May 4, 1923, p. 13.
104. "63,000 pay $390,000 to see Big Boxers Fight for Charity," *The New York Times*, May 13, 1923, p. 1.
105. "Scored 'Come-Back' Says Jess Willard," *The New York Times*, May 13, 1923, p. S1; W. O. McGeehan, "Drops Johnson in 11th After Uphill Battle," *The Washington Post*, May 13, 1923, p. 57.
106. "Remarkable Comeback is staged by Willard," *The Los Angeles Times*, May 13, 1923, p. I 1.
107. "Willard and Firpo Will Confer Today," *The New York Times*, May 14, 1923, p. 12.
108. "Willard and Firpo Will Confer Today," *The New York Times*, May 14, 1923, p. 12.)
109. "Jess in Shape, but no Match for Jack," *The Chicago Daily Tribune*, May 14, 1923, p. 18.
110. "Jess Willard Signs for Bout with Firpo," *The New York Times*, May 16, 1923, p. 12; "Luis Firpo Signs for Willard Bout," *The New York Times*, May 24, 1923, p. 15.
111. "Willard too Old Says Boxing Board," *The New York Times*, May19, 1923, p. 10; "Firpo to meet Willard July 7, Site Not Chosen," *The Washington Post*, May 24, 1923, p. 19; "Jersey Will not Bar Willard if he is Fit," *The New York Times*, May 24, 1923, p. 15.
112. "Legion Not Behind Bout, Says Owsley," *The New York Times*, May 17, 1923, p. 16.
113. "Jess Willard Rescues Women and Children in Flood," *The New York Times*, June 13, 1923, p. 1.
114. Robert Edgren, "Sports through Edgren's Eyes," *The Washington Post*, June 3, 1923, p. 51.
115. "Boxing Notes," *The Washington Post*, June 5, 1923, p. 23.
116. "Demands Willard Prove his Fitness," *The New York Times*, June 22, 1923, p. 14.
117. "Jersey Physicians Pass Jess Willard" *The New York Times*, June 26, 1923, p. 16.
118. "Officials Examine Jersey City Arena," *The New York Times*, July 3, 1923, p. 9; "Willard-Firpo Bout Arena Ruled Unsafe," *The Washington Post*, July 3, 1923, p. 14.
119. "Arena to be in Condition for Willard-Firpo Battle," *The Washington Post*, July 4, 1923, p. 8.
120. "Jeffries to Referee Willard-Firpo Fight," *The Washington Post*, July 4, 1923, p. 8; "Jeffries Referee for Willard Bout," *The New York Times*, July 4, 1923, p. 10.
121. "Lewis to referee Willard-Firpo Bout," The New York Times, July 7, 1923, p. 8.
122. Hugh Fullerton, "Dempsey Retains World's Heavyweight Crown, Winning Decision over Gibbons in 15-round

Bout," *The Washington Post*, July 5, 1923, p. 1; "Rickard Hails Bout as Gibbons Triumph," *The New York Times*, July 5, 1923, p. 4; "New York Praises Gibbons, the Loser," *The New York Times*, July 6, 1923, p. 9.

123. "Willard and Firpo are both Confident," *The New York Times*, July 8, 1923, p. 24; "Willard and Firpo may Draw 80,000," *The New York Times*, July 8, 1923, p. 24; "Willard and Firpo Ease Up in Work," *The New York Times*, July 11, 1923, p. 15.

124. "Argentina Wild with Excitement," *The New York Times*, July 12, 1923, p. 13; "Willard and Firpo in Clash Tonight," *The New York Times*, July 12, 1923, p. 13.

125. "Wills Picks Willard," *The New York Times*, July 12, 1923, p. 13; W.O. McGeehan, "90,000 Expected at Firpo-Willard Ringside Tonight," *The Washington Post*, July 12, 1923, p. 13; Harry Newman, "Firpo Looks Far Better than Old Jess in Jersey," *The Chicago Daily Tribune*, July 11, 1923, p. 17.

126. "Crowd at Fight a World Record," *The New York Times*, July 13, 1923, p. 2.

127. According to *Time Magazine*, vol. 1, no. 21 (July 23, 1923), p. 25 Firpo received $110,000 and Willard received $185, 000.

128. "Betting Goes to Even as Men Enter the Ring," *The New York Times*, July 13, 1923, p. 2.

129. According to the report in *Time Magazine* vol. 1, no.21 (July 23, 1923), p. 25 Willard reported that he had injured his left hand three days before the fight. "My hand pained me frightfully whenever I hit Firpo with it. I do not wish to appear as if I am alibi-ing, but I feel sure I could have defeated Firpo had my hand been all right."

130. "Firpo Beats Willard," *The Los Angeles Times*, July 12, 1923, p. 11 and the fight films; "Firpo Knocks Out Willard in 8 Rounds; 100,000 See Fight," *The New York Times*, July 13, 1923, p. 1.

131. W. O. McGeehan, "Kansan Battered to Ring in Eighth by Sledge Blows," *The Washington Post*, July 13, 1923, p. 1, 13. According to *Time Magazine*, v. 1, no. 21 (July 23, 1923), p. 25 "It was generally conceded that Firpo won because he can punch hard, and that Willard lost because he is too old."

Chapter 11

1. I owe the family information to James Willard Mace and those of his cousins who were kind enough to respond to my requests.

2. James Willard Mace, *The Life and Times of Jess Willard* (1980) unpublished typescript, p. 220.

3. Mace, *The Life and times of Jess Willard*, p. 221.

4. Mace, *The Life and Times of Jess Willard*, pp. 221–222.

5. Mace, *The Life and Times of Jess Willard*, p. 236.

6. Mace, *The Life and Times of Jess Willard*, pp. 222–223.

7. Frederic Mullally, *Primo: The Story of "Man Mountain" Carnera* (London: Robson Books, 1991), pp. 126–146.

8. Mace, *The Life and Times of Jess Willard*, p. 224.

9. *Dempsey* by Dempsey, p. 230.

10. *Dempsey* by Dempsey, p. 231.

11. Mace, *The Life and Times of Jess Willard*, p. 235.

12. Mace, *The Life and Times of Jess Willard*, p. 248.

13. Mace, *The Life and Times of Jess Willard*, p. 250.

14. Mace, *The Life and Times of Jess Willard*, p. 236.

Bibliography

Newspapers

Afro-American Weekly
Atlanta Constitution
Beloit Daily News
Billboard
Boston Herald
Boston Journal
Bridgeport Evening Post
Buffalo Evening News
Buffalo Evening Times
Buffalo Sunday Times
Cadillac Evening News
Chicago Broadax
Chicago Daily News
Chicago Daily Tribune
Chicago Defender
Chicago Evening American
Chicago Inter-Ocean
Chicago Record-Herald
Chillicothe Constitution
Cincinnati Enquirer
Cincinnati Post
Colorado Statesman Daily Constitution
Daily Oklahoman
Daily Post and Record
Denver Express
Duluth Herald
Duluth News-Tribune
Elk City Daily News
Elk City Record
Emmett Citizen
Eureka Herald
Evening News (Ada, OK)
Evening Star (KS)
Fargo Courier-News
Florida Metropolis
Fort Wayne Daily News
Fort Wayne Journal-Courier
Fort Wayne Journal-Gazette
Fort Wayne News
Fort Wayne News Sentinel
Fort Worth Star-Telegram
Grand Rapids Press
Hammon News
Havana Daily Post
Illustrated Record
Indianapolis Freeman
Indianapolis Star
Jacksonville Florida Times-Union
Joplin Globe
Joplin News Herald
Junction City Daily Union
Kansas City Journal
Kansas City Post
Kansas City Star
Kansas City Times
Lake County Times
Las Vegas Optic (NM)
Lawrence Daily Gazette
Lawrence Daily Journal-World
London Times
Los Angeles Examiner
Los Angeles Record
Los Angeles Times
Manhattan Daily Nationalist
Marion Daily Star (OH)
Matagorda County Tribune (TX)
Miami Herald
Miami Metropolis
Milwaukee Free Press
Morning Albertan
Moving Picture World
National Police Gazette
Nevada State Journal
New Castle News
New York Evening Journal
New York Herald
New York Times and *Magazine*
New York Tribune
New York World
Oklahoma City Times
Oklahoma News
Omaha World-Herald
Philadelphia Inquirer
Pueblo Chieftain
Pueblo Star-Journal
St. Louis Daily Globe
St. Louis Globe-Democrat
St. Louis Post-Dispatch
St. Louis Times
St. Marys Star
St. Paul Pioneer Press
St. Petersburg Independent
Salt Lake Telegram
Salt Lake Tribune
San Francisco Chronicle
Sapulpa Evening Light
Sayre Record
Shawnee Daily Herald (OK)
Shawnee Daily News (OK)
Sports Illustrated
Springfield Missouri Republican (MO)
Springfield Daily Leader (MO)
Time Magazine
Times-Picayune(New Orleans)
Topeka Daily Capital
Topeka Daily State Journal
Trenton Evening Times
Tulsa Daily World
Universal Weekly
Variety
Washington Post
Washington Times
Westmorland Recorder
Wheeling West Virginia Sunday Register
Wichita Beacon
Wichita Eagle
Winnipeg Tribune
Wilkes-Barre Times
Youngstown Daily Vindicator
Youngstown Telegram

Books and Other Sources

Abitiz, Lynette. "A History of St. Clere." A 4-H Self-Determined Project, August 2, 1991.

"An Act Concerning Crimes and Punishments (Apr. 16, 1850)." *The Statutes of California Passed at the First Session of the Legislature* (San Jose: J. Winchester, State Printer, 1850), chapter 99, sec. 44: 233.

Administrator's Bonds. Estate of M.B. Willard, November 4, 1881 and November 9, 1881. Probate Court, Pottawatomie County, Westmoreland, Kansas.

Alcon, Manuel. *Lo de Mora*. Victoria, BC: Trafford Publishing, 2005.

Allen, Anne Beiser. "Fred Fulton, the Rochester Plasterer." *Minnesota History* (Summer 2004): 74–87.

Allen, Arly. "The Boxer and the Duelist: The Origins of the Missouri Prizefight Law of 1874." *Missouri Historical Review* 104, no. 4 (July 2010): 213–232.

Allen, Arly. "The Early Boxing Career of Jess Willard (1910–1911)." *The Journal of the International Boxing Research Organization (IBRO)*, no. 84 (December 20, 2004): 39–46.

Allen, Arly. "The Early Boxing Record of Joe Cox, the Missouri White Hope (1911)." *The Journal of the International Boxing Research Organization (IBRO)*, no. 84 (December 20, 2004): 52–55.

Allen, Arly. "Jess Willard and Carl Morris: Heavyweight Boxing in Oklahoma." *The Chronicles of Oklahoma* 83, no. 4 (Winter 2005–2006): 432–451.

Allen, Arly. "Seeking 'The Great White Hope': Heavyweight Boxing in Springfield, 1910–1912." Pt. 1, *Missouri Historical Review* 100, no. 3 (April 2006): 159–173; and Pt. 2, no. 4 (July 2006): 212–223.

Allen, Arly. "The Thirteen Party and the Boxing Deaths of Luther McCarty and John 'Bull' Young (May to Aug. 1913)." Pt. 1: "The Boxing Death of Luther McCarty (May 24, 1913)." *The Journal of the International Boxing Research Organization (IBRO)*, no. 98 (June 15, 2008): 6–19 and Pt. 2: "The Boxing Death of Bull Young (August 23, 1913)." *The Journal of the International Boxing Research Organization (IBRO)*, no. 99 (September 2008): 7–15.

Aycock, Colleen, and Mark Scott. *The First Black Champions: Essays on Fights of the 1800s to the 1920s*. Jefferson, NC: McFarland, 2011.

Aycock, Colleen, and Mark Scott. *Tex Rickard: Boxing's Greatest Promoter*. Jefferson, NC: McFarland, 2012.

Baer, Judith A. "Edward Douglass White." *The Supreme Court Justices: A Biographical Dictionary*. Edited by Melvin I. Urofsky. New York: Garland, 1994.

Barr, Thomas P. "The Pottawatomie Baptist Manual Labor Training School." *Kansas Historical Quarterly* XLIII, no. 4 (Winter 1977): 377–431.

Barry, John M. *The Great Influenza: The Epic Story of the Deadliest Plague in History*. New York: Viking, 2004.

Baughman, Robert W. *Kansas in Maps*. Topeka: Kansas State Historical Society, 1961.

Billings, Molly. "The Influenza Pandemic of 1918." http://virus.stanford.edu/uda/.

Blackett, Michael. "A Helping Hand." *Jeff Mayweather: Proboxinginsider*, September 25, 2012. http://proboxinginsider.com/a-helping-hand/.

Blackmar, Frank W. "Pottawatomie County." *Kansas a Cyclopedia of State History* (1912): 490–492.

Bottjer, Eric. "Jack Dempsey KO3 Jess Willard, July 4, 1919, Bay View Park Arena, Toledo, Ohio." *The Ring Magazine* (March 1997): 32–33.

Bunk, Brian D. "Harry Wills and the Image of the Black Boxer from Jack Johnson to Joe Louis." *Journal of Sport History* 39, no.1 (Spring 2012): 63–79.

Burke, James M., Rev., S.J. "Early Years at St. Mary's Pottawatomie Mission." *Kansas Historical Quarterly* XX, no. 7 (August 1953): 501–529.

Byerly, Carol R. "The U.S. Military and the Influenza Pandemic of 1918–1919." *Public Health Report* 2010, 125 (Suppl. 3): 82–91.

Callis, Tracy, and Chuck Johnston. *Boxing in the Los Angeles Area: 1880–2005*. Victoria, BC: Trafford Publishing, 2009.

Casey, Orben J. "Governor Lee Cruce and Law Enforcement, 1911–1915." *Chronicles of Oklahoma* 54, no. 4 (Winter 1976–1977): 435–460.

Clayborn, Colleen. *Historic Matagorda County*, v. 1 (Houston: D. Armstrong Co., 1986), pp. 367–384.

Cohan, George M. "Over There." *Wikipedia*. Accessed Nov. 8, 2014.

Cohn, Alfred, and Joe Chisholm. *"Take the Witness!"* Garden City, NY: Doubleday, 1934.

Collings, Ellsworth, and Alma Miller England. *The 101 Ranch*. Norman: University of Oklahoma Press, 1971 [1937].

Cone, Carl B. "The Molineaux-Cribb Fight, 1810: Wuz Tom Molineaux Robbed?" *Journal of Sports History* 9, no. 3 (Winter 1982).

Corri, Eugene. *Refereeing 1000 Fights: Reminiscences of Boxing*. London: C. Arthur Pearson, Ltd., 1919.

Cox, Monte. "Were Dempsey's Gloves Loaded? You Decide!" December 1, 2004. http://coxscorner.tripod.com/dempsey_gloves.html).

"The Culliton Papers: Willard's Side." http://www.wildabouthoudini.com/2001/08/culliton-papers-willards-side.html.

Curley, Jack. "Memoirs of a Promoter, as told to Frank Graham." *Ring Magazine* (April 1931, September 1931 and October 1931).

Cushman, Clare. "Edward Douglass White, 1894–1910, 1910–1921." *The Supreme Court Justices: Illustrated Biographies*, 1789–1993. Edited by Clare Cushman. Washington, D.C. Congressional Quarterly, 1993.

Dana, Henry Wadsworth Longfellow. "'Sail on, O Ship of State!' How Longfellow Came to Write These Lines 100 Years Ago." *Colby Library Quarterly*, series 2, no. 13 (February 1950):209–214

De Arment, Robert K. *Alias Frank Canton*. Norman: University of Oklahoma Press, 1997.

Deed Record no. 133 and Mortgage Record, no. 128 in the Half-Breed Survey, No. 9 and No. 8, Register of Deeds, Oskaloosa, Jefferson County, Kansas.

Dempsey, Jack, and Barbara Piattelli Dempsey. *Dempsey*. New York: Harper & Row, 1977.

Dickinson, Emily. "Success is Counted Sweetest." *Selected Poems and Letters of Emily Dickinson*. Edited by Robert N. Linscott. New York: Doubleday Anchor Books, 1959.

Dorinson, Joseph. "Black Heroes in Sport: From Jack Johnson to Muhammad Ali." *Journal of Popular Culture* 31, no. 3 (Winter 1997): 115–135.

Earl of Halsbury [Giffard, Hardinge Stanley]. *The laws of England: being a complete statement of the whole law of England* by the Right Honourable the Earl of Halsbury ... and other lawyers, v. 9. London: Butterworth, 1909.

Edgren, Robert. "Champions I Have Known." *Jess Willard [Archive]—Boxing Forum* http://www.boxingscene.com/forums/archive/. Accessed July 26, 2014.

Edmonds, I.G. *The Big U: Universal in the Age of Silent Films*. South Brunswick, NJ: A.S. Barnes and Co., 1977.

"Edward Douglass White." *Wikipedia*. Accessed June 13, 2014.

Egan, Pierce. *Boxiana: Or Sketches of Ancient and Modern Pugilism From the Days of the Renowned Broughton and Slack to the Championship of Cribb* 1. Brighton, MA: Elibron Classics, 2006 [1830].

"Elisha Leonard Stalker." 1900 Census. Ancestry.com.

Fleisher, Nat. *Jack Dempsey: The Idol of Fistiana*. New York: Bantam Books, 1949.

Gee, Tony. *John L. Sullivan: Cradle to Grave*. Romford, Essex: Sporting Profiles, 1998.

Greenwood, Robert. *Jack Johnson vs. James Jeffries: The Prize Fight of the Century: Reno, Nevada, July 4, 1910*. Reno: Jack Bacon & Company, 2004.

Half-Breed Survey. General Land Office, August 13, 1869. Register of Deeds, Oskaloosa, Jefferson County, Kansas.

Harris, Leslie M. *In the Shadow of Slavery: African Americans in New York City, 1626–1863*. Chicago: University of Chicago, 2003.

Hollis, John. "Were Dempsey's Fists Loaded in Toledo?" *Boxing Illustrated* (May 1964): 20–24, 66.
"Houdini Unchained." http://www.boxing.com/houdini_unchained.html.
Inventory and Appraisement of the Estate of M.B. Willard, W-78, November 4 and November 24, 1881. Probate Court, Pottawatomie County, Westmoreland, Kansas.
Isenberg, Michael T. *John L. Sullivan and His America*. Urbana: University of Illinois Press, 1994 [1988].
Jack London Reports: War Correspondence, Sports Articles, and Miscellaneous Writings. Edited by King Hendricks and Irving Shepard. Garden City, NY: Doubleday, 1970.
Jess Willard, et al. vs. Charles F. Knoblauch, 8th Circuit Court of Appeals, Case no. 6061, Court of Civil Appeals, El Paso, TX. Part of Case no. 890, Civil Court of Appeals. Box No. H45 in the C.L. Sonnichsen Special Collections Department of the University of Texas at El Paso Library.
Jobert, Timothee. "Paris et la Revanche de l'Homme 'Blanc' (1908–1915)." *Stadion* 28, no. 2 (2002).
Johnson, Jack. *My Life and Battles*. Edited and translated by Christopher Rivers. Westport, CT: Praeger, 2007.
Justice's Court of Los Angeles City, Case no. 5808, *The People of the State of California, Plaintiff vs. Jess Willard, et al, Defendants* (August 23, 1913).
Kahn, Roger. *A Flame of Pure Fire: Jack Dempsey and the Roaring 20s*. New York: Harcourt Brace & Company, 1999.
Kammer, David. "TKO in Las Vegas: Boosterism and the Johnson-Flynn Fight." *The New Mexico Historical Review* 61 (1986): 301–318.
Kearns, Jack "Doc" with Oscar Fraley. *The Million Dollar Gate*. New York: Macmillan, 1966.
Khayyam, Omar. *The Rubaiyat of Omar Khayyam*. Translated by Edward T. FitzGerald. New York: St. Martin's Press, 1983.
Kilty, James. *Leonis of Vernon*. New York: Carlton Press, 1963.
L. Lawrence Weber, Appt. v. Frederick S. Freed, Deputy Collector of United States Customs in Charge of the Port of Newark, N.J., Supreme Court of the United States (Oct. Term, 1915): 239, 240, 241, U.S. Book 60. Rochester: Lawyers Cooperative Publishing Company, 1916.
LaForce, Christopher. *The Choynski Chronicles: A Biography of Hall of Fame Jewish Boxer Joe Choynski*. Iowa City: Win by KO Publications, 2013.
Lardner, John. *White Hopes and Other Tigers*. Philadelphia: J.B. Lippincott 1951.
Litwack, Leon F. *North of Slavery: The Negro in the Free States, 1790–1860*. Chicago: University of Chicago Press, 1961.
London Prize Ring Rules of 1838, 1853. Cyberboxingzone.com.
Lucas, John A., and Ronald A. Smith. *Saga of American Sport*. Philadelphia: Lee & Febiger, 1978.
Mace, James Willard. *The Life and Times of Jess Willard*. 1980. Unpublished manuscript, 2003.
Manz, William H. "Benjamin Cardozo Meets Gunslinger Bat Masterson." *New York State Bar Association Journal* (July-August 2004): 10–17.
Marquess of Queensberry. *The Sporting Queensberrys by the 10th Marquess of Queensberry*. London: Hutchinson, 1942.
Marquis [sic] *of Queensberry Rules Governing Contests for Endurance, 1865*. Cyberboxingzone.com.
McCaffery, Dan. *Tommy Burns: Canada's Unknown World Heavyweight Champion*. Toronto: James Lorimer and Company, Ltd., 2000.
McCallum, John D. *The World Heavyweight Boxing Championship: A History*. Radnor, PA: Chilton Books, 1974.
Meier, August, and Elliott Rudwick. *From Plantation to Ghetto*. New York: Hill and Wang, 1976 [1966].
Mercante, Arthur. *Inside the Ropes*. Ithaca: McBooks Press, Inc., 2006.
Mortgage Records no. 72/309 and 72/310 Warranty Deed Records 77/568 and 77/ 569. Register of Deeds, Holton, Jackson County, Kansas.
Moyle, Clay. *Sam Langford: Boxing's Greatest Uncrowned Champion*. Seattle: Bennett and Hastings Publishing, 2006.
Mullally, Frederic. *Primo: The Story of "Man Mountain" Carnera*. London: Robson Books, 1991.
Mutual Film Corporation, Appt. v. Industrial Commission of Ohio et al., The Supreme Court Reporter 35 (Oct. Term, 1914) (Dec. 1914–Aug. 1915). St. Paul: West Publishing Co., 1915.
"Myron B. Willard." 1850, 1870, 1880, Census Records. Ancestry.com.
Nicholson, Kelly Richard. *A Man Among Men*. Draper, UT: Homeward Bound Publishing, 2002.
"No Opponents for Willard and Crown." Carl Morris vs. Fred Fulton, *Boxrec Boxing Encyclopedia*, http://boxrec.com.
Oklahoma County Common Pleas Book, Docket 2491, Book 5, March 25, 1911.
Out of the Shadows. Edited by David K. Wiggins. Fayetteville: University of Arkansas Press, 2006.
Peterson, Nancy M. "Buffalo Bill's Legacy." *American History* 38, no. 4 (October 2003): 51–56, 80.
Petition for Letters of Administration, Nov. 9, 1881. Probate Court, Pottawatomie County, Westmoreland, Kansas.
Pollack, Adam J. *In the Ring with James J. Jeffries*. Iowa City: Win by KO Publications, 2009.
Radford, Peter. *The Celebrated Captain Barclay*. London: Headline Book Publishing, 2001.
Roberts, Randy. *Jack Dempsey: The Manassa Mauler*. New York: Grove Press, 1979.
Runstedtler, Theresa. *Jack Johnson, Rebel Sojourner*. Berkeley: University of California Press, 2012.
Rush, Barbara Williams. "The 101 Ranch Wild West Show, 1904–1932." *Chronicles of Oklahoma* 43, no. 4 (Winter 1965–1966): 416–431.
St. Johns, Adela Rogers. *Final Verdict*. Garden City, NY: Doubleday, 1962.
Samuels, Charles. *The Magnificent Rube: The Life and Gaudy Times of Tex Rickard*. New York: McGraw-Hill 1957.
Second Annual Report of the State Athletic Commission. Albany: J.B. Lyon Company Printers, 1912. Reprinted in the *Journal of the International Boxing Research Organization (IBRO)*, no. 97, March 12, 2008: 71–72.
Session Laws, 1901, State of Kansas. Topeka: W.Y. Morgan, State Printer, 1901.
Silverman, Kenneth. *Houdini!!! The Career of Ehrich Weiss*. New York: HarperCollins, 1996.
Somrack, F. Daniel. *Boxing in San Francisco*. Charleston, SC: Arcadia Publishing, 2005
Sowell, Mike. "Nellie Bly's Forgotten Stunt: As the First Woman to Cover a Championship Prize Fight, She Claimed to Have Gained Rare Access to Jack Dempsey." *American Journalism* 21, no. 3: 55–76.
Stratmann, Linda. *The Marquess of Queensberry: Wilde's Nemesis*. New Haven: Yale University Press, 2013.
Streeter, Floyd Benjamin. *The Kaw: The Heart of a Nation*. New York: Farrar and Rinehart, 1941.

Streible, Dan. *Fight Pictures: A History of Boxing and Early Cinema*. Berkeley: University of California Press, 2008.

Superior Court, County of Los Angeles, The People of the State of California against Jess Willard, et al. Case no. 8740 (October 13, 1913); Demurrer (October 14, 1913); Decision (January 13, 1914); Instructions to the jury by Judge Gavin W. Craig. Jr. (January. 7–13, 1914) and Opinion of the Court (Oct. 21, 1913).

The Supreme Court Reporter 36 (October Term, 1915) (December 1915–July 1916) St. Paul: West Publishing Co. 1916.

Tabor, Bob. "Jess Willard: Prize Fighter, Wild West Attraction, Circus Owner." *The White Tops, Worlds Foremost Publication Devoted Exclusively to the Circus.* 38, no. 2 (March–April 1965): 3–8.

Tocqueville, Alexis de. *Democracy in America*. Edited by Harvey C. Mansfield and Delba Winthrop. Chicago: University of Chicago Press, 2000 [1835].

Trope, Michael Lance. *Once Upon a Time in Los Angeles: The Trials of Earl Rogers*. Spokane: Arthur H. Clark Co., 2001.

Tuchman, Barbara. *The Zimmerman Telegram*. New York: Macmillan, 1958.

Uhlig, Frank Jr. "The Great White Fleet." *American Heritage* XV, no. 2 (February 1964).

The United States of America vs. John Arthur Johnson, United States District Court, Northern District of Illinois, Case no. 5166, April 30, 1913.

Ward, Geoffrey C. *Unforgivable Blackness: The Rise and Fall of Jack Johnson*. New York: Alfred K. Knopf, 2004.

Wallis, Michael. *The Real Wild West: The 101 Ranch and the Creation of the American West*. New York: St. Martin's Press, 1999.

Warranty Deed nos. 53 and 373, *Book V*, Oct. 25, 1880. Register of Deeds Office, Pottawatomie County, Westmoreland, Kansas.

Warranty Deed no. 99 and 111; Mortgage Record no. 60, 238. Register of Deeds, Lawrence, Douglas County, Kansas.

"Was Morris-Fulton Bout on Square? There are Doubts." Carl Morris vs. Fred Fulton, *Boxrec Boxing Encyclopedia*. http://boxrec.com.

Wells, Jeff. *Boxing Day: The Day That Changed the World*. Sydney: HarperSports, 1998.

Wiggins, David K. "Peter Jackson and the Elusive Heavyweight Championship: A Black Athlete's Struggle Against the Late Nineteenth Century Color-Line." *Journal of Sport History* 12, no. 2 (Summer 1985).

Willard, Jess. *Here's My Story*. 1967. Unpublished Typescript Dictated by Jess Willard to John Patrick and Provided to Author by James Willard Mace.

Wilson, Raymond. "Another White Hope Bites the Dust: The Jack Johnson-Jim Flynn Heavyweight Fight in 1912." *Montana: Magazine of Western History* 29, no. 1 (1979): 30–39.

W-124. Westmoreland County Court House, Westmoreland, Kansas.

The World Almanac and Encyclopedia, 1908. New York: Press Publishing Co. New York World, 1907.

Index

www.ingramcontent.com/pod-product-compliance
Ingram Content Group UK Ltd.
Pitfield, Milton Keynes, MK11 3LW, UK
UKHW060612180726
13836UKWH00012B/2512